GRATIA ET CERTAMEN

BIBLIOTHECA EPHEMERIDUM THEOLOGICARUM LOVANIENSIUM

CLXIX

GRATIA ET CERTAMEN

THE RELATIONSHIP BETWEEN GRACE AND FREE WILL
IN THE DISCUSSION OF AUGUSTINE
WITH THE SO-CALLED SEMIPELAGIANS

BY

D. OGLIARI

LEUVEN
UNIVERSITY PRESS

UITGEVERIJ PEETERS
LEUVEN - PARIS - DUDLEY, MA

2003

ISBN 90 5867 357 X (Leuven University Press)
D/2004/1869/9
ISBN 90 429 1351 7 (Peeters Leuven)
D/2003/0602/104
ISBN 2 87723 741 9 (Peeters France)

Library of Congress Cataloging-in-Publication Data

Ogliari, Donato.
    Gratia et certamen: the relationship between grace and free will in the
discussion of Augustine with the so-called semipelagians / Donato Ogliari.
       p. cm. -- (Bibliotheca Ephemeridum theologicarum Lovaniensium; 169)
    Includes bibliographical references and index.
    ISBN 90-429-1351-7 (alk. paper)
    1. Augustine, Saint, Bishop of Hippo. 2. Grace (Theology)--History of
doctrines--Early church, ca. 30-600. 3. Free will and determinism--Religious
aspects--Christianity--History of doctrines--Early church, ca. 30-600.
4. Predestination--History of doctrines--Early church, ca. 30-600.
I. Title. II. Series.

BR65.A9G79 2003
234'.9'09014--dc21
                                                              2003050577

Leuven University Press / Presses Universitaires de Louvain
Universitaire Pers Leuven
Blijde Inkomststraat 5, B-3000 Leuven-Louvain (Belgium)

© 2003, Peeters, Bondgenotenlaan 153, B-3000 Leuven (Belgium)

FOREWORD

"Sheets of paper covered with words pile up in archives sadder than cemeteries, because no one ever visits them, not even on All Souls' Day. Culture is perishing in overproduction, in an avalanche of words, in the madness of quantity" (M. Kundera, *The Unbearable Lightness of Being*). I cannot foresee whether Kundera's words will prove the fate of this publication, but I nourish the hope that this undertaking might contribute to the field of 5th century history of theology, shedding in particular more light upon the topic of grace, free will, predestination and their related issues.

However, and this is the main reason for this foreword, I must acknowledge that the present work (a doctoral dissertation presented at the Louvain Faculty of Theology in June 2002) is not the result of a solitary journey. On the contrary, several people accompanied me and made the outcome possible by their assistance. First and foremost, I owe a debt of gratitude to my promoter, Prof. Dr. Mathijs Lamberigts. His guidance and supervision during the developmental period of these pages was invaluable. His suggestions, his critical remarks (which conceded nothing to "taken-for-granted" positions) have been of great help and have often been the cause of enlightening insights. Some of the remarks of the members of the Reading Committee, Prof. Dr. Jan van Oort, Dr. Josef Lössl and Dr. Johan Leemans, have also been taken into account in the present publication in as far as the structural coherence of the work allowed it.

It goes without saying that during my somewhat erratic sojourn in Louvain and during the period of research I received help from many quarters: not just on an intellectual level, but from the encouragement and friendship that came from several institutions and many good people. To begin with I am sincerely indebted to the Right Rev. Ab. Guido Bianchi OSB and my monastic community of Madonna della Scala Abbey in Noci (I) on one hand, and on the other to the Right Rev. Ab. Kris op de Beeck OSB and the monastic community of Keizersberg Abbey in Louvain. If my confrères of Noci allowed me to complete my studies, those of Keizersberg provided me with a "natural" home in all senses, making it possible for me to enjoy the undisturbed environment, so necessary for any intellectual endeavour. My special thanks go to the librarian, Dom Guibert Michiels OSB, for his constant and fraternal availability. A word of gratitude also goes to Prior Fr. Bernard Bruning OSA and the Augustinian community in Heverlee-Louvain, whose library, besides being a haven for Augustinian "learners", is also a place where one always feels welcome. Likewise, a word of gratitude must go to the staff of the Library of the Louvain Faculty of Theology, and to Prof. Dr. Gilbert Van Belle, Editor of the "Bibliotheca Ephemeridum Theologicarum Lovaniensium" for accepting and including this present work in such a prestigious series.

I am also very grateful for the support (especially precious in the inevitable dark days of the journey) that I have received from many people, among whom I would especially like to mention the following: my mother Bruna Martarello-Ogliari and my family in Italy, for their constant closeness, and the De Winter-Coppens family in Belgium, whose home became a true "Bethany" for me.

Finally, my deep gratitude goes to my old friend Fr. James McGrath SMM who took upon himself the task of going through large sections of the present work in order to make my English more presentable. Thanks too go to Mrs. Sally Williams and Mrs. Helena Schröder, who were valuable co-operators in this task. The final, polishing touches are due to the generosity of my confrères of Pluscarden Abbey (Scotland), namely the Righ Rev. Ab. Dom Hugh Gilbert OSB and Dom Benedict Hardy OSB, to whom the expression of my fraternal friendship and gratitude is but the feeble echo of my debt. Last but not least, a word of thanks goes also to Prof. Em. Dr. Margherita M. D'Aprile who has painstakingly checked the Latin and Greek quotations in the footnotes. Naturally, any remaining mistakes, *quos aut incuria fudit aut humana parum cauit natura*, are my responsibility, and mine alone.

UT IN OMNIBUS GLORIFICETUR DEUS

TABLE OF CONTENTS

CHAPTER III

GRACE, FREE WILL AND THE STRUGGLE FOR PERFECTION

CHAPTER IV

THE *UEXATA QUAESTIO* OF PREDESTINATION

CONCLUSION

EPILOGUE

INDEXES

ABBREVIATIONS

AAWG.PH	Abhandlungen der Akademie der Wissenschaften in Göttingen. Philologisch-historische Klasse
ACO	Acta conciliorum oecumenicorum
ACW	Ancient Christian Writers
AFM	Archives de la France monastique
AGWG.PH	Abhandlungen der Gesellschaft der Wissenschaften zu Göttingen. Philologisch-historische Klasse
AMRG	Arbeitsmaterialen zur Religionsgeschichte
AnBib	Analecta biblica
ATA	Année théologique augustinienne
Aug	Augustinianum
AugL	Augustinus-Lexikon
Aug(L)	Augustiniana (Louvain)
AugMag	Augustinus Magister
AugSt	Augustinian Studies
AUU	Acta Universitatis Upsaliensis
BAMA.H	Bibliotheca augustiniana medii aevi – Sectio historica
BA	Bibliothèque augustinienne
BAC	Biblioteca de autores cristianos
BECNT	Baker Exegetical Commentary of the New Testament
BEFAR	Bibliothèque des écoles françaises d'Athènes et de Rome
Ben	Benedictina
BETL	Bibliotheca Ephemeridum Theologicarum Lovaniensium
BFCL	Bulletin des Facultés catholiques de Lyon
BGAM	Beiträge zur Geschichte des Alten Mönchtums und des Benediktinerorderns
BGrL	Bibliothek der griechischen Literatur
BHT	Beiträge zur historischen Theologie
BiToTe	Bible de tous les temps
BKAW	Bibliothek der klassischen Altertumswissenschaften
BLE	Bulletin de littérature ecclésiastique
BMus	Bibliothèque du Muséon
BSGRT	Bibliotheca scriptorum graecorum et romanorum teubneriana
BSS	Bibliotheca sanctorum
Cass.	Cassiciacum. Würzburg
Cath	Catholicisme. Paris
CCist	Collectanea cisterciensia
CCL	Corpus Christianorum – Series latina
CClCr	Civiltà classica e cristiana
CDios	La ciudad de Dios
CEAug.SA	Collection des études augustiniennes, Série antiquité

CiSt	Cistercian Studies
CollAug	Collectanea augustiniana
CorLat	Corona lateranensis
CSCO	Corpus scriptorum christianorum orientalium
CSEL	Corpus scriptorum ecclesiasticorum latinorum

DBS	Dictionnaire de la Bible. Supplément
DHGE	Dictionnaire d'histoire et de géographie ecclésiastiques
DIP	Dizionario degli istituti di perfezione
Div	Divinitas
DoC	Doctor communis
DPAC	Dizionario patristico e di antichità cristiane
DS	Enchiridion symbolorum (Ed. Heinrich Denzinger/A. Schönmetzer)
DSBP	Dizionario di spiritualità biblico-patristica
DSp	Dictionnaire de spiritualité, ascétique et mystique
DT	Divus Thomas (Freiburg i. Br.)
DTC	Dictionnaire de théologie catholique
DTI	Dizionario teologico interdisciplinare

| EC | Enciclopedia cattolica |
| EE | Estudios ecclesiasticos |

FC	Fontes christiani
FaCh	Fathers of the Church
FKDG	Forschungen zur Kirchen und Dogmengeschichte
FZPT	Freiburger Zeitschrift für Philosophie und Theologie

GCS	Die Griechischen christlichen Schriftsteller der ersten drei Jahrhunderte
GuL	Geist und Leben
Greg	Gregorianum

HDG	Handbuch der Dogmengeschichte
HTK	Herders theologischer Kommentar zum neuen Testament
HTR	The Harvard Theological Review

| IJPR | International Journal for Philosophy of Religion |
| ITQ | Irish Theological Quarterly |

JECS	Journal of Early Christian Studies
JEH	Journal of Ecclesiastical History
JHI	Journal of History of Ideas
JTS	Journal of Theological Studies

| KKTS | Konfessionskundliche und kontroverstheologische Studien |
| Kl | Klerenomia (Thessaloniki) |

| Lat | Lateranum |
| LCC | Library of Christian Classics |

LCL	The Loeb Classical Library
LCP	Latinitas christianorum primaeva
LCPM	Letture cristiane del primo millennio
LouvSt	Louvain Studies
LTK	Lexikon für Theologie und Kirche
MA	Miscellanea agostiniana
MBT	Münsterische Beiträge zur Theologie
MSR	Mélanges de science religieuse
MySal	Mysterium salutis
NBA	Nuova biblioteca agostiniana
NHMS	Nag Hammadi and Manichaean Studies
NPNF	A Select Library of the Nicene and post-Nicene (Christian) Fathers
NRT	Nouvelle revue théologique
NTSt	New Theology Studies
OCA	Orientalia christiana analecta
OCP	Orientalia christiana periodica
OC(R)	Orientalia christiana
ÖBFZPT	Ökumenische Beihefte zur Freiburger Zeitschrift für Philosophie und Theologie
OCPM	Oxford Classical and Philosophical Monographs
OECS	Oxford Early Christian Studies
ÖF.S	Ökumenische Forschungen. II. Soteriologische Abteilung
OSHT	Oxford Studies in Historical Theology
OTM	Oxford Theological Monographs
PatMS	Patristic Monograph Series
PatSor	Patristica sorbonensia
PatSt	Patristic Studies
PerkJ	Perkins Journal
PL	Patrologiae cursus completus (accurante Jacques-Paul Migne). Series latina.
PLS	PL. Supplementum (accurante A. Hamman)
PG	Patrologiae cursus completus (accurante Jacques-Paul Migne). Series graeca.
PO	Patrologia orientalis
ProvHist	Provence historique
PSB	The Princeton Seminary Bulletin
PTS	Patristische Texte und Studien
PuP	Päpste und Papsttum
RAC	Reallexicon für Antike und Christentum
RAM	Revue d'ascétique et de mystique
RBen	Revue bénédictine
RE	Realencyklopädie für protestantische Theologie und Kirche
REAug	Revue des études augustiniennes
RechAug	Recherches augustiniennes

REG	Revue des études grecques
REL	Revue des études latines
RevPhil	Revue de philosophie
RevAg	Revista agustiniana
RevSR	Revue des sciences religieuses
RGG	Religion in Geschichte und Gegenwart
RHE	Revue d'histoire ecclésiastique
RHLR	Revue d'histoire et de littérature religieuses
RMab	Revue Mabillon
RMÂL	Revue du moyen âge latin
RPL	Revue philosophique de Louvain
RSLR	Rivista di storia e letteratura religiosa
RSPT	Revue des sciences philosophiques et théologiques
RSR	Recherches de science religieuse
RSSR.M	Recherches et synthèses de sciences religieuses. Section de morale
RTAM	Recherches de théologie ancienne et médiévale
RTHP	Recueil des travaux d'histoire et de philologie (3ème série).
RTP	Revue de théologie et de philosophie
SBEC	Studies in the Bible and Early Christianity
SC	Sources chrétiennes
SCA	Studies in Christian Antiquity
ScEc	Sciences ecclésiastiques
SE	Sacris erudiri
SEAug	Studia ephemeridis "Augustinianum"
SHR	Studies in the History of Religions
SM	Sacramentum mundi
SMSR	Studi e materiali di storia delle religioni
SPAW.PH	Sitzungsberichte der Preußischen Akademie der Wissenschaften. Philosophisch-Historische Klasse
SPMed	Studia patristica mediolanensia
SpOr	Spiritualité orientale
SRS	Studies in Religion and Society
SSAM	Settimane di studio del Centro Italiano di studi sull'alto medioevo
SSRel	Studi storico religiosi
StAns	Studia anselmiana
StEv	Studia evangelica
StMon	Studia monastica
StOr	Studies in Oriental Religions
StPatr	Studia patristica
StSSpTh	Studien zur systematischen und spirituellen Theologie
StTL	Studia theologica lundensia
SVigChr	Supplements to Vigiliae Christianae
SVSL	Skrifter Utgivna av Vetenskaps–Societeten i Lund
TaS	Texts and Studies
TGL	Tijdschrift voor geestelijk leven
Theol(P)	Théologie
ThH	Théologie historique

ThPS	Théologie, pastorale et spiritualité
Trad	Traditio. Studies in Ancient and Medieval History, Thought and Religion
TRE	Theologische Realenzyklopädie
TTS	Tübinger theologischen Studien
TU	Texte und Untersuchungen
TVGMS	TVG-Monographien und Studienbücher
TWNT	Theologisches Wörterbuch zum Neuen Testament
VC	Verbum caro
VieMon	Vie monastique
VigChr	Vigiliae christianae
WSt	Wiener Studien
ZKG	Zeitschrift für Kirchengeschichte
ZKT	Zeitschrift für katolische Theologie
ZNW	Zeitschrift für die neutestamentliche Wissenschaft und die Kunde der älteren Kirche
ZPE	Zeitschrift für Papyrologie und Epigraphik
ZTK	Zeitschrift für Theologie und Kirche

BIBLIOGRAPHY

I. PRIMARY SOURCES

1. Augustine

Confessiones, ed. Verheijen (CCL, 27), Turnhout, 1981.
Contra aduersarium Legis et Prophetarum, ed. Daur (CCL, 49), Turnhout, 1985, pp. 35-131.
Contra Cresconium, ed. Petschenig (CSEL, 52), Vienna, 1908, pp. 323-582.
Contra duas epistulas Pelagianorum, ed. Vrba – Zycha (CSEL, 60), Vienna, 1913, pp. 421-570.
Contra epistulam Parmeniani, ed. Petschenig (CSEL, 51), Vienna, 1908, pp. 17-141.
Contra Faustum Manichaeum, ed. Zycha (CSEL, 25/1), Vienna, 1891, pp. 249-797.
Contra Felicem Manichaeum, ed. Zycha (CSEL, 25/2), Vienna, 1892, pp. 799-852.
Contra Fortunatum Manichaeum, ed. Zycha (CSEL, 25/1), Vienna, 1891, pp. 81-112.
Contra Iulianum, ed. Maurini (PL, 44), cc. 641-874.
Contra litteras Petiliani, ed. Petschenig (CSEL, 52), Vienna, 1909, pp. 1-227.
Contra secundam Iuliani responsionem imperfectum opus, Books 1-3, ed. Zelzer (CSEL, 85/1), Vienna, 1974; Books 4-6, ed. Maurini (PL, 45), cc. 1337-1608.
Contra Secundinum Manichaeum, ed. Zycha (CSEL, 25/2), Vienna, 1892, pp. 903-947.
De baptismo contra Donatistas, ed. Petschenig (CSEL, 51), Vienna, 1908, pp. 143-375.
De bono coniugali, ed. Zycha (CSEL, 41), Vienna, 1900, pp. 185-231.
De catechizandis rudibus, ed. Bauer (CCL, 46), Turnhout, 1969, pp. 121-178.
De ciuitate Dei, ed. Dombart – Kalb (CCL, 47-48), Turnhout, 1955.
De continentia, ed. Zycha (CSEL, 41), Vienna, 1900, pp. 139-183.
De correptione et gratia, ed. Folliet (CSEL, 92), Vienna, 2000, pp. 219-280.
De diuersis quaestionibus ad Simplicianum, ed. Mutzenbecher (CCL, 44), Turnhout, 1970.
De diuersis quaestionibus lxxxiii, ed. Mutzenbecher (CCL, 44A), Turnhout, 1975, pp. 1-249.
De doctrina christiana, ed. Martin (CCL, 32), Turnhout, 1962, pp. 1-167.
De dono perseuerantiae, ed. Maurini (PL, 45), cc. 993-1034.
De duabus animabus, ed. Zycha (CSEL, 25/1), Vienna, 1891, pp. 49-80.
De Genesi ad litteram, ed. Zycha (CSEL, 28/1), Vienna, 1894, pp. 1-435.
De Genesi contra Manichaeos, ed. Weber (CSEL, 91), Vienna, 2000.
De gestis Pelagii, ed. Vrba – Zycha (CSEL, 42), Vienna, 1902, pp. 49-122.
De gratia Christi et de peccato originali, ed. Vrba – Zycha (CSEL, 42), Vienna, 1902, pp. 123-206.

De gratia et libero arbitrio, ed. MAURINI (PL, 44), cc. 881-912.

De haeresibus, ed. VANDER PLAETSE – BEUKERS (CCL, 46), Turnhout, 1969, pp. 286-345.

De libero arbitrio, ed. GREEN (CCL, 29), Turnhout, 1970, pp. 205-321.

De moribus Ecclesiae catholicae et de moribus Manichaeorum, ed. BAUER (CSEL, 90), Turnhout, 1992.

De musica, ed. MAURINI (PL, 32), cc. 1081-1194.

De natura et gratia, ed. VRBA – ZYCHA (CSEL, 60), Vienna, 1913, pp. 231-299.

De natura et origine animae, ed. VRBA-ZYCHA (CSEL, 60), Vienna, 1913, pp. 301-419.

De nuptiis et concupiscentia, ed. VRBA-ZYCHA (CSEL, 42), Vienna, 1902, pp. 209-252.

De opere monachorum, ed. ZYCHA (CSEL, 41), Vienna, 1900, pp. 529-596.

De peccatorum meritis et remissione et de baptismo paruulorum, ed. VRBA – ZYCHA (CSEL, 60), Vienna, 1913, pp. 1-151.

De perfectione iustitiae hominis, ed. VRBA – ZYCHA (CSEL, 42), Vienna, 1902, pp. 1-48.

De praedestinatione sanctorum, ed. MAURINI (PL, 44), cc. 959-992.

De quantitate animae, ed. HÖRMANN (CSEL, 89), Vienna, 1986, pp. 129-231.

De sancta uirginitate, ed. ZYCHA (CSEL, 41), Vienna, 1900, pp. 233-302.

De spiritu et littera, ed. VRBA – ZYCHA (CSEL, 60), Vienna, 1913, pp. 153-229.

De Trinitate, ed. MOUNTAIN-GLORIE (CCL, 50-50A), Turnhout, 1968.

Enarrationes in psalmos, ed. DEKKERS – FRAIPOINT (CCL, 38-40), 2nd ed., Turnhout, 1990.

Enchiridion ad Laurentium, seu de fide, spe et caritate, ed. EVANS (CCL, 46), Turnhout, 1969, pp. 49-114.

Epistula ad Catholicos de secta Donatistarum seu *De unitate Ecclesiae*, ed. PETSCHENIG (CSEL, 52), Vienna, 1908, pp. 229-322.

Epistolae ex duobus codicibus nuper in lucem prolatae, ed. DIVJAK (CSEL, 88), Vienna, 1981.

Epistulae, ed. GOLDBACHER (CSEL, 34/1-2; 44; 57; 58), Vienna, 1895, 1898, 1904, 1911, 1923.

Epistulae ad Galatas expositio, ed. DIVJAK (CSEL, 84), Vienna, 1971, pp. 53-141.

Epistulae ad Romanos inchoata expositio, ed. DIVJAK (CSEL, 84), Vienna, 1971, pp. 143-181.

Expositio quarumdam propositionum ex epistula ad Romanos, ed. DIVJAK (CSEL, 84), Vienna, 1971, pp. 1-52.

In Ioannis epistulam ad Parthos tractatus, ed. MAURINI (PL, 35), cc. 1977-2062.

Quaestionum in Heptateuchum, ed. FRAIPONT (CCL, 33), Turnhout, 1958, pp. 1-377.

Retractationes, ed. MUTZENBECHER (CCL, 57), Turnhout, 1974.

Sermones 1-50, ed. LAMBOT (CCL, 41), Turnhout, 1961; 51ff, ed. MAURINI (PL, 38-39), cc. 332-1638 and ed. MORIN-WILMART-LAMBOT (PLS, 2), cc. 417-840.

Tractatus in Euangelium Ioannis, ed. WILLEMS (CCL, 36), Turnhout, 1954.

Works of Augustine, with Translation, Introduction, Commentary we
have referred to in the text

An Simplicianus zwei Bücher über verschiedene Fragen, ed. T.G. Ring,
Schriften gegen die Pelagianer. Schriften über die Gnade, Bd. III,
Würzburg, 1991.

Answer to the Pelagians. IV: To the Monks of Hadrumetum and Provence.
Translation, introduction and notes by R.J. Teske (The Works of Saint
Augustine, I/26), New York, 1999.

Aux moines d'Adrumète et de Provence: De gratia et libero arbitrio – De correptione et gratia – De praedestinatione sanctorum – De dono perseverantiae. Introduction, Traduction et Notes par J. Chéné – J. Pintard, Œuvres
de Saint Augustin (BA, 24), Paris, 1962.

De dono perseverantiae. A translation with an introduction and a commentary
by M.A. Lesousky (PatSt, 91), Washington, DC, 1956.

Exposés généraux de la foi: De fide et symbolo – Enchiridion. Traduction et
notes par J. Rivière – F.-J. Thonnard, Œuvres de Saint Augustin (BA, 9),
Paris, 1947.

Four Anti-Pelagian Writings: On Nature and Grace. On the Proceedings of
Pelagius. On the Predestination of the Saints. On the Gift of Perseverance.
Translated by J.A. Mourant – W.J. Collinge. With Introduction and
Notes by W.J. Collinge (FaCh, 86), Washington, DC, 1992.

Grace and Free Will. Translated by R.P. Russell (FaCh, 59), Washington, DC,
1968.

Grazia e libertà. La grazia e il libero arbitrio. La correzione e la grazia. La
predestinazione dei santi. Il dono della perseveranza. Introduzione e Note
di A. Trapè. Traduzione di M. Palmieri (NBA, 20), Rome, 1987.

La crise pélagienne. I: Epistula ad Hilarium Syracusanum – De perfectione
iustitiae hominis – De natura et gratia – De gestis Pelagii. Introduction,
traduction et notes par G. de Plinval – J. de la Tullaye, Œuvres de Saint
Augustin (BA, 21), Paris, 1966.

La crise pélagienne. II: De gratia Christi et de peccato originali. De natura et
origine animae. Introduction, traduction et notes par J. Plagnieux – F.-J.
Thonnard, Œuvres de Saint Augustin (BA, 22), Paris, 1975.

Les Révisions. Introduction, traduction et notes par G. Bardy, Œuvres de Saint
Augustin (BA, 12), Paris, 1950.

Lettere. Introduzione e commento a cura di M. Pellegrino (NBA, 21), Rome,
1969.

Logik des Schreckens. Augustinus von Hippo De diversis quaestionibus ad Simplicianum I 2, ed. K. Flasch – W. Schäfer (Excerpta classica, Bd. VIII),
Mainz, 1990.

Mélanges doctrinaux: Quaestiones 83 – Quaestiones VII ad Simplicianum –
Quaestiones VIII dulcitii – De divinatione daemonum. Introduction, traduc-
tion et notes par G. Bardy – J.-A. Beckaert – J. Boutet, Œuvres de Saint
Augustin (BA, 10), Paris, 1952.

Natura e grazia. Il castigo e il perdono dei peccati ed il battesimo dei bambini
– Lo Spirito e la lettera – La natura e la grazia – La perfezione della gius-
tizia dell'uomo. Introduzione e note di A. Trapè. Traduzione di I. Volpi
(NBA, 17/1), Rome, 1981.

Premières polémiques contre Julien: De nuptiis et concupiscentia – Contra duas epistulas Pelagianorum. Introduction, traduction et notes par F.-J. THONNARD – E. BLEUZEN – A.C. VEER, *Œuvres de Saint Augustin* (BA, 23), Paris, 1974.

Schriften gegen die Semipelagianer: Gnade und freier Wille. Zurechtweisung und Gnade (ed. S. KOPP); *Die Vorherbestimmung der Heiligen. Die Gabe der Beharrlichkeit* (ed. A. ZUMKELLER), Würzburg, 1955.

Six traités anti-Manichéens: De duabus animabus – Contra Fortunatum – Contra Adimantum – Contra Epistulam Fundamenti – Contra Secundinum – Contra Felicem Manichaeum. Introduction, traduction et notes par J. JOLIVET – M. JOURION, *Œuvres de Saint Augustin* (BA, 17), Paris, 1961.

The Retractations, ed. M.I. BOGAN (FaCh, 60), Washington, DC, 1968.

Tratados sobre la gracia: Del espíritu y de la letra – De la naturaleza y de la gracia – De la gracia de Jesucristo y del pecado original – De la graciay del libre albedrío – De la corrección y de la gracia – De la predestinación de los santos – Del don de perseverancia. Version, Introduccion y Notas de V. CAPANAGA *et al., Obras de San Augustin,* T. VI (BAC, 50), 2nd ed., Madrid, 1956.

2. OTHERS

AESCHYLUS, *Eumenides,* ed. LLOYD-JONES (LCL), London-Cambridge, MA, repr. 1963.

AMBROSE, *De Abraham,* ed. SCHENKL (CSEL, 32/1), Vienna, 1897, pp. 501-638.

—, *De Cain et Abel,* ed. SCHENKL (CSEL, 32), Vienna, 1897, pp. 339-409.

—, *De fide,* ed. FALLER (CSEL, 78), Vienna, 1962.

—, *De fuga saeculi,* ed. SCHENKL (CSEL, 32/2), Vienna, 1897, pp. 163-207.

—, *De Iacob et uita beata,* ed. SCHENKL (CSEL, 32/2), Vienna, 1897, pp. 1-70.

—, *De interpellatione Job et David,* ed. SCHENKL (CSEL, 32/2), Vienna, 1897, pp. 211-296.

—, *De paenitentia,* ed. GRYSON (SC, 179), Paris, 1971.

—, *De Spiritu sancto,* ed. FALLER (CSEL, 79), Vienna, 1964, pp. 1-222.

—, *De uirginibus,* ed. GORI (Opera omnia di Sant'Ambrogio, 14/1), Milan, 1989, pp. 100-240.

—, *Epistulae,* ed. FALLER (CSEL, 82/1); ed. FALLER – ZELZER (CSEL, 82/2); ed. ZELZER (CSEL, 82/3), Vienna, 1968, 1990, 1982.

—, *Exameron,* ed. SCHENKL (CSEL, 32/1), Vienna, 1897, pp. 3-261.

—, *Exhortatio uirginitatis,* ed. GORI (Opera omnia di Sant'Ambrogio, 14/2), Milan, 1989, pp. 198-270.

—, *Expositio de psalmo cxviii,* ed. PETSCHENIG (CSEL, 62), Vienna, 1913.

—, *Expositio euangelii secundum Lucam,* ed. ADRIAEN (CCL, 14), Turnhout, 1957, pp. 1-400.

AMBROSIASTER, *Commentarius in xiii epistulas Paulinas,* ed. VOGELS (CSEL, 81,1-3), Vienna, 1966/1969.

Apophthegmata Patrum (Collectio alphabetica) (PG, 65), cc. 72-440.

ARISTOTLE, *Ethica Nicomachea,* ed. RACHAM (LCL), London-Cambridge, MA, repr. 1968.

—, *Metaphysica,* ed. TREDENNICK (LCL), London-Cambridge, MA, repr. 1975.

—, *Physica*, ed. WICKSTEED-CORNFORD (LCL, 228), London-Cambridge, MA, 1957.

—, *Politica*, ed. RACKHAM (LCL), London-Cambridge, MA, repr. 1972.

ARNOBIUS IUNIOR (attributed to), *Praedestinatus*, ed. GORI (CCL, 25B), Turnhout, 2000.

ATHANASIUS, *De decretis Nicaenae synodi*, ed. OPITZ (Athanasius Werke, Bd. II/1), 3. Lieferung, Berlin-Lipsia, 1935.

—, *Epistulae ad Serapionem*, ed. MAURINI (PG, 26), cc. 529-676.

—, *Oratio de incarnatione uerbi*, ed. KANNENGIESSER (SC, 199), Paris, 1973.

—, *Orationes contra Arianos* 1-3, ed. METZLER, revised by SAVVIDIS (Athanasius Werke, Bd. I/1: Die dogmatischen Schriften), 2. Lieferung: *Orationes* 1-2; 3. Lieferung: *Oratio* 3, Berlin-New York, 1998 and 2000; *Oratio* 4, ed. MAURINI (PG, 26), cc. 468-525.

—, *Vita Antonii*, ed. BARTELINK (SC, 400), Paris, 1994.

BASIL OF CAESAREA, *Asceticon magnum* siue *Quaestiones (Regulae fusius tractatae)*, ed. MAURINI (PG, 31), cc. 889-1052.

—, *De Spiritu sancto*, ed. PRUCHE (SC, 17bis), Paris, 1968.

—, *Epistulae*, ed. COURTONNE, Tomes I-III (Les Belles Lettres), Paris, 1957, 1961, 1966.

—, *Homiliae in Exaemeron*, ed. AMAND DE MENDIETA – RUDBERG (GCS, n.f., Bd. II), Berlin, 1997.

—, *Homiliae super psalmos*, ed. GARNIER (PG, 29), cc. 209-494.

—, *Quod Deus non est auctor malorum*, ed. MAURINI (PG, 31), cc. 329-353.

BENEDICT OF NURSIA, *Regula monachorum*, ed. DE VOGÜÉ (SC, 181-182), Paris, 1972.

CAELESTINUS, *Epistula ad episcopos Galliarum*, ed. MAURINI (PL, 45), cc. 1755-1760.

—, *Epistulae*, ed. COUSTANT (PL, 50), cc. 417-558.

CASSIAN, *De incarnatione Domini contra Nestorium*, ed. PETSCHENIG (CSEL, 17), Vienna, 1888, pp. 235-391.

—, *De institutis coenobiorum*, ed. PETSCHENIG (CSEL, 17), Vienna, 1888, pp. 3-231; ed. GUY (SC, 109), Paris, 1965.

—, *Conlationes*, ed. PETSCHENIG (CSEL, 13), Vienna, 1886; ed. PICHERY (SC, 42, 54, 64) Paris, 1955, 1958, 1959.

CASSIODORUS, *Institutiones*, ed. GABETII (PL, 70), cc. 1105-1150.

CICERO, *De diuinatione*, ed. FALCONER (LCL), London-Cambridge, MA, repr. 1964.

—, *De finibus*, ed. RACKHAM (LCL), London-Cambridge, MA, repr. 1967.

—, *Tusculanae*, ed. KING (LCL), London-Cambridge, MA, repr. 1966.

CLEMENT OF ALEXANDRIA, *Excerpta e Theodoto*, ed. STÄHLIN (GCS, 17/2), Berlin, 1970, pp. 105-133.

—, *Qui diues saluetur*, ed. STÄHLIN – FRÜCHTEL – TREU (GCS, 17/2), Berlin, 1970, pp. 161-191.

—, *Paedagogus*, Book 1, ed. MARROU – HARL (SC, 70); Book 2, ed. MONDÉSERT – MARROU (SC, 108); Book 3, ed. MONDÉSERT – MATRAY – MARROU (SC, 158), Paris, 1960, 1965, 1970.

—, *Protrepticus*, ed. MONDÉSERT – PLASSART (SC, 2), 2nd ed., Paris, 1976.

—, *Stromata*, Book 1, ed. MONDÉSERT – CASTER (SC, 30); Book 2, ed. MONDÉSERT – CAMELOT (SC, 38); Book 4, ed. VAN DEN HOEK (SC, 463);

Book 5, ed. LE BOULLUEC – VOULET (SC, 278-279), Paris, 1951, 1954, 2001, 1981; Books 7-8, ed. STÄHLIN – FRÜCHTEL – TREU (GCS, 17/2), Berlin, 1970, pp. 3-102.

CLEMENT OF ROME, *Epistula ad Corinthios*, ed. JAUBERT (SC, 167), Paris, 1971.

Codex canonum ecclesiasticorum, ed. BALLERINI (PL, 56), cc. 359-746.

Concilia Africae A. 345–A. 525, ed. MUNIER (CCL, 149), Turnhout, 1974.

Concilia Galliae A. 314–A. 506, ed. MUNIER (CCL, 148), Turnhout, 1963.

Concilia Galliae A. 511–A. 695, ed. DE CLERCQ (CCL, 148A), Turnhout, 1963.

CYPRIAN, *Ad Demetrianum*, ed. HARTEL (CSEL, 3/1), Vienna, 1868, pp. 349-370.

—, *Ad Donatum*, ed. HARTEL (CSEL, 3/1), Vienna, 1868, pp. 3-16.

—, *Ad Quirinum (Testimoniorum l. iii)*, ed. SIMONETTI (CCL, 3A), Turnhout, 1976, pp. 3-13.

—, *De bono patientiae*, ed. HARTEL (CSEL, 3/1), Vienna, 1868, pp. 395-415.

—, *De catholicae ecclesiae unitate*, ed. BÉVENOT (CCL, 3), Turnhout, 1972, pp. 207-233.

—, *De dominica oratione*, ed. MORESCHINI (CCL, 3A), Turnhout, 1976, pp. 90-113.

—, *De habitu uirginum*, ed. HARTEL (CSEL, 3/1), Vienna, 1868, pp. 185-205.

—, *De mortalitate*, ed. HARTEL (CSEL, 3/1), Vienna, 1868, pp. 295-314.

—, *De opere et eleemosynis*, ed. HARTEL (CSEL, 3/1), Vienna, 1868, pp. 371-394.

—, *Epistulae*, ed. DIERCKS (CCL, 3B-C), Turnhout, 1994 and 1996.

CYRIL OF ALEXANDRIA, *Explanatio in epistulam ad Romanos*, ed. AUBERT (PG, 74), cc. 773-856.

EPICTETUS, *Diatribae*, ed. OLDFATHER (LCL), Vols. I-II, London-Cambridge, MA, repr. 1967 and 1966.

Expositio fidei catholicae, ed. MONACHI CASINENSES (PLS, 1), cc. 1683-1685.

EUCHERIUS, *De laude heremi* (PL, 50), cc. 701-712.

EUSEBIUS OF CAESAREA, *Demonstratio euangelica*, ed. HEIKEL (GCS, 23), Lipsia, 1913.

EVAGRIUS PONTICUS, *Ad monachos*, ed. GREßMANN (TU, 39), Lipsia, 1913, pp. 153-165.

—, *De malignis cogitationibus* (PG, 40), cc. 1237-1244.

—, *De octo uitiosis cogitationibus* (PG, 40), cc. 1272,1276.

—, *Gnosticus*, ed. A. and C. GUILLAUMONT (SC, 356), Paris, 1989.

—, *Kephalaia gnostica*, ed. GUILLAUMONT (PO, 28), pp. 15-263.

—, *Practicus*, ed. A. and C. GUILLAUMONT (SC, 170-171), Paris, 1971.

—, *Sermo siue dogmatica epistula de sanctissima Trinitate* (Ps.-BASIL, *Epistula 8*), in Y. COURTONNE (ed.), *S. Basile, Lettres*, T. I, Paris, 1957, pp. 22-37.

EVODIUS, *Epistula ad abbatem Valentinum*, ed. MORIN (PLS, 2), cc. 332-334.

FAUSTUS OF RIEZ, *De gratia*, ed. ENGELBRECHT (CSEL, 21), Vienna, 1891, pp. 3-96.

FULGENTIUS OF RUSPE, *Ad Monimum*, ed. FRAIPONT (CCL, 91), Turnhout, 1968, pp. 1-64.

—, *De ueritate praedestinationis ad Ioannem presbyterum et Venerium diaconum*, ed. FRAIPONT (CCL, 91), Turnhout, 1968, pp. 458-548.

GENNADIUS, *De uiris inlustribus*, ed. RICHARDSON (TU, 14), Lipsia, 1896.

GREGORY OF NAZIANZUS, *In laudem funebrem s. Basilii (Oratio 43)*, ed. BERNARDI (SC, 384), Paris, 1993.

—, *Orationes* 1-3, ed. BERNARDI (SC, 247); *Orationes* 32-37, ed. MORESCHINI (SC 318); *Orationes* 38-41, ed. GALLEY – MORESCHINI (SC, 358), Paris, 1978, 1985, 1990.

GREGORY OF NYSSA, *Antirrheticus aduersus Apolinarium*, ed. MÜLLER (Gregorii Nysseni opera, 3/1, pp. 131-233), Leiden, 1958.

—, *Contra Eunomium*, ed. JAEGER (Gregorii Nysseni opera, 1-2), Leiden, 2nd ed., 1960.

—, *Contra fatum*, ed. MCDONOUGH (Gregorii Nysseni opera, 3/2), Leiden, 1987, pp. 29-63.

—, *De beatitudinibus*, ed. CALLAHAN (Gregorii Nysseni opera, 7/2), Leiden-New York-Cologne, 1992, pp. 75-170.

—, *De instituto christiano*, ed. JAEGER (Gregorii Nysseni opera, 8/1), Leiden, 1952.

—, *De opificio hominis*, ed. FORBES (*S.P.N. Gregorii Nysseni, Basilii M. fratris*), T. I, Burntisland, 1855, pp. 96-319.

—, *De oratione dominica*, ed. CALLAHAN (Gregorii Nysseni opera, 7/2), Leiden, 1992, pp. 5-74.

—, *De perfectione*, ed. JAEGER (Gregorii Nysseni opera, 8/1), Leiden, 1952, pp. 173-214.

—, *De uirginitate*, ed. AUBINEAU (SC, 119), Paris, 1966.

—, *De uita Moysis*, ed. DANIÉLOU (SC, 1bis), Paris, 3rd ed. revised and corrected, 2000.

—, *Dialogus de anima et resurrectione* (PG, 46), cc. 12-160.

—, *In Canticum canticorum homiliae*, ed. LANGERBECK (Gregorii Nysseni opera, 6), Leiden, 1960.

—, *In inscriptione Psalmorum*, ed. MCDONOUGH (Gregorii Nysseni opera, 5), Leiden, 1962, pp. 24-175.

—, *Oratio catechetica*, ed. MÜHLENBERG (Gregorii Nysseni opera, 3/4), Leiden-New York-Cologne, 1996.

HILARY OF ARLES, *Sermo de uita S. Honorati Arelatensis episcopi*, ed. VALENTIN (SC, 235), Paris, 1977.

HILARY OF POITIERS, *Tractatus super psalmos*, ed. MILHAU (SC, 344 and 347), Paris, 1988.

HILARY (of Provence), *Epistula* 226 [among the Augustinian letters] (CSEL, 57), pp. 468-481.

HERODOTUS, *Historiae*, ed. GODLEY (LCL), London-Cambridge, MA, repr. 1961.

HINCMARUS OF REIMS, *De praedestinatione Dei et libero arbitrio*, iuxta editionem SIRMONDIANAM (PL, 125), cc. 65-474.

Historia Monachorum and *Historia Lausiaca*, ed. REITZENSTEIN, Göttingen, 1916.

HOMERUS, *Iliad*, ed. GOOLD (LCL), London-Cambridge, MA, repr. 1999.

HONORATUS OF MARSEILLES, *Vita S. Hilarii Arelatensis*, ed. JACOB (SC, 404), Paris, 1995.

HONORIUS AUGUSTUS, *Sacrum Rescriptum* (PL, 45), cc. 1726-1728.

—, *Epistula ad Aurelium* [Ep. 201 among the Augustinian letters] (CSEL, 57), pp. 296-299.

IANUARIANUS, *Epistula ad abbatem Valentinum* ed. MORIN (PLS, 2), cc. 335-341.

IRENAEUS, *Aduersus haereses*, Books 1-3, ed. ROUSSEAU – DOUTRELEAU (SC, 263-264; 293-294; 210-211); Book 4, ed. ROUSSEAU et al. (SC, 100*-

100**); Book 5, ed. Rousseau – Doutreleau – Mercier (SC, 152-153), Paris, 1979, 1982, 1974, 1965, 1969.

—, *Demonstratio praedicationis apostolicae (Epideixis)*, ed. Rousseau (SC, 406), Paris, 1995.

Jerome, *Aduersus Iouinianum*, ed. Martianaei *et al.* (PL, 23), cc. 221-352.

—, *Commentarii in Esaiam*, ed. Adriaen (CCL, 73A), Turnhout, 1963, pp. 465-799.

—, *Commentarii in iv epistulas Paulinas*, ed. Martianaei *et al.* (PL, 26), cc. 331-656.

—, *Contra Vigilantium*, ed. Martianaei *et al.* (PL, 23), cc. 353-368.

—, *Dialogi contra Pelagianos*, ed. Moreschini (CCL, 80), Turnhout, 1990.

—, *Epistulae*, ed. Hilberg (CSEL, 54-56), Vienna, 1910, 1912, 1918.

John Chrysostom, *Ad Demetrium de compunctione*, ed. de Montfaucon (PG, 47), cc. 393-409.

—, *De mutatione nominum*, ed. de Montfaucon (PG, 51), cc. 113-156.

—, *De uerbis apostolis: Habentes autem eumdem spiritum*, ed. de Montfaucon (PG, 51), cc. 271-302.

—, *De uirginitate*, ed. Musurillo – Grillet (SC, 125), Paris, 1966.

—, *Homilia habita postquam presbyter Gothus*, ed. de Montfaucon (PG, 63), cc. 499-510.

—, *Homiliae in Oziam*, ed. Dumortier (SC, 277), Paris, 1981.

—, *In epistulam ad Ephesios argumentum et homiliae*, ed. de Montfaucon (PG, 62), cc. 9-176.

—, *In epistulam ad Hebraeos argumentum et homiliae*, ed. de Montfaucon (PG, 63), cc. 9-236.

—, *In epistulam ad Philippenses*, ed. de Montfaucon (PG, 62), cc. 177-298.

—, *In epistulam ad Romanos homiliae*, ed. de Montfaucon (PG, 60), cc. 391-682.

—, *In epistulam II ad Corinthios argumentum et homiliae*, ed. de Montfaucon (PG, 61), cc. 381-610.

—, *In Genesim homiliae*, ed. de Montfaucon (PG, 54), cc. 385-580.

—, *In Iohannem homiliae*, ed. de Montfaucon (PG, 59), cc. 23-482.

—, *In Matthaeum homiliae*, ed. de Montfaucon (PG, 57).

—, *Quod regulares feminae uiris cohabitare non debeant*, ed. Dumortier (Les Belles Lettres), Paris, 1955, pp. 95-137.

John of Damascus, *De haeresibus*, ed. Lequien (PG, 94), cc. 677-780.

—, *Dialogus contra Manichaeos*, ed. Lequien (PG, 94), cc. 1505-1584.

—, *Expositio fidei*, ed. Kotter (PTS, 12), Berlin, 1973.

Julian of Aeclanum, *Ad Turbantium*, ed. De Coninck (CCL, 88), pp. 340-396.

—, *Expositio libri Iob. Tractatus Prophetarum Osee. Iohel et Amos. Accedunt operum deperditorum fragmenta post Albertum Bruckner denuo collecta aucta ordinata*, ed. De Coninck, auxiliante M.J. D'Hont (CCL, 88), Turnhout, 1977.

Julian Pomerius, *De uita contemplativa*, ed. Marsi (PL, 59), cc. 415-520.

Justin, *Apologia*, ed. Marani (PG, 6), cc. 328-470.

—, *Dialogus cum Tryphone Iudaeo*, ed. Marani (PG, 6), cc. 472-800.

Leo the Great, *Epistulae*, ed. Ballerini (PL, 54), cc. 593-1218.

Manichaica, Codex Manichaicus Coloniensis, in A. HEINRICHS – L. KOENEN (eds.), *Der Kölner Mani-Kodex (P. Colon. inv. nr. 4780)*, in *ZPE* 19 (1975) 1-85.

—, *Kephalaia*, Bd. I/1, ed. BÖHLIG – POLOTSKY (Manichäische Handschriften der Staatlichen Museen Berlin, 1), Stuttgart, 1940.

—, *Manichaean Psalm-Book. Part II*, ed. ALLBERRY, with a contribution of IBSCHER (Manichaean Manuscripts in the Chester Beatty Collection, 2), Stuttgart, 1938.

—, *Turfanfragment* M 2, in F.C. ANDREAS – W.B. HENNING (eds.), *Mitteliranische Manichaica aus Chinesisch-Turkestan* III (SPAW.PH, 2), Berlin, 1934; *Turfanfragment* M 17, in F.W. MÜLLER (ed.), *Handschriften-Reste in Estrangelo-Schrift aus Turfan, Chinesich-Turkestan* II (SPAW.PH, 2), Berlin, 1904.

MARCIANUS (PS.-NYLUS), *Tractatus moralis et multifarius*, ed. ALLATII (PG, 79), cc. 1280-1285.

MARIUS MERCATOR, *Commonitorium super nomine Caelestii*, ed. SCHWARTZ (ACO, 1/5), Berlin and Lipsia, 1924-1926, pp. 65-70.

—, *Commonitorium aduersum haeresim Pelagii et Caelestii*, ed. SCHWARTZ (ACO, 1/5), Berlin – Lipsia, 1924-1926, pp. 5-23.

—, *Nestorii capitula a Cyrillo excerpta et a Mario Mercatore translata*, ed. SCHWARTZ (ACO, 1/5), Berlin and Lipsia, 1924-1926, pp. 55-60.

METHODIUS OF OLYMPUS, *Conuiuium decem uirginum*, ed. MUSURILLO – DEBIDOUR (SC, 95), Paris, 1963.

—, *De libero arbitrio*, ed. VAILLANT (PO, 22), pp. 726-833.

MINUCIUS FELIX, *Octauius*, ed. HALM (CSEL, 2), Vienna, 1867, pp. 3-56.

OPTATUS OF MILEVI, *Contra Parmenianum Donatistam*, ed. ZIWSA (CSEL, 26), Vienna, 1893.

ORIGEN, *Commentarii in epistulam ad Romanos*, ed. HEITHER (FC, Bd. 2,1-6), Berlin, 1991-1996.

—, *Commentarii in Iohannem*, ed. BLANC, Books 1-5 (SC, 120); Books 6-9 (SC, 157); Books 13 (SC, 222); Books 19-20 (SC, 290), Paris, 1966, 1970, 1975, 1982.

—, *Contra Celsum*, ed. BORRET, Books 1-2 (SC, 132); Books 3-4 (SC, 136); Books 5-6 (SC, 147); Books 7-8 (SC, 150), Paris, 1967-1969.

—, *De oratione*, ed. KOETSCHAU (GCS, 3), Lipsia, 1899, pp. 297-403.

—, *De principiis*, ed. CROUZEL – SIMONETTI, Books 1-2 (SC, 252); Books 3-4 (SC, 268); Paris, 1978, 1980.

—, *Fragmenta in diuersos Psalmos*, ed. DELARUE (PG, 12), cc. 1085-1320, 1409-1686.

—, *In Exodum homiliae*, ed. BORRET (SC, 321), Paris, 1985.

—, *In Iesu Naue homiliae*, ed. JAUBERT (SC, 71), Paris, 1960.

—, *In librum Iudicum homiliae*, ed. MESSIÉ – NEYRAND – BORRET (SC, 389), Paris, 1993.

—, *In Lucam homiliae*, ed. PÉRICHON (SC, 87), Paris, 1962.

—, *Philocalia* 21-27 (On Free Will), ed. JUNOD (SC, 226), Paris, 1976.

OROSIUS, *Historiarum aduersum paganos*, ed. ZANGEMEISTER (CSEL, 5), Vienna, 1882, pp. 1-600.

OVIDIUS, *Metamorphoses*, ed. MILLER (LCL), T. II, London-Cambridge, Ma, repr. 1964.

PAULINUS OF NOLA, *Carmina*, ed. HARTEL (CSEL, 30), Vienna, 1894, pp. 1-338.
—, *Epistulae*, ed. HARTEL (CSEL, 29), Vienna, 1894, pp. 1-425.
PELAGIUS, *De possibilitate non peccandi*, ed. HAMMAN (PLS, 1), cc. 1457-1464.
—, *De diuina lege*, ed. MARTIANAEI (PL, 30), cc. 105-116.
—, *Epistula ad adolescentem*, ed. HAMMAN (PLS, 1), cc. 1375-1380.
—, *Epistula ad Demetriadem*, ed. MARTIANAEI (PL, 30), cc. 15-45.
—, *Expositiones xiii epistularum Pauli*, ed. HAMMAN (PLS, 1), cc. 1110-1374.
(Ps.)-PELAGIUS, *De induratione cordis Pharaonis*, ed. HAMMAN (PLS, 1), cc. 1506-1539.
PHILO OF ALEXANDRIA, *De praemiis et poenis*, ed. BECKAERT (Les Œuvres de Philo d'Alexandrie, 27), Paris, 1961.
—, *De sacrificiis Abelis et Caini*, ed. MÉASSON (Les Œuvres de Philon d'Alexandrie, 4), Paris, 1966.
—, *De somniis*, ed. SAVINEL (Les Œuvres de Philo d'Alexandrie, 19), Paris, 1962.
—, *Quod Deus sit immutabilis*, ed. MOSÈS (Les Œuvres de Philo d'Alexandrie, 7-8), Paris, 1963, pp. 58-151.
PHILOXENUS OF MABBUG, *Homiliae*, ed. LEMOINE (SC, 44), Paris, 1956.
PHOTIUS, *Myriobiblon siue Bibliotheca*, ed. WOLFII *et al.* (PG, 103).
PLATO, *Gorgias*, ed. BURNET (LCL/Platonis opera, T. III), Oxford, repr. 1968.
—, *Leges*, ed. BURNET (LCL/Platonis opera, T. V), Oxford, repr. 1967.
—, *Phaedo*, ed. BURNET (LCL/Platonis opera, T. I), Oxford, repr. 1967.
—, *Phaedrus*, ed. BURNET (LCL/Platonis opera, T. II), Oxford, repr. 1967.
—, *Politicus*, ed. DUKE *et al.* (LCL/Platonis opera, T. I), Oxford, repr. 1995.
—, *ResPublica*, ed. BURNET (LCL/Platonis opera, T. IV), Oxford, repr. 1968.
—, *Theaetetus*, ed. DUKE *et al.* (LCL/Platonis opera, T. I), Oxford, repr. 1995.
—, *Timaeus*, ed. BURNET (LCL/Platonis opera, T. IV), Oxford, repr. 1968.
PLINIUS SECUNDUS, *Historia naturalis*, ed. K. MAYHOFF (BSGRT), Lipsia, 1875-1906.
PROSPER OF AQUITAINE, *De gratia Dei et libero arbitrio contra Collatorem* (PL, 51), cc. 213-276.
—, *De uocatione omnium gentium* (PL, 51), cc. 647-722.
—, *Epistula* 225 [among the Augustinian letters] (CSEL, 57), pp. 454-468.
—, *Epistula ad Rufinum [De gratia et libero arbitrio]* (PL, 51), cc. 77-90.
—, *Epitoma Chronicorum* (PL, 51), cc. 535-606.
—, Περὶ ἀχαρίστων sive *De ingratis* (PL, 51), cc. 91-148.
—, *Poema coniugis ad uxorem*, ed. HARTEL (CSEL, 30), Vienna, 1894, pp. 344-348.
—, *Pro Augustino responsiones ad capitula obiectionum Gallorum calumni-antium* (PL, 51), cc. 155-174.
—, *Pro Augustino responsiones ad capitula obiectionum Vincentianarum* (PL, 51), cc. 177-186.
—, *Pro Augustino responsiones ad excerpta Genuensium* (PL, 51), cc. 187-202.
PS.-MACARIUS/SYMEON, *Homiliae spiritales [Collectio III]*, ed. DESPREZ (SC, 275), Paris, 1980.
—, *Sermones et epistulae (Reden und Briefe. Die Sammlung I des Vaticanus Graecus 694 B)*, ed. BERTHOLD (GCS, 55,1-2), Berlin, 1973.
Regulae SS. Patrum, ed. DE VOGÜÉ (SC, 297-298), Paris, 1982.
REMIGIUS OF LYON, *De tenenda immobiliter Scripturae ueritate* (PL, 121), cc. 1083-1134.

RUTILIUS NAMATIANUS, *De reditu suo siue Iter Gallicum*, ed. DOBLHOFER, Heidelberg, 1972.
SALVIAN, *De gubernatione Dei*, ed. LAGARRIGUE (SC, 220), Paris, 1975.
SENECA, *Ad Lucilium epistulae morales*, ed. GUMMERE (LCL), T. III, London-Cambridge, MA, repr. 1962.
—, *De tranquillitate animi*, ed. BASORE (LCL), London-Cambridge, MA, repr. 1965.
Sermo in Sanctum Pascha [HIPPOLYTUS/*Spuria*], ed. NAUTIN (SC, 27), Paris, 1950.
SIDONIUS APOLLINARIS, *Carmina*, ed. MANSI (PL, 58), cc. 639-748.
—, *Epistulae*, ed. MANSI (PL, 58), cc. 443-640.
SOCRATES, *Historia ecclesiastica*, ed. VALESIUS, cuius editionem criticis obser- vationibus locupletavit G. READING (PG, 67), cc. 29-841.
Stoicorum Veterum Fragmenta, ed. ARNIM, 4 Vols., Lipsia, 1921, 1923-1924.
STRABO, *Geographica*, ed. MEINEKE (BSGRT), Lipsia, 1904-1909.
SULPICIUS SEVERUS, *Epistulae*, ed. FONTAINE (SC, 133), Paris, 1967, pp. 316-344.
—, *Vita Martini*, ed. FONTAINE (SC, 133), Paris, 1967, pp. 248-316.
SVETONIUS, *Tiberius*, ed. ROLFE (LCL), T. I, London-Cambridge, MA, repr. 1979.
TERTULLIAN, *Ad martyras*, ed. DEKKERS (CCL, 1), Turnhout, 1954, pp. 1-8.
—, *Aduersus Marcionem*, ed. BRAUN (SC, 365, 368-369), Paris, 1990/1994.
—, *Apologeticum*, ed. DEKKERS (CCL, 1), Turnhout, 1954, pp. 77-171.
—, *De anima*, ed. WASZINK, Amsterdam, 1947.
—, *De anima*, ed. GERLO (CCL, 2), Turnhout, 1954, pp. 781-869.
—, *De baptismo*, ed. BORLEFFS (CCL, 1), Turnhout, 1954, pp. 277-295.
—, *De fuga in persecutione*, ed. THIERRY (CCL, 2), Turnhout, 1954, pp. 1135-1155.
—, *De uirginibus uelandis*, ed. DEKKERS (CCL, 2), Turnhout, 1954, pp. 1207-1226.
VALENTINUS, *Epistula* 216 [among the Augustinian letters] (CSEL, 57), pp. 396-402.
VETTIUS VALENS, *Anthologiarum libri novem*, ed. PINGREE (BSGRT), Lipsia, 1986.
VINCENT OF LÉRINS, *Commonitorium*, ed. DEMEULENAERE (CCL, 64), Turnhout, 1985, pp. 147-195.
—, *Excerpta [e S. Augustino]*, ed. DEMEULENAERE (CCL, 64), Turnhout, 1985, pp. 199-231.
ZOSIMUS, *Epistula* 45 *(Magnum pondus)*, ed. GUENTHER (CSEL, 35/1), Vienna, 1895, pp. 99-103.
—, *Epistula* 46 *(Postquam a nobis)*, ed. GUENTHER (CSEL, 35/1), Vienna, 1895, pp. 103-108.

ANCIENT WORKS, WITH TRANSLATION, INTRODUCTION, COMMENTARY WE HAVE REFERRED TO IN THE TEXT

Apophthegmata Patrum The Sayings of the Desert Fathers. The Alphabetical Collection, ed. B. WARD, London-Oxford-Kalamazoo, MI, 1975.
ATHANASIUS, *Lettres festales et pastorales en copte*, ed. L.-TH. LEFORT (CSCO, 151), Louvain, 1955.

—, *Select Writings and Letters of Athanasius, Bishop of Alexandria*, ed. A. ROBERTSON (NPNF, 2nd ser., 4), Edinburgh, 1897, repr. Edinburgh-Grand Rapids, MI, 1991.

—, *The Life of Saint Anthony*, ed. R.T. MEYER (ACW, 10), Westminster, MD, 1950.

CASSIAN, *Conferences*, ed. C. LUIBHEID, New York-Mahwah, 1985.

—, *The Conferences*, ed. G. RAMSEY (Ancient Christian Writers, 57), New York-Mahwah, 1997.

—, *The Monastic Institutes consisting of On the Training of a Monk and The Eight Deadly Sins in Twelve Books*, ed. J. BERTRAM, Oxford, 1999.

—, *Traité de l'incarnation contre Nestorius*, ed. M.-A. VANNIER, Paris, 1999.

Early Monastic Rules. The Rules of the Fathers and the Regula Orientalis, ed. V. FRANKLIN – I. HAVENER – J.A. FRANCIS, Collegeville, MN, 1982.

EVAGRIUS PONTICUS, *Briefe aus der Wüste* (Sophia, 24), ed. G. BUNGE, Trier, 1986.

—, *Praktikos oder der Mönch. Hundert Kapitel über das geistliche Leben*, ed. G. BUNGE, Köln, 1989.

GREGORY OF NYSSA, *Saint Gregory of Nyssa. Ascetical Works*, ed. V. WOODS-CALLAHAN [FaCh, 58], Washington, DC, 1967.

—, *The Great Catechism*, ed. W. MOORE (NPNF, 2nd ser., 5), Edinburgh, 1892, repr. Edinburgh-Grand Rapids, MI, 1994, pp. 471-509.

Historia Lausiaca. The Lausiac History of Palladius, ed. C. BUTLER (TaS, 6/1-2), Cambridge, 1898-1904.

JOHN CHRYSOSTOM, *The Homilies of St. John Chrysostom on the Epistle of St. Paul the Apostle to the Romans*, ed. J.B. MORRIS – W.H. SIMCOX (NPNF, first ser., 11), n.p.,n.d., repr. Grand Rapids, MI, 1979, pp. 335-564.

ORIGEN, *Commentary on the Gospel according to John. Books 1-10*, ed. R.E. HEINE (FaCh, 80), Washington, DC, 1989.

—, *Contra Celsum*, ed. H. CHADWICK, Cambridge, 1953.

—, *I principi*, ed. M. SIMONETTI, Turin, 1968.

PSEUDO-MACARIUS, *Reden und Briefe*, ed. K. FITSCHEN (BGrL, 52), Stuttgart, 2000.

VINCENT OF LÉRINS, *Commonitorio-estratti. Tradizione e novità nel cristianesimo*, ed. L. LONGOBARDO, Rome, 1994.

II. MODERN LITERATURE

ABEL, F.-M., *Le* Praedestinatus *et le pélagianisme*, in *RTAM* 35 (1968) 5-25.

ADAM, A., *Das Fortwirken des Manichäismus bei Augustin*, in *ZKG* 69 (1958) 1-25.

—, *Der manichäische Ursprung der Lehre von den zwei Reichen bei Augustin* (1952), in ID., *Sprache und Dogma. Untersuchungen zu Grundproblemen der Kirchengeschichte*, Gütersloh, 1969, pp. 133-140.

—, *Lehrbuch der Dogmengeschichte*, Bd. I: *Die Zeit der Alten Kirche*, 5th ed., Gütersloh, 1985.

ALEXANDER, J.S., *Lérins*, in *TRE* 21 (1991) 10-16.

ALFARIC, P., *L'évolution intellectuelle de saint Augustin*. T. I: *Du Manichéisme au Néoplatonisme*, Paris, 1918.

ALSZEGHY, Z., *Fuite du monde*, in *DSp* 5 (1964) 1593-1599.

AMAND, D., *Fatalisme et liberté dans l'antiquité grecque. Recherches sur la survivance de l'argumentation morale antifataliste de Carnéade chez les philosophes grecs et les théologiens chrétiens des quatre premiers siècles* (RTHP, 3ème série, 19), Louvain, 1945.

AMANN, É., *Lucidus*, in *DTC* 9 (1926) 1020-1024.

—, *Praedestinatus*, in *DTC* 12/2 (1935) 2775-2780.

—, *Semi-Pélagiens*, in *DTC* 14/2 (1941) 1796-1850.

AMARGIER, P., *Marseille*, in *Cath* 8 (1979) 714-722.

ANATOLIOS, K., *Athanasius. The coherence of his thought*, London-New York, 1998.

ARBESMANN, R., *The concept of* Christus medicus *in St. Augustine*, in *Trad* 10 (1954) 1-28.

ARMAS, G., *Tergiversaciones en la soteriologìa agustiniana*, in *Augustinus* 6 (1961) 499-512.

ARNOLD-DÖBEN, V., *Die Bildersprache des Manichäismus* (AMRG,3), Cologne, 1978.

ASMUSSEN, J.P., *Die Gnosis*. Bd. III: *Der Manichäismus*, Zürich-München, 1980.

AUBERT, R., *Honorat (Saint) de Lérins*, in *DHGE* 24 (1993) 1029.

—, *Honorat (Saint), évêque d'Arles*, in *DHGE* 24 (1993) 1027-1028.

AUDOLLENT, A., *Afrique*, in *DHGE* 1 (1912) 705-861.

AUER, J., *Militia Christi*, in *DSp* 10 (1980) 1210-1123.

BABCOCK, W.S., *Augustine and Paul: the Case of Romans IX*, in *StPatr* 16 (TU, 129), Berlin, 1985, pp. 473-479.

—, *Augustine's interpretation of Romans (A.D. 394-396)*, in *AugSt* 10 (1979) 55-74.

—, *Grace, Freedom and Justice: Augustine and the Christian Tradition*, in *PerkJ* 27 (1973) 1-15.

—, *Introduction*, in ID. (ed.), *Paul and the Legacies of Paul*, Dallas, 1990, xiii-xxviii.

—, *Sin and Punishment. The Early Augustine on Evil*, in J.T. LIENHARD – E.C. MULLER – R.J. TESKE (eds.), *Augustine*. Presbyter Factus Sum (CollAug, 2), New York, 1993, pp. 235-248.

BAILLEUX, E., *La liberté augustinienne et la grâce*, in *MSR* 19 (1962) 30-48.

BALL, J., *Les développements de la doctrine de la liberté chez saint Augustin*, in *RPL* 55 (1957) 404-413.

BAMMEL, C.P., *Augustine, Origen and the Exegesis of St. Paul*, in *Aug* 32 (1992) 341-368.

BARDY, G., *Cassien (Jean)*, in *Cath* 2 (1949) 616-617.

—, *Prosper d'Aquitaine (saint)*, in *DTC* 13 (1936) 846-850.

—, *Saint Augustin. L'homme et l'oeuvre*, 6th ed., Paris, 1946.

—, *Vincent de Lérins*, in *DTC* 15/2 (1950) 3045-3055.

BARTELINK, G., *Die Beeinflussung Augustins durch die griechischen Patres*, in J. DEN BOEFT – J. VAN OORT (eds.), *Augustiniana Traiectina. Communications présentées au Colloque International d'Utrecht 13-14 novembre 1986*, Paris, 1987, pp. 9-24.

BASTIAENSEN, A., *Les prédécesseurs latins chrétiens*, in J. DEN BOEFT –J. VAN OORT (eds.), *Augustiniana Traiectina. Communications présentées au Colloque International d'Utrecht 13-14 novembre 1986*, Paris, 1987, pp. 25-57.

BATAILLE, G., *Castore*, in *BSS* 3 (1963) 941.

BAUCKHAM, R., *Scripture, Tradition and Reason. A study in the Criteria of Christian Doctrine, Essays in Honour of Richard P.C. Hanson*, Edinburgh, 1988.

BAUDRY, G.-H., *Libre arbitre*, in *Cath* 7 (1975) 707-710.

BAUMGARTNER, C., *La grâce du Christ*, Paris, 1963.

BAVAUD, G., *La doctrine de la prédestination et de la réprobation d'après saint Augustin et Calvin*, in *REAug* 5 (1959) 431-438.

BAVEL, T.J., VAN, *Correctio, corrigere*, in *AugL* 2 (1996) 22-27.

—, *Correptio, corripere*, in *AugL* 2 (1996) 35-39.

—, *Love*, in A.D. FITZGERALD (ed.), *Augustine through the Ages. An Encyclopedia*, Grand Rapids, MI-Cambridge, 1999, pp. 509-516.

BAVEL, T.J. VAN – BRUNING, B., *Die Einheit des "Totus Christus" bei Augustinus*, in C.P. MAYER – W. ECKERMANN (eds.), Scientia Augustiniana. *Festschrift P. Dr. theol. Dr. phil. Adolar Zumkeller OSA zum 60. Geburtstag* (Cass., 30), Würzburg, 1975, pp. 43-75.

BEATRICE, P.F., *Porphyrius*, in *TRE* 27 (1997) 54-59.

—, *Tradux Peccati. Alle fonti della dottrina agostiniana del peccato originale* (SPMed, 8), Milan, 1978.

BENJAMINS, H.S., *Eingeordnete Freiheit. Freiheit und Vorsehung bei Origenes*, Leiden, 1994.

—, *Origen's Concept of Free Will in Relationship to the Fight against Opposing Powers* (de Principiis III.2-3), in *StPatr* 26, Louvain, 1993, pp. 217-220.

BERNARD, R., *La prédestination du Christ total selon saint Augustin*, in *RechAug* 3 (1965) 1-58.

BERROUARD, M.F., *L'exégèse augustinienne de Rom. 7,7-25 entre 396 et 418*, in *RechAug* 16 (1981) 101-196.

BESSE, J.-M., *Le monachisme africain (du IVᵉ au VIᵉ siècle)*. Extrait de la *Revue du Monde Catholique*, Paris-Poitiers, 1900.

—, *Les moines de l'ancienne France. (Période Gallo-Romaine et Mérovingienne)* (AFM, 2), Paris, 1906.

BIANCHI, U., *Sur le dualisme de Mani*, in A. VAN TONGERLOO – S. GIVERSEN (eds.), Manichaica Selecta. *Studies presented to Professor Julien Ries on the occasion of his seventieth birthday* (Manichaean Studies, 1), Louvain, 1991, pp. 9-17.

BIARNE, J., *Moines et rigoristes en Occident*, in J.-M. MAYEUR et al. (eds.), *Histoire du Christianisme des origines à nos jours. T. II: Naissance d'une Chrétienté (250-430)*, Paris, 1995, pp. 747-768.

BLAISE, A., *Dictionnaire latin-français des auteurs chrétiens*, Turnhout, 1954.

BOCHET, I., *Saint Augustin et le désir de Dieu*, Paris, 1982.

BÖHLIG, A. (ed.) in collaboration with J.P. ASMUSSEN, *Die Gnosis*. Bd. III: *Der Manichäismus*, Zürich-Münich, 1980.

BOHLIN, T., *Die Theologie des Pelagius und ihre Genesis* (AUU, 9), Upsala, 1957.

BOK, N.W. DEN, *Freedom of the Will. A Systematic and Biographical Sounding of Augustine's Thoughts on Human Will*, in *Aug(L)* 44 (1994) 237-270.

BONNER, G., *Adam*, in *AugL* 1 (1986) 63-87.

—, *Augustine and Modern Research on Pelagianism* (The Saint Augustine Lecture Series, Villanova University 1970), Villanova, 1972.

—, *Augustine on Romans 5,12*, in *StEv* 5 (1968) 242-247.

—, *Caelestius*, in *AugL* 1 (1986-1994) 693-698.

—, *Les origines africaines de la doctrine augustinienne sur la chute et le peché originel*, in *Augustinus* 12 (1967) 97-116.

—, *Pelagianism Reconsidered*, in *StPatr* 27, Louvain, 1993, pp. 237-241.

—, *'Rufinus of Syria and African Pelagianism'*, in *AugSt* 1 (1970) 31-47.

—, *St Augustine of Hippo. Life and Controversies*, London, 1963, 2nd ed., Norwich, 1986.

—, *The Desire for God and the Need for Grace in Augustine's Theology*, in *Congresso Internazionale su S. Agostino nel XVI Centenario della Conversione, Roma, 15-20 settembre 1986*, Atti, Vol. I (SEAug, 24), Rome, 1987, pp. 203-215.

BOSSUET, J.B., *Traité sur le libre arbitre*, in *Œuvres complètes*, T. II (ed. MIGNE), Paris, 1856, cc. 715-756.

BOSTOCK, G., *The Influence of Origen on Pelagius and Western Monasticism*, in W.A. BIENERT – U. KÜHNEWEG (eds.), Origeniana Septima. *Origenes in den Auseinandersetzungen des 4. Jahrhunderts* (BETL, 137), Louvain, 1999, pp. 381-396.

BOUBLÍK, V., *La predestinazione. S. Paolo e S. Agostino* (CorLat, 3), Rome, 1961.

BOUILLARD, H., *Saint Thomas et le Semi-Pélagianisme*, in *BLE* 43 (1942) 181-209.

BOUMAN, J., *Augustinus. Lebensweg und Theologie. Glaubenskrise– Glaubensgewissheit im Christentum und im Islam*, Bd. I (TVG, 333), Giessen – Basel, 1987.

BOUYER, L., *La vie de S. Antoine. Essai sur la spiritualité du monachisme primitif* (SpOr, 22), Bégrolles en Mauges, 1977.

—, *The Spirituality of the New Testament and the Fathers* (A History of Christian Spirituality, 1), New York, 1982.

BOYD, W.J.P., *Origen and Pharaoh's Hardened Heart. A Study on Justification and Election in St. Paul and Origen*, in *StPatr* VII (TU, 92), Berlin, 1966, pp. 434-442.

BOYER, C., *Dieu pouvait-il créer l'homme dans l'état d'ignorance et de difficulté?* in *Greg* 11 (1930) 32-57.

—, *Jean Calvin et saint Augustin*, in *AugSt* 3 (1972) 15-34.

—, L'adiutorium sine quo non. *Sa nature et son importance dans la doctrine de saint Augustin*, in *DoC* 13 (1960) 5-18.

BRAEM, E., *Christus als model en genadebron van onze praedestinatie volgens Sint Augustinus*, in *Aug(L)* 4 (1954) 353-361.

BRAKKE, D., *Athanasius and the Politics of Asceticism*, Oxford, 1995.

BRARD, M.-B., *Lérins*, in *Cath* 7 (1975) 435-437.

BROGLIE, G. DE, *Pour une meilleure intelligence du "De correptione et gratia"*, in *AugMag*, T. III, Paris, 1955, pp. 317-337.

BROUETTE, E., *Honoratus*, in *LTK* 5 (1960) 472-473.

BROWN, P., *Asceticism: Pagan and Christian*, in A. CAMERON – P. GARNSEY (eds.), *The Cambridge Ancient History*, Vol. XIII: *The Late Empire, A.D. 337-425*, Cambridge, 1998, pp. 601-631.

—, *Augustine of Hippo. A Biography*, London, 1967.

—, *Pelagius and His Supporters: Aims and Environment*, in *JTS*, N.S. 19 (1968) 93-114.

—, *Religion and Society in the Age of St. Augustine*, London, 1972.

—, *The Making of Late Antiquity*, London, 1978.

BRUNING, B., Otium *and* negotium *within the one Church*, in *Aug(L)* 51 (2001) 105-149.

—, *De l'astrologie à la grâce*, in *Aug(L)* [*Mélanges T.J. van Bavel*, T. II] 41 (1991) 575-643.

BRUNNER, E., *Dogmatik*, Bd. I: *Die christliche Lehre von Gott*, Zurich, 1946.

BUCHER, T.G., *Zur formalen Logik bei Augustinus*, in *FZPT* 29 (1982) 3-45.

BUONAIUTI, E., *Manichaeism and Augustine's Idea of "massa perditionis"*, in *HTR* 20 (1927) 117-127.

BURNABY, J., Amor Dei. *A Study of the Religion of Saint Augustine*, London, 1938.

BURNS, J.P., *A Change in Augustine's Doctrine of Operative Grace in 418*, in *StPatr* 16/2 (TU,129), Berlin, 1985, pp. 491-496.

—, *Augustine's Role in the Imperial Action against Pelagius*, in *JTS* 30 (1979) 77-83.

—, *The Atmosphere of Election: Augustinianism as Common Sense*, in *JECS* 2 (1994) 325-339.

—, *The Development of Augustine's Doctrine of Operative Grace*, Paris, 1980.

—, *The Interpretation of Romans in the Pelagian Controversy*, in *AugSt* 10 (1979) 43-54.

BURTON-CHRISTIE, D., *The Word in the Desert. Scripture and the Quest for Holiness in Early Christian Monasticism* (OECS), New York-Oxford, 1993.

CALONNE, R., *Le libre arbitre selon le Traité des Principes d'Origène*, in *BLE* 89 (1988) 243-262.

CANÉVET, M., *Le 'De instituto christiano' est-il de Grégoire de Nysse?*, in *REG* 82 [1969] 404-423.

CAPPONI, F., *"Insuperabiliter" o "Inseparabiliter"?*, in *Latomus* 28 (1969) 681-684.

CAPPUYNS, M., *Cassien (Jean)*, in *DHGE* 11 (1949) 1319-1349.

—, *L'auteur du* De vocatione omnium gentium, in *RBen* 39 (1927) 198-226.

—, *Le premier représentant de l'augustinisme médiéval. Prosper d'Aquitaine*, in *RTAM* 1 (1929) 309-337.

CAREFOOTE, P.J., *Augustine, the Pelagians and the Papacy. An Examination of the Political and Theological Implications of Papal Involvement in the Pelagian Controversy* (unpublished doctoral dissertation, Faculty of Theology, K.U.Leuven), 2 Vols., Louvain, 1995.

CASEY, P., *Clement of Alexandria and the Beginnings of Christian Platonism*, in *HTR* 18 (1925) 39-101.

CASIDAY, A.M.C., *Cassian, Augustine, and* De Incarnatione, in *StPatr* 38, Louvain, 2001, pp. 41-47.

CAVALLIN, S., *Vitae Sanctorum Honorati et Hilarii Episcoporum Arelatensium* (SVSL, 40), Lund, 1952.

CAYRÉ, F., *La Prédestination dans Saint Augustin. Notes générales*, in *ATh(A)* 2 (1941) 42-63.

CHADWICK, H., *The Early Church*, London, 1967.

—, *The Sentences of Sextus: A Contribution to the History of Early Christian Ethics* (TaS, New Series, 5), Cambridge, 1959.

CHADWICK, N.K., *Poetry and Letters in Early Christian Gaul*, London, 1955.

CHADWICK, O., *Cassianus, Johannes*, in *TRE* 7 (1981) 650-657.
—, *Euladius of Arles*, in *JTS* 46 (1945) 200-205.
—, *Introduction*, in C. LUIBHEID (ed.), *John Cassian. Conferences*, New York–Mahwah, 1985.
—, *John Cassian. A Study in Primitive Monasticism*, 2nd ed., Cambridge, 1968.
—, *Western Asceticism. Selected Translations with Introductions and Notes* (LCC, 12), London, 1958.
CHARY, T., *Aggée-Zacharie-Malachie*, Paris, 1969.
CHÉNÉ, J., *La théologie de saint Augustin. Grâce et prédestination*, Le Puy–Lyon, [1962].
—, *Le Semipélagianisme du Midi de la Gaule d'après les lettres de Prosper d'Aquitaine et d'Hilaire à saint Augustin*, in *RSR* 43 (1955) 321-341.
—, *Les origines de la controverse semi-pélagienne*, in *ATA* 13 (1953) 56-109.
—, *Que signifiaient "initium fidei" et "affectus credulitatis" pour les Semi-pélagiens?*, in *RSR* 35 (1948) 566-588.
—, *Saint Augustin enseigne-t-il dans le "De Spiritu et littera" l'universalité de la volonté salvifique de Dieu?*, in *RSR* 47 (1959) 215-224.
—, *Sur un texte du "De dono perseverantiae" (Cap. XIX, n. 49)*, in *REAug* 6 (1960) 309-313.
CHITESCU, N., *Saint Jean Cassien était-il semi-pélagien?*, in G.D. DRAGAS (ed.), *AksumThyateira. A Festschrift for Archbishop Methodius of Thyateira and Great Britain*, London, 1985, pp. 579-589.
CHITTY, D.J., *The Desert a City*, Oxford, 1966.
CIPRIANI, N., *Un'altra traccia dell'Ambrosiaster in Agostino (De pecc. Mer. et rem. 2,36,58-59)*, in *Aug* 24 (1984) 515-525.
CLARK, E.A., *Asceticism*, in A.D. FITZGERALD (ed.), *Augustine through the Ages. An Encyclopedia*, Grand Rapids, MI-Cambridge, 1999, pp. 67-71.
—, *Asceticism, Pre-Augustine*, in A.D. FITZGERALD (ed.), *Augustine through the Ages. An Encyclopedia*, Grand Rapids, MI-Cambridge, 1999, pp. 71-76.
—, *Clement's use of Aristotle. The Aristotelian Contribution to Clement of Alexandria's Refutation of Gnosticism*, New York, 1977.
—, *From Origenism to Pelagianism: Elusive Issues in an Ancient Debate*, in *PSB* 12 (1991) 283-303.
—, *Origenist Controversy*, in A.D. FITZGERALD (ed.), *Augustine through the Ages. An Encyclopedia*, Grand Rapids, MI-Cambridge, 1999, pp. 605-607.
—, *The Origenist Controversy. The Cultural Construction of an Early Christian Debate*, Princeton, 1992.
CODINA, V., *El aspecto cristologico en la espiritualidad de Juan Casiano* (OCA, 175), Rome, 1966.
CODY, A., *Haggai, Zechariah, Malachi*, in R.E. BROWN – J.A. FITZMYER – R.E. MURPHY (eds.), *The New Jerome Biblical Commentary*, Englewood Cliffs, NJ, 1990, pp. 349-361.
COLISH, M.L., *The Stoic Tradition from Antiquity to the Early Middle Ages*. Vol. I: *Stoicism in Classical Latin Literature*; Vol. II: *Stoicism in Christian Latin Thought through the Sixth Century*, Leiden, 1990, second impression with addenda and corrigenda.
COLLIN, L., *Prosper d'Aquitaine*, in *Cath* 12 (1990) 38-39.
COLOMBAS, G.M., *Asceti e ascete*, in *DIP* 1 (1974) 917-926.
—, *El monacato primitivo*, 2 Vols. (BAC, 351 and 376), Madrid, 1974-1975.
CONZELMANN, H., art. χάρις, *D. Neues Testament*, in *TWNT* 9 (1969) 381-390.

COURCELLE, P., *Les Lettres grecques en Occident, de Macrobe à Cassiodore*, 2nd ed., Paris, 1948.
—, *Recherches sur les Confessions de saint Augustin*, 2nd ed., Paris, 1968.
COURTOIS, C., *L'évolution du monachisme en Gaule de St Martin à St Colomban*, in *Il Monachesimo nell'Alto Medioevo e la formazione della civiltà occidentale* (SSAM, 4), Spoleto, 1957, pp. 47-72
COUSIN, P., *Précis d'histoire monastique*, Tournai, 1956.
COYLE, J.K., *Healing and the 'Physician' in Manichaeism*, in J.K. COYLE – S.C. MUIR (eds.), *Healing in Religion and Society from Hippocrates to the Puritans. Selected Studies* (SRS, 43), New York, 1999.
—, *Mani, Manicheism*, in A.D. FITZGERALD (ed.), *Augustine through the Ages. An Encyclopedia*, Grand Rapids, MI-Cambridge, 1999, pp. 520-525.
—, *What Did Augustine Know about Manichaeism when he Wrote his Two Treatises* De moribus?, in J. VAN OORT – O. WERMELINGER – G. WURST (eds.), *Augustine and Manichaeism in the Latin West. Proceedings of the Fribourg-Utrecht Symposium of the International Association of Manichaean Studies* (NHMS, 49), Leiden-Boston-Cologne, 2001, pp. 43-56.
CRISTIANI, L., *Jean Cassien. La spiritualité du désert*, 2 Tomes, S. Wandrille, 1946.
CROUZEL, H., *Origène*, Paris, 1985.
—, *Origène, précurseur du monachisme*, in *Théologie de la vie monastique. Études sur la Tradition patristique* [Theol(P), 49], Paris, 1961, pp. 15-38.
—, *Theological Construction and Research: Origen on Free Will*, in B. DREWERY – R. BAUCKHAM (eds.), *Scripture, Tradition and Reason. A Study in the Criteria of Christian Doctrine. Essays in honour of Richard P.C. Hanson*, Edinburgh, 1988, pp. 239-265.
—, *Thélogie de l'image de Dieu chez Origène* (Théol[P], 34), Paris, 1956.

DALMAU, J.M., *"Praedestinatio, Electio" en el libro "De praedestinatione Sanctorum"*, in *AugMag*, T. I, Paris, 1955, pp. 127-136.
DAL TOSO, G., *La nozione di* proairesis *in Gregorio di Nissa. Analisi semiotico-linguistica e prospettive antropologiche* (Patrologia. Beiträge zum Studium der Kirchenväter, 5), Frankfurt am Main-Berlin-Bern-New York-Paris-Vienna, 1998.
DAMIAN, T., *Some Critical Considerations and New Arguments Reviewing the Problem of St. John Cassian's Birthplace*, in *OCP* 57 (1991) 257-280.
DANIÉLOU, J., *Orientations actuelles de la recherche sur Grégoire de Nysse*, Leiden, 1971.
—, *Platonisme et théologie mystique. Essai sur la doctrine spirituelle de saint Grégoire de Nysse* (Théol[P], 2), 2nd ed., Paris, 1954.
DANIÉLOU, J. – MARROU, H.I. (eds.), *The Christian Centuries*, Vol. I: *The First Six Hundred Years*, 2nd impression, London, 1978.
DASSMANN, E., *Ambrosius*, in *AugL* 1 (1986) 270-285.
—, *Ambrosius von Mailand*, in *TRE* 2 (1978) 362-386.
—, *Cyprian*, in *AugL* 2 (1996) 196-211.
—, *Die Frömmigkeit des Kirchenvaters Ambrosius von Mailand. Quellen und Entfaltung* (MBT, 29), Münster Westfalen, 1965.
—, *Hiob (Job)*, in *RAC* 15 (1989) 366-442.

—, «*Tam Ambrosius quam Cyprianus*» *(c. Iul. imp. 4,112). Augustins Helfer im pelagianischen Streit*, in D. PAPANDREOU – W.A. BIENERT – K. SCHÄFERDIEK (eds.), Oecumenica et Patristica. *Festschrift für Wilhelm Schneemelcher zum 75. Geburtstag*, Chambésy-Gerf, 1989.

DAWSON, D., *Figure, Allegory*, in A.D. FITZGERALD (ed.), *Augustine through the Ages. An Encyclopedia*, Grand Rapids, MI-Cambridge, 1999, pp. 365-368.

DECELLES, D., *Divine Prescience and Human Freedom in Augustine*, in *AugSt* 8 (1977) 151-160.

DECRET, F., *Aspects du manichéisme dans l'Afrique romaine. Les controverses de Fortunatus, Faustus et Felix avec saint Augustin*, Paris, 1970.

—, *Le manichéisme présentait-il en Afrique et à Rome des particularismes régionaux distinctifs?*, in *Aug* 34 (1994) 5-40.

DELAROCHE, B., *Saint Augustin lecteur et interprète de saint Paul dans le* De peccatorum meritis et remissione *(hiver 411-412)* (CEAug.SA, 146), Paris, 1996.

DEMARIA, S., *I capitoli LXIX e LXX dei Kephalaia copti manichei. Traduzione e commento* (Archeologia e Storia della Civiltà Egiziana e del Vicino Oriente Antico–Materiali e studi, 3), Imola/Bologna, 1998.

DESPREZ, V., *Les origines du monachisme occidental. I. Italie, Palestine, Gaule; II. Afrique et Espagne*, in *Lettre de Ligugé* n. 204 (1980) 6-18; n. 209 (1981) 9-31.

—, *Règles monastiques d'Occident*, Bégrolles-en-Mauges, 1980.

DEWART, J. MC W., *The Christology of the Pelagian Controversy*, in *StPatr* 17/3, Oxford, 1982, pp. 1221-1244.

DIEM, H., *Augustins Interesse in der Prädestinationslehre*, in *Theologische Aufsätze Karl Barth zum 50. Geburtstag*, München, 1936, pp. 362-381.

DIHLE, A., *Liberté et destin dans l'antiquité tardive*, in *RTP* 121 (1989) 129-147.

—, *The Theology of Will in Classical Antiquity*, Los Angeles, 1982.

DITTMANN, H., *Gnade. A. Nichtchristlich, II. Israelitisch-jüdisch*, in *RAC* 11 (1980) 333-351.

DJUTH, M., *Initium fidei*, in A.D. FITZGERALD (ed.), *Augustine through the Ages. An Encyclopedia*, Grand Rapids, MI-Cambridge, 1999, pp. 447-451.

—, *Royal Way*, in A.D. FITZGERALD (ed.), *Augustine through the Ages. An Encyclopedia*, Grand Rapids, MI-Cambridge, 1999, pp. 735-737.

—, *Stoicism and Augustine's Doctrine of Human Freedom after 396*, in J.C. SCHNAUBELT – F. VAN FLETEREN (eds.), *Augustine: Second Founder of the Faith* (CollAug, 1), New York-Bern-Frankfurt a. M.-Paris, 1990, pp. 387-401.

—, *The Hermeneutics of* De libero arbitrio III: *Are There Two Augustines?*, in *StPatr* 27, Louvain, 1993, pp. 281-289.

DÖRRIE, H. – DÖRRIES, H., *Erotapokriseis*, in *RAC* 6 (1966) 342-370.

DÖRRIES, H., *Die Theologie des Makarios/Symeon* (AGWG.PH, 3. Folge, 103), Göttingen, 1978.

DOIGNON, J., *Hilaire de Poitiers avant l'exil*, Paris, 1971.

DOREN, R. VAN, *Castor*, in *DHGE* 11 (1949) 1455-1456.

DOUCET, L., *L'exégèse augustinienne de I Tim. 2,4: "Dieu veut que tous les hommes soient sauvés"?*, in *BFCL* 73 (1984) 43-61.

DRECOLL, V.H., *Die Entstehung der Gnadenlehre Augustins* (BHT, 109), Tübingen, 1999.

DRIJVERS, H.J.W., *Conflict and Alliance in Manichaeism*, in H.G. KIPPENBERG (ed.), *Struggles of Gods*, Berlin-New York-Amsterdam, 1984.

DUFFY, S.J., *Anthropology*, in A.D. FITZGERALD (ed.), *Augustine through the Ages. An Encyclopedia*, Grand Rapids, MI-Cambridge, 1999, pp. 24-31.

—, *The Dynamics of Grace. Perspectives in Theological Anthropology* (New Theology Studies, 3), Collegeville, 1993.

DUNPHY, W., *Marius Mercator on Rufinus the Syrian. Was Schwartz mistaken?*, in *Aug* 32 (1992) 279-288.

DUCHESNE, L., *Fastes épiscopaux de l'ancienne Gaule*. T. I: *Provinces du Sud-Est*, 2nd ed., Paris, 1907.

—, *Histoire ancienne de l'Église*, T. III, 3rd ed., Paris, 1910.

—, *Le* Liber Pontificalis, T. I., Paris, 1955.

EIJK, P.J. VAN DER, *Origenes' Verteidigung des freien Willens*, in *VigChr* 42 (1988) 339-351.

ELM, S., *Virgins of God: the Making of Asceticism in Late Antiquity* (OCPM), Oxford, 1994.

EMERY, P.-Y., *Le Christ notre récompense: Grâce de Dieu et responsabilité de l'homme*, Neuchâtel, 1962.

ESTAL, J.-M. DEL, *Sobre los comienzos de la vida común entre las virgines de África*, in *CDios* 73 (1957) 335-360.

—, *Testimonio positivo de Petiliano sobre la inexistencia del monacato en África antes de S. Agustin*, in *StMon* 3 (1961) 123-136.

—, *Un cenobitismo preagustiniano en África?*, in *CDios* 72 (1956) 375-403 and 74 (1958) 161-195.

EVANS, G.R., *Augustine on Evil*, Cambridge, 1982.

—, *Neither a Pelagian nor a Manichee*, in *VigChr* 35 (1981) 232-244.

EVANS, R.F., *Pelagius: Inquiries and Reappraisals*, New York, 1968.

FARRELLY, M.J., *Predestination, Grace and Free Will*, Westminster, MD, 1964.

FASCHER, E., *Erwählung*, in *RAC* 6 (1966) 409-436.

FERRIER, F., *Prédestination*, in *Cath* 11 (1988) 764-781.

FITSCHEN, K., *Messalianismus und Antimessalianismus: ein Beispiel ostkirchlicher Ketzergeschichte* (FKDG, 71), Göttingen, 1998.

FITZMYER, J.A., *Romans. A New Translation with Introduction and Commentary*, New York, 1993.

FLETEREN, F. VAN, *Augustine's Principles of Biblical Exegesis,* De doctrina christiana *Aside: Miscellaneous Observations*, in *AugSt* 27 (1996) 107-128.

FLOËRI, F., *Le pape Zosime et la doctrine augustinienne du péché originel*, in *AugMag*, T. II, Paris, 1955, pp. 755-761.

FOLLIET, G., *Aux origines de l'ascétisme et du cenobitisme africain*, in *Saint Martin et son temps. Mémorial du XVIᵉ centenaire des débuts du monachisme en Gaule, 361-1961* (StAns, 46), Rome, 1961.

—, *Certus est numerus electorum: de Agustín a Tomás de Aquino*, in *Augustinus* 43 (1998) 215-227.

—, *«(Deus) omnia cooperatur in bonum»*, Rom. 8,28. *Les citations du verset chez Augustin*, in *SE* 37 (1997) 33-55.

—, *Le monachisme en Afrique de saint Augustin à saint Fulgence*, in *Il monachesimo occidentale dalle origini alla* Regula Magistri. *XXVI Incontro di studiosi dell'antichità cristiana, Roma, 8-10 maggio 1997* (SEAug, 62), Rome, 1998, pp. 291-315.

—, *"Massa damnata"*, *"Massa sanctorum" chez saint Augustin*, in *RevAg* 33 (1992) 95-109.

FONTAINE, J., *France. I. Antiquité chrétienne*, in *DSp* 5 (1964) 785-805.

—, *L'aristocratie occidentale devant le monachisme aux IVème et Vème siècles*, in *RSLR* 15 (1979) 28-53.

—, *L'ascétisme chrétien dans la litterature gallo-romaine d'Hilaire à Cassien*, in *Atti del Colloquio sulla Gallia Romana, Accademia Nazionale dei Lincei, Roma 10-11 maggio 1971*, Rome, 1973, pp. 87-115.

FONTAINE, J. – PIETRI, L., *Les grandes Églises missionaires: Hispanie, Gaule, Bretagne*, in J.-M. MAYEUR et al. (eds.), *Histoire du Christianisme*. T. II: *Naissance d'une Chrétienté (250-430)*, Paris, 1995, pp. 813-860.

FORMAN M. – SULLIVAN T., *The Latin Cenobitic Rules: AD 400-700: Editions and Translations*, in *ABenR* 48 (1997) 52-68.

FORTIN, E.L., *Christianisme et culture philosophique au cinquième siècle. La querelle de l'âme humaine en Occident* (CEAug.SA, 10), Paris, 1959.

—, *Civitate Dei, De*, in A.D. FITZGERALD (ed.), *Augustine through the Ages. An Encyclopedia*, Grand Rapids, MI-Cambridge, 1999, pp. 196-202.

FRANK, K.S., *Johannes Cassianus*, in *RAC* 18 (1997) 414-426.

—, *Johannes Cassianus, De institutis coenobiorum. Normativer Erzähltext, präskriptiver Regeltext und appellative Du-Anrede*, in T. KÜHN – U. SCHAEFER (eds.), *Dialogische Strukturen. Dialogic Structures. Festschrift für Willi Erzgräber*, Tubingen, 1996, pp. 7-16.

—, *John Cassian on John Cassian*, in *StPatr* 33, Louvain, 1997, pp. 418-433.

FRANSEN, P., *Augustine, Pelagius and the Controversy on the Doctrine of Grace*, in *LouvSt* 12 (1987) 172-181.

—, *Dogmengeschichtliche Entfaltung der Gnadenlehre*, in *MySal*, Bd. IV/2: *Das Heilsgeschehen in der Gemeinde. Gottes Gnadenhandeln*, Einsiedeln-Zürich-Cologne, 1973, pp. 631-765.

FREND, W.H.C., *Manichaeism in the Struggle between Saint Augustine and Petilian of Constantine*, in *AugMag*, T. II, Paris, 1955, pp. 859-866.

FRITZ, G., *Pomère*, in *DTC* 12/2 (1935) 2537-2543.

GARRIGOU-LAGRANGE, R., *Prédestination*, in *DTC* 12/2 (1935) 2809-3022.

GAVIGAN, J.J., *De vita monastica in Africa Septentrionali inde a temporibus S. Augustini usque ad invasiones Arabum* (BAMA, Series II/1), Turin, 1962.

GAZEAU, R., *Honorat (Saint) d'Arles*, in *Cath* 5 (1962) 918-919.

GEARY, J., *Before France and Germany: The Creation and Transformation of the Merovingian World*, Oxford, 1988.

GEERLINGS, W., *Christus exemplum. Studien zur Christologie und Christuverkündigung Augustins* (TTS, 13), Tübingen, 1978.

—, *Römisches Recht und Gnadentheologie. Eine typologische Skizze*, in C. MAYER (ed.), Homo Spiritalis. *Festgabe für Luc Verheijen OSA, zu seinem 70. Geburtstag* (Cass., 38), Würzburg, 1987, pp. 357-377.

—, *Zur Frage des Nachwirkens des Manichäismus in der Theologie Augustins*, in *ZKT* 93 (1971) 45-60.

GILSON, É., *Introduction à l'étude de saint Augustin*, 3rd ed., Paris, 1949.

GIRARDET, K., *Filologos und filologein*, in *Kl* 2 (1970) 323-333.

GOBRY, I., *Les moines en Occident*. T. II: *De saint Martin à saint Benoît. L'enracinement*, Paris, 1995.

GODET, P., *Cassien Jean*, in *DTC* 2 (1910) 1823-1829.

GOEHRING, J.E., *Ascetics, Society, and the Desert. Studies in Early Egyptian Monasticism*, Harrisburg, 1999.

GOLDENBERG, R., *Gnade. II. Judentum*, in *TRE* 13 (1984) 465-467.

GORDAY, P.J., Paulus Origenianus: *The Economic Interpretation of Paul in Origen and Gregory of Nyssa*, in W.S. BABCOCK (ed.), *Paul and the Legacies of Paul*, Dallas, 1990, pp. 141-163.

GOUGAUD, L., *Les critiques formulées contre les premiers moines d'occident*, in *RMab* 24 (1934) 145-163.

GOULD, G., *The Desert Fathers on Monastic Community* (OECS), Oxford, 1993.

GOULD, J.B., *The Stoic Conception of Fate*, in *JHI* 35 (1974) 17-32.

GRABOWSKI, S.J., *The Church. An Introduction to the Theology of St. Augustine*, St. Louis, MO – London, 1957.

GRAF REVENTLOW, H., *Gnade. I. Altes Testament*, in *TRE* 13 (1984) 459-464.

GRANT, F.C. (ed.), *Hellenistic Religions: The Age of Syncretism*, New York, 1953.

GRECH, P., *I principi ermeneutici di S. Agostino*, in *Lat* 28 (1982) 209-223.

GRESHAKE, G., *Gnade als konkrete Freiheit. Eine Untersuchung zur Gnadenlehre des Pelagius*, Mainz, 1972.

—, *Geschenkte Freiheit. Einführung in die Gnadenlehre*, Freiburg i. Br.-Basel-Vienna, 1992.

GRIBOMONT, J., *Basilio*, in *DIP* 1 (1974) 1101-1109.

—, *Gioviniano*, in *DIP* 4 (1977) 1300-1301.

—, *Naissance et développements du monachisme chrétien (II.)*, in A. SOLIGNAC et al., *Monachisme*, in *DSp* 10 (1980) 1524-1617, cc. 1536-1547.

GRIFFE, É., *La Gaule chrétienne à l'époque romaine*. T. II: *L'Église des Gaules au Vᵉ siècle*, 2nd ed., Paris, 1966; T. III: *La cité chrétienne*, Paris, 1965.

—, *Saint Martin et le monachisme gaulois*, in *Saint Martin et son temps. Mémorial du XVIᵉ Centenaire des débuts du monachisme en Gaule, 361-1961* (StAns, 46), Rome, 1961, pp. 3-24.

GRILLMEIER, A., *Christ in Christian Tradition. From the Apostolic Age to Chalcedon (451)*, London, 1965.

GROSS, H., *Gnade im Alten Testament*, in *MySal*, Bd. IV/2: *Das Heilsgeschehen in der Gemeinde. Gottes Gnadenhandeln*, Einsiedeln-Zürich-Cologne, 1973, pp. 599-610.

GROSS, J., *Entstehungsgeschichte des Erbsündendogmas. Von der Bibel bis Augustinus* (Geschichte des Erbsündendogmas, Bd. I), München-Basel, 1960.

—, *Entwicklungsgeschichte des Erbsündendogmas im nachaugustinischen Altertum und in der Vorscholastik (5.-11. Jahrhundert)* (Geschichte des Erbsündendogmas, Bd. II), München-Basel, 1963.

GROSSI, V., *Correptio–correctio–emendatio in Agostino d'Ippona. Terminologia penitenziale e monastica*, in *Aug* 38 (1998) 215-222.

—, *Il porsi della questione della "voluntas salvifica" negli ultimi scritti di Agostino (a. 420-427) I.*, in J.C. SCHNAUBELT – F. VAN FLETEREN (eds.), *Augustine: Second Founder of the Faith*, (CollAug, 1), New York-Bern-Frankfurt a. M.-Paris, 1990, pp. 315-328.

—, *Il termine* "Praedestinatio" *tra il 420-435: dalla linea agostiniana dei "Salvati" a quella di "Salvati e dannati"*, in *Aug* 25 (1985) 27-64.

—, *La crisi antropologica nel monastero di Adrumeto*, in *Aug* 19 (1979) 103-133.

—, *L'antropologia agostiniana. Note previe*, in *Aug* 22 (1982) 456-467.

—, *L'antropologia cristiana negli scritti di Agostino* ("De gratia et libero arbitrio", "De correptione et gratia"), in *SSRel* 4 (1980) 89-113.

—, *La predestinazione in S. Agostino*, in *DSBP* 15: *Elezione-Vocazione-Predestinazione*, Rome, 1997, pp. 341-367.

—, *Pelagio*, in *DIP* 6 (1980) 1327-1330.

GROSSI, V. – SESBOÜÉ, B., *Grâce et justification: du témoignage de l'Écriture à la fin du Moyen-Âge*, in B. SESBOÜÉ (ed.), *Histoire des Dogmes*. T. II: *L'homme et son salut*, Paris, 1995, pp. 269-324.

GRÜTZMACHER, F., *Cassianus, Johannes*, in *RE* 3 (1897) 746-749.

GUILLAUMONT, A., *Aux origines du monachisme chrétien. Pour une phénoménologie du monachisme* (SpOr, 30), Bégrolles en Mauges, 1979.

—, *Les 'Képhalaia gnostica' d'Évagre le Pontique et l'histoire de l'Origénisme chez les Grecs et chez les Syriens* (PatSor, 5), Paris, 1962.

GUY, J.-C., *Écriture sainte et vie spirituelle, 4: Le monachisme*, in *DSp* 4 (1958) 159-164.

—, *Jean Cassien. Vie et doctrine spirituelle* (ThPS, Recherches et Syntheses, 9), Paris, 1961.

HAARDT, R., *Gnosis und Freiheit.* »*Die Gnosis ist Freiheit*« *(Evangelium nach Philippus 132,10). Einige bemerkungen zur Exposition des problems*, in Ex orbe religionum. *Studia Geo Widengren*, Vol. I (SHR, 21), Leiden, 1972.

HAIGHT, R., *The Experience and Language of Grace*, Dublin, 1979.

HAMMAN, A.G., *Prosper von Aquitanien*, in *TRE* 27 (1997) 525-526.

—, *Semipélagianisme*, in *Cath* 13 (1993) 1073-1075.

—, *Scrittori della Gallia*, in A. DI BERARDINO (ed.), *Patrologia*. Vol. III: *Dal Concilio di Nicea (325) al Concilio di Calcedonia (451). I Padri latini*, Turin, 1978, pp. 477-532.

HARL, M., *La mort salutaire du Pharaon selon Origène*, in *Studi in onore di Alberto Pincherle* (SMSR, 38/1), Rome, 1967, pp. 260-268.

HARNACK, A. VON, *Monasticism: Its Ideals and History*, New York, 1895.

—, *Lehrbuch der Dogmengeschichte*, Bd. III, 4th ed., Tübingen, 1920 (Anastatischer Neudruck).

HARRISON, C., *Delectatio Victrix: Grace and Freedom in Saint Augustin*, in *StPatr* 27, Louvain, 1993, pp. 298-302.

HARRISON, V., *Grace and Human Freedom According to St. Gregory of Nyssa* (SBEC, 30), Lewiston (N.Y.), 1992.

HAUKE, M., *Heilsverlust in Adam. Stationen griechischer Erbsündenlehre: Irenäus-Origenes-Kappadozier* (KKTS, 58), Paderborn, 1993.

HAUSHERR, I., *Aphraate*, in *DSp* 1 (1937) 746-752.

—, *L'erreur fondamentale et la logique du Messialinisme*, in *OCP* 1 (1935) 328-360.

—, *Les orientaux connaissent-ils les "nuits" de Saint Jean de la Croix?*, in *OCP* 12 (1946) 5-46.

—, *L'origine de la théorie orientale des huit péchés capitaux*, in *OCP* 86 (1933) 164-175.

—, *Spiritualité monachale et unité chrétienne*, in *Il monachesimo orientale. Atti del Convegno di Studi Orientali, Roma, 9-12 aprile 1958* (OCA, 153), Rome, 1958.

HELLEGOUARC'H, J., *Le vocabulaire latin des relations et de partis politiques sous la république*, 2nd ed., Paris, 1972.

HEUSSI, K., *Der Ursprung des Mönchtum*, Tübingen, 1936.

HOBBEL, A.J., *The Imago Dei in the writings of Origen*, in *StPatr* 21, Louvain, 1989, pp. 301-307.

HOCH, A., *Lehre des J. Cassianus von Natur und Gnade. Ein Beitrag zur Geschichte des Gnadenstreites im 5. Jahrhundert*, Freibourg i. Br., 1895.

HOLZE, H., *Die Bedeutung der experientia in der monastischen Theologie Johannes Cassians*, in *StPatr* 20, Louvain, 1989, pp. 256-263.

HOMBERT, P.-M., *Augustin, prédicateur de la grâce au début de son épiscopat*, in G. MADEC (ed.), *Augustin prédicateur (395-411), Actes du Colloque International de Chantilly (5-7 septembre 1996)* (CEAug.SA, 159), Paris, 1998, pp. 217-245.

—, *Gloria gratiae. Se glorifier en Dieu, principe et fin de la théologie augustinienne de la grâce*, Paris, 1996.

HONNAY, G., *Caelestius, discipulus Pelagii*, in *Aug(L)* 44 (1994) 271-302.

HOPKINS, J., *Augustine on Foreknowledge and Free Will*, in *IJPR* 8 (1977) 111-126.

HOWARD COLLINS, R.J., *Faustus von Reji*, in *TRE* 11 (1983) 63-67.

—, *Fulgentius von Ruspe*, in *TRE* 11 (1983) 723-727.

HUFTIER, M., *Libre arbitre, liberté et péché chez saint Augustin*, in *RTAM* 33 (1966) 187-281.

JACQUIN, A.M., *À quelle date apparaît le terme «Semipélagien»?*, in *RSPT* 1 (1907) 506-508.

—, *La prédestination d'après saint Augustin*, in *MA*, Vol. II, Rome, 1931, pp. 853-878.

—, *La question de la prédestination aux V et VI siècles*, in *RHE* 5 (1904) 265-283; 725-754; 7 (1906) 269-300.

JAEGER, W., *Das frühe Christentum und die griechische Bildung*, Berlin, 1963.

—, *Paideia Christi*, in *ZNW* 50 (1959) 1-14.

—, *Paideia: The Ideals of Greek Culture*, 3 Vols., New York, 1945.

—, *Two Rediscovered Works of Ancient Christian Literature: Gregory of Nyssa and Macarius*, Leiden, 1954.

JOEST, C. *Die Bedeutung von Akedia und Apatheia bei Evagrios Pontikos*, in *StMon* 35 (1993) 7-53.

JOURION, M., *Honorat d'Arles*, in *DSp* 7/1 (1969) 717-718.

KÄHLER, E., *Prädestination*, in *RGG* 5 (1961³) 483-487.

KARAVITES, P., *Evil, Freedom and the Road to Perfection in Clement of Alexandria* (SVigChr, 43), Leiden-Boston-Cologne, 1999.

KASPER, C.M., *Der Beitrag der Mönche zur Entwicklung des Gnadenstreites in Südgallien, dargestellt an der Korrespondenz des Augustinus, Prosper und Hilarius*, in A. ZUMKELLER (ed.), *Signum Pietatis. Festgabe für Cornelius Petrus Mayer osa zum 60. Geburtstag*, Würzburg, 1989, pp. 153-182.

—, *Theologie und Askese. Die Spiritualität des Inselmönchtums von Lérins im 5. Jahrhundert* (BGAM, 40), Münster, 1991.

KELLY, J.N.D., *Early Christian Doctrines*, London, 1958.
KEMMER, A., Charisma Maximum. *Untersuchung zu Cassians Vollkommen-heitslehre und seiner Stellung zum Messalianismus*, Louvain, 1938.
—, *Gregorius Nyssenus estne inter fontes Joannis Cassiani numerandus?*, in *OCP* 21 (1955) 451-466.
KENNY, A., *Was St. John Chrysostom a Semi-Pelagian?*, in *ITQ* 27 (1960) 16-29.
KERMIT SCOTT, T., *Augustine. His Thought in Context*, New York, 1995.
KNOCH, O. – SCHINDLER, A., *Gnade. B. Christlich*, in *RAC* 11 (1980) 351-446.
KRAUS, G., *Vorherbestimmung. Traditionelle Prädestinationslehre im Licht gegenwärtiger Theologie* (ÖF.S, 5), Freiburg i. Br., 1977.
KRAUS, J., *Hilarius*, in *LTK* 5 (1986) 335.
KUNZELMANN, A., *Die Chronologie der Sermones des Hl. Augustinus*, in *MA*, Vol. II, Rome, 1931, pp. 417-520.

LA BONNARDIERE, A.-M., *Augustin, ministre de la parole de Dieu*, in ID. (ed.), *Saint Augustin et la Bible* (BiToTe, 3), Paris, 1986, pp. 53-57.
—, *Biblia Augustiniana. A.T. Le livre de la Sagesse*, Paris, 1970.
—, *Bible et polémiques*, in ID. (ed.), *Saint Augustin et la Bible* (BiToTe, 3), Paris, 1986, pp. 329-352.
—, *Le verset paulinien Rom 5,5 dans l'oeuvre de saint Augustin*, in *AugMag*, T. II, Paris, 1954, pp. 657-665.
—, *Quelques remarques sur les citations scripturaires du «De gratia et libero arbitrio»*, in *REAug* 9 (1963) 77-85.
—, *Recherches de chronologie augustinienne*, Paris, 1965.
LABRIOLLE, P. DE, *La réaction païenne. Étude sur la polémique antichrétienne du Ier au VIe siècle*, Paris, 1934.
—, *Les débuts du monachisme*, in A. FLICHE – V. MARTIN (eds.), *Histoire de l'Église*. T. III: *De la paix constantinienne à la mort de Théodose*, Paris, 1936, pp. 299-369.
—, *Rutilius Namatianus et les Moines*, in *REL* 6 (1928) 30-41.
LABROUSSE, M., *Saint Honorat fondateur de Lérins et évêque d'Arles. Étude et traduction de textes d'Hilaire d'Arles, Fauste de Riez et Césaire d'Arles* (VieMon, 31), Bégrolles-en-Mauges, 1995.
LACHELIER, J., *[Note sur] Nature*, in A. LALANDE (ed.), *Vocabulaire technique et critique de la philosophie*, 6th ed., Paris, 1951.
LAGARRIGUE, G., *La spiritualité de J. Cassien (360-435), élève en orient et maître en occident*, in *Compte Rendue des Séances du groupe strasbur-geois. I Séance du 17 mars 1984*, in *REL* 62 (1984) 17-18.
LAMBERIGTS, M., *Augustine and Julian of Aeclanum on Zosimus*, in *Aug(L)* 42 (1992) 311-330.
—, *Augustine, Julian of Aeclanum and E. Pagels' Adam, Eve, and the Serpent*, in *Aug(L)* 39 (1989) 393-435.
—, *Caelestius*, in A.D. FITZGERALD (ed.), *Augustine through the Ages. An Ency-clopedia*, Grand Rapids, MI-Cambridge, 1999, pp. 114-115.
—, *De polemiek tussen Julian van Aeclanum en Augustinus van Hippo. Een bij-drage tot de theologiegeschiedenis van de tweede pelagiaanse controverse (418-430)* (unpublished doctoral dissertation, Faculty of Theology, K.U.Leuven), 4 Vols., Louvain, 1988.
—, *Julian of Aeclanum: a Plea for a Good Creator*, in *Aug(L)* 38 (1988) 5-24.

—, *Julien d'Éclane et Augustin d'Hippone: deux conceptions d'Adam*, in *Aug(L)* [*Mélanges T.J. van Bavel*, T. I] 40 (1990) 373-440.

—, *Julian of Aeclanum on Grace: Some Considerations*, in *StPatr* 27, Louvain, 1993, pp. 342-349.

—, *Julianus IV (Iulianus von Aeclanum)*, in *RAC* 19 (1999) 483-505.

—, *Le mal et le péché. Pélage: la réhabilitation d'un hérétique*, in *RHE* 95 (2000) 97-111.

—, *Les évêques pélagiens déposes: Nestorius et Éphèse*, in *Aug(L)* 35 (1985) 264-280.

—, *Predestination*, in A.D. FITZGERALD (ed.), *Augustine through the Ages. An Encyclopedia*, Grand Rapids, MI-Cambridge, 1999, pp. 677-679.

—, *Some Critiques on Augustine's View of Sexuality Revisited*, in *StPatr* 33, Louvain, 1997.

—, *Was Augustine a Manichaean? The Assessment of Julian of Aeclanum*, in J. VAN OORT – O. WERMELINGER – G. WURST (eds.), *Augustine and Manichaeism in the Latin West. Proceedings of the Fribourg-Utrecht Symposium of the International Association of Manichaean Studies* (NHMS, 49), Leiden-Boston-Cologne, 2001, pp. 113-136.

LANCEL, S., *Saint Augustin*, Paris, 1999.

LANCEL, S. – AUBERT, R., *Hadrumète*, in *DHGE* 22 (1988) 1493-1496.

LANGLOIS, P., *Fulgentius*, in *RAC* 8 (1972) 632-661.

LARCHER, C., *Études sur le livre de la Sagesse* (Études bibliques), Paris, 1969.

LAWLESS, G., *Augustine of Hippo and his Monastic Rule*, Oxford, 1987.

LE BOULLUEC, A., *La place de la polémique antignostique dans le* Peri Archon, in H. CROUZEL (ed.), *Origeniana*, Bari, 1975, pp. 47-61.

LEBOURLIER, J., *Essai sur la responsabilité du pécheur dans la réflexion de saint Augustin*, in *AugMag*, T. III, Paris, 1955, pp. 287-300.

—, *Grâce et liberté chez saint Augustin*, in *AugMag*, T. II, Paris, 1955, pp. 789-793.

LEBRETON, J., *Saint Vincent de Lérins et Saint Augustin*, in *RSR* 30 (1940) 368-369.

LECLERCQ, J. *et al.*, *Monachesimo*, in *DIP* 5 (1978) 1672-1742.

LECLERCQ, J. – GRIBOMONT, J. – VOGÜÉ, A. DE, *Monachisme*, in *Cath* 9 (1982) 505-535.

LEE, K.-L.E., *Augustine, Manichaeism, and the Good* (Patristic Studies, 2), New York, 1999.

LEEMING, B., *Augustine, Ambrosiaster and the* massa perditionis, in *Greg* 11 (1939) 58-91.

LEKKERKERKER, A.F.N., *Römer 7 und Römer 9 bei Augustin*, Amsterdam, 1942.

LEMONNYER, A., *Prédestination, I: La prédestination dans la sainte Écriture*, in *DTC* 12/2 (1935) 2809-2815.

LEPELLEY, C. – LANCEL, S., *Africa*, in *AugL* (1 (1986) 180-219.

LETTER, P. DE, *"Gratia generalis" in the "De vocatione omnium gentium" and in St. Augustine*, in *StPatr* 14 (TU, 117), Berlin, 1976, pp. 393-401.

LETTIERI, G., *Fato e predestinazione in* De civ. Dei *V,1-11 e* C. duas ep. Pelag. *II,5,9-7,16*, in *Aug* 35 (1995) 457-496.

LEYS, R., *L'image de Dieu chez saint Grégoire de Nysse*, Brussels-Paris, 1951.

LEYSER, C., *Semi-Pelagianism*, in A.D. FITZGERALD (ed.), *Augustine through the Ages. An Encyclopedia*, Grand Rapids, MI-Cambridge, 1999, pp. 761-766.

LIÉBAERT, J., *La tradition patristique jusqu'au Ve siècle*, in P. GUILLUY (ed.), *La culpabilité fondamentale. Péché originel et anthropologie moderne* (RSSR.M, 11), Gembloux-Lille, [1975], pp. 34-55.

LIEU, S.N.S., *Manichaeism in the Later Roman Empire and Medieval China*, 2nd ed. revised and expanded, Tübingen, 1992.

LIMBERIS, V., *The Concept of 'freedom' in Gregory of Nyssa's* De instituto Christiano, in *StPatr* 27, Louvain, 1993, pp. 39-41.

LOGAN, A.H.B., *Gnostic Truth and Christian Heresy. A Study in the History of Gnosticism*, Edinburgh, 1996.

LOHSE, B., *Askese und Mönchtum in der Antike und in der alten Kirche*, München-Vienna, 1969.

LONERGAN, B., *Grace and freedom: operative grace in the thought of St. Thomas Aquinas*, London-New York, 1971.

LOOFS, F., *Augustinus*, in *RE* 1 (1897) 257-285.

LORENZ, R., *Die Anfänge des abendländischen Mönchtums im 4. Jahrhundert*, in *ZKG* 77 (1966) 1-61.

LORIÉ, L.T.A., *Spiritual Terminology in the Latin Translations of the* Vita Antonii (LCP, 11), Nijmegen, 1955.

LÖSSL, J., Intellectus Gratiae. *Die erkenntnistheoretische und hermeneutische Dimension der Gnadenlehre Augustins von Hippo* (SVigChr, 38), Leiden-New York-Cologne, 1997.

—, *Julian von Aeclanum. Studien zu seinem Leben, seinem Werk, seiner Lehre und ihrer Überlieferung* (SVigChr, 60), Leiden-Boston-Cologne, 2001.

—, *Mt 6:13 in Augustine's Later Works*, in *StPatr* 33, Louvain, 1997, pp. 167-171.

LUBAC, H. DE, *Surnaturel. Études historiques* (Theol[P], 8), Paris, 1946.

—, *Le mystère du surnaturel* (Théol[P], 64), Paris, 1965.

LÜTCKE, K.-H., *Auctoritas*, in *AugL* 1 (1990) 498-510.

LYONNET, S., *Études sur l'Épître aux Romains* (AnBib, 120), Rome, 1989.

—, *Péché, IV. Dans le Nouveau Testament*, in *DBS* 7 (1966) 486-567.

MACQUEEN, D.J., *John Cassian on Grace and Free Will. With Particular Reference to* Institutio XII *and* Collatio XIII, in *RTAM* 44 (1977) 5-28.

McHUGH, M.P., *Prosper of Aquitaine*, in A.D. FITZGERALD (ed.), *Augustine through the Ages. An Encyclopedia*, Grand Rapids, MI-Cambridge, 1999, pp. 685-686.

MADEC, G., *Petites études augustiniennes* (CEAug.Sa, 142), Paris, 1994.

—, *Saint Augustin: du libre arbitre à la liberté par la grâce de Dieu*, in O. FATIO – G. BEDOUELLE (eds.), *Liberté chrétienne et libre arbitre* (ÖBFZPT, 24), Fribourg, 1994, pp. 31-45.

MADOZ, J., *El Concepto de la Tradicion en S. Vicente de Lerins*, Rome, 1933.

MAGRIS, A., *Augustins Prädestinationslehre und die manichäischen Quellen*, in J. VAN OORT – O. WERMELINGER – G. WURST (eds.), *Augustine and Manichaeism in the Latin West. Proceedings of the Fribourg-Utrecht Symposium of the International Association of Manichaean Studies* (NHMS, 49), Leiden-Boston-Cologne, 2001, pp. 148-160.

—, *La logica del pensiero gnostico*, Brescia, 1997.

—, *L'idea di destino nel pensiero antico*. Vol. II: *Da Platone a S. Agostino*, Udine, 1985.

MALONE, E.E., *The Monk and the Martyr* (SCA, 12), Washington, 1950.
MANDOUZE, A., *Saint Augustin. L'aventure de la raison et de la grâce*, Paris, 1968.
MANDOUZE, A. et al., *Prosopographie chrétienne du Bas-Empire*. T. I: *Prosopographie de l'Afrique Chrétienne (303-533)*, Paris, 1982.
MANRIQUE, A., *La vida monástica en San Agustin*, El Escorial-Salamanca, 1959.
—, *San Agustin y el monaquismo africano*, in *CDios* 173 (1960) 118-138.
MARA, M.G., *Paolo di Tarso e il suo epistolario. Ricerche storico-esegetiche*, L'Aquila, 1983.
—, *Agostino interprete di Paolo* (LCPM, 16), Milan, 1993.
MARAFIOTI, D., *Alle origini del teorema della predestinazione (Simpl. 1,2,13-22)*, in *Congresso Internazionale su S. Agostino nel XVI Centenario della Conversione, Roma, 15-20 settembre 1986*, Vol. II (SEAug, 25), Rome, 1987, pp. 257-277.
—, *Il problema dell' "Initium Fidei" in sant'Agostino fino al 397*, in *Aug* 21 (1981) 541-565.
—, *L'uomo tra legge e grazia. Analisi del* De spiritu et littera *di S. Agostino*, Brescia, 1983.
MARKUS, R.A., *Life, Culture, and Controversies of Augustine*, in A.D. FITZGERALD (ed.), *Augustine through the Ages. An Encyclopedia*, Grand Rapids, MI-Cambridge, 1999, pp. 498-504.
—, *Pelagianism: Britain and the Continent*, in *JHE* 37 (1986) 191-204.
—, *The End of Ancient Christianity*, Cambridge, 1990.
—, *The Legacy of Pelagius: Orthodoxy, Heresy and Conciliation*, in R. WILLIAMS (ed.), *The Making of Orthodoxy. Essays in Honour of Henry Chadwick*, Cambridge, 1989, pp. 214-234.
MARROU, H.-I., *Jean Cassien à Marseille*, in *RMÂL* 1 (1945) 5-26.
—, *La patrie de Jean Cassien*, in *OCP* 13 (1947) 588-599.
—, *Le fondateur de Saint-Victor de Marseille: Jean Cassien*, in *ProvHist* 16 (1966) 297-308.
—, *Nouvelle Histoire de l'Église*. T. I: *Des origines à Grégoire le Grand*, 2nd ed., Paris, 1985.
—, *Patristique et Humanisme. Mélanges* (PatSor, 9), Paris, 1976.
—, *Saint Augustin et la fin de la culture antique* (BEFAR, 145 and 145bis), 4th ed., Paris, 1958.
MARROU, H.-I., en collaboration avec A.-M. LA BONNARDIERE, *Saint Augustin et l'augustinisme*, Paris, [1955].
MARSILI, S., *Giovanni Cassiano ed Evagrio Pontico. Dottrina sulla carità e contemplazione* (StAns, 5), Rome, 1936.
MARTINETTO, G., *Les premières réactions antiaugustiniennes de Pélage*, in *REAug* 17 (1971) 83-117.
MASOLIVER, A., *Historia del Monacato cristiano*. T. I: *Desde los orígines hasta san Benito*, Madrid, 1994.
MASSEIN, P., *Le phénomène monastique dans les religions non chrétiennes (I.)*, in A. SOLIGNAC et al., *Monachisme*, in *DSp* 10 (1980) 1524-1617, cc. 1525-1536.
MATHISEN, R.W., *Ecclesiastical Factionalism and Religious Controversy in Fifth- Century Gaul*, Washington, D.C., 1989.
—, *For Specialists Only: The Reception of Augustine and His Teachings in Fifth-Century Gaul*, in J.T. LIENHARD – E.C. MULLER – R.J. TESKE (eds.),

Augustine. Presbyter Factus Sum (CollAug, 2), New York, 1993, pp. 29-41.

MATHON, G., *Onorato*, in *BSS* 9 (1967) 1202-1203.

MAYER, C., *Adiutorium quo, adiutorium sine quo non*, in *AugL* 1 (1986) 95.

MEER, F. VAN DER, *Augustinus de zielzorger*, 2 Vols., 3rd ed., Utrecht, 1957.

MEREDITH, A., *Gregory of Nyssa*, London-New York, 1999.

MICHEL, A., *Volonté de Dieu, VI: Volonté salvifique*, in *DTC* 15 (1950) 3356-3374, cc. 3362-3363.

MIQUEL, P., *Signification et motivations du monachisme (III.)*, in A. SOLIGNAC *et al.*, *Monachisme*, in *DSp* 10 (1980) 1524-1617, cc. 1547-1557.

—, *Un homme d'expérience: Cassien*, in *CCist* 30 (1968) 131-146.

MONCEAUX, P., *St. Augustin et St. Antoine*, in *MA*, Vol. II, Rome, 1931, pp. 61-89.

MONTCHEUIL, L. DE, *L'hypothèse de l'état originel d'ignorance et de difficulté d'après le "De libero arbitrio" de saint Augustin*, in *RScR* 23 (1933) 197-221.

MONTGOMERY HITCHCOCK, F.R., *Irenaeus of Lugdunum. A Study of his Teaching*, Cambridge, 1914.

MOO, D.J., *The Theology of Romans 9-11*, in D.M. HAY – E.E. JOHNSON (eds.), *Pauline Theology*. Vol. III: *Romans*, Minneapolis, 1995.

MORARD, F.E., *Monachos, Moine. Histoire du terme grec jusqu'au 4e siècle*, in *FZPT* 20 (1973) 332-411.

MOREMBERT, T. DE, *Saint-Victor de Marseille*, in *Cath* 13 (1993) 605-606.

MORRIS, L. *The Epistle to the Romans*, Grand Rapids, MI, 1988.

MOUSSY, C., *Gratia et sa famille*, Paris, 1966.

MUNIER, C., *Zosime (1)*, in *DSp* 16 (1994) 1651-1658.

MUNZ, P., *John Cassian*, in *JEH* 11 (1960) 1-22.

MUSSNER, F., *Die Neutestamentliche Gnadentheologie in Grundzügen*, in *MySal*, Bd. 4/2: *Das Heilsgeschehen in der Gemeinde. Gottes Gnadenhandeln*, Einsiedeln-Zürich-Cologne, 1973, pp. 611-629.

MUYLDERMANS, J., *À travers la tradition manuscrite d'Evagre le Pontique. Essai sur les manuscrits grecs conservés à la bibliothèque nationale de Paris* (BMus, 3), Louvain, 1932.

NAGEL, P., *Die Motivierung der Askese in der alten Kirche und der Ursprung des Mönchtums*, Berlin, 1966.

NOUAILHAT, R., *Saints et Patrons. Les premiers moines de Lérins*, Paris, 1988.

NÜRNBERG, R., *Askese als sozialer Impuls. Monastisch-asketische Spiritualität als Wurzel und Triebfeder sozialer Ideen und Aktivitaten der Kirche in Sudgallien im 5. Jahrhundert*, Bonn, 1988.

—, *Johannes Cassianus*, in *LTK* 5 (1996) 888-889.

NUVOLONE, F.G., *Pélage et Pélagianisme, I. Les écrivains*, in *DSp* 12/2 (1986) 2880-2923.

—, *Problèmes d'une nouvelle édition du* De Induratione Cordis Pharaonis *attribué à Pélage*, in *REAug* 26 (1980) 105-117.

NYGREN, G., *Das Prädestinationsproblem in der Theologie Augustins* (StTL, 12), Lund, 1956.

OBERLINNER, L., *Die Pastoralbriefe*. Bd. I: *Kommentar zum ersten Timotheusbrief* (HTK, 11/2/1/), Freiburg, 1994.

O'CONNELL, R.J., *"De libero arbitrio I"*, in *AugSt* 1 (1970) 49-68.

O'CONNOR, W., *Saint Vincent of Lérins and Saint Augustine. Was the* Commonitorium *of Saint Vincent of Lérins intended as a Polemic Treatise against Saint Augustine and his Doctrine on Predestination?*, in DoC 16 (1961) 123-257.

O'DALY, G., *Anima, animus*, in AugL 1 (1986-1988) 315-340.

—, *Predestination and Freedom in Augustine's Ethics*, in G. VESEY (ed.), *The Philosophy in Christianity*, Cambridge, 1989, pp. 85-97.

O'DONNELL, *The Authority of Augustine*, in AugSt 22 (1991) 7-35.

OERTER, W.B., *Mani als Arzt? Zur Deutung eines manichäischen Bildes*, in V. VAVRINEK (ed.), *From Late Antiquity to Early Byzantium. Proceedings of the Byzantinological Symposium in the 16ᵗʰ Eirene Conference*, Prague, 1985.

O'KEEFE, J.J., *Sin, ἀπάθεια and Freedom of the Will in Gregory of Nyssa*, in StPatr 23, Louvain, 1989, pp. 52-59.

O'LOUGHLIN, T., *Caesarius of Arles*, in A.D. FITZGERALD (ed.), *Augustine through the Ages. An Encyclopedia*, Grand Rapids, MI-Cambridge, 1999, pp. 115-116.

OLPHE-GALLIARD, M., *Cassien (Jean)*, in DSp 2 (1953) 214-276.

OORT, J. VAN, *Augustine and Mani on* concupiscentia sexualis, in J. DEN BOEFT – J. VAN OORT (eds.), *Augustiniana Traiectina. Communications présentées au Colloque International d'Utrecht 13-14 novembre 1986*, Paris, 1987, pp. 137-152.

—, *Augustine on Sexual Concupiscence and Original Sin*, in StPatr 22, Louvain, 1989, pp. 382-386.

—, *Augustinus und der Manichäismus*, in A. VAN TONGERLOO (ed.), in collaboration with J. VAN OORT, *The Manichaean* ΝΟΥΣ. *Proceedings of the International Symposium organized in Louvain from 31 July to 3 August 1991* (Manichaean Studies, 2), Louvain, 1995, pp. 289-307

—, *Jerusalem and Babylon. A Study into Augustine's* City of God*, and the Sources of his Doctrine of the Two Cities* (SVigChr, 14), Leiden-New York-Copenhagen-Cologne, 1991.

—, *Mani, Manichaeism and Augustine. The Rediscovery of Manichaeism & its Influence on Western Christianity. Lectures delivered at the State University of Tbilisi & the K. Kekelidze Institute of Manuscripts of the Georgian Academy of Sciences, Tbilisi, Georgia, 26-29 September, 1995*, 3ʳᵈ rev. ed., Tbilisi (Georgia), 1998.

—, *Manichaeism in Augustines's* De civitate Dei, in E. CAVALCANTI (ed.), *Il* 'De civitate Dei'*: l'opera, le interpretazioni, l'influsso*, Roma-Freiburg-Vienna, 1996, pp. 193-214.

OPELT, I., *Die Polemik in der christlichen lateinischen Literatur von Tertullian bis Augustin* (BKAW, Neue Folge: Reihe 2, 63), Heidelberg, 1980.

OROZ RETA, J., *Predestinación, vocación y conversión según san Agustín*, in J.C. SCHNAUBELT – F. VAN FLETEREN (eds.), *Augustine: Second Founder of the Faith* (CollAug, 1), New York-Bern-Frankfurt a. M.-Paris, 1990, pp. 29-43.

ORT, L.J.R., *Mani: a Religio-historical Description of his Personality*, Leiden, 1967.

OTTO, S., *Die Antike im Umbruch* (List Taschenbücher der Wissenschaft; Geschichte des politischen Denkens, 1513), Münich, 1974.

PAGELS, E., *The Johannine Gospel in Gnostic Exegesis. Heraclon's Commentary on John*, Nashville, 1973.

PALANQUE, G.-R., *Les évêchés provençaux à l'époque romaine*, in ProvHist 1 (1951) 103-143.

PANG, A.A., *Augustine on Divine Foreknowledge and Human Free Will*, in REAug 40 (1994) 417-431.

PAREDI, A., *Paulinus of Milan*, in SE 14 (1963) 206-230.

PARMA, C., *Pronoia* und Providentia*: der Vorsehungsbegriff Plotins und Augustins*, Leiden, 1971.

PASTORINO, A., *I "temi spirituali" della vita monastica in Giovanni Cassiano*, in CClCr 1 1980) 123-172.

PEIFER, C., *Pre-Benedictine Monasticism in the Western Church*, in T. FRY et al. (eds.), *RB 1980. The Rule of St. Benedict*, Collegeville, MN, 1981, pp. 42-64.

—, *The Biblical Foundation of Monasticism*, in CiSt 1 (1966) 7-31.

PENCO, G., *Il concetto di monaco e di vita monastica in Occidente nel sec. VI*, in StMon 1 (1959) 7-50.

—, *Storia del monachesimo in Italia dalle origini alla fine del Medio Evo*, Rome, 1961.

PERLER O. – MAIER J.-L. *Les voyages de st. Augustin*, Paris, 1969.

PERRONE, L. (ed.), *Il cuore indurito del Faraone. Origene e il problema del libero arbitrio*, Genua, 1992.

—, *Libero arbitrio*, in A. MONACI CASTAGNO (ed.), *Origene. Dizionario, la cultura, il pensiero, le opere*, Rome, 2000, pp. 237-243.

PESCH, O.H. – PETERS, A., *Einführung in die Lehre von Gnade und Rechtfertigung*, Darmstadt, 1981.

PIETRI, C., *Esquisse de conclusion. L'aristocratie chrétienne entre Jean de Constantinople et Augustin d'Hippone*, in C. KANNENGIESSER (ed.), *Jean Chrysostome et Augustin. Actes du Colloque de Chantilly 22-24 septembre 1974* (ThH, 35), Paris, 1975.

—, *Les difficultés du nouveau système (395-431). La première hérésie d'Occident: Pélage et le refus rigoriste*, in J.-M. MAYEUR et al. (eds.), *Histoire du christianisme des origines à nos jours. T. II: Naissance d'une chrétienté (250-430)*, Paris, 1995, pp. 453-479.

—, *Roma Christiana. Recherches sur l'Église de Rome, son organisation, sa politique, son idéologie de Miltiade à Sixte (311-440)*, T. II (BEFAR, 224), Rome, 1976.

PIETRI C. and L. (eds.), *Prosopographie chrétienne du Bas-Empire*. T. II: *Prosopographie de l'Italie chrétienne (313-604)*, Vol. I: A-K, Rome, 1999.

PIETRI, L., *Martin von Tours*, in TRE 22 (1992) 194-196.

PINCHERLE, A., *La formazione teologica di Sant'Agostino*, Rome, 1947.

PIPER, J., *The Justification of God: An Exegetical and Theological Study of Romans 9:1-23*, Grand Rapids, MI, 1993.

PIRENNE, R., *La morale de Pélage. Essai historique sur le rôle primordial de la Grâce dans l'enseignement de la théologie morale* (Excerpta ex Dissertatione ad Lauream), Rome, 1961.

PIZZOLATO, L.F., *L' "induramento" del cuore del Faraone: tra Gregorio di Nissa e Agostino*, in Aug 35 (1995) 511-525.

PLAGNIEUX, J., *Le grief de complicité entre erreurs nestorienne et pélagienne d'Augustin à Cassien par Prosper d'Aquitaine?*, in REAug 2 (1956) [Mémorial Bardy] 391-402.

PLATZ, P., *Der Römerbrief in der Gnadenlehre Augustins*, Würzburg, 1938.
PLINVAL, G. DE, *Aspects du déterminisme et de la liberté dans la doctrine de saint Augustin*, in *REAug* 1 (1955) 345-378.
—, *Le luttes pélagiennes*, in A. FLICHE – V. MARTIN (eds.), *Histoire de l'Église*. T. IV: *De la mort de Théodose à l'election de Grégoire le Grand*, Paris, 1937, pp. 79-128.
—, *Pélage, ses écrits, sa vie et sa réforme. Étude d'histoire litteraire et religieuse*, Lausanne, 1943.
—, *Prosper. Interprète de s. Augustin*, in *RechAug* 1 (1958) 336-355.
—, *Semipelagianesimo*, in *EC* 11 (1953) 286-288.
POHLENZ, M., *L'uomo greco* (Il pensiero storico, 44), Florence, 1962.
—, *Griechische Freiheit. Wesen und Werden eines Lebensideal*, Heidelberg, 1955.
POLLMANN, K., *Hermeneutical Presuppositions*, in A.D. FITZGERALD (ed.), *Augustine through the Ages. An Encyclopedia*, Grand Rapids, MI-Cambridge, 1999, pp. 426-429.
PONTET, M., *L'exégèse de S. Augustin prédicateur* (Theol [P], 7), Paris, [1945].
POQUE, S., *Le language symbolique dans la prédication d'Augustin d'Hippone. Images héroïques*, 2 Tomes, Paris, 1984.
PRAET, D., *Explaining the Christianization of the Roman Empire. Older Theories and Recent Developments*, in *SE* 33 (1992-1993) 5-119.
PRICOCO, S., *Monaci, Filosofi e Santi. Saggi di storia della cultura tardoantica*, Messina, 1992.
—, *Il monachesimo occidentale dalle origini al Maestro. Lineamenti storici e percorsi storiografici*, in *Il monachesimo occidentale dalle origini alla Regula magistri. XXVI Incontro di studiosi dell'antichità cristiana, Roma, 8-10 maggio 1997* (SEA, 62), Rome, 1998, pp. 7-22.
—, *L'isola dei santi. Il cenobio di Lerino e le origini del monachesimo gallico*, Rome, 1978.
PRINZ, F., *Askese und Kultur. Vor-und frühbenediktinisches Mönchtum an der Wiege Europas*, München, 1980.
—, *Cassiano*, in *DIP* 2 (1975) 633-638.
—, *Frühes Mönchtum im Frankenreich. Kultur und Gesellschaft in Gallien, den Rheinlanden und Bayern am Beispiel der monastischen Entwicklung (4. bis 8. Jahrhundert)*, München, 1965.
PRISTAS, L., *The Theological Anthropology of John Cassian* (unpublished doctoral dissertation, Boston College), Boston, 1993.
PUECH, H.C., *Das Evangelium des Mani*, in W. SCHNEEMELCHER (ed.), *Neutestamentliche Apokryphen in deutscher Übersetzung*. Bd. I: *Evangelien*, 6th ed., Tübingen, 1990.
—, *Le Manichéisme. Son fondateur–sa doctrine*, Paris, 1949.

QUASTEN, J., *Initiation aux Pères de l'Église*, T. II, Paris, 1957.
QUISPEL, G., *Mani et la tradition evangélique des judéo-chrétiens*, in *RSR* 60 (1972) 143-150.

RAHNER, K., *Augustin und der Semipelagianismus*, in *ZKT* 62 (1938) 171-196.
—, *Heilswille Gottes, Allgemeiner H.G.*, in *LTK* 5 (1960) 165-168.

RAMSEY, B., *Cassian, John*, in A.D. FITZGERALD (ed.), *Augustine through the Ages. An Encyclopedia*, Grand Rapids, MI-Cambridge, 1999, pp. 133-135.
—, *John Cassian: Student of Augustine*, in *CiSt* 28 (1993) 5-15.
REBILLARD, E., Quasi funambuli. *Cassien et la controverse pélagienne sur la perfection*, in *REAug* 40 (1994) 197-210.
REES, B.R., *Pelagius. A reluctant Heretic*, Woodbridge/Suffolk, 1988.
REFOULÉ, F., *Datation du premier concile de Carthage contre les Pélagiens et du "Libellus fidei" de Rufin*, in *REAug* 9 (1963) 41-49.
REMY, G., *Le Christ médiateur dans l'oeuvre de saint Augustin*, 2 Tomes, Lille-Paris, 1979.
RICHÉ, P., *Education et culture dans l'Occident barbare (VI-VIII siècles)*, Paris, 1962.
RIGBY, P., *Original Sin*, in A.D. FITZGERALD (ed.), *Augustine through the Ages. An Encyclopedia*, Grand Rapids, MI-Cambridge, 1999, pp. 607-614.
—, *Original Sin in Augustine's Confessions*, Ottawa, 1987.
RING, T.G., *Electio*, in *Aug(L)* 2 (2001) 741-752.
—, *"Electio" in der Gnadenlehre Augustins*, in A. ZUMKELLER – A. KRUEMMEL (eds.), Traditio Augustiniana: *Studien über Augustinus und seine Rezeption. Festgabe für Willigis Eckermann OSA zum 60. Geburtstag* (Cass., 46), Würzburg, 1994, pp. 39-79.
RIST, J.M., *Augustine: Ancient Thought Baptized*, Cambridge, 1994.
—, *Augustine on Free Will and Predestination*, in *JTS* 20 (1969) 420-447.
—, *Stoic Philosophy*, Cambridge-London-New York-Melbourne, 1969.
ROLDANUS, J., *Origène, Antoine et Athanase. Leur interconnexion dans la Vie et les Lettres*, in *StPatr* 26, Louvain, 1993, pp. 389-314.
RONDET, H., Gratia Christi. *Essai d'histoire du dogme et de théologie dogmatique*, Paris, 1948.
—, *La liberté et la grâce dans la théologie augustinienne*, in ID. *et al.* (eds.), *Saint Augustin parmi nous*, Le Puy-Paris, 1954, pp. 199-222.
—, *La prédestination augustinienne. Genèse d'une doctrine*, in *ScEc* 18 (1966) 229-251.
—, *Le péché originel dans la tradition patristique et théologique*, Paris, 1966.
—, *Prédestination, grâce et liberté*, in *NRT* 69 (1947) 449-474.
RONDET, H. – RAHNER, K., *Predestination*, in *SM* 5, New York-London, 1970, pp. 88-91.
RORDORF, W., *Saint Augustin et la tradition philosophique antifataliste: A propos de* De civitate Dei *5,1-11*, in *VC* 28 (1974) 190-202.
ROSE, E., *Die manichäische Christologie* (StOr, 5), Wiesbaden, 1979.
ROTTMANNER, O., *Der Augustinismus. Ein dogmengeschichtliche Studie*, München, 1892.
ROTUREAU, G., *Ame (Thélogie)*, in *Cath* 1 (1948) 430-434.
ROUSSEAU, P., *Ascetics, Authority, and the Church in the Age of Jerome and Cassian*, Oxford, 1978.
—, *Basil of Caesarea*, Berkeley-Los Angeles-Oxford, 1994.
—, *Cassian, Contemplation and the Cenobitic Life*, in *JEH* 26 (1975) 113-126.
—, *Cassian: Monastery and World*, in M. FAIRBURN – W.H. OLIVER (eds.), *The Certainty of Doubt. Tributes to Peter Munz*, Wellington, 1995, pp. 68-89.
RUCKSTUHL, E., *Gnade. III: Neues Testament*, in *TRE* 13 (1984) 467-476.
RUDOLPH, K., *Augustinus Manichaicus. Das Problem von Konstanz und Wandel*, in J. VAN OORT – O. WERMELINGER – G. WURST (eds.), *Augustine and*

Manichaeism in the Latin West. Proceedings of the Fribourg-Utrecht Symposium of the International Association of Manichaean Studies (NHMS, 49), Leiden-Boston-Cologne, 2001, pp. 1-15.

RUIZ PASQUAL, J., *San Agustin y la salvación de los gentiles. Voluntad salvifica universal de Dios*, in *Augustinus* 38 (1993) 379-430.

SAGE, A., *De la grâce du Christ, modèle et principe de la grâce*, in *REAug* 7 (1961) 17-34.

—, *La Règle de saint Augustin commentée par ses écrits*, Paris, 1961.

—, *Faut-il anathématiser la doctrine augustinienne de la prédestination?*, in *REAug* 8 (1962) 233-242.

—, *La volonté salvifique universelle de Dieu dans la pensée de saint Augustin*, in *RechAug* 3 (1965) 107-131.

—, *Les deux temps de la grâce*, in *REAug* 7 (1961) 209-230.

—, *Péché originel. Naissance d'un dogme*, in *REAug* 13 (1967) 211-248.

—, *"Praeparatur voluntas a Domino"*, in *REAug* 10 (1964) 1-20.

SAINT-MARTIN, J., *Prédestination, III. La prédestination d'après les Pères latins, particulièrment d'après saint Augustin*, in *DTC* 12/2 (1935) 2832-2896.

SALAMITO, J.-M., *Excellence chrétienne et valeurs aristocratiques: la morale de Pélage dans son contexte ecclésial et social*, in G. FREYBURGER – L. PERNOT (eds.), *Du Héros Païen au Saint Chrétien* (CEAug.SA, 154), Paris, 1997, pp. 139-157.

SAXER, V., *Marsiglia*, in *DPAC* 2 (1983) 2127-2129.

SCHEFFCZYK, L., *Die Heilsverwirklichung in der Gnade. Gnadenlehre* (Katholische Dogmatik, 6), Aachen, 1998.

—, *Urstand, Fall und Erbsünde von der Schrift bis Augustinus*, in M. SCHMAUS et al. (eds.), *Handbuch der Dogmengeschichte*, Bd. II/3a (1. Teil), Freiburg-Basel-Vienna, 1981.

SCHINDLER, A., *Augustin/Augustinismus I*, in *TRE* 4 (1979) 646-698.

—, *Gnade und Freiheit. Zum Vergleich zwischen den griechischen und lateinischen Kirchenväter*, in *ZTK* 62 (1965) 178-195.

SCHLIER, H., *Der Römerbrief* (HTK, 6), Freiburg-Basel-Vienna, 1977.

SCHOCKENHOFF, E., *Zum Fest der Freiheit. Theologie des christilichen Handelns bei Origenes* (TTS, 33), Mainz, 1990.

SCHREINER, T.R., *Romans* (BECNT, 6), Grand Rapids, MI, 1998.

SCHRÖDER, H.O., *Fatum (Heimarmene)*, in *RAC* 7 (1969) 524-636.

SCHWAGER, R., *Der wunderbare Tausch. Zur Geschichte und Deutung der Erlösungslehre*, München, 1986.

SERENTHÀ, L., *Predestinazione*, in *DTI* 2 (1977) 759-774.

SERTILLANGES, D., *Agnosticisme et anthropomorphisme (Réponse à M. Gardair)*, in *RevPhil* 5 (1906) 158-181.

SEVERUS, E. VON, *Zu den biblischen Grundlagen des Mönchtums*, in *GuL* 26 (1953) 113-122.

SHERIDAN, M., *The Controversy over ἀπάθεια: Cassian's Sources and his Use of Them*, in *StMon* 39 (1997) 287-310.

—, *The Origins of Monasticism in the Eastern Church*, in T. FRY et al. (eds.), *RB 1980. The Rule of St. Benedict*, Collegeville, MN, 1981, pp. 3-41.

SIMON, P., *Aurelius Augustinus. Sein geistiges Profil*, Paderborn, 1954.

SIMONETTI, M., *Fausto di Riez*, in *DPAC* 1 (1983) 1336-1338.

SIMONIN, H.D., *Prédestination, II. La prédestination d'après les Pères grecs*, in *DTC* 12/2 (1935) 2815-2832.

SMALBRUGGE, M.A., *La prédestination entre subjectivité et language. Le premier dogme moderne*, in *RTP* 127 (1995) 43-54.

—, *Rupture dans l'homme, rupture dans la culture. Quelques réflexions sur le thème de la prédestination chez Augustin*, in *Aug(L)* 50 (2000) 235-256.

SMITH, T.A., *Agonism and Antagonism: Metaphor and the Gallic Resistance to Augustine*, in *StPatr* 38, Louvain, 2001, pp. 283-289.

—, *"De Gratia": Faustus of Riez's Treatise on Grace and Its Place in the History of Theology*, Notre Dame, IN, 1990.

—, *Fulgentius of Ruspe*, in A.D. FITZGERALD (ed.), *Augustine through the Ages. An Encyclopedia*, Grand Rapids, MI-Cambridge, 1999, pp. 373-374.

SMOLAK, K., *'Skytische Schriftsteller in der lateinischen Literatur der Spätantike'*, in V. GJUZELEV – R. PILLINGER (eds.), *Das Christentum in Bulgarien und auf der übrigen Balkanhalbinsel in der Spätantike und im frühen Mittelalter*, Vienna, 1987, pp. 23-29.

SOLIGNAC, A., *Autour du* De natura *de Pélage*, in M. SOETARD (ed.), *Valeurs dans le stoïcisme. Du Portique à nos jours (Textes rassemblés en hommage à Michel Spanneut)*, Lille, 1993, pp. 181-192.

—, *Le salut des païens d'après la prédication d'Augustin*, in G. MADEC (ed.), *Augustin prédicateur (395-411), Actes du Colloque International de Chantilly (5-7 septembre 1996)* (CEAug.SA, 159), Paris, 1998, pp. 419-428.

—, *Les excès de l' "intellectus fidei" dans la doctrine d'Augustin sur la grâce*, in *NRT* 110 (1988) 825-849.

—, *Liberté-Libération, III: Pères de l'Église*, in *DSp* 9 (1976) 809-824.

—, *[Introduction]*, in ID. et al., *Monachisme*, in *DSp* 10 (1980) 1524-1617, cc. 1524-1525.

—, *Pélage et Pélagianisme, II: Le mouvement et sa doctrine*, in *DSp* 12/2 (1986) 2889-2942, cc. 2923-2936.

—, *Prosper d'Aquitaine (saint)*, in *DSp* 12/2 (1986) 2446-2456.

—, *Semipélagiens*, in *DSp* 14 (1990) 556-568.

SOMOS, R., *Origen, Evagrius Ponticus and the Ideal of Impassibility*, in W.A. BIENERT – U. KÜHNEWEG (eds.), Origeniana Septima. *Origenes in den Auseinandersetzungen des 4. Jahrhunderts*, Louvain, 1999, pp. 365-373.

SOUTER, A., *Pelagius' Expositions of Thirteen Epistles of St. Paul* (TaS, 9,1-3), Cambridge, 1922, 1926, 1931 (also in PLS, 1, cc. 1110-1374).

—, *The Earliest Latin Commentaries on the Epistles of st. Paul: a Study*, Oxford, 1927, anastatic impression, 1999.

SPANNEUT, M., *Le stoïcisme des Pères de l'Église. De Clement de Rome à Clément d'Alexandrie* (PatSor, 1), Paris, 1957.

SPINELLI, M., *Teologia e "Teoria" nella* Conlatio De Protectione Dei *di Giovanni Cassiano*, in *Ben* 31 (1984) 23-35.

STAATS, R., *Gregor von Nyssa und die Messalianer: die Frage der Priorität zweier altkirchlicher Schriften* [PTS, 8], Berlin, 1968.

—, *Makarios-Symeon. Epistola Magna. Eine messalianische Mönchsregel und ihre Unschrift in Gregors von Nyssa "De instituto christiano"* [AAWG.PH, dritte Folge, 134], Göttingen, 1984.

STEWART, C., *Cassian the Monk* (Oxford Studies in Historical Theology), Oxford-New York, 1998.

—, *Working the Earth of the Heart: the Messalian Controversy in History, Texts and Language to AD 431* (OTM), Oxford, 1991.

STRAND, N., *Augustine on Predestination and Divine Simplicity: the Problem of Compatibility*, in *StPatr* 38, Louvain, 2001, pp. 290-305.

STROHEKER, K.F., *Der senatorische Adel im spätantiken Gallien*, Tübingen, 1948 (reprint, Darmstadt, 1970).

STUMP, E., *Augustine on Free Will*, in E. STUMP – N. KRETZMANN (eds.), *The Cambridge Companion to Augustine*, Cambridge, 2001, pp. 124-147.

SUMMA, G., *Geistliche Unterscheidung bei Johannes Cassian* (StSSpTh, 7), Würzburg, 1992.

TEJERINA ARIAS, G., *La eclesiología agustiniana del Christus Totus*, in *Aug(L)* 42 (2001) 1139-1179.

TELFER, W., *The Origins of Christianity in Africa*, in *StPatr* 4 (TU, 73), Berlin, 1961, pp. 512-517.

TESELLE, E., *Augustine the Theologian*, New York, 1970.

—, *Pelagius, Pelagianism*, in A.D. FITZGERALD (ed.), *Augustine through the Ages. An Encyclopedia*, Grand Rapids, MI-Cambridge, 1999, pp. 633-640.

—, *Rufinus the Syrian, Caelestius, Pelagius: Explorations in the Prehistory of the Pelagian Controversy*, in *AugSt* 3 (1972) 61-95.

THIER, S., *Kirche bei Pelagius* (PTS, 50), Berlin-New York, 1999.

THOMAS, J.-F., *Saint Augustin s'est-il trompé? Essai sur la prédestination*, Paris, 1959.

THONNARD, F.-J., *La notion de nature chez saint Augustin. Ses progrès dans la polémique antipélagienne*, in *REAug* 11 (1965) 239-265.

—, *La prédestination augustinienne et l'interprétation de O. Rottmanner*, in *REAug* 9 (1963) 259-287.

—, *La prédestination augustinienne. Sa place en philosophie augustinienne*, in *REAug* 10 (1964) 97-123.

TIBILETTI, C., *Giovanni Cassiano. Formazione e dottrina*, in *Aug* 17 (1977) 355-380.

—, *La salvezza umana in Fausto di Riez*, in *Orpheus* n.s. 1 (1980) 371-390.

—, *Libero arbitrio e grazia in Fausto di Riez*, in *Aug* 19 (1979) 259-285.

—, *Note sulla teologia del* "Carmen de providentia Dei", in *Aug* 30 (1990) 453-476.

—, *Pagine monastiche provenzali. Il monachesimo nella Gallia del quinto secolo*, Rome, 1990.

—, *Polemiche in Africa contro i teologi provenzali*, in *Aug* 26 (1986) 499-517.

—, *Rassegna di studi e testi sui «Semipelagiani»*, in *Aug* 25 (1985) 507-522.

—, *Valeriano di Cimiez e la teologia dei Maestri Provenzali*, in *Aug* 22 (1982) 513-532.

TILLEMONT, LENAIN L.-S. DE, *Mémoires pour servir à l'histoire ecclésiastique des six premiers siècles*, T. XII, Paris, 1701; T. XIII: *La vie de saint Augustin*, Paris, 1702.

TIXERONT, J., *Histoire des dogmes dans l'antiquité chrétienne*. T. II: *De saint Athanase à saint Augustin (318-430)*, 9th ed., Paris, 1908.

TONGERLOO, A. VAN, *Reflections on the Manichaean* ΝΟΥΣ, in ID. (ed.), in collaboration with J. VAN OORT, *The Manichaean* ΝΟΥΣ. *Proceedings of the International Symposium organized in Louvain from 31 July to 3 August 1991* (Manichaean Studies, 2), Louvain, 1995, pp. 309-315.

TRAPÈ, A., *A proposito della predestinazione: S. Agostino e i suoi critici moderni*, in *Div* 7 (1963) 243-284.

—, *Libertà e grazia*, in *Congresso internazionale su S. Agostino nel XVI centenario della conversione, Roma, 15-20 settembre 1986*, Vol. I (SEAug, 24), Rome, 1987, pp. 189-202.

—, *S. Agostino*, in A. DI BERARDINO (ed.), *Patrologia*. Vol. III: *Dal Concilio di Nicea (325) al Concilio di Calcedonia (451)*. *I Padri latini*, Casale Monferrato, 1978, pp. 323-434.

—, *S. Agostino esegeta: teoria e prassi*, in *Lat* 28 (1982) 224-237.

—, *S. Agostino. L'uomo, il pastore, il mistico*, 5th ed., Fossano/Cuneo, 1987.

TRIGG, J.W., *Origen. The Bible and Philosophy in the Third-century Church*, Atlanta, 1983.

TURMEL, J., *Histoire des dogmes*. T. I: *Le péché originel. La rédemption*, Paris, 1931.

—, *Histoire de l'interpretation de I Tim. II,4*, in *RHLR* 5 (1900) 385-415.

VAGANAY, L., *Porphyre*, in *DTC* 12/II, cc. 2555-2590.

VALENTIN, L., *Saint Prosper d'Aquitaine. Étude sur la littérature ecclésiastique au cinquième siècle en Gaule*, Paris-Toulouse, 1900.

VALERO, J.B., *El estoicismo de Pelagio*, in *EE* 57 (1982) 39-63.

—, *Las bases antropologicas de Pelagio en su tratado de las* Expositiones (Estudios, 18), Madrid, 1980.

VANNESTE, A., *Nature et grâce dans la théologie de saint Augustin*, in *RechAug* 10 (1975) 143-169.

VERHEIJEN, L., *La règle de saint Augustin*. T. II: *Recherches historiques*, Paris, 1967.

—, *Nouvelle approche de la Règle de Saint Augustin*. T. II: *Chemin vers la vie heureuse*, Louvain, 1988.

—, *Saint Augustin*, in *Théologie de la vie monastique. Études sur la Tradition patristique* [Theol(P), 49], Paris, 1961, pp. 201-212.

—, *Saint Augustine: monk, priest, bishop*, Villanova, 1978.

VESSEY, M., Opus Imperfectum. *Augustine and His Readers, 426-435 A.D.*, in *VigChr* 52 (1998) 264-285.

—, *Vincent of Lérins*, in A.D. FITZGERALD, *Augustine through the Ages. An Encyclopedia*, Grand Rapids, MI-Cambridge, 1999, p. 870.

VILLER, M., *Aux sources de la spiritualité de saint Maxime. Les œuvres d'Évagre le Pontique*, in *RAM* 11 (1930) 156-184; 239-268; 331-336.

—, *Le martyr et l'ascèse*, in *RAM* 6 (1925) 105-142.

VILLER, M. – OLPHE-GALLIARD, M., *L'ascèse chrétienne, A. Les origines scripturaires – B. La période patristique (III.)*, in J. DE GUIBERT et al., *Ascèse, Ascétisme*, in *DSp* 1 (1937) 936-1010, cc. 960-977.

VILLER, M. – RAHNER, K., *Aszese und Mystik in der Väterzeit. Ein Abriß der frühchristlichen Spiritualität*, Unveränderte Neuausgabe mit eunem Vorwort von K.H. Neufeld, Freiburg i. Br., 1939 (reprint, Darmstadt, 1989).

VÖGTLE, A., *Achtlasterlehre*, in *RAC* 1 (1950) 74-79.

VOGÜÉ, A. DE, *Histoire littéraire du mouvement monastique dans l'antiquité*, Tomes I-V, Paris, 1991-1998.

—, *Il monachesimo prima di San Benedetto* (Orizzonti Monastici, 18), Seregno/Milan, 1998.

—, *Pour comprendre Cassien. Un survol des Conférences*, in *CCist* 39 (1977) 250-272.

—, *Sur la patrie d'Honorat de Lérins, évêque d'Arles*, in *RBen* 88 (1978) 290-291.

WAGENAAR, K., *De Bijbel bij de oude monniken*, in *TGL* 27 (1971) 532-553; 607-620.

WANG, TCH'ANG-TCHE, J., *Saint Augustin et les vertus des païens*, Paris, 1938.

WEATHERFORD, R.C., *Compatibilism and Incompatibilism*, in T. HONDERICH [ed.], *The Oxford Companion to Philosophy*, Oxford-New York, 1995, p. 144.

—, *Determinism*, in T. HONDERICH (ed.), *The Oxford Companion to Philosophy*, Oxford-New York, 1995.

—, *Fatalism*, in T. HONDERICH (ed.), *The Oxford Companion to Philosophy*, Oxford-New York, 1995, p. 270.

—, *Libertarianism*, in T. HONDERICH [ed.], *The Oxford Companion to Philosophy*, Oxford-New York, 1995, p. 485.

WEAVER, R.H., *Augustine's Use of Scriptural Admonition Against Boasting in His Final Arguments on Grace*, in *StPatr* 27, Louvain, 1993, pp. 424-430.

—, *Divine Grace and Human Agency. A Study of the Semi-Pelagian Controversy* (PatMS, 15), Macon, 1996.

WEBER, H.-O., *Die Stellung des Johannes Cassianus zur Ausserpachomianischen Mönchstradition: Eine Quellenuntersuchung* (BGAM, 24), Münster, 1959.

WEISMANN, F.J., *The problematic of freedom in St. Augustine: towards a new hermeneutics*, in *REAug* 35 (1989) 104-119.

WEISS, J.-P., *Le semi-pélagianisme se réduit-il à une réaction contre Augustin et l'augustinisme de la première génération?*, in *Congresso Internazionale su S. Agostino nel XVI Centenario della Conversione, Roma, 15-20 settembre 1986*, Atti I (SEAug, 24), Rome, 1987, pp. 465-481.

WERMELINGER, O., *Neuere Forschungskontroversen um Augustinus und Pelagius*, in C. MAYER – K.H. CHELIUS (eds.), *Internationales Symposion über den Stand der Augustinus-Forschung. Vom 12. bis 16. April 1987 im Schloß Rauischholzhausen der Justus-Liebig-Universität Gießen* (Cass., 39/1), Würzburg, 1989.

—, *Rom und Pelagius. Die theologische Position der römischen Bischöfe im pelagianischen Streit in den Jahren 411-432* (PuP, 7), Stuttgart, 1975.

WETZEL, J., *Pelagius Anticipated: Grace and Election in Augustine's Ad Simplicianum*, in J. MC WILLIAM (ed.), *Augustine. From Rethor to Theologian*, Toronto, 1992, pp. 121-132.

—, *Predestination, Pelagianism and Foreknowledge*, in E. STUMP – N. KRETZMANN (eds.), *The Cambridge Companion to Augustine*, Cambridge, 2001, pp. 49-58.

WICKHAM, L., *Pelagianism in the East*, in R. WILLIAMS (ed.), *The Making of Orthodoxy. Essay in honour of Henry Chadwick*, Cambridge, 1989, pp. 200-213.

WILKEN, R.L., *Free Choice and Divine Will in Greek Christian Commentaries on Paul*, in W.S. BABCOCK (ed.), *Paul and the Legacies of Paul*, Dallas, 1990, pp. 123-140.

WRZOL, L., *Die Psychologie des Johannes Cassianus*, in *DT*, 2nd series, 5 (1918) 181-231; 425-456; 7 (1920) 70-96; 9 (1922) 269-294.

YATES, J.P., *Was there "Augustinian" Concupiscence in pre-Augustinian North Africa?*, in *Aug(L)* 51 (2001) 39-56.

ZACHHUBER, J., *Human Nature in Gregory of Nyssa. Philosophical Background and Theological Significance* (SvigChr, 46), Leiden-Boston-Cologne, 2000.

ZANANIRI, M., *La controverse sur la prédestination au Ve siècle: Augustin, Cassien et la Tradition*, in P. RANSON (ed.), *Saint Augustin, s.l.*, 1988, pp. 248-261.

ZARB, S.M., *Chronologia operum sancti Augustini*, Rome, 1934.

ZELZER, K., 'Cassianus natione Scytha, ein Südgallier', in *WSt* 104 (1991) 161-168.

ZIESLER, J.A., *Paul's Letter to the Romans*, Philadelphia, PA, 1989.

ZIMMERLI, W., art. χάρις, B. *Altes Testament*, in *TWNT* 9 (1969) 366-377.

ZUMKELLER, A., *Augustinus über die Zahl der Guten bzw. Auserwählten*, in *Aug* 10 (1970) 421-457.

—, *Correptione et gratia (De-)*, in *AugL* 2 (1996) 39-47.

—, *Das Mönchtum des heiligen Augustinus*, Würzburg, 1950.

—, *Dono perseuerantiae (De)*, in *AugL* 2 (2001) 650-660.

—, ‹Propositum› *in seinem spezifisch christlichen und theologischen Verständnis bei Augustinus*, in C. MAYER (ed.), Homo Spiritalis. *Festgabe für L. Verheijen zu seinem 70. Geburtstag*, Würzburg, 1987, pp. 295-310.

INTRODUCTION

From the Pelagian controversy at the beginning of the 5th century to the *De auxiliis* and the Jansenist controversies in the 16th and 17th centuries, to name only the most well known, disputes over the relationship between grace and free will have left a definite mark on the history of the Western Church. These disputes, and the attempts made at the level of theological reflection to rationalize such a relationship, are clear evidence of the impossibility of finding a definitive and satisfactory solution. Such a solution, in fact, would need to reconcile two apparently irreconcilable principles, and would also have to be capable of balancing, in a fair and constructive manner, faith and reason, revelation and human experience.

When St Paul wrote to the Christians of Philippi: "Work out your own salvation with fear and trembling; for it is God who is at work in you, enabling you both to will and to work for his good pleasure" (Phil 2,12-13), he was expressing, in a balanced way, the need of a synergism between the acceptance and the offer of salvation. He could not possibly have imagined at the time just how much concern a passage like this would give future generations. During the first centuries, the relationship and co-operation between grace and human agency was not regarded as a problem. The Church Fathers, particularly those of the Eastern Church, simply took it for granted, and did not feel compelled to engage in speculation about their interaction, spiritual or otherwise. This irenic vision was shattered by the collision of two different streams of thought: the Pelagian, emphasizing the possibilities of the human will, and the Augustinian, stressing the sovereign and unrestrained activity of divine grace.

The Pelagian movement takes its name from its eponymous founder, Pelagius, a lay ascetic from Roman Britain, who was active in Rome before the city was sacked by Alaric's hordes in 410. Whilst in the eternal city, Pelagius preached a strong asceticism and a severe moral commitment as the necessary means to attain salvation. His preaching and the high moral standard of his life (recognized by Augustine himself)[1]

---

1. At least until 415 Augustine praised Pelagius' own zealous commitment to the cause of a coherent Christian life. Cf. Augustine, *De natura et gratia* 1,1 (CSEL, 60), p. 233.

made an impression, particularly in the milieu of the Christian aristocracy, where the ancient aspirations to a virtuous life and to the heroic
ideals of the past could be channelled through an ascetic engagement
based on the demands of Christian revelation[2]. Pelagius had fled Rome
before the city was taken and after a brief stay in Northern Africa he
established himself in the Holy Land. One of his followers, the Roman
aristocrat Caelestius[3], while in Carthage, aroused the suspicion and the
anger of the African Church by preaching that infant baptism could be
supported even without appealing to the doctrine of original sin, since
the fall of Adam affected no one other than Adam himself. Caelestius
had adopted this notion (in opposition to that of the transmission of
Adam's sin) from Rufinus the Syrian[4], whom he had met in Rome
around 399. Whereas Caelestius was denounced as heretic at an episcopal gathering in Carthage in 411, Pelagius (meanwhile in Palestine)
escaped the same fate after he was acquitted at the Palestinian Council
of Diospolis in 415, where he dissociated himself from Caelestius and
from what he was accused of[5]. The condemnation of Pelagius came in

---

2. See C. PIETRI, *Les difficultés du nouveau système (395-431). La première hérésie
d'Occident: Pélage et le refus rigoriste*, in J.-M. MAYEUR, *et al.* (eds.), *Histoire du christianisme des origines à nos jours*. T. II: *Naissance d'une chrétienté (250-430)*, Paris,
1995, pp. 453-479, esp. 453-454.

3. See G. BONNER, *Caelestius*, in *AugL* 1 (1986) 693-698; G. HONNAY, *Caelestius,
discipulus Pelagii*, in *Aug(L)* 44 (1994) 271-302; M. LAMBERIGTS, *Caelestius*, in A.D.
FITZGERALD (ed.), *Augustine through the Ages. An Encyclopedia*, Grand Rapids, MI –
Cambridge, 1999, pp. 114-115; C. and L. PIETRI (eds.), *Caelestius*, in *Prosopographie
chrétienne du Bas-Empire. 2. Prosopographie de l'Italie chrétienne (313-604)*. I: *A-K*,
Rome, 1999, pp. 357-375.

4. Cf. Augustine, *De gratia Christi et de peccato originali* 2,3,3 (CSEL, 42), p. 168.
See F.G. NUVOLONE, *Pélage et Pélagianisme. I: Les écrivains*, in *DSp* 12/2 (1986) 2889-
2923, cc. 2890-2891. "L'Oriental apportait à Pélage et plus encore à Célestius, le
témoignage d'une tradition proche de la leur, mais pourvue d'une armature conceptuelle
plus ferme" (PIETRI, *Les difficultés du nouveau système* [n. 2], p. 455). Marrou writes that
Rufinus supplied Pelagius and Caelestius with "la dogmatique optimiste que réclamait
leur théologie morale" (H.-I. MARROU, *Les attaches orientales du Pélagianisme*, in
Patristique et Humanisme [PatSor, 9], Paris, 1976, pp. 331-344, p. 343). Marius Mercator's suggestion that Rufinus should be regarded as the inspirer of the Pelagian movement
in Rome ("... Romam primus inuexit": Marius Mercator, *Commonitorium aduersum
haeresim Pelagii et Caelestii*, *Prol.* 1 [ACO, 1/5], p. 5), should be put in perspective. The
tendency of the movement, in fact, was essentially ascetic, and in respect to this Pelagius'
inspiration and role cannot be doubted. See also, E. TESELLE, *Rufinus the Syrian, Caelestius, Pelagius: Explorations in the Prehistory of the Pelagian Controversy*, in *AugSt* 3
(1972) 61-95; W. DUNPHY, *Marius Mercator on Rufinus the Syrian: Was Schwartz Mistaken?*, in *Aug* 32 (1992) 279-288.

5. See S. THIER, *Kirche bei Pelagius* (PTS, 50), Berlin-New York, 1999, p. 323;
O. WERMELINGER, *Rom und Pelagius. Die theologische Position der römischen Bischöfe
im pelagianischen Streit in der Jahren 411-432* (PuP, 7), Stuttgart, 1975, pp. 82ff;
ID., *Neuere Forschungskontroversen um Augustinus und Pelagius*, in C. MAYER –

416 at the councils of Carthage and Milevis, and was ratified by pope Innocent I in 417. Caelestius and Pelagius appealed to Rome and their defence did not fall on deaf ears for they succeeded in being acquitted by the new pope, Zosimus. The bishops of the African Church, under the leadership of Augustine, counterattacked with intensified efforts, until in the spring of 418 they managed to secure the condemnation of the Pelagian teaching by means of the joint action of imperial and papal power[6]. This joint action, however, did not settle the controversy once and for all, either on the level of theological discussion[7] or of historical development. As a matter of fact, the Pelagian resistance was kept alive by 19 Italian bishops (led by Julian of Aeclanum) who did not accept the condemnation[8], and by some other pockets of resistance in Gaul and Britain, which only gradually faded through political enforcement or exile. Julian of Aeclanum, the most powerful theologian of the Pelagian movement, was eventually banished to the East, and was condemned again at the Council of Ephesus (431)[9]. Once his last appeal for clemency to pope Sixtus in 439 was refused[10], he vanished from the scene, much as Pelagius had done after his own condemnation in 418.

This "bird's-eye" introduction to the Pelagian movement and controversy cannot, of course, give the exact idea of the complexity of this multifaceted reality. It is only in the 20th century that such complexity has been acknowledged, and some attempts to tackle it as objectively as possible have been undertaken[11], particularly on a double front: on the

---

K.H. CHELIUS (eds.), *Internationales Symposion über den Stand der Augustinus-Forschung. Vom 12. bis 16. April 1987 im Schloß Rauischholzhausen der Justus-Liebig-Universität Gießen* (Cass., 39/1), Würzburg, 1989, p. 212; NUVOLONE, *Pélage et Pélagianisme. I: Les écrivains* (n. 4), c. 2896.

6. See *infra*, pp. 21ff.

7. Zosimus' *Epistula tractoria* is not fully African (or Augustinian) in its formulation. Concerning it and the initial pro-Pelagian attitude of Zosimus, see *infra* pp. 22-24.

8. As it has been rightly noted, their resistance was a clear sign that "Italian Christianity, like European Christianity as a whole, simply did not possess the coherent doctrinal tradition against which Pelagian views could be measured unambiguously" (R.A. MARKUS, *Pelagianism: Britain and the Continent*, in *JHE* 37 [1986] 191-204, pp. 197-198). A further sign of the non-compact theological horizon in Europe can be found also in the fact that the accuser of Caelestius at Carthage in 411 was Paulinus of Milan. See A. PAREDI, *Paulinus of Milan*, in *SE* 14 (1963) 206-230.

9. See J. LÖSSL, *Julian von Aeclanum. Studien zu seinem Leben, seinem Werk, seiner Lehre und ihrer Überlieferung* (SVigChr, 60), Leiden-Boston-Cologne, 2001, pp. 311-319.

10. See M. LAMBERIGTS, *Julian of Eclanum*, in FITZGERALD (ed.), *Augustine through the Ages* (n. 3), pp. 478-479; C. and L. PIETRI (eds.), *Iulianus 9*, in *Prosopographie chrétienne du Bas-Empire. 2. Prosopographie de l'Italie chrétienne* (n. 3), pp. 1175-1186.

11. From the pioneering work of A. SOUTER, *Pelagius' Expositions of Thirteen Epistles of St. Paul* (TaS, 9,1-3), Cambridge, 1922; 1926; 1931 (also in PLS, 1, cc.

one hand the attempt to disentangle the Pelagian thought from the interpretation of the opposition[12], and on the other the endeavour to distinguish between that which was written by Pelagius and that which was
the product of his followers[13], viz. between that which is *pelagisch* and
that which is *pelagianisch*[14]. The fact that a considerable part of the *corpus Pelagianum* has come down to us through the works of Augustine[15]
is, to a great extent, the reason why the "Augustinian" reception and
understanding of Pelagian texts have proved so influential to subsequent
judgements[16], contributing, for instance, to attribute to Pelagius some
positions which were not genuinely his[17]. Furthermore, in Augustine's
writings, the Pelagian texts were disembodied in short formulas and
then, once extrapolated from the context they belonged to, refuted, piece
by piece, in a theoretical and systematic way[18].

Of immediate interest to our enquiry is the recognition of the clash
between Pelagianism and Augustinianism; a clash which resulted in a
one-sided solution. In point of fact, the winning party, led by the bishop
of Hippo, arrived at such an uncompromising stance on the exalted function and supremacy of divine grace that there seemed little or no room
for the action of human will. The co-operation between God's intervention and the human being's desire, will and action, kept in theological
balance during the first centuries, was undone in favour of a notion
of God's infinite and absolute omnipotence; an omnipotence whose

110-1374), to G. DE PLINVAL, *Pélage, ses écrits, sa vie et sa réforme. Étude d'histoire littéraire et religieuse*, Lausanne, 1943; T. BOHLIN, *Die Theologie des Pelagius und ihre
Genesis* (AUU, 9), Upsala, 1957; and the more recent works of WERMELINGER, *Rom und
Pelagius* (n. 5); G. GRESHAKE, *Gnade als konkrete Freiheit. Eine Untersuchung zur
Gnadenlehre des Pelagius*, Mainz, 1972; J.B. VALERO, *Las bases antropologicas de Pelagio en su tratado de las Expositiones*, Madrid, 1980. For a thorough *status quaestionis*
of the *Pelagiusforschung*, see WERMELINGER, *Neuere Forschungskontroversen* (n. 5),
pp. 191-198.
   12. "Le pélagianisme pour une bonne part est une construction dans laquelle Pélage
lui-même ne se reconnaissait pas!" (M. LAMBERIGTS, *Le mal et le péché. Pélage: la réhabilitation d'un hérétique*, in *RHE* 95 [2000] 97-111, p. 108).
   13. For a comprehensive view of the different Pelagian works and their autorship, see
NUVOLONE, *Pélage et Pélagianisme. I: Les écrivains* (n. 4).
   14. GRESHAKE, *Gnade als konkrete Freiheit* (n. 11), p. 27, n. 3.
   15. "Augustinus bleibt weiterhin Hauptquelle zur Rekonstruierung der pelagianischen
Streitigkeiten" (WERMELINGER, *Neuere Forschungskontroversen* [n. 5], p. 217).
   16. See *Ibid.*, pp. 190-191.
   17. "Bereits Augustinus ist mit einer Vielfalt von Schriften pelagianischer Provenienz
konfrontiert. Schon bei ihm findet sich die Tendenz ... Pelagius mehr zuzuschreiben, als
ihm tatsächlich zugehört" (*Ibid.*, p. 216). For some examples, see LAMBERIGTS, *Le mal et
le péché* (n. 12), pp. 101ff.
   18. "Augustin s'est occupé en d'autres mots de rassembler en une synthèse dogmatique une littérature pélagienne cependant très variée, le tout pour ensuite pouvoir la
réfuter" (*Ibid.*, p. 106).

primacy and freedom of intervention could not be questioned or jeopardized by mankind's use of free will, whatever its potential.

After the Pelagian movement had been condemned, the Augustinian position on grace was openly challenged within the *Catholica*, and, even more remarkable, on African soil, by a group of monks from the monastery of Hadrumetum, on the coast of Northern Africa. Subsequently, the challenge was taken up (and this time with more intellectual vigour) by the monks of the monastic settlements in Southern Gaul. Although both the African and the Gallic monks were at one with the bishop of Hippo on the necessity of a grace bestowed upon the believer by the redemptive act of Christ, they could not accept the idea that the human person was somehow deprived of a genuinely independent role in the process of allegiance to God's design. If Augustine preferred to stress the second verse of the Pauline passage quoted above ("it is God who is at work in you") in order to safeguard the supremacy of God's grace, the monks would quote both verses without stressing one above the other. They suggested, for instance, that the initial movement of man in turning to God, or in ultimately rejecting the offer of grace, could be ascribed to the function of human will independent of any divine intervention. Above all, they reacted to Augustine's predestinarian theory which, in their eyes, not merely nullified the significance of human action, but also introduced what was to them an incomprehensible arbitrariness into God's activity. The debate around these and other related issues took place in ca. 426-428, not long before Augustine's death, and was carried on for several decades by the admirers and defenders of Augustine, on the one hand, and by those connected with the monastic establishment of Southern Gaul, on the other. It was eventually settled at the Council of Orange, in 529, where the Augustinian doctrine was declared part of the Church's teaching, although the notion of absolute grace was softened and the predestinarian theory left aside.

The resistance against Augustinian views on grace (from 426 to 529) has improperly been called "Semipelagianism", a name that is foreign to the actual historical and theological context in which this resistance developed. At the time of Augustine, but also in the decades that followed (during which representatives of both sides, in Gaul and Africa, continued the confrontation), no one ever thought of addressing the monks and divines of Hadrumetum and of Southern Gaul as "Semipelagian". Prosper of Aquitaine, an admirer of the bishop of Hippo[19], and a defender of his views on grace, calls one of the two groups in which he

---

19. See *infra*, p. 91, n. 4.

classified the Gallic monks, as *Pelagianae reliquiae prauitatis*[20]. This expression, however, never occurs again, and is not used by Augustine who, on the contrary, considered and called the monks of Hadrumetum and Provence *fratres*[21], *dilectissimi*[22], *nostri*[23]. In the eyes of the bishop of Hippo they were not so much adversaries as brethren who needed correct instruction in what he believed to be the right interpretation of pertinent theological issues. It is for this reason that in the main body of our research we shall avoid the expression "Semipelagianism" and replace it with more suitable terms. Expressions such as the monks/monastic community of Hadrumetum, in as much as African resistance to Augustine is concerned, and Massilians/Massilianism, as a blanket term[24] for the monks belonging to the monastic settlements in Southern Gaul at the beginning of the 5th century, will be used. But where did the term "Semipelagian" come from[25]? And why, more precisely, is it inappropriate?

No mention of it can be found either in ancient Christian literature[26] or in medieval theological production[27]. It is during the agitation caused by the teachings of Baius on grace and free will, that the expressions *Pelagianorum reliquiae* and *Massilienses* were developed and used to distinguish the teaching of the monks of Southern Gaul from that of the Pelagians[28]. The term "Semipelagianism" made a timid appearance in the second half of the 16th century, during the so-called *De auxiliis* controversy; a controversy provoked by the vehement reaction of the Dominican theologian D. Bañez to the publication of the Jesuit theologian L. de Molina's *De Concordia liberi arbitrii cum gratiae donis* (1588). In the meetings of the *Congregatio de auxiliis* the term "Semipelagianism" was used to describe the teaching of the monks of Southern

20. Prosper of Aquitaine (= Prosper), *Ep.* 225,7 (CSEL, 57), p. 465.
21. Cf., for instance, Augustine, *De gratia et libero arbitrio* 1,1 and 24,46 (PL, 44), cc. 881 and 911; *De correptione et gratia* 1,1 (CSEL, 92), p. 219; *De praedestinatione sanctorum* 1,2 (PL, 44), c. 961.
22. Cf. Augustine, *De gratia et libero arbitrio* 1,1 (PL, 44), c. 881.
23. Cf. Id., *De dono perseuerantiae* 24,66 (PL, 45), c. 1033.
24. Although not only the monks from Marseilles (= *Massilia*), but also those from Lérins, from the islands of Hyères and from other monastic settlements (see *infra*, pp. 111-118), were involved in the anti-Augustinian reaction, we will make use of the terms "Massilians/Massilianism" as blanket terms for the Gallic critics and their movement.
25. See A.M. JACQUIN, *À quelle date apparaît le terme "Semipélagien"?*, in *RSPT* 1 (1907) 506-508.
26. See É. AMANN, *Semi-Pélagiens*, in *DTC* 14/2 (1941) 1796-1850, c. 1796.
27. H. BOUILLARD, *Saint Thomas et le Semi-Pélagianisme*, in *BLE* 43 (1942) 181-209.
28. See JACQUIN, *À quelle date apparaît le terme "Semipélagien"?* (n. 25), p. 507.

Gaul[29]. The expression, however, was still limited in its usage, and it was only in the 17th century that theologians became increasingly familiar with it, to the point where it was finally adopted as a technical term and added to the theological vocabulary of the day. It was used to describe the initial opposition to Augustine's doctrine on grace and free will by the monks of Hadrumetum and Provence (when Augustine was still alive), and subsequently to describe the opposition by Gallic clerics to later defenders of the bishop of Hippo's ideas.

The term "Semipelagianism" has remained in use until today, and is still used because of its evocative power. In that respect it has become a *nom commode*, a compact party label it is not easy to displace, in spite of its ambiguous[30] and unjust[31] connotations. In point of fact, the designation "Semipelagianism" gives the false impression of an existing and "unified movement" connecting Africa with Gaul, and gives also rise to the idea that the monks were acquiescent with the Pelagian tenets on grace and free will[32]. Furthermore, we can add a "historical" reason why the monks of Hadrumetum and Southern Gaul were not deserving of such an unjust misnomer. Historically speaking, the nature of the polemic between the monks of Hadrumetum and Southern Gaul on one hand, and Augustine, on the other, was *not* a Pelagian one[33]. Even though their reaction to the bishop of Hippo had occurred in the aftermath of the Pelagian controversy, it was nevertheless independent of it, although we cannot rule out that at least an echo of the whole discussion must have reached the monks, particularly the more cultivated ones in Southern Gaul. As to the monks of Hadrumetum, in fact, we have the

29. "C'est, semble-t-il, durant les discussions de la Congregation *de auxiliis* que le terme a fait son apparition. Un des consulteurs signale l'existence, chez Molina, de l'erreur de Cassien et des autres Gaulois, qu'il appelle un peu plus loin la *sententia semipelagianorum*" (AMANN, *Semi-Pélagiens* [n. 26], c. 1796).

30. Cristiani speaks of the term Semipelagianism as a "nom commode mais tendancieux" (L. CRISTIANI, *Jean Cassien. La spiritualité du désert*, S. Wandrille, 1946, T. II, p. 237).

31. "To apply the term to the monks of Africa or of Gaul who had difficulties with Augustine's views is both anachronistic and unjust" (R.J. TESKE, *General Introduction*, in ID. [ed.], *Answer to the Pelagians. IV: To the Monks of Hadrumetum and Provence* [The Works of Saint Augustine, I/26], New York, 1999, p. 11).

32. The term "Semi-Pelagianism ... is uselessly pejorative and suggests a direct link with Pelagius" (J. DANIÉLOU – H.I. MARROU [eds.], *The Christian Centuries*. Vol. I: *The First Six Hundred Years*, 2nd impression, London, 1978); "The name is wrong. The leaders of the school were not half-way to being disciples of Pelagius" (O. CHADWICK, *John Cassian. A Study in Primitive Monasticism*, 2nd ed., Cambridge, 1968, p. 127).

33. "Quanto all'uso del termine "semipelagianesimo" e affini ..., pensiamo che non debba essere più usato ..., perché storicamente la natura della polemica non era quella pelagiana" (V. GROSSI, *La predestinazione in S. Agostino*, in *DSBP* 15: *Elezione-Vocazione-Predestinazione*, Rome, 1997, pp. 341-367, p. 346, n. 7).

clear impression that they seemingly ignored, and remained outside, the
theological debate produced by the Pelagian controversy. This is why (in
our eyes) they were taken aback by the content of a letter that Augustine
had written to Sixtus several years earlier, in 418, soon after the condemnation of Pelagianism. The bewilderment and the uproar that the
content of that letter (which recalls, against Pelagianism, the main points
of the Augustinian doctrine on grace) provoked in the African monks,
show that they were ignorant of the exact development of the issues at
stake in the Pelagian controversy. Not possessing a sufficient acquaintance with the terms of the confrontation nor a precise judgement, they
really "risked being hoist by their own reading"[34]. What actually triggered the resistance of the monks who were living in two geographically
different and distant areas, viz. the opposite sides of the Mediterranean,
was the fear that some of Augustine's statements on grace would endan-
ger the practice of Christian asceticism and the moral effort that lay at
the core of their monastic commitment. It is therefore misleading to
interpret the discussion between Augustine and the monks of Hadrumetum and Provence as merely the bishop of Hippo's final answer to the
Pelagian question[35].

Various proposals have been put forward to obviate the ambiguity of
the term Semipelagianism. It has been suggested, for instance, that, at
least in the case of the Massilians, it would be fairer to call them "Semiaugustinians"[36], a term which would imply that they had a penchant for
Augustinianism rather than Pelagianism. However, the very name
"Semiaugustinians" is, in our opinion, somewhat ambiguous too in that
it does not take into account the substratum upon which the opposition
of the Massilians to Augustine's views on grace, free will and predestination was based. This substratum, in fact, ought to be considered in
close connection with the traditional (pre-Augustinian) views held by
the Church (more specifically by the Church of the *pars Orientis*) and
with the rapid expansion and influence of Eastern asceticism in the

34. M. VESSEY, Opus Imperfectum. *Augustine and His Readers, 426-435* A.D., in
VigChr 52 (1998) 264-285.
35. Quite recently, in two American English translations the works of Augustine
addressed to the monks of Hadrumetum and Provence were referred to as "Anti-Pelagian
Writings" or "An Answer to the Pelagians": see J.A. MOURANT – W.J. COLLINGE (eds.),
*Saint Augustine. Four Anti-Pelagian Writings: On Nature and Grace, On the Proceed-
ings of Pelagius, On the Predestination of the Saints, On the Gift of Perseverance* (FaCh,
86), Washington, 1992; TESKE (ed.), *Answer to the Pelagians. IV: To the Monks of
Hadrumetum and Provence* (n. 31). Also the entry *Semipelagianismus* in *TRE* 31 (2000)
143, refers back to the article *Pelagius/Pelagianischer Streit*.
36. This suggestion was forwarded in F. GRÜTZMACHER, *Cassianus, Johannes*, in *RE*
3 (1897) 746-749, p. 747.

Western Church. Another term that has been suggested as a substitute for "Semipelagianism" is that of "Antiaugustinianism"[37]. It is a term which, rather than emphasizing the views that the monks of Hadrumetum and Provence shared with Augustine, would in fact emphasize the reasons for the monks' resistance and opposition to the bishop of Hippo's doctrine of grace. It seems that this term can more adequately explain the reaction of the monks, although it should only be applied *stricto sensu*, namely as referring only to the particular theological discussion concerning the relationship between grace, free will and predestination, and to no other issues. From all this, however, it becomes clear that the blanket terms Massilians and Massilianism remain the best available option.

The need for a historical and theological reappraisal of the positions held by the monks of Hadrumetum and by the Massilians has been met by a number of studies, either in connection with Augustine's works addressed respectively to the African and Gallic monks or with the writings of Cassian (the spokesperson of the Massilian reaction to the bishop of Hippo) and his followers. As to Augustine's specific treatises, it suffices to mention some studies in the form of long "Introductions" to bilingual editions[38] or to vernacular translations[39]. The setting of these studies is undoubtedly the reason why the problems that Augustine had to tackle are approached and commented within a predominant "Augustinian" perspective. The position of the bishop of Hippo's interlocutors,

---

37. See, for instance: "Pour nous, le sémi-pélagianisme est essentiellement un antiaugustinisme exacerbé" (AMANN, *Semi-Pélagiens* [n. 26], c. 1796); "The doctrine *[Semipelagianism]* is in fact Anti-Augustinianism" (DANIÉLOU – MARROU [eds.], *The Christian Centuries*. Vol. I [n. 32], p. 407); "A more accurate term ... is anti-Augustinian" (CHADWICK, *John Cassian* [n. 32], p. 113). See also PIETRI, *Les difficultés du nouveau système* [n. 2], p. 453.

38. See, for instance, S. KOPP – A. ZUMKELLER (eds.), *Aurelius Augustinus, Schriften gegen die Semipelagianer: Gnade und freier Wille, Zurechtweisung und Gnade, Die Vorherbestimmung der Heiligen, Die Gabe der Beharrlichkeit*, Würzburg, 1955, pp. 11-75; V. CAPANAGA, *et al.*, *Obras de San Agustín.* T. VI: *Tratados sobre la gracia: Del espíritu y de la letra. – De la naturaleza y de la gracia. – De la gracia de Jesucristo y del pecado original. – De la gracia y del libre albedrío. – De la corrección y de la gracia. – De la predestinación de los santos. – Del don de perseverancia* (BAC, 50), 2nd ed., Madrid, 1956, pp. 27-46; J. CHÉNÉ – J. PINTARD, *Œuvres de Saint Augustin. Aux moines d'Adrumète et de Provence: De gratia et libero arbitrio – De correptione et gratia – De praedestinatione sanctorum – De dono perseverantiae* (BA, 24), Paris, 1962, pp. 9-28; 74-83; 246-260; 436-453; A. TRAPÈ (ed.), *Sant'Agostino. Grazia e libertà: La grazia e il libero arbitrio, La correzione e la grazia, La predestinazione dei santi, Il dono della perseveranza* (NBA, 20), Rome, 1987, pp. IX-CXCII; 3-17; 99-113; 193-219.

39. See, for instance, MOURANT–COLLINGE (eds.), *Saint Augustine* (n. 35), pp. 181-217; TESKE (ed.), *Answer to the Pelagians. IV: To the Monks of Hadrumetum and Provence* (n. 31), pp. 11-37.

in fact, is treated briefly, and mainly in order to delineate the historical context in which the discussions with Augustine took place, but little or no attention is paid to the goodness of their ultimate concern and to the premises from which such concern was engendered. Although in varied degrees, the main preoccupation that emerges from these "Introductions" to Augustine's writings addressed to the monks of Hadrumetum and Southern Gaul concerns the interpretation/explanation of the bishop of Hippo's views, undertaken in the attempt to fit them into the general development of Augustine's thought, above all in the light of the coherence of his theological construction as a whole[40]. A more "critical" approach to Augustine's view on the issues raised by the African and Gallic monks can be found interspersed in books, or in scholarly articles dealing specifically with both sides of the confrontation[41].

The person and thought of Cassian, the most outspoken representative of the anti-Augustinian, viz. Massilian, reaction has been approached in several studies and with different emphases. Godet, for instance, stressed Cassian's aversion to what the author (without nuances) defined as Pelagian "naturalism", but at the same time he believed that the divine of Marseilles can indeed be regarded as a Semipelagian[42]. Kemmer's study on the relationship between Cassian's teaching on the ascetic struggle for perfection and analogous views held by the Messalian monks on the same issue, was important in that it retraced, and focused on, the notion of the goodness of nature as it was understood in Eastern theology. He pointed out that the latter optimistic understanding of nature, still considered a source of goodness in spite of Adam's fall, comes into conflict with the concept of sin, regarded as being in contradiction with the very definition of nature. In so doing Kemmer brought to the surface one of the pivotal points of Cassian's theology of grace and free will[43]. Cristiani[44], on the contrary, ignored the eastern concept of nature and its influence on Cassian, and passed judgement on the work of the divine of Marseilles from a dogmatic-Augustinian perspective, rather than from a

---

40. Chéné's synthesis-introduction to a collection of Augustinian texts that deal with the issues of grace, free will and predestination is still very valuable. See J. CHÉNÉ, *La théologie de saint Augustin. Grâce et prédestination*, Le Puy-Lyon, [1962].

41. See, for instance, the article of K. RAHNER, *Augustin und der Semipelagianismus*, in *ZKT* 62 (1938) 171-196. Other articles and books will be mentioned in the following footnotes and/or in the course of the study.

42. See P. GODET, *Cassien Jean*, in *DTC* 2 (1910) 1823-1829. "L'adversaire décidé de Pélage ... n'a pas laissé, quoi qu'en aient dit ses apologistes, anciens et modernes, de toucher sur l'écueil du semipélagianisme" (*Ibid.*, c. 1826).

43. See A. KEMMER, *Charisma Maximum. Untersuchung zu Cassians Vollkommenheitslehre und seiner Stellung zum Messalianismus*, Louvain, 1938.

44. See CRISTIANI, *Jean Cassien* (n. 30).

historical point of view. Moreover, he introduced the distinction between natural and supernatural order, which was not in use at the time of Augustine and Cassian. Cappuyns underlined the contacts that Cassian entertained with the works (or with the teaching) of eastern theologians such as Origen and Evagrius Ponticus. He was convinced of the perfect orthodoxy of Cassian's spiritual doctrine as well as of the fact that the roots of the so-called Semipelagianism should be retraced in pre-Cassian (eastern) history of ascesis and theology[45]. Olphe-Galliard too reiterated Cassian's attachment to eastern theological tradition and pointed out the influence that Stoicism, Aristotelianism and Neoplatonism have exercised on his literary production. He affirmed, however, that Cassian was not an original thinker and theologian in that he merely reproduced the thought of the Church of the *pars Orientis* he came in contact with during his long stay in the East. Above all Olphe-Galliard was at pains to free Cassian from Pelagian connections and interpreted the "formules erronées" (as he defined them) of *Conlatio* 13 as an attempt to adapt the eastern thought to preoccupations which were of the Western Church. He also stressed Cassian's asceticism, calling attention on the fact that it is in virtue of his monastic experience that he was led to give precedence to psychological/moral solutions rather than to abstract intellectual formulations[46]. Guy described Cassian as wanting to occupy a middle position between Augustine and Pelagius, a position which was not dependent on Pelagianism but on Eastern monastic theology and its emphasis on religious experience[47]. The work of O. Chadwick on John Cassian[48] remains a very valuable and balanced study. The author pin-points the differences and the similarities between Augustine on one side, and Cassian and the Gallic monks on the other. He shows clearly how great a role a different intellectual and spiritual background can play in the formation of theological opinions and in the unfolding of a theological discussion. He also shows how the points in which the bishop of Hippo and the divine of Marseilles agreed were eventually more than those upon which they were in disagreement[49]. The way Chadwick approaches the differences between Augustine and Cassian is

45. See M. CAPPUYNS, *Cassien (Jean)*, in *DHGE* 11 (1949) 1319-1348. "Cassien n'a certainement pas inventé ce qu'on appelle aujourd'hui le semipélagianisme. Les origines en remontent très haut dans l'histoire de l'ascèse et de la théologie. Origène et S. Jean Chrysostome en ont esquissé inconsciemment les premières ébauches doctrinales" (*Ibid.*, c. 1345).

46. See M. OLPHE-GALLIARD, *Cassien (Jean)*, in *DSp* 2 (1953) 214-276.

47. See J.-C. GUY, *Jean Cassien. Vie et doctrine spirituelle*, Paris, 1961.

48. See CHADWICK, *John Cassian* (n. 32).

49. *Ibid.*, pp. 127ff.

a very objective one, serene, bereft of that suspicion and recrimination of which, particularly the monks of Southern Gaul, had been the object over the last centuries. In Tibiletti's studies about the monks of Provence, the insistence on the eastern background of Cassian's thought and on his intellectual connections with Stoicism constitute the main concern[50]. Stewart's monograph[51], the first major study on Cassian after Chadwick's, focuses, as the title clearly suggests, on Cassian's familiarity with monastic literary sources and on his personal experience as a monk, which is what makes his monastic teaching trustworthy. Against this background much attention is paid to Cassian's spiritual theology, the eschatological perspective of the monastic journey, the Christological basis of biblical interpretation, the teaching on continence/chastity and on prayer/contemplation. It is Stewart's contention that the way Cassian deals with the issue of the relationship between grace and free will should be understood in the light of the necessity of divine intervention, as is clearly evident in the experience of continence and chastity, in whose framework such a relationship should be set.

Other studies have taken into account the whole span of the so-called Semipelagian controversy, stretching from the first African reaction in 426 (the *terminus a quo*) to the decrees of the 2nd Council of Orange of 529 (the *terminus ad quem*), the council where the disputed problems of grace, free will and predestination, were eventually settled and whose decisions became normative for the Church. Some of these studies deserve a mention here. The long article of Amann[52], whose conviction that the African and Gallic monks' position should be referred to as Antiaugustinianism rather than Semipelagianism[53], made it clear that some affirmations of the monks can indeed acquire a Pelagian flavour whenever they are taken as single units, that is, extrapolated from their historical and literary context. He admitted quite openly that the monks' reaction against the rigidity of Augustine's theory of predestination is praiseworthy. What he judged unfavourably, however, is their over-estimation of the goodness of nature and their concept of *initium fidei*, which, according to Amann, constituted the pivotal point of their optimistic notion of nature[54]. He also failed to recognize the eastern connections

50. See C. TIBILETTI, *Giovanni Cassiano. Formazione e dottrina*, in *Aug* 17 (1977) 355-380; ID., *Rassegna di studi e testi sui "Semipelagiani"*, in *Aug* 25 (1985) 507-522; ID., *Pagine monastiche provenzali. Il monachesimo nella Gallia del quinto secolo*, Rome, 1990, pp. 27-59.
51. See C. STEWART, *Cassian the Monk* (OSHT), New York-Oxford, 1998.
52. See AMANN, *Semi-Pélagiens* (n. 26).
53. See *supra*, n. 37.
54. Cf. AMANN, *Semi-Pélagiens* (n. 26), cc. 1849-1850.

of the monks' theological views, assuming that they were Antiaugustin-
ian on account of their independent theoretical stand. Chéné[55], on the
contrary, pointed out in his study on the origins of Semipelagianism the
eastern theological views with which the Massilians seemed to be well
acquainted[56]. He also delineated the network of "monastic" Antiaugus-
tinian alliance of which Marseilles and Lérins were the strongholds.
With regard to the specific concept of *initium fidei*, however, he asserted
that the impact of this error is more wide-ranging and serious than it is
usually suggested[57]. Solignac's article, while referring to the studies of
Amann and Tibiletti for the historical setting of Semipelagianism, concentrates on the doctrinal aspects of Semipelagianism in as much as they
affected (or were the result of) a specific view on spiritual/religious
commitment[58]. He too stresses the Massilians' eastern monastic background and the latter focus on prayer and ascesis as means to combat
fatalism. Unlike Chéné, Solignac believes that the critical judgement on
the monks' standpoint on the issue of the *initium fidei* should not be
over-emphasized, but rather nuanced in virtue of the fact that the interplay of grace and free will was not seen by them in antithetic terms but
in the light of *cas concrets* drawn from Scripture[59]. Weaver's study on
Semipelagianism[60] is the last well-constructed attempt to explore the historical development and the theological significance of the Semipelagian
controversy, from its outset to the 2nd Council of Orange (529). She proceeds with her enquiry at a threefold level corresponding to three main
working hypotheses[61]: first, the conviction that divine grace and human
agency operate from different frameworks, each with its own set of
issues where overlapping may cause confusion and misunderstanding;
second, the importance to be given to the social and religious (monastic)
setting; third, the different theological background nurtured by different
theological traditions. In this respect, the general direction of Weaver's
work has been of some inspiration to our own research, since it seems to
us that Weaver's work takes up the best intuitions of the aforementioned
scholars and brings them together in an attempt to give a coherent

---

55. J. Chéné, *Les origines de la controverse semi-pélagienne*, in *ATA* 13 (1953) 56-
109.
56. Cf. Id., *Notes complémentaires* 16 (BA, 24), pp. 806-807.
57. Cf. Id., *Que signifiaient "initium fidei" et "affectum credulitatis" pour les Semi-
pélagiens?*, in *RSR* 35 (1948) 566-588, p. 588.
58. A. Solignac, *Semipélagiens*, in *DSp* 14 (1990) 556-568.
59. *Ibid.*, c. 566.
60. R.H. Weaver, *Divine Grace and Human Agency. A Study of the Semi-Pelagian
Controversy* (PatMS, 15), Macon, GA, 1996.
61. Cf. *Ibid.*, pp. IX-X.

structure to the emergence and development of a debate that involved Augustine and the Augustinian party on one hand, and the monks of Hadrumetum and Southern Gaul and their later followers on the other, from the late twenties of the 5th century to the late twenties of the 6th century.

It is necessary at this stage to clarify the method and the specific aim(s) of the present work. First of all, our investigation is restricted in time and range in that it is limited to the initial stage of the controversy, namely to the time in which the issues on grace, free will and predestination were tackled in Africa and Gaul during Augustine's life time. We will not take into consideration the second and longer stage of the controversy, which stretched into the 6th century, right up to the 2nd Council of Orange (529). This second stage will be referred to in the *Epilogue*, in which we will give a brief summary of the *Nachgeschichte* of the controversy up to 529.

One of our main purposes is to assess the historical and theological framework in which the debate started and developed, yielding a unique contribution to Western theology and culture, the repercussions of which continue up to this day. For this reason a genetic methodology will be applied to help us retrace the *Sitz-im-Leben* in which the discussions between Augustine and the monks of Hadrumetum, and those between Augustine and the monks of Provence, took place. It is clear to us that Augustine was rather alien to some teachings and attitudes which were part of Eastern Christian and monastic culture and with which, conversely, the monastic settlements (particularly in Southern Gaul) were conversant. Since we are convinced – as Aristotle once pointed out – that when things are observed from their origins and followed through in their development, they can be perceived and elucidated more clearly[62], we have deemed it necessary to retrace on a larger scale (when that is possible) the influences that have determined the line of thought of the two parties at the beginning of the so-called Semipelagian controversy. Analogously, and on a smaller scale, this genetic methodology will be applied to the literary production of the *dramatis personae*, according to a chronological order. This has been somehow more evident with regard to Augustine's vast literary output, in which possible developments of thought (where a development is present at all)[63] can be detected and

---

62. "Εἰ δὴ ἐξ ἀρχῆς τὰ πράγματα φυόμενα βλέψειεν, ὥσπερ ἐν τοῖς ἄλλοις, καὶ ἐν τούτοις κάλλιστ' ἂν οὕτω θεωρήσειεν" (Aristotle, *Politica* I,1252a,3).

63. Augustine himself, referring to his *Retractationes*, recognised that he had not always been consistent with regard to some issues, but that such "inconsistency" should be considered a sign of further development and progress in his thought: "Nam propterea

reasoned in the light of a historical and logical approach. The relatively modest literature produced by the monks of Hadrumetum and Southern Gaul, among which the works of Cassian occupy a prominent place, does not lend itself to an "inward" genetic methodology. For this reason we will try to understand the position of the African and Gallic monks in the light of the insights that their writings disclose, particularly in the light of the ascetic and theological connections they enjoyed with the *pars Orientis*.

The Massilians' link with the eastern thought in the matters of theology and asceticism brings us to the other important, not to say central, aim of our research, namely the conviction (perceivable in various ways all throughout the pages of the present work) that the ascetic/monastic perspective of the anti-Augustinian party played a major role in the so-called Semipelagian controversy. We believe that the debate between Augustine and the African and Gallic monks was not so much affected by theoretical premises or pre-suppositions about the relationship between grace and free will as by the attempt to define the potentialities and/or the limits of human effort within the framework of the Christian "struggle" for perfection. In fact, as we have hinted at in the title of this work, we believe that the underlying concern that runs across the debated issues finds its full expression in the way in which the relationship between divine benevolence (*gratia*) and spiritual struggle (*certamen*) is understood. Such a concern pertains primarily to the very meaning and "function" of "agonism", viz. ascetic and monastic effort, in the life of the believer. In our opinion, it is precisely through the rationale of the ascetic/monastic undertaking and the struggle for perfection that the position of the African and Gallic monks vis-à-vis Augustine's concept of grace, faith and predestination, can be properly assessed, both intellectually and spiritually.

Attention will be also paid to the Pelagian tenets, at least in as far as the monks' attitude intersected with them, particularly in questions strictly connected with the ascetic drive and the moral commitment demanded by it. Even if the African and Gallic monks considered themselves anti-Pelagian, we cannot rule out the existence of an "ascetic thread" that, more or less unconsciously, made for a mutual sympathy and understanding when it came to actual involvement in Christian life. We thus surmise that the monks of both Hadrumetum and Southern Gaul

nunc facio libros *[Retractationes]*, in quibus opuscula mea retractanda suscepi, ut nec me ipsum in omnibus me secutum fuisse demonstrem, sed proficienter me existimo Deo miserante scripsisse, non tamen a perfectione coepisse" (Augustine, *De dono perseuerantiae* 21,55 [PL, 45], c. 1028).

had probably shared the ascetic endeavour characteristic of Pelagianism, without having to share the doctrine that it purported, for, as it has been suggested, it was perfectly "possible to reject the letter of Pelagianism but still be seduced unawares by its spirit"[64]. It is not at all unlikely, in fact, that the high moral standard and the masculine spirituality encouraged by Pelagianism may have had a positive impact on our monks. Nevertheless, we should not expect to find direct, literal influences. As for the relationship with Eastern theology, also with regard to Pelagianism we can detect some affinities, reminiscences and parallels which, in this particular case, probably go back to a common background. At times, however, the result of the comparison between the arguments will simply confront us with their irreconcilability or with the impossibility of finding a coherent and unassailable solution. Like a jig-saw puzzle, some of the pieces may turn out to be missing whilst others simply do not fit, leaving us with the inkling of a possible (but still pending) solution. Furthermore, we must acknowledge that when the history and development of monastic asceticism and culture cut across the path of complex theological problems, the latter are not simply viewed or solved from a dogmatic point of view. On the contrary, they are approached from within a specifically monastic ethos, an ethos which besides tending to the preservation of the riches of tradition (even in matter of doctrine), tries to assimilate these riches in a manner that nowadays would probably be defined as "practical" theology. This is an attitude which maintains all its relevance in a monastic setting.

Last but not least, we have deemed it necessary, in the course of the present work, to deal with the "re-discovery" of Paul's letters[65] (above all his letter to the Romans), which from the second half of the 4th century began to play an increasing role in theological discussions, including that between Augustine and the Massilians. Although the Christological debate was not over (the dogma of the theandric nature of Christ will be solemnly proclaimed at the Council of Chalcedon, in 451) the Christian writers were confronted with the re-emergence of

---

64. J. WETZEL, *Predestination, Pelagianism and Foreknowledge*, in E. STUMP – N. KRETZMANN (eds.), *The Cambridge Companion to Augustine*, Cambridge, 2001, pp. 49-58, p. 52.

65. "It comes as something of a surprise – writes Babcock – to discover just how central Paul was to the theological developments of this era and just how important he was for the definition of Christianity's distinctive identity over against its cultural and intellectual environment in late antiquity. Nor was the Paul who had this import for patristic Christianity a Paul whose theology of divine grace and divine election was deliberately factored out or quietly ignored. Instead that theology had a decisive impact" (W.S. BABCOCK [ed.], *Paul and the Legacies of Paul*, Dallas, TX, 1990, p. xx).

vital questions linked with the "absolute" mediation of Christ for the attainment of salvation, and its significance for the life of the believer, vis-à-vis the understanding of God's grace, his universal salvific will and his gratuitous election, on one hand, and the "relative" mediation of the Church, on the other. Paul will become more and more a privileged *locus* in which to look for enlightenment and solutions to the understanding of God, the divine direction of the cosmos and the meaning of man's life both in this world and in the next.

Regarding the more concrete application of our research, we will initially focus our attention on the content of the writings that deal with the relationship between grace and free will, both in Augustine and the monks of Hadrumetum, who were the first to react openly to some aspects of the bishop of Hippo's doctrine of grace, vis-à-vis the role of free will (*Chapter 1*). The historical and theological background will be analysed with the aim of better understanding the significance of the African monks' reaction to the bishop of Hippo. The following issues will be developed: the particular quest for perfection that was built into the ascetic-monastic ideal, its rise and diffusion, and the propagation of an Augustinian monasticism existing beside a non-Augustinian monasticism, of which the monastery of Hadrumetum was an example. Apart from the *Ep.* 217, written by Augustine to Vitalis, a cleric of Carthage, who had raised problems similar to those that the monks of Hadrumetum would eventually raise, the starting-point of the controversy must be seen as the vivid disagreement provoked in the community of Hadrumetum by Augustine's letter-treatise to Sixtus (*Ep.* 194), a former supporter of the Pelagian movement. The handling of the crisis is well known, thanks to the survival of an epistolary exchange between the bishop of Hippo and the superior of the community of Hadrumetum (*Epp.* 214-216). Augustine's treatises *De gratia et libero arbitrio*[66] and *De correptione et gratia*[67], in which the bishop of Hippo directly addresses the problems raised by the monks, contained an expounded explanation of the role of free will, the nature and necessity of grace, the need for and the meaning of reproof (vis-à-vis God's gift of perseverance), the significance of predestination, the emphasis on God's role in redemption, the issue of Adam's non-perseverance and the question of the two economies of grace, concerning respectively the first Adam, and the second Adam, Jesus Christ.

66. Augustine, *De gratia et libero arbitrio* (PL, 44), cc. 881-912.
67. Id., *De correptione et gratia* (CSEL, 92), pp. 219-280.

Our investigation will then concentrate on the rise of Massilianism, seen from its historical and theological background (*Chapter 2*). The rise and development of monasticism in Provence, especially in Marseilles and Lérins, will be studied with particular reference to John Cassian, the most representative spokesman of the Massilian communities at the time of the debate with Augustine. Close attention will be paid to Cassian's view on grace and free will, as it is to be found in his monastic writings, the *De institutis coenobiorum* and the *Conlationes*, and more specifically in his *Conlatio* 13. We will attempt to prove that this particular conference was written in direct reaction to some of the assertions made in Augustine's *De correptione et gratia*, the work held responsible for fuelling the opposition in Southern Gaul. Mention will then be made of the two Gallic laymen Prosper and Hilary and the information they passed on to Augustine concerning the Massilian position (cf. *Epp.* 225 and 226); information which in turn caused the bishop of Hippo to reply in the *De praedestinatione sanctorum*[68] and the *De dono perseuerantiae*[69]. In these two writings Augustine comes to terms with such questions as the role of grace with regard to the beginning of faith (*initium fidei*), the teaching on predestination (with a particular focus on the example of the gratuitous predestination applied to Christ and the baptized infants), and the grace of final perseverance.

After having set both the works of Augustine and Cassian in their own context, and after having revisited their content, the next step will be to retrace the pre-history or the theological background that made the Massilian resistance to Augustine possible (*Chapter 3*), seen through a "bird's-eye" view of the mutual interplay of grace and free will in the pre-Augustinian theological tradition. This overview is meant to give us a better insight into how these concepts have influenced Christian doctrine and affected its development, and to contextualize Augustine's "innovative" position and the more traditional position held by the Massilians. Our survey will emphasize the synergetic teaching of the Eastern theologians whose influence, through Origen and Evagrius, had reached Cassian and the Gallic monastic communities. As mentioned above, in fact, one of our main goals will be to show how much the monks of Provence, through the mediation of Cassian, owe to Eastern theological tradition; their comprehension of the co-operation of divine grace and human agency, considered within the framework of the ascetic/monastic struggle for perfection, should be understood in this light. Our attention

---

68. Id., *De praedestinatione sanctorum* (PL, 44), cc. 959-992.
69. Id., *De dono perseuerantiae* (PL, 45), cc. 993-1034.

will eventually be drawn to the specific issues that reveal a substantial difference between Augustine's and Cassian's approach, namely the questions of the *naturae bonum* and the *initium fidei*. Whereas Augustine's main concern was to deal with the issues at stake by endeavouring to answer the question of "how" decayed man might become free, Cassian continued to adopt the eastern viewpoint, according to which, God's saving activity takes place within a "cosmic", "unitarian" and "paideutic" process in which mankind takes an active part. The influences on Cassian's thought, gleaned from his theological, monastic and cultural background, particularly the Origenian-Evagrian theological systems, the spirituality of the Fathers of the desert, and the philosophy of the Stoa, will be investigated and taken into account.

Strictly speaking, the relationship of grace and free will cannot be divorced from the problem of predestination, and apart from the specific writing devoted to it (the *De praedestinatione sanctorum*), this problem also appears in several other of Augustine's works. We will devote a special section (*Chapter 4*) to this controversial issue. It is well known that the bishop of Hippo developed an independent thinking on this subject, quite apart from the traditional teaching of the Church. In fact, in the eyes of his adversaries (and the Massilians too shared their view), his approach smacked of fatalism and was reminiscent of his earlier adhesion to Manichaeism. For that reason we will attempt to re-discover the original understanding of predestination and divine election in the early Christian tradition as it appears in Scripture, but particularly as it was understood by Paul. A comparison will then be drawn between Augustine's novel view, based on the sister doctrine of original sin, and the doctrine of irresistible sovereign grace. Some of the problems ensuing from Augustine's concept of predestination, will be taken into consideration and discussed: the interplay of prescience and predestination (which, in Augustine's view could no longer be seen as synonyms), the inference of a *praedestinatio gemina* and a consequent asymmetrical theological determinism, the meaning of such concepts as *massa damnata / massa sanctorum* and *certus numerus electorum*, the problem of divine justice vis-à-vis divine mercy, and the restricted interpretation of 1 Tim 2,4 over and against the indisputable proclamation of God's universal salvific will.

The *Conclusion* or final evaluation (*Chapter 5*) will highlight once more the differences of approach between Augustine and the monks of Hadrumetum and Southern Gaul. We will pin-point the difficulties they were confronted with in attempting to solve the questions in debate, and the impasse they eventually led to. We will also try to show how the different attitudes held before scriptural revelation, the received tradition of the Church, as well as the social and ecclesiastical climate of the times and the monastic phenomenon, influenced and shaped the theological thought of both Augustine and the Massilians.

Finally, those who have some familiarity with Augustine's works are all too well aware of the obstacles the reader is sometimes confronted with. The lack of systematisation, the tortuousness of his thought, often interrupted by long parentheses or by the introduction of other issues, and the many repetitions in his writing, frequently frustrate any expectation of finding a linear explanation. On the other hand, we must also acknowledge that such "interference" prevents the enquirer from making hasty judgements, or reaching apodictic and one-sided conclusions. It also acts as a reminder that the author's reiteration might well represent his insistence on the importance of some of his insights. Moreover, it must be said that the repetitions occasionally give birth to some significant nuance eventually seen as important to the understanding of a particular thought. Guided by this concern, the content of the primary sources related to our topic will be presented following the layout allotted them by their respective authors, even though we are aware that, at times, this might give the impression of a lack of order and a repetitiveness to the work.

NOTA BENE

1. In the body of the text, the Latin quotations and the titles of the works of Augustine and Cassian, as well as those of other Church fathers or Latin writers, and the Latin scriptural references, the consonant "v" is rendered as "u", except for the passages quoted in the footnotes, where we have respected the editor's choice.

2. Scriptural quotations in English are taken from the *New Revised Standard Version – Anglicized Edition* (Oxford, 1998).

3. Translations from Greek and Latin texts, when not otherwise indicated, are personal ones.

CHAPTER ONE

THE AFRICAN "RESISTANCE" TO AUGUSTINE
HISTORICAL AND THEOLOGICAL FRAMEWORK

Towards the end of his life, although still engaged in a bitter dispute
with Julian of Aeclanum – the most powerful defender of Pelagianism –
Augustine could confidently root his staunch belief about the role of
original sin and the place of God's grace in the life of faith in the pro-
nouncements that had been formulated at the height of the Pelagian controversy at the plenary council of the African Church, held in Carthage
on the 1st May 418[1]. This council, which gathered over two hundred
African bishops[2], had approved a series of canons against Pelagianism in
which the essential tenets about original sin, the function and efficacy of

1. For a survey of the Pelagian controversy, see G. DE PLINVAL, *Les luttes pélagiennes*, in A. FLICHE – V. MARTIN (eds.), *Histoire de l'Église. IV: De la mort de Théodose à l'élection de Grégoire le Grand*, Paris, 1937, pp. 79-128; ID., *Pélage, ses écrits,
sa vie et sa réforme. Étude d'histoire littéraire et religieuse*, Lausanne, 1943, pp. 252-
384; C. MUNIER, *Introduction*, in *La crise pélagienne. II: De gratia Christi et de peccato
originali, De natura et origine animae* (BA, 22), pp. 9-24; O. WERMELINGER, *Rom und
Pelagius. Die theologische Position der römischen Bischöfe im pelagianischen Streit in
der Jahren 411-432* (PuP, 7), Stuttgart, 1975, pp. 134-219; C. PIETRI, *Roma Christiana.
Recherches sur l'Église de Rome, son organisation, sa politique, son idéologie de Miltiade à Sixte (311-440)* (BEFAR, 224), T. II, Rome, 1976, pp. 1222-1244; G. BONNER,
St Augustine of Hippo. Life and controversies, London, 1963, 2nd ed., Norwich, 1986,
pp. 312-351; B. REES, *Pelagius. A Reluctant Heretic*, Woodbridge, 1988; E. TESELLE,
Pelagius, Pelagianism, in A.D. FITZGERALD (ed.), *Augustine through the Ages. An Encyclopedia*, Grand Rapids, MI – Cambridge, 1999, pp. 633-640.
2. According to *Concilium Carthaginense A. 418*, in *Concilia Africae A. 345 – A. 525*
(CCL, 149), p. 69: 203 bishops. According to *Concilium Carthaginense A. 418 (sec. rec.
gallicas)*, p. 74; Prosper, *De gratia Dei et libero arbitrio contra Collatorem* 5,3 (PL, 51),
c. 227; Id., *Responsiones ad capitula Gallorum* 8 (PL, 51), c. 164: 214 bishops. According to Photius, *Myriobiblon siue Bibliotheca* 53 (PG, 103), c. (92) 91: 224 bishops.
According to Wermelinger, the variant number of bishops can be explained by the fact
that two different gatherings of the African bishops took place in Carthage one shortly
after the other: that of the *Concilium Africanum* held in November 417 (where 214 bishops were assembled) and that of the *Concilium plenarium* of 1st May 418 (which gathered
205 bishops). The number of 214 was however attested to in a letter sent to Zosimus by
the *Concilium plenarium* of 418, to indicate that the content of the letter had been subscribed by more bishops (*i.e.*, all those who were present at the previous council of
November 417) than those who were actually present at the council of 1st May 418 (cf.
WERMELINGER, *Rom und Pelagius* [n. 1], p. 150). The number suggested by Photius "mag
auf einem Schreibfehler beruhen" (*Ibid.*, p. 120, n. 86). For the various attempts at reconciling the variant number of bishops, cf. *Ibid.*, pp. 149-150.

grace and the need for asking forgiveness for one's own sins, had eventually been established[3]. Besides, Augustine could rely on the condemnation issued almost simultaneously against Pelagianism by the emperor Honorius and by pope Zosimus[4]. The emperor Honorius, with a rescript issued on the 30th April, condemned all those who denied the Fall and banished Pelagius and Caelestius[5], whereas in the summer of the same year 418[6], pope Zosimus wrote his so-called *Epistula tractoria*[7] to all the

3. A series of eight or, according to some manuscripts, nine canons was approved: *Can. 1*: Adam's mortality is not a necessity of nature but the consequence of original sin. *Can. 2*: Adam's sin is inherited by his posterity: this is the *regula fidei* that the Church has always professed and according to which "etiam parvuli, qui nihil peccatorum in se ipsis adhuc committere potuerunt, ideo in peccatorum remissionem veraciter baptizantur, ut in eis regeneratione mundetur, quod generatione traxerunt". *Can. 3*: A place of eternal bliss does not exist for children who die without baptism. *Can. 4*: Grace is not only necessary for the remission of sins, but also for their prevention. *Can. 5*: Grace not only helps man to discern what to do and what to avoid, but also makes him capable of lovingly doing what he knows to be right. *Can. 6*: Grace is not given to man merely as an external help to free will so that he might follow God's commandments. *Can. 7*: No one can pretend to be sinless, nor can anybody consider himself a sinner only for the sake of a supposed humility. *Can. 8 and 9*: The words of the Lord's prayer: "Forgive us our trespasses" must not be applied to others but to oneself. Only in this sense, are the words said truthfully. Cf. *DS* 222-230; *Concilia Africae A. 345 – A. 525* (n. 2), pp. 67-73; WERMELINGER, *Rom und Pelagius* (n. 1), pp. 166-168; 169-196; A. AUDOLLENT, *Afrique*, in *DHGE* 1 (1912) 705-861, cc. 819-822.
    4. C. MUNIER, *Zosime (1)*, in *DSp* 16 (1994) 1651-1658.
    5. Cf. Honorius Augustus, *Sacrum Rescriptum* (PL, 45), cc. 1726-1728.
    6. See O. PERLER – J.L. MAIER, *Les voyages de st. Augustin*, Paris, 1969, pp. 340-345.
    7. For the extant fragments, see: Augustine, *Ep.* 190,6,23 (CSEL, 57), p. 159; see also *DS* 231; Prosper, *De gratia Dei et libero arbitrio contra Collatorem* 5,3 (PL, 51), c. 228; Caelestinus, *Ep. ad episcopos Galliarum* (PL, 45), c. 1758; *DS* 231; WERMELINGER, *Rom und Pelagius* (n. 1), pp. 307-308. For an analysis of the content of the *Tractoria* see *ibid.*, pp. 209-218; see also PIETRI, *Roma Christiana* (n. 1), II, pp. 1237-1244. For a presentation of Zosimus' position during the Pelagian controversy, see WERMELINGER, *Rom und Pelagius* (n. 1), pp. 134-164. In particular, for Zosimus' attitude in relation to his predecessor Innocent I and the *affaire* of Caelestius vis-à-vis the position of the African Church, see PIETRI, *Roma Christiana* (n. 1), II, pp. 1212-1230; P.J. CAREFOOTE, *Augustine, the Pelagians and the Papacy: An Examination of the Political and Theological Implications of Papal Involvement in the Pelagian Controversy* (unpublished doctoral dissertation, K.U. Leuven), 2 Vols., Louvain, 1995, pp. 177ff. The lack of documents makes it impossible to know what part the emperor's rescript and the doctrinal decisions of the Council of Carthage of 418 played in the drafting of the *Tractoria*. Some think that the latter was inspired by the pronouncements of the African episcopacy (cf., *e.g.*, MUNIER, *Introduction*, in *La crise pélagienne II* [n. 1], p. 23). Along the same line is Amann who writes "que la *Tractoria* de Zosime s'inspirait, au point de vue doctrinal, des décisions exprimées par le grand Concile de Carthage" (É. AMANN, *Zosime*, in *DTC* 15 [1950] 3708-3716, c. 3714). Furthermore, it has been maintained that the fact that the *Tractoria* had to be imposed on reluctant bishops ought to be interpreted as "significative de son [Zosimus'] ralliement à la théologie africaine" (MUNIER, *Zosime* [n. 4], c. 1655). A confirmation of this, continues Munier, is given by Augustine himself in his *Ep.* 190,6,22-23 (CSEL, 57, pp. 157-160), and by the explicitly dissatisfied reaction of some bishops, like those belonging to the ecclesiastical province of Aquileia, or that of Julian of Aeclanum.

bishops of the Christian world. This letter (whose name has been handed down by Mercator[8]) sketched the history of the events concerning the Pelagian controversy; it affirmed the doctrine of grace, of original sin and of the efficacy of baptism; it formally excommunicated both Pelagius and Caelestius and, finally, it showed gratitude to the African bishops for the decisive role they had played in the controversy[9]. It must be

The latter's reaction, above all, indicated clearly that "le document pontifical ne demandait pas seulement la condamnation des erreurs de Pélage et de Célestius, mais l'acceptation de certaines propositions favorables à la doctrine africaine, pour ce qui concerne le péché originel" (MUNIER, Zosime [n. 4], c. 1655). On the other hand, as Floëri has shown, there are enough grounds to assert that Zosimus did not capitulate entirely under the pressure of the combined action of Ravenna and the African Church (see F. FLOERI, Le pape Zosime et la doctrine augustinienne du péché originel, in AugMag, T. II, Paris, 1955, pp. 755-761). In fact, although "la doctrine d'ensemble affirmée à cette occasion... n'est pas très éloignée de celle des évêques africains" (A. MANDOUZE, L'aventure de la raison et de la grâce, Paris, 1968, p. 449, n. 7), it appears that Zosimus did not completely align with the African canons of the Council of Carthage of 418. As a matter of fact, it should not be forgotten that Zosimus was of Greek origin (natione graecus: L. DUCHESNE, Le Liber Pontificalis. Texte, introduction et commentaire, T. I, Paris, 1955, p. 225) and that his attitude towards the whole affaire reflected both his preoccupation with remaining faithful to the Eastern theology with which he was conversant and his uneasiness towards the pessimistic anthropology of the African Church. Thus, as Floëri contends, the Tractoria was not merely an approval or echo of the nine anti-Pelagian canons of the Council of Carthage of 418. He proves his argument by comparing an extant fragment of the Tractoria on the subject of original sin with the correspondent second canon of Carthage. Whereas the latter speaks of a peccatum being present in infants awaiting expiation (expietur) through baptism, Zosimus' Tractoria speaks of infants being slaves of sin in the sense that they have inherited both physical and spiritual death (mors); it does not speak of a real peccatum ex traduce as an ontological feature of infancy. According to Floëri there are "des divergences significatives, qui prouvent que le pape est resté réticent jusqu'au bout vis-à-vis de la doctrine africaine" (FLOËRI, Le pape Zosime, p. 755). It is clearly evident that Zosimus wanted to remain faithful to the Eastern theology. Floëri's argument is shared by WERMELINGER, Rom und Pelagius (n. 1), p. 174, n. 187. G. Bonner, in his turn, writes that "the Africans, supported by the emperor, were able to maintain their own extreme traducian position, even if they were unable to constrain Zosimus to reproduce it exactly in his Epistola tractoria" (G. BONNER, Pelagianism reconsidered, in StPatr 27, Leuven, 1993, pp. 239-240). A different opinion is given by Pietri (cf. PIETRI, Roma Christiana [n. 1], II, p. 1223, n. 1). Perler prefers to speak of "une différence de terminologie à propos d'une même réalité" (O. PERLER, in Discussion autour de la communication de F. Floëri, in AugMag, T. III, Paris, 1955, pp. 261-263, p. 263).

8. Marius Mercator, Commonitorium super nomine Caelestii 3,1 (ACO, 1/5), p. 68.

9. Cf. Prosper, De gratia Dei et libero arbitrio contra Collatorem 5 (PL, 51), c. 228. See also the words of praise addressed by an enthusiastic Prosper to the African Church, a Church which decrees what Rome at a second stage approves (decernis quod Roma probet): "Tu causam fidei flagrantius, Africa, nostrae/ Exsequeris; tecumque suum jungente vigorem/ Juris apostolici solio, fera viscera belli/ Conficis, et lato prosternis limite victos./ Convenere tui de cunctis urbibus almi/ Pontifices, geminoque senum celeberrima coetu" (Id., Περὶ ἀχαρίστων sive De ingratis 1,72-78 [PL, 51], c. 100). According to De Plinval, however, "il faut ... reconnaître que la position doctrinale de Zosime ne s'est pas calquée rigoureusement sur celle des Pères africains, en dépit des allégations insuffisamment

remembered, however, that despite his formal pronouncement, the position of Zosimus towards the Pelagian movement (especially in the person of Caelestius) had been rather lenient[10]. His attitude changed at the height of the controversy, when the pressure of the imperial court of Ravenna, acting in strict collaboration with the African episcopacy, became unbearable[11]. As a result of this concerted action, Zosimus found himself isolated and "was obliged to give in"[12]. He was *de facto* "defeated by the co-operation between Africa and Ravenna"[13].

Many of the results obtained against Pelagianism were no doubt due to Augustine[14] and his prominent position within the theological thinking

nuancées et tendancieuses de Prosper" (G. DE PLINVAL, *Discussion autour de la communication de F. Floëri* [n. 7], p. 262). See also MANDOUZE, *L'aventure de la raison et de la grâce* (n. 7), p. 427, n. 3.

10. Cf., for instance, the rehabilitation of Pelagius and Caelestius by Zosimus' letters *Magnum pondus* (*Ep.* 45 [CSEL, 35/1], pp. 99-103) and *Postquam a nobis* (*Ep.* 46 [CSEL, 35/1], pp. 103-108).

11. For the interwoven discussions and negotiations between the African Church and Rome and the African Church and the imperial court of Ravenna, see WERMELINGER, *Rom und Pelagius* (n. 1), pp. 146-164; 197-201. Cf. also M. LAMBERIGTS, *Augustine and Julian of Aeclanum on Zosimus*, in *Aug(L)* 42 (1992) 311-330, pp. 322, 328, 330.

12. *Ibid.*, p. 322.

13. *Ibid.*, p. 322, n. 73. "Cette coalition fit capituler Zosime" (PIETRI, *Roma Christiana* [n. 1], II, p. 1230). And again: "Innocent, un an plus tôt, avait esquivé l'appel africain: Zosime s'inclinait et, pour mieux envelopper sa défaite dans les apparences orgueilleuses de la grandeur, il prenait une position solennelle et catégorique. C'était un triomphe africain: une victoire réelle contre la procédure pontificale, un succès plus considérable, puisque le siège de Rome proclamait, sans aucune réserve désormais, contre Pélage et contre Coelestius, la foi d'Aurelius, d'Augustin et de tout leur collège" (*Ibid.*, p. 1241). A proof of the hectic diplomatic activity between the African Church and the political power at Ravenna, can be found in Augustine's letter to count Valerius, a very influential officer at the imperial court. Augustine thanked him for his contribution in the defeat of the Church's new enemies (*recentioribus inimicis*: Augustine, *Ep.* 200,2 [CSEL, 57], p. 294). Still more allusive to the African bishops' pressure is the letter of the emperors Honorius and Theodosius to Aurelius, bishop of Carthage: "Secuta est clementia nostra iudicium sanctitatis tuae, quo constat eos *[Pelagius and Caelestius]* ab universis iusta sententiae examinatione damnatos" (*Ep.* 201 [among the Augustinian ones], [CSEL, 57], p. 296). See also J.P. BURNS, *Augustine's Role in the Imperial Action against Pelagius*, in *JTS* 30 (1979) 77-83. It must be added, however, that the strength of the co-operation of Ravenna with the African Church was not only based on political reasons (the necessity of assuring the loyalty of the African provinces and their troops was certainly an important feature: cf. PIETRI, *Roma Christiana* [n. 1], II, p. 1171), but also on genuinely Christian feelings and piety on the side of Honorius, his sister Galla Placidia and the imperial *entourage* (cf. P. BROWN, *Religion and Society in the Age of St. Augustine*, London, 1972, p. 317).

14. "Pareille convergence ou plutôt pareille émulation ne se fût point produite si, de part et d'autre de la Méditerranée, à Rome et à Ravenne comme à Carthage et en Numidie, le terrain n'avait pas été méticuleusement préparé par l'homme qui, ayant pressenti du premier coup la gravité de l'enjeu, a rassemblé patiemment toutes les pièces du procès, autant dire tous les éléments d'une solution radicale. Pour accepter de telles responsabilités, il fallait être Augustin" (MANDOUZE, *L'aventure de la raison et de la grâce* [n. 7], pp. 449-450).

process of the Church of his time. He could certainly look back with sat-isfaction at the defeat of the movement which stemmed from Pelagius, despite the fierce and continuing opposition and resistance of the afore-mentioned Julian of Aeclanum. The reality of original sin, the need for baptism at any stage of life (childhood or adulthood) as a condition for being saved, the necessity and gratuity of grace over and against a reli-gion based upon merits, was defended to demonstrate that fallen man can do nothing and cannot be saved outside God's gratuitous mercy. These central truths, and all that follows from them, had not only been defended but also officially stated by the African Church under Augus-tine's untiring solicitation and personal involvement.

Yet, in the heat of the theological fight, and probably encouraged by the victory over Pelagianism, Augustine made some assertions with regard to the consequences of original sin, the necessity of grace and its dispensation, its inner efficacy and its relationship with free will, that would somehow go beyond the previously commonly shared belief of the Church. This being the case, it is not surprising to discover that cer-tain affirmations by the bishop of Hippo were received with amazement, hesitation, and even resistance by some Christians, whose main goal was to live out an integral faith. They, on the whole, had no prejudices what-soever against the theological system of Augustine; on the contrary, they were among those who had sincerely supported and endorsed his struggle against Pelagianism, accepting the ecclesiastical decisions that were taken against the errors of the movement[15].

The starting point of Augustine's clear-cut doctrine of grace was the status in which humanity finds itself because of the consequences of the original sin of its ancestors. Fallen humanity, he would declare, forms a *massa damnata* from which only God's bountiful and merciful justice is able to save those He wishes to save. Everything depends on God's absolute and free choice. In this respect, human merit cannot claim any right to salvation. Augustine was, of course, well aware of the scriptural texts teaching either the universal salvation of mankind (*e.g.* 1 Tim 2,4) or the necessity of faith in God and in his Son Jesus Christ the Media-tor[16], together with the consequent need for baptism as a basic condition

---

15. See É. AMANN, *Semi-Pélagiens*, in *DTC* 14/2 (1941) 1796-1850, cc. 1797-1798; J. CHÉNÉ, *Les origines de la controverse semi-pélagienne*, in *ATA* 13 (1953) 56-109, p. 58; ID., *Introduction générale* [BA, 24], p. 26.

16. According to the bishop of Hippo, faith in Christ the Mediator must be explicit in order to attain salvation (cf., for instance, Augustine, *Confessiones* 10,43,68 [CCL, 27], p. 192; *De ciuitate Dei* 18,47 [CCL, 48], p. 645; *Ep.* 194 [to Sixtus], 6,23 [CSEL, 57], p. 194 *et passim*).

for being introduced into the sphere of salvation (*e.g.*, Heb 11,6; Gal 2,16; Jn 3,5). Yet, from these two different, but equally fundamental truths about the mystery of salvation, the bishop of Hippo felt inclined to stress the more severe one, concerned as he was with the maintainance of the *conditions* attached to salvation (faith and baptism), rather than stress the universality of Redemption. His belief was based mainly on his daily experience of the conspicuous number of children, as well as adults, who die without faith in the God-Christ and without having received the sacrament of baptism. Thus, Augustine's conclusion was that, within the universal plan of salvation for mankind, there must be a divine *oeconomia*, albeit a mysterious one, which allows that a certain number of people are not reached by the redemptive act of Christ by means of faith and baptism.

What is necessary, at this point, is to introduce and consider attentively the reactions caused in some clerical and monastic circles by the implacable Augustinian logic of the mystery of grace and its relationship with free will and predestination.

1. AUGUSTINE'S LETTER TO VITALIS

First of all, we have a letter[17] written by Augustine to a certain Vitalis, qualified as *frater*[18] and belonging to the Church of Carthage[19]. Whether Vitalis simply held some erroneous views on the theology of grace without being in total opposition to Augustine's doctrine on the same subject (as it has been suggested[20]), cannot be proved with certainty. It is certain that the bishop of Hyppo was worried about Vitalis' unsound understanding of grace. Augustine, in fact, felt it his duty to intervene and correct the position of the *frater* of Carthage after receiving information describing it as unorthodox and streaked with Pelagian views. Written some time after the summer of 416[21], this letter tackles the question of

---

17. Id., *Ep.* 217 [CSEL, 57]; pp. 403-425.
18. *Ibid.* titulus, p. 403; 217,2,4, p. 406; 217,2,5, p. 407; 217,5,17, p. 416; 217,7,30, p. 425. "Cette insistance au vocatif (sans possessif d'accompagnement) et plus encore l'emploi... de la formule *frater Vitalis* suggère que V. pourrait être un moine (d'autant que le 'semi-pélagianisme' a fleuri volontiers dans ce milieu)" (A. MANDOUZE, *Vitalis* 8, in ID., *et al.*, *Prosopographie chrétienne du Bas-Empire*, T. I: *Prosopographie de l'Afrique Chrétienne [303-533]*, Paris, 1982, pp. 1222-1223).
19. "In Carthaginensi eruditus Ecclesia" (Augustine, *Ep.* 217,1,2 [CSEL, 57], p. 404).
20. "Cette lettre – affirms Chéné – nous met en présence d'une erreur plutôt que d'une opposition aux doctrines augustiniennes" (CHÉNÉ, *Les origines de la controverse semi-pélagienne* [n. 15], p. 94, n. 1). Cf. AMANN, *Semi-Pélagiens* (n. 15), cc. 1798f.
21. The *terminus post quem* (as suggested in MANDOUZE, *Vitalis* 8 [n. 18], p. 1222), should be the anti-Pelagian Council of Milevis of 416, a date by which Augustine did not

the *initium fidei*, which will become one of the main issues in the discussions between Augustine and the monks of Southern Gaul. Vitalis' standpoint on this matter is clearly stated in the letter. Although convinced that divine grace plays an essential role in the life of faith, he was upholding the view that the *initium fidei* was not God's gift, but a possibility resulting from a personal act of assent and adhesion, viz. the initiative of the creature's autonomous will in saying "yes" or "no" to God's gift of faith[22].

No doubt, to the bishop of Hippo such a position smacked of Pelagianism[23]. The stress, would he contend, should be laid upon God's grace, which not only precedes and sustains any good will[24] but which is also the cause of the *initium fidei* itself. Furthermore, grace should not be identified merely with revealed truth, nor considered as if it were simply acting from without (*e.g.* by means of the law, of Scripture or of doctrine[25]). Grace, continues Augustine, has to do with a *uocatio* which is

possess as yet the Acts of the Council of Diospolis to which he refers in his letter to Vitalis (cf. Augustine, *Ep*. 217,2,4 [CSEL, 57], p. 406; *ibid*. 217,6,18, p. 417) and which he speaks of in a letter addressed to Paolinus in 417 (cf. Id., *Ep*. 186,1,2 [CSEL, 57], p. 47). Moreover, "cette même lettre ne faisant pas explicitement allusion à la condamnation ultérieure de Pélage par Rome, il ne paraît pas prudent de décaler ce terminus, comme le fait Goldbacher (cf. A. GOLDBACHER, *Index* III [CSEL, 58], pp. 57-58), jusqu'aux années où se développe la discussion sur l'*initium fidei*" (MANDOUZE, *Vitalis* 8 [n. 18], p. 1222). Goldbacher, in fact, placed the *Ep*. 217 in ca. 427.

22. "Quo modo dicis quod te audio dicere, ut recte credamus in Deum et evangelio consentiamus, non esse donum Dei, sed hoc nobis esse a nobis, id est ex propria voluntate, quam nobis in nostro corde non operatus est ipse? Et ad hoc, cum audieris: Quid est ergo quod ait Apostolus: *Deus in uobis operatur et uelle [et perficere]?* Respondes per legem suam, per scripturas suas Deum operari, ut uelimus, quas uel legimus uel audimus; sed eis consentire uel non consentire ita nostrum est, ut, si uelimus, fiat, si autem nolimus, nihil in nobis operationem Dei ualere faciamus. Operatur quippe ille, dicis, quantum in ipso est, ut uelimus, dum nobis nota fiunt eius eloquia; sed si eis acquiescere nolumus, nos, ut operatio eius nihil in nobis prosit, efficimus" (Augustine, *Ep*. 217,1,1 [CSEL, 57], pp. 403-404). Cf. also *Ibid*. 217,7,29, p. 424: "Tu autem, si ea, quae de te audio, vera sunt, initium fidei, ubi est etiam initium bonae, hoc est piae voluntatis, non vis donum esse Dei, sed ex nobis nos habere contendis, ut credere incipiamus". As it has been rightly pointed out, "il faut ne pas perdre de vue les conditions générales du temps, où ce sont principalement des païens qui se présentent à l'Église pour lui demander la foi" (AMANN, *Semi-Pélagiens* [n. 15], c. 1798).

23. "Haec est illa Pelagianorum mala male diffamata meritoque reprobata et ab ipso etiam Pelagio timente damnari in orientalium episcoporum iudicio damnata sententia" (Augustine, *Ep*. 217,2,4 [CSEL, 57], p. 406). It seems, however, that Augustine was convinced that Vitalis' erroneous opinions were held in good faith, and that he should not be considered a follower of Pelagianism: "Ego enim haereticum quidem Pelagianum te esse non credo, sed ita te esse nolo, ut nihil illius ad te transeat uel in te relinquatur erroris" (*Ibid*. 217,6,25, p. 421).

24. "Quia praeuenit hominis uoluntatem bonam, nec eam cuiusquam inuenit in corde, sed facit" (*Ibid*. 217,2,5, p. 406). Cf. also *Ibid*. 217,6,25, p. 421.

25. Cf. *Ibid*. 217,3,11ff, pp. 412f.

alta atque secreta[26], something very profound and mysterious which exercises a strong power of attraction with regard to the creature's consciousness and will. Witness against the priority of natural assent over the power of grace in provoking the *initium fidei* can also be found in prayer, since prayers are offered to God for the conversion of heathens. There would be no point in such prayer if faith were merely and effectively embraced through the choice of natural will[27]. Augustine then synthesizes in twelve sentences (*Duodecim sententiae contra Pelagianos*)[28] the teaching, opposed to the Pelagian view, that Vitalis should make his own: a teaching in which one easily detects the imprint of the bishop of Hippo's personal and powerful theological construction.

We do not know what the reaction of Vitalis was, since we have no reply from him, and the argument from silence is never conclusive. Did he revise, under Augustine's urging, his position on the absolute autonomy of the will with respect to the *initium fidei*, or did he simply refuse to engage himself in discussions with the bishop of Hippo, thus maintaining his opposition to Augustine's views on this particular matter?[29] Any attempt to answer to this question is reduced to conjecture.

2. AUGUSTINE'S *EP*. 194 (TO SIXTUS)
AND THE *AFFAIRE* OF HADRUMETUM

It was in the monastery of Hadrumetum[30] that some of Augustine's statements on grace and its relation to free will met with a frontal attack. This opposition would eventually develop (although in an independent way) into a movement originating in some of the monastic foundations of Southern Gaul.

The incident that occurred in Hadrumetum is well documented in an epistolary exchange that took place in 426 between Augustine and Valentinus, the superior of the monastery[31]. From this correspondence, we learn that the

---

26. *Ibid.* 217,2,5, p. 406.

27. Cf. *Ibid.* 217,2,4, pp. 405-406.

28. Cf. *Ibid.* 217,5,16, pp. 414-416.

29. We might well suppose that Augustine's initial words in the letter to Vitalis (*rogo ut litteras meas nec aspernanter sumas, et salubriter legas*: *Ibid.* 217,1,1, p. 403) were not simply a literary device, but possibly hinted at a clear-cut mental attitude of the *frater* of Carthage on the issue at stake.

30. Hadrumetum (today's town of Sousse, in Tunisia) was a maritime city of Africa which became the provincial capital of the Byzacena province during the time of the Diocletian reforms. So are we informed by the mid-6th century Byzantine historian Procopius of Caesarea in his *De aedificiis Justiniani* VI. See S. LANCEL, *Hadrumète*, in *DHGE* 22 (1988) 1493-1496, cc. 1493-1494; C. LEPELLEY – S. LANCEL, *Africa*, in *AugL* 1 (1986) 180-219, c. 188.

31. Augustine, *Ep.* 214 and 215 (CSEL, 57), pp. 380-396; Valentinus, *Ep.* 216 (among the Augustinian letters) (CSEL, 57), pp. 396-402. See A. MANDOUZE, *Valentinus*

monastic peace of Hadrumetum was shattered by the long letter (the *Ep.* 194) written by Augustine (towards the end of 418 or the beginning of 419[32]) to Sixtus, the Roman priest who eventually became pope Sixtus III[33].

3, in ID. *et al.*, *Prosopographie chrétienne du Bas-Empire*, T. I: *Prosopographie de l'Afrique Chrétienne [303-533]*, Paris, 1982, pp. 1133-1134. It seems that Valentinus was not a priest and that he was the head of a *monasterium laicorum* (cf. J.J. GAVIGAN, *De vita monastica in Africa Septentrionali inde a temporibus S. Augustini usque ad invasiones Arabum* [BAMA.H, 1], Turin, 1962, p. 130). This is inferred by the words that Valentinus used to explain the request he addressed to the priest Sabinus for an explanation of the *Ep.* 194: "Ad maiorem auctoritatem rogauimus" (Valentinus, *Ep.* 216,3 [CSEL, 57], p. 398). Furthermore, there is nothing certain to back up the hypothesis (cf. L. VERHEIJEN, *La règle de saint Augustin*, T. II, Paris, 1967, p. 99) that identifies abbas Valentinus with a priest of the monastery holding the same name, and who is also mentioned in a document of 523/525 as the first of a series of four priests belonging to the community of Hadrumetum (cf. MANDOUZE, *Valentinus 3*, p. 1134; see also ID., *Valentinus 5*, in ID. *et al.*, *Prosopographie chrétienne du Bas-Empire*, T. I: *Prosopographie de l'Afrique Chrétienne [303-533]*, Paris, 1982, p. 1135). Cf. J. CHÉNÉ, *Introduction générale* [BA, 24], p. 44-45.

32. Goldbacher dates it very shortly after the *Ep.* 191, also sent to Sixtus, which was most probably written in the last months of 418 (cf. A. GOLDBACHER, *Index* III [CSEL, 58], pp. 49-50).

33. Augustine, *Ep.* 194 (CSEL, 57), pp. 176-214. The *Ep.* 194 is a "letter of instruction", a sort of *uademecum*, sent in order to help Sixtus to counter Pelagian errors. It also gently chastises Sixtus' "Pelagian past" which was perceived by Augustine as lingering somewhat in the attitude of the Roman priest. This at least was the impression of the African bishop (bishops?): "Quod enim fatendum est ... inimicis christianae gratiae te fauere" (*Ibid.* 194,1,1, p. 176). Must we interpret the African opinion as a fear of a possible "duplicity" in Sixtus' behaviour? In that regard, we are reminded of a short, earlier letter of Augustine, the *Ep.* 191 (CSEL, 57, pp. 163-165), existing in mutilated form (see A. GOLDBACHER, CSEL, 58, p. 50, n. 1), that was sent to Sixtus during the last months of 418, through the acolyte Albinus (cf. Augustine, *Ep.* 194,1,1 [CSEL, 57], p. 176). This was in reply to a letter sent by the Roman priest (and unfortunately lost). In it Augustine had promised another longer and more detailed letter (the actual *Ep.* 194), which would eventually be sent to Sixtus through Firmus (cf. *Ibid.* 194,1,1, p. 176). Moreover, in *Ep.* 191, Augustine congratulated Sixtus on his recantation of Pelagianism and on the fact that he had sided with pope Zosimus' *Tractoria* (cf. *Ep.* 191,2 [CSEL, 57], p. 164). It must not be forgotten that previously Zosimus too had not only been a sympathizer or an associate of the Pelagian movement in Rome but, more than that, its *patronus* ("Quid enim gratius legi uel audiri potest, quam gratiae Dei tam pura defensio aduersus inimicos eius ex ore eius, qui eorundem inimicorum magni momenti patronus ante iactabatur?": *Ibid.* 191,1, pp. 163-164). See also: "Quod enim fatendum est caritati tuae, tristes eramus nimis, cum fama iactaret inimicis Christianae gratiae te fauere" (*Ep.* 194,1,1 [CSEL, 57], p. 176). Most probably Sixtus had met Pelagius in Rome at the time when, as a young Roman, he was pursuing a higher education, the very education which would allow him to become part of the "aristocratie sacerdotale" that played a decisive role in the Church of Rome and in the papal household in particular (cf. DE PLINVAL, *Pélage, ses écrits, sa vie et sa réforme* [n. 1], p. 232). It seems, however, that Sixtus became a strong adversary of Pelagianism only after the latter's condemnation had been proclaimed. The change was so remarkable that Augustine himself felt it necessary to remind him of the profitability of instructing those who had been associated with the Pelagian movement in the true faith, rather than merely terrifying them ("Qui tamen lenius sunt profecto tractandi; quid enim eos terreri opus est...? Etsi enim terrendi non sunt, tamen docendi sunt": Augustine, *Ep.* 191,2 [CSEL, 57], p. 165). See also: "Aliquanto diutius tecum sermocinamur admo-

It happened like this[34]. Florus[35], a monk of Hadrumetum, came across the *Ep.* 194 while visiting his hometown of Uzalis; he copied it with the help (*deuote dictante*)[36] of Felix[37], a fellow monk, and sent the copy through him to the monastery of Hadrumetum (*uentum est ad monasterium cum eodem libello*)[38] as a "blessed bread (*eulogias*)"[39], while he himself continued his journey to Carthage.

In short, the content of this *Ep.* 194[40] is as follows: first of all, basing himself on the scriptural quotation of Pr 8,35 (*preparatur enim uoluntas a Domino*: LXX[41]), Augustine affirms that free will is not nullified by

nentes, ut docendis instes, quibus terrendis satis, quantum comperimus, institisti" (*Ep.* 194,1,2, p. 177).

34. For an account of those events, see Valentinus, *Ep.* 216 (CSEL, 57), p. 397ff.

35. See A. MANDOUZE, *Florus* 2, in ID. *et al.*, *Prosopographie chrétienne du Bas-Empire*, T. I: *Prosopographie de l'Afrique Chrétienne [303-533]*, Paris, 1982, pp. 478-479.

36. Valentinus, *Ep.* 216,2 (CSEL, 57), p. 397.

37. See A. MANDOUZE, *Felix* 57, in ID. *et al.*, *Prosopographie chrétienne du Bas-Empire*, T. I: *Prosopographie de l'Afrique Chrétienne [303-533]*, Paris, 1982, pp. 429-430.

38. Impersonal construction which most likely refers to the return of Felix to Hadrumetum (cf. *Ibid.*, p. 430).

39. Valentinus, *Ep.* 216,2 (CSEL, 57), p. 397.

40. In one of his letters to Valentinus and the monks of Hadrumetum, Augustine calls the *Ep.* 194 "librum uel epistulam meam" (Augustine, *Ep.* 214,2 [CSEL, 57], p. 381), although soon afterwards he refers to it with the words: "supra dictam epistulam ad Sixtum" (*Ibid.* 214,3, p. 382). "La lunghezza (17 colonne) e soprattutto l'importanza degli argomenti trattati, in polemica con i Pelagiani, dovettero suggerire la denominazione *liber*, sebbene l'intestazione rechi il nome del destinatario e dello scrivente" (M. PELLEGRINO, *Introduzione*, in *Sant'Agostino, Lettere* [NBA, 21], Rome, 1969, I-CVIII, p. XI).

41. See especially A. SAGE, *Preparatur voluntas a Domino*, in *REAug* 10 (1964) 1-20. The passage of Pr 8,35 (used by Augustine respectively once in the *De gratia et libero arbitrio*, twice in the *De correptione et gratia* and in the *De praedestinatione sanctorum*, and once in the *De dono perseuerantiae*) helps to illustrate, through the image of the rock, the effects of grace. Appearing for the first time at the beginning of the Pelagian controversy (cf. Augustine, *De peccatorum meritis et remissione et de baptismo paruulorum* 2,18,30 [CSEL, 60], pp. 101-102), this quotation is repeated several times in Augustine's anti-Pelagian polemic; in his *Contra secundam responsionem Iuliani opus imperfectum*, for instance, it is employed ten times (see A.M. LA BONNARDIERE, *Quelques remarques sur les citations scripturaires du "De gratia et libero arbitrio"*, in *REAug* 9 [1963] 77-85, p. 78). Speaking against the Pelagian belief that it is the will that enables man to choose good or evil, Augustine opposes the view that free will can only be exercised in the matter of sinfulness. If man's free will could also be exercised in the decision to do good, a lesser role would then be ascribed to God. God's will could then be seen as simply "neutral" whilst man possessed greater capacity for choice. Augustine argues that man's propensity for doing good comes solely from God. More precisely, only the *uoluntas* that is prepared by God is the *bona uoluntas* (cf. Augustine, *De peccatorum meritis et remissione et de baptismo paruulorum* 2,18,30 [CSEL, 60], p. 102). Augustine's interpretation of Pr 8,35 remained substantially the same until the end of his life and in his last writings, when the use of this scriptural passage became more noticeable. Moreover, in Augustine's eyes, Pr 8,35 had the advantage of speaking in favour of both

the help of God. On the contrary, not only are both good will and free will helped and strengthened by God, but they are ultimately made possible and sustained by his grace, on which they are firmly anchored as on a solid rock[42]. The will left to itself is, in fact, condemned to float among vanities (*per inania feratur*). Moreover, since all men, because of original sin, belong to the *massa damnationis*, no one can claim the right to salvation. Salvation rests only on God's mercy which, being absolutely sovereign, is not "due" to anybody. In fact God saves those He wishes to save and does it freely, without taking into account any human merit whatsoever, and also without feeling hindered in his saving action by man's faults[43]. Augustine's response to the Pelagian problem of God's action in the lives of sinful people, some of whom would be saved, some of whom condemned, is to say that, however incomprehensible it might be, God grants the means of salvation to whom He chooses, and does so in a way that is both free and just[44].

To the objection that sinners could justify their obstinacy by the conviction that they could do nothing against God's refusal to bestow his grace upon them (cf. Rom 9,18), Augustine says that the ultimate cause of this obstinacy, which is permitted by God, must again be found in the just condemnation of the *uniuersa massa damnata*[45]. Man's obstinacy and disobedience are inexcusable, for they are caused solely by his *pessima uoluntas*[46]. God is not the cause of evil doing. What He certainly does, is to make possible a change in the life of the sinner, even though such merciful intervention belongs solely to his just and unknowable design, including his right to abstain if necessary: *nec obdurat Deus*

---

grace and free will. In fact, in the light of grace, the free will too would be delivered from the bondage of sin and reestablished within the range of action that leads to perfection (cf. SAGE, *Preparatur voluntas a Deo*, p. 16).

42. Cf. Augustine, *Ep.* 194,2,3 (CSEL, 57), p. 178. Cf. also Id., *De spiritu et littera* 30,52 (CSEL, 60), p. 208.

43. "Quod autem personarum acceptorem Deum se credere existimant, si credant, quod sine ullis praecedentibus meritis, *cuius uult, miseretur* et, quos dignatur, uocat et, quem uult, religiosum facit, parum adtendunt quod debita reddatur poena damnato, indebita gratia liberato, ut nec ille se indignum queratur nec dignum se iste glorietur, atque ibi potius acceptionem nullam fieri personarum, ubi una eademque massa damnationis et offensionis inuoluit, ut liberatus de non liberato discat, quod etiam sibi supplicium conueniret, nisi gratia subueniret; si autem gratia, utique nullis meritis reddita sed gratuita bonitate donata" (Id., *Ep.* 194,2,4 [CSEL, 57], pp. 178-179).

44. "Ubi quia uniuersa ista massa merito damnata est, contumeliam debitam reddit iustitia, honorem donat indebitum gratia non meriti praerogatiua, non fati necessitate, non temeritate fortunae sed altitudine *diuitiarum sapientiae et scientiae Dei [Rom 11,33]*" (*Ibid.* 194,2,5, p. 179). See also *Ibid.* 194,6,23, p. 194.

45. *Ibid.* 194,3,14, p. 187.

46. *Ibid.* 194,6,24, p. 195.

impertiendo malitiam, sed non impertiendo misericordiam[47]. In other words, if some are condemned through their hardness of heart, this occurs not because of any divine activity; God's apparent lack of mercy being in accordance with his own hidden design. Augustine illustrates, through references to certain passages in Paul's letter to the Romans, the inscrutability of God's judgements and actions: God's endurance and patience when dealing with the objects of wrath made for destruction (Rom 9,22-23); the potter's right over the clay he is moulding (Rom 9,20-21); the inscrutability of God's judgement and will (Rom 11,33-36). Augustine continues to show that in God there is no partiality with regard to the *massa damnata* in which all men are included. Divine justice accomplishes what has been truly deserved by sinful men, whereas their potential election and justification is brought about simply by God's gratuitous and merciful grace[48].

Countering the Pelagian belief that grace could be equated with "human nature", flowing as it does from the hands of the Creator, Augustine affirms that Christian grace is the means whereby sinful men are justified and saved, rather than anything pertaining to their creation as human beings. Man's salvation, therefore, is the "meritorious" act of Christ[49]. Sins are forgiven and good actions accomplished through faith, which is a gift of God's merciful intervention[50]. Prayer too, sustained as it is by God's grace and spirit, is able to bring about this merciful intervention[51].

We must conclude that there is no merit in man which is not the effect of the power of grace. This conviction is expressed by Augustine through an aphorism which became famous because of the incisive manner with which it defined what we tautologically refer to as the "gratuity of grace": *Cum Deus coronat merita nostra, nihil aliud coronet quam munera sua*[52]. Grace is thus accorded to the man who lives a

---

47. *Ibid.*

48. Cf. *Ibid.* 194,2,5, pp. 179ff. Also: "Quae tamen misericordia et ueritas ita sibi occurrunt, quia scriptum est: Misericordia et ueritas occurrerunt sibi, ut nec misericordia impediat ueritatem, qua plectitur dignus, nec ueritas misericordiam, qua liberatur indignus" (*Ibid.* 194,3,6, p. 181).

49. "Etenim Christus non pro nullis, ut homines conderentur, sed pro impiis mortuus est, ut iustificarentur" (*Ibid.* 194,3,8, p. 182), and again: "Nosse uel credere, quod neminem Deus liberet nisi gratuita misericordia per Dominum nostrum Iesum Christum et neminem damnet nisi aequissima ueritate per eundem Dominum nostrum Iesum Christum" [cf. Rom 1,17; Gal 3,11; Heb 10,38; Hab 2,4] (*Ibid.* 194,6,23, p. 194). See also *Ibid.* 194,6,28ff, pp. 198f.

50. Cf. *Ibid.* 194,3,9-15 *passim*, pp. 183-188 *passim*.

51. Cf. *Ibid.* 194,4,16f, pp. 188f.

52. *Ibid.* 194,5,19, p. 190. This epigrammatic statement occurred already in the *Confessiones*. Referring to God, Augustine asked: "Quisquis autem enumerat uera merita sua, quid tibi enumerat nisi munera tua?" (Id., *Confessiones* 9,13,34 [CCL, 27], p. 152).

life of faith and justice. But such a life, meritorious as it may be, is only made possible by grace. Likewise, eternal life, which presupposes man's meritorious life, is nothing other than the fruit of grace itself which makes the merits possible thus allowing the just and faithful man to enter eternity[53]. Thus grace itself becomes a "rewarding" grace. The gratuity of divine election is shown even more clearly by the fate of the many infants dying without baptism over and against those who have indeed been baptized. Man cannot but recognize, in the light of faith, the incomprehensibility of God's design and profess the certainty that in him there can be no iniquity or partiality[54]. Finally, Augustine considers absurd the Pelagian idea of the so-called *futuribilia,* according to which babies dying before baptism receive the deserved punishment for evil actions that they, had they lived, would have performed at some future date[55].

As soon as the copy of Augustine's *Ep.* 194 reached Hadrumetum and was read in the monastic community (without abbot Valentinus being informed), it became clear that the majority of its members being simple men, were unable to grasp the difficult questions contained therein. Many of them were thrown into confusion and reacted accordingly[56]. The way Augustine rejected the idea of independence of human merit from the action of grace, the decisive manner by which he described

53. Cf. Id., *Ep.* 194,5,20-21 (CSEL, 57), pp. 191-193.
54. Cf. *Ibid.* 194,7,31ff, pp. 200ff.
55. Cf. *Ibid.* 194,9,41ff, pp. 209ff.
56. Abbot Valentinus calls these brothers *imperiti* (Valentinus, *Ep.* 216,2 [CSEL, 57], p. 397) and *ignari* (*Ibid.* 216,6, p. 402). As Rees puts it, the disturbance at Hadrumetum "had arisen in the first place because the majority of the monks were simple men, dedicated to the pursuit of the ascetic life and holding uncomplicated Christian beliefs, so that much of the great battle which had been waged in the more subtle atmosphere of the theologians had passed over their heads almost unnoticed" (REES, *Pelagius. A Reluctant Heretic* [n. 1], p. 103). As an analogy, we are reminded of the Origenist or "anthropomorphite" controversy that occurred in the Egyptian desert towards the end of the 4th century, one of the causes of which was the opposition taken between the more sophisticated and better educated monks of Greek origin and the majority of the monks, of mostly Coptic origin, who were simple men. Their opposition, in fact, was not simply the result of nationalist feelings, nor of different theological perspectives, but of the divergent levels of learning. With regard to this, we find an allusion in the historian Socrates: "Πολλοὶ τῶν ἁπλοϊκῶν ἀσκητῶν: Multi quidem ex simplicioribus monachi" (Socrates, *Historia ecclesiastica* 6,7 [PG, 67], c. 684 [683]). Cassian himself suggests that the anthropomorphic view held by the majority of the monks of the Egyptian desert was due to their *simplicitas* (Cf. Cassian, *Conlatio* 10,2 [SC, 54], p. 76). It should not surprise us, therefore, to learn that there were simple, unlearned monks at Hadrumetum as well as others of the intellectual standing of Florus and Felix. Moreover, by the time the disturbance took place, monasticism as a whole had already become a mass-phenomenon, hosting people from all levels of society. As Augustine himself writes: "Nunc autem ueniunt plerumque ad hanc professionem seruitutis Dei et ex condicione seruili, uel etiam liberti uel propter hoc a dominis liberati siue liberandi et ex uitia rusticana et ex opificum exercitatione et plebeio labore" (Augustine, *De opere monachorum* 22,25 [CSEL, 41], p. 570).

faith as being an absolutely gratuitous gift of God, and the predestinarian consequences derived from this theological principle, all caused argument and friction among the monks. Some of them took Augustine's views to extremes, inferring that the overwhelming power of grace could annihilate free will. A further logical step, they argued, was that there was no point in considering final judgement as an event in which man would eventually be rewarded according to his good deeds[57]. Conversely, those monks who were sensitive to the ascetic demands of monastic life and the daily effort it required, were unable to understand a position they thought would mean a nullification of the free will that chose goodness as well as of the merit stemming from it[58]. They preferred the view that free will is operative, although still realizing it could not exist without the help of grace; the latter giving man the capability of knowing and choosing what is good in the light of the promise of eventual reward[59].

Abbot Valentinus only became aware of what was happening in his community when Florus returned home from Uzalis-Carthage. His arrival, in fact, provoked such a great uproar that it could not pass unnoticed. Florus was judged responsible for this situation, particularly since some of the monks thought that the *Ep.* 194 was a forgery, and that it could not possibly be ascribed to Augustine. In order to restore peace among his flock, Valentinus sent a delegation of monks (bearers of a letter now alas missing) to Evodius[60], the bishop of Uzalis and an old friend of Augustine, asking him to intervene by writing a more confident and sound explanation of *Ep.* 194 (*aliquid certius [...] de hoc sacrosancto libro*)[61].

---

57. Cf. Id., *Ep.* 214,1 (CSEL, 57), p. 380.

58. Augustine, however, will point out the possible risks of such an awareness. Cf. Id., *De gratia et libero arbitrio* 4,6 (PL, 44), c. 885. See *infra*, n. 136.

59. "Quidam in uobis sic gratiam praedicent, ut negent hominis esse liberum arbitrium et, quod est grauius, dicant, quod in die iudicii non sit redditurus Deus unicuique secundum opera eius. Etiam hoc tamen indicauerunt, quod plures uestrum non ita sentiant, sed liberum arbitrium adiuuari fateantur per Dei gratiam, ut recta sapiamus atque faciamus et cum uenerit Dominus reddere unicuique secundum opera eius, inueniat opera nostra bona, *quae praeparauit Deus, ut in illis ambulemus*. Hoc qui sentiunt, bene sentiunt" (Id., *Ep.* 214,1 [CSEL, 57], p. 380-381). Cf. Mt 16,27; Rom 2,6; Rev 22,12; Eph 2,10.

60. Cf. A. MANDOUZE, *Evodius* 1, in ID. et al., *Prosopographie chrétienne du Bas-Empire*. T. I: *Prosopographie de l'Afrique Chrétienne [303-533]*, Paris, 1982, pp. 366-373.

61. Valentinus, *Ep.* 216,3 (CSEL, 57), p. 398. The embassy sent to Evodius may be explained, as Brown suggests, not only by the friendship the bishop of Uzalis shared with Augustine, but also by the fact that the *Ep.* 194 had probably been found and copied by Florus and Felix in the library of Evodius' episcopal house (see P. BROWN, *Augustine of Hippo. A Biography*, London 1967, p. 399).

Evodius' intervention[62] showed his concern about restoring reconciliation, peace and harmony in the monastic community, worried, as he was,
about the consequences an uprising might cause to religious practice.
Regarding the theological problems raised by the monks about divine
justice and mercy and the relationship between grace and free will, however, he contented himself with showing meekness and resignation
before so great a mystery[63]. His recommended course of action to the
monks of Hadrumetum was to follow the road of *pietas*, on which to
build a zealous religious life, rather than that of *contentio*[64]. He finally

62. Evodius' letter (*Ep. ad abbatem Valentinum*) can be found in PLS, 2, cc. 331-334.
It reproduces the second updated edition of the text of the letter brought to light and published in G. MORIN, *Lettres inédites de saint Augustin et du prêtre Januarien dans
l'affaire des moines d'Adrumète*, in *RBen* 18 (1901) 241-256, pp. 253-256.

63. "Si quid minus liquet de liberi arbitrii et gratiae munere exitu, vel de iudicii
secreta altitudine atque hominum diversorum ordinatione sive occultissima dispensatione,
nemo perturbetur, si non intelligit... et quod non in ista vita intelligitur, ad illam vitam
servetur" (Evodius, *Ep. ad abbatem Valentinum* [PLS, 2], cc. 332-333). Evodius' letter is
indeed striking for its lack of involvement and insight into the question with which he
was confronted. Known to Augustine since the latter's baptism in 387, Evodius shared his
friend's second stay in Rome (387-388) before reaching Africa (see PERLER–MAIER, *Les
voyages de st. Augustin* [n. 6], pp. 146-147). During their stay in Rome, where they led a
sort of common life, Evodius became Augustine's interlocutor in the discussions/dia-
logues over the soul (*De animae quantitate*) and free will (*De libero arbitrio*: here
Evodius took an active part in the first book and a small one in the second), as the bishop
of Hippo himself recalls in one of his letters to his friend (cf. Augustine, *Ep.* 162,2
[CSEL, 44], p. 513). To judge from the questions put to Augustine by Evodius in both
dialogues, we are left with the impression that Evodius took part in the debate with "une
curiosité passionné" (MANDOUZE, *Evodius* 1 [n. 60], p. 367), and a certain independence
of thought and cautiousness in accepting Augustine's explanations. See, for instance:
"[*Interim*] accipio, unde sit anima; quae mecum sedulo retractabo et, si quid me moverit,
post requiram" (Augustine, *De quantitate animae* 2,3 [CSEL, 89], p. 133), where the sentence is cautiously tempered by the adverb *interim*; or the *non intellego* (cf. *Ibid.* 4,6,
p. 137). Finally, as Mandouze has rightly pointed out: "Dans l'un et l'autre dialogue,
E. apparaît comme un jeune homme autrement mieux doué qu'on ne l'a souvent prétendu
et de toute façon intensément préoccupé de problèmes métaphysiques" (MANDOUZE,
Evodius 1 [n. 60], p. 368). The same can also be affirmed with regard to the surviving
four letters written by Evodius to Augustine (cf., among the Augustinian letters: Evodius,
Ep. 158 [CSEL, 44], pp. 488-497; *Ep.* 160, *Ibid.*, pp. 503-506; *Ep.* 161, *Ibid.*, pp. 507-
511; *Ep.* 163, *Ibid.*, pp. 520-521) where Evodius "s'y montre aussi vivement préoccupé
de questions métaphysiques et théologiques" (MANDOUZE, *Evodius* 1 [n. 60], p. 369). If
that is so, we are indeed surprised by the somewhat superficial and reluctant explanation
with which Evodius met the request of Valentinus and his monks over the *affaire* that had
stirred the monastery of Hadrumetum. Although unable to judge the real intentions of
Evodius, we are nevertheless left with some doubts: did his hesitation in engaging himself deeply with the question of the relationship between grace and free will depend on
his not wanting to seem to question the authority of his powerful friend, the bishop of
Hippo?

64. "Laudamus quidem studium vestrum, sed nolumus esse contentiosum; contentio
enim perturbationem excitat, studium pietatem requirit" (Evodius, *Ep. ad Valentinum*
[PLS, 2], c. 332). Also: "Cum pietate, non cum contentione... nemo perturbetur, si non
intelligit" (*Ibid.*).

exhorted them to avoid the sin of pride which could lead to the criticism
of the Church Fathers on the subject of the dispensation of grace (the
implicit reference to Augustine is quite clear) and to the refusal of the
definitions of the plenary council (he is most likely thinking of canons
from 4 to 6 of the Council of Carthage of 418)[65]. Such was the content
of Evodius' letter to Valentinus and his monks. Although a moderate
one, the generic answers that the bishop of Uzalis gave to the community of Hadrumetum, together with the final exhortation against pride,
did not satisfy the monks nor did it help to appease their spirits. The
instruction fell on deaf ears. The intervention of a well respected priest,
a certain Sabinus, who was consulted on the matter after Evodius' letter
proved ineffective, failed as well. Although he read and explained
clearly (*cum liquidis interpretationibus*)[66] the content of Augustine's *Ep.*
194 to the monks, Sabinus succeeded neither in appeasing nor reconciling their minds[67].

As a last resort Valentinus was persuaded to give way to the rough
insistence (*rusticitas*) of those in opposition to Augustine's views. These
monks were convinced that Augustine himself should be consulted, for
only he could give a correct and suitable explanation of the points that

---

65. "Superbum est autem, tantorum et tam sanctorum ecclesiae magistrorum de
divinae gratiae dispensatione sapienter libros conscriptos a nobis parvulis, cum pie intellegere nolumus, velle culpari vel in aliquo reprehendi, et, quod plus abominandum est, de
hac quaestione plenarii concilii diffinitas sententias nolle accipere" (*Ibid.*, pp. 333-334).
    66. Valentinus, *Ep.* 216,3 (CSEL, 57), p. 399.
    67. There is also a letter from the *presbyter* Januarianus (or, according to some vari-
ants in the manuscript discovered by Morin, *Ianuarius* and *Ianuarinus*) written to Valentinus in answer to a letter (missing) handed to him by a delegation of monks from
Hadrumetum (cf. A. MANDOUZE, *Ianuarianus* 5, in ID. *et al.*, *Prosopographie chrétienne
du Bas-Empire*, T. I: *Prosopographie de l'Afrique Chrétienne [303-533]*, Paris, 1982,
p. 581). We are, however, unable to pin-point the exact time when this occurred, nor are
we able to relate the content of Januarianus' letter to those of Evodius and Sabinus, or to
judge the weight that his answer might have had upon the development of the events (see
MANDOUZE, *Valentinus* 3 [n. 31], p. 1133). Januarianus' letter (*Ep. de Dei gratia*) can be
found in PLS, 2, cc. 334-342. It reproduces the text published in MORIN, *Lettres inédites*
(n. 62), pp. 247-253. In it Januarianus offers to Valentinus some useful advice on how to
handle the crisis at Hadrumetum, and gives a summary of the main points of the doctrine
of grace, closely following Augustine's views. "Cet exposé doctrinal – writes Chéné – est
augustinien d'un bout à l'autre" (J. CHÉNÉ, *Notes complémentaires* [BA, 24], p. 213).
Januarius must have been a careful student of Augustine's thought and a docile recipient
and propagator of his teaching on grace. Like Evodius he did not encourage discussion,
but pointed to a submissive acceptance of Augustine's intellectual achievements. "His
deferential attitude both to Augustine and to the tradition of the church – Weaver writes
– provides us with two significant clues as to the character of the North African church,
as do the somewhat similar attitudes of Evodius and Valentinus" (R.H. WEAVER, *Divine
Grace and Human Agency. A Study of the Semi-Pelagian Controversy* [PatMS, 15,
Macon, GA, 1996, p. 11).

were discussed at Hadrumetum. Reluctantly[68], Valentinus allowed two monks, Cresconius and Felix[69], to go to Hippo, but without charging them with an official mission and consequently without providing them with letters of recommendation[70]. The abbot, in fact, disapproved of this mission, probably because he did not want to seem to share the same doubts as the monks with regard to Augustine's view on grace[71].

Augustine warmly welcomed the two visitors from Hadrumetum, as well as a third monk who joined them later. This was the other Felix, who at Uzalis dictated the *Ep.* 194 to Florus. Since they were impatient to return to the monastery of Hadrumetum by Easter[72], Augustine wrote a letter addressed to abbot Valentinus (*Ep.* 214) in which he returned to the difficult issue at stake (*difficillima quaestio*)[73]. After the letter had

---

68. "Inordinata profectione" (Valentinus, *Ep.* 216,1 [CSEL, 57], p. 397). "Arripuerunt profectionem nobis taliter non optatam" (*Ibid.*, p. 398).

69. Cresconius and Felix were probably two of those "five or more brethren" (*quinque enim, uel eo amplius*: *Ibid.* 216,3; p. 399) whose animosity was at the origin of the bitter dispute brought about by Augustine's *Ep.* 194, and who held Florus responsible for all that had happened.

70. Letters of recommendation were compulsory for clerics (and therefore also for monks) who moved or travelled from one diocese to another (see the 2nd Council of Milevis of 416, can. 20, entitled: "Vt sine formatis nemo ad comitatum proficiscatur, et qualiter fiant formatae", in *Concilia Africae A. 345 – A. 525* [n. 2], pp. 366-367). *Formata* was the technical word for "lettre de recommandation" (A. BLAISE, *Dictionnaire latin-français des auteurs chrétiens*, Turnhout, 1954, p. 360). Cf. also: "Epistulas communicatorias quas formatas dicimus" (Augustine, *Ep.* 44,2,3 [CSEL, 34/2], p. 111). See *Codex canonum ecclesiasticorum* 63 (*Regula formatarum*) [PL, 56], c. 730; PIETRI, *Roma Christiana* (n. 1), II, p. 1262, n. 3.

71. "Ne dum per dubitantes et de ueritate fluctuantes scriberemus, de dictis sapientiae tuae, quae est sicut angeli Dei, dubitare cum dubitantibus uideremur" (Valentinus, *Ep.* 216,1 [CSEL, 57], p. 397).

72. Cf. Augustine, *Ep.* 214,5 (CSEL, 57), p. 384. The *terminus ad quem* must be set at Easter of either 426 or 427. In fact, the *De gratia et libro arbitrio* and the *De correptione et gratia* are the last two works revised by Augustine in his *Retractationes*, a book which was completed in 427.

73. "Difficillimam quaestionem et paucis intellegibilem" (*Ibid.* 214,6, p. 385). Cf. also Id., *Ep.* 215,2 (CSEL, 57), p. 389. The first paragraphs the *Ep.* 214 show how the problems discussed in the letter to Sixtus (*Ep.* 194) should be approached and understood. The Lord Jesus, says Augustine, did not come into the world to judge it but to save it (cf. Jn 3,17; 12,47). And yet the same Lord, as it is believed by the Church, will come at the end of time to judge both the living and the dead (cf. *Symbolum Nicaenum–Constantinopolitanum*; 2 Tim 4,1; 1 Pet 4,5; Rom 3,6). Thus, if on the one hand grace is needed to save the world, on the other hand free will is also required as a condition of its judgement. Both are necessary, and if grace cannot be denied, free will cannot be overrated to the point of making it independent of God's grace: "Si ergo non est Dei gratia, quo modo saluat mundum? et si non est liberum arbitrium, quo modo iudicat mundum? Proinde librum uel epistulam meam, quam secum ad nos supra dicti adtulerunt, secundum hanc fidem intellegite, ut neque negetis Dei gratiam, neque liberum arbitrium sic defendatis, ut a Dei gratia separetis, tamquam sine illa uel cogitare aliquid uel agere secundum Deum ulla ratione possimus, quod omnino non possumus" (Augustine, *Ep.* 214,2 [CSEL,

been written, Cresconius and the two Felixes changed their minds and
remained at Hippo for a longer time, deciding to take the opportunity of
being in Augustine's presence and of hearing and better understanding
his arguments against those whom the bishop of Hippo had labelled as
the "new Pelagian heretics"[74]. This, at least, is the reason for their delay
given by Augustine to Valentinus in his second letter (*Ep.* 215)[75]. Such
a delay, however, was judged positively by the bishop of Hippo, who
was thus inspired to write a small treatise on grace and free will, the *De
gratia et libero arbitrio*[76]. This small treatise he handed on to the monks
on their way home, together with the aforementioned letters (*Epp.* 214
and 215) and a copy of the ecclesiastical documents containing the pro-
nouncements against Pelagianism. Augustine had long desired such an
opportunity[77]. He provided an accurate list of this material in his second
letter to Valentinus[78].

57], pp. 381-382). In this sense, the letter sent to Sixtus opposed the Pelagian belief which
attributed the bestowal of God's grace to man's merits. On the contrary, continues Augustine, there is nothing of merit that is not granted by God, and therefore nothing of good
that man can boast about (cf. 1 Cor 4,7). Human merits are, in fact, the result of divine
mercy and grace (cf. Id., *Ep.* 214,3ff, pp. 382ff). Augustine also indicates that the principal source of his thinking is Holy Scripture. It is in Scripture, above all, that we learn
about the existence of both grace and free will (cf. *Ibid.* 214,4.7, pp. 383.386).

74. "Ut instructiores ad uos redirent aduersus nouos haereticos Pelagianos" (Id., *Ep.*
215,1 [CSEL, 57], p. 388). Under the direction and supervision of Augustine, the monks
worked on the *Ep.* 194, on Cyprian's *De dominica oratione* and on various other ecclesiastical documents (cf. *infra* n. 78).

75. This second letter gave Augustine the opportunity to reiterate some of his key
concepts on grace and free will. He affirmed that only unbaptized children are condemned
because of original sin, whereas those who have been baptized and possess free will will
have to take responsibility for their own personal sins (cf. *Ibid.* 215,1, p. 388). Referring
to Cyprian's work on the Lord's prayer, he also reiterated the necessity of praying to God
both for ourselves, in order to do his will, and for the pagans, so that his grace might lead
them to conversion (cf. *Ibid.* 215,3, p. 390). It followed an exhortation not to turn neither
right nor left (cf. Pr 4,26 [LXX]), that is, neither to rely on free will as if in itself it were
sufficient for good works, nor to abandon it on the premise that grace can operate in us
despite our evil deeds (cf. Rom 3,8): "Hoc est, nec sic defendatis liberum arbitrium, ut ei
bona opera sine Dei gratia tribuatis, nec sic defendatis gratiam, ut quasi de illa securi,
mala opera diligatis; quod ipsa gratia Dei auertat a uobis" (*Ibid.* 215,8, p. 395).

76. "Et scripsi ad uos etiam librum, quem si adiuuante Domino diligenter legeritis et
uiuaciter intellexeritis, nullas existimo inter uos de hac re dissensiones ulterius iam
futuras" (*Ibid.* 215,2, p. 389).

77. Cf. Id., *Ep.* 214,5 (CSEL, 57), p. 384.

78. "Quod enim scriptum est ad papam Innocentium, Romanae urbis episcopum, de
concilio prouinciae Carthaginensis et de concilio Numidiae *[Epp. 175-176]* et aliquanto
diligentius a quinque episcopis *[Ep. 177; the five bishops are: Aurelius, Augustine, Alip-
ius, Euodius and Possidius]* et quae ipse ad tria ista rescripsit *[Epp. 181-183]* item quod
papae Zosimo de Africano concilio scriptum est *[it is gone lost]*, eiusque rescriptum ad
uniuersos totius orbis episcopos missum *[the Tractoria]* et quod posteriori concilio ple-
nario totius Africae contra ipsum errorem breuiter constituimus *[the Council of
Carthage of May 1ˢᵗ, 418]* et supra memoratum librum meum, quem modo ad uos scripsi

Had Augustine believed abbot Valentinus' report on the way the monks of his community had received and welcomed the *De gratia et libero arbitrio*[79], he would almost certainly have been content with the result. But something else was disturbing the atmosphere in the monastic community, something that escaped the attention of the superior and which, for that reason, was not drawn to the attention of Augustine. The monk chosen to go and deliver the letter to the bishop of Hippo was Florus, a name already familiar to us: the Florus who had unconsciously caused the quarrel at Hadrumetum. His learning and intelligence were not the only reason for sending him on this mission; Augustine had himself requested his presence. He wanted to check personally if the unease caused by the *Ep.* 194 that Florus had copied and sent to his community by means of Felix, was due to any misunderstanding of Augustine's thought on the *difficillima quaestio* of grace and free will[80]. Or, more simply, if the tensions were merely to be ascribed to Florus' incapacity to explain a difficult matter in a correct and plain way to a community of monks which numbered within itself simple brethren (*animae innocentes*)[81], unable to grasp complicated theological issues because of their little learning (*imperiti [...] non intellegentes*)[82].

On his arrival at Hippo, Florus found Augustine in bad health, as we read in a short note addressed to Valentinus and forwarded to him through the same Florus on his way back home[83]. Florus reassured the old bishop about his own orthodoxy by providing an interpretation on the subject of grace in line with that of Augustine, who was very satisfied

[*De gratia et libero arbitrio*]; haec omnia et in praesentia legimus cum ipsis et per eos misimus uobis" (Id., *Ep.* 215,2 [CSEL, 57], pp. 389-390). As to the episcopal councils, he must have sent an extract of the most significant parts: "Ad concilia episcopalia novissima necessitate peruentum est; unde vobis, non quidem omnia, sed tamen aliqua legenda direxi" (Id., *De gratia et libero arbitrio* 4,6 [PL, 44], c. 886).

79. "Sed quia interdum, domine papa, prouenit gaudium ex tristitia, non adeo maestificamur, quia per ignaros et curiosos suauissimis monitionibus tuae sanctitatis inluminari meruimus" (Valentinus, *Ep.* 216, 4 [CSEL, 57], p. 399).

80. "Melius autem facietis, quod multum rogo, si ipsum, a quo dicunt se fuisse turbatos, ad me mittere non grauemini. Aut enim non intellegit librum meum aut forte ipse non intellegitur, quando difficillimam quaestionem et paucis intellegibilem soluere atque enodare conatur" (Augustine, *Ep.* 214,6 [CSEL, 57], p. 385). See also: "Si quid de uobis mereor, ueniat ad me frater Florus" (Id., *Ep.* 215, 8 [CSEL, 57], p. 396).

81. Valentinus, *Ep.* 216,3 (CSEL, 57), p. 398.

82. *Ibid.* (see *supra* n. 56).

83. This note, found by Morin (cf. MORIN, *Lettres inédites* [n. 62], p. 243), is reproduced in CSEL, 58, praef., p. XCIII; *BA* 24, p. 228; NBA, 23, p. 562. With regard to his illness, Augustine writes: "Praesente quippe ipso me imbecillitas corporis et talis et tam multis diebus tenuit, ut cum illo esse non possem" (Augustine's *Note* [CSEL, 58], p. XCIII). He then asks Valentinus' permission for Florus to return to Hippo for further intensive instruction ("abundantiorem instructionem": *Ibid.*).

with the evidence[84]. Moreover, Florus informed him about the recent happenings and developments in his monastic community, especially about a doubt, which appears not to have been apparent to abbot Valentinus, since the superior did not mention it in his letter to Augustine. This doubt concerned "rebuke" and whether or not it was necessary. Florus must have reported that someone (*ibi quendam*) in the monastery had made the comment that according to the views expounded by Augustine in his *De gratia et libero arbitrio,* no one ought to be rebuked for not keeping God's commandments. On the contrary, all that could be done for a brother straying from the divine precepts, was to pray that he might keep them in future. This piece of information alarmed Augustine. He could see the danger that could be drawn from such an objection. Thus he decided to write a second book addressed to Valentinus and his community, the *De correptione et gratia*[85].

Even though difficult to ascertain, it is generally believed that Florus himself went back to Hadrumetum with both the aforementioned note and with the new treatise on rebuke and grace[86]. In default of documentation,

84. "Talem repperi, qualem optaveram" (*Ibid.*). See also: "Hanc fidem, quae sine dubio uera et prophetica et apostolica et catholica fides est, etiam in fratre nostro Floro inuenisse me gaudeo" (Id., *De correptione et gratia* 1,2 [CSEL, 92], p. 220). Augustine's positive judgement meets with the favourable recommendation of Florus made by his superior Valentinus: "Serui tui Flori haec fides est, pater, non sicut fratres isti sunt locuti" (Valentinus, *Ep.* 216,4 [CSEL, 57], p. 400). It is likely that Cresconius and the two Felixes, in their previous visit to Augustine, had not introduced Florus in a favourable light.

85. "Rursus ad eosdem [*the monks of Hadrumetum*] scripsi alterum librum quem *De correptione et gratia* praenotaui, cum mihi nuntiatum esset dixisse ibi quendam, neminem corripiendum si Dei praecepta non facit, sed pro illo ut faciat tantummodo orandum" (Augustine, *Retractationes* 2,67 [CCL, 57], p. 142).

86. See, for instance, MORIN, *Lettres inédites* (n. 62), p. 244; cf. J. CHÉNÉ, *Seconde réponse d'Augustin aux moines d'Adrumète (Introduction)* (BA, 24), pp. 213. 215, n. 1 (cf. also *Ibid.* p. 27). More cautiously, Mandouze writes: "C'est très probablement F.*(lorus)* qui, rentrant à *Hadrumetum,* rapporte à Valentinus une lettre (215A) d'Augustin ainsi que le second ouvrage rédigé par ce dernier à l'intention de la communauté, le *De correptione et gratia*" (MANDOUZE, *Florus* 2 [n. 35], p. 479). Some legitimate skepticism is allowed regarding this. If, due to his illness (*imbecillitas corporis*), Augustine had had little opportunity either to entertain or converse with Florus, how had he found the physical and intellectual strength to write the exacting piece of work that the *De correptione et gratia* undoubtedly is? Moreover, this treatise is not mentioned at all in the note delivered by Florus to Valentinus. We might, therefore, question whether the bearer of the treatise *De correptione et gratia* was indeed Florus, and whether the treatise might have not been delivered at a later date. If it was delivered by Florus, it could still have been delivered at a later date, possibly after a second visit to Hippo, made at the express wish of Augustine himself in the note to Valentinus: "Unde iterum rogo, ut iam non meum solum sed utriusque nostrum desiderium implere digneris et eum rursus mittere, ut aliquamdiu nobiscum sit" (Augustine's *Note* to Valentinus [CSEL, 58], *Praef.*, p. XCIII). If then the note was delivered to Valentinus by Florus after his first visit to Hippo, the *De correptione et gratia* must have reached Hadrumetum after Florus' second visit to Augustine had taken place.

we suppose that the newly written treatise must have been favourable, and that their minds must have been eventually been placated. At least, there were no further adverse reactions to the delicate subject of grace and free will from the monastery of Hadrumetum. Augustine's second treatise must indeed have been on target and helped solve the problems which were at the origin of the *perturbatio* of the monastic community[87].

However, before summarizing the content of the works addressed by Augustine to the abbot and the monks of Hadrumetum, namely the *De gratia et libero arbitrio* and the *De correptione et gratia*, it might be useful at this stage to briefly describe the *Sitz-im-Leben* of the Hadrumetum monastery as seen against the wider background of the monastic phenomenon.

3. THE *SONDERWELT* OF MONASTICISM: THE AFRICAN CONTEXT AND THE COMMUNITY OF HADRUMETUM

Whether or not Augustine should be considered the patriarch of African monasticism[88] depends a great deal on the meaning we assign to the term "patriarch". If by it we mean that Augustine was the first to introduce monasticism in Africa[89], then we cannot make such an affirmation with absolute certainty. Yet, the term "patriarch" could certainly be applied to him, if by it we mean that his inclination to this form of life, his personal experience and his *Rule* were determining factors in the spread and development of African monasticism[90]. That Augustine contributed in a decisive way to the expansion of the monastic ideal in Africa is in fact indisputable, even if we must surmise that some form of monastic life was already being lived on African soil[91] before the

87. From Prosper's letter to his friend Rufinus we can infer that the outburst that occurred at Hadrumetum had come to an end: "Confide ergo in virtute misericordiae Dei, quoniam haec contradictio, sicut in aliis mundi partibus, ita et in his regionibus conquiescet" (Prosper, *Ep. ad Rufinum [De gratia et libero arbitrio]* [PL, 51], cc. 88-89).
88. "Usque ad dies nostros consideratur patriarcha vitae monasticae africanae" (GAVIGAN, *De vita monastica in Africa Septentrionali* [n. 31], p. 31).
89. This is the firm conviction, for example of Monceaux: "Au temps de la conversion d'Augustin, certain pays, comme l'Afrique, n'avaient encore jamais vu un moine"; "Pour toute l'Afrique latine, Augustin a été l'initiateur et le maître du monachisme" (P. MONCEAUX, *St. Augustin et St. Antoine. Contribution à l'histoire du monachisme*, in *MA*, T. II, Rome, 1931, pp. 61-89, pp. 65 and 72). See also GAVIGAN, *De vita monastica in Africa Septentrionali* (n. 31), pp. 30-31; A. ZUMKELLER, *Das Mönchtum des heiligen Augustinus*, Würzburg, 1950, pp. 104-105.
90. "Le monachisme africain doit principalement à saint Augustin la forme qu'il gardera jusqu'à la conquête arabe" (V. DESPREZ, *Les origines du monachisme occidental. II Afrique et Espagne*, in *Lettre de Ligugé* n. 209 [1981] 9-31, p. 9).
91. "Like every other aspect of the Church's life and thought in North Africa, the development of monasticism there was dominated by the genius and sanctity of St.

appearance of the *monastica uiuendi forma* of Augustinian imprint. Doubtlessly, before Augustine's return to his home town Thagaste in 388 and the establishment of a small community whose monastic features were inchoately shaped by him[92]; even before his genius and

Augustine. It is not likely, however, that monastic life in Roman Africa only began with the efforts of Augustine" (C. PEIFER, *Pre-Benedictine monasticism in the Western Church*, in T. FRY, *et al.* [eds.], *RB 1980. The Rule of St. Benedict*, Collegeville, MN, 1981, p. 59). "En realidad, sería muy sorprendente que no hubiera habido monjes, incluso cenobitas, en el norte de Africa antes de una fecha tan tardía como el año 388. Dada la rápida expansión del monacato en todos los países del Mediterráneo y la proximidad de Egipto, 'paraíso de los monjes', podríamos decir a priori que los hubo" (G.M. COLOMBAS, *El monacato primitivo*, T. I [BAC, 351], Madrid, 1974, p. 274). Cf. J. BIARNE, *Moines et rigoristes en Occident*, in J.-M. MAYEUR, *et al.* (eds.), *Histoire du Christianisme des origines à nos jours*. T. II: *Naissance d'une Chrétienté (250-430)*, Paris, 1995, p. 757; A. MANRIQUE, *San Agustín y el monaquismo africano*, in *CDios* 173 (1960) 118-138.

92. Whether or not Thagaste was Augustine's first monastery after his return to Africa in 388, has been a *quaestio disputata* for a long time (see a brief account in G. LAWLESS, *Augustine of Hippo and his Monastic Rule*, Oxford, 1987, pp. 45-58). Although Thagaste cannot be regarded as being a "monastic" foundation in a technical sense, there is evidence to support the conviction that it was indeed Augustine's "first monastery" (and not a mere replica of the philosophical-like circle of Cassiciacum) wherein life was already characterized by those "monastic" features furthered developed in Hippo: surrender of property and possession (at least in Augustine's case), fasting, fraternity, dialogue, spiritual reading (*lectio diuina*), work of an intellectual bent (cf. *Ibid.*, pp. 46.48-50). "The group of like-minded enthusiasts – writes Brown – that had gathered round him in his retirement *[at Thagaste]*, came, by slow and subtle stages, to resemble a 'monastery', with Augustine as 'spiritual father' " (BROWN, *Augustine of Hippo* [n. 61], p. 136). "The life of Augustine and his friends at Thagaste already resembled that of the monks of Capraria, as described in *Letter* 48" (L. VERHEIJEN, *Saint Augustine: Monk, Priest, Bishop,* Villanova, PA, 1978, p. 25). Finally, we agree with Lawless when he concludes: "When we read Augustine on Augustine, there is to my knowledge no passage which militates against calling Thagaste a monastery in a bona fide sense. This is not to say that Augustine's monasticism awaited no further development. Contrariwise, everything we read in Augustine's writings on monastic life corroborates our knowledge about the years 388-391" (LAWLESS, *Augustine of Hippo*, p. 50). See also ZUMKELLER, *Das Mönchtum des heiligen Augustinus* (n. 89), pp. 46-57. Furthermore, it must be noted that the project of leading a monastic life after the example of the Egyptian monks, goes back to the time of Augustine's conversion. He was, in fact, enthused by Ponticianus' account of how two friends of his had been converted and had become *serui Dei* after reading Athanasius' *Vita Antonii* which they had found in a hermit's hut, during a stroll outside Trier (cf. Augustine, *Confessiones* 8,6,14-15 [CCL, 27], pp. 121-123; see ZUMKELLER, *Das Mönchtum des heiligen Augustinus*, pp. 27ff). Augustine's decision to become Christian is closely connected to his resolve also to become a monk: "Dans sa vie personnelle ..., il y a eu un lien très étroit entre sa résolution de devenir chrétien baptisé et celle de devenir religieux: les deux ont coïncidé" (L. VERHEIJEN, *Saint Augustin*, in *Théologie de la vie monastique. Études sur la Tradition patristique* [Theol(P), 49], Paris, 1961, pp. 201-212, p. 201). "Il s'est converti à l'Église catholique, mais aussi à un projet de vie monastique, projet qu'il est allé réaliser dans son pays natal, à Thagaste d'abord et surtout à Hippone" (ID., *Le monachisme de saint Augustin*, in ID., *Nouvelle approche de la Règle de saint Augustin*. T. II: *Chemin vers la vie heureuse*, Louvain, 1988, pp. 13-29, p. 14); "... ils s'étaient faits baptiser avec un projet de vie monastique" (*Ibid.*, p. 16). See also B. BRUNING, *Otium and* negotium *within the one Church*, in *Aug(L)* 51 (2001) 105-149.

sanctity provided impetus to the spread of monastic ideals, "groups" of *uirgines* and *continentes* were already in existence in Roman Africa. They were witnesses to a very successful ascetic and pre-cenobitic tradition, focused on perfect chastity. Originally independent from cenobitism[93], these ascetics began, during the 4th century, to look for some form of organization whereby attempts were made at living together along the lines of a cenobitic style. This is certainly one of the features marking the transition from a "Christian" asceticism to a "monastic" asceticism[94].

During the 3rd century two great and prominent African leaders, Tertullian (†220 ca.) and Cyprian (†258), added their own impetus to the quest for perfection within the African Church. They upheld enthusiastically, both in their lives and with their teaching[95], the ideal of Christian perfection, and thanks to their exhortations many men and women embraced the way of life of the *uirgines* and *continentes*. The former, in particular, had grown in number to such an extent that towards the end

93. *Virgines* and *continentes* used to live in the world, in their own houses and with their own relatives, namely in their own *milieu*, and kept the administration of their own goods (cf. M. VILLER – M. OLPHE-GALLIARD, *L'ascèse chrétienne. A. Les origines scripturaires – B. La période patristique [III.]*, in J. DE GUIBERT, *et al.*, *Ascèse, Ascétisme*, in *DSp* 1 [1937] 936-1010, cc. 960-977, c. 967; G.M. COLOMBAS, *Asceti e ascete*, in *DIP* 1 [1974] 917-926, c. 919). The asceticism of some wealthy Roman women, widows and virgins alike, is well known in the West. Marcella's house, for instance, was the meeting place for noble women interested in studying the bible. When Jerome arrived in Rome, in 381, he soon became their spiritual father. A similar type of commitment was also present in the Christian East. An example can be found in the so-called "Sons and Daughters of the Covenant" (*benai qejâmâ*), who occupied a place at the very heart of the Syriac-speaking Church of upper Mesopotamia. To them was addressed Aphraates' *Demonstrationes (takhwjâtâ)* (cf. I. HAUSHERR, *Aphraate*, in *DSp* 1 [1937] 746-752, c. 747).

94. For an historical overview of the origins and the initial inspiration and ideals of monasticism both in the East and in the West, see D.J. CHITTY, *The Desert a City*, Oxford, 1966; M. SHERIDAN, *The Origins of Monasticism in the Eastern Church*, in FRY, *et al.* (eds.), *RB 1980* [n. 91], pp. 3-41; C. PEIFER, *Pre-Benedictine Monasticism in the Western Church*, in *Ibid.*, pp. 42-64; G. GOULD, *The Desert Fathers on Monastic Community* (OECS), Oxford, 1993; D. BURTON-CHRISTIE, *The Word in the Desert. Scripture and the Quest for Holiness in Early Christian Monasticism* (OECS), New York-Oxford, 1993; S. ELM, *Virgins of God: the Making of Asceticism in Late Antiquity* (OCPM), Oxford, 1994; J.E. GOEHRING, *Ascetics, Society, and the Desert. Studies in Early Egyptian Monasticism*, Harrisburg, PA, 1999. The first "institutional" forms of communal/monastic asceticism are associated with Pachomius in Egypt, and with Basil the Great in central Asia Minor (cf. CHITTY, *The Desert a City*, pp. 20-38; PEIFER, *Pre-Benedictine Monasticism*, pp. 24-34).

95. Cf. Tertullian, *De uirginibus uelandis* (CCL, 2), pp. 1207-1226; Cyprian, *De habitu uirginum* (CSEL, 3/1), pp. 185-205. Texts from these works are collected in J.M. DEL ESTAL, *Sobre los comienzos de la vida común entre las vírgines de África*, in *CDios* 170 (1957) 335-360. On asceticism in Tertullian and Cyprian see also B. LOHSE, *Askese und Mönchtum in der Antike und in der alten Kirche*, München – Wien, 1969, pp. 160-162.

of the 4th century some of them started gathering together and forming small cenobitic communities. Evidence of this can be traced back in one canon of a council held at Hippo in October 393 (and later inserted in the legislative *corpus* of the Council of Carthage of 397) which prescribes that girls without parents be entrusted to the care of women known for their austerity and virtue[96]. We can confidently argue that a similar process to that of the *uirgines* which gave origin to a feminine cenobitism must have occurred also among the ranks of the African *continentes* some of whom started gradually to form male cenobitic communities[97] whose influence must have reached Augustine[98].

The *Entwicklung* from an ascetic form of life to a cenobitic monasticism has led some scholars to conclude that the latter had developed naturally from the first[99], and that the difference between an ascetic and a monk existed only in degree rather than in nature[100]. Although we

96. "Ut uirgines sacrae,…, prouidentia grauioribus feminis commendentur" (*Concilia Africae A. 345 – A. 525* [n. 2], p. 42).

97. Cf. COLOMBAS, *El monacato primitivo*. T. I (n. 91), p. 274. "Il serait bien téméraire de dire qu'aucune tentative de vie commune entre continents n'ait été encore réalisée avant le retour d'Augustin en Afrique" (G. FOLLIET, *Aux origines de l'ascétisme et du cenobitisme africain*, in *Saint Martin et son temps. Mémorial du XVIe centenaire des débuts du monachisme en Gaule, 361-1961* [StAns, 46], Rome, 1961, p. 34). And more assertively: "Nul doute que le cénobitisme a fait son apparition en Afrique avant l'arrivée d'Augustin" (*Ibid.*, p. 43). See also M. VILLER – K. RAHNER, *Askese und Mystik in der Väterzeit. Ein Abriß der frühchristlichen Spiritualität*, Freiburg i. Br., 1939 (reprint, Darmstadt, 1989), pp. 43-49; A. MASOLIVER, *Historia del Monacato cristiano*. T. I: *Desde los orígines hasta san Benito*, Madrid, 1994; J.-M. BESSE, *Le monachisme africain (du IVe au VIe siècle)*, extrait de la *Revue du Monde catholique*, Paris-Poitiers, 1900; I. GOBRY, *Les moines en Occident*. T. II: *De saint Martin à saint Benoît. L'enracinement*, Paris, 1995; R. LORENZ, *Die Anfänge des abendländischen Mönchtums im 4. Jahrhundert*, in *ZKG* 77 (1966) 1-61.

98. Undoubtedly, the ascetic tradition present on the soil of Africa, whether in its individual or in its incipient cenobitc form, must have exercised its influence on Augustine and must have contributed to his idea of cenobitism: "Augustin a trouvé en Afrique des traditions d'ascétisme chrétien sans lesquelles il n'aurait probablement pas pu en aussi peu de temps 'inventer' et divulguer la forme de cénobitisme qui porte effectivement sa marque" (MANDOUZE, *L'aventure de la raison et de la grâce* [n. 7], p. 174, n. 1). Moreover, we should not forget the positive impact exercised on Augustine after his conversion by the male and female communities of Milan and Rome: "Vidi ego sanctorum diuersorium Mediolani non paucorum hominum, quibus unus presbyter praeerat uir optimus et doctissimus. Romae etiam plura cognoui… Neque hoc in uiris tantum sed etiam in feminis; quibus item multis uiduis et uirginibus simul habitantibus". (Augustine, *De moribus ecclesiae catholicae et de moribus Manichaeorum* 1,33,70 [CSEL, 90], pp. 74-75).

99. "It is … clear that the monasteries were a growth, in new circumstances, from already existing groups of virgins or male ascetics" (O. CHADWICK, *John Cassian. A Study in Primitive Monasticism*, 2nd ed., Cambridge, 1968, p. 55). "The monks were the successors of the groups of virgins and celibates in the churches during the age of persecution" (*Ibid.*, pp. 65-66).

100. Cf. for instance J. FONTAINE, *L'ascétisme chrétien dans la littérature gallo-romaine d'Hilaire à Cassien*, in *Atti del Colloquio sulla Gallia romana. Accademia Naz.*

cannot deny that individual ascetic life served as a *terreau* to cenobitic monasticism[101], we must nevertheless point out that the two forms of life were not exactly the same[102], even if it is sometimes difficult to make a readily recognizable distinction between the two[103]. First of all, Christian asceticism is as old as the Church, for the simple fact that it was always part of the evangelical message itself, whereby the believer is invited to attain a life of perfection through self-discipline, by mastering those basic impulses of the *condition humaine,* such as hunger, sleep, sexuality. The rigorous *modus uiuendi* of the ascetic movement constituted a reminder of this truth over and against a general relaxation of the life of Christian communities[104]. Since monks were people who took the

---

dei Lincei, 10-11 maggio 1971, Rome, 1973, 87-115, p. 90. It must be said, at this point, that problems of interpretation with regard to the rise of monasticism are often caused by an improper and vague use of the term. In fact, it would be very misleading to consider monasticism as a synonym of cenobitism *tout court.* Not only because some of the features of "communal" life could be found in some ascetic milieux as well, but also because monasticism itself had acquired from the very beginning a comprehensive meaning reaching out to anchoretic and semi-eremitical life alike. Thus monasticism must not be considered merely as an equivalent of cenobitism. The same term μόναχος-*monachus* is ambivalent because it can mean both solitude and unity (cf. F.E. MORARD, *Monachos, Moine. Histoire du terme grec jusqu'au 4ᵉ siècle,* in *FZPT* 20 [1973] 332-411; see also L.T.A. LORIÉ, *Spiritual terminology in the Latin Translations of the Vita Antonii* [LCP, 11], Nijmegen, 1955, pp. 25-34).

101. Cf. BIARNE, *Moines et rigoristes en Occident* (n. 91), p. 750.

102. "Si la virginité consacrée remonte aux origines mêmes du christianisme, le monachisme est une institution originale qu'il ne faut pas confondre avec la précédente" (H.-I. MARROU, *Nouvelle Histoire de l'Église,* I/2, 2ⁿᵈ ed., Paris, 1985, p. 310).

103. At a certain point, with the affirmation of cenobitism, "le affinità tra gli asceti premonastici e i monaci medesimi e le loro istituzioni sono tali, che è difficile dire con certezza se certi individui o gruppi debbano classificarsi tra i primi o tra i secondi.... è indubitabile che fu lungo questa linea e a conclusione d'una evoluzione omogenea di tali gruppi di asceti che nacque quel grande movimento, così vario e dalle manifestazioni più diverse, che noi oggi designiamo con un nome che mai ebbe un significato del tutto univoco: il monachesimo" (COLOMBAS, *Asceti e ascete* [n. 93], c. 922).

104. Pietri speaks of *zelanti,* a term which he applies specifically to all those Roman women and men (*uirgines* and *continentes*) striving to be *integri christiani,* but which can be applied to all those in the Christian world who were aiming at such a goal (cf. PIETRI, *Roma Christiana* [n. 1], I, pp. 432ff). We should remember too that the Pelagians were very similar to such *zelanti.* Like all ascetics, they too assumed an attitude that "was always thought of as being a reaction, an act of self-definition, the establishment of a discontinuity between the 'authentic' Christian and the rank-and-file of Christians in name only" (P. BROWN, *Pelagius and his Supporters: Aims and Environment,* in *JTS,* n.s., 19 [1968] 93-114, p. 104). "What characterizes Roman Pelagianism in its formative years is its combination of asceticism and moralism" (G. BONNER, *Augustine and modern Research on Pelagianism* [The Saint Augustine Lecture Series, Villanova University 1970], Villanova, PA, 1972, p. 11). The rigorism of the Pelagians, however, was so natural a part of their quest for Christian perfection that their ascetic discipline and aims were "the least original aspect of the movement" (BROWN, *Pelagius and his Supporters,* pp. 104-105). According to Pelagius, in fact, the Christian *lex* ought to be imposed in all

Gospel message seriously and desired to put it into practice *sine glossa*, we can affirm without further ado that asceticism, as an important feature of Christian faith and religion, would *ipso facto* be regarded as an integral part of the monastic life too. This cannot, however, be taken to mean that the monastic phenomenon ought only to be reduced to the practice of an ascetic life, as if monks should be identified *sic et simpliciter* with the top representatives of asceticism. But if this is not so, what is then the *nouum* of monasticism?

If it is always difficult and delicate to set limits to a spiritual phenomenon (especially if that is done through the lens of a mere sociological analysis!), this holds true even with regard to the task of illustrating and defining the originality and the meaning of the rise and spread of the monastic movement (be it in its anchoretic, semi-eremitical or cenobitic form) on the scene of 4th century Christianity[105]. This becomes even more evident if one takes into account the fact that alongside Christian ascetic endeavours there were similar currents that had been existing for centuries within the pagan world[106] and the non-Christian religions[107].

---

its rigours on every baptized person, regardless of his status, and there should be no loopholes in as far as Christian commitments were concerned. He was for a sort of *reductio ad unum*, "one" law for everybody: "In causa iustitiae omnes unum debemus: virgo, vidua, nupta, summus, medius, et imus gradus, aequaliter iubentur implere praecepta" (Pelagius, *Ep. ad Demetriadem* 10 [PL, 30], c. 25).

105. As it has been justly remarked: "Le monachisme, dans le christianisme (et même en dehors), est un mouvement essentiellement spirituel. Les analyses ou classifications d'ordre sociologique ne l'atteignent que de l'estérieur, et toujours de manière partielle" (P. MIQUEL, *Signification et motivations du monachisme*, in A. SOLIGNAC, *et al.*, *Monachisme*, in *DSp* 10 [1980] 1524-1617, cc. 1547-1557, c. 1547). Besides, as Gribomont puts it: "Le monachisme n'est pas un système théorique qui tiendrait son unité de la cohérence de ses principes; il n'est pas non plus issu d'un fondateur déterminé, qui l'aurait marqué à son image. Dès l'origine, il se manifeste spontanément en diverses provinces; des formes analogues existent en diverses religions et cultures non chrétiennes. Il semble donc difficile de l'analyser comme un phénomène unitaire" (J. GRIBOMONT, *Naissance et développements du monachisme chrétien*, in A. SOLIGNAC, *et al.*, *Monachisme*, in *DSp* 10 [1980] 1524-1617, cc. 1536-1547, c. 1536). As a matter of fact, any definition of monasticism shows itself as being "toujours trop étroite" (A. SOLIGNAC, *[Introduction]*, in ID. *et al.*, *Monachisme*, in *DSp* 10 [1980] 1524-1617, cc. 1524-1525, c. 1524). See also COLOMBÁS, *El monacato primitivo*. T. I (n. 91), p. 36ff; J. LECLERCQ *et al.*, *Monachesimo*, in *DIP* 5 (1978) 1672-1742; P. DE LABRIOLLE, *Les débuts du monachisme*, in A. FLICHE – V. MARTIN (eds.), *Histoire de l'Église*. T. III: *De la paix constantinienne à la mort de Théodose*, Paris, 1936, pp. 299-369, especially pp. 348-354; K. HEUSSI, *Der Ursprung des Mönchtums*, Tübingen, 1936, pp. 280-304.

106. See P. BROWN, *Asceticism: Pagan and Christian*, in A. CAMERON – P. GARNSEY (eds.), *The Cambridge Ancient History*. Vol. XIII: *The Later Empire, A.D. 337-425*, Cambridge, 1998, pp. 601-631. The author concentrates mainly on the differences in meaning attached by differing groups to their understanding of asceticism.

107. See, for instance, P. MASSEIN, *Le phénomène monastique dans les religions non chrétiennes (I.)*, in A. SOLIGNAC, *et al.*, *Monachisme*, in *DSp* 10 (1980) 1524-1617,

That deep transformations of the human person were made possible by ascetic discipline, was not a conviction relevant only to Christian asceticism and monasticism, but also to ancient philosophical tradition and non-Christian milieux. It is in fact against the background of commonplace ascetic practices and privations, such as fasting, sexual renunciation, poverty and the like, that Christian monasticism flourished with its own distinctive mark and aim.

Simply put (within the restricted purpose of this section), the rise of Christian monasticism, be it in its anchoretic, semi-eremitical or cenobitic form, rests on several reasons. These testify both to the variety and complexity of a phenomenon which had a considerable impact on society, both in the East and in the Christian West[108], and to the consequent impossibility of connecting or reducing it to one cause alone. Most scholars see the rise of the Christian monastic movement as an attempt to represent a paradigm of Christian life which ideally reflected the purity and fervour of primitive Christianity. Not surprisingly, in a period in which the relaxation of the Church had become apparent (the natural result of the Constantinian toleration [Edict of Milan of 313] towards the Christian religion), such an attempt was not easily accepted. In a world that had become friendlier and less hostile towards the followers of Christ than it had been in previous centuries, there was a reaction on the part of the monastic movement where it was felt that the Christian message faced the very real risk of being watered down and deprived of the revolutionary strength of its intramundane perspectives. The *fuga mundi*[109], that is the physical separation of the monks from the world, was a clear sign of contradiction with respect to the *illusio saeculi* which had also eventually found a hearing within the Church[110]. The need for "setting apart", so as to find a more favourable milieu in which to live their particular calling, was in fact the spontaneous reaction of many to

---

cc. 1525-1536. The author treats of ascetic/monastic phenomena present in ancient religions such as Induism, Buddhism and Judaism (the sect of the Essenes) as well as in the ancient Greek world (*e.g.*, the Pythagoreans).

108. According to Brown, for instance, in the great process of cultural transformation which marked the making of Late Antiquity, the monks of Egypt played "a role more enduring than that of Constantine" (P. BROWN, *The Making of Late Antiquity*, London, 1978, p. 80). See also S. PRICOCO, *Aspetti culturali del primo monachesimo d'Occidente*, in *Monaci, Filosofi e Santi. Saggi di storia della cultura tardoantica*, Messina, 1992, pp. 9-37.

109. See Z. ALSZEGHY, *Fuite du monde*, in *DSp* 5 (1964) 1593-1599.

110. The rise of monasticism as a "reform movement", providing an outlet for all those who felt estranged in a Church besieged by mediocrity and laxity, is an explanation which has been adopted by several historians since it was given its classic formulation in A. VON HARNACK, *Monasticism, Its Ideals and History*, New York, 1895.

a diminished religious and moral consciousness within the Church. It is
on this level, above all, that the monks distinguished themselves from
the ascetics[111]. Naturally, their radical life style and determination to live
out Gospel values contrasted unfavourably when compared with the life
style of the majority of Christians, causing relationships between the
groups to become strained[112]. Their withdrawal from the world did in
fact raise some perplexities, particularly because it came to be regarded
as a sign of separatism and individualism, not to say (in some cases at
least) of extravagance! Were the monks only pursuing their own salvation? Or did their choice of lifestyle have a social purpose too? These
were the basic questions the monastic movement was confronted with
vis-à-vis the distrust and criticism of many outside[113] the Church as well
as inside it[114].

    111. Marginality seems to be the distinguishing mark of monasticism. "The criterion
for distinguishing monastic life in the strict sense from ... pre-monastic forms of asceticism can only be that of living separately from the rest of the Christian community"
(C. PEIFER, *Pre-Benedictine Monasticism* [n. 94], p.43). "Ciò che distingue il monaco dal
semplice asceta è pertanto unicamente il fatto che egli pratica l'ascetismo non in seno a
una communità cristiana, ma in un mondo separato, nella solitudine del deserto o in seno
a una comunità costituita esclusivamente di asceti" (COLOMBAS, *Asceti e ascete* [n. 93],
c. 923).
    112. See H. CHADWICK, *The Early Church*, London, 1967, American ed. New York,
1986, pp. 176ff.
    113. The pagan poet Ausonius, for instance, reproached his former disciple and friend
Paulinus of Nola because he was convinced that his monastic retirement was a choice dictated by laziness, madness and misanthropy. This we infer from Paulinus' "apology" (cf.
Paulinus of Nola, *Carmina* 10 and 11 [CSEL, 30], pp. 24-42). That the monastic call of
Paulinus, a man belonging to the highest ranks of society, had provoked a scandalous
reaction, is witnessed also by Ambrose, *Ep.* 27 *[Ad Sabinum]* (CSEL, 82), pp. 180ff.
    114. The criticism ensuing from the Christian milieu was more nuanced. Often the
monastic choice was disdained for its provocative way of life. The election of Martin to
bishop of Tours, for instance, was the cause of no little opposition on the part of some lay
people and bishops who disapproved of it on the ground of Martin's "ascetic look":
"Pauci tamen, et nonnulli ex episcopis qui ad constituendum antistitem fuerant euocati,
impie repugnabant, dicentes scilicet contemptibilem esse personam, indignum esse epis-
copatu hominem uultu despicabilem, ueste sordidum, crine deformem" (Sulpicius
Severus, *Vita Martini* 4,1 [SC, 133], pp. 270-272). In Rome, the premature death of the
young lady Blesilla was attributed to excessive austerity and fasting by the Roman mob
who rose against the "genus detestabile monachorum", intending to chase them out of the
town and stone or drown them (cf. Jerome, *Ep.* 39,6 [CSEL, 54], p. 306). The following
description by Salvian (between 440-450) is also of interest: "Ita igitur et in monachis, id
est, sanctis Dei, Afrorum probatur odium,... Itaque eos non sine causa, ut dixi, oderunt,
in quibus omnia sibi aemula atque inimica cernebant. Illi enim uiuebant jugiter in nequitia
isti in innocentia, illi in libidine isti in castitate, illi in lustris isti in monasteriis, illi prope
jugiter cum diabolo isti sine cessatione cum Christo" (Salvian, *De gubernatione Dei*
8,4,19.21 [SC, 220], pp. 522.524). See also the encouraging exhortation addressed by
Augustine to several monks who had been attacked on account of their ascetic and vir-
ginal life (cf. Augustine, *Sermo* 354 *[Ad continentes]* [PL, 39], cc. 1563-1569). Criticism
of monasticism was also directed against an extravagant and false imitation of monastic

A second opinion sees a direct connection between the rise of monasticism and the anti-Christian persecutions that had caused many to flee and hide themselves in the desert, thus constituting the first colonies of hermits or semi-eremitical groups. A third and contrasting opinion sees the rise of popularity of the monastic life, at a time when persecution had ceased, as the desire by many to "give up" their life in a martyrdom of sorts. This was seen, in the language of Christendom, as the most powerful witness to faith. In other words, the fact that persecution had ended meant that monastic life, including the ascetic notion of Christian life as a fight or warfare (= *militia*)[115], became in the eyes of many a surrogate martyrdom[116]. Monasticism came to be considered a "white" martyrdom as opposed to the "red" one of a former time of persecution, when witness to one's faith often meant the shedding of one's own blood. The idea of comparing monastic life to a *martyrium sine cruore* or *sine sanguine,* was very popular in 4th century Christian literature[117]. This means that even when peace was assured within the Church, martyrdom remained the *mensura* whereby faith and religion were qualified and weighed, especially in the field of asceticism, virginity and above all

life. Jerome criticised the so called *remnuoth* (monks living according to their own taste) with his usual verve and bitter sarcasm (cf. Jerome, *Ep.* 22,34 [CSEL, 54], pp. 196-197). See also Augustine, *De opere monachorum* 30,38 (CSEL, 41), p. 589. Monks were further criticised for their withdrawal from the world because their departure was seen as a weakening of the ordinary Christian communities. An instance of this social-pastoral argument can be found in Vigilantius's criticism of monasticism, as it is reported by Jerome: "Si omnes se clauserint, et fuerint in solitudine, quis celebrabit ecclesias? Quis saeculares homines lucrifaciet? Quis peccantes ad virtutes poterit cohortari?" (Jerome, *Contra Vigilantium* 15 [PL, 23], c. 366). However, regarding the social connotation of monasticism, we should avoid the temptation of homologising its manifold expressions. Basilian monasticism in Cappadocia, for instance, was marked from the beginning by a social connotation and an openness to the sorrounding world and its needs. A connotation which, rather than a reaction to the *fuga mundi* of the "Egyptian way", as some have thought, was directly derived from the evangelical ideal of love (cf. J. GRIBOMONT, *Basilio,* in *DIP* 1 [1974] 1101-1109, cc. 1106-1107).

115. See J. AUER, *Militia Christi,* in *DSp* 10 (1980) 1210-1223.

116. Cf. VILLER – RAHNER, *Askese und Mystik in der Väterzeit* (n. 97), p. 38, where we meet the expression "Der Ersatz des Martyriums".

117. Antony, the great forerunner of monasticism, remains paradigmatic in regard to this: "When the persecution finally ceased and bishop Peter of blessed memory has suffered martyrdom, he [*Antony*] left and went back to his solitary cell; and there he was a daily martyr to his conscience (και ἦν ἐχεῖ καϑ᾽ ἡμέραν μαρτυρῶν τῇ συνειδήσει), ever fighting (ἀγωνιζόμενος) the battles of faith. For he practised a zealous and more intense ascetic life (Καὶ γὰρ καὶ ἀσκήσει πολλῇ καὶ συντονωτέρα ἐκέκρητο)" (Athanasius, *Vita Antonii* 47,1 [SC, 400], p. 262; English tr. by R.T. MEYER [ed.], *St. Athanasius. The Life of Saint Antony* [ACW, 10], Westminster, MD, 1950, p. 60). The expression μαρτυρῶν τῇ συνειδήσει (cf. 2 Cor 1,12: τὸ μαρτύριον τῆς συνειδήσεως ἡμῶν) indicates that the monk's life, with its day-to-day ascesis, was considered to be the equivalent of martyrdom.

monasticism[118]. Other hypotheses could be used to explain the rise of monasticism, such as a desire to "do battle" with the devil in the desert; the search for paradise lost, or the much more down to earth notion of escape from socio/economic situations – a "freedom from slavery, from debt, from parental pressure or from a woman's anger"[119].

All these reasons, and more[120], can be adduced to explain the monastic phenomenon from a "phenomenological" point of view, and they are certainly plausible in some particular cases. Yet, beyond all these and their theological interpretation, there remains an ultimately fundamental aim which was at the core of the monastic call and of the movement it generated: the desire to live the purity of the Gospel message in its entirety. Such a desire becomes reality through a process of radical detachment from earthly things, and the total renunciation of human ambitions and affections (= *fuga mundi*) in order to devote oneself entirely to the quest for holiness[121]. Such holiness may well be seen in terms of the quest for "unity" of life, which is sought by committing oneself entirely to the service of God[122].

118. We can synthesize the many patristic references to the equation of monasticism with martyrdom by a sentence of Cassian: "Illos [*the cenobites and the hermits*] patientia atque districtio, qua sic deuote in hac quam semel adripuerunt professione perdurant, ut numquam suas expleant uoluntates, crucifixos huic mundo cotidie uiuosque martyras facit" (Cassian, *Conlationes* 18,7 [SC, 64], p. 21). Cf. also: "Deuotae... mentis seruitus quotidianum martyrium est" (Jerome, *Ep.* 108, 31 [CSEL, 55], p. 349); "Non enim ideo laudabilis uirginitas, quia et in martyribus repperitur, sed quia ipsa martyres faciat" (Ambrose, *De uirginibus* 1,3,10, *Opera omnia di Sant'Ambrogio* 14/1, p. 110); "Sed quamquam ista non tulerit, inpleuit tamen sine cruore martyrium" (Sulpicius Severus, *Ep.* 2,12 [SC, 133], p. 330); see G.M. COLOMBAS, *El monacato primitivo*, T. II (BAC, 376), Madrid, 1975, pp. 228-278; M. VILLER, *Le martyr et l'ascèse*, in *RAM* 6 (1925) 105-142; E.E. MALONE, *The monk and the martyr* (SCA, 12), Washington, 1950.
    119. Cf. Philoxenus of Mabbug, *Homiliae* 3 (SC, 44), pp. 84-85.
    120. See MIQUEL, *Signification et motivations du monachisme* (n. 105), cc. 1547-1557; P. NAGEL, *Die Motivierung der Askese in der alten Kirche und der Ursprung des Mönchtums*, Berlin, 1966, pp. 81-107.
    121. "Le mobile qui est à l'origine du monachisme, c'est assurément le besoin qui pousse les âmes à fuir le monde pour se consacrer plus librement au service de Dieu seul. Elles veulent rompre d'une façon plus décisive encore que par la simple profession de virginité avec l'ambiance profane dissolvante ou, pour le moins, trop absorbante" (VILLER–OLPHE-GALLIARD, *L'Ascèse chrétienne* [n. 93], c. 968). The theological background was provided by Origenian spirituality, which greatly influenced the beginning of monasticism (see H. CROUZEL, *Origène, précurseur du monachisme*, in *Théologie de la vie monastique* [n. 92], pp. 15-38).
    122. Cf. A. GUILLAUMONT, *Esquisse d'une phénoménologie du monachisme*, in ID., *Aux origines du monachisme chrétien. Pour une phénoménologie du monachisme* (SpOr, 30), Bégrolles en Mauges, 1979, pp. 228-239, p. 228. However rooted in Scripture, Guillaumont sees the convergence of the Judeo-Christian ideal of "unity" as similar to the theory of unification stemming from Platonic and Neo-Platonic views, and largely developed by gnostic systems (cf. *Ibid.*). In this respect, the portrait of Antony's spiritual development as it is described in Athanasius' *Vita Antonii* (SC, 400) has always existed as the

For the sake of completeness, some allowance should be made at this point for the virtuous life pursued by lay people outside a monastic setting. This is clear indication that the ideal of committing oneself entirely to God belongs to the core of the Gospel that each Christian should try to live up to the full. In this regard the *Festal Letters*[123] of Athanasius provide us with an interesting case in which ordinary believers (viz. not belonging to the categories of virgins and monks) were urged to pursue the Christian ideal of *arètè*. Besides his practical attempt to integrate into a comprehensive Church (viz. the Alexandrian Church) all those who, within it, had devoted themselves to ascetic life, Athanasius attempted also to integrate asceticism into a comprehensive theoretical view of Christian faith and life[124]. He wanted to demonstrate that ascetic values were not the prerogative of virgins and monks alone, and that, on the contrary, such values could be assimilated into a vision encompassing ordinary Christians. They too are called to a life of renunciation, even though their "ascetic" life must be envisaged as taking place at different levels. In the eyes of Athanasius, this multifarious way of living out the ascetic values attests to the diversity of the Church's members who, beyond their specific commitment, are held together by a shared "way of life" (πολιτεία). More precisely, this way of life is formed through imitation of the saints' discipline of the body and of their renunciation of the world[125]. Thus, in his *Festal Letters* the bishop of Alexandria considered the "paschal discipline an intensified version of the regime that ordinary Christians should practise throughout the year: during Lent and Easter, Christians should increase (αὐξάνειν) the

paradigm for the monastic world to follow. With regard to this, we cannot underrate the importance of the role played by Athanasius, bishop of Alexandria, in enthusiastically propagating the monastic ideal in the West during his exile at Trier (336-338) and Rome (340). His laudatory description of the Egyptian monks made a profound impression on his listeners. But, above all, his *Vita Antonii*, purposely written for admirers across the Mediterranean sea, became higly popular in the West (where it was already translated into Latin by 370) and strongly influenced the growth and development of Western monasticism. As to the question of the historical value of the details found in the *Vita Antonii*, see *Ibid.*, p. 42. Bartelink notes that as far as Athanasius is concerned, it is practically impossible to separate fact and idea. However, this is not to imply that Antony was merely a literary creation, and that his *Vita* is nothing but an object of enquiry in the field of the *Ideengeschichte*. On the contrary, Athanasius and his hero appear to be both influencing and absorbing one another (see J. ROLDANUS, *Origène, Antoine et Athanase. Leur interconnexion dans la Vie et les Lettres*, StPatr 26, Louvain, 1993, pp. 389-314).

123. In his *Festal Letters*, written during the seasons of Lent and Easter, Athanasius developed an ascetic program for ordinary Christians. These letters survive fragmentarily in Greek, Syriac and Coptic.

124. See D. BRAKKE, *Athanasius and the Politics of Asceticism*, Oxford, 1995, pp. 12f.

125. See *Ibid.*, pp. 142-200.

discipline (ἄσκησις) all the more"[126]. What Athanasius concretely recommended in his *Festal Letters* was an ascetic regime including prayers, vigils, renunciation of sex, fasting, study of Scriptures, making peace with others, almsgiving and hospitality, a regime which (although not undertaken in a cenobitic context) was indeed very close to what was habitually pursued in specialized ascetic/monastic settings[127].

To go back to the rise and development of monasticism in the African context, we must infer that the ideal of committing oneself entirely to God, along the lines sketched above, must have been shared by all those men and women who had dedicated themselves to the ascetic life. They must have tried, at a certain point, to apply these ideals to monastic/cenobitic living forms, before the return of Augustine to Thagaste in

126. *Ibid.*, p. 183.
127. Some concrete examples of this ascetic regime can be found in the English translation of Athanasius' *Festal Letters* from Greek and Syriac fragments: A. ROBERTSON (ed.), *Select Writing and Letters of Athanasius, Bishop of Alexandria* (NPNF, 2nd ser., 4), Edinburgh 1897, repr. Edinburgh-Grand Rapids/MI, 1991, pp. 506-553 *passim*. A French translation of the Coptic fragments can be found in L.-TH. LEFORT (ed.), *S. Athanase. Lettres festales et pastorales en copte* (CSCO, 151), Louvain, 1955, *passim*. A translation of some of the Coptic fragments is provided by BRAKKE, *Athanasius and the Politics of Asceticism* (n. 124), *Appendix F (Festal Letters 24 [2], 29, 39, 40)*, pp. 320-334.
128. It seems that Augustine's silence before the Donatist bishop Petilian's assertion that the bishop of Hippo was responsible for the establishment and spread of monastic life in Africa should be interpreted in this sense (cf. Augustine, *Contra litteras Petiliani* 3,39,48 [CSEL, 52], p. 201: "Deinceps perrexit ore maledico in uituperationem monasteriorum et monachorum, arguens etiam me quod hoc genus uitae a me fuerit institutum; quod genus uitae omnino quale sit nescit uel potius toto orbe notissimum nescire se fingit". The existence of some pre-Augustinian monastic forms must have been known and given for granted, which is why Augustine did not think it necessary to reply to Petilian's provocation. It is precisely in this direction that Folliet interprets the second part of the above quotation: "Si le rôle d'Augustin dans la diffusion du monachisme y est incontestablement attesté, son prétendu titre de fondateur du monachisme n'y est pas moins clairement récusé par Augustin lui-même" (G. FOLLIET, *Compte rendu* of J.-M. DEL ESTAL, *Testimonio positivo de Petiliano sobre la inexistencia del monacato en África antes de S. Agustín*, in *REAug* 10 [1964] p. 225, n° 156). Del Estal believed, on the contrary, that the quotation from Augustine's *Contra litteras Petiliani* 3,39,48 should be read in the light of the thesis which favoured the non existence of monasticism in Africa before Augustine (cf. J.-M. DEL ESTAL, *Testimonio positivo de Petiliano sobre la inexistencia del monacato en África antes de S. Agustín*, in *StMon* 3 [1961] 123-136). Such an article is the logical sequence of del Estal's thesis on the vow of virginity and cenobitism in the primitive African Church (cf. ID., *Sobre los comienzos de la vida común entre las vírgines de África*, in *CDios* 73 [1957] 335-360; ID., *Un cenobitismo preagustiniano en África?* in *CDios* 72 [1956] 375-403 and 74 [1958] 161-195). On the other hand, the conviction that Augustine played an important role in the spreading of African monasticism is not without foundation, and such a role was undoubtedly recognized by his contemporaries. He enjoyed, after all, "la réputation d'être fort engagé dans la vie monastique et d'avoir beaucoup fait pour elle" (A. DE VOGÜÉ, *Histoire littéraire du mouvement monastique dans l'antiquité. T. III/1: Le monachisme latin, Jérome, Augustin et Rufin au tournant du siècle [391-405]*, Paris, 1996, p. 214).

388[128]. Among the African ascetic/monastic communities existing beside Augustinian monasticism, and maintaining their independence and autonomy even after the spread of the latter at the turn of the 5th century[129], must be numbered the community at Hadrumetum. We have no precise information about the beginnings of this monastery[130], even though some scholars believe that it was of Italian origin[131]. Nevertheless, a direct indication that the monastic community of Hadrumetum did not belong to the Augustinian circle, seems apparent from the concluding words of Valentinus' letter to the bishop of Hippo. After having expressed his concern about the problems that had arisen in his monastery, the abbot takes advantage of the unforeseen epistulary contact with Augustine to ask him for some useful advice about governing the monastic community[132]. From this request we can infer that Hadrumetum was in no way related to Augustine and to his monastic views, not to say to his *Rule*. Furthermore, there are other details which favour the idea that the monastery of Hadrumetum was, in fact, independent from the Augustinian monastic circle[133]. For instance, if Hadrumetum was a foundation ensuing from Hippo or attached to it, abbot Valentinus would have immediately asked Augustine for advice

129. Groups of monks of Messalian trend, against which Augustine wrote his polemic work *De opere monachorum*, bear witness, for instance, to an ascetic life which had developed independently of Augustine.

130. "Rien n'est particulièrement attesté de l'histoire de l'Église d'Hadrumète tout au long du IVᵉ s…. On ne sait rien non plus du premier essor de la communauté monastique dans la capitale byzacénienne, vraisemblablement vers la fin du IVᵉ s." (S. LANCEL – R. AUBERT, *Hadrumète*, in *DHGE* 22 [1988] 1493-1496, c. 1494). See also BESSE, *Le monachisme africain* (n. 97), p. 30.

131. Cf. A. MANRIQUE, *San Augustin y el monaquismo africano*, in *CDios* 173 (1960) 117-138; COLOMBAS, *El monacato primitivo*. T. I (n. 91), p. 274.

132. "Si quid autem famulus tuae sanctitatis frater suggesserit Florus, pro regula monasterii, digneris, pater, petimus, libenter accipere, et per omnia nos infirmos instruere" (Valentinus, *Ep.* 216,6 [CSEL, 57], p. 402). Some scholars (e.g. A. SAGE, *La Règle de saint Augustin commentée par ses écrits*, Paris, 1961, pp. 260-263; A. MANRIQUE, *La vida monástica en San Agustín*, El Escorial-Salamanca, 1959, pp. 457-458) believed that it was on the basis of this request that Augustine composed and addressed his *Rule* for the community of Hadrumetum (or as a *complément* to Hadrumetum's own Rule), which is known as the *Regula ad seruos Dei*. The critical study of L. Verheijen, however, shows that the *Regula ad seruos Dei* or *Praeceptum* was written by Augustine at the time of the foundation of the lay monastery at Hippo in ca. 391 (cf. L. VERHEIJEN, *La Règle de saint Augustin*. T. II: *Recherches historiques*, Paris, 1967, pp. 87-116; see also LAWLESS, *Augustine of Hippo* [n. 92], p. 60). The arguments of Manrique, and especially of Sage (who speaks of Hadrumetum as already having its own Rule), do eventually presuppose that Hadrumetum was not an Augustinian foundation.

133. Cf. J. FOLLIET, *Le monachisme en Afrique de saint Augustin à saint Fulgence*, in *Il monachesimo occidentale dalle origini alla Regula Magistri. XXVI Incontro di studiosi dell'antichità cristiana, Roma, 8-10 maggio 1997* (SEA, 62), Rome, 1998, pp. 291-315, pp. 300-302.

instead of addressing himself first to Evodius and then to Sabinus and Januarianus. Contact with Augustine was eventually established only on request of some of the recalcitrant monks. Even the fact that the community of Hadrumetum was still ignoring the existence of the *Ep.* 194 (seven or eight years after it had been written), as well as the existence of the Pelagian controversy documentation for which Augustine had been principally responsible, shows that there was no regular exchange between Hippo and the monastery of Hadrumetum, as one would expect if the latter had been a branch of the former. Besides, the monastic foundations of Augustinian imprint had spread in Africa through Augustine's disciples who, in their turn, had become bishops and had founded monasteries after the pattern of Hippo. Interestingly, Valentinus does not mention any connection with the bishop of Hadrumetum; on the contrary, his first thought when trouble arose in his monastery, was to ask advice from bishop Evodius, a friend of Augustine, in whose library the *Ep.* 194 was found. Finally, another indication of Hadrumetum's independence from Augustinian influence is seen in the fact that the title *abbas* with which Augustine addresses Valentinus, is not typical of Augustinian monastic spirituality. We are led to conclude that even if the monks of Hadrumetum were admiring Augustine's leading position within the African Church, this could not be taken *per se* as a guarantee of the monks' total approval of his theological ideas. On the contrary, the fact that the community of Hadrumetum was neither rooted in nor inspired by Augustinian monastic ideals meant that it was exposed to a wider range of external influences, including the ascetic appeal of the Pelagian movement[134], whose positive view on the resources of human will and nature would not be lost on those accustomed to the effort of daily asceticism.

It is hardly surprising that devout monks of genuine vocation grew in the conviction, consciously or unconsciously, that they were a steely nucleus, a specialized body of heroes in the midst of a somewhat relaxed body of Christians[135]. Likewise, it is not inconceivable to imagine that, in monastic circles, the echo of Pelagius' voluntaristic doctrine

---

134. It is generally accepted that Pelagius himself, although a layman and not a monk, was recognized as being a champion of asceticism. The example of his life and the spread of his writings, in which he stressed the value of asceticism and human effort for all the baptized, could not but find a favourable welcome in monastic circles.

135. Jerome, for instance, had plainly given way to this conviction. According to him, to rally to the rigorous demands of asceticism and to persevere in them in a perceptible way amongst the mass of superficial Christians, was a sign of election and *superbia sancta*: "Disce in hac parte superbiam sanctam, scito te illis esse meliorem" (Jerome, *Ep.* 22,16 [CSEL, 54], p. 163).

of salvation, interwoven with a confident vision of the possibilities inherent in human nature, must have been welcomed – especially regarding the Pelagian defence of continence, a subject about which the monks were particularly concerned and sensitive[136]. In point of fact, it should not be forgotten that the Pelagian stress on asceticism and continence played also an important role in the controversy with the unorthodox Jovinian[137]. Although both Pelagius and Jovinian opposed the idea of a division in the Church between an ascetic/monastic élite craving for sanctity and a mass of simple believers with minimal demands, their methods were opposed. Countering the view that the continent state, lived by monks, virgins and even some married couples, was superior and therefore worthy of greater reward, Jovinian promoted the Christian ideal of marriage. He disparaged any elitistic form of asceticism and strongly defended as sufficient for salvation the grace of faith and baptism common to all Christians. In his eyes, those who had chosen to live under the *sanctum propositum* of continence could not claim any superiority at all over the ordinary baptized believer. Pelagius, who agreed with Jovinian that perfection was a goal for all the baptized, was convinced that asceticism was precisely the means by which that goal could be reached. He therefore defended the ascetic life vigorously, not merely as a theoretical possibility, ultimately confined to a small group of strongly determined believers, but as an urgent claim to be laid on every Christian[138]. With similar forcefulness he upheld the possibility of a continent and chaste life, undertaken in the name of the Gospel and

136. Unlike Jerome's invitation to consider the quest for perfection with *superbia sancta*, Augustine prefers to warn the monks of Hadrumetum against feeling satisfied with their personal efforts to which they might attribute their desire to live justly: "Et audeat miser homo, quando bene vivit et bene operatur, vel potius bene vivere et bene operari sibi videtur, in se ipso, non in Domino gloriari, et spem recte vivendi in se ipso ponere" (Augustine, *De gratia et libero arbitrio* 4,6 [PL, 44], c. 885). Augustine carefully avoids any possible hint that might put into jeopardy the gratuity and necessity of grace: see *Ibid.* 4,7, c. 886, where Augustine makes a specific reference to monastic continence.

137. Pelagius "repoussait, malgré la rigueur de son ascèse, les excès de Jérôme, sans rien concéder à Jovinien. Il prêche la réforme, l'exercice, à Rome, de l'ascèse, et d'une active charité" (PIETRI, *Roma Christiana* [n. 1], I, pp. 450-451). See J. GRIBOMONT, *Gioviniano*, in *DIP* 4 (1977) 1300-1301; A. DE VOGÜÉ, *Histoire littéraire du mouvement monastique dans l'antiquité*. T. II: *Première partie: le monachisme latin. De l'Itinéraire d'Egérie à l'éloge funèbre de Népotien (384-396)*, Paris, 1993, p. 273ff. Jerome and Augustine also reacted negatively to Jovinian ideas (cf. Jerome, *Aduersus Iouinianum* [PL, 23], cc. 211-338; Augustine, *De bono coniugali* [CSEL, 41], pp. 185-231; Id. *De sancta uirginitate* [CSEL, 41], pp. 233-302).

138. Pelagius' desire not to use a designation other than "Christian", can be found in the following exhortation: "Ego te christianum volo esse, non monachum dici, et virtutem propriae laudis possidere magis quam nomen alienum" (Pelagius, *De diuina lege* 9 [PL, 30], c. 119).

enhanced by means of man's free will[139]. The stress on human freedom and will, which constituted the kernel of Pelagian anthropology, must have been regarded by the monks (including those of Hadrumetum) as an incentive to continue following the ideals of perfection within the monastery and through that very same *propositum*, so depreciated by Jovinian[140].

Within this framework, we can understand the unease felt by those brethren of Hadrumetum who were inclined to think of themselves as specialists in asceticism, when faced with Augustine's views on grace. They felt threatened in their monastic *Weltanschauung* by the ideas on divine predestination and absolute gratuity of grace that Augustine had expounded in his *Ep.* 194, and summarized so well when he said: *Cum Deus coronat merita nostra, nihil aliud coronet quam munera sua*[141]. These words sounded like a serious challenge to their monastic undertaking, the achievement of which rested on the central role played by human agency. It was their conviction that the pattern of their daily living, together with the spiritual scope offered by monastic life, would form a tension resulting in evangelical perfection.

Other monks, beside those at Hadrumetum, must have had the same difficulty in harmonizing the idea of free will and divine grace; at least in as far as grace was regarded as an overwhelming cause in the annihilation of human effort. If everything was ultimately the work of grace, what then would be the point of leading an ascetic life? If in crowning human merit God merely crowns his divine gifts, what then was the purpose of fasting, nightwatches, obedience and all the other practices that make up an integral and essential part of monastic life? These were the kind of questions the monks were asking themselves, driven by a real concern about the meaningfulness of their way of life. Questions such as these would necessarily raise problems that could only be met by deep and subtle insight and distinctions. Augustine was as well aware of this challenge, as he was to admit the difficulty of reconciling, on a conceptual level, the truth of grace with the truth of free will[142]. Nevertheless,

---

139. See Id., *Ep. ad Demetriadem* 9-13 [PL, 30], cc. 25-29, where Pelagius insists that commitment to virginity is a super-rogatory one, ranking above the commitments required of all Christians, and that those who choose it as their particular state in life will merit a special reward.

140. "I *fratres* di Adrumeto avevano recepito, del pelagianesimo, qualche principio inerente al loro sforzarsi nello scegliere e portare avanti il *propositum* di vivere in monastero" (V. GROSSI, *La crisi antropologica nel monastero di Adrumeto*, in *Aug* 19 [1979] 103-133, p. 118). See also *Ibid.*, pp. 105ff and p. 126.

141. Augustine, *Ep.* 194,5,19 (CSEL, 57), p. 190.

142. Cf. Id., *Ep.* 214,6-7 (CSEL, 57), pp. 385-386; *Ep.* 215,2 (CSEL, 57), p. 389; *De gratia Christi et de peccato originali* 1,47,52 (CSEL, 52), p. 163.

he could not retreat before such fundamental issues. He felt it was his duty to try to illuminate and solve them, both as a theologian and as a bishop.

4. AUGUSTINE'S *DE GRATIA ET LIBERO ARBITRIO*

In the *Retractationes* Augustine presents and sums up the content of the *De gratia et libero arbitrio* with the following words[143]:

> I wrote a book whose title is *On Grace and Free Choice* because of those persons who, by thinking that free choice is denied when the grace of God is defended, defend free will in such a manner as to deny the grace of God by affirming that it is bestowed according to our merits. I addressed it, however, to those monks of Hadrumetum in whose monastery the controversy on this subject started; as a result, some of them were compelled to consult me[144].

The insistence on free will and human merit, must not be seen as detrimental to the necessity and gratuity of grace, as if the latter were incompatible with the former. This was the issue at stake, and Augustine's purpose was to show how the two poles, grace and free will, could be kept together. The necessity of the first and the existence of the second constitute two inseparable truths (*utrumque uerum est*)[145] whose coexistence must be safeguarded despite the difficult problems that such an attempt would inevitably raise[146]. Nonetheless, we cannot avoid an

143. English translation in M.I. BOGAN (ed.), *Augustine. The Retractations* (FaCh, 60), Washington, DC, 1968, p. 268.

144. "Propter eos qui, cum defenditur Dei gratia, putantes negari liberum arbitrium sic ipsi defendunt liberum arbitrium, ut negent Dei gratiam, asserentes eam secundum merita nostra dari, scripsi librum cuius est titulus *De gratia et libero arbitrio*. Ad eos autem scripsi monachos Adrumetinos, in quorum monasterio de hac re coeperat esse contentio, ita ut me consulere eorum aliqui cogerentur" (Augustine, *Retractationes* 2,66 [CCL, 57], p. 141). Cf. Id., *Ep.* 214,1 (CSEL, 57), p. 380-381; *Ep.* 215,1 (CSEL, 57), p. 388.

145. Id., *De gratia et libero arbitrio* 21,42 (PL, 44), c. 907. "Si sa – writes Trapè – che la dottrina agostiniana della grazia è la teologia dei grandi binomi che accompagnano la sintesi del pensiero del vescovo d'Ippona dall'inizio alla fine. Alcuni non lo notano o non lo tengono presente, ma questo non toglie che il merito del dottore della grazia sia stato proprio quello di averli intuiti, illustrati, difesi; e di aver insegnato a tenerli fermamente insieme" (A. TRAPÈ, *Introduzione* to *La grazia e il libero arbitrio*, in ID. (ed.), *Sant'Agostino. Grazia e libertà: La grazia e il libero arbitrio, La correzione e la grazia, La predestinazione dei santi, Il dono della perseveranza* [NBA, 20], Rome, 1987, pp. 3-17, p. 6).

146. Cf. G. BARDY, *Saint Augustin. L'homme et l'œuvre*, 6th ed., Paris, 1946, p. 430. On the philosophical side it is most likely that the inspiration for the harmony that Augustine sees between grace and human freedom was provided by Stoic compatibilism. See M. DJUTH, *Stoicism and Augustine's Doctrine of Human Freedom after 396*, in J. SCHNAUBELT – F. VAN FLETEREN (eds.), *Augustine: Second Founder of the Faith* (CollAug, 1), New York-Frankfurt a. Mainz-Paris, 1990, pp. 387-401.

uneasy feeling when we realize that the explanation of precisely "how" the two poles can effectively be reconciled and kept in balance in such a way that neither is highlighted to the detriment of the other is missing[147].

No doubt the necessity of grace and the existence of free will are defended and treated by Augustine as two fundamental and binding truths, convinced, as he was, that neither of them could be done away with. Also, the scriptural references he gives speak of the power of grace as well as of the importance of free will and good works. Moreover, the same biblical passages that exalt grace do sometimes contain an explicit or implicit reference to man's free will. And yet, in spite of the possible risk of seeming to lay too much weight on meritorious acts, Augustine ends by overstressing the power of grace whose sovereignty reaches out to the very core of free will. In point of fact, his demonstration of the coexistence of divine grace and human free will seems to rest on the presupposition that the role of grace is of paramount importance, although its role – Augustine agrees – has to be defended without denying the role of free will[148].

It is true that in the *De gratia et libero arbitrio* there is a kind of "front reversal"[149] with regard to the way Augustine approached the problem of nature and grace during the Pelagian controversy. Apart from the polemic context in which what had to be safeguarded were the prerogatives of grace, the bishop of Hippo could now pay greater attention to resisting the denial of the existence of free will. Yet this is not enough to modify Augustine's fundamental arguments, which are ultimately inspired and led by the concern of safeguarding the necessity, gratuity and the sovereignty of grace[150]. The second part of the *De gratia et*

147. Cf. J. CHÉNÉ, *Introduction générale* (BA, 24), p. 74.

148. Augustine is well aware that to deny the existence of free will would be absurd ("quod absurdissime dicitur": Augustine, *Contra secundam Iuliani responsionem imperfectum opus* 2,157 [CSEL, 85/1], p. 279) since it falls so obviously into the sphere of our daily experience.

149. "Agostino osserva che ha scritto molto contro quelli che esaltavano il libero arbitrio – i pelagiani –, ma negavano la grazia ... Ora invece era sorta la necessità di *rovesciare il fronte*: difendere cioè il libero arbitrio contro coloro che, affermando la grazia, negavano l'altro polo del mistero della salvezza" (TRAPÈ, *Introduzione* to *La grazia e il libero arbitrio* [n. 145], p. 6). See also *Ibid.* p. 21 (text-note n. 2).

150. "Rien dans ce traité – writes Amann – qui rappelle nos modernes tentatives de 'concilier la grâce avec le libre arbitre'. C'est avant tout l'affirmation de la grâce et – ce qui est un pléonasme – de son caractère absolument gratuit. Cela n'empêche pas, certes, d'affirmer la liberté de l'homme sous l'influx divin; mais visiblement ce n'est pas ce problème qui préoccupe Augustin. S'il est question du libre arbitre dans le traité, c'est surtout de son incapacité radicale à assurer le début, la continuation, la persévérance de la vie surnaturelle dont l'aboutissement est le ciel" (AMANN, *Semi-Pélagiens* [n. 15], c. 1800).

libero arbitrio, which is entirely devoted to the question of the nature of grace, supports this line of thought and its consequences. This alone speaks volumes about what continues to be the greatest concern of the bishop of Hippo.

The methodology underlying this treatise, viz. a constant use of Sacred Scripture, has always been a familiar one to the Church Fathers. Augustine is no exception. By his frequent and substantial recourse to Scripture[151], Augustine shows how much he relies on the *diuina auctoritas*[152], and how massively he appeals to it in order to root his theological views on solid and unquestionable ground: the very word of God[153]. There Augustine finds the *testimonia*, the scriptural proofs he needs in

151. Out of 7.230 lines, distributed in 32 columns of PL, 44, ca. 2.580 contain scriptural quotations. That means that the presence of scriptural passages amounts to ca. 35% (equal to over one third) of the entire text of the *De gratia et libero arbitrio*.

152. By *diuina auctoritas* Augustine means that God is the principal author (*auctor*) of the Bible, and that all "events recorded in Scripture have meanings intended by God" (F. VAN FLETEREN, *Augustine's Principles of Biblical Exegesis*, De doctrina christiana *Aside: Miscellaneous Observations*, in *AugSt* 27 [1996] 107-128, p. 126). Augustine's thorough knowledge of Scripture appears in all its evidence in the way he masters intertextual criticism, viz. in the way he criticizes or enlightens a scriptural text in term of another (or more). This method was very common in the ancient Church, and it has been practised up to the present. As to Augustine's exegesis, it is often thought that he was a proponent of allegorical exegesis, and in a sense he was because many of his works contain this type of exegesis, and yet his preference went to the literal and historical meaning of the text. See *Ibid.*, p. 127; D. DAWSON, *Figure, Allegory*, in FITZGERALD (ed.), *Augustine through the Ages* (n. 1), pp. 365-368; K. POLLMANN, *Hermeneutical Presuppositions*, in FITZGERALD (ed.), *Augustine through the Ages* (n. 1), pp. 426-429. According to Van Fleteren, Augustine's apparent contradiction deriving from the fact that he extensively used allegorical exegesis, although he had opted for a more scientific method, can be explained as follows: "First of all, literal and allegorical meaning are not contradictory, but rather complementary. Secondly, literal meanings of Scripture are more obvious; allegorical meanings are not. The exegete's task is to disclose an underlying spiritual meaning in Scripture, when one exists. Thirdly, the task of uncovering allegorical meanings in certain literary genres, for example the Psalms, had not been completed in Scripture itself. Augustine applies himself to this unfinished enterprise. Fourthly, the nature of human understanding, that man can not intuit truth directly, demanded that God speak to man by sign and symbol and that someone uncover and promulgate the hidden meaning of the scriptural record. Augustine no doubt saw himself as completing work begun by Christ himself, Paul, and John" (VAN FLETEREN, *Augustine's Principles of Biblical Exegesis*, p. 128).

153. "Et sic disputasse, ut non magis ego, quam divina ipsa Scriptura vobiscum locuta sit evidentissimis testimoniis veritatis" (Augustine, *De gratia et libero arbitrio* 20,41 [PL, 44], c. 905-906). Moreover, Augustine's concern for truth, when the latter is questioned by its adversaries, becomes even deeper and his inquiry into God's word more diligent: "Haereticorum quippe inquietudine, ut scripturas uigilantius perscrutemur... tamquam de somno ignauiae nostra excitatur industria" (Id., *Ep.* 194,10,47 [CSEL, 57], p. 213, p. 213). For Augustine's approach to Sacred Scripture, see the still very valuable work of M. PONTET, *L'exégèse de S. Augustin prédicateur* (Theol[P], 7), Paris, 1945, especially pp. 111-253; VAN FLETEREN, *Augustine's Principles of Biblical Exegesis* (n. 152).

order to formulate his explanation of the co-presence of grace and free will in Christian life[154]. Moreover, his insistence on Scripture, in the first part of the *De gratia et libero arbitrio*, is appropriate for another reason. It must not be forgotten, in fact, that the bishop of Hippo was dealing with monks, viz. with men who had devoted themselves to the service of God, and for whom Holy Scripture was the great code upon which their *conuersatio* was based. That means that their familiarity with the Bible would make them turn naturally to it as the source of enlightenment and inspiration for their daily monastic commitment[155]. For the same reason, Augustine's recourse to Scripture, in order to substantiate both the existence of free will and the necessity of grace, was an obligatory move.

a) The Recognition of Free Will and the Necessity of Grace

Biblical revelation constitutes, therefore, the first and main point of reference that Augustine uses to prove the reality and necessity of human free will. He argues that if the observance of divine revelation was entrusted to human beings, then it follows that they would be capable of adhering to it and fulfilling it through the proper use of free will. Moreover, the teaching of revelation is offered to mankind so that they not adduce the pretext of ignorance with regard to God's will, nor justify their bad conduct by attributing its ultimate cause to God himself[156]. Having quoted many biblical passages from both the Old and the New Testament to illustrate the point that free will and the ability to choose

154. "Proinde, carissimi, sicut superioribus testimoniis sanctarum Scripturarum probavimus, ad bene vivendum et recte agendum esse in homine liberum voluntatis arbitrium, sic etiam de gratia Dei, sine qua nihil boni agere possumus, quae sint divina testimonia videamus" (Augustine, *De gratia et libero arbitrio* 4,7 [PL, 44], c. 886).
155. As Trapè has rightly noted, these monks were "docili, in linea di principio, all'insegnamento della Scrittura. È da questa dunque che bisognava argomentare per illuminarli. Così fa Agostino" (Trapè, *Introduzione* to *La grazia e il libero arbitrio* [n. 145], p. 7). Cf. also Augustine, *De correptione et gratia* 1,1 [CSEL, 92], p. 219. That the Bible was really the book of the monks there is no doubt. It was the nourishment of their life, their mirror and the rule to which they would refer before all others, the instrument without which their monastic formation was unthinkable. With reason Athanasius calls the monks "lovers of the word [of God]" (Athanasius, *Vita Antonii* 4 and 44 [SC, 400], pp. 140 and 254). Φιλολογεῖν in Christian-monastic milieux became a technical term meaning: "reading/studying the Bible". See K. Girardet, "*Filologos und filologein*", in *Kl* 2 (1970) 323-333. Much has been written on the relationship between the Bible and monasticism. See, for instance, Colombas, *El monacato primitivo*. T. II (n. 118), pp. 75-94; E. von Severus, *Zu den biblischen Grundlagen des Mönchtums*, in *GuL* 26 (1953) 113-122; J.-C. Guy, *Écriture sainte et vie spirituelle. 4: Le monachisme*, in *DSp* 4 (1958) 159-164; C. Peifer, *The Biblical Foundation of Monasticism*, in *CiSt* 1 (1966) 7-31; K. Wagenaar, *De Bijbel bij de oude monniken*, in *TGL* 27 (1971) 532-553; 607-620.
156. Augustine, *De gratia et libero arbitrio* 2,3 (PL, 44), cc. 883f (cf. Jas 1,13-15; Pr 19,3; Ec 15,11-18).

have both been taken into account[157], Augustine resumes his discourse on God's teaching and precepts. He affirms, without any doubt on his part, that the latter needs the endorsement of human free will. Sinful actions, however, must be attributed entirely and solely to man's free will, whereas those actions which are in line with God's commandments are the result of both operative grace and the active participation of human will[158]. Moreover, the punishment of the *sempiternus ignis* is not only deserved by those who have known or have come into contact with divine precepts and refused to embrace them, but also (although in a mitigated form) by those who have ignored these commandments for the simple reason that they have never heard of them[159]. Besides, if one

157. Cf. *Ibid.* 2,4, c. 883.

158. "Nempe ubi dicitur: Noli hoc, et noli illud, et ubi ad aliquid faciendum vel non faciendum in divinis monitis opus voluntatis exigitur, satis liberum demonstratur arbitrium. Nemo ergo Deum causetur in corde suo, sed sibi imputet quisque, cum peccat. Neque cum aliquid secundum Deum operatur, alienet hoc a propria voluntate" (*Ibid.* 2,4, c. 884).

159. Cf. *Ibid.* 3,5, cc. 884f. Several times Augustine faced the problem of sin being caused by ignorance, a problem which he raises here in relation to the heathen. In short, it is a question that must be seen and understood in close connection with his doctrine of *peccatum originale*, which is the real cause of the transmission of both *ignorantia* and *concupiscentia* to humanity. In Augustine's eyes this constitutes the just punishment for original sin, and its immediate moral consequences after the fall. In fact, on the one hand, man finds himself unable (because of *ignorantia*) to know God and his revelation, and on the other he is prevented (by *concupiscentia*) from accomplishing that which is good, even when he is aware of it. This is the state in which unbaptized heathen find themselves. Furthermore, *ignorantia* and *concupiscentia* do not belong to the category of punishement alone (as the result of original sin), but also to a *tertium quid* which simultaneously comprises both punishment (*poena*) and guilt (*reatus/peccatum*). This is clearly stated in one of Augustine's last works: "Tertium uero genus, ubi peccatum ipsum est et poena peccati, potest intellegi in eo qui dicit: *Quod nolo malum, hoc ago*; ad hoc pertinent etiam omnia, quae per ignorantiam, cum agantur mala, non putantur mala uel etiam putantur bona" (Id., *Contra secundam Iuliani responsionem imperfectum opus* 1,47 [CSEL, 85/1], p. 35). Thus, in an unbaptized person, viz. a heathen person who has never heard of God's doctrine and commandments, ignorance (but it applies also to concupiscence) is both *reatus/peccatum* (as an extension of Adam's voluntary original sin in which all men have sinned and for which all are morally responsible) and *poena peccati* (see J. CHÉNÉ, *Notes complementaires* [BA, 24], pp. 769-771). Augustine summarizes this problem in a clear-cut way: "Illud *[peccatum]* ex uno in omnes pertransiit, in quo ante propria in singulis quibusque peccata omnes communiter peccauerunt. Ac per hoc inexcusabilis est omnis peccator uel reatu originis uel additamento etiam propriae uoluntatis, sive qui nouit siue qui ignorat siue qui iudicat siue qui non iudicat, quia et ipsa ignorantia in eis, qui intellegere noluerunt, sine dubitatione, peccatum est, in eis autem, qui non potuerunt, poena peccati. Ergo in utrisque non est iusta excusatio sed iusta damnatio" (Augustine, *Ep.* 194,6,27 [CSEL, 57], p. 197). Cf. also: Id., *De correptione et gratia* 10,28 (CSEL, 92), pp. 252-253; *De libero arbitrio* 3,18,51 (CCL, 29), p. 8; *De peccatorum meritis et remissione et de baptismo paruulorum* 1,36,58-59 (CSEL, 60), pp. 126-127; *De spiritu et littera* 36,64 (CSEL, 60), pp. 223f; *De natura et gratia* 17,19; 67,81 (CSEL, 60), pp. 245, 194-296; *Contra secundam Iuliani responsionem imperfectum opus* 1,105 (CSEL, 85/1), pp. 121-123. See A. TRAPÈ, *Introduzione generale*, in *Sant'Agostino,*

affirms that in following God's precepts, man's incapability ought to be ascribed to *concupiscentia*, then one is left with no other alternative than to acknowledge that man himself, and only man, is responsible for evil doing[160].

Yet Scripture reminds us too that we can overcome evil with good (cf. Rom 12,21), which means that free will is a reality and not merely an hypothesis. In a nutshell, as Augustine powerfully affirms, *uelle enim et nolle propriae uoluntatis est*[161]. Nevertheless, if free will has a role to play in the life of the faithful, it is only in the light of faith and thanks to divine grace that free will becomes effective with regard to the choice and accomplishment of what is good. The bishop of Hippo regards grace as necessary for the positive exercise of free will, by referring to Holy Scripture on a threefold level: that of religious/monastic continence, that of conjugal continence and that of concupiscence in general. Neither perfect continence nor conjugal chastity, nor an effective struggle against concupiscence, are possible without the coexistence and co-operation of grace and free will[162], or without the agency of the *uoluntas bona*, viz. the will guided by divine grace[163].

Natura e grazia (NBA, 17/1), Rome, 1981, pp. VII-CXCIX, pp. LXXVIff.; J. CHÉNÉ, *Notes complementaires* (BA, 24), pp. 769ff. Unlike the unbaptized, the presence of ignorance and concupiscence in the believers cannot be considered a *reatus/peccatum* (baptism, in fact, has washed away original sin) but a *poena peccati*, the punishment resulting from original sin. In this sense alone, *ignorantia* and *concupiscentia* subsist in a certain measure even in Christian people. The cause of their faults continues to reside in *ignorantia* and *infirmitas* (or *concupiscentia*): "Duabus ex causis peccamus: aut non uidendo quid facere debeamus, aut non faciendo quod debere fieri iam uidemus; quorum duorum illud ignorantiae malum est, hoc infirmitatis" (Augustine, *Enchiridion ad Laurentium, seu de fide, spe et caritate* [= *Enchiridion ad Laurentium*] 22,81 [CCL, 46], p. 94).

160. Id., *De gratia et libero arbitrio* 3,5 (PL, 44), c. 885.

161. *Ibid.*

162. "Et Dei donum... et liberum arbitrium" (*Ibid.* 4,7, c. 886). See also: "Ergo et victoria qua peccatum vincitur, nihil aliud est quam donum Dei, in isto certamine adiuvantis liberum arbitrium" (*Ibid.* 4,8, c. 887).

163. "Non autem intrat in tentationem, si voluntate bona vincat concupiscentiam malam. Nec tamen sufficit arbitrium voluntatis humanae, nisi a Domino victoria concedatur oranti, ne intret in tentationem" (*Ibid.* 4,9, c. 887). Cf. *Ibid.* 20,41, cc. 905-906. The expression "non autem intrat in tentationem" is an allusion to Mt 6,13. See J. LÖSSL, *Mt 6:13 in Augustine's Later Works*, in *StPatr* 33, Louvain, 1997, pp. 167-171, pp. 169f. We may as well point out that *uoluntas* and *(liberum) arbitrium uoluntatis*, although closely related and somehow interchangeable, are in point of fact relatively distinct terms. The *liberum arbitrium* can be seen as the "judging power" of the will, the personal centre of freedom and responsibility where both discerning and choosing take place. In this sense the *liberum arbitrium* guides our will, but is not exactly identical with it. Grace, for instance, addresses the *arbitrium* in order to operate on the level of the *uoluntas*, inclining it and making it consent to truth and goodness (the *uoluntas bona*). Although Augustine operates a "contraction" as it were, in that he is mainly concerned with the willing or not willing of the *uoluntas*, his preoccupation also implicitly highlights

Opposing the Pelagians' focus on man's agency and merit, Augustine goes on to illustrate three stages in which free will is exercised through the enlightenment of grace: conversion, good works and eternal life. The concrete example he refers to in support of his theses is that of the apostle Paul. To start with, the life of the great Apostle clearly demonstrates that conversion is not the result of one's previous merit (intending by it what one actually deserves), for, as Augustine states, Paul's only merit at the time of his conversion was as persecutor of the Church! The change produced in his life did not depend on him at all, but on the work of grace alone. At the moment of Paul's conversion on the road to Damascus *gratia Dei erat sola*[164]. No one turns towards God without grace, which provides the necessary strength to do so. Neither can one claim good works as the fruit of one's merit and capability. In fact, even a virtuous and just man, living in accordance with God's plan and commandments, still needs God's sustaining grace. Left to his own free will he would be unable to stand upright in faith and would inevitably fall[165]. Paul himself, whilst acknowledging the merit that enabled him to "fight" the good fight, and keep the faith until the race was finished (cf. 2 Tim 4,7), and whilst looking forward to receiving the crown of righteousness as a reward, was well aware that all this was only made possible by God's grace. God is, in fact, both the judge who justly rewards man's conduct and the merciful father who makes this same conduct possible: *Cui redderet coronam iustus iudex, si non donasset gratiam misericors pater?*[166]. Finally, eternal life itself is not accorded by God on the basis of man's merit, unless this merit is believed, as it actually is, to be God's gift. It follows that between God's agency and man's there exist an incommensurable difference[167], which Augustine's famous aphorism stresses very well: *Si ergo Dei dona sunt bona merita tua,*

the areas in which the *arbitrium* has actually vested its consent. See N.W. DEN BOK, *Freedom of the Will. A Systematic and Biographical Sounding of Augustine's Thoughts on Human Willing*, in *Aug (L)* 44 (1994) 237-270, pp. 241-243.

164. Augustine, *De gratia et libero arbitrio* 5,12 (PL, 44), c. 889. For the gratuitous character of conversion, see J.P. BURNS, *The Development of Augustine's Doctrine of Operative Grace*, Paris, 1980, pp. 168.176.179.181.185.

165. "Nam si se illa subtraxerit, cadit homo, non erectus, sed praecipitatus libero arbitrio" (Augustine, *De gratia et libero arbitrio* 6,13 [PL, 44], c. 889). See also: "[Ideo necessarium est homini, ut] ambulet cum illo gratia, et incumbat super ipsam ne cadat" (*Ibid.* 6,13, c. 890).

166. *Ibid.* 6,14, c. 890. See *Ibid.* 7,16-18, cc. 891-892.

167. Émery speaks of "hétérogénéité qui existe entre l'œuvre de Dieu et celle de l'homme" (P.-Y. ÉMERY, *Le Christ notre récompense: Grâce de Dieu et responsabilité de l'homme*, Neuchâtel, 1962, p. 143).

non Deus coronat merita tua tamquam merita tua, sed tamquam dona sua[168].

In this way Augustine solves what may, at first sight, appear to be a contradiction, namely: how can eternal life be considered a gift of grace if, in the words of Scripture, God "will render to every man according to his works" (Rom 2,6)? The answer rests precisely on the conviction that good works themselves, although belonging to human agency, are brought about and made possible by God's grace: *ipsa bona opera nostra quibus aeterna redditur uita, ad Dei gratiam pertinere*[169]. Thus, eternal life is a gratuitous gift, because the good works which have "merited" it are themselves the fruit of God's grace. Drawing from the gospel of John (cf. 1,16) Augustine comes thus to the conclusion that everlasting life, as the *praemium* of good works, *gratia est pro gratia*[170].

b) The Nature of Grace

In the second part of the *De gratia et libero arbitrio*, Augustine discusses again the nature of grace while keeping in the foreground (in order to refute it) the Pelagians' view on the subject. To begin with, the bishop of Hippo specifies what grace is not, by affirming that it cannot merely be identified with the law[171]. The latter, in fact, only provides a knowledge of what is evil or sinful, but is *per se* of no help whatsoever in avoiding them. Still less is one able to draw from the law the strength necessary to fight sin efficaciously. Saint Paul affirmed: "The written code kills, but the Spirit gives life" (2 Cor 3,6) – Christians must realize that without God's grace the "letter of the law" remains powerless, or, if it has any power at all, it is a power that brings about death. Man is not justified by it[172]. The law alone is useless, only the Spirit of the Lord

---

168. Augustine, *De gratia et libero arbitrio* 6,15 (PL, 44), c. 891. A similar expression was employed by Augustine in his *Confessiones* and in his letter to Sixtus (cf. *supra*, n. 52). See also: "Ac per hoc et ipsum hominis meritum donum est gratuitum" (Id., *Ep.* 186,3,10 [CSEL, 57], pp. 53-54).

169. Id., *De gratia et libero arbitrio* 8,20 (PL, 44), c. 892.

170. *Ibid.* 8,20, c. 893. Also *Ibid.* 9,21 *passim*, cc. 893-894.

171. As a matter of fact, Pelagius did not make any radical distinction between law and grace. He considered the law an expression of divine justice and in itself divine grace, a sort of *lex naturae* implanted in all people by God (cf. T. BOHLIN, *Die Theologie des Pelagius und ihre Genesis* [AUU, 9], Upsala, 1957, pp. 100ff). According to Pelagius Paul also described the law as grace (cf. Pelagius, *Expositiones xiii epistularum Pauli [Com. in Rom. 8,2]* [PLS, 1], c. 1145; *Ibid. [Com. in Gal. 6,2]* [PLS, 1], c. 1286). The purely spiritual experience of external grace, dependent on Christ's redemption and so central in the theology of Augustine, seems to be ignored by Pelagius who refuses to see grace as a distinct and utterly transcendent power (see *infra*, pp. 230ff.).

172. "Non quia lex mala est, sed quia sub illa sunt quos reos facit iubendo, non adiuvando. Gratia quippe adiuvat ut legis quisque sit factor, sine qua gratia sub lege positus

can assist man's will in its attempt to pursue and accomplish the content of the law in accordance with divine will. Likewise, continues Augustine, grace cannot be considered as the mere equivalent of nature *in qua creati sumus, ut habeamus mentem rationalem, qua intellegere ualeamus, facti ad imaginem Dei*[173]. Even if nature, itself a gift of God, may in some way be called grace[174], it could never be equal to *the* grace that comes to us through Christ. Indeed, nature is shared by humanity as a whole, including the pagans and the evildoers, whereas Christ's saving grace is given only to those who believe in him. Besides, if grace were to be reduced either to law or nature, Christ's redeeming death would be null and void. Finally, argues the bishop of Hippo, grace cannot only be viewed as a divine intervention that washes away the sins of the past. Its power with regard to man is not limited to that action alone. It also helps him to avoid any future failings and to tackle efficaciously anything that would hinder such a process[175]. After all, this is what we ask in the Lord's prayer, as it has been painstakingly illustrated by Cyprian in his commentary on the "Our Father"[176]. Augustine concludes thus: *Neque scientia diuinae legis, neque natura, neque sola remissio peccatorum est illa gratia, quae per Iesum Christum Dominum nostrum datur, sed ipsa facit ut lex impleatur, ut natura liberetur, ne peccatum dominetur*[177].

After having explained what grace is not, Augustine refutes what he regards as a mitigated form of Pelagianism, namely the opinion of those who believe that grace is given according to good will which precedes, through faith and prayer, the bestowal of grace itself. Augustine shows, with the help of scriptural references, how it is that grace precedes faith, prayer and good will, and not viceversa[178]. Moreover, if faith and prayer

tantummodo erit legis auditor" (Augustine, *De gratia et libero arbitrio* 12,24 [PL, 44], c. 896).

173. *Ibid.* 13,25, c. 896. Cf. Id., *Ep.* 194,3,8 (CSEL, 57), p. 182.

174. Augustine affirms that whereas by our first creation we are made men, by the second one we are made Christians. Even creation is a gift, in that it is given gratuitously, but it is different from that grace by which we become Christians. In the first instance no personal merit makes us worthy of the gift and in the second instance we are, in fact, always unworthy of it. For this reason creation can only be called a grace in a general sense, whereas real grace comes from the redemptive act of Christ. Cf. Id., *Sermo* 26,5 (CCL, 41), pp. 351f.

175. Id., *De gratia et libero arbitrio* 13,26 (PL, 44), cc. 896-897. See can. 3 of the Council of Carthage (1st May, 418) in *Concilia Africae A. 345 – A. 525* (n. 2), p. 70 (recensio Quesnelliana) and p. 75 (recensio Gallica).

176. Cyprian, *De dominica oratione* (CCL, 3A), pp. 90-113. See also Augustine, *Ep.* 215,3 (CSEL, 57), p. 388; Id., *De dono perseuerantiae* 2,4-5,9 (PL, 44), cc. 996-999.

177. Id., *De gratia et libero arbitrio* 14,27 (PL, 44), c. 897.

178. "Ergo spiritus gratiae facit ut habeamus fidem, ut per fidem impetremus orando, ut possimus facere quae iubemur" (*Ibid.* 14,28, c. 898). Cf. Id., *Ep.* 194,3,9ff and 4,16f (CSEL, 57), pp. 183ff and 188f.

were only dependent on man's good will, what need would there be in praying for the conversion of unbelievers, or for those of corrupt will and obstinate opposition to faith? To rely on God for all of the above, means to believe in the truthfulness of the words that the prophet Ezechiel put into God's mouth: "I will take the stony heart out of their flesh and give them a heart of flesh" (Ez 11,19). Divine intervention is completely gratuitous and does not depend on man's good will. The latter, together with faith and prayer, is in itself a gift of God[179]. To avoid such a conclusion leading to serious misunderstanding about the actual role played by free will, Augustine affirms that any real transformation occurs with the help of free will also, as it is stressed in another passage of the prophet Ezechiel: *Et* faciam *ut in iustificationibus meis ambuletis, et iudicia mea* obseruetis *et* faciatis (Ez 36,27). In other words, God does not work in man as if the latter were a passive beneficiary, unable to co-operate through the exercise of his will. God works both *in* man (*et faciam*) and *with* man (*ut [...] obseruetis et faciatis*). To man God *dat quod iubet, cum adiuuat ut faciat cui iubet*[180].

To the Pelagian objection that God would not command what He knew man would be incapable of observing (meaning that all precepts can be met by man's autonomous will and agency and without the help of grace), Augustine replies by emphasizing his conviction that God's commandments are indeed beyond human capacity. Faith and prayer, both gifts of grace, are the means by which man is able to secure and perform what the law of God requires: *Ipsa est enim fides, quae orando impetrat quod lex imperat*[181]. The good that man desires rests solely on the efficacy of God's intervention[182]. God gives man the necessary strength to transform a *uoluntas* that is *bona* but *parua* and *inualida*, into a *uoluntas* that is *magna* and *robusta,* able to desire and to fulfil what is good, namely God's commandments[183].

179. Cf. ID., *De gratia et libero arbitrio* 14,29-30 (PL, 44), cc. 898-899.
180. *Ibid.* 15,31, c. 899. Cf. the Augustinian formulation: "Da quod iubes et iube quod vis" (Id., *Confessiones* 10,29,40; 10,31,45 and 10,37,60 [CCL, 27], pp. 176, 179 and 188). For Augustine's use of this formulation and other similar expressions, see the list of the Augustinian *loci* in the *Appendix* of: P.-M. HOMBERT, *Gloria gratiae. Se glorifier en Dieu, principe et fin de la théologie augustinienne de la grâce*, Paris, 1996, pp. 493-494.
181. Augustine, *De gratia et libero arbitrio* 16,32 (PL, 44), c. 900.
182. "Certum est enim nos mandata servare, si volumus; sed quia praeparatur voluntas a Domino, ab illo petendum est ut tantum velimus, quantum sufficit ut volendo faciamus. Certum est nos velle, cum volumus: sed ille facit ut velimus bonum, de quo dictum est... *Praeparatur voluntas a Domino*" (*Ibid.*). "Certum est nos facere, cum facimus: sed ille facit ut faciamus, praebendo vires efficacissimas voluntati" (*Ibid.* 16,32, cc. 900-901).
183. "Qui ergo vult facere Dei mandatum et non potest, iam quidem habet voluntatem bonam, sed adhuc parvam et invalidam; poterit autem, cum magnam habuerit et robustam" (*Ibid.* 17,33, c. 901).

The *magna uoluntas*, continues Augustine, coincides with the *magna caritas*, because it is through love especially that good will manifests itself to the full. Charity, in fact, is a will burning with divine love (*diuino amore ardentissima uoluntas*)[184]. God's grace, which prepares the will by inclining it from the beginning towards all that is good (that is towards charity), is the same grace that now co-operates with the will, sustaining and strengthening it in such a way that it may accomplish efficaciously what is longed for and willed[185]. At this point Augustine takes the opportunity to show, with a great many biblical quotations taken from Paul, Peter, James, John and the Synoptics, that charity is the central truth of Christian life; grace leads to this truth as to its very essence[186]. In its twofold and inseparable movement, the love for God and for one's neighbour, charity represents the fulness of the law. Of course, the precepts concerning charity would be useless if man was lacking free will, but the latter too would be fruitless if charity (in

184. *Ibid.* 17,34, c. 902.
185. Based on two scriptural passages ("Deus est enim qui operatur in uobis et uelle" [Phil 2,13] and "Scimus quoniam diligentibus Deum omnia cooperantur in bonum" [Rom 8,28]) Augustine makes a distinction between the two forms of grace which later theology will name "operative" and "co-operative grace". The case of Peter whose will (charity), although small and imperfect, allowed him to say to the Lord: "Animam meam pro te ponam" (Jn 13,37), is an example of the grace that prepares man's will before bringing it to fulfilment: "Et quis istam etsi parvam dare coeperat caritatem, nisi ille qui praeparat voluntatem [*cf. Pr 8,35, LXX*], et cooperando perficit, quod operando incipit? Quoniam ipse ut velimus operatur incipiens, qui volentibus cooperatur perficiens. Propter quod ait Apostolus: *Certus sum quoniam qui operatur in vobis opus bonum, perficiet usque in diem Christi Iesu*. Ut ergo velimus, sine nobis operatur; cum autem volumus, et sic volumus ut faciamus, nobiscum cooperatur: tamen sine illo vel operante ut velimus, vel cooperante cum volumus, ad bona pietatis opera nihil valemus" (*Ibid.* 17,33 [PL, 44], c. 901). This same distinction appears under different terminology (that of "prevenient" and "subsequent" grace) in the *Enchiridion*: "Nolentem [*gratia*] praeuenit ut uelit; uolentem subsequitur ne frustra uelit" (Id., *Enchiridion ad Laurentium* 9,32 [CCL, 46], p. 67). Thus, operative grace prepares our will (cf. Pr 8,35, LXX) by allowing us to will, although in a still inchoative way, whereas co-operative grace makes possible the concrete and efficacious accomplishment of one's good will. For instance, it is thanks to this second form of grace that martyrs were able to shed their blood for Christ (cf. Id., *De gratia et libero arbitrio* 17,33 [PL, 44], c. 901). According to Augustine, not only is the universality and sovereignty of grace underlined in both forms of grace, but also the existence and agency of man's free will is safeguarded. It must not be forgotten, however, that the distinction between "operative" and "co-operative" grace is not always a clearcut one. It may happen, in fact, that the first form of grace (regardless of whether the person involved is aware of it or not) is immediately transformed into the second one and brought to fulfilment, as in the case of saint Paul's conversion (cf. *Ibid.* 5,12, cc. 888f).
186. *Ibid.* 17,34-36, cc. 902-903. That *caritas* constitutes the centre of Christian life and the essence of that grace that inflames man's will ("Istam caritatem, id est divino amore ardentissimam voluntatem" [*Ibid.* 17,34, c. 902]), is one of Augustine's most cherished ideas. Cf. Id., *Contra duas epistulas Pelagianorum* 4,5,11 (CSEL, 60), p. 532, where Augustine describes helping grace as the *inspiratio dilectionis*.

exactly the same way as the will) were not bestowed and increased by God himself[187]. Charity, in fact, is not an autarchical virtue. It too is a gift of God, poured into man's heart by the Holy Spirit (cf. Rom 5,5)[188].

In the last part of the *De gratia et libero arbitrio* Augustine emphasizes the power of God's grace, whose sovereignty reaches out to good and wicked wills alike. He considers too the problem of baptized and unbaptized children. Regarding the first subject, and recalling that God inclines man's will towards good and helps him to accomplish and persevere in it until the eventual reward of eternal life, Augustine states that even those whose will remains attached to wordly and sinful habits and who refuse conversion, are in God's hands. God continues to exercise an absolute power over them in such a way that certain sins can be considered punishment for other sins, as it is instanced in the *uasa irae* of which Paul speaks as "ready for destruction" (Cf. Rom 9,22), or in the hardening of Pharaoh's heart (cf. Ex 9,16)[189], which was meant to make God's power manifest in him[190]. It goes without saying, however, that God can incline man's heart and will whenever He wishes and in whatever way He thinks best. Whatever the reason behind his intervention in whatever sense, what really matters is the belief that God's decision

---

187. "Quod quidem sine suo fructu prorsus admoneretur, nisi prius acciperet aliquid dilectionis, ut addi sibi quaereret unde quod iubebatur impleret" (Id., *De gratia et libero arbitrio* 18,37 [PL, 44], c. 904).

188. Cf. *Ibid.* 18,38-19,40, cc. 904-905.

189. *Ibid.* 20,41, c. 906. As Chéné has pointed out, this sentence should not be understood to mean that God positively "wills" one sin as a punishment for another (see J. CHÉNÉ, *Notes complementaires* [BA, 24], p. 778). It should rather be interpreted in line with the *enduratio* of Pharaoh's heart which Augustine mentions immediately afterwards. See the following note.

190. By *enduratio* Augustine means the non-intervention of God's grace with regard to some, according to his own inscrutable design (cf. Augustine, *Expositio quarumdam propositionum ex Epistola ad Romanos* 62 [CSEL, 84], p. 43; *Ep.* 194,3,14 [CSEL, 57], p. 187; *De gratia et libero arbitrio* 23,45, cc. 910f). It should be added that Augustine had initially made a distinction between those who were justified and those who were not, by invoking the notion of prior worthiness or unworthiness (cf. Id., *De diuersis quaestionibus lxxxiii* 68,5 [CCL, 44A], p. 181). In that context, the hardening of Pharaoh's heart was the result of his refusal to acknowledge God. That merit-based distinction is now dropped. In the *De diuersis quaestionibus ad Simplicianum* Augustine defined his position; the hardening of Pharaoh's heart is the result of God withholding his mercy: "...ut obduratio Dei sit nolle misereri" (Id., *De diuersis quaestionibus ad Simplicianum* 1,2,15 [CCL, 44], p. 40). See V.H. DRECOLL, *Die Entstehung der Gnadenlehre Augustins* (BHT, 109), Tübingen, 1999, pp. 214-215; 237. Although Augustine tries to keep the balance by pointing out that Pharaoh also had some responsibility for the hardening of his own heart ("Ac per hoc [...] et ipse Pharao per liberum arbitrium": Augustine, *De gratia et libero arbitrio* 23,45 [PL, 44], c. 911) more emphasis is laid on the gratuitous manner by which divine grace operates. Eventually, it was God himself who hardened Pharaoh's heart; an outcome of his just judgement.

always corresponds to a just design[191]. Unquestionably, of course, Augustine did not believe that God positively provokes man's "inclination" to evil doing[192]. He had already stressed at the beginning of the *De gratia et libero arbitrio* how inconceivable it would be to attribute to God the cause of one's own faults[193]. In stating that God inclines man to evil, Augustine had in mind the withdrawal of divine mercy, and the consequent abandonment of man to the depravity of his will and to his deserved punishment. Augustine recalls several examples of this, mainly quoting from the Old Testament.

The second issue tackled in this final part of the treatise concerns a problem of Pelagian thought, viz. the problem of baptized children. It

---

191. Cf. *Ibid.* 21,42-43, cc. 908-909. See also: "Fons autem iustitiae quis est, nisi Deus? Primum ergo fundamentum fidei pone: *Numquid iniquitas apud Deum?* Latere te aequitas potest, esse ibi iniquitas non potest" (Id., *Sermo* 27,3 [CCL, 41], p. 362). It is interesting to note that in *De gratia et libero arbitrio* 21,42 we are in the presence of a "dossier clos", as it is called by La Bonnardière. In this dossier there are references to biblical books that are rarely quoted by Augustine and that are here assembled to reinforce a particular point of a controversy, namely the justice of God's designs. "Telle page du *De gratia et libero arbitrio* – writes La Bonnardière – présente un étonnant florilege *[3 Kings (1 Kg) 12,15; 2 Paral (2 Chr) 21,16-17; 2 Paral (2 Chr) 25,7-8; 4 Kings (2 Kg) 14,9-10; 2 Paral (2 Chr) 25,20; Ez 14,9; Est 15,4-19; Pr 21,1; Ps 104,25; Rom 1,24.26.28; 2 Thes 2,10-11]*, très nouveau dans l'oeuvre d'Augustin et, tel qu'il est constitué, unique, même si l'un ou l'autre de ses fragments est cité par Augustin un peu auparavant dans le *Contra Iulianum* V.... Nous avons ici la preuve, et ce n'est pas la seule, d'une étude par Augustin, étude toujours structurée, mais tout à fait nouvelle, de thèmes scripturaires qui, en effet, n'ont pas de pierres d'attente dans son oeuvre, avant la discussion polémique sur la Bible avec Julien d'Eclane, et avec les moines d'Adrumète et de Marseille. Ces thèmes son des 'questions disputées' entre doctes théologiens: ils n'ont jamais appartenu à la catéchèse et à la pastorale d'Augustin" (A.-M. LA BONNARDIERE, *Bible et polémiques*, in EAD. [ed.], *Saint Augustin et la Bible* [BiToTe, 3], Paris, 1986, pp. 329-352). See also EAD., *Quelques remarques sur les citations scripturaires du "De gratia et libero arbitrio"* (n. 41), *passim*, where the author studies the rare biblical quotations used by Augustine in the *De gratia et libero arbitrio*.

192. See how Augustine specifies the meaning of *inclinare* in his comment on the sin of Shimei (= *filius gemini*) who cursed king David: "Eius voluntatem proprio vitio suo malam in hoc peccatum iudicio suo iusto et occulto inclinavit... Nec causa tacita est, cur ei Dominus isto modo dixerit maledicere David, hoc est, cor eius malum in hoc peccatum miserit vel dimiserit: *ut videat*, inquit, *Dominus humilitatem meam, et retribuat mihi bona pro maledicto eius in die isto [2 Kg 16,12]*" (Augustine, *De gratia et libero arbitrio* 20,41 [PL, 44], cc. 906-907). It is not a question of God inducing man to evildoing (which in Augustine's eyes would be inconceivable), but of God allowing man to will, choose and perform evil deeds. Or, as it is said in another paragraph, God restrains himself from guiding the false prophet and allows him to go astray: "Quando ergo auditis dicentem Dominum: *Ego Dominus seduxi prophetam illum [Ez 14,9]* ... in eo quem seduci permittit ... mala eius merita credite" (*Ibid.* 23,45, cc. 910-911). See also: "Ac per hoc quando legitis in Litteris veritatis, a Deo seduci homines, aut obtundi vel obdurari corda eorum, nolite dubitare praecessisse mala merita eorum, ut iuste ista paterentur" (*Ibid.* 21,43, c. 909). See J. CHÉNÉ, *Notes complémentaires* (BA, 24), pp. 779-780.

193. Cf. Augustine, *De gratia et libero arbitrio* 2,3 (PL, 44), c. 883.

goes without saying that these children cannot be said to receive the
grace of baptism on the basis of any previously earned merit, derived
from their own will[194]. In the case of these infants, therefore, grace is
quite simply the gift of God; even more so, when the grace of baptism
is bestowed on the child of a pagan family, whilst the child of Christian
parents is not similarly graced, because death occurred before baptismal
regeneration could take place. In this latter case the child would receive
just judgement (punishment). To cite another instance of the gratuity of
divine grace, Augustine considers the case of two children, who, despite
similar circumstances, receive different treatment, in that one is baptized, whilst the other is not[195]. Here too, the unfathomable grace of God
can be seen at work, both gratuitously and in just manner[196], even if, in
his foreknowledge, God foresees the baptized child's eventual lapse into
wickedness. Augustine is at pains to point out that the sovereign action
and the complete freedom of God in bestowing his mercy and grace on
mankind in no way hinders man's exercise of free will: this fact is quite
evident from our daily experience of life.

We are left with the impression that the *De gratia et libero arbitrio*
ends without ultimately solving the difficult issues in question regarding
the relationship between grace and free will. The real challenge that the
bishop of Hippo faced lay not simply in attempting to describe the existence of the two realities or stressing one to the detriment of the other,
but in describing the relationship and interconnectedness of these realities in such a way as to be fair to both. Augustine's attempt at finding a
conciliatory solution clashes with his own inner conviction of the overwhelming power of God's grace.

5. AUGUSTINE'S *DE CORREPTIONE ET GRATIA*

As stated previously, the *De correptione et gratia* was occasioned by
a report, presumably given to Augustine by the monk Florus, of a further
objection which had arisen in the community of Hadrumetum. Somebody (*quendam*), after the reading of the *De gratia et libero arbitrio*, had
openly registered his anxiety regarding the need for rebuke. Accepting

---

194. Cf. *Ibid.* 22,44, c. 909.

195. Cf. *Ibid.* 22,44-23,45, cc. 909-911.

196. "Reddet omnino Deus et mala pro malis, quoniam iustus est; et bona pro malis,
quoniam bonus est; et bona pro bonis, quoniam bonus et iustus est; tantummodo mala pro
bonis non reddet, quoniam iniustus non est. Reddet ergo mala pro malis, poenam pro
iniustitia; et reddet bona pro malis, gratiam pro iniustitia; et reddet bona pro bonis,
gratiam pro gratia" (*Ibid.* 23,45, c. 911). Cf. also Id., *Contra Iulianum* 3,18,35 (PL, 44),
cc. 720-721; *Ep.* 186,6,20 (CSEL, 57), pp. 61-62.

the idea that the ability, both to desire and accomplish God's will is in itself a gift of God, he then concluded that "no one should be admonished for not observing the commandments of God, but that prayer alone should be offered for him so that he would observe them"[197].

Augustine did not shrink from answering this objection, and the accurate and elaborate way he did so reveals his eagerness to discuss theological matters, as well as his real concern for the spiritual well-being of the monks of Hadrumetum[198]. The desire to make his point as clear as possible to his interlocutors urged him to restate his view of grace and free will in a more thorough way. For this reason, the *De correptione et gratia* was described in the 17th century, perhaps not without slight exaggeration, as the key to understanding Augustine's doctrine of grace and free will[199]. It is nevertheless true, as remarked more recently, that in the *De correptione et gratia* we have the integral Augustinian view on grace[200]. Augustine himself affirms that nowhere has he stressed the all-encompassing power of grace so clearly and decisively as in this work[201]. The term "rebuke" (*correptio*)[202] which appears together with that of "grace" in the title, is in fact misleading. The objection over the necessity of rebuke, raised by the anonymous monk of Hadrumetum, is dealt with in a few paragraphs and is eventually taken up again in the conclusion of the first part of the treatise, and summarized again at the very end of it. Apart from this, Augustine's energy was directed towards deeper discussion of the more fundamental issues arising from the nature

197. "Neminem corripiendum si Dei praecepta non facit, sed pro illo ut faciat tantummodo orandum" (Id., *Retractationes* 2,67 [CCL, 57], p. 142).

198. "Rarement la charité d'Augustin s'était montrée si aimable, si patiemment condescendante que dans l'affaire des moines d'Hadrumète" (BARDY, *Saint Augustin* [n. 146], p. 431). It is quite likely that Augustine's promptness in helping the monks of Hadrumetum was also due to the love he had always cherished for monastic life.

199. "Clavis qua ad universam Augustini de divina gratia et libero arbitrio doctrinam aditus aperitur" (H. NORIS, *Historia Pelagiana* I,23, Padua, 1677, p. 92).

200. "Nous avons donc dans ce livre de la correction et de la grâce, la vision augustinienne de la grâce en son originalité irréductible et sous sa forme intégrale. Nous ne remercierons jamais assez le moine inconnu dont l'objection futile nous a valu une oeuvre de ce prix" (CHÉNÉ, *Les origines de la controverse semi-pélagienne* [n. 15], p. 100).

201. Cf. Augustine, *De dono perseuerantiae* 21,55 (PL, 45), c. 1027.

202. *Correptio* should not be confused with *correctio*. "Pour Augustin les deux notions sont nettement distinctes, la *correptio* étant à ses yeux comme un remède, alors que la *correctio* est liée à l'idée de sanction, et la *correptio* doit toujours précéder la *correctio*" (G. FOLLIET, *Introduction: Notes à l'edition* [of the *De correptione et gratia*], [CSEL, 92], p. 175). See also, T.J. VAN BAVEL, *Correptio, corripere*, in *AugL* 2 (1996) 35-39; ID., *Correctio, corrigere*, in *Ibid.*, cc. 22-27; V. GROSSI, *Correptio–correctio–emendatio in Agostino d'Ippona. Terminologia penitenziale e monastica*, in *Aug* 38 (1998) 215-222.

of grace, its meaning, dispensation and action, together with the questions of predestination and perseverance.

Broadly speaking, we can divide the *De correptione et gratia* into two
parts. The first deals with the question of rebuke in the larger context of
God's gift of perseverance and the mystery of his prescience and predestination; the second tackles the big question of Adam's non-perseverance.

a) The Necessity of Rebuke vis-à-vis God's Gift of Perseverance and
   Predestination

Augustine starts his *De correptione et gratia* by recalling the central
point of his previous treatise (*De gratia et libero arbitrio*), viz. the sovereignty of grace. Not only does grace enable free will to do good, but
it is also the condition inherent in the desire to will and choose what is
good[203]. Grace acts as an inner force or inspiration. It makes human
beings desire its inspirational help, so that they may be led to act in
accordance with God's commandments[204]. Furthermore, it is by God's
grace, acting through Jesus Christ, that men are delivered from evil.
Without such grace they are incapable of doing good. On the other
hand, divine grace does not override human capacity and effort: on the
contrary, it enables them to be effective and makes them operative[205].
However, the power of prayer should always be resorted to when one is
not able to act in accordance with grace, so that the spiritual strength
might be received in order to do so. All that man has, comes in fact from
God (cf. 1 Cor 4,7)[206].

---

203. Little wonder that Augustine's main ideas, within the fundamental relationship
of grace and free will, are interwoven and repeated over and over again in these two treatises. This repetition was meant to ensure that these important truths would be readily and
easily absorbed by the minds of his readers.

204. Cf. Augustine, *De correptione et gratia* 1,2 (CSEL, 92), p. 220. After having
quoted several scriptural passages of the Old Testament illustrating God's grace at work
in the heart of his people, Augustine concludes by emphasizing the sovereignty of grace
in the following unequivocal way: "Intus egit, corda tenuit, corda mouit, eosque uoluntatibus eorum, quas ipse in illis operatus est, traxit" (*Ibid.* 14,45, p. 275).

205. "Intelligant si filii Dei sunt, spiritu Dei se agi *[Rom.* 8,14*]*, ut quod agendum est
agant; et cum egerint, illi a quo aguntur gratias agant; aguntur enim ut agant, non ut ipsi
nihil agant" (*Ibid.* 2,4, p. 221). See, further on, this beautiful synthesis: "Voluntas quippe
humana non libertate consequitur gratiam sed gratia potius libertatem, et ut perseueret
delectabilem perpetuitatem, et insuperabilem fortitudinem" (*Ibid.* 8,17, p. 238). See also
Id., *De peccatorum meritis et remissione et de baptismo paruulorum* 2,5,6 (CSEL, 60),
pp. 76-77.

206. As to the importance of this scriptural text in Augustine's thought on grace, see
HOMBERT, *Gloria gratiae* (n. 180), *passim*.

At this point Augustine introduces the objection made by the *frater* of Hadrumetum: why should superiors rebuke faulty brethren if the reason for failure is that they have not received the enabling power of grace? Superiors should limit themselves to directing the brethren in what should be done, and then pray that they might be enabled to do it. Augustine replies to this objection by pointing to the behaviour of the Apostles who acted in a threefold way: by prescribing, rebuking and praying. It is necessary to prescribe in order to make known what should be done; to rebuke so that one might understand that his inability to do good depends on evil will; to pray, in order to receive the grace needed to desire what is good and act accordingly[207]. The fact that the *uoluntas* is prepared by God does not exclude the necessity of rebuke which has, and continues to have, a healing or remedial action, in that it is directed towards the evildoer's eventual repentance and conversion, by guiding him to the realization that evil is the result of misdirected free will, detached, as it is, from the inspiration of divine grace[208]. For this reason, rebuke should be constantly exercised. It should not be neglected on the presupposition that God's direct intervention can heal some situations without the interference of the superiors' reproach. In both cases, however, the intervention of God's grace is absolutely necessary to bring man into the sphere of salvation[209].

Furthermore, Augustine makes a distinction between those who do not obey God's commandments because they have not received regeneration through baptism, and those who have been baptized but have fallen away from God through disobedience and actual sin. In the first instance, those who ignore God's teaching and commit sin are not exempt from reproach simply because they are still prey to the corruption inherited by original sin, and are therefore unable either to know or recognize the grace of Christ. According to the bishop of Hippo, rebuke is just as necessary for them, since the pain deriving from it might have a regenerative effect leading to a desire for Christian conversion. On the other hand, Christians who, in spite of past regeneration through baptism, fall into sin through wilfulness and lack of perseverance, cannot be said to be ignorant of God's commandments and will. Rebuke is necessary for them so that they may be encouraged and helped in their

---

207. Augustine, *De correptione et gratia* 3,5 (CSEL, 92), pp. 222-223.

208. "Tuum quippe uitium est quod malus es, et maius uitium corripi nolle quia malus es" (*Ibid.* 5,7, p. 224).

209. "Tunc autem correptione proficit homo, cum miseretur atque adiuuat, qui facit quos uoluerit etiam sine correptione proficere" (*Ibid.* 5,8, pp. 225-226). See also *Ibid.* 6,9, p. 226.

ongoing conversion toward God[210]. Christians who lead a sinful life, however, might object that, even though they have been regenerated through baptism and justified by divine grace through the *fidem, quae per dilectionem operatur* (cf. Gal 5,6)[211], they were not given sufficient grace for unfailing final perseverance (*sed in illa usque in finem perseuerantiam non accepi*)[212]. Augustine affirms that perseverance too is a gift of God. Yet he still sees rebuke as useful and necessary in the life of those who lack perseverance, because, if it is in accordance with God's plan, they might eventually receive the further grace of repentance. This is borne out by many scriptural references pointing out the useful-ness both of rebuke and prayer in guiding the evildoer towards the grace of repentance (cf 2 Tm 2,25; Lk 22,32; 2 Cor 13,17; Phil 1,3-6, etc.)[213]. Moreover, those who do not persevere and relapse into sin, although jus-tified by baptism, are compared to the heathens and unbaptized infants who have not received the sacrament of regeneration. God makes no exception in either case, as far as the damnation deserved by all human beings is concerned[214], for it is only He, in his mercy and through the mediation of Jesus Christ[215], who is able to separate from the *massa perditionis* those he has predestined to final perseverance and salvation.

The question of perseverance leads Augustine to speak spontaneously of the mystery of predestination. Basing himself on the evangelical say-ing: *Multi uocati, pauci electi* (Mt 20,16; 22,14)[216], he affirms with

---

210. Cf. *Ibid.* 6,9, pp. 226-227; see also *Ibid.* 7,11, p. 231.

211. *Ibid.* 6,10, p. 228.

212. *Ibid.* Here Augustine begins to pay special attention to the grace of perseverance, an issue which he will further elaborate in his *De praedestinatione sanctorum* and *De dono perseuerantiae*. According to Burns, the treatment of the grace of perseverance rep-resents Augustine's final stage in the development of his doctrine of operative grace. Analogously to the way he worked out the operative grace of conversion in the *Ep.* 194, he would now identify a distinct operative grace of perseverance which, while producing in the believer the desire to will and perform good actions through charity, preserves him from the sin which would exclude him from eternal life (cf. BURNS, *The Development of Augustine's Doctrine of Operative Grace* [n. 164], pp. 172-173). As Burns justly remarks, Augustine "asserted that this grace of perseverance is given without regard for the prior merits of good willing and performance based on charity. Thereby he defined a fully gra-tuitous predestination, distinct and separable from the prior gifts of faith and charity" (*Ibid.*, p. 176). Cf. also Augustine, *De correptione et gratia* 8,17 (CSEL, 92), pp. 237-238.

213. See *Ibid.* 6,10, pp. 227-231.

214. "Non sunt ab illa conspersione discreti, quam constat esse damnatam" (*Ibid.* 7,12, p. 232). See also *Ibid.* 8,16, pp. 236-237.

215. As to the place and role of Christ's mediation with regard to the predestination of the elect, see *infra*, pp. 353ff.

216. Cf. Augustine, *De diuersis quaestionibus ad Simplicianum* 1,2,10 (CCL, 44), p. 35; see also Id., *Contra Iulianum* 5,4,14 (PL, 44), c. 792; Id., *De praedestinatione sanctorum* 16,32-33 (PL, 44), cc. 983f.

absolute certainty that those who have been called according to the divine election (*secundum propositum*) will be saved[217]. Why some people, the *electi*, receive the will to persevere from God, and others, who are also *uocati* but not *electi*, do not receive it, is a question that is destined to remain unanswered[218]. The answer belongs to the mysterious but just judgement of God. On this very point Augustine recognizes the limits of his investigation by recalling the Apostle's words: *O homo, tu quis es qui respondeas Deo?* (Rom 9,20), and: *O altitudo diuitiarum sapientiae et scientiae Dei! quam inscrutabilia sunt iudicia eius, et inuestigabiles uiae eius* (*Ibid.* 11,33)[219]. Even the shock and difficulty encountered in accepting the fact that unbaptized children of Christian parents die and are condemned, whereas the baptized infants of non Christian parents are bestowed with divine grace, has to be seen against the background of God's unfathomable and inscrutable design. Similarly, one cannot pretend to understand why God allows some people who have led a good life to fall into evil doing and to die without the gift of final perseverance (viz. without attaining salvation), whilst He allows others to die before they are deceived by guile (cf. Wis 4,11) and so be saved[220].

Thus, only those who have been inscribed in the Father's memory with unshakable steadiness (*inconcussa stabilitas*), viz. only those who have been foreknown and predestined by God, do receive the gift of perseverance and can be truly said to be sons of God[221]. All others are not considered so. Even sincere and just people might not be saved, if according to God's foreknowledge and predestination it is seen that they

217. "Illi ergo electi, ut saepe dictum est, *qui secundum propositum uocati*, qui etiam praedestinati atque praesciti" (Id., *De correptione et gratia* 7,14 [CSEL, 92], p. 234); "Non enim sunt a massa illa perditionis praescientia Dei et praedestinatione discreti, et ideo nec *secundum propositum uocati* ac per hoc nec electi, sed in eis uocati de quibus dictum est: *multi uocati*, non in eis de quibus dictum est: *pauci uero electi*" (*Ibid.* 7,16, pp. 236-237). Cf. also Id., *De dono perseuerantiae* 14,35 (PL, 45), c. 1014.

218. What counts for Augustine is the conviction that God's grace is absolutely necessary in order to persevere in faith. Thus, for instance, Christ himself prayed that Peter's faith might not fail at the moment of his trial (cf. Lk 22,32). Peter's perseverance was therefore due to the gratuitous intervention of divine grace, which acted on his will by "preparing" it (cf. Pr 8,35, LXX), that is by making it *liberrima, fortissima, inuictissima, perseuerantissima* (Id., *De correptione et gratia* 8,17 [CSEL, 92], p. 238).

219. Cf. *Ibid.* 8,17, p. 237. See also *Ibid.* 8,18, p. 239.

220. "Et cur aliis detur, aliis non detur, sine murmure aduersus Deum dignentur ignorare nobiscum" (*Ibid.* 8,19, p. 241).

221. "...iam filii Dei erant in memoriali Patris sui inconcussa stabilitate conscripti. (...) Qui uere filii sunt, praesciti et praedestinati sunt conformes imaginis Filii eius, et secundum propositum uocati sunt ut electi essent. Non enim perit filius promissionis, sed filius perditionis *[cf. Jn 17,12]*" (*Ibid.* 9,20, p. 243).

will fail in perseverance[222]. They are among the *uocati*, but not among the *electi*, and therefore are destined to perish[223]. Those instead who *in Dei prouidentissima dispositione praesciti, praedestinati, uocati, iustificati, glorificati sunt*[224] (cf. Rom 8,28-30), have always been God's sons, not only before they were regenerated, but before they were even born. For that very reason they cannot perish, and nothing will be able to hinder their salvation. In fact, for the *electi,* truly everything (*prorsus omnia*)[225], even the experience of sin and evil, is turned into good by God's Providence. Their faults become, as it were, a means by which they grow into the awareness that persevering in what is good is exclusively a gift of God.

At this point Augustine concludes the first part of the *De correptione et gratia* by reiterating his ideas on the need for rebuke, by stating that it is indeed necessary in some cases, but that it should always be exercised with charity. No one, in fact, can know whether the erring brother now reproached, belongs to the *electi* or merely to the *uocati*, namely whether he will receive the grace of perseverance or not. Thus, bearing in mind the absolute freedom of God, who applies his mercy or his severe judgement in a way known only to himself[226], those in charge of their brethren, are duty bound and responsible for rebuking those who err, in order to bring them back to the right path.

222. "Non quia iustitiam simulauerunt, sed quia in ea non permanserunt" (*Ibid.* 9,20, p. 242).
223. "Appellamus ergo nos et electos et Christi discipulos et Dei filios, quia sic appellandi sunt, quos regeneratos pie uiuere cernimus; sed tunc uere sunt quod appellantur, si manserint in eo propter quod sic appellantur. Si autem perseuerantiam non habent, id est, in eo quod coeperunt esse non manent, non uere appellantur quod appellantur et non sunt; apud eum enim hoc non sunt, cui notum est quod futuri sunt, id est, ex bonis mali" (*Ibid.* 9,22, p. 245).
224. *Ibid.* 9,23, p. 246.
225. *Ibid.* 9,24, p. 247. See, for instance, the utility for a proud man – whom God has predestined to salvation – to fall into a manifested sin in order to learn how to be humble: "Et audeo dicere superbis esse utile cadere in aliquod apertum manifestumque peccatum, unde sibi displiceant, qui iam sibi placendo ceciderant" (Id., *De ciuitate Dei* 14,13 [CCL, 48], p. 436).
226. "Faciat ipse cum caritate quod scit esse faciendum; scit enim talem corripiendum, facturo Deo aut misericordiam aut iudicium, misericordiam quidem, si a massa perditionis ille qui corripitur gratiae largitate discretus est, et non est inter uasa irae quae perfecta sunt in perditionem sed inter uasa misericordiae quae praeparauit Deus in gloriam *[cf. Rom. 9,22.23]*, iudicium uero, si in illis est damnatus, in his non est praedestinatus" (Id., *De correptione et gratia* 9,25 [CSEL, 92], p. 249).

b) The Problem of Adam's Non-Perseverance. The Two Economies:
The Grace of the First Man and the Grace of Christ

The true novelty of the *De correptione et gratia* comes to the fore in the following chapters in which Augustine replies to a further objection, this time even more exacting and fundamental than that on rebuke. Coming undoubtedly from the community of Hadrumetum, where fervent discussion must have brought it to the surface, the objection concerned Adam's non-perseverance before his fall (prelapsarian status) as distinct from Adam's (viz. humanity's) condition after the fall (infralapsarian status)[227].

If Adam had been created upright (*rectus*) and without defects (*sine ullo uitio*), how could he possibly lack the gift of final perseverance? Augustine responds by saying that Adam was not lacking in this respect, but that he lost that gift when he fell from the state of grace in which God had created him[228]. Moreover, the real difficulty arises as the logical consequence of the first statement, viz.: if Adam was perfect, how could he, in fact, lose his perfection, and sin against God? Given the importance of this objection, we shall quote the way Augustine himself has formulated it:

> If he had perseverance in that rectitude in which he was created without defect, he undoubtedly persevered in it, and if he persevered, he, of course, did not sin, nor did he abandon his rectitude and God. The truth, however, cries that he sinned and abandoned the good. He, therefore, did not have perseverance in that good, and if he did not have it, he, of course, did not receive it. For how could he both have received perseverance and yet not have persevered? But, if the reason he did not have it is that he did not receive it, how did he sin by not persevering since he had not received perseverance? For one cannot say that he did not receive it because he was not set apart from the mass of perdition by the generosity of grace. Before he

227. For this discussion cf. also Id., *Enchiridion ad Laurentium* 28,105-107 (CCL, 46), pp. 106-107. Although the aim of the *Enchiridion* differs from that of the *De correptione et gratia*, there are similarities, especially in Augustine's comparison of Adamitic and Christian grace. It is as if, when writing chapters 10-12 of the *De correptione et gratia*, Augustine had before him a copy of the *Enchiridion*. In this work he perceived God's will as benign or positive, in an attempt to explain the nature and origin of evil, and it is within this framework that he tackled the case of Adam. God, he wrote, sent his Son, Jesus Christ to bring salvation, whereas Adam's fall brought only condemnation. God foresaw Adam's fall from the state of perfection in which he had been created ("in ea salute in qua conditus erat" [*Ibid.* 28,104, p. 106]), but permitted it in order that his gift of freedom to mankind would remain intact. However, the perfection of God's plan is still apparent in spite of Adam's disobedience. See also Id., *De ciuitate Dei* 14,27 (CCL, 48), pp. 450-451.

228. Cf. Id., *De correptione et gratia* 10,26 (CSEL, 92), pp. 249-250.

sinned, there was, of course, not yet the mass of perdition in the human
race from which our damaged origin is derived[229].

With this general approach to the divine economy of salvation, both
before and after Adam's fall, Augustine sets himself the task of explaining what is already an accepted part of the *depositum fidei* (*quod rectis-
sime credimus*)[230]. We can be certain that the Lord did, in fact, create
everything good, but foresaw the possibility that evil would interfere
with this creation. We also know that in his omnipotent wisdom and
love He is able to retrieve some good even out of evil situations. Thus it
is that both angels and men experience the power of free will and exercise it accordingly, for good or evil. They can receive the beneficial
power of divine grace which enables them to exercise this free will
towards righteousness. When their free will is exercised without regard
to divine will, they experience divine justice. We know that, due to a
maladjusted use of free will, some of the angels fell from grace and were
eternally damned, whilst others, standing firmly by divine truth, entered
a state of eternal bliss[231]. Analogously, the first man, had he so willed,
could have remained in his original state of uprightness (*rectitudo*) and
bliss (*beatitudo*) without any defects or faults[232]. Had he stood firm,
using his free will in accordance with God's plan, instead of abusing the
gift God had given, he too would have received, like the angels who did
not rebel against God, eternal, perfect bliss and the happiness of remaining in God's beneficent regard[233]. Having freely abandoned God, Adam
was condemned to be abandoned by God, together with his heirs who
share in his sin.

---

229. "Si in illa rectitudine in qua sine uitio factus est, habuit perseuerantiam, procul
dubio perseuerauit in ea, et si perseuerauit, utique non peccauit nec illam suam recti-
tudinem Deumque deseruit. Eum autem peccasse et desertorem boni fuisse, ueritas cla-
mat. Non ergo habuit in illo bono perseuerantiam, et si non habuit non utique accepit.
Quomodo enim et accepisset perseuerantiam et non perseuerasset? Porro, si propterea
non habuit quia non accepit, quid ipse non perseuerando peccauit, qui perseuerantiam non
accepit? Neque enim dici potest ideo non accepisse, quia non est discretus a massa perditionis gratiae largitate. Nondum quippe erat illa in genere humano perditionis massa, antequam peccasset ex quo tracta est origo uitiata" (Id., *De correptione et gratia* 10,26
[CSEL, 92], p. 250). The English translation is taken from R.J. TESKE (ed.), *Answer to the
Pelagians. IV: To the Monks of Hadrumetum and Provence* (The Works of Saint Augustine, I/26), New York, 1999, p. 127.
    230. Augustine, *De correptione et gratia* 10,27 (CSEL, 92), c. 932.
    231. Cf. *Ibid.*
    232. We find this same doctrine explained by Augustine in a sermon: "Creatus est
primus homo in natura sine culpa, in natura sine uitio. Creatus est rectus... Voluit
deserere a quo factus erat. Permisit Deus, tamquam dicens: 'Deserat me et inueniat se, et
miseria sua probet quia nihil potest sine me'" (Id., *Sermo* 26,2-3 [CCL, 41], p. 349).

Since the time of Adam's fall and condemnation, in which all men became *obstricti*, only Christ's redemptive and gratuitous death is able to save those predestined, through God's design, for salvation[234]. This redemptive grace is great but at the same time different (*magna, sed disparem*)[235] from the *gratia laeta* Adam benefited from in the bliss of Eden[236]. In fact, unlike Adam, humanity is confronted with evil in this world, and experiences the constant struggle between the spirit and the flesh (cf Rom 7,23-25)[237]. Mankind then requires not so much a *laetior gratia* as a *potentior gratia*, a more powerful grace than that given to Adam, namely the grace that comes only from the incarnate Son of God, Christ the Saviour, through whom human beings are enabled to overcome the sinful desires of the flesh[238]. By misusing his free will Adam

233. Cf. Id., *De correptione et gratia* 10,28 (CSEL, 92), pp. 252-253.
234. Cf. *Ibid.*, p. 253.
235. *Ibid.* 11,29, p. 253.
236. "In illo beatitudinis loco sua secum pace fruebatur" (*Ibid.*).
237. This passage of Paul (to be seen in the broader context of Rom 7,7-25) had already acquired in Augustine its definitive meaning by 418/419 (see Id., *De nuptiis et concupiscentia* 1,27,30-31,37 [CSEL, 42], pp. 242-248). By that time, in fact, Augustine was convinced that in Rom 7,7-25 Paul spoke of himself, describing his own personal struggle against concupiscence in such a way that he saw himself as already being *totus sub gratia*. As Babcock has noted, the bishop of Hippo eventually came to this understanding of Rom 7,25 in the light of man's constitutional weakness: "For the first time – he writes – Augustine has pictured a human state in which a person must struggle against a self which is not merely resistant to the will, but is actually beyond his own control, which conquers him rather than being conquered by him" (W.S. BABCOCK, *Augustine's interpretation of Romans [A.D. 394-396]*, in *AugSt* 10 [1979] 55-74, p. 61). From here on Augustine makes use of this scriptural quotation with reference to all Christians who, although regenerated by grace, continue to struggle with evil in their daily lives. Augustine, in a previous interpretation of this pericope, implied that man is subject to the law (*sub lege*), viz. a human being, as yet untouched by grace and acting with a certain amount of autonomy in his or her choice between good or the contrary forces of concupiscence. Cf. Augustine, *Expositio quarumdam propositionum ex epistula ad Romanos* 41 and 44-46 (CSEL, 84), pp. 22-23 and 24-30; Id., *De diuersis quaestionibus lxxxiii* 66,5-6 (CCL, 44A), pp. 155-162; Id., *De diuersis quaestionibus ad Simplicianum* 1,1,1-16 (CCL, 44), pp. 19-20; cf. M.-F. BERROUARD, *L'exégèse augustinienne de Rom. 7,7-25 entre 396 et 418*, in *RechAug* 16 (1981) 101-196; J.P. BURNS, *The interpretation of Romans in the Pelagian controversy*, in *AugSt* 10 (1979) 43-54.
238. Augustine, *De correptione et gratia* 11,30 (CSEL, 92), pp. 254-255. As it has been rightly underlined: "L'idée du developpement qui suit est que la puissance de la grâce reçue par les rachetés est celle-là même qui conférait au Christ-homme, de par son union avec le Verbe de Dieu, une indéfectible rectitude, ou du moins elle en est une participation" (M.J. PINTARD [ed.], *Augustin, De correptione et gratia* [texte et notes], in *BA* 24, pp. 334-335). According to Augustine, the impotence of human nature (when not enlightened and sustained by grace) is a necessary assumption in order to save the position of Christ's unique mediatorship between man and God. Inspired by 1 Tim 2,5 ("Unus mediator Dei et hominum homo Christus Iesus"), Augustine stressed that Christ is the only source of salvation for mankind. If man were capable of good without the aid of Christ's grace, then Christ's coming would have been unnecessary and his death and

abandoned that grace that would have prevented his sin, and was in turn abandoned by that very grace (*deseruit et desertus est*)[239]. The grace accorded to Adam was ultimately dependent on his own free will which, having been perfectly created, was able to decide whether to remain in that perfection and persevere in justice or to abandon it[240]. The grace accorded to Adam's heirs through Christ, instead, is more powerful (*plus potest*), not only because it gives man the possibility of doing good and persevering in it, but above all because it makes him desirous of that same good[241]. God grants mankind both the capacity of desiring virtue and of doing God's will[242]. Adam, on the other hand, only received the gift of *posse si uellet, sed non habet uelle quod posset; nam si habuisset, perseuerasset*[243]. His free will was "totally free", to the point that he was able to choose between good and evil. Had he made the choice to persevere in the good (like the angels who did not disobey), such good would have been regarded as meritorious. Conversely, in Adam's heirs, delivered from sin by Christ, the capacity of desiring and persevering in good, cannot be attributed to man, but is solely the fruit of God's efficacious grace. In fact, because of the *poena peccati* in which all humanity finds itself (as a consequence of Adam's fall), the grace of perseverance is given by the beneficence of God, and through Jesus' mediation, to those God chooses.

It was Augustine's conviction that the only way to account for Adam's responsibility in the fall, was to introduce a "double economy"

resurrection would be nullified (cf., for instance, Augustine, *De gratia Christi et de peccato originali* 2,26,31 [CSEL, 42], pp. 190-191; Id., *De natura et gratia* 2,2; 6,6; 7,7; 9,10; 34,39; 40,47; 41,48; 44,51; 50,58, 53,61; 60 and 70 [CSEL, 60], pp. 231-299 *passim*; Id., *Contra duas epistulas Pelagianorum* 1,7,12; 1,21,39; 4,4,6 [CSEL, 60], pp. 432-433; 457; 527-528). For the emphasis on Christ's saving mediatorship, see: G. RÉMY, *Le Christ médiateur dans l'œuvre de saint Augustin*, 2 Tomes, Lille-Paris, 1979; J. PLAGNIEUX – F.J. THONNARD, *Notes complémentaires*, in *BA* 22, pp. 729-732. For the opposition Adam-Christ, see RÉMY, *Le Christ médiateur dans l'oeuvre de saint Augustin*, T. I, pp. 395ff; 644-648; G. BONNER, *Adam*, in *AugL* 1 (1986) 63-87, cc. 84-86.

239. "Nec ipsum ergo Deus esse uoluit sine sua gratia, quem reliquit in eius libero arbitrio. Quoniam liberum arbitrium ad malum sufficit, ad bonum autem parum est, nisi adiuuetur ab omnipotenti bono. Quod adiutorium si homo ille per liberum non deseruisset arbitrium, semper esset bonus; sed deseruit, et desertus est" (Augustine, *De correptione et gratia* 11,31 [CSEL, 92], p. 256).

240. "Tunc ergo dederat homini Deus bonam uoluntatem, in illa quippe eum fecerat qui fecerat rectum; dederat adiutorium, sine quo in ea non posset permanere si uellet, ut autem uellet in eius libero reliquit arbitrio" (*Ibid.* 11,32, p. 257).

241. "Prima est enim qua fit ut habeat homo iustitiam si uelit; secunda ergo plus potest, qua etiam fit ut uelit, et tantum uelit, tantoque ardore diligat, ut carnis uoluptatem contraria concupiscentem uoluntate spiritus uincat" (*Ibid.* 11,31, p. 256).

242. "Non solum posse quod uolumus, uerum etiam uelle quod possumus" (*Ibid.* 11,32, p. 258).

243. *Ibid.*

of grace. The reason for this disparity in the bestowal of grace is to be found in Adam's inborn ability and power to act in accordance with God's will, whilst his fragile and sinful heirs require continuous support. Therefore, man, being completely dependent on God's mercy (also in his free will), is never able to boast of his performance. In other words, if Adam was granted the grace of a free will offered without any restraint, his fallen but redeemed heirs are offered a grace that operates "irresistibly" both at the level of their desire and performance. The problem, however, is the exact interpretation of such double economy. It has been suggested, for instance, that Augustine would have considered it unthinkable to attribute to Adam the responsibility for his sin, had he committed it under the economy of a "Christic" grace[244]. Such literal and historical interpretation, it seems to us, does little or no justice to Augustine's thought. Is it really possible that he believed the first man less dependent on God, as far as the power of his free will was concerned, than fallen but redeemed man? Did Augustine not hold, as one of the essential tenets of his theology, that the sovereignty of God's grace over the human will should be maintained, regardless of its pre- or infralapsarian status?

In reality, the sovereignty of God's grace, at work both in Adam and fallen man, is not, as Augustine would explain in the distinction made between *adiutorium sine quo* and *audiutorium quo*[245], a question of divine grace being less operative in the first case and unfailingly effective in the second one. In Augustine's eyes, divine grace is "one", even though it operates on different levels (or *régimes*, *temps*)[246], and is *per se* efficacious at any stage. Adam was left completely free in his decision

---

244. See J. LEBOURLIER, *Grâce et liberté chez saint Augustin*, in *AugMag*, T. II, Paris, 1955, pp. 789-793, p. 792; H. RONDET, *La liberté et la grâce dans la théologie augustinienne*, in ID. *et al.* (eds.), *Saint Augustin parmi nous*, Le Puy-Paris, 1954, pp. 199-222, p. 222. This interpretation was put forward in the 18th century by theologians of the Augustinian school, like card. Noris, L. Berti e F. Belleli (cf. J. CHÉNÉ, *Notes complémentaires* [BA, 24], pp. 790-791) and by the Jansenists.

245. Cf. *infra*, n. 251.

246. The subsequent Scholastic distinction between sufficient and efficacious grace does not really explain Augustine's thought, as expressed in chapters 10-12 of the *De correptione et gratia*. For Augustine it is simply a question of grace being operative in different contexts, or within different frameworks or stages: the stage that is "prior (*prius*)", viz. the Adamitic one, and that which comes "after (*deinde*)", viz. the Christian one (cf. Augustine, *De correptione et gratia* 10,27 [CSEL, 92], p. 251). See also: "prius ... postea" (Id., *Enchiridion ad Laurentium* 28, 105 [CCL, 46], p. 106). De Broglie calls these two different stages *régimes* (cf. G. DE BROGLIE, *Pour une meilleure intelligence du "De correptione et gratia"*, in *AugMag*, T. III, Paris, 1955, pp. 317-337, p. 317), whereas Sage speaks of them as two *temps* (cf. A. SAGE, *Les deux temps de la grâce*, in *REAug* 7 [1961] 209-230, pp. 211-214 *passim*).

for good or evil, and yet he could not have desired and chosen good, nor
persevered in it, except under the sovereign influence of God's bountiful
grace. On the other hand, the internal action exercised by Christ's grace
on Adam's descendants, an action which has to be sought "plus loin, –
et plus bas"[247], possesses the prodigious feature of providing fallen
human nature with the capability of following righteousness in an
unquestionable and unfailing manner[248]. This does not mean that the
human being remains passive before grace[249], but certainly, *de facto*, he
remains a secondary co-operator, subordinate and subservient to the
agency of grace. However, even if we agreed with the interpretation of
the two *régimes* or *temps* existing in one grace (not two different types
of grace!) and operating at two different stages of salvation history, the
prelapsarian and the infralapsarian, we would be left with an open tension that Augustine did not actually solve. In fact, on an operational
level, the unity of grace does not really seem to be safeguarded. Whereas
in the first stage, divine grace is in full harmony with Adam's unblem-
ished free will and the full range of freedom that he enjoyed, in the
second stage, grace adapts itself to a flawed free will in need of a more
powerful, enlightening and sustaining grace, namely the grace of Christ
acting directly in man from within. In other words, if primordial operative grace did preserve intact the human (and angelic) ability to obey or
disobey the will of God, in Adam's heirs, this ability would seem to be
overshadowed from the beginning by "Christic" grace, the direct cause
of mankind's desire for good and of its perseverance in it. Augustine is
very clear in differentiating between the fact that in Adam's freedom and
our freedom there exists a substantial new set of circumstances. On one
hand, Adam's *prima libertas uoluntatis* consisted in the *posse non peccare*, his *prima immortalitas* in the *posse non mori*, and his *prima
perseuerantiae potestas* in the *bonum posse non deserere*. On the other
hand, the *nouissima libertas*, to be found in all those (among the descendants of Adam) who have been reached by the redemptive grace of
Christ, is much greater. It consists in the *non posse peccare*, with regard
to the will; in the *non posse mori*, with regard to mortality; and in

---

247. H. DE LUBAC, *Surnaturel. Études historiques* (Theol[P], 8), Paris, 1946, p. 52.
    248. Cf. *infra*, n. 258. "Le prodige c'est que cette action s'accommode désormais à la
condition propre de notre nature déchue, de notre intelligence aveugle, de notre volonté
divisée, débile, inconstante: en sorte que ces misérables organes d'action, dont on serait
fondé à n'attendre plus rien de solidement bon, se voient pris en main par le Créateur et
maintenus par Lui dans la voie du bien, avec une puissance, une constance et une sûreté
sans égales" (DE BROGLIE, *Pour une meilleure intelligence du "De correptione et gratia"*
[n. 246], p. 335). Cf. Augustine, *De correptione et gratia* 12,38 (CSEL, 92), pp. 265ff.
    249. "Aguntur enim ut agant, non ut ipsi nihil agant" (*Ibid.* 2,4, p. 221).

the *bonum non posse deserere*, with regard to the capacity of perseverance[250].

In this way Augustine is able to introduce his famous distinction between the two different types of assistance, the *adiutorium sine quo aliquid non fit* and the *adiutorium quo aliquid fit*[251]. He illustrates this distinction with the following example: man cannot live without food (food is the *adiutorium sine quo non*), but without the will to live (the *adiutorium quo*) food is of no use whatsoever. But, when man receives the *beatitudo*, he becomes *ipso facto beatus*, because therein is contained both the assistance without which such a *beatitudo* could not become reality, and the assistance in which this *beatitudo* becomes indeed reality[252]. Adam, who was created righteous and was able to enjoy happiness in that he possessed the freedom from sin and death and the possibility of perseverance, received the *adiutorium sine quo non*, namely the assistance without which he would have been powerless. Adam's possession of this gift of judgement, enabling him to choose good and avoid evil, did not render him forever incapable of sin. The propensity for sin, or "metaphysical weakness" (which does not entail any necessity for Adam to sin, but rather his ability to choose evil over good and virtue) was caused by the fact that, like all creatures, he was originally created *ex nihilo*[253]. Conversely, those who have been predestined, receive the

250. Cf. *Ibid.* 12,33, p. 259. See also: "Sed ordo praetermittendus non fuit, in quo Deus uoluit ostendere quam bonum sit animal rationale quod etiam non peccare possit, quamuis sit melius quod peccare non possit; sicut minor fuit immortalitas, sed tamen fuit, in qua posset etiam non mori, quamuis maior futura sit in qua non possit mori" (Id., *Enchiridion ad Laurentium* 28,105 [CCL, 46], p. 106). "Notre grâce des derniers temps est une grâce non d'eschatologie conséquente, mais d'eschatologie déjà présente. La grâce du Christ, qui retire de l'esclavage du péché est une grâce de victoire sur le péché, de vie éternelle qui demeure en nous, de félicité dans le Christ ressuscité. Elle ne nous place pas comme la grâce adamique, simplement à la jonction des voies du bien et du mal; elle nous engage déjà dans la voie royale de la béatitude" (SAGE, *Les deux temps de la grâce* [n. 246], p. 219); "L'*adiutorium quo* est donc bien la grâce des derniers temps, grâce qui culmine dans le don de la persévérance finale" (*Ibid.*, p. 230).
251. "Itemque ipsa adiutoria distinguenda sunt. Aliud est adiutorium sine quo aliquid non fit, et aliud est adiutorium quo aliquid fit" (Augustine, *De correptione et gratia* 12,34 [CSEL, 92], p. 259).
252. Cf. *Ibid.* 12,34, p. 260.
253. Augustine sums up this theory in a passage of the *De ciuitate Dei*. After having explained that Adam's fall was caused by *superbia*, viz. the inherent or ontological weakness of both men and angels, he says: "Ac per hoc ut natura sit, ex eo habet quod a Deo facta est; ut autem ab eo quod est deficiat, ex hoc quod *de nihilo facta est [Italics mine]*. Nec sic defecit homo, ut omnino nihil esset, sed ut inclinatus ad se ipsum minus esset, quam erat, cum ei qui summe est inhaerebat" (Id., *De ciuitate Dei* 14,13 [CCL, 48], pp. 434-435). Cf. *Ibid.* 12,6, p. 361; *Contra secundam Iuliani responsionem opus imperfectum* 5,39 (PL, 45), cc. 1475-1476. See BONNER, *Adam* (n. 238), cc. 78-80; ID., *St Augustine of Hippo* (n. 1), p. 369. "Both Satan and Adam – writes Rist – are free of all

gift of perseverance, which works in them not only as an *adiutorium sine quo non*, but also as an *adiutorium quo*, due to whose infallibility they cannot help but persevere.

As Augustine emphasizes, there is no doubt that human beings need a *maior libertas* other than that possessed and enjoyed by Adam in Paradise. Unlike Adam in the garden of Eden, human beings are now faced with the temptations and allurements of this world. A freedom *munita atque firmata*[254] by the gift of perseverance, viz. a freedom fortified and sustained by that operative grace which is given to those predestined by God, now enables the *electi* to overcome innumerable worldly passions and hindrances, and so reach eventual salvation[255]. The grace which the

---

moral evil before they fall. They have the choice and the power to avoid sin. Their weakness, therefore, the weakness by which they choose death rather than life, sin rather than God, can only be explained metaphysically. ... It appears to be Augustine's view that the free choice given to Adam and to Satan is incompatible with the impossibility of sinning except in the case of God himself. All created beings which are endowed with the power of choice will be liable to sin, and therefore it is likely that some of them will sin in fact. Such sins, it must be repeated, are not the result of the *moral* weakness of the individual, nor of a conflict between concupiscence and moral knowledge, for such a struggle exists only in fallen humanity; rather they spring from a metaphysical weakness endemic in all creatures that are at the same time endowed with a genuine power of choosing" (J.M. RIST, *Augustine on Free Will and Predestination*, in *JTS* 20 [1969] 420-447, p. 433).

254. Augustine, *De correptione et gratia* 12,35 (CSEL, 92), p. 261.

255. L'*adiutorium quo* finds its climax in final perseverance, the mystery of which was questioned within the monastic community of Hadrumetum. But this final perseverance, an example of which is to be found in the lives of the martyrs, is the prerogative of the *electi* (cf. Id., *De correptione et gratia* 12,35 [CSEL, 92], pp. 261ff), whose option in dying for Christ, though freely taken, is at the same time only made possible by Christ's most powerful grace. According to Burns we have here the last and most elaborate stage of the three phases of the development of Augustine's thought on grace: *1.* In the *De diuersis quaestionibus ad Simplicianum* (A.D. 396/397), grace operates through environmental factors which appeal to man's disposition and encourages him to embrace faith. Augustine spoke of a *uocatio congrua* (cf., *e.g.*, Id., *De diuersis quaestionibus ad Simplicianum* 1,2,13 [CCL, 44], p. 38), an expression that underlines his conviction that man is moved to faith by divine grace. The latter operates through a calling (*uocatio*) and by manipulating external and environmental circumstances in such a way as to make them adapt (*congruere*) to man's prior disposition. Man is then able to "respond" to God's call by his own free will. *2.* In the *Ep.* 194 (A.D. 418/419) grace is presented as acting from within by reversing evil tendencies (see Paul's conversion: cf. Id., *De gratia et libero arbitrio* 5,12 [PL, 44], c. 889). It is by operative grace, namely by the Holy Spirit acting from within the human will, that man is brought to conversion and faith, and is made capable of answering to God's call. *3.* In the *De correptione et gratia* the first two phases are combined in order to illustrate the fact that God maintains the *electi* in the good, enabling them to persevere to the end (cf. BURNS, *The Development of Augustine's Doctrine of Operative Grace* [n. 164], pp. 7-9; 39-44; 141-158 *passim*). As to this thesis we share the disagreement expressed by Grossi: "La tesi di J. Patout Burns sullo sviluppo della dottrina della grazia in Agostino: *Vocatio congrua* fino all'anno 418; grazia interiore o efficace (*interior grace, operative grace*) relativamente all'inizio della fede o alla

Lord accords to his faithful through Christ is thus *maior* in comparison to Adam's *magna libertas*. Whereas Adam's *magna libertas* (originally due to a sinless will, unstained by concupiscence) contained within it the possibility of perseverance, even though he eventually failed in this respect, the predestined faithful are granted a *maior* and infallible grace, which is always efficacious in aiding man's weakness (a weakness which is the result of Adam's loss of the *magna libertas*). In addition, they receive from Christ the grace of final perseverance and the reward of eternal salvation. Without such powerful grace, the human being is indeed powerless, and possesses nothing he can boast of before God[256]. Therefore, those who receive the grace of Christ are in an advantageous position compared to that of Adam. In fact, their will, weakened (*infirma, inualida et imbecilla*) as the result of Adam's sin, is now rejuvenated by the agency of divine grace itself, and this leads the will to persevere[257] *indeclinabiliter et insuperabiliter*[258].

conversione dall'anno 418 con l'opera *De gratia Christi*; e relativamente alla perseveranza finale dall'anno 427 col *De correptione et gratia*, è impostata nel suo assieme al di fuori dell'ottica agostiniana sul rapporto della libertà con la grazia, risente ancora dello schema giansenista della 'grazia efficace'" (V. GROSSI, *L'antropologia agostiniana. Note previe*, in *Aug* 22 [1982] 456-467, p. 466, n. 13). From the following quotation we can realize that Augustine's position on the question of the relationship between grace and free will was already decided from the year 396/397: "...ubi satis ostendit etiam ipsam bonam uoluntatem in nobis operante Deo fieri" (Augustine, *De diuersis quaestionibus ad Simplicianum* 1,2,12 [CCL, 44], p. 36).

256. Cf. Id., *De correptione et gratia* 12,37 (CSEL, 92), p. 265.

257. "Ut quoniam non perseuerabunt, nisi et possint et uelint, perseverandi eis et possibilitas et uoluntas diuinae gratiae largitate donetur. Tantum quippe Spiritu sancto accenditur uoluntas eorum, ut ideo possint quia sic uolunt, ideo sic uelint quia Deus operatur ut uelint" (*Ibid.* 12,38, pp. 265-266).

258. "Subuentum est igitur infirmitati uoluntatis humanae, ut diuina gratia indeclinabiliter et insuperabiliter agretur, et ideo quamuis infirma non tamen deficeret, neque aduersitate aliqua uinceretur. Ita factum est ut uoluntas hominis inualida et imbecilla in bono adhuc paruo perseueraret per uirtutem Dei, cum uoluntas primi hominis fortis et sana in bono ampliore non perseuerauerit, habens uirtutem liberi arbitrii" (*Ibid.*, p. 266). The reading *insuperabiliter* was already established by the Theologi Lovanienses and the Maurini. Although it was recognized that all the MSS have *insuperabiliter*, the option of *PL* 44 for *inseparabiliter* was clearly dictated for reasons of apologetics, in that the term *insuperabiliter* was thought to favour "les erreurs nouvelles" [*viz. Jansenism*] (PL, 44, c. 940, n. 1). The reading *insuperabiliter* is nowadays accepted by all. See G. FOLLIET, *Introduction. Notes à l'edition* (of the *De correptione et gratia*) (CSEL, 92), pp. 201-202; J. CHÉNÉ, *Notes complémentaires* (BA, 24), p. 784ff; F. CAPPONI, *"Insuperabiliter"* o *"Inseparabiliter"*?, in *Latomus* 28 (1969) 681-684. The Christological background is of course of paramount importance for a correct understanding of the expression "indeclinabiliter et insuperabiliter". As it has rightly been stated: "Les mots *indeclinabiliter* et *insuperabiliter* ... ne prennent tout leur sens qu'en référence à la volonté sainte et indéclinable du Christ" (HOMBERT, *Gloria gratiae* [n. 180], pp. 498-499).

It should not be forgotten, and Augustine is quite adamant here, that the grace of perseverance is reserved for the *praedestinati-electi*, whose number has been decided upon by God from all eternity and is therefore unalterable, namely it cannot be either increased or decreased (*neque augendum neque minuendum*)[259]. This *numerus clausus* is hidden to the world, so that no one, not even those *qui bene currunt* and whose salvation is assured by God, may take pride in being counted among the elect. God does not reveal the number of those to be saved on purpose so that all men may hold to a *saluberrimum timorem, quo uitium elationis opprimitur*[260]. This uncertainty of salvation is undoubtedly meant to encourage man to live in trembling fear and in the light of that faith which operates through charity. The *electi*, however, set apart by God for salvation, remain the object of God's mercy, thanks to which they eventually gain the reward of eternal life. Their good deeds are themselves the result of God's mercy, a mercy always at work in the life of the elect. It is divine grace, in fact, which makes possible and crowns their fidelity[261]. Thus, continues Augustine, the reward of eternal life can be considered a *gratia pro gratia* (Jn 1,16), because it is given to the faithful according to the merits that divine grace itself has bestowed on them. As for those not belonging to the *certissimus et felicissimus numerus*[262] of the elect, they are to be justly judged by God according to their status and behaviour. As well as those not regenerated by baptism, there are those who, although baptized, have misused their free will and become the slave of sin; and we should not forget those who, having lived under the influence of grace for a certain time, have abandoned it and so, in their turn, been abandoned by it (*deserunt et deseruntur*[263]). For all these categories of people, the exclusion from salvation and eternal life rests in God's justice.

At this point, Augustine again takes up the question of rebuke, which was the initial reason for writing the *De correptione et gratia*. He stresses anew the necessity of charitable reproving for all those in need of censure, regardless of the fact that this reproof might also be used against those who have been predestined by God. In this specific case,

---

259. Augustine, *De correptione et gratia* 13,39 (CSEL, 92), p. 267.
260. *Ibid.* 13,40, p. 269.
261. Cf. *Ibid.* 13,41, pp. 269ff.
262. *Ibid.* 13,42, p. 271.
263. *Ibid.* Cf. also: "*[Deus] non deserit, nisi deseratur*" (Id., *De natura et gratia* 26,29 [CSEL, 60], p. 255). Yet, how this happens, remains wrapped in mystery: "Mais ceux qui l'abandonnent ne l'abandonneraient pas, s'il ne les laissait à l'infirmité de leur libre arbitre; et c'est cet "abandonnement" divin qui est tout mystérieux" (M.J. PINTARD, *Footnotes* to the text of the *De correptione et gratia*, in *BA* 24, p. 367, n. 1).

God himself will assuredly bring about fruitfulness from the rebuke in a way that is irresistible[264]. It is evident that although he stresses the necessity of rebuking, Augustine does not ultimately solve the concrete problem of brotherly *correptio*. He leaves us without a real answer, stating, coherently with his theological system, that the conversion of sinners does not ultimately depend on reproof, but on God's mercy alone that grants the grace of conversion to those he favours. At times, however, God also makes use of reproof to facilitate his eternal design, as part of a process where grace interacts with human co-operation. But it goes without saying that God's design is effective in itself, regardless of his having recourse to rebuke. The latter, *stricto sensu*, is not really necessary for the accomplishment of God's intentions.

Augustine is now faced with the problem of harmonizing his conclusions with the call to universal salvation, as expressed in the words of the Apostle: *[Deus] uult omnes homines saluos fieri* (1Tm 2,4). Having said that there are many ways of interpreting this passage, Augustine makes a shift from the general understanding of the principle concerning God's desire for man's salvation to a more restricted interpretation of it. He clearly states that the term *omnes* must not be understood as referring to "all men", but to "all the predestined"[265]. Augustine's peculiar understanding of the word *omnes* acquires a different semantic meaning in this particular context: a context which only applies to those who have been *mis-à-part* by God's mysterious and inscrutable design[266]. In

---

264. "... cui uolenti facere saluum nullum hominum resistit arbitrium? Sic enim uelle seu nolle in uolentis aut nolentis est potestate, ut diuinam uoluntatem non impediat nec superet potestatem. Etiam de his enim qui faciunt quae non uult, facit ipse quae uult" (Augustine, *De correptione et gratia* 14,43 [CSEL, 92], p. 272). Cf. also: "Non est itaque dubitandum, uoluntati Dei qui in coelo et in terra omnia quaecumque uoluit fecit *[cf. Ps 134,6]* et qui etiam illa *quae futura sunt fecit (Is 45,11 [LXX])*, humanas uoluntates non posse resistere, quominus faciat ipse quod uult, quandoquidem etiam de ipsis hominum uoluntatibus quod uult cum uult, facit" (*Ibid.* 14,45, p. 273).

265. "Et quod scriptum est, quod *omnes homines uult saluos fieri*, nec tamen omnes salui fiunt, multis quidem modis intelligi potest, ex quibus in aliis opusculis nostris aliquos commemorauimus, sed hic unum dicam. Ita dictum est: *Omnes homines uult saluos fieri*, ut intelligantur omnes praedestinati quia omne genus hominum in eis est" (*Ibid.* 14,44, p. 272).

266. Although Augustine never intended to contradict the biblical affirmation of 1 Tm 2,4, the latter became, towards the end of his life, the object of a restricted exegesis. This was a vision which could be defined as the logical consequence of Augustine's views on grace and its limited dispensation. If, before 397, he thought that the effectiveness or not of God's universal salvation depended mainly on man's good or malajusted will (cf. for instance: "Nostrum est enim credere et velle": Id., *Expositio quarumdam propositionum ex epistula ad Romanos* 54 [61] [CSEL, 84], p. 36; cf. also *Ibid.* 66 [74], p. 46), after 397 Augustine began to stress the incapacity of man to access faith without the help of grace. As a consequence of this, salvation too would no longer depend on human will, but on God's will and predilection alone. From then on Augustine would remain steadily

88   CHAPTER ONE

other words, Augustine bends the objective meaning of 1 Tm 2,4 to safeguard his personal theological view. A further confirmation of the
change of perspective in the interpretation of this Pauline passage is the
bishop of Hippo's contention that God allows us to will what He himself
wills, in the same way that He sends the Spirit which makes us cry:
"Abba! Father" (cf Rom 8,15). Precisely as the Spirit cries in and
through us, so God, in willing the salvation of all mankind, makes
mankind desirous of it[267].

Towards the end of the treatise, the bishop of Hippo again reminds his
readers of the need for reproof and the way it should be applied, *i.e.*,
with the solicitude of charity. It is the *pastoralis necessitas* of superiors
to be concerned for all those who are found to be at fault. The certainty
that God will not let his chosen people perish (*Sciuit Dominus qui sunt
eius*: 2 Tim 2,19) should not be seen as an excuse by those superiors
who, *pigri et negligentes*, do not reprove those who deserve it. It must be
quite clear, that according to Augustine, reproof falls into the sphere of
their direct responsibility, which should not be abdicated on the grounds
that, ultimately, efficacious grace alone is responsible for man's well
being[268]. Without knowing who will be saved and who condemned, but
aware that God's decisions are always right and that He can always
intervene, even unexpectedly, it should be the earnest duty of superiors
to care for the spiritual well-being of the flock entrusted to them. Led
by the desire that all might be saved, they should do everything in their
power (including rebuke) to bring sinners back to God or, as it is
specifically stated in this treatise, to help those monks who behave in
a regrettable manner, failing to live up to the ideals of their monastic
profession[269]. Furthermore, to a reproach applied *medicinaliter*, together
with the "prescription" given to the person reproached to aid his resolve
to improve, a superior should also add his prayers, imploring the help of

anchored to this position, emphasizing the words *Deus uult* at the expense of the term
omnes. Rivière has tried to justify Augustine's approach by describing it as "une objection contre l'infaillibilité du plan divin qu'il se propose d'écarter, non une thèse qu'il veut
établir sur la façon d'en concevoir l'object" (J. RIVIÈRE, *Notes complementaires*, in *BA* 9,
Paris, 1947, p. 410). We cannot agree, however, that, in order to save the theological significance of God's supreme and infallible governance, Augustine consciously minimized
the difference of the domains to which exegesis and doctrine both belong from a methodological and epistemological point of view. For the development of Augustine's exegesis
of 1 Tm 2,4, see *infra*, pp. 357ff.

267. "Si ergo clamantem Spiritum recte dixit Scriptura a quo efficitur ut clamemus,
recte etiam uolentem Deum a quo efficitur ut uelimus" (Augustine, *De correptione et
gratia* 15,47 [CSEL, 92], p. 277).

268. Cf. *Ibid.* 15,48, p. 278.

269. Cf. *Ibid.* 15,46, pp. 275ff.

God's grace. Prayer becomes, as it were, the expression of one's awareness that both grace and reproof are necessary and should be kept
together in positive tension: since grace does not prohibit rebuke, neither does the latter abolish the necessity of the former:

> And since these things are so, grace neither restrains rebuke, nor does
> rebuke restrain grace; and on this account righteousness is so to be pre-
> scribed that we may ask in faithful prayer, that, by God's grace, what is
> prescribed may be done; and both these things are done in such a way that
> righteous rebuke may not be neglected. But let all these things be done
> with love, since love both does not sin and does cover the multitude of
> sins[270].

Thus far we could indeed say that the content of the *De correptione et
gratia*, a work whose aim was to offer a synthesis of the relationship
between God's *gratia* and man's *liberum arbitrium*, is the most important and probably the most difficult theological writing on Christian
grace and anthropology of the 5th century.

We do not have any record as to the reactions from Hadrumetum. We
may well surmise that the treatise somehow appeased the monks who
had raised doubts over the need for rebuke vis-à-vis the sovereignty of
grace. However, if that was the case in the monastery of Hadrumetum,
where the disputes and divisions were eventually overcome (probably
thanks to Augustine's teaching "authority"), it was certainly not the case
across the *mare nostrum*, in the monastic milieu of Southern Gaul,
where the *De correptione et gratia* would cause harsh and bitter reactions provoking a new dispute. This time, however, the Gallic monks,
more conversant with the dilemma of grace and free will than their
African confrères, were more prepared to defend their position. This is
what we shall soon realize, by sailing to Marseilles and Lérins.

---

270. "Quae cum ita sint, nec gratia prohibet correptionem nec correptio negat gratiam; et ideo sic est praecipienda iustitia, ut a Deo gratia, qua id quod praecipitur fiat,
fideli oratione poscatur; et hoc utrumque ita faciendum est ut neque iusta correptio negle-
gatur. *Omnia* uero haec *cum caritate fiant*, quoniam caritas nec facit peccatum et *cooperit
multitudinem peccatorum*" (*Ibid.* 16,49, p. 280).

CHAPTER TWO

THE RISE OF "MASSILIANISM" IN GAUL
HISTORICAL AND THEOLOGICAL FRAMEWORK

The monks of Southern Gaul, undoubtedly more learned than their African confrères in Hadrumetum, whose disturbance hardly ranks as a controversy, found that some of Augustine's assertions on the question of grace were intransigent and unacceptable. For that reason they opposed Augustine's description of grace as an inner force or inspiration which moves man's will *indeclinabiliter et insuperabiliter*; his distinction between the status of Adam before and after the fall (a distinction in which he tried to prove the absolute gratuity and sovereignty of grace in the life of fallen humanity) and his clear-cut view on predestination to salvation, a view which takes predestination to grace to an extreme consequence. All these views, conveyed by Augustine's *De correptione et gratia*[1], did provoke negative judgement from the monks of Southern Gaul[2]. We learn of this opposition from letters[3] sent to the bishop of Hippo from two Gallic admirers, Prosper[4] and

1. "Quand ils eurent entre les mains le livre *De la correction et de la grace*, ils virent clairement qu'une radicale antinomie séparait leur pensée de la pensée d'Augustin et déclarèrent se refuser à une théologie aussi excessive et aussi périlleuse" (J. CHÉNÉ, *Les origines de la controverse semi-pélagienne*, in *ATA* 13 [1953] 56-109, p. 101).
2. See R.W. MATHISEN, *Ecclesiastical Factionalism and Religious Controversy in Fifth-Century Gaul*, Washington, D.C., 1989, pp. 123-124.
3. Prosper, *Ep.* 225 (CSEL, 57) (among the Augustinian letters), pp. 454-468; Hilary, *Ep.* 226 (CSEL, 57) (among the Augustinian letters), pp. 468-481.
4. Prosper was a layman from Aquitaine ("Prosper, homo Aquitanicae regionis": Gennadius, *De uiris inlustribus* 85 [TU, 14], p. 90). This is the only piece of information we have about his life, with the exception of what we can deduce from his writings. See L. VALENTIN, *Saint Prosper d'Aquitaine. Étude sur la littérature ecclésiastique au cinquième siècle en Gaule*, Paris-Toulouse, 1900; G. BARDY, *Prosper d'Aquitaine (saint)*, in *DTC* 13 (1936) 846-850; A. SOLIGNAC, *Prosper d'Aquitaine (saint)*, in *DSp* 12 (1986) 2446-2456; L. COLLIN, *Prosper d'Aquitaine*, in *Cath* 12 (1990) 38-39; A.-G. HAMMAN, *Scrittori della Gallia. Prospero di Aquitania*, in A. DI BERARDINO (ed.), *Patrologia*, Vol. III: *Dal Concilio di Nicea (325) al Concilio di Calcedonia (451). I Padri latini*, Turin, 1978, pp. 522-528; ID., *Prosper von Aquitanien*, in *TRE* 27 (1997) 525-526; M.P. McHUGH, *Prosper of Aquitaine*, in A.D. FITZGERALD (ed.), *Augustine through the Ages. An Encyclopedia*, Grand Rapids, MI – Cambridge, 1999, pp. 685-686. Prosper must have been born towards the end of the 4th century. After receiving a classical education, he moved to Marseilles, probably attracted by the lively theological and monastic atmosphere of that town, which at the beginning ot the 5th century was called the "New Athens". It is probable that he lived in a monastic environment although not a monk

Hilary[5], anxious to acquaint him with the latest developments. It was at their request, in fact, that Augustine wrote his final works: the *De praedestinatione sanctorum* and the *De dono perseuerantiae*.

himself, an hypothesis still supported by Collin (cf. COLLIN, *Prosper d'Aquitaine*, c. 38). If the *Poema coniugis ad uxorem* [PL, 51], cc. 611-616) was really his, then he must have been married for a certain time (see SOLIGNAC, *Prosper d'Aquitaine*, c. 2447; HAMMAN, *Prosper van Aquitanien*, p. 525). Whilst at Marseilles, from about 426 on, he was involved in the controversy between the monks of the region and Augustine whose views he strongly defended and whose intervention at a certain point he warmly solicited. Before writing to the bishop of Hippo, Prosper had already written a long letter to a certain Rufinus (Prosper, *Ep. Ad Rufinum* [PL, 51], cc. 77-90) in which he dealt with the Augustinian doctrine of grace and, through scriptural argumentation, attacked both Pelagian and Massilian views. Rufinus was probably seeking clarification about the twofold criticism (which Prosper also reported in his letter to Augustine) which must have been current in ecclesiastical and monastic milieux of Southern Gaul. On one hand, Augustine was believed to teach fatalism disguised as grace ("Dicentes eum liberum arbitrium penitus submovere, et sub gratiae nomine necessitatem praedicare fatalem": *Ibid.* 3,4, c. 79), whereas on the other, he was accused of dividing humanity into two *massae* of different natures, as the pagans and the Manichaeans would do ("Duas illum humani generis massas, et duas credi velle naturas: ut scilicet tantae pietatis viro paganorum et Manichaeorum ascribatur impietas": *Ibid.*). Beneath this criticism, the point at stake was the problem of predestination and of the fixed number of elect (cf. *Ibid.* 11,12, c. 84). It was on these grounds that Augustine's understanding was criticized and opposed. Prosper's letter to Rufinus represented, as it were, "il primo impasto dei suoi futuri trattati" (HAMMAN, *Prospero di Aquitania*, p. 523). As the confrontation did not produce any positive result, Prosper decided to call on Augustine's help in an effort to receive further explanation and enlightenment on the problem of grace (cf. Prosper, *Ep.* 225 [CSEL, 57], pp. 454-468). At the same time he wrote the Περὶ ἀχαρίστων sive *De ingratis carmen* [PL, 51], cc. 91-148) where he versified in 1002 hexameters the doctrinal arguments already put forward in his letter to Rufinus, refuting both Pelagianism and Massilianism. After the death of the bishop of Hippo, Prosper "devient aux yeux de tous le continuateur attitré de son combat" (COLLIN, *Prosper d'Aquitaine*, c. 39; cf. VALENTIN, *Saint Prosper d'Aquitaine*, pp. 368ff.), although, it seems, in a very intransigent way ("Il défendit sa mémoire *[of Augustine]* et ses idées avec une fougue où la charité n'est pas en excès": J. CHÉNÉ, *Notes complémentaires* [BA, 24], p. 389); see also M. CAPPUYNS, *Le premier représentant de l'augustinisme médiéval. Prosper d'Aquitaine*, in *RTAM* 1 (1929) 309-337; G. DE PLINVAL, *Prosper. Interprète de s. Augustin*, in *RechAug* 1 (1958) 336-355. Prosper travelled to Rome with his friend Hilary (the author of *Ep.* 226) to inform pope Caelestinus I about the continuing controversy in Southern Gaul, and to ask him to condemn the views on grace professed at Marseilles and Lérins. The pope eventually wrote a letter to the Gallic bishops (cf. Caelestinus I, *Ep. ad episcopos Galliarum* [PL, 50], cc. 528-530) which was more of a reprimand addressed to the anti-Augustinian party than a condemnation. It also encouraged them to hold in great esteem the African bishop and master who had done so much for the well being of the Church. Disappointed at the tenor of the letter, the intransigent Prosper returned to Marseilles to fight even more vigorously against the Massilian party. Between 432 and 434 he wrote his main works: *Pro Augustino responsiones ad capitula obiectionum Gallorum calumniantium* (PL, 51), cc. 155-174; *Pro Augustino responsiones ad capitula obiectionum Vincentianarum* (PL, 51), cc. 77-186; *Pro Augustino responsiones ad excerpta Genuensium* (PL, 51), cc. 187-202; *De gratia Dei et libero arbitrio liber contra Collatorem* (= Cassian) (PL, 51), cc. 213-276. The polemic ceased with the death of John Cassian (ca. 435) who was considered, as we shall see, the principal exponent of the anti-Augustinian opposition (as to the issue of

1. PROSPER'S AND HILARY'S LETTERS TO AUGUSTINE
(EPP. 225 AND 226): THE PROBLEM OF THEIR DATING

We can assume that the objections coming from the monastic élite of Southern Gaul to some aspects of Augustine's theology of grace were reported to the bishop of Hippo by Prosper and Hilary in 427, rather than in the year 429, which has been traditionally accepted until now. The assumption that Prosper's and Hilary's letters were written in 429 comes from an explicit reference to *sanctum Hilarium, Arelatensem episcopum*[6] in all but one manuscript containing Prosper's *Ep*. 225. This assumption was enforced by the conviction that Hilary had succeeded Honoratus to the see of Arles in January 429. This was taken for granted until an article by O. Chadwick challenged it by focusing on the MS *Parisinus nov. acq. 1449* as a reliable source. This MS uses the name *Elladium* instead of *Hilarium*[7]. The dyptics of an ancient episcopal catalogue of the see of Arles, which dates back to the 9th century, support this challenging theory. In it we find the name of a certain Euladius, in the genitive form *Euladii*, between Patroclus and Honoratus[8]. Elected to the see of Arles after the murder of Patroclus, this Euladius or Helladius[9] must have been

grace) in Southern Gaul. Thereafter, Prosper established himself in Rome where he co-operated with pope Leo the Great. It is probably thanks to the latter (an ancient friend of Cassian) that Prosper's attacks on Cassian ceased and his "Augustinianism" became more flexible. It was in Rome, in fact, that Prosper passed from a staunchly rigid and militant theology, regarding the question of the absolute gratuity of grace, to a more moderate and open-minded approach. The latter resulted in the *De uocatione omnium gentium* (PL, 51), cc. 647-722, a work which, because it differed from Prosper's other works, was considered by many as being foreign to his thought (see BARDY, *Prosper d'Aquitaine [saint]*, c. 848; M. CAPPUYNS, *L'auteur du De uocatione omnium gentium*, in *RBen* 39 [1927] 198-226). Prosper must have died around 455, because the content of the *Epitoma Chronicorum* (PL, 51), cc. 535-606, on which he worked until the end of his life, extends to that year.

5. Hilary, a friend of Prosper, was also a layman (see a hint to this in Hilary, *Ep*. 226,6 [CSEL, 57], p. 478; cf. also J. KRAUS, *Hilarius*, in *LTK* 5 [1986] c. 335). Tillemont believed that this Hilary was the same person who wrote a short letter to Augustine about the Pelagians in Sicily in 414-415 (cf. Hilary, *Ep*. 156 [among the Augustinian letters] [CSEL, 44], pp. 448-449: L.-S. LENAIN DE TILLEMONT, *Mémoires pour servir à l'histoire ecclésiastique des six premiers siècles*. T. XIII: *La vie de saint Augustin*, Paris, 1702, art. 243, p. 640). Unlike Prosper (who had never met Augustine) Hilary had the chance of enjoyning his company at Hippo ("Sufficiat mihi poena mea, quod a praesentiae tuae deliciis exsulatus, ubi salubribus tuis uberibus nutriebar, non solum absentia tua crucior...": Hilary, *Ep*. 226,10 [CSEL, 57], p. 480).

6. Cf. Prosper, *Ep*. 225,9 (CSEL, 57), p. 467.

7. O. CHADWICK, *Euladius of Arles*, in *JTS* 46 (1945) 200-205 (the same standpoint is taken up in his book *John Cassian. A Study in Primitive Monasticism*, 2nd ed., Cambridge, 1968, p. 128).

8. Cf. L. DUCHESNE, *Fastes épiscopaux de l'ancienne Gaule*. T. I: *Provinces du Sud-Est*, 2nd ed., Paris, 1907, pp. 5, 250, 251 and 254.

9. Since *Elladium* and *Euladii* are probably a scribal contraction of *Helladius*, we will continue to use the latter spelling.

governing his diocese for a short time, presumably from the end of 426 to the end of 427/beginning of 428. But the general assumption that Honoratus was the immediate successor of Patroclus, made the presence of the name Helladius in the catalogue obtrusive. So much so that even Duchesne, at the beginning of the 20th century, hastily and self-assuredely dismissed the hypothesis of a certain Helladius having been bishop of Arles, and expunged his name from the episcopal list on the ground that it had been unreasonably added[10]. After Chadwick's article, however, an increasing number of scholars have come to accept the reading "Helladius" (instead of "Hilary")[11] on the ground that the general rule of the *lectio difficilior* should be preferred[12]. Moreover, the fact that MS *Parisinus nov. acq. 1449* bears traces of complete independence from the other manuscripts which, although earlier, belong to the same family[13], is a further indication that *Elladium* must be a genuine reading and not a mere copyist's error. For this reason J.-R. Palanque has retained the name of bishop Helladius in the episcopal list of Arles[14], whereas

10. "Après Patrocle [*Patruli*, n° 15], on trouve un *Euladius*, qui n'a nul droit de figurer ici, car Patrocle eut sûrement saint Honorat pour successeur immédiat" (DUCHESNE, *Fastes épiscopaux* [n. 8], p. 253).

11. Chadwick's conclusion has been endorsed by, among others, Cavallin, who writes: "O. Chadwick... optimo ut videtur iure contendit inter Patroclum et Honoratum Euladium quendam sedem Arelatensem occupavisse" (S. CAVALLIN, *Vitae Sanctorum Honorati et Hilarii Episcoporum Arelatensium* [SVSL, 40], Lund, 1952, p. 13). See also É. GRIFFE, *La Gaule chrétienne à l'époque romaine*. T. II: *L'Église de Gaule au Vème siècle*, 2nd ed., Paris, 1966, p. 121 and above all pp. 191-193; G. BONNER, *St Augustine of Hippo. Life and Controversies*, London, 1963, 2nd ed., Norwich, 1986, p. 350; C. PIETRI, *Roma Christiana. Recherches sur l'Église de Rome, son organisation, sa politique, son idéologie de Miltiade à Sixte (311-440)* (BEFAR, 224), T. II, Rome, 1976, p. 1028, n. 3; B. REES, *Pelagius. A Reluctant Heretic*, Woodbridge, 1988, p. 104; S. PRICOCO, *L'isola dei santi. Il cenobio di Lerino e le origini del monachesimo gallico*, Rome, 1978, pp. 36 and 43; W.J. COLLINGE, *Introduction*, in J.A. MOURANT – W.J. COLLINGE (eds.), *Saint Augustine. Four Anti-Pelagian Writings: On Nature and Grace, On the Proceedings of Pelagius, On the Predestination of the Saints, On the Gift of Perseverance* (FaCh, 86), Washington, 1992, pp. 179-217, pp. 186-187; J. FONTAINE – L. PIETRI, *Les grandes Églises missionaires: Hispanie, Gaule, Bretagne*, in J.-M. MAYEUR et al. (eds.), *Histoire du Christianisme*. T. II:. *Naissance d'une Chrétienté, chrétienté (250-430)*, Paris, 1995, pp. 813-860. Valentin considers as plausible the episcopate of Helladius in Arles, (cf. M.-D. VALENTIN, *Introduction*, in Hilary of Arles, *Sermo de uita S. Honorati Arelatensis episcopi* [SC, 235], p. 22). Rousseau also believes that Chadwick was right (cf. P. ROUSSEAU, *Cassian: Monastery and World*, in M. FAIRBURN – W.H. OLIVER [eds.], *The Certainty of Doubt. Tributes to Peter Munz*, Wellington, 1995, pp. 68-89, p. 70).

12. "Il serait surprenant – it has been written – que le copiste ait changé un nom aussi courant qu' "Hilarius" [ou "Hillarius"] pour un nom aussi rare que celui d'Helladius: la *lectio difficilior* est préférable" (P.-A. JACOB, *Introduction*, in Honoratus of Marseilles, *Vita S. Hilarii Arelatensis* [SC, 404], p. 29).

13. Cf. A. GOLDBACHER (ed.), Augustine, *Epistulae* (CSEL, 58), *Praef.*, pp. xliii, lxx, lxxiii.

14. Cf. G.-R. PALANQUE., *Les évêchés provençaux à l'époque romaine*, in *Provence historique* 1 (1951) 103-143, p. 132.

Duchesne's peremptory conviction that the name of Helladius had been added to the list together with the names of other bishops not belonging to the see of Arles, is counteracted by Griffe[15]. If Helladius did actually occupy the see of Arles, then the death of Honoratus, which occurred in mid-January after a couple of years of episcopate[16], ought to be moved forward from January 429 (the traditionally accepted date)[17] to January 430[18].

From the above arguments, we conclude that if Prosper's letter to Augustine mentioned bishop Hilary of Arles, then we should place it in 430, within the few months between the accession of Hilary to the see of Arles (January 430) and Augustin's death (August 430); a very short time indeed for Augustine, aged and infirm, to sit down and write the *De praedestinatione sanctorum* and the *De dono perseuerantiae*. Moreover, the sailing time from Gaul to Africa, and the limitations imposed by the *mare clausum* (11 November–10 March)[19], together with the fact that communications with some parts of Africa, at that time, were already affected by the Vandal invasion (Hippo would be besieged in June of the

---

15. "Les noms ajoutés – he writes – sont le plus souvent des noms de personnages illustres: Martin, Ambroise, Augustin. Le nom d'Euladius n'entre pas dans cette categorie. Cela seul mérite qu'on ne l'exclue pas aussi facilment que l'a fait Mgr Duchesne" (GRIFFE, *La Gaule chrétienne à l'époque romaine*, T. II [n. 11], p. 192, n. 10).

16. Cf. Hilary of Arles, *Sermo de uita S. Honorati Arelatensis episcopi* 29,3 (SC, 235), p. 150.

17. Cf. *e.g.*, DUCHESNE, *Fastes épiscopaux de l'ancienne Gaule* (n. 8), p. 250; A. GOLDBACHER, *Index III* (CSEL, 58), pp. 60-61; J. CHÉNÉ, *Introduction* to *Réponses d'Augustin aux moines de provence et de Provence* (BA, 24), pp. 383-390, p. 390.

18. Cf., *e.g.*, CHADWICK, *Euladius of Arles* (n. 7), p. 205; GRIFFE, *La Gaule chrétienne à l'époque romaine*. T. II (n. 11), p. 242; H.-I. MARROU, *Nouvelle Histoire de l'Église*. T. I: *Des origines à Grégoire le Grand*, Paris, 1963, p. 481; VALENTIN, *Introduction* (n. 11), p. 9; M. LABROUSSE, *Saint Honorat fondateur de Lérins et évêque d'Arles. Étude et traduction de textes d'Hilaire d'Arles, Fauste de Riez et Césaire d'Arles* (VieMon, 31), Bégrolles-en-Mauges, 1995, p. 15; "Hilaire... lui succède [to Honoratus] en 430" (PIETRI, *Roma Christiana* [n. 11], p. 1030). Other scholars content themselves with giving a vague reference (429/430), as to the date of Honoratus' death: cf., *e.g.*, R. GAZEAU, *Honorat (Saint) d'Arles*, in *Cath* 5 (1963) 918-919, c. 918. Jourion writes: "Nous savons ... qu'immediatement après l'intermède d'un nommé Euladius ou Helladius, le choix d'un successeur de Patrocle au siège d'Arles se porta sur l'abbé de Lérins. Honorat ne fut pas longtemps évêque: en 430, au plus tard, et dès le début de l'année, il s'éteignit" (M. JOURION, *Honorat d'Arles*, in *DSp* 7/1 [1969] 717-718, c. 717). See also R. AUBERT, *Honorat (Saint), évêque d'Arles*, in *DHGE* 24 (1993) 1027-1028, c. 1027.

19. See O. PERLER – J.-L. MAIER, *Les voyages de saint Augustin*, Paris, 1969, pp. 68-74. Of course the *mare clausum*-rule should not be taken too rigidly. Ships would in fact sail also in the winter if urgent affairs called for it, and enterprising sailors could always be found. That was, for instance, the case in the years 417-418, when the Pelagian controversy had reached its zenith and matters had to be handled swiftly between the African Church and both the pope and the emperor in Italy (cf. *Ibid.*, p. 71). Augustine's discussion with the Massilians, however, cannot be ranked as a most urgent matter requiring immediate action.

same year), plus the danger imposed by travel, would further restrict the chances of a written exchange between Prosper and Augustine. Finally, it should be born in mind that during the very last years of his life Augustine was not only engaged in writing the *De haeresibus* (in 429), but was also working (probably since 428) on his ponderous *Contra secundam Iuliani responsionem imperfectum opus*, which remained unfinished at the time of his death. If we hold to the hypothesis that Prosper's reference in his letter to Augustine was not to Hilary but to Helladius, the *Ep.* 225 (and Hilary's *Ep.* 226) ought then to be placed somewhere near the middle of Helladius' episcopate (end of 426–end of 427/beginning of 428).

Furthermore, the presence of Helladius in the see of Arles, between Patroclus and Honoratus, would throw light on three factors. First of all, it would enable us to identify the two Helladius' that are mentioned respectively in the preface to the first set of *Conlationes* as a monk (*frater*) and in the preface to the second collection as a bishop (*episcopus*) as being the same person. The monk to whom Cassian addressed his first ten conferences in 425/426, was bishop of Arles in 427, at the time in which Cassian was still writing the second set of conferences where the *Conlatio* 13 is to be found[20]. Secondly, from Prosper's complaint about bishop Helladius' request for clarification from Augustine on some of the more controversial points of the *De correptione et gratia*[21], we can infer that Helladius was in fact fully in agreement with the views professed by Cassian and the Massilians. By the fact that he is mentioned twice in the preface of both the two first sets of Cassian's *Conlationes*, we can assume that the ties between the two divines were friendly and based on mutual esteem. These ties can be interpreted as the result of a convergence of monastic ideals and perspectives, as well as of a common agreement upon theological issues such as the relationship between grace and free will, developed by Cassian in his *Conlatio* 13. Thirdly, it is worth noticing that there is no specific reference or allusion to Cassian's *Conlatio* 13 in Prosper's *Ep.* 225, nor are there any recorded verbal similarities. This means that by the time Prosper wrote to the bishop of Hippo (ca. 427)[22], *Conlatio* 13 was still being written.

20. Cf. *infra*, n. 155.
21. "Sanctum Helladium, Arelatensem episcopum, sciat beatitudo tua admiratorem sectatoremque in aliis omnibus tuae esse doctrinae et de hoc, quod in querelam trahit, iam pridem apud sanctitatem tuam sensum suum per litteras uelle conferre" (Prosper, *Ep.* 225,9 [CSEL, 57], p. 467).
22. And not in 429 as it was traditionally thought. By 429, in fact, such a crucial and relevant piece of work as the *Conlatio* 13, could not have escaped the watchful and careful inquisition of Prosper, nor would he have failed to mention it in his letter to his African heros!

Moreover, the teaching attributed to the Massilians by Prosper appears to be more Pelagian in content and much less nuanced than that forwarded by Cassian's *Conlatio* 13. In fact, whereas in Prosper's letter it is reported that, according to the Massilians, the first stage of faith in God must be attributed to human will, in Cassian the first step in the process of faith is alternated between God's initiative and man's agency[23]. Besides, it is noteworthy that Prosper never mentions Cassian's arguments on *torpor*[24] and *tepor*[25] which, in the mind of the divine of Marseilles, is the subtle and insidious consequence of a predestinarian view. Similarly, unlike the interpretation put forward in Prosper's letter[26], Cassian's own interpretation of Rom 9,16[27] is not seen as relating to predestination, but as a testimony to the power of grace that exists alongside man's free will. Furthermore, Prosper speaks of the "hypothetical merits" of unbaptized infants, a subject which is never dealt with in *Conlatio* 13. This means that it had not yet been published, and it is therefore possible that Prosper was simply referring to the ongoing discussions that were taking place in the monastic and ecclesial milieu of Provence.

We can conclude then that, since the *De correptione et gratia* had probably come to the notice of the monks of Provence before mid 427[28], viz. during Helladius' episcopate, the two separate responses to it also developed some time in 427: one being Cassian's *Conlatio* 13, a reasoned reaction to Augustine's extreme views on grace and predestination as contained in the *De correptione et gratia*[29], the other Prosper's and Hilary's letters to Augustine. In other words, we can assume that the relationship between the *De correptione et gratia* and the *Conlatio* 13 was not merely accidental. The latter was indeed very relevant to the controversy and stood out as a sort of manifesto on the theological view of grace held by the monks and churchmen of Southern Gaul.

---

23. See *infra*, particularly pp. 133-153 *passim*.
24. Cf. Cassian, *Conlatio* 13,13 (SC, 54), p. 168.
25. Cf., for instance: "Si nos nolle uel *intepuisse* perspexerit" (*Ibid.* 13,11, p. 164), and the *tepidus* in Id., *De insitutis coenobiorum* 4,33 (SC, 109), p. 172.
26. Cf. Prosper, *Ep.* 225,3 (CSEL, 57), p. 459.
27. Cf. Cassian, *Conlatio* 13, 9 (SC, 54), p. 159.
28. That the *De gratia et libero arbitrio* and the *De correptione et gratia*, were written in 425/426 is upheld, for instance, by S.M. ZARB, *Chronologia operum sancti Augustini*, Rome, 1934, p. 73; J. CHÉNÉ, *Introduction(s)* (BA, 24), pp. 44-45; 214-215. They must have reached the monasteries of Provence either in the second half of 426 or, at the latest, in the first half of 427. Instead, the *De praedestinatione sanctorum* and the *De dono perseuerantiae* must have been written by Augustine, on the request of Prosper and Hilary, in 428, and not in 429 or in the last months of 430, as argued, for instance, by J. CHÉNÉ, *Augustin aux moines de Provence* (BA, 24), pp. 436-461, p. 438, and by PERLER – MAIER, *Les voyages de saint Augustin* (n. 19), p. 475.
29. See *infra* n. 197.

Massilianism through the Eyes of Prosper and Hilary[30]

Prosper introduced Augustine (whom he calls *patronum fidei*[31]) to the opinion (*definitio atque professio*)[32] of the Massilians by reminding him that their differences regarding some of his views were not unknown, although the disagreement was, up to then, expressed in a respectful and hesitant way. But once Augustine's *De correptione et gratia* had reached the coast of Provence, the uneasiness provoked by its content burst into an open and *abrupta dissensio*[33]. The main reason was the pre-destination theory that Augustine expounded, viz. the call of the elect according to God's decree (*de uocatione electorum secundum Dei propositum*)[34] and its relation to God's universal salvific will.

From the discussions held in the monastic circles of Provence, it was possible (as Prosper leads us to understand) to distinguish between the two groups who were approaching the same problem at different levels. The first group of Massilians always professed the anti-Pelagian belief that all men are sinners, and that no one could possibly presume to save himself by his own deeds. Man can be saved only through the power bestowed on him by baptismal regeneration, and it is thanks to the redeeming blood of Christ that the possibility of obtaining God's for-giveness and mercy (*propitiatio*) is offered to all[35], so that all those who wish to embrace faith and be baptized may be saved. However, this group of Massilians contended that God has always foreknown those believers who would persevere in faith. At a second stage (*deinceps*), they will be accorded the help of grace. God's foreknowledge has there-fore predestined to his eternal kingdom, since the very beginning and after having called them gratuitously to faith, all those whom he has foreseen to be worthy of being elected[36]. What this group among the Massilians wished so vividly to convey was their refusal of the Augus-tinian discriminatory system according to which some were predestined to be counted among the elect (*eligendi*) and to be saved from the begin-ning of time, whilst others were destined for final rejection (*reiciendi*). In other words, they opposed a discrimination between those who,

30. See J. CHÉNÉ, *Le Semipélagianisme du Midi de la Gaule d'après les Lettres de Prosper d'Aquitaine et d'Hilaire à saint Augustin*, in *RSR* 43 (1955) 321-341.
31. Prosper, *Ep.* 225,1 (CSEL, 57), p. 455.
32. *Ibid.* 225,3, p. 457.
33. *Ibid.* 225,2, p. 455.
34. *Ibid.*
35. "Uniuersis tamen hominibus propitiationem, quae est in sacramento sanguinis Christi, sine exceptione esse propositam" (*Ibid.* 225,3, p. 457).
36. *Ibid.*

according to God's decision, will be *uasa honoris* or *uasa contumeliae*[37]. In the eyes of the Massilian monks a predestinarian doctrine such as this would inevitably lead to a sort of fatalism (*fatalem quandam necessitatem*)[38] which would deprive sinners of the hope of being saved and would make the elect's efforts superfluous. It would also enhance the belief that it was part of God's design to create human beings with different natures (and this is Manichaeism!). In fact, if every man's future has already been decided before his creation, and if man's will is preceded by God's *propositum* in such a way that he could never become anything different from what he has been created for, then there is no place for any commitment whatsoever[39]. These monks justified their standpoint by appealing to the tradition of the Church Fathers who, were they at pains to stress, had never interpreted as predestinarian the scriptural passage in question, viz. Rom 9,14-21[40].

Furthermore, according to Prosper, a second group existed among the Massilians, whose opinions seemed to link them very closely to Pelagianism[41]. They held as fact the Pelagian distinction between the grace of the Creator (*gratia Creatoris*) and the grace of Christ through which we are reborn and redeemed (*gratia qua in Christo renascimur*)[42]. They gave priority to the idea of a grace that belonged to the act of creation through which men, created as free rational beings with the capability of obeying God's commandments and distinguishing between good and evil, would eventually obtain the grace of regeneration through the blood of Christ. All this could be attained by man's natural efforts, enlightened by the good use of an initial grace (*initialis gratia*) bestowed on everyone at the moment of creation. Thus *petendo, quaerendo, pulsando*, he can obtain the redeeming grace of Christ (*saluans gratia*)[43]. As to the

37. *Ibid.* 225,3, pp. 457-458.
38. *Ibid.*, p. 458.
39. "Quoquo enim modo se egerint, non posse aliud erga eos, quam Deus definiuit, accidere..... Remoueri itaque omnem industriam tollique uirtutes, si Dei constitutio humanas praeueniat uolutates, et sub hoc praedestinationis nomine fatalem quandam induci necessitatem aut diuersarum naturarum dici Dominum conditorem, si nemo aliud possit esse, quam factus sit" (*Ibid.*).
40. "A nullo umquam ecclesiasticorum ita esse intellecta" (*Ibid.*, p. 459).
41. "In tantum a Pelagianis semitis non declinant" (*Ibid.* 225,4, p. 460).
42. *Ibid.*
43. "Ad condicionem hanc uelint uniuscuiusque hominis pertinere, in qua eum nihil prius merentem quia nec existentem liberi arbitrii et rationalem gratia creatoris instituat, ut per discretionem boni ac mali et ad cognitionem Dei et ad oboedientiam mandatorum eius possit suam dirigere uoluntatem atque ad hanc gratiam, qua in Christo renascimur, peruenire per naturalem scilicet facultatem petendo, quaerendo, pulsando, ut ideo accipiat, ideo inueniat, ideo introeat, quia bono naturae bene usus ad istam saluantem gratiam initialis gratiae ope meruerit peruenire" (*Ibid.*).

propositum through which God calls men to salvation through his grace (*uocans gratia*), they affirm that it concerns everyone. No one, in fact, is excluded from the gift of salvation which is offered to all, either through natural or written law, or by the preaching of the Gospel[44]. However, only those who are baptized are welcomed into God's kingdom, for only those who want to become (*qui uoluerint*) children of God will be saved. On the other hand, those who refuse to believe (*qui noluerint*) will be condemned for ever, for it is up to them to accept the offer of salvation given by God to everybody. The Massilians belonging to this second group referred, for verification, to several scriptural passages in which man is invited to make a choice, either by obeying God's saving will or by disobeying to it. Everyone, in fact, is imbued with the same power or impulse (*momentum*) to choose and ultimately to move either towards virtue or vice[45]. In addition to that, the explanation given by this second group of Massilians, as to why children, unbaptized and bereft of Christ's message at the time of death, should suffer perdition, is that God in his foreknowledge foresaw what they would eventually become had they reached the age of reason (and responsibility). In other words, because God foresees that some children (if they lived) would have made a bad use of their free will, He refuses them the sacrament of regeneration[46]. God's refusal of salvation to these infants depends, therefore, on

---

44. "Quod Deus constituerit nullum in regnum suum nisi per sacramentum regenerationis adsumere et ad hoc salutis donum omnes homines uniuersaliter siue per naturalem siue per scriptam legem siue per euangelicam praedicationem uocari" (*Ibid.*). We agree with Chéné's opinion in considering too hasty Prosper's conclusion that the second group of Massilians was crypto-Pelagian. In fact, despite a similar language, there are important divergencies between their affirmations and the Pelagian tenets. As Chéné writes: "L'assertion que les hommes sont invités au salut ou par la loi naturelle, ou par la Loi écrite, ou par l'Évangile, n'implique pas qu'ils aient pu, avant l'avènement de la Loi ou de l'Évangile se sauver *sans aucune foi*, par la seule droiture de leur conscience.... D'ailleurs, loi de nature ne s'oppose pas en ce texte à loi révélée, mais à loi écrite; et on peut croire que dans l'esprit de ces maîtres *[les Massilienses]*, cette loi naturelle comportait un certain contenu de révélation dérivant de la Révélation primitive, de sorte que l'adhésion qu'on y donnait n'était pas un act rationnel seulement, mais un acte de foi. Le contexte, loin de contredire cette interprétation, la confirmerait plutôt, puisque la phrase en question se termine par ces mots: 'ut et, qui uoluerint, fiant filii Dei et inexcusabiles sint, qui *fideles* esse noluerint'" (J. CHÉNÉ, *Notes complémentaires* [BA, 24], pp. 801-802).
45. "Quantum quisque ad malum tantum habeat facultatis ad bonum parique momento animum se uel ad uitia uel ad uirtutes mouere; quem bona appetentem gratia Dei foveat" (Prosper, *Ep.* 225,4 [CSEL, 57], p. 461). However, man's capability in taking the first step (by either obeying or disobeying the God who invites him to believe) does not imply, in the view of the Massilians, that human will is in itself sufficient to reach salvation. In fact, once man's desire is manifested and the first step taken in the direction of salvation, man feels the need of God's sustaining grace.
46. "Tales aiunt perdi talesque saluari, quales futuros illos in annis maioribus, si ad actiuam seruarentur aetatem, scientia diuina praeuiderit" (*Ibid.* 225,5, p. 461).

their hypothetical future demerits[47]. This assertion, too, is applied to those pagan peoples that have refused the preaching of the gospel (and in consequence of that, the admittance to salvation) by their unwillingness to believe and receive the sacrament of baptism[48]. In conclusion, these Massilians would affirm that God offers eternal life to all men, without exception, but leaves them the freedom of will to believe spontaneously in him and by doing so to receive by their own merit, namely through their own will and faith, the help of God's grace[49].

The view of this second group of Massilians is born of the uneasiness felt over the Augustinian doctrine of an absolutely gratuitous grace; a grace which precedes human effort and is already in place at the moment of man's creation. It is precisely this idea of grace that the monks of Marseilles could not accept. It was their conviction that the merit of the saints cannot be attributed solely to God's grace, and that the number of elect cannot be fixed beforehand either, because if that were the case, there would be no point in exhorting and encouraging either Christians or non-believers to further effort. And yet they all need exhortation and encouragement, because it is through their will and application (*diligentia*) that they are enabled to follow the divine commandments and to merit God's help. Two things are needed in order to obtain salvation: God's grace and man's obedience, although the latter, would they insist, precedes the former. Thus, the initiative in adhering to salvation (the *initium fidei*) depends on the one who wishes salvation, viz. man, and not on the One who has the power to actually save him, namely God. The decision for a life of faith and the desire for salvation begins with the human will. Only at a second stage man's will is granted the gift of saving grace; not that grace inspires and subdues human will from the very beginning[50]. After having summed up the somewhat controversial

47. "Sed in tantum quibuscumque commenticiis meritis electionem Dei subiciunt, ut, quia praeterita non extant, futura, quae non sint futura, confingant nouoque apud illos absurditatis genere et non agenda praescita sint et praescita non acta sint" (*Ibid.* 225,5, p. 462). This very strange hypothesis was not new. It had already been advanced by some Pelagians (cf. Augustine, *Ep.* 194,9,42 [CSEL, 57], pp. 209-210). The peculiarity of laying a "responsibility" upon someone to whom the grace of salvation has not been offered on account of a future refusal or abuse of it is also what makes this hypothesis unacceptable. Of course not all the Massilians were holding this explanation. In Hilary's letter, for instance, the problem of the salvation of unbaptized infants seems to be left open to a sort of intermediary solution (cf. Hilary, *Ep.* 226,8 [CSEL, 57], pp. 477-478).

48. Cf. Prosper, *Ep.* 225,5-6 (CSEL, 57), pp. 462-463.

49. "Quantum ad Deum pertinet, omnibus paratam uitam aeternam, quantum autem ad arbitrii libertatem, ab his eam adprehendi, qui Deo sponte crediderint et auxilium gratiae merito credulitatis acceperint" (*Ibid.* 225,6, p. 463).

50. "Cum duo sint, quae humanam operentur salutem, Dei scilicet gratia et hominis oboedientia, priorem uolunt oboedientiam esse quam gratiam, ut initium salutis ex eo, qui

ideas forwarded by both groups of Massilians, ideas in which he thinks some remains of the Pelagian errors can be detected[51], Prosper is confident in asking Augustine for clarification.

Hilary's letter, in its turn, informed Augustine of the theories on divine election and predestination held especially by the second group of Massilians; theories that seemed to be shared not only by the monks and clergy of Marseilles, but by other communities in Gaul also[52]. According to Hilary's report, they would agree on the fact that fallen man is unable to save himself by his own efforts, and yet they clung to the conviction that divine salvation (which is offered to all) does not become effective unless man is awakened to his capability of willing to be saved and of believing in this possibility. This awakening of man's will and faith (the *initium fidei*) is a kind of *conditio sine qua non* for obtaining the *augmentum fidei*, which leads to a real and complete salvation[53]. The Massilians' opinion was based on the Pauline text of Rom 10,9: *Crede, ut saluus eris*. They contended that, whereas the first part of the quotation (the imperative *crede*) points to faith as a required condition (*exigi*) in man, the second part (*ut saluus eris*) concerns salvation which is offered (*offerri*) as a consequence of his faith. Therefore, what is first asked of man is that he make his faith manifest. This is made possible by the fact that human nature has been created good, viz. capable of willing and

saluatur, non ex eo credendum sit stare, qui saluat, et uoluntas hominis diuinae gratiae sibi pariat opem, non gratia sibi humanam subiciat uoluntatem" (*Ibid.* 225,6, p. 464). Cf. also Id., *Ep. ad Rufinum* 7,8 (PL, 51), c. 82; Περὶ ἀχαρίστων sive *De ingratis* 2, 459-463 (PL, 51), c. 119. Prosper's description would lead us to believe that for the Massilians the *initium fidei* was completely independent of God's sovereign grace. Yet, the words "si originaliter malus receptionem boni non a summo Bono, sed a semetipso inchoare male creditur" (Id., *Ep.* 225,7 [CSEL, 57], p. 465) could also be interpreted in the light of the influence that divine grace exercises on every good action (including the *initium fidei*) without preventing, however, any good action being performed *naturaliter* (see *infra*, pp. 272-302 *passim*).

51. "In istis Pelagianae reliquiis prauitatis" (*Ibid.* 225,7, p. 465). The distinction between the two groups of Massilians is not apparent in Hilary's letter, nor in Augustine's reply to the two laymen of Provence, and does not reappear in Prosper's later writings. The controversy continues to focus on the question of the *initium fidei* (in the framework of the necessity of grace) and on the doctrine of predestination. Prosper himself, in his later writings, judges the position of the Massilians a *tertium quid*: "...ut nulla eorum quae excisa sunt, asserat, et quaedam ex his quae defensa sunt, respuat" (Id., *De gratia Dei et libero arbitrio liber contra Collatorem* 1,2 [PL, 51], c. 217). In his eyes such compromise could not be in full harmony either with the Pelagian nor with the Catholic view: "Nec cum haereticis tibi, nec cum catholicis plena concordia est" (*Ibid.* 3,1, c. 221).

52. Hilary, *Ep.* 226,2 (CSEL, 57), p. 469.

53. "Id conueniens adserunt ueritati uel congruum praedicationi, ut, cum prostratis et numquam suis uiribus surrecturis adnuntiatur obtinendae salutis occasio, eo merito, quo uoluerint et crediderint a suo morbo se posse sanari, et ipsius fidei augmentum et totius sanitatis suae consequantur effectum" (*Ibid.*).

believing. This capability has never been totally corrupted or extinguished (*deprauatam uel extinctam*) by the fall of the first man; on the contrary, even after Adam's fall, human nature has maintained this power to some degree. Thus, the grace of salvation has never been denied; it is simply believed to be preceded by man's desire and will to raise himself to the level of faith[54]. Besides which, another Pauline passage, viz. Rom 12,3 (*Sicut unicuique partitus est mensuram fidei*), is interpreted to mean that only the one who has started to will and to believe, will receive the divine help he needs for eventual salvation[55]. As to the question of predestination, it is quickly explained in terms of God's foreknowledge. What is noteworthy here, is that the Massilians did not simply refer to the witness of the Catholic Fathers only, but also to the works that Augustine wrote himself at the beginning of his pastoral ministry[56]. Relying upon these sources, they affirmed that grace is bestowed on man only when God is able to foresee his future commitment through faith. Thus, as a result, the gospel is preached to certain peoples only (and not to all men) and at a particular time (and not earlier), according to God's foreknowledge of how his word of salvation will be eventually received and welcomed[57]. In other words, the Massilians believed that divine foreknowledge and predestination should be understood in the sense that God knows in advance and predestines (by his eternal decree, *propositum*) all those who will eventually believe in

---

54. "Quod enim dicitur: *Crede et saluus eris*, unum horum exigi adserunt aliud offerri, ut propter id, quod exigitur, si redditum fuerit, id, quod offertur, deinceps tribuatur. unde consequens putant exhibendam ab eo fidem, cuius naturae id uoluntate conditoris concessum est, et nullam ita deprauatam uel extinctam putant, ut non debeat uel possit se uelle sanari" (*Ibid.* 226,2, pp. 469-470). "Nec negari gratiam, si praecedere dicatur talis uoluntas, quae tantum medicum quaerat, non autem quicquam ipsa iam valeat" (*Ibid.* 226,2, p. 470).

55. "Ut iuuetur, qui coeperit uelle" (*Ibid.*). The beginning of willing and believing (*initium fidei*) was conceived by the Massilians, in a very broad sense, as a synonym of the *initium salutis*. As Chéné has rightly endorsed, in holding man capable of making the first step towards faith "ils n'entendaient pas seulement la foi au sens de croyance, mais la foi-confiance dans les promesses du salut, et d'une manière plus générale, tout l'ensemble des dispositions religieuses qui naissent spontanément da la foi dans une âme ouverte à Dieu: prière, repentir ou commencement de repentir, crainte des jugements de Dieu, espérance de rénovation et de salut – toutes choses, précise la lettre d'Hilaire au même endroit (n. 2), qui n'entrent pas à proprement parler dans l'oeuvre de guérison, mais y préparent seulement. C'était dire que l'homme, malgré sa déchéance, est capable d'accomplir *tous les actes préparatoires à sa justification*" (J. CHÉNÉ, *Notes complémentaires* [BA, 24], p. 810).

56. Cf. *e.g.*, Augustine's *Expositio quarumdam propositionum ex epistula ad Romanos* (cit. in Hilary, *Ep.* 226,3 [CSEL, 57], pp. 471. 472; *Ibid.* 226,6, p. 475), and Augustine's *De libero arbitrio* (cit. in *Ibid.* 226,8, p. 477).

57. Cf. *Ibid.*, 226,3, pp. 470f.

him and be saved[58]. Likewise, final perseverance[59] is given only to those
who have made a good use of their free will, because it is up to man,
through his free will, to welcome or to refuse the remedy offered by
God. The grace of perseverance is, in fact, a gift that can be merited by
desire and prayer[60]. Moreover, continues Hilary, the Massilians did not
accept the division of mankind into two categories, nor did they believe
that, once this separation is established, nothing can be added or sub-
tracted. Unlike Augustine's view on predestination, they held that the
number of those who have been elected and those who have been condemned has not been fixed once and for all. This opinion, based on the
conviction that God wills the salvation of all mankind, explains the use
of both exhortations and reproof[61]. Finally, the Massilians disagreed
with Augustine's position on two other issues: one was the distinction,
made by the bishop of Hippo, between Adam's grace and the grace
accorded to all mankind after the fall of its forefather[62], and the other
was the fate of unbaptized children, who, according to Augustine, are
destined for eternal damnation.

In spite of some exaggeration in the way both Prosper and Hilary
depicted the Massilians' position, it is clear from their reports that the
defenders of Augustine were consistent in pointing out the main objections raised against the bishop of Hippo by the monks and clerics of
Provence[63]. Such objections were directed against Augustine's most rigid
doctrines, such as that of predestination and that of the limited dispensation of grace, both doctrines which, in their eyes, would dangerously

58. "Ceterum praescientiam et praedestinationem uel propositum ad id ualere con-
tendunt, ut eos praescierit uel praedestinauerit uel proposuerit eligere, qui fuerant credituri" (*Ibid.* 226,4, p. 472).

59. If gratuitous predestination, accomplished regardless of human efforts, is ultimately the crux of the matter in Prosper's letter, in Hilary's there is a specific reference
to the question of perseverance of which Augustine had spoken in his *De correptione et
gratia*.

60. "Nolunt autem ita hanc perseuerantiam praedicari, ut non uel suppliciter emereri
uel amitti contumaciter possit" (*Ibid.* 226,4, p. 473). Unlike Augustine, it seems that the
Massilians did not believe in unfailing perseverance. They did not consider it invincible
and it could indeed be lost, either because of man's laziness or because of his resistance
(*contumaciter*) to God. Besides, in their eyes, perseverance could not guarantee any
exemption from the failings of human frailty: "Nec cuiquam talem dari perseuerantiam,
a qua non permittatur praeuaricari, sed a qua possit sua uoluntate deficere et infirmari"
(*Ibid.*).

61. Cf. *Ibid.*, 226,5, p. 474; also 226,7, p. 476.

62. Cf. *Ibid.*, 226,6, p. 475.

63. "À supposer qu'en décrivant des doctrines que certainement ils détestaient, Prosper et Hilaire en aient exagéré ou durci certains traits, on n'admettrait pas sans une
extrême invraisemblance qu'ils en ont altéré la physionomie générale" (CHÉNÉ, *Introduction* to *Réponses d'Augustin aux moines de Provence* [n. 17], p. 389).

open the way to annihilation of man's free will and the improper restriction of universal salvation.

Moreover, the impact that Augustine's views had on the Massilians could not simply be reckoned on the level of abstract theological discussions. There were at least two important features of Christian life and faith that seemed threatened. First of all the legitimacy (particularly on the side of the monks) of an ascetic life, whereby the effort and the commitment of the will were regarded as constituting one of the main components of the quest of perfection. Secondly, the safeguarding of the authority of the Church's tradition whose inner continuity seemed to be undermined by the *nouum*[64] of Augustine's argumentation. As a matter of fact, the issue of "authority"[65], linked to that of "tradition"[66] (the latter being the *conditio sine qua non* of the former), comes to the fore at this point as one of the most significant keys of interpretation in the whole controversy in which the bishop of Hippo and the Massilians were involved. As we shall have the opportunity to stress[67], the authoritative Fathers held in particular consideration by the monks of Southern Gaul were not exactly those Augustine was referring to. Besides, much of the latter's theological thinking was the product of his own intellectual search, often enhanced under the pressure of disputes and polemics! So, although held in great esteem in the Western Church as a whole, including Gaul, Augustine was certainly not followed blindly when it came to some of the questions concerning grace and predestination[68]. On the other hand, Prosper and Hilary's appeal to Augustine's teaching and authority was an expression of their conviction that also the "new"

64. "Nouum et inutile esse praedicationi, quod quidam secundum propositum eligendi dicantur, ut id nec arripere ualeant nec tenere nisi credendi uoluntate donata" (Hilary, *Ep.* 226,2 [CSEL, 57], p. 469).

65. Augustine was pushed to a *redde rationem*, namely to give evidence that his views were in line with the authoritative teaching of the Church by and large: "Cui ego iam parum prodesse existimo te reddere rationem, nisi et addatur auctoritas" (cf. *Ibid.* 226,9, p. 479).

66. See, for instance: "Multi ergo seruuorum Christi, qui in Massiliensi urbe consistunt, in sanctitatis tuae scriptis quae aduersus Pelagianos haereticos condidisti, contrarium putant Patrum opinioni et ecclesiastico sensui quicquid in eis de uocatione electorum secundum Dei propositum disputasti" (Prosper, *Ep.* 225,2 [CSEL, 57], p. 455). Cf. also *Ibid.* 225,3 and 8, pp. 459 and 466.

67. See chs. III and IV, *passim*.

68. As Mathisen puts it: "Gaul's categorical rejection of one of Augustine's main teachings meant that Augustine never could have the status in Gaul of an unquestioned theological authority. This does not mean to say, however, that Augustine was not admired and respected" (R.W. MATHISEN, *For Specialists Only: The Reception of Augustine and His Teachings in Fifth-Century Gaul*, in G.T. LIENHARD – E.C. MULLER – R.J. TESKE [eds.], *Augustine. Presbyter Factus Sum*, New York, 1993, pp. 29-41, p. 34).

theories of the bishop of Hippo had to be regarded as being linked with the Church's tradition.

Furthermore, as well as the issue of the "authority" of the Church's tradition, Prosper and Hilary's appeal to Augustine also raised the issue of "institutional" authority. The fact that they had to defend the views of the bishop of Hippo before prominent figures, in both the monastic and ecclesiastical environments of Provence, was of no little significance for the outcome of the discussions that were going on within the local Church. We must assume that a reverential assent to the leading monks and clergymen of Southern Gaul, who professed their divergencies with Augustine regarding his concept of grace, was spontaneously elicited by their authority, an authority resting on either their sanctity (*e.g.*, Cassian and the monks of Southern Gaul) or rank (*e.g.*, Helladius of Arles), or both. No doubt, this state of affairs must have prompted Prosper and Hilary (at a disadvantage because of their "lay" status) to appeal to the authority of the bishop of Hippo in order to defend their own views[69].

2. The Centre of the Opposition to Augustine's Views on Grace: The Monastic Milieu of Southern Gaul

As we have seen, the reactions of the religious élite in Southern Gaul to Augustine's views on grace, simply voiced an uneasiness which was already present in differing degrees and which was originally triggered by the reading of *De correptione et gratia*. Surely, as Prosper and Hilary hinted at on several occasions, the Massilians' opposition must not have been totally immune to the influence of Pelagian ideas. The latter, we believe, must have penetrated, more easily than anywhere else, the monastic circles of the Western Christian Church. Although we do not possess a positive proof either of the extent and depth of the spread of the Pelagian ideas in the Northern regions of the Roman Empire, or of a hypothetical *lien historique*[70] between Pelagianism and the monastic

69. "Although a bishop, simply by virtue of his position, had authority as a teacher, Prosper respected the present occupant of the see of Arles as theologically knowledgable, and he understandably believed that Augustine could explain his own work far more convincingly to his episcopal counterpart than he himself could" (R.H. WEAVER, *Divine Grace and Human Agency. A Study of the Semi-Pelagian Controversy* [PatMS, 15], Macon, GA, 1996, p. 45).

70. With regard to a possible historical tie between Pelagianism and Massilianism, Solignac writes that "dans l'état actuel des recherches, on ne peut donner une réponse décisive à cette question" (A. SOLIGNAC, *Semipélagiens*, in *DSp* 14 [1990] 556-568, c. 557). Although it is certain that, after Pelagianism was condemned in 418, a number of bishops hesitated or openly refused to accept such condemnation, it is not clear to what extent Gaul, and especially Provence, were affected by such a reaction. This vagueness, together with the fact that none of the dissenting bishops sought refuge in Gaul, leads us

movement that was being shaped in Southern Gaul, we may surmise that some of Pelagius' writings (especially the more "monastic" in content, such as the aforementioned *Epistula ad Demetriadem*) must have been known to the monks of Provence[71].

That the main opposition came from the monastic community of Marseilles is inferred from Prosper's letter, in which he speaks specifically of *multi seruorum Christi, qui in Massiliensi urbe consistunt*[72]. These "servants", without any doubt, are to be identified with the monks of the monastery of St. Victor, founded in ca. 415/416 in Marseilles by John Cassian[73]. Because of his ascetic and virtuous life, he was a man of outstanding spiritual authority, which is probably why Prosper does not expressly mention him in his letter as the coryphaeus of the anti-Augustinian party. His influence was great and far reaching and the esteem, in

---

to conclude that the Rescript of Valentinian III issued on the 9th July 425 against the bishops who still sided with Pelagian errors ("Diversos vero episcopos nefarium Pelagiani et Caelestiniani dogmatis errorem sequentes": *Constitutio VII Valentiniani* [PL, 48], cc. 410-411) and addressed to Amatius, prefect of the *praetorium* of Gaul, should be taken cautiously. De Plinval remarks that Valentinian's rescript was probably intended to be an official and authoritative intervention directed at consolidating the integrity of the faith rather than chasing out possible "Pelagian bishops". By that time, in fact, the Pelagian movement no longer constituted a genuine threat (see G. DE PLINVAL, *Pélage, ses écrits, sa vie et sa réforme. Étude d'histoire littéraire et religieuse*, Lausanne, 1943, p. 348). It has also been suggested that the imperial intervention may have been dictated by the fact that, in some minds, a connection between the doctrines of Pelagius and the opinions of the Massilians had already been made, and that there was sufficient ground to justify the fear of the Pelagian spectre, at least on the part of the pope and of the emperor (cf. P.J. CAREFOOTE, *Augustine, the Pelagians and the Papacy: An Examination of the Political and Theological Implications of Papal Involvement in the Pelagian Controversy* [unpublished doctoral dissertation, K.U. Leuven], 2 Vols., Louvain, 1995, p. 312). However intriguing such a hypothesis may be, we should hesitate in adopting it, on the ground that the discussion between the Massilians on one side and Augustine and his supporters on the other only came into the open in 427, independently of the Pelagian controversy (see *supra*, Introduction). Maybe Valentinian's rescript should indeed "be considered a preemptive strike, rather than reactionary" (*Ibid.*, p. 313).

71. "D'autre part, les moines provençaux disposaient d'une information indirecte sur les doctrines pélagiennes par les oeuvres d'Augustin, dont ils possédaient les plus importantes" (SOLIGNAC, *Semipélagiens* [n. 70], c. 557). An indirect admission that the works of Augustine were read in Provence can be found in the letter of Prosper. In speaking of Helladius bishop of Arles, he writes: "...sanctum Helladium, Arelatensem episcopum,... admiratorem sectatoremque in aliis omnibus tuae esse doctrinae..." (Prosper, *Ep.* 225,9 [CSEL, 57], p. 467).

72. *Ibid.* 225,2, p. 455

73. According to Wermelinger, western reaction to some of Augustine's expressions coincided with the arrival of Cassian in Marseilles: "Diese antiaugustinische Bewegung kann im südlichen Gallien bis in den Pontifikat des Zosimus zurückverfolgt werden und fällt vielleicht mit der Ankunft des Cassian in Marseille zusammen" (O. WERMELINGER, *Rom und Pelagius. Die theologische Position der römischen Bischöfe im pelagianischen Streit in der Jahren 411-432* (PuP, 7), Stuttgart, 1975, p. 245).

which he was held, so high that a direct attack on Cassian would have
been regarded as particularly unpleasant and distasteful. Hilary, for his
part, told Augustine that the opposition to his views on grace had spread
also outside Marseilles: *Haec sunt itaque, quae Massiliae uel etiam
aliquibus locis in Gallia uentilantur*[74]. We can conclude, therefore, that
besides Marseilles, other monasteries in Provence, especially along the
Mediterranean coast, were involved. Among them was the monastic settlement which would eventually become very famous: the monastery of
Lérins. Like Marseilles, Lérins was a *foyer* of opposition to the Augustinian view of grace[75]; an opposition which would continue through the
activity of those monks who would be chosen to become bishops in the
various dioceses of Southern Gaul[76]. For this reason, it is important, at
this stage, to recall the substratum of the two monastic settlements of
Lérins and Marseilles. It was in these communities, in fact, that reaction
to Augustine's doctrine of grace was engendered, and it was in the fertile soil of these communities, and in their local Churches, that such a
reaction continued to gain shape and find support. Thus, it is only after
having sketched the features of Gallic monasticism, that we will be able
to focus on Cassian's work, which constitutes, as it were, *la tête du pont*
of the anti-Augustinian position in Gaul.

a) The Development of Monasticism in Gaul

J.M. Besse has often underlined, in his systematic history of ancient
monastic France, the impossibility of reconstructing a unitary vision of
the birth and development of Gallic monasticism. The variety of forms
which gave it shape and the lack of data in the field of the *événementiel*,
preclude a thorough investigation into early monasticism in Gaul[77]. In

74. Hilary, *Ep.* 226,2 (CSEL, 57), p. 469.
75. Lérins was second only to Marseilles as a stronghold of resistance to Augustine's
inflexible doctrine of grace. Cf. CHÉNÉ, *Les origines de la controverse sémi-pelagienne*
(n. 1), p. 108.
76. "Presque toute la promotion d'évêques qui s'était instruite à Lérins, et qui, de 430
à 480, occupera les chaires du midi de la Gaule, avait été formée dans un esprit de
défiance à l'égard de l'augustinisme" (G. DE PLINVAL, *L'activité doctrinale dans l'Église
gallo-romaine*, in A. FLICHE – V. MARTIN [eds.], *Histoire de l'Église*. T. IV: *De la mort
de Théodose à l'élection de Grégoire le Grand*, Paris, 1937, p. 400).
77. J.-M. BESSE, *Les moines de l'ancienne France (Période Gallo-Romaine et
Mérovingienne)* (AFM, 2), Paris, 1906, pp. 1ff. See also C. COURTOIS, *L'évolution du
monachisme en Gaule de St Martin à St Colomban*, in *Il Monachesimo nell'Alto Medioevo
e la formazione della civiltà occidentale* (SSAM, 4), Spoleto, 1957, pp. 47-72; F. PRINZ,
*Frühes Mönchtum im Frankenreich. Kultur und Gesellschaft in Gallien, den Rheinlanden
und Bayern am Beispiel der monastischen Entwicklung (4. bis 8. Jahrhundert)*, München,
1965; R. LORENZ, *Die Anfänge des abendländischen Mönchtums im 4. Jahrhundert*,
in *ZKG* 77 (1966) 1-61, pp. 12-18; É. GRIFFE, *La Gaule chrétienne*. T. III: *La cité*

spite of a shortage of concrete facts, however, one thing is certain, namely the fact that despite the regular contact existing during the 4th century between the Churches of the Eastern and Western part of the Roman Empire, the ascetic/monastic ideals of Egypt and Palestine did not exercise great influence in the ecclesiastical milieux of Gaul. On the contrary, such influence was rather negligible in the beginning, and it spread relatively slowly, probably because of the effective and strongly structured Church life in this part of the Roman Empire[78]. A looser form of monasticism made its appearance with Martin of Tours (316/17–397)[79]. A remarkable ascetic, he was undoubtedly the first great, conscious propagator of this way of life. Initially, he embraced monastic life as a hermit, at first somewhere in the surrounding area of Milan and then on the island of Gallinaria off the Ligurian coast[80]. Only after having reached Gaul, in the second half of the 4th century, did he finally establish a cenobitic form of monastic life at Ligugé and Marmoutier, respectively, in the regions of Poitiers and Tours[81]. However,

chrétienne, Paris, 1965, pp. 299-352; G.M. COLOMBAS, El monacato primitivo, T. I (BAC, 351), Madrid, 1974, pp. 237-249; S. PRICOCO, Il monachesimo occidentale dalle origini al Maestro. Lineamenti storici e percorsi storiografici, in Il monachesimo occidentale dalle origini alla Regula Magistri. XXVI Incontro di studiosi dell'antichità cristiana, Roma, 8-10 maggio 1997 (SEA, 62), Rome, 1998, pp. 7-22.

78. BESSE, Les moines de l'ancienne France (n. 77), p. 35. "It is possibly because of the strength of the classical tradition, and the effectiveness of Church life in this area that monasticism was relatively late in obtaining an important position. We have no clear evidence of organized monasticism in southern Gaul before the fifth century" (N.K. CHADWICK, Poetry and Letters in Early Christian Gaul, London, 1955, p. 142).

79. Even though it is with Martin that "beginnt in Gallien die Geschichte des Mönchtums" (PRINZ, Frühes Mönchtum im Frankenreich [n. 77], p. 19; see also L. PIETRI, Martin von Tours, in TRE 22 [1992] 194-196), the monasticism he encouraged "gives no impression of an elaborate organized economy, or regular discipline, and his monastery left no permanent monastic tradition" (CHADWICK, Poetry and Letters in Early Christian Gaul [n. 78], p. 143).

80. Cf. Sulpicius Severus, Vita Martini 6,4-5, T. I (SC, 133), Paris, 1967, p. 266.

81. Cf. É. GRIFFE, Saint Martin et le monachisme gaulois, in Saint Martin et son temps. Mémorial du XVIe centenaire des débuts du monachisme en Gaule, 361-1961 (StAns, 46), Rome, 1961, pp. 3-24. The foundation near Poitiers owes much to Hilary, the bishop of that city. After an exile of five years in Phrygia, he had returned to Gaul, not only more conversant in Greek theology (which he would transmit to the West), but also permeated with the ascetic and monastic ideals he came into contact with. Although it seems that Hilary's personal inclination towards such ideals was already present before his exile, the direct acquaintance he made with monasticism while in Asia Minor must have positively influenced his decision to allow Martin to start a monastic community at Ligugé, near Poitiers (cf. Sulpicius Severus, Vita Martini 7,1, T. I (SC, 133), p. 266; J. DOIGNON, Hilaire de Poitiers avant l'exil, Paris, 1971, pp. 380-384). As to the existence of a Christian Gallic asceticism that might have influenced and shaped the form of monasticism inaugurated by Martin, see J. FONTAINE, L'ascétisme chrétien dans la litterature gallo-romaine d'Hilaire à Cassien, in Atti del Colloquio sulla Gallia Romana. Accademia Nazionale dei Lincei, Roma 10-11 maggio 1971, Rome, 1973, pp. 87-115.

apart from this high profile monk-missionary figure, who was committed to the evangelization of a countryside still very much under the influence of paganism[82], we must wait until the first decades of the 5th century to find any decisive spread in monastic ideals. This spread was brought about, to some extent, by the pressure of barbaric invasion[83], and found its outcome in several foundations in Southern Gaul[84]. It is no

Furthermore, it is worth noticing that Sulpicius Severus' *Vita Martini* depicts Martin as having always lived an ascetic life, whether he was involved in the organization of monastic communities or served as a bishop, in the government of the Church of Tours. According to his biographer, Martin's inner life never ceased to be ascetic in character, and he was able to keep this attitude in his day-to-day episcopal commitments ("Idem enim constantissime perseuerabat qui prius fuerat ": Sulpicius Severus, *Vita* Martini 10 [SC, 133], T. I, p. 272). The consistency of his asceticism and its interaction with his pastoral life has been recalled by Martin's biographer with a terminology borrowed from the desert Fathers. Like the virtuous monks of the desert Martin stands out for his humility, poverty, fasting, penitence, prayer and love for solitude (cf. *Ibid.* 10, pp. 272.274). Beside both the literary style (*e.g.*, the stress on the ideal of *constantia*, a recurrent feature in classical biography) and the underlying apologetical intention of Sulpicius who had to explain to his readers why Martin was engaged in pastoral activity (cf. J. FONTAINE, *Commentaire*, in Sulpicius Severus, *Vita Martini*, T. II [SC, 134], Paris, 1968, pp. 661-663), the point was clearly made about him having remained an ascetic interiorly and exteriorly alike (see P. ROUSSEAU, *Ascetics, Authority, and the Church in the Age of Jerome and Cassian*, Oxford, 1978, pp. 148-151). Finally, it has been suggested that Martin's voluntary ascetic life, which was so much in contrast with the ostentation and privileges of the bishops descended from the local Gallo-Roman aristocracy, brought about a confrontation between the two types of Gallic bishops. There were those who, through their position of authority, considered themselves the guardians of Gallo-Roman ideals, and those whose self-identity and authority was instead based on their asceticism and on their quest of holiness. Martin is portrayed by his biographer as the ideal model of a succesful symbiosis of monastic life together with the role and the task of bishop (see J. GEARY, *Before France and Germany: the Creation and Transformation of the Merovingian World*, Oxford, 1988, pp. 140-143).

82. "Martin war mehr praktischer Christ, Missionar und Tempelzerstörer" (PRINZ, *Frühes Mönchtum im Frankenreich* [n. 77], p. 94, n. 28).

83. While other provinces in the Roman Empire were overrun by barbarian hordes and the Rhine frontiers shattered, Provence remained fairly safe, "the one retreat – as Salvian writes emphatically – that still lives in a dead Roman commonwealth" (paraphrase of *De gubernatione* 4,6,30 [SC, 220], p. 254: "Cum Romana respublica uel iam mortua, uel certe extremum spiritum agens"). Many people migrated from Northern and Central Gaul to the South in search of a secure and peaceful haven. But many also came from other parts of the Roman Empire: "When the Visigothic leader Alaric sacked Rome in 410 – writes O. Chadwick –, many prominent men fled to Provence" (O. CHADWICK [ed.], *Western Asceticism. Selected Translations with Introductions and Notes* [The Library of Christian Classics, XII], London, 1958, p. 190).

84. The pressure of barbaric invasion was not extraneous to the growth of the ascetic/monastic phenomenon. Such a "menace not only increased the population of the south [*of Gaul*], but provided an apocalyptic background to the growth of the monastic movement" (O. CHADWICK, *John Cassian. A Study in Primitive Monasticism*, 2nd ed., Cambridge, 1968, p. 34). The dislocation of so many people, especially from Northern and Central Gaul, also contributed to a concentration in the south and a considerable amount of human intellectual potential. There were those from the Gallic aristocracy who

exaggeration to say that among these foundations, those of Lérins and St. Victor of Marseilles were so outstanding that the Gallic monasticism of the 5th century has to be identified with the history of these two coenobiums, and only partly with that of the monastic settlement in the Jura[85].

b) Lérins

The monastic community of Lérins[86] was founded some time between 400 and 410[87] by Honoratus who settled on the island with his friend Caprasius and some other companions who, desiring a life of perfection, entrusted themselves to his direction. The solitude and *insularis relegatio*, which of itself would accentuate the *fuga mundi*, constituted an

had suffered a sudden loss of riches and who were now looking for a new meaning to life, often attracted by the strong appeal that the monastic call exercised on their minds (cf. FONTAINE, *L'ascétisme chrétien dans la litterature gallo-romaine d'Hilaire à Cassien* [n. 81], pp. 89, 106). Thus, beside those members of the aristocracy who considered monastic life a repudiation, not only of the privileges inherent to their status, but also of traditional Roman values, there were some among them who found that the monastic ideal represented, in its Christianized form, a way of life akin to the classical/philosophical ideal of *otium*. There is no doubt that the input into Gallic monasticism of well educated and refined aristocrats added some sophistication to the monastic environment, and must have set the conditions for the increasing appeal of monastic ideals to the élite of Western society (cf. J. FONTAINE, *L'aristocratie occidentale devant le monachisme aux IVème et Vème siècles*, in *RSLR* 15 [1979] 28-53).

85. Cf. J. BIARNE, *Moines et rigoristes en Occident*, in J.-M. MAYEUR, *et al.* (eds.), *Histoire du Christianisme des origines à nos jours*. T. II: *Naissance d'une Chrétienté (250-430)*, Paris, 1995, p. 763.

86. Lérins, today Île Saint-Honorat, was called *Lerina* or *Lerinus* (cf. Plinius Secundus, *Historia naturalis* 3,79 [ed. MAYHOFF, p. 263]) or *Planasia*, because of its flatness (cf. Strabo, *Geographica* 4,1,10 [ed. MEINEKE, p. 251]). Lérins is the smallest of the two islands forming the small archipelago off the French coast near Cannes. The other island, today Île Saint-Marguerite, was called *Lero* (cf. Plinius Secundus, *Historia naturalis* 3,79, p. 263) and it was home only to a few anchorites, the most famous of which was Eucherius, a monk of Lérins and the future bishop of Lyon. For information on the monastic settlement of Lérins see above all: PRICOCO, *L'isola dei santi* (n. 11); GRIFFE, *La Gaule chrétienne*, T. III (n. 77), pp. 332-341; PRINZ, *Frühes Mönchtum im Frankenreich* (n. 77), pp. 47-87; M.-B. BRARD, *Lérins*, in *Cath* 7 (1975) 435-437; COURTOIS, *L'évolution du monachisme en Gaule de St Martin à St Colomban* (n. 77); J.S. ALEXANDER, *Lérins*, in *TRE* 21 (1991) 10-16; R. NOUAILHAT, *Saints et Patrons. Les premiers moines de Lérins*, Paris, 1988; R. NÜRNBERG, *Askese als sozialer Impuls. Monastisch-asketische Spiritualität als Wurzel und Triebfeder sozialer Ideen und Aktivitaten der Kirche in Sudgallien im 5. Jahrhundert*, Bonn, 1988; C.M. KASPER, *Theologie und Askese. Die Spiritualität des Inselmönchtums von Lérins im 5. Jahrhundert* (BGAM, 40), Münster, 1991.

87. There is no certainty among modern scholars as to the exact date of the foundation, although they seem to agree with the suggestion already advanced by Tillemont who dated the beginning of the monastic life on the island between 400 and 410 (cf. L.-S. LENAIN DE TILLEMONT, *Mémoires pour servir à l'histoire ecclésiastique des six premiers siècles*, T. XII, Paris, 1701, pp. 675f).

excellent milieu for a monastic undertaking that aimed at fully concentrating on the *quaerere Deum*, and was certainly not an unusual feature in Western monasticism, both in its anchoretic and cenobitic form[88]. Martin of Tours himself, as mentioned above, spent some time as a hermit on Gallinaria, an island off the Ligurian coast. On the island of Hyères (*Stoechades*) there were several monastic communities which were on friendly terms with John Cassian[89]. A letter from Jerome exalts the life of his friend Bonosus who retired to a desert island[90], and another letter tells of islands in the Tyrrhenian sea (*Etruscum mare*) inhabited by groups of monks (*monachorum chori*) who were frequently helped by the generosity of the noblewoman Fabiola[91]. At Capraria, an island between Corsica and the Italian coast, there existed a monastic community to which Augustine addressed a strong letter calling the monks to faithfully live up to the demands of their particular vocation[92].

88. See the lyrical way in which Ambrose of Milan speaks of the monks' preference for the deep solitude of the islands: "Quid enumerem insulas, quas uelut monilia plerumque praetexit, in quibus ii qui se abdicant intemperantiae saecularis inlecebris fido continentiae proposito eligunt mundo latere, et uitae huius declinare dubios anfractus? Mare est ergo secretum temperantiae, exercitium continentiae, graiitatis secessus, portus securitatis, tranquillitas saeculi, huius mundi sobrietas, tum fidelibus uiris atque deuotis incentiuum deuotionis, ut cum undarum leniter adluentium sono certent cantus psallentium, plaudant insulae tranquillo fluctuum sanctorum choro, hymnis sanctorum personent" (Ambrose, *Hexameron* 3,5,23 [CSEL, 32/1], pp. 74-75). There were however quite down-to-earth reasons for choosing an island: "Per l'insicurezza causata dall'anarchia imperiale e dalle conseguenti invasioni barbariche le isole parevano offrire un asilo più ospitale e tranquillo" (G. PENCO, *Storia del monachesimo in Italia dalle origini alla fine del Medio Evo*, Rome, 1961, p. 21).

89. Cassian would, in fact, dedicate his last seven *Conlationes* to them: "Ad sanctos qui in Stoechadibus consistunt insulis" (Cassian, *Conlatio* 11, *Praefatio* [SC, 54], p. 99). These same monks, continues Cassian, have caused the islands to flourish by attracting many other brothers to the *monastica conuersatio*: "Insulas maximis fratrum cateruis fecistis florere" (*Ibid.* 18, *Praefatio* [SC, 64], p. 9).

90. "(Bonosus)...contempta matre, sororibus et carissimo sibi germano, insulam pelago circumsonante nauifragam, cui asperae cautes et nuda saxa et solitudo terrori est, quasi quidam nouus paradisi colonus insedit" (Jerome, *Ep.* 3,4 [CSEL, 54], pp. 15f). See C. and L. PIETRI (eds.), *Bonosus 1*, in *Prosopographie chrétienne du Bas-Empire. 2. Prosopographie de l'Italie chrétienne (313-604)*, Vol. I: *A-K*, Rome, 1999, p. 344.

91. Cf. Jerome, *Ep.* 77,6,5 (CSEL, 55), p. 44.

92. Augustine, *Ep.* 48 (CSEL, 34), pp. 137-140. Unlike Augustine, Orosius speaks highly of these monks, with terms of great esteem: cf. Orosius, *Historiarum aduersum paganos* 7,36,5 (CSEL, 5), p. 534. The monks of Capraria were, on the contrary, contemptuously described by the pagan Gallic poet Rutilius Namatianus as *lucifugi uiri*: "Squalet lucifugis insula plena uiris" (Rutilius Namatianus, *De reditu suo sive Iter Gallicum* 1,440 [ed. DOBLHOFER, p. 120]). See also P. DE LABRIOLLE, *Rutilius Namatianus et les Moines*, in *REL* 6 (1928) 30-41; L. GOUGAUD, *Les critiques formulées contre les premiers moines d'Occident*, in *RMab* 24 (1934) 145-163. Namatianus thought one of his friends, who had established himself on the Island of Gorgona, off the Tuscan coast, an *exul* who had embraced a *turpem latebram* (Rutilius Namatianus, *De reditu suo sive Iter Gallicum* 1,515-526, p. 128).

The choice of the island of Lérins was therefore not a casual one. It met the desire of Honoratus and his friends who longed to set themselves apart from the world in an isolated place where they could fully devote themselves to the quest for God. At the same time, it was a choice perfectly in line with the canons of the monastic life led in the deserts of Egypt or Palestine, which Honoratus took as his model[93]. In point of fact, it was the longing to conform to the example of the desert Fathers[94] that had pushed Honoratus, his friend Caprasius and their other companions, to eventually establish themselves in the solitude of Lérins[95]. There, Honoratus acted as superior of the monastic community until his election to the see of Arles (end of 427/beginning of 428). When he died at the beginning of 430, he was succeded by his young relative and future biographer, Hilary.

Monastic life at Lérins must have been mixed: although cenobitic in character, it was open to the possibility of an eremitical way of life that could be fully embraced and lived out in the surrounding areas of the monastery[96]. The debate as to whether there was a written rule for the community of Lérins continues without a definitive conclusion. Some scholars still believe that rather than a rule *stricto sensu*, the monks of Lérins must have followed some *consuetudines*, modelled on the

93. According to Hilary of Arles, Honoratus had attempted to visit the desert Fathers together with his brother Venantius and his friend Caprasius, but the goal was never reached. The *peregrinatio* was first stranded off the coast of Greece and then came to a definitive standstill after the death of Venantius (cf. Hilary of Arles, *Sermo de uita S. Honorati Arelatensis episcopi* 11-15 [SC, 235], pp. 96-110). Lérins – writes Prinz – "erwies sich als eine Art 'Relaisstation' für den Einfluß des monastischen Orientis" (PRINZ, *Frühes Mönchtum im Frankenreich* [n. 77], p. 94). Moreover, "die Anwesenheit Cassians in Marseille und seine enge Verbindung mit Lerinum verbürgt den Einfluß des Orients in diesem Kloster" (*Ibid.*, p. 95). See also *Ibid.* pp. 90-101 *passim*.

94. "La vie des moines orientaux était alors, autant et plus qu'elle l'a jamais été, le type sur lequel les moines de partout cherchaient à modeler leur existence" (BESSE, *Les moines de l'ancienne France* [n 77], p. 47). In the second series of the *Conlationes*, dedicated to Honoratus and Eucherius, the first is described by Cassian as wanting to form his community on the school of the Fathers of monastic life: "Illorum quoque patrum praeceptis optet institui" (Cassian, *Conlatio* 11, *Praefatio* [SC, 54], p. 97). Later on Sidonius Apollinaris would write that the monks of Lérins followed the tradition of the "Memphiticos et Palaestinos archimandritas" (Sidonius Apollinaris, *Ep.* 8,14 [PL, 58], c. 612).

95. Probably the choice of this particular island was also motivated by the friendly ties existing between Honoratus and Leontius, bishop of the neighbouring Fréjus (Cf. Hilary of Arles, *Sermo de uita S. Honorati Arelatensis episcopi* 15,2 [SC, 235], p. 108).

96. "Hallamos en Lérins una combinación de cenobitismo y eremitismo que recuerda la organización de las lauras de Palestina. Los monjes jóvenes vivían en comunidad; los adultos y bien probados, en celdas individuales separadas entre sí. Pero, en realidad, dominaba el cenobitismo" (COLOMBAS, *El monacato primitivo*, T. I [n. 77], pp. 255-256).

fervent, austere and disciplined life of the eastern monks[97]. The majority
of scholars, however, postulate the existence of a written rule which has
now been lost[98], though this conviction is not unanimously shared[99]. For
instance, de Vogüé, in a critical edition of the so-called *Regulae Sanctorum Patrum*, suggests that the rule followed at Lérins should be identified with this enigmatic set of rules[100].

97. "Nous ne possedons pas le texte de la règle de Lérins. On peut même se demander si l'auteur s'est donné la peine de la rédiger. Il a dû se contenter d'un enseignement
oral et de cet autre enseignement plus efficace, qui réalise une doctrine dans l'organisation stable d'une communauté religieuse" (BESSE, *Les moines de l'ancienne France*
[n. 77], p. 48). See BRARD, *Lérins* (n. 86), c. 436; PRICOCO, *L'isola dei santi* (n. 11),
pp. 77ff; ALEXANDER, *Lérins* (n. 86), pp. 11f.
98. "Die Regel von Lérins ist nicht überliefert; daß sie existierte, wird durch zeit-
genössische Quellen bezeugt. Wahrscheinlich wurde sie im Kloster mündlich tradiert"
(PRINZ, *Frühes Mönchtum im Frankenreich* [n. 77], p. 95; cf. *Ibid.*, pp. 69f. and 72). See
also COURTOIS, *L'évolution du monachisme en Gaule de St Martin à St Colomban* (n. 77),
pp. 58 and 64f.; G. PENCO, *Il concetto di monaco e di vita monastica in Occidente nel sec.
VI*, in *StMon* 1 (1959) 7-50, p. 43. Some were led to believe that there was a written rule
at Lérins, on the evidence of the words of the *Institutio* of the 3rd council of Arles
(between 449 and 461): "Regulae quae a fundatore ipsius monasterii dudum constituta
est in omnibus custodita" (*Concilia Galliae A. 314-A. 506* [CCL, 148], p. 134).
99. See, for instance, ALEXANDER, *Lérins* (n. 86), pp. 11f.
100. Cf. *Regulae SS. Patrum* (SC, 297-298); especially SC, 297, pp. 10-11, 22-26,
125, 155. "La fondation du monastère de Lérins semble avoir donné lieu à la rédaction
d'un écrit volontairement énigmatique: la 'Règle des saints Pères Sérapion, Macaire,
Paphnuce et l'autre Macaire'.... Si, comme nous le pensons, il représente la législation
primitive de Lérins, on peut y voir le point de rencontre des deux séries de règles monastiques.... Par son apparence orientale, il se place dans le prolongement de la Règle
basilienne traduite par Rufin et de la Règle pachômienne traduite par Jérôme, tandis que
son origine probablement latine l'apparente à l'*Ordo monasterii* augustinien et au *Praeceptum* d'Augustin" (A. DE VOGÜÉ, *Histoire littéraire du mouvement monastique dans
l'antiquité*. T. V: *Le monachisme latin. De l'épitaphe de sainte Paule à la consécration
de Démétriade [404-414]*, Paris, 1998, p. 55); cf. ID., *Il monachesimo prima di San
Benedetto* (Orizzonti Monastici, 18), Seregno/Milan, 1998, pp. 51-64. The characteristic
pattern of the Rules handed down under the name *Regulae Sanctorum Patrum* is that they
appear to be strictly related to one another. De Vogüé has, in fact, demonstrated that they
belong to the same lineage and form a clearly recognizable family whereby each rule
engenders the other in succession. His analysis has also shown that their content recalls
the Lérinian environment. According to the Benedictine scholar, the first rule, the *Regula
Quattuor Patrum* (= RQP) goes back to the first decade of the 5th century, namely to the
beginning of the foundation of Lérins. The *Secunda Regula Patrum* (= 2RP) should be
regarded as an updated text composed at the time of Honoratus' election to the see of
Arles, with the goal of responding to the new needs of the growing community. The *Regula Macharii* and the *Regula orientalis* were composed at the end of the 5th century,
whereas the *Tertia Regula Patrum* (= 3RP) is due (as an aside) to the work of the Council of Clermont of 535. The three rules, the RQP, the 2RP and the 3RP, also share the
same form. They are minutes or deliberations of gatherings of the abbots in charge of
communities still developing a fully cenobitic life style. From this we gather that the
monastic community of Lérins did not simply rely on a set of *consuetudines*, nor did it
provide a "once-and-for-all" and thoroughly "thought out" rule. It is most likely, in fact,
that "the purpose of these abbatial synods was not to provide complete monastic rules,

Lérins soon became a very renowned and influential religious centre[101]. Not only was it the place where a community of holy monks lived their confined life, but it also became the nursery of a long line of scholars and bishops[102]. Most important, is the fact that the intellectual formation of its members was seen as a service to "theological life" rather than a simple "theological thought process". Put another way, the *monastica congregatio* of Lérins was not so much an *école de lettres* as an *école de théologie monastique*[103] where theological learning was ancillary to asceticism[104]. Undoubtedly, those who joined the monastery having already received a high education[105], could take advantage of the learned atmosphere to increase their theological formation, but their ideal, as for all at Lérins, was the wisdom of the divine service to which they had entirely devoted themselves. Eucherius' writings, the *De contemptu mundi* and the *De laude eremi*, are very eloquent on this matter,

---

but rather to frame partial regulations, directed by immediate experience and necessity" (C.V. FRANKLIN – I. HAVENER – J.A. FRANCIS [eds.], *Introduction*, in *Early Monastic Rules. The Rules of the Fathers and the Regula Orientalis*, Collegeville, 1982, p. 9). Finally, as de Vogüé points out, the *Regulae Sanctorum Patrum* seem to be "à quelques années de distance, la réponse du monachisme de la Gaule à celui de l'Afrique. C'est dire l'intérêt peu commun d'un texte qui nous fait assister à l'éclosion de la vie cénobitique en Provence" (DE VOGÜÉ, *Histoire littéraire du mouvement monastique dans l'antiquité*. T. V [n. 100], p. 55). This view is also shared by Pricoco who writes: "Queste regole attesterebbero il grande ruolo avuto dal modello lerinese nello sviluppo del primo cenobitismo europeo e colmerebbero il fossato di circa un secolo e mezzo che intercorre tra la legislazione che all'Occidente arriva dall'Oriente, dall'Egitto, dalla Numidia di Agostino e le grandi regole del VI secolo" (PRICOCO, *Il monachesimo occidentale dalle origini al Maestro* [n. 77], p. 12).

101. For Lérins' influence see: COURTOIS, *L'évolution du monachisme en Gaule de St Martin à St Colomban* (n. 77), pp. 57ff.; J. FONTAINE, *France. I. Antiquité chrétienne*, in *DSp* 5 (1964) 785-805, cc. 797-805.

102. "Lérins... fut pour une grande partie de la Gaule, une véritable pépinière d'évêques et de saints" (L. DUCHESNE, *Histoire ancienne de l'Église*. T. III, 3rd ed., Paris, 1910, p. 272). Among the most prominent scholars (most of whom became also bishops) must be mentioned: Hilary bishop of Arles (403-449), Vincent (the author of the *Commonitorium*, who died between 435-450), Lupus bishop of Troyes (395-479), Faustus bishop of Riez (ca. 408-ca. 490), Caesarius bishop of Arles (ca. 470-542). See CHADWICK, *Poetry and Letters in Early Christian Gaul* (n. 78), pp. 142-169.

103. BRARD, *Lérins* (n. 86), c. 436; see also KASPER, *Theologie und Askese* (n. 86), pp. 181ff.

104. "Una escuela de ascetismo" (COLOMBAS, *El monacato primitivo*, T. I [N. 77], p. 258). See also KASPER, *Theologie und Askese* (n. 86), pp. 181ff. The same applies, as we shall see, to Cassian's monastic foundation at Marseilles.

105. It should be noted that the celebrated Lérinian writers (Vincent, Hilary, Maximus, Faustus, Lupus, Eucherius, Salvian and Caesarius) were monks who had received their classical formation before joining the monastery. It is remarkable that all of them (with the exception of the most famous one, Vincent, the writer of the *Commonitorium*) wrote their works while they were engaged as bishops in the different episcopal sees of Gaul (see COLOMBAS, *El monacato primitivo*, T. I [n. 77], p. 258).

as well as Honoratus' request to Cassian for a copy of that practical code of monastic life, which is the *De institutis coenobiorum*. In addition, Cassian's dedication of his last seven *Conlationes* to Honoratus attests to the intimate relationship (*freundschaftliche Verbindung*[106]) that existed between the two founders with regard to the aim of monastic life and its underlying ascetical motivations, which they both drew from the tradition of the Eastern Church. It is also interesting to note that in the mid-5th century, whilst recalling the monastic life of Lérins, Sidonius Apollinaris speaks of fasting, vigils, psalmody[107] and the rigours of discipline rather than a theological school[108]. Even the election of a number of Lérinian monks to bishoprics seems to be due, first and foremost, to their spiritual qualities and sanctity of life, and only in the second place to their doctrinal knowledge[109].

At least two peculiarities characterized Lérins from its very beginning and should be taken into account. First the provenance of its members: many, including its founder Honoratus, a native of the *Gallia belgica*, came from regions outside Provence. They were probably refugees who had fled the northern and central regions of Gaul, when these areas were conquered and ravaged by barbaric invasion[110]. Secondly, many of these refugees belonged to the *genus clarus* of Roman-Gallic aristocracy and were often related to each other through family ties[111]. Against this background of the social and political instability (due to the decadence of the Roman Empire and to increasing invasions from the North-East), Prinz's conclusion that the monastic community of Lérins was in fact a *Flüchtlingskloster*[112], a refuge for the fleeing aristocracy of Northern Gaul, is no doubt of great interest, but should be seen from the right perspective. This sociological interpretation, in fact, is only a partial truth and cannot be taken and applied *sic et simpliciter* to the entire

---

106. PRINZ, *Frühes Mönchtum im Frankenreich* (n. 77), p. 50.
107. Sidonius Apollinaris, *Carmina* 16, vv. 104-108 (PL, 58), c. 720.
108. Id., *Ep.* 9,3 (PL, 58), c. 618.
109. Cf. P. RICHÉ, *Education et culture dans l'Occident barbare (VI-VIII siècles)*, Paris, 1962, p. 145.
110. Cf. PRINZ, *Frühes Mönchtum im Frankenreich* (n. 77), pp. 45-58.
111. Cf. PRICOCO, *L'isola dei santi* (n. 11), pp. 69ff.
112. Prinz entitles the first paragraph of the chapter devoted to Lérins and its influence in Gaul: "Lerinum als Flüchtlingskloster der nordgallischen Aristokratie" (PRINZ, *Frühes Mönchtum im Frankenreich* [n. 77], p. 47). Prinz arrives at this conclusion on the wave of Stroheker's explanation of the meaning of abbatial and episcopal offices in 5th century Gaul, offices which he interpretes as a political compensation and an instrument of secular power for the senatorial and landowning aristocracy. Cf. K.F. STROHEKER, *Der senatorische Adel im spätantiken Gallien*, Tübingen, 1948 (reprint, Darmstadt, 1970), pp. 71ff., 92ff.

Lérins-event as if it were the only hermeneutical category. Apart from the necessary inner conviction and Christian motivation of those aristocratic "refugees" who joined Lérins[113], we cannot ignore other external circumstances, such as the intermediary role that the geographical position of Provence played in spreading the Christian message and in favouring the rise and development of a "Gallic" monastic phenomenon. Nevertheless, the presence of cultured people and, in some cases, people with a solid experience in military or civil administration[114], must have contributed greatly to its formation and must have been decisive ingredients in the religious and cultural reform that Lérins, together with Marseilles, was going to undergo, particularly with regard to other monastic expressions already existing in Gaul, such as the Martinian one[115]. Certainly, *l'école* of Lérins would exercise a great influence in

113. Cf. PRICOCO, *L'isola dei santi* (n. 11), pp. 71ff. In a more objective and nuanced way, Kasper distinguishes between an "outer" and "inner" motivation for the ascetical life of the Lérinian monks: 1) Die äußere Motivation: Lérins als "Flüchtlingskloster" oder Stütze der *via regia* in Theologie und Askese? 2) Die innere Motivation: Zwischen *contemptus mundi* und Gottesliebe (KASPER, *Theologie und Askese* [n. 86], pp. 147ff. 152ff.).

114. As was the case, for instance, of Vincent of Lérins who joined Lérins after having been engaged in wordly affairs, perhaps in the military service: cf. Vincent of Lérins, *Commonitorium* 1 (CCL, 64), p. 147.

115. "Personalità di tal genere erano destinate a primeggiare nella Chiesa di quei tempi e a fare di Lerino un centro fervido di cultura religiosa e di attività ecclesiastica. Per il loro impulso Lerino maturò una cultura religiosa e monastica specifica, che conferì caratteri tipici al "monachesimo del Rodano", meglio organizzato, più colto, meno aperto al folklore del miracoloso e del meraviglioso rispetto ad altri centri monastici della Gallia" (PRICOCO, *L'isola dei santi* [n. 11], p. 73). The reforming fervour of the Lérinian monks was also maintained by those, among them, who would eventually become bishops. Thus, as Pietri writes: "Honorat, puis Hilaire, ont quitté Lérins pour le siège épiscopal d'Arles et, dans l'enthousiasme d'une foi brûlante, ils considèrent assez vite que leur Eglise peut conduire la réforme: le groupe ascétique, à la conquête de l'épiscopat, impose des évêques intègres, recrutés dans ce groupe d'hommes qui donnent à leur convictions le vêtement du 'philosophe' chrétien" (PIETRI., *Roma Christiana* [n. 11], T. II, p. 1029). It should not be forgotten, however, that even though intellectual endeavour was certainly present, the effort to reform the Church of Provence remained essentially ascetic in character (cf. *Ibid.*). At Lérins, as well as at Marseilles, a better organized and culturally "higher-level" monasticism was being developed, when compared with the earlier monastic tradition associated with Martin of Tours. It is from Cassian, above all, that comes an explicit reaction to the *fabulosa* literary construction of Martin's *Vita* where thaumaturgy stands out as "le principe d'organisation" (J. FONTAINE, *Introduction*, in Sulpicius Severus, *Vita Martini*, T. I [SC, 133], p. 85). In fact, Cassian's *De institutis coenobiorum*, with its concentration on the traditional/ascetic teaching of the desert Fathers, rather than on miraculous and fabulous stories, could be considered as a criticism of Martinian monasticism as depicted in Sulpicius' *Vita* and *Dialogi*, where wondrous deeds abound. "Propositum siquidem – wrote Cassian – mihi est non de mirabilibus Dei, sed de correctione morum nostrorum et consummatione uitae perfectae secundum ea, quae a senioribus nostris accepimus, pauca disserere" (Cassian, *De institutis coenobiorum*, Praef. 8 [SC, 109], p. 30). As Stewart puts it: "The *Institutes* are inescapably a

the Gallic Church as a whole and, more specifically, in many monasteries of the region[116]. Its religious and cultural activity would become, in fact, the means of friendly *liaisons* with other important monastic centres, such as those located on the Islands of Hyères (of which very little is known) and above all the Cassianic foundation of St. Victor in Marseilles. Together with the latter, Lérins would contribute to the elaboration of a "theological thought process" on the anti-Augustinian position in the matter of grace and predestination, that would form a reference point for years to come[117].

c) Marseilles and Its "Star": John Cassian[118]

In 415, with the support of Proculus, the bishop of Marseilles, who favoured the spread of monasticism in his ecclesiastical province[119],

critique of the native monastic tradition associated especially with Martin of Tours" (C. STEWART, *Cassian the Monk* [OSHT], New York-Oxford, 1998, p. 17). Fontaine, however, prefers to underline the continuity between Cassian's and Martin's formulae of monasticism and speaks of a "logical development" of Cassian's reforming endeavours with regard to earlier Gallic monasticism, rather than a rejection of it (cf. J. FONTAINE, *L'ascétisme chrétien dans la littérature gallo-romaine d'Hilaire à Cassien* [n. 81], pp. 105-113).

116. "Le rayonnement spirituel et intellectuel de Lérins a été immense" (BIARNE, *Moines et rigoristes en Occident* [n. 85], p. 763). "Lérins eut une influence sur de nombreux monastères gaulois" (BRARD, *Lérins* [n. 86], c. 436).

117. With regard to this question, the two most representative writers are Vincent of Lérins and Faustus of Riez. That the argumentation of Vincent's *Commonitorium* was an indirect answer to Augustine's views on grace (see especially Vincent of Lérins, *Commonitorium* 26,8-9 (CCL, 64), pp. 184-185, which is a clear allusion to Augustine, *De dono perseuerantiae* 23,64 [PL, 45], c. 1032) is a thesis which had already been defended in G.J. Vossius' *Historia de controversiis* I,9 (1618) and in E. Noris' *Historia pelagiana* II (1673), and which was taken up anew in J. MADOZ, *El Concepto de la Tradicion en S. Vicente de Lerins*, Rome, 1933, above all pp. 59-89. See J. LEBRETON, *Saint Vincent de Lérins et Saint Augustin*, in *RSR* 30 (1940) 368-369. However, apart from the different approach to some of the questions concerning grace, Vincent (and the school of Lérins) was an admirer of Augustine's doctrine of the Trinity and of the Incarnation, as is shown by a florilegium (announced in Vincent of Lérins, *Commonitorium* 16,9 [CCL, 64], p. 169) discovered by J. Madoz in the library of Ripoll, in Northern Catalonia (see Id., *Excerpta [e S. Augustino]* [CCL, 64], pp. 199-231). Only the introduction and the epilogue are written by Vincent. The rest is an Augustinian *Summa* against the doctrine of Nestorius. See also G. BARDY, *Vincent de Lérins*, in *DTC* 15/2 (1950) 3045-3055, c. 3048. As well as Vincent of Lérins, another writer of note, Faustus of Riez, will contribute to the opposition to Augustine's doctrine of grace in the 5th century (cf. C. TIBILETTI, *Libero arbitrio e grazia in Fausto di Riez*, in *Aug* 19 [1979] 259-285; M. SIMONETTI, *Fausto di Riez*, in *DPAC* 1 [1983] 1336-1338, c. 1337).

118. On Cassian see, above all: S. MARSILI, *Giovanni Cassiano ed Evagrio Pontico* (StAns, 5), Rome, 1936; P. GODET, *Cassien Jean*, in *DTC* 2 (1910) 1823-1829; L. CRISTIANI, *Jean Cassien. La spiritualité du désert*, S. Wandrille, 1946, T. II; G. BARDY, *Cassien (Jean)*, in *Cath* 2 (1949) 616-617; M. CAPPUYNS, *Cassien (Jean)*, in *DHGE* 11 (1949) 1319-1348; M. OLPHE-GALLIARD, *Cassien (Jean)*, in *DSp* 2 (1953) 214-276;

John Cassian founded twin monasteries, both male and female, in this coastal city[120]. The male monastery was called St. Victor, after the martyr's burial place which was located in a cemetery site outside the walls of the city, by the river Lacydon[121]. The site of the female community remains uncertain, although tradition has identified it with a monastery within the city walls, later dedicated to the Holy Saviour[122]. There is no doubt that among the literary and institutional events of the first quarter of the 5th century, the foundation of the monastery of St. Victor, together with the great influence of its founder, shines forth as a *lumière*[123] which has continued to enlighten Western monasticism ever since.

Cassian was born around 360-365 in *Scythia minor*[124], in what is nowadays Dobrudjia, on the west coast of the Black Sea in Romania.

E. PICHERY, *Introduction*, in Jean Cassien, *Conférences* (SC, 42), pp. 7ff; J.-C. GUY, *Jean Cassien. Vie et doctrine spirituelle*, Paris, 1961; H.O. WEBER, *Die Stellung des J. C. zur ausserpachomianischen Mönchstradition. Eine Quellenuntersuchung*, Münster i. W., 1961; GRIFFE, *La Gaule chrétienne*, T. III (n. 77), pp. 305-313; 341-344; F. PRINZ, *Cassiano*, in *DIP* 2 (1975) 633-638; HAMMAN, *Scrittori della Gallia* (n. 4), pp. 486-495; ROUSSEAU, *Ascetics, Authority and the Church* (n. 81), *passim*; ID., *Cassian, Contemplation and the Cenobitic Life*, in *JEH* 26 (1975) 113-126; A. MASOLIVER, *Historia del Monacato cristiano*. T. I: *Desde los orígines hasta san Benito*, Madrid, 1994, pp. 70-76; COLOMBAS, *El monacato primitivo*, T. I (n. 77), pp. 249-253; C. TIBILETTI, *Giovanni Cassiano. Formazione e dottrina*, in *Aug* 17 (1977) 355-380; CHADWICK, *John Cassian* (n. 84); ID., *Cassianus*, in *TRE* 7 (1981) 650-657; R. NÜRNBERG, *Johannes Cassianus*, in *LTK* 5 (1996) 888-889; WEAVER, *Divine Grace and Human Agency* (n. 69), *passim*; K.S. FRANK, *Johannes Cassianus*, in *RAC* 18 (1997) 414-426; STEWART, *Cassian the Monk* (n. 115).

119. Cf. P. AMARGIER, *Marseille*, in *Cath* 8 (1979) 714-722, c. 714. That Proculus, bishop of Marseilles from 381 to after 418, was monastically minded, can be inferred from a letter that Jerome sent to the monk Rusticus (later bishop of Narbonne) in 411/412, in which Jerome greatly praises Proculus (cf. Jerome, *Ep.* 125,20,2 [CSEL, 56], p. 141). Since Rusticus lived in a monastery in Marseilles along with Venerius (Proculus' successor to the episcopal see), we also suppose that a monastically structured community of clerics, very similar to that founded by Augustine at Hippo, must have existed (cf. STEWART, *Cassian the Monk* [n. 115], p. 16).

120. "Apud Massiliam presbyter *[Cassian]* condidit duo id est virorum et mulierum monasteria, quae usque hodie extant" (Gennadius, *De uiris inlustribus* 62 [ed. RICHARDSON, P. 82]).

121. Cf. T. DE MOREMBERT, *Saint-Victor de Marseille*, in *Cath* 13 (1993) c. 605.

122. BESSE, *Les moines de l'ancienne France* (n. 77), p. 36.

123. Cf. A. DE VOGÜÉ, *Occident chrétien*, in J. LECLERCQ – J. GRIBOMONT – A. DE VOGÜÉ, *Monachisme*, in *Cath* 9 (1982) 505-535, c. 516.

124. Although some modern scholars still opt for Provence (cf., for instance, M. PETSCHENIG, *Johannis Cassiani opera*. *Prolegomena* [CSEL, 13], pp. II-IV; CAPPUYNS, *Cassien [Jean]* [n. 118], cc. 1320f.; CRISTIANI, *Jean Cassien. La spiritualité du désert*, S. Wandrille, 1946 [n. 118], T. I, pp. 36ff.; K. ZELZER, *'Cassianus natione Scytha, ein Südgallier'*, in *WSt* 104 [1991] 161-168; K.S. FRANK, *John Cassian on John Cassian*, in *SP* 33, Louvain, 1997, pp. 418-433, p. 425), the reasons given for agreeing with those who believe that Gennadius' expression *natione Scytha* ("Cassianus natione Scytha": Gennadius, *De uiris inlustribus* 62 [ed. RICHARDSON, p. 82]) should be taken to indicate

After receiving a classical education, Cassian was attracted to monastic ideals and travelled with his friend Germanus to Palestine where, in 378-380, they joined a monastic community in Bethlehem with the clear aim of acquainting themselves with the *militia spiritalis*[125]. The fame of the desert Fathers pushed them on towards Egypt; at first for only a brief stay in Pannefisi, but a second time for a much longer sojourn in the desert of Scetis. From there, where they had joined a colony of monks under the spiritual guidance of abba Pafnutius, Cassian and Germanus visited the other famous monastic centres of Nitria and Cells. At Cells they met and associated with Evagrius Ponticus (346-399), the "philosopher of the desert", and with his companions, all fervent sympathizers of Origen's spiritual theology[126]. Evagrius Ponticus would profoundly influence Cassian's future writings[127].

Cassian's stay in the Egyptian desert ended with the outbreak of the Origenist controversy[128], which eventually saw the then bishop of Alexandria, Theophilus, and a number of Origenist monks in bitter opposition to each other. The Origenist controversy was shaped by the

the eastern region of the Roman empire, are more compelling (cf., for instance, T. DAMIAN, *Some critical considerations and new arguments reviewing the problem of St. John Cassian's birthplace*, in *OCP* 57 [1991] 257-280). According to Stewart, Cassian's "bilingualism makes the most compelling argument for the Balkan hypothesis: in Cassian's day Scythia Minor was a bilingual region where Greek had a strong presence" (STEWART, *Cassian the Monk* [n. 115], p. 6). See also CHADWICK, *John Cassian* (n. 84), p. 9.

125. Cf. Cassian, *Conlatio* 16,1 (SC, 54), p. 223.

126. "In those parts of Egypt where Cassian had dwelt Origen was a dominant influence" (C. BUTLER, *The Lausiac History of Palladius* [TaS, 6/1-2], Cambridge, 1898-1904, Vol. I, p. 205).

127. "Cassian relied heavily on Evagrius' writings and on those of their common master, Origen" (STEWART, *Cassian the Monk* [n. 115], p. 36). Although nowhere in the *De institutis coenobiorum* or in the *Conlationes* is the name of Evagrius explicitly mentioned (except maybe for the story of the monk *de prouincia Ponti* who burnt the letters he had received from his relatives and friends after fifteen years, without even having read them: cf. *De institutis coenobiorum* 5,32,1-3 [SC, 109], p. 240) Cassian reproduces the teaching that the great disciple of Origen and of the desert Fathers elaborated at Cells. If Cassian avoids any explicit reference to Evagrius, never mentioning him by name, this is due mainly to the fact that at the time when he wrote the *De institutis coenobiorum* and the *Conlationes*, the echoes of the Origenist controversy, which ended with the condemnation of Origenism by Theophilus of Alexandria in 400 (as a result of which also Evagrius' works were discredited), were still very much in the air. In such a scenario it would have been "politically inexpedient to advertise connections with Evagrius, the great theoretician of monastic Origenism" (STEWART, *Cassian the Monk* [n. 115], p. 11).

128. Cf. CHADWICK, *John Cassian* (n. 84), pp. 28-32; STEWART, *Cassian the Monk* (n. 115), p. 12. See also E.A. CLARK, *The Origenist Controversy. The Cultural Construction of an Early Christian Debate*, Princeton, 1992, especially pp. 11-84. For a short introduction to the complexity of the Origenist controversy and to the network of issues that it raised, see EAD., *Origenist Controversy*, in FITZGERALD (ed.), *Augustine through the Ages* (n. 4), pp. 605-607.

disputes over two seemingly unconnected issues, viz. Trinity and asceticism, and was mainly marked by contemporary and more radical Origenist speculation for which Evagrius Ponticus was held to be responsible. Questions such as the Son's subordination or not to the Father, and the quest for a definition of the Spirit's status (godhead or creaturehood?), which had come to the fore in the last quarter of the 4th century, were mingled with more practical questions concerning theodicy, viz. the attempt to reconcile God's justice and goodness with the presence of evil and inequalities in the world and in human history, and the significance of human freedom in its relationship with divine benevolence. All these issues were mostly tackled in Origen's *De principiis*, and some of them would come to the fore also during the Pelagian controversy[129], as well as during the discussion between Augustine and the Massilians. The immediate reason of the outbreak of the Origenist controversy among the monks of Egypt was the so-called "anthropomorphite" problem, which can be formulated as follows: could God possibly and actually be "imaged" in human beings or in other ways? Or, as Clark, puts it: "Were images of *any* sort conducive to spiritual progress, or was the Christian's goal a kind of 'mental iconoclasm'?"[130]. Because of such controversy, in 400, Cassian and Germanus were among those who had to flee from Egypt[131]. Whereas the majority of them travelled to Palestine, another group, including the two Gallic friends, sailed for Constantinople where they were welcomed by John Chrysostom, the bishop of that town. John Chrysostom himself had previoulsy been a monk and was somewhat suspect regarding Origenist association[132]. In Constantinople, under the protection of John (whom Cassian would one day describe as his mentor[133]) Cassian and Germanus were ordained

129. Very interestingly, it must be noted that by re-focusing on issues related to theology/theodicy, the Origenist controversy can be considered as having contributed, both culturally and spiritually, to the Pelagian debate that would start not before long. For instance, as Clark argues, "Augustine's theory of original sin becomes the functional equivalent of Origen's notion of the precosmic sin and 'fall' of the rational creatures.... The dispute between Pelagians and Augustinians is thus a latter-day episode in the Origenist controversy... or, conversely, Origenism stands as the prehistory of the Pelagian debate" (CLARK, *The Origenist Controversy* [n. 128], p. 6).

130. *Ibid.*, p. 4. See also *Ibid.*, ch. 2: *Image and Images. Evagrius Ponticus and the Anthropomorphite Controversy*, pp. 43ff.

131. An incident recorded in the *Conlationes* indicates that Cassian sided with Evagrius on the anthropomorphite question: "Quamquam non dubitem etiam ex hoc ipso non minimam instructionem super omnipotentis Dei quae in Genesi legitur imagine quibusque simplicioribus conferendam" (Cassian, *Conlatio* 10,1 [SC, 54], p. 75). In the meantime, it must be noted, Evagrius had died. His death, in fact, occurred in 399.

132. Cf. CAPPUYNS, *Cassien (Jean)* (n. 118), c. 1325.

133. Cassian used words of high praise in favour of John Chrysostom whom he calls *magister* (cf. Cassian, *De incarnatione Domini contra Nestorium* 7,31 [CSEL, 17], pp. 389-391).

respectively deacon and priest. In 405, following the decree of expulsion promulgated by emperor Arcadius in 404 against the partisans of John Chrysostom, Cassian and Germanus went to Rome. John Chrysostom, in the meantime had been deposed and exiled twice, in 403 and in 404. In Rome, the two friends handed pope Innocent I a letter from the clergy of Constantinople, defending bishop John who had become the target of the anti-Origenist party[134]. We do not know whether Cassian returned to the East (according to some, to Antioch)[135] with the pope's answer, but it is quite likely that he remained in Rome for some years and that he was ordained priest there, although in a way that was free of juridical obligation to the local Church[136]. As to Germanus, he must have died in Rome, since he is mentioned no longer.

In ca. 415/417 we find Cassian in Marseilles. This destination is wrapped in mystery, as we do not know the reasons, personal or political, that induced Cassian to travel to the South of Gaul[137]. It was here, however, that he founded the twin monasteries we have already spoken of. The male monastery, just like Lérins, soon became a renowned spiritual and theological centre[138] from where several monks were eventually chosen as bishops of Marseilles and other episcopal sees in Southern Gaul[139]. Contacts were soon made, not only with the major monastic

134. "Presumably their facility with Latin made them likely candidates for this important (and sensitive) appeal to the papacy, just as Cassian's knowledge of Greek would later recommend him as a critic of Nestorius" (STEWART, *Cassian the Monk* [n. 115], p. 14). Cf. *infra*, n. 144.

135. For discussions on the hypothesis of Cassian's return to the East, see STEWART, *Cassian the Monk* (n. 115), pp. 14-15. However, as Guy affirms, it is not easy nor necessary to choose between his return to the East or his stay at Rome (GUY, *Jean Cassien* [n. 118], p. 27).

136. K.S. FRANK, *John Cassian on John Cassian* (n. 124), p. 420.

137. According to Marrou (who believes that Cassian returned to the East after his mission to Rome), the decision to travel to Provence was taken by Cassian during his stay at Antioch, where he met the deposed bishop of Aix, Lazarus. The latter (who was allowed to return to Gaul in 416) would have convinced Cassian to travel to Provence, after having recommended him to his friend Proculus, bishop of Marseilles (cf. H.-I. MARROU, *Jean Cassien à Marseille*, in *RMÂL* 1 [1945] 5-26, pp. 5f.; see also ID., *La patrie de Jean Cassien*, in *OCP* 13 [1947] 588-599, pp. 588ff). There seems to be no sufficient ground for supposing that at the origin of Cassian's journey to Provence was his meeting with Lazarus at Antioch. If that were the case, it could be inferred that already at this stage Cassian had some anti-Pelagian connections, viz. Lazarus who was one of Pelagius' accusers at the Council of Diospolis in 415. As to Proculus, there can be no doubt that he was one of the western bishops who were already associated with the ascetic movement of that time (see *supra*, n. 119).

138. "Tout comme à Lérins, une école de théologie cristallisa autour de l'école spirituelle représentée par la fondation cassianite. Les oeuvres de Cassien en furent le ferment" (AMARGIER, *Marseille* [n. 119], c. 715).

139. See V. SAXER, *Marsiglia*, in *DPAC* 2 (1983) 2127-2129.

settlements off the coast of Southern Gaul, like the *ingens coenobium* of Lérins and the communities on the islands of Hyères, but also with other monastic foundations of Provence, *e.g.*, the *nouellum monasterium* founded by Castor of Apt, the bishop to whom Cassian would address his *De institutis coenobiorum*[140]. At Marseilles, beside the *De institutis coenobiorum*, Cassian also wrote the *Conlationes* and the polemical, rather than doctrinal, and somewhat inaccurate work *De incarnatione Domini contra Nestorium*[141]. This work (at least according to Cassian) was prepared for publication at the request of Leo, then archdeacon of Rome and later pope (440-461)[142]. It seems, however, that the initial task required of Cassian was simply to translate into Latin[143] the documents concerning the Christological controversy in which Nestorius was involved. That being the case, Cassian was not chosen for his expertise in matters of dogmatics, but rather because of his knowledge of Greek and of the Church of Constantinople[144] whose patriarch was under fire. More-over, it seems that the fact of not addressing the Christological question in a dogmatic fashion and of ending up with writing a pamphlet intended to ruin Nestorius' theses[145] (a pamphlet in which he makes a groundless Christological connection between Pelagianism and Nestorianism[146]),

---

140. Cf. Cassian, *De institutis coenobiorum, Praef.* 2 (SC, 109), p. 23.

141. Id., *De incarnatione Domini contra Nestorium* (CSEL, 17), pp. 235-391.

142. Cf. *Ibid., Praefatio, passim*, pp. 235-236.

143. Cf. M.-A. VANNIER, *Introduction*, in EAD. (ed.), *Jean Cassien. Traité de l'incarnation contre Nestorius*, Paris, 1999, p. 31.

144. "Cassian war einer der ganz wenigen Kirchenschriftsteller im Westen, die griechische Sprache voll beherrschten" (PRINZ, *Frühes Mönchtum im Frankenreich* [n. 77], p. 471).

145. "Cassian provides a campaign piece rather than a theological assessment" (STEWART, *Cassian the Monk* [n. 115], p. 22). Moreover, as it has been noted, "it was not the intention of the monk of St. Victor to recognize the difficulties of his opponent and to cure them, but to oppose what seemed to him to be an already established heresy.... He is not a doctor,..., but a judge" (A. GRILLMEIER, *Christ in Christian Tradition. From the Apostolic Age to Chalcedon [451]*, London, 1965, p. 390).

146. "The most distinctive aspect of his defense *[Cassian's]* of the divinity of Christ is a connection he makes between Pelagianism and Nestorianism. This odd linkage may arise from the fact that Julian of Eclanum and Pelagius' disciple Celestius had sought refuge in Constantinople" (STEWART, *Cassian the Monk* [n. 115], p. 22). "Son accusation de pélagianisme *[against Nestorius]* n'est guère fondée" (VANNIER, *Introduction* [n. 143], p. 63). Even if there are evidences of a historical link between Pelagianism and Nestori-anism, probably due to the initial solidarity of Nestorius in the face of the fate of Julian and his associates who had sought refuge in Constantinople after their condemnation (cf. Marius Mercator, *Nestorii capitula et sermones a Mario Mercatore translati* [ACO, 1/5], p. 60; J. LÖSSL, *Julian von Aeclanum. Studien zu seinem Leben, seinem Werk, seiner Lehre und ihrer Überlieferung* [SVigChr, 60], Leiden-Boston-Cologne, 2001, pp. 309-311) no real dogmatic connections can be established among them. One of Cassian's groundless claims, for instance, was that Nestorius shared the Pelagian heresy of the *soli-tarius homo*, viz. Christ viewed as a mere example of good deeds and not as a Saviour (cf.

was also tainted with some personal grudges[147], an attitude which would make the *De incarnatione Domini contra Nestorium* still more untrust-worthy. The date of Cassian's death is not known. It is likely that he finally reached the *tutissimum silentii portum* some time in the mid-430s[148].

d) Cassian's Monastic Literature

The presence of Cassian in the West, but above all his two most important writings, the *De institutis coenobiorum* and the *Conlationes,* forming, as they do, a complete code of primitive monasticism[149], a doc-trinal and practical *summa* which was never to be equalled in monastic literature, were to produce a wide and profound echo in the monastic world both of the time and in centuries to come[150]. The *De institutis coenobiorum,* written between 419-426, is made up of two parts: the first (books I-IV) describes the external life of the monks, namely the monastic and liturgical institutions that Cassian experienced among the eastern monks, especially those of Egypt; the second part (books V-XII)

Cassian, *De incarnatione Domini contra Nestorium* 6,14 [CSEL, 17], p. 341). Moreover, one cannot rule out that the accusation of Pelagianism brought against Nestorius by Cassian might have been a move, made in order to prevent the same accusation of Pelagianism being eventually laid on him. Cf. VANNIER, *Introduction* (n. 143), p. 62; J. PLAGNIEUX, *Le grief de complicité entre erreurs nestorienne et pélagienne d'Augustin à Cassien par Prosper d'Aquitaine?*, in REAug 2 (1956) 391-402, pp. 391-392. About Nestorius' somewhat ambiguous attitude with regard to Pelagianism, and the absence of any mention of the Pelagians in the imperial decree of 428 against the heretics, see M. LAMBERIGTS, *Les évêques pélagiens déposes: Nestorius et Éphèse*, in Aug(L) 35 (1985) 264-280, pp. 269-271.

147. Vannier suggests that one of the reasons behind Cassian's attack to Nestorius had nothing to do with the intellectual domain; it was rather "une rancoeur personnelle à l'encontre de l'un des successeurs de Jean Chrysostome qui a entrepris des répresailles contre un group dont il faisait partie, celui des partisans de l'ancien évêque de Constan-tinople" (VANNIER, *Introduction* [n. 143], pp. 32, 57ff).

148. Cassian, *Conlatio* 24,26 (SC, 64), p. 206.

149. Cf. GODET, *Cassien Jean* (n. 118), c. 1825; STEWART, *Cassian the Monk* (n. 115), pp. 29f.

150. Their reading and assimilation would be warmly recommended, for instance, by St. Benedict: "...sedeant omnes in unum et legat unus Collationes uel Vitas Patrum..."; "...dicta uespera paruo interuallo mox accedant ad lectionem Collationum..."; "Necnon et Collationes Patrum et Instituta et Vitas eorum... quid aliud sunt nisi bene uiuentium et oboedientium monachorum instrumenta uirtutum?" (Benedict of Nursia, *Regula mona-chorum* 42,3.5 and 73,5 [SC, 182], pp. 584 and 672). See also: "Cassianum presbyterum, qui conscripsit de Institutione fidelium monachorum sedulo legite, et libenter audite" (Cassiodorus, *Institutiones* 29 [PL, 70], c. 1144). As Rousseau writes: "The *Institutes* and *Conferences* stand as a complete and entirely literary creation, exerting upon their readers the influence of a rule of life. For this reason, the study of early monastic history reaches, with Cassian, a *point de départ*, rather than a conclusion" (ROUSSEAU, *Ascetics, Authority and the Church* [n. 81], p. 236).

deals more explicitly with the spiritual and inner life of the monks and tackles the presence of the eight principal vices, together with the remedies for fighting them. The struggle against vices, whose aim is to purify the soul in view of the contemplation of God, is made possible by the cenobitic discipline. Such discipline constitutes the ascetic framework within which the *uita actiua*, viz. the disciplining of oneself, is lived out. Once this task of purification is accomplished, the monk gains access to the *uita contemplatiua* where the ideal framework is now provided by eremitical life. The 24 *Conlationes*, as Cassian himself underlines, are, in fact, about the *uita contemplatiua*[151]. They present, in a dialogical form[152], the *inlustrium patrum scientiam atque doctrinam*[153], a teaching that Cassian had assimilated through his contacts with the anchorites living in the deserts of Egypt; a teaching which he, no doubt, elaborated upon on the basis of his personal experience and convictions[154]. The *Conlationes* were written at different periods, from 425/426 to 428[155].

---

151. Cf. Cassian, *Praef.* (to *Conlatio* 1-10) 5 (SC, 42), pp. 75-76.

152. Generally speaking, the style is that of the classical dialogue or *erotapokriseis* (question and answer session): see H. DÖRRIE–H. DÖRRIES, *Erotapokriseis*, in *RAC* 6 (1966) 342-370. Most of the conversations in the *Conlationes* begin with a question or a topic that Cassian and his friend Germanus submitted to the various elders.

153. Cassian, *Conlatio* 17,30 (SC, 54), p. 283.

154. What is certain is that "Cassiano intendeva trasmettere dottrine monastiche, d'origine principalmente egiziana. Tuttavia non si dice per ciò stesso che tutto quel che da Cassiano ci vien presentato, raccontato e riferito, sia sempre quel che egli ha udito e visto nella sua dimora in Egitto. Prima di tutto per uno che scrive dopo circa venti anni non sarebbe stato facile ricordare tutto e solo il sentito dei monaci Egiziani...; secondo, bisogna pensare che la materia che egli ci dà, è elaborata in una forma tutta personale, e perciò anche il pensiero ivi riprodotto può avere, e molto probabilmente ha subito modificazioni...; e terzo, non si deve omettere che alcune Collazioni sono semplicemente programmatiche: hanno cioè una determinata posizione da chiarire e da difendere" (MARSILI, *Giovanni Cassiano ed Evagrio Pontico* [n. 118], p. 79).

155. The writing of the *Conlationes* has usually been placed in 425-426 (cf. *e.g.* CAPPUYNS, *Cassien [Jean]* [n. 118], c. 1331) or in 426-427 (cf. E. PICHERY, *Introduction*, in Jean Cassien, *Conférences* [SC, 42], pp. 28-30) following the traditional assumption that Honoratus had been elected bishop of Arles in 426, and relying on the piece of information given by Cassian himself in the preface to the third and last series of his *Conlationes* where Honoratus is addressed as a bishop: " beato episcopo... Honorato " (Cassian, *Praefatio* to *Conlationes* 18-24 [SC, 64], p. 8). However, if we accept as genuine the reading of *elladium* of MS *Parisinus nov. acq. 1449* containing Prosper's *Ep.* 225, instead of "Hilarium" (see *supra*, pp. 93ff.), we can confidently maintain that Helladius, bishop of Arles, and the Helladius who is mentioned twice in Cassian's *Conlationes* (first as a hermit, and a second time as a bishop) are the same person. That being the case, we can then date the different sets of Cassian's *Conlationes* with a high degree of certainty. In fact, when Helladius, who would have become bishop of Arles at the end of 426, was mentioned in the *Preface* to the first set of *Conlationes*, he was still an anchorite and was called *frater* ("sancte frater Helladi": Id., *Praefatio* to *Conlationes* 1-10 [SC, 42], pp. 74-75); which means that Cassian must have ended his *Conlationes* 1-10 by 426, before Helladius' election to the see of Arles. In the same year, Castor, the bishop of Apt (419-426)

The first group of conferences (1-10), which reports the teaching of the Fathers of the desert of Scetis, was meant to be a continuation of the *De institutis coenobiorum*. In point of fact this first series was devoted to Castor, the bishop of Apt who had commissioned the *De institutis coenobiorum*. However, since Castor's death occurred in the interim, Cassian dedicated this first set of conferences to the late bishop's brother, Leontius, and to Helladius. The second group of conferences (11-17), dedicated to Honoratus and Eucherius of Lérins, contains the teaching acquired during the first period of Cassian's sojourn in Egypt, at Pannefisi. Finally, the third group of conferences (18-24), is devoted to the four abbots of Lérins: Jovinian, Minervius, Leontius and Theodor, and recalls several themes which were the subject of different conversations held with the desert Fathers at different stages[156].

Whether or not Cassian's two works, the *De institutis coenobiorum* and the *Conlationes*, highlight his vocation as reformer[157]; whether or not they illustrate his "intention" of reforming Western monasticism[158], it is certainly true that he identified *tout court* monastic life with what he saw and learned during his stay in Palestine and especially in Egypt. In

---

died (cf. R. VAN DOREN, *Castor*, in *DHGE* 11 [1949] 1455-1456, c. 1455; G. BARDY, *Castor*, in *Cath* 2 [1949] c. 623; G. BATAILLE, *Castore*, in *BSS* 3 [1963] c. 941), which is why the first set of *Conlationes* was dedicated to Leontius (probably the bishop of Fréjus [419-432/33]: see CHADWICK, *John Cassian* (n. 84), p. 38; PIETRI, *Roma Christiana*. T. II [n. 11], p. 1037, n. 1) and to Helladius, and not to Castor, as Cassian had originally intended (cf. Cassian, *Praefatio* to *Conlationes* 1-10 [SC, 42], p. 74). The second series of *Conlationes* (11-17) ought, instead, to be placed during the time of Helladius' episcopate (in 427), since in the *Preface* to this second collection, Cassian speaks of him as having become *episcopus* ("sanctis Helladio et Leontio episcopis ": Id., *Praefatio* to *Conlationes* 11-17 [SC, 54], p. 99), whereas Honoratus is addressed as abbot ("ingenti ... coenobio praesidens congregationem": *Ibid.*, p. 98). The third series of *Conlationes* must have followed quite quickly the second one, for in the *Preface* to the second set of *Conlationes* Cassian mentioned another collection of seven conferences on which he was presumably already working ("septem aliae conlationes, quae ad sanctos qui in Stoechadibus consistunt insulis emittendae sunt fratres, desiderium ut arbitror uestri ardoris explebunt": *Ibid.*, p. 99). A possible date for this third series could therefore be 428, namely after Helladius's death and the election of Honoratus of Lérins to the see of Arles who, in the preface to the third collection of *Conlationes* is reported as having already become bishop (see *supra* in this same note).

156. See A. DE VOGÜÉ, *Pour comprendre Cassien. Un survol des Conférences*, in *CCist* 39 (1977) 250-272.

157. Cf. COLOMBAS, *El monacato primitivo*, T. I (n. 77), p. 253.

158. "Son programme monastique était audacieux et précis: réformer le monachisme occidental, – qu'il critique volontiers, – par le retour éclairé aux traditions des temps apostoliques – *ab exordio praedicationis apostolicae* – tout en adaptant l'austérité des Orientaux aux exigences particulières de l'Occident" (CAPPUYNS, *Cassien (Jean)* [n. 118], c. 1327). "Personne n'a autant que lui *[Cassian]* contribué à la formation et au développement du monachisme occidental" (BESSE, *Les moines de l'ancienne France* [n. 77], p. 50).

both these works one is aware of Cassian's eagerness, and his earnest desire to put his first hand knowledge of monasticism at the disposal not only of Castor's *nouellum monasterium* of Apt but also of the other monasteries of Provence. In so doing, Cassian, a disciple in the East and a master in the West[159], was able to conform and adapt the spiritual treasure of the desert Fathers to western mentality and practice[160]. By transposing the essentials of Egyptian and Palestinian eremitical life into the cenobitic settlements of Southern Gaul[161], he consolidated the monastic institution, which was characterized at that time, according to Cassian's own statement, by a looseness (*arbitrium*) mainly due to the absence of binding norms and regulations[162]. That this action constituted indeed Cassian's greatest intuition[163] is shown by the great influence that his literary works on monasticism exercised upon the growth and co-ordination of Western cenobitism. In this sense we can truly regard him as the chief organizer of pre-Benedectine cenobitism in the West[164], not only because he can indeed be considered *le législateur et le peintre*[165] of monastic life in Southern Gaul, but above all, as already hinted at, because of the role he played as *porte-parole*[166], as *liaison exceptionnelle*[167],

159. We find this very appropriate expression in the title of the following communication: G. LAGARRIGUE, *La spiritualité de J. Cassien (360-435), élève en Orient et maître en Occident*, in *Compte Rendu des Séances du groupe strasbourgeois. I. Séance du 17 mars 1984*, in *REL* 62 (1984) 17-18, p. 17.

160. Cf. Cassian, *De institutis coenobiorum*, Praef. 9 (SC, 109), pp. 30. 32.

161. As to the Eastern monastic traditions and customs introduced by Cassian in Provence, see A. PASTORINO, *I "temi spirituali" della vita monastica in Giovanni Cassiano*, in *CClCr* 1 (1980) 123-172.

162. "Si quid forte non secundum typum maiorum antiquissima constitutione fundatum, sed pro arbitrio uniuscuiusque instituentis monasterium uel deminutum uel additum in istis regionibus conprobauero, secundum eam quam uidimus monasteriorum regulam per Aegyptum uel Palaestinam antiquitus fundatorum fideli sermone uel adiciam uel recidam, nequaquam enim credens rationabilius quippiam uel perfectius nouellam constitutionem in occiduis Galliarum partibus repperire potuisse quam illa sunt instituta..." (Cassian, *De institutis coenobiorum*, Praef. 8 [SC, 109], p. 30). Cf. PRICOCO, *L'isola dei santi* (n. 11), pp. 93f.

163. His "grande trouvaille", as it has been defined (CAPPUYNS, *Cassien [Jean]* [n. 118], c. 1327). See also: "Redevenu cénobite par conviction, après une longue expérience de la vie solitaire, il élabore la synthèse des deux états et jette les bases spirituelles d'une réforme monastique qui trouvera son couronnement dans l'oeuvre de S. Benoît" (*Ibid.*, c. 1347).

164. "Kassian... ist der große Ordner des abendländischen Cönobitentums vor Benedikt" (M. VILLER – K. RAHNER, *Askese und Mystik in der Väterzeit. Ein Abriß der frühchristlichen Spiritualität*, Freiburg i. Br., 1939 [reprint, Darmstadt, 1989], p. 185).

165. GODET, *Cassien Jean* (n. 118), c. 1823.

166. A. DE VOGÜÉ, *Histoire littéraire du mouvement monastique dans l'antiquité*. T. III/1: *Le monachisme latin, Jérome, Augustin et Rufin au tournant du siècle [391-405]*, Paris, 1996, p. 90.

167. P. COUSIN, *Précis d'histoire monastique*, Tournai, 1956, p. 48.

Bindeglied[168], *intermédiaire*[169] between Eastern monasticism and the monastic world of the West. Moreover, it is recognized that his *De institutis coenobiorum* and *Conlationes* have imposed themselves since their appearance as classics of Christian spirituality. Their influence has not only been incalculable in Western monasticism (which has been affected in a profound and lasting manner[170]) but has also been felt in an enduring and impressive way, across the centuries, in the Western Church as a whole[171].

Among the various aspects of Christian thought where Cassian was most influential in Gaul, during the 5th century, we must mention his doctrine of grace. Seen against the backdrop of his own monastic communities, where the monks, motivated by a masculine spirituality, lived an ascetic life founded on the pragmatic ideals of the desert Fathers and their quest of virtue and perfection, Cassian's doctrine of grace cannot simply be considered a reaction to Augustine's more extreme conclusions on the same subject. More importantly, Cassian's views, influenced as they were by his monastic experience in Palestine and Egypt, can only be properly understood against this Eastern theological background. There is no doubt that he was heavily dependent upon it[172], also for his interpretation of the doctrine of grace and free will. In fact,

---

168. VILLER–RAHNER, *Askese und Mystik in der Väterzeit* (n. 164), p. 186.

169. "Cassien fut à cette époque, le principal intermédiaire entre l'Orient et l'Occident. Il chercha surtout, dans ses *Institutions*, à mettre la vie des Pères du désert à la portée des Gallo-Romains ses compatriotes" (BESSE, *Les moines de l'ancienne France* [n. 77], p. 50). It is difficult to assess whether or not the ascetic/monastic life already present in Gaul exercised some influence on the monastic ideas of Cassian. On the one hand, the communities of Lérins and those of the Islands of Hyères had only recently been founded, and lacked the rich, first-hand knowledge of Eastern monasticism which Casssian possessed, and because of which he was able to set in motion the monastic renewal in Southern Gaul. On the other, saint Martin's foundations in Ligugé and Marmoutier, almost a half century earlier, represented too loose a form of monasticism to appeal to Cassian's formation. "Deshalb blieb der Orient für ihn *[Cassian]* aber doch das Vorbild, während man im martinischen Mönchtum kaum Spuren der monastischen Regularität des christlichen Ostens findet" (PRINZ, *Frühes Mönchtum im Frankenreich* (n. 77), p. 96, n. 34).

170. For a brief overview of the influence exercised by Cassian's work upon Western monasticism, see CHADWICK, *John Cassian* (n. 84), pp. 148-162; CAPPUYNS, *Cassien (Jean)* (n. 118) , cc. 1343-1347; OLPHE-GALLIARD, *Cassien (Jean)* (n. 118), cc. 267-274; STEWART, *Cassian the Monk* (n. 115), 24.

171. See GODET, *Cassien Jean* (n. 118), c. 1825. M. Cappuyns even compares Cassian's influence to that of some Church Fathers: "Par la profondeur et la pérennité de son influence, il appartient au petit groupe de Pères occidentaux qui ont marqué d'une empreinte originale la vie de l'Eglise, les Jérôme, les Augustin, les Grégoire le Grand" (CAPPUYNS, *Cassien [Jean]* [n. 118], c. 1347).

172. "Doch sind es daneben auch Cassians eigene Gedanken, die er bewußt oder unbewußt mit der Autorität der Orientalen ausstattet" (PRINZ, *Frühes Mönchtum im Frankenreich* [n. 77], p. 471).

although the monastic communities of Marseilles and Lérins showed
Augustine great respect and payed homage to his work[173], they were particularly dissatisfied with the content of the *De correptione et gratia*[174];
more precisely with his theories on predestination, irresistible grace and
God's salvific will. The Massilians regarded such theories as disturbing
to the very *raison d'être* of their *monastica uiuendi forma*, not to say
annihilating of the need for the ascetic efforts they considered indispensable in their striving for perfection and acquisition of virtue[175]. In
the monastic communities where an active participation of the will in the
process of salvation was regarded as the norm, and deathbed conversion
was judged with suspicion and considered ineffective[176], Augustine's
statement that perseverance was purely a divine gift provoked great
uneasiness. Furthermore, it was suspected that the theory of predestination, coupled with a restricted vision of universal salvation, would lead

173. See, for instance: "Sed plane illud tacere non debeo, quod se dicant tuam sanctitatem hoc excepto in factis et dictis omnibus admirari" (Hilary, *Ep.* 226,9 [CSEL, 57],
p. 479). Cf. also: "Sanctum Helladium, Arelatensem episcopum, sciat beatitudo tua admiratorem sectatoremque in aliis omnibus tuae esse doctrinae et de hoc quod in querelam
trahit, iam pridem apud sanctitatem tuam sensum suum per litteras uelle conferre" (Prosper, *Ep.* 225,9 [CSEL, 57], p. 467). Without doubt Cassian too never failed to admire the
depth of, and make use of the insights of some of Augustine's ideas. See B. RAMSEY,
John Cassian: Student of Augustine, in *CiSt* 28 (1993) 5-15; A.M.C. CASIDAY, *Cassian,
Augustine, and* De Incarnatione, in *StPatr* 38, Louvain, 2001, pp. 41-47. However, that
Augustine was not Cassian's pet theologian, nor his own monastic reference, can be
inferred by the fact that the bishop of Hippo is not granted any of the fulsome praise that
Cassian's other sources receive. Cassian's "monastic remarks on Augustine in *De Inc.*
7.27.1 are markedly less effusive than those about the other western authorities he is quoting" (STEWART, *Cassian the Monk* [n. 115], p. 154, n. 173). The "Augustinus Hipponae
Regiensis oppidi sacerdos" (Cassian, *De incarnatione Domini contra Nestorium* 7,27
[CSEL, 17], p. 385) can hardly be compared, for instance, with: "Hilarius, uir uirtutum
omnium atque ornamentorum et sicut uita, ita etiam eloquentia insignis" (*Ibid.* 7,24,
p. 382), or with: "Ambrosius, eximius Dei sacerdos, qui a manu Domini non recedens
in Dei semper digito quasi gemma rutilavit" (*Ibid.* 7,25, p. 383), or "Hieronymus,
catholicorum magister, cuius scripta per uniuersum mundum quasi diuinae lampades
rutilant" (*Ibid.* 7,26, p. 384).
        174. If Cassian and the Massilians' unease with some of Augustine's views on grace
can be "immediately" linked to their reaction to the *De correptione et gratia*, we can presume that this conclusion was also reached thanks to a knowledge of Augustine's earlier
works, where some of these thoughts had already begun to emerge. Discussion with
regard to such views was probably going on before the appearance of the *De correptione
et gratia*, the appearance of which must have represented the proverbial "straw that broke
the camel's back", as far as the Massilians were concerned.
        175. "Leur intention profonde est de défendre la légitimité de leur effort ascétique,
menacée à leurs yeux par les conséquences extrêmes des théories augustiniennes" (SOLI-
GNAC, *Semipélagiens* [n. 70], c. 559). "Partnership between divine grace and human will
which they had always hitherto taken for granted was in danger of being undermined"
(REES, *Pelagius. A Reluctant Heretic* [n. 11], p. 105).
        176. Cf. Caelestinus, *Ep. ad episcopos per Viennensem et Narbonensem prouincias*
(PL, 50), cc. 431f; Leo the Great, *Ep.* 108 (PL, 54), cc. 1012f.

to a fatalistic attitude and to a state of inertia. It is not surprising that
these ideas were disturbing to people who made pragmatic virtue a way
of life[177]. It is against this background that Cassian, ever conscious of his
spiritual authority, stands out. He was a most outspoken representative
of the views circulating in both the monastic and ecclesiastical circles of
Southern Gaul, and of the great uneasiness caused in these same circles
by the way in which Augustine had treated questions related to grace.
We can now turn our attention to Cassian's *De institutis coenobiorum*
and *Conlationes*. Here traces of the Massilian views on the question of
the relationship between grace and free will can be detected in several
places, and above all in *Conlatio* 13.

e) Grace and Free Will in Cassian's De institutis coenobiorum and Conlationes

At the very beginning of the second section of the *De institutis coenobiorum* (books 5-12), Cassian affirms that the first step for a monk
endeavouring to reach perfection consists in engaging himself in a "psy-
chomachy", that is in fighting against those passions which are identified with the eight principal vices[178]. Man should recognize them, discover their cause and then find the remedy needed in order to overcome
them. The way Cassian deals with the last of these principal vices, viz.
the *spiritus superbiae*, in the twelfth book of the *De institutis coenobiorum*[179], is interesting in its doctrinal implications. From the chronological point of view, this vice comes first. In fact, Lucifer's fall and ban-
ishment from heaven were due to his *superbia*; he believed that the
perfection he possessed pertained to his own nature and was not the

177. See also, in this regard, Prosper, *Ep. ad Rufinum* (PL, 51), cc. 77-90.

178. They are: 1) *gastrimargia* or *gulae concupiscentia*, 2) *fornicatio*, 3) *filargyria* or
auaritia, 4) *ira*, 5) *tristitia*, 6) *acedia* or *anxietas siue taedium cordis*, 7) *cenodoxia* or
uana seu inanis gloria, 8) *superbia*, (cf. Cassian, *De institutis coenobiorum* 5,1 [SC, 109]
p. 190). A summary of these eight vices can be found in *Conlatio* 5 (abba Serapion), SC
42, pp. 188-217. This list of vices is probably taken from Evagrius Ponticus, *De octo
uitiosis cogitationibus* (PG, 40), cc. 1272-1276, a work which, in its turn, was influenced
by Origen and Stoicism. See I. HAUSHERR, *L'origine de la théorie orientale des huit
péchés capitaux*, in *OC(R)* 30 (1933) 164-175; A. VÖGTLE, *Achtlasterlehre*, in *RAC* 1
(1950) 74-79. The influence of Stoicism should be taken into account, especially when
Cassian deals with the "connections between ethics and anthropology that mark the original Stoic position. He is interested in the genesis and dynamics of the vices, the virtues
and the passions as well as in practical guidelines for applying ethical principles in daily
life. Cassian has learned much from Stoic psychology and casuistry alike" (M.L. COLISH,
The Stoic Tradition from Antiquity to the Early Middle Ages. Vol. II: *Stoicism in Christian Latin Thought through the Sixth Century*, Leiden, 1990, p. 115).

179. See D.J. MACQUEEN, *John Cassian on Grace and Free Will. With particular Reference to Institutio XII and Collatio XIII*, in *RTAM* 44 (1977) 5-28.

result of God's gratuitous gift (*gratia*). Consequently he was also convinced that he could procure and enjoy perfect virtue and eternal bliss merely by trusting in his own free will (*liberi scilicet arbitrii facultate confisus*[180]). Lucifer is an outstanding example, albeit a negative one, for mankind who, due to the weakness of the flesh and the impossibility of reaching the state of perfection by any human effort, constantly experiences the need for God's merciful protection. To stress this point Cassian quotes a sentence that was also dear to Augustine: *Quid habes quod non accepisti?* (1Cor 4,7)[181]. The episode of the thief, who was hanged with Jesus on Calvary and was saved after his last minute repentance, perfectly demonstrates the role God's mercy plays in the work of salvation, completely independent of any human merit[182]. On the other hand, at pains to avoid devaluing human effort, Cassian points out the wisdom and tradition of the Fathers and adds that God's grace and mercy are accorded to those who labour and strive for perfection[183]. In other words, God's grace is always ready to intervene and lead to perfection those who implore it and seek it with good will. God is ready to grant all these things if man "affords" him the opportunity[184]. Human good will would seem, therefore, to retain an initial active power independent of God's grace filled action.

Since the *Conlationes* were meant to be "the indispensable complement and crowning"[185] of the *De institutis coenobiorum*, and since the first series of the *Conlationes* was composed when the writing of the *De institutis coenobiorum* was still being formed, we might well expect nothing substantially new from Cassian other than that already expressed in his other monastic work. In point of fact, in the *Conlationes*, Cassian does develop themes similar to those tackled in the second part of his *De institutis coenobiorum*. Thus, the *Conlatio* 3 (*De tribus abrenuntiationibus*)[186], which reports the conversation of Cassian

180. Cassian, *De institutis coenobiorum* 12,4 (SC, 109), p. 454.
181. Cf. *Ibid.* 12,10 (SC, 109), p. 464.
182. Cf. *Ibid.* 12,11, p. 464.
183. "Vt enim dicimus conatus humanos adprehendere eam per se ipsos non posse sine adiutorio Dei, ita pronuntiamus laborantibus tantum ac desudantibus misericordiam Dei gratiamque conferri et, ut uerbis Apostoli loquar, uolentibus et currentibus inpertiri" (*Ibid.* 12,14, p. 468).
184. "Dicimus enim secundum Saluatoris sententiam dari quidem petentibus, aperiri pulsantibus et a quarentibus inueniri, sed petitionem et inquisitionem et pulsationem nostram non esse condignam, nisi misericordia Dei id quod petimus dederit uel aperuerit quod pulsamus uel illud quod quaerimus fecerit inueniri. Praesto est namque, occasione sibi tantummodo a nobis bonae uoluntatis oblata, ad haec omnia conferenda" (*Ibid.*).
185. "Le complément indispensable et le couronnement" (CAPPUYNS, *Cassien [Jean]* [n. 118], cc. 1329-1330).
186. Cassian, *Conlatio* 3 (SC, 42), pp. 138-165.

and Germanus with abba Pafnutius, establishes the idea that the triple
abrenuntiatio to wordly riches and goods, to spiritual and fleshly passions of the past, and to the visible and material things (all of them
thought to impede the mind from raising itself to the higher and invisible plane of eternal goods)[187] was a "must" for all who wished to attain
a perfect life. Abba Pafnutius concludes by saying that it is God himself
who makes this possible, for it is He who calls man to conversion, who
guides him along the path to salvation, who crowns him with final perseverance, and, finally, who introduces him to eternal bliss[188]. The
beginning and the accomplishment of the good will are both the work of
grace, and the striving undergone by human efforts must be placed
within this framework, provided by grace itself. At this point, Cassian's
friend, Germanus, asks abba Pafnutius what the actual role of free will
and human effort is, and whether they have any purpose at all, given that
it is God who initiates and brings to fulfilment the work of man's perfection[189]. The reply of the venerable abba is unequivocal. There is, he
says, an intermediary stage (*quaedam medietas*) which pertains to man,
where he is asked to give his assent to God's call[190]. No doubt, Cassian
felt it his duty to stress the necessity of God's grace. For that reason he
underlines, through scriptural quotations, the fact that human efforts
alone are not enough to bring about salvation. God is and remains the
guide and the master of man's efforts. He is the one who guides his foot-
steps and gives him the grace of faith and perseverance[191]. In fact, free

187. "Prima est qua corporaliter uniuersas diuitias mundi facultatesque contemnimus,
secunda qua mores ac uitia affectusque pristinos animi carnisque respuimus, tertia qua
mentem nostram de praesentibus uniuersis ac uisibilibus euocantes futura tantummodo
contemplamur et ea quae sunt inuisibilia concupiscimus" (*Ibid.* 3,6, p. 145).
188. "Quemadmodum inspiratione Domini prouocati ad uiam salutis adcurrimus, ita
etiam magisterio ipsius et inluminatione deducti ad perfectionem summae beatitudinis
peruenimus" (*Ibid.* 3,10, p. 155).
189. "In quo ergo liberum consistit arbitrium nostraeque quod laudabiles sumus
reputatur industriae, si Deus in nobis omnia quae ad nostram perfectionem pertinent et
incipit et consummat?" (*Ibid.* 3,11, p. 155).
190. "Hoc uos recte mouisset, si in omni opere uel disciplina principium tantum esset
ac finis et non etiam quaedam medietas interesset. Itaque sicut occasiones salutis diuersis
modis Deum cognoscimus operari, ita nostrum est occasionibus a diuinitate concessis uel
enixius uel remissius famulari" (*Ibid.* 3,12, p. 155).
191. "Certos tamen esse nos conuenit, quod omnem uirtutem indefessis conatibus
exercentes nequaquam diligentia uel studio nostro perfectionem possimus adtingere nec
sufficiat humana sedulitas laborum merito ad tam sublimia beatitudinis praemia peruenire,
nisi ea Domino nobis cooperante et cor nostrum ad id quod expedit dirigente fuerimus
indepti" (*Ibid.* 3,12, p. 156). Cf. also: "Quamobrem certos esse nos conuenit tam ipsis
rerum experimentis quam innumeris scripturae testimoniis eruditos, nostris nos uiribus,
nisi Dei solius auxilio fulciamur, tantos hostes superare non posse et ad ipsum cotidie
summam uictoriae nostrae referre debere" (*Ibid.* 5,15, pp. 206-207).

will, left to its own devices, would spontaneously veer towards evil, rather than towards good[192]. Yet, even though divine action is believed to be present at the beginning and end of man's good will[193], Cassian reiterates that there is a very short interval belonging to man's initiative. This interval is located between the *initium uoluntatis bonae*, inspired by God, and the *perfectio uirtutum*, which is also the work of God in various ways[194]. Man's capability in enthusiastically accepting or ignoring the invitation of grace is contained in this short interval or time span. Reward or punishement follow as a direct consequence of man's use of moral responsibility. He has a choice, at this level, to pursue or to refuse the demands of God's kingdom.

f) The Conlatio *13: A Practical Ethos and a Conciliatory Approach*

It is in *Conlatio* 13 (*De protectione diuina*)[195], however, that Cassian fully develops the theme of grace and free will begun in the second part of *Conlatio* 3. But the emphasis is now different. Whereas in *Conlatio* 3 Pafnutius desired, above all, to demonstrate the necessity of divine aid, now, in *Conlatio* 13, Chaeremon's aim is to try to delimit the place and role of both grace and free will, in a way that might be seen as conciliatory and fair to both. It is for this very reason that *Conlatio* 13 has received so much attention since its appearance. It is there, in fact, that we find Cassian's attempt to define a coherent doctrine of grace in relationship to free will, a doctrine in which, on some points at least, he shows his reaction to, and his distance from, Augustine's views contained in the *De correptione et gratia*. Supported by the opinion of many scholars we believe, in fact, *saluo meliori iudicio*, that Cassian's *Conlatio* 13 was written under the direct stimulus of Augustine's *De correptione et gratia*[196]. Other scholars, nevertheless, reject this hypothesis

192. "Nostrum arbitrium... procliuius uel ignoratione boni uel oblectatione passionum fertur ad uitia" (*Ibid.* 3,12, p. 156).

193. Cf. *Ibid.* 3,12-18 *passim*, pp. 156ff.

194. "Quibus manifestissime perdocemur et initium uoluntatis bonae nobis Domino inspirante concedi, cum aut per se aut per exhortationem cuiuslibet hominis aut per necessitatem nos ad salutis adtrahit uiam, et perfectionem uirtutum ab eodem similiter condonari, nostrum uero hoc esse, ut adhortationem auxiliumque Dei uel remissius uel enixius exsequamur, et pro hoc nos uel remunerationem uel supplicia dignissime promereri, quod eius dispensationi ac prouidentiae erga nos benignissima dignatione conlatae uel negleximus uel studuimus nostrae oboedientiae deuotione congruere" (*Ibid.* 3,19, p. 162). Cf. *Ibid.* 13,3.7.8.9 (SC, 54), pp. 151.155.158.160.

195. *Ibid.* 13 (SC, 54), pp. 147-181.

196. See, for instance: "It seems extremely probable that Cassian's thirteenth Conference was written in 427 under the direct stimulus of the *De correptione*" (CHADWICK, *Poetry and Letters in Early Christian Gaul* [n. 78], p. 179); "In his *[Cassian's]* opposition

(namely that Cassian wrote his *Conlatio* 13 as a rebuttal of Augustine's *De correptione et gratia*) and believe that the second series of Conferences (to which *Conlatio* 13 belongs) were written around 426-427, before the *De correptione et gratia* arrived in Gaul[197]. What seems unacceptable to us, however, is the suggestion advanced by Markus according to which the controversial passages of *Conlatio* 13 should not so much be interpreted as a reaction to some of Augustine's views on grace, as an attack to Pelagianism, which appears to have found support in Gaul even after the rescript of Valentinian III in 425, and which Cassian must have been forced to counter[198]. It is our contention that such an

comes the explicit rejection of the... doubtful theology contained in *De correptione et gratia*" (CHADWICK, *John Cassian* [n. 84], p. 126). And again: "The accepted chronology places the publication of *Coll.* XIII in 426, before the controversy broke out. I regard this dating as erroneous and consider *Coll.* XIII to have been a work evoked by the controversy" (*Ibid.*, p. 129, n. 1); "Contro l'opera di Agostino *De correptione et gratia* è diretta la *Conlatio XIII* di C." (PRINZ, *Cassiano* [n. 118], c. 637). According to Kemmer, the *Conlatio* 13 "zeigt sich unverkennbar die polemische Tendenz gegen Augustin" (A. KEMMER, *Charisma Maximum. Untersuchung zu Cassians Vollkommenheitslehre und seiner Stellung zum Messalianismus*, Louvain, 1938, p. 30). See also Butler who affirms: "I am ready... to believe that the thirteenth Conference was written to combat some of St Augustine's positions on free-will, grace and predestination" (BUTLER, *The Lausiac History of Palladius* [n. 126], Vol. I, p. 205), and L. WRZOL, *Die Psychologie des Johannes Cassianus*, in *DT* 7 (1920) 70-96, p. 74; PIETRI, *Roma Christiana* (n. 11), T. II, p. 1028, n. 3 and p. 1029.

197. See, for instance, CHÉNÉ, *Origines de la controverse semipélagienne* (n. 1), p. 102; GODET, *Cassien Jean* (n. 118), c. 1825; SOLIGNAC, *Semipélagiens* (n. 70), c. 559; HAMMAN, *Scrittori della Gallia* (n. 4), p. 489. It has also been argued that, since *Conlatio* 13 ties up naturally with the preceding twelfth conference on chastity, and fits so well into the overall scheme of the conferences, it should be regarded as "a general response to aspects of Augustine's thought – already well known in Gaul – rather than as a tactical move in response to Augustine's latest works.... It is the culmination of Cassian's teaching on grace and free will, not an initial foray" (STEWART, *Cassian the Monk* [n. 115], p. 20). This view, already advanced by Amann ("Tout l'ensemble de cette littérature ascétique *[Institutiones* and *Conlationes]* était composée avant l'apparition du *De correptione et gratia* d'Augustin. Mais Cassien avait certainement eu connaissance d'autres ouvrages du maître africain": É. AMANN, *Semi-Pélagiens*, in *DTC* XIV/2 [1941] 1796-1850, c. 1803), is shared by other scholars like: R.A. MARKUS, *The End of Ancient Christianity*, Cambridge, 1990, pp. 177-179; ROUSSEAU, *Cassian: Monastery and World* (n. 11), pp. 82-83; WEAVER, *Divine Grace and Human Agency* (n. 69), pp. 96-97. Stewart, however, avows that "the interplay of these events *[the relations between the* De correptione et gratia *and* Conlatio *13]* remains unclear" (STEWART, *Cassian the Monk* [n. 115], p. 154, n. 176). By saying so he does not rule out the feasibility of an alternative explanation.

198. Markus writes: "It seems more natural to interpret the *Conference* in the context of the Pelagian views apparently held in Gaul which were condemned by legislation in 425..., as an attack not on Augustine's, but on Pelagian, views, albeit from a point of view more in line with a pre-Augustinian theological tradition than with Augustine's anti-Pelagian theology" (MARKUS, *The End of Ancient Christianity* [n. 197], p. 178); see also ID., *The Legacy of Pelagius: Orthodoxy, Heresy and Conciliation*, in R.D. WILLIAMS (ed.), *The Making of Orthodoxy*, Cambridge, 1989, pp. 214-234. According to Markus,

argument is untenable and that *Conlatio* 13, imbedded as it is in the second series of conferences written in 427[199], should be considered a reaction on Cassian's part and also from the monastic environments of Provence, to Augustine's *De correptione et gratia*, written in 426/427. We can assume, in other words, that the composition of *Conlatio* 13 took place in the heat of the controversy, and that the relationship between the *De correptione et gratia* and the *Conlatio* 13 were not merely accidental, but consequential.

The protagonist of *Conlatio* 13, abba Chaeremon, who in *Conlatio* 12 (*De castitate*) stressed the necessity of divine action and protection as a *conditio sine qua non* in attaining and maintaining the state of chastity[200], is now faced with Germanus' question, a question very similar in content to that addressed to abba Pafnutius[201]: if chastity can only be lived out with the help of God's gratuitous mercy, what part does human effort play? Would not mankind lose all inner motivation and be reduced to the practice of a vain and valueless exercise whose eventual success could only be dependent on God? Would that not destroy man's free will[202]? And we can also ask ourselves why pagans, with no knowledge of God or grace, manage to live chastely[203]? The objections made by Germanus to abba Chaeremon bear the imprint of Cassian's reaction

the passages of *Conlatio* 13 dealing with the relationship between grace and free will had become part of the antipredestinarian attack (viz. against Augustine's predestinarian views) only after the controversy had arisen in the monastic environments of Southern Gaul. We believe, however, that such a conjecture can be rejected on account of Cassian own's uneasiness (as it clearly emerges from *Conlatio* 13) with regard to Augustine's view of encompassing grace and the predestinarian shape that ultimately ensues from it. In such a context, Cassian's efforts were not so much directed towards restoring the necessity of God's acting grace against Pelagianism (as Markus argues) as towards the recognition of the value and the role that the agency of free will, in its relationship with grace, can and should play within a framework that safeguards and enhances its goodness.

199. As to the conclusion we arrived at in establishing the dating of Cassian's *Conlationes*, cf. *supra*, pp. 93ff and n. 155.

200. "Certos tamen esse nos conuenit, quod, licet omnem continentiae districtionem, famem scilicet ac sitem, uigilias quoque et operis iugitatem atque incessabile subeamus studium lectionis, perpetuam tamen castimoniae puritatem horum laborum merito contingere nequeamus, nisi in his iugiter desudantes experientiae magisterio doceamur incorruptionem eius diuinae gratiae largitate concedi. Ob hoc sane solummodo se unusquisque infatigabiliter in his exercitiis perdurare debere cognoscat, ut per illorum adflictionem misericordiam Domini consecutus de inpugnatione carnis ac dominatione praepotentium uitiorum diuino mereatur munere liberari, non quo adepturum se per illa confidat istam quam cupit inuiolatam corporis castitatem" (Cassian, *Conlatio* 12,4 [SC, 54], pp. 124-125).

201. Cf. *supra*, n. 189.

202. "Illud uidetur obsistere quod ad destructionem liberi tendit arbitrii" (Cassian, *Conlatio* 13,4 [SC, 54], p. 151).

203. Cf. *Ibid.* 13,4, pp. 151-152.

to Augustine[204] (although the bishop of Hippo is never mentioned[205]) and introduce the topic that would be developed in *Conlatio* 13, viz. the conciliation of grace with man's free will. Previously, Chaeremon had underlined the fact that God's grace inspires the beginning of man's good will (*initia sanctae uoluntatis*) and aids its fulfilment[206]; not in a way that is irresistible but in a way that leaves the ultimate choice to man[207]. Chaeremon, in replying to Germanus' question, reiterates the principle by pointing out that perfect purity belongs only to Christian chastity (*summa castimoniae puritas*)[208] and is always the result of God's gift. The chastity of the pagan philosophers, such as Socrates and Diogenes, was only a discipline, a fragile and provisional continence[209].

204. "Bien que ce ne soit pas lui *[Cassian]* qui parle en cette XIIIe Conférence, mais le très vénérable Chérémon, il est permis de lui attribuer les propos de cet entretien, en ce sens tout au moins qu'il les approuve sans réserve; mais en outre il est sûr qu'il a mêlé ses pensées personnelles aux siennes: les allusions à l'hérésie de Pélage et aux exagérations de saint Augustin son trop transparentes pour qu'on puisse douter de cette osmose" (CHÉNÉ, *Les origines de la controverse semipélagienne* [n. 1], p. 103). "He *[Cassian]* set out his counter-propositions on the vexed question of grace and free will, placing them in his *Conlatio* XIII in the mouth of the abbot Cheremon of Panephysis in the Delta of Egypt. This was a mere literary device: in reality he was tilting at St Augustine" (J. DANIÉLOU – H. MARROU [eds.], *The Christian Centuries*, Vol. I: *The First Six Hundred Years*, 2nd impression, London, 1964, 1978, p. 406).
205. The opposition that took shape against Augustine's doctrine of grace was in fact generally respectful of his person and of the role that he played within the Church. See G. DE PLINVAL, *Les luttes pélagiennes*, in FLICHE – MARTIN (eds.), *Histoire de l'Église.* T. IV (n. 76), p. 116.
206. "Initia sanctae uoluntatis inspirat... qui et incipit quae bona sunt et exsequitur et consummat in nobis" (Cassian, *Conlatio* 13,3 [SC, 54], p. 151). Cf. *Ibid.* 13,7.8.9, pp. 155.158.160; *Ibid.* 3,19 (SC, 42), p. 162. Prosper promptly qualified this formulation a *definitio catholicissima* (Prosper, *De gratia Dei et libero arbitrio contra Collatorem* 2,2 [PL, 51], c. 218).
207. "Nostrum uero est, ut cotidie adtrahentem nos gratiam Dei humiliter subsequamur, uel certe... eidem resistentes..." (Cassian, *Conlatio* 13,3 [SC, 54], p. 151). Augustine had instead stressed the invincibility of grace acting through the will of those who had been elected. See, for instance: "Subuentum est igitur infirmitati uoluntatis humanae, ut diuina gratia indeclinabiliter et insuperabiliter ageretur; et ideo, quamuis infirma, non tamen deficeret, neque aduersitate aliqua uinceretur" (Augustine, *De correptione et gratia* 12,38 [CSEL, 92], p. 266).
208. Cassian, *Conlatio* 13,4 (SC, 54), p. 152.
209. They only possessed – says Cassian – a partial chastity (*portiuncula castitatis*), viz. the continence of the flesh and not that of the soul (cf. *Ibid.*, 13,5, p. 152). "Cassian affirms a qualified natural capacity for good. The pagans, by refraining from immoral behavior, are doing good inasmuch as they restrain their evil impulses. There is no question here, however, of acts tending toward salvation" (L. PRISTAS, *The Theological Anthropology of John Cassian* [unpublished doctoral dissertation, Boston College], Boston, 1993, p. 276). It is in this sense that the possibility of the existence of virginity among the pagans was raised and dismissed by other Church Fathers. Cf., for instance, John Chrysostom, *De uirginitate* 1,1 (SC, 125), p. 92; Id., *Quod regulares feminae uiris cohabitare non debeant* 1,5 (PG, 47), c. 514.

Chastity is, in fact, an area where human frailty is fully apparent and where it is clearly seen that, without God's grace, success would be difficult to achieve. Even more so with regard to salvation, where one's own efforts alone are certainly not sufficient[210]. God's immutable plan that nobody should perish and that all should be saved accounts for his gratuitous intervention on behalf of mankind, without exception[211]. All human beings, in fact, live with the burden of either original or actual sin[212] and can only be delivered from it by the saving power of Christ. This power is always at their disposal[213] and can even act independently of their consciousness[214]. Certainly, the allusion to original sin in the light of the universal call to salvation (rather than the sinfulness shared by all humanity), and Cassian's optimistic and all-embracing interpretation of the double quotation of 1 Tim 2,4, are evidence of his explicit reaction to Augustine's predestinarian views[215].

According to the divine of Marseilles, all who opt for perdition, do so against the will of God[216], who desires the salvation of all mankind. For that very reason God never ceases to come to their aid, being always ready to enkindle, with his grace, any small hint or beginning of good

---

210. "Et idcirco licet in multis, immo in omnibus possit ostendi semper auxilio Dei homines indigere nec aliquid humanam fragilitatem quod ad salutem pertinet per se solam, id est sine adiutorio Dei posse perficere, in nullo tamen euidentius quam in adquisitione atque custodia castitatis ostenditur" (Cassian, *Conlatio* 13,6 [SC, 54], pp. 153-154). "Nec sufficere nobis id quod possumus certum est, nisi etiam oportunitas peragendi ea quae nobis utique possibilia sunt a Domino tribuatur" (*Ibid.*, p. 155).

211. "Propositum namque Dei, quo non ob hoc hominem fecerat ut periret, sed ut in perpetuum uiueret, manet inmobile... *uolens omnes homines saluos fieri*" (*Ibid.* 13,7, p. 155). "Qui enim ut pereat unus ex pusillis non habet uoluntatem, quomodo sine ingenti sacrilegio putandus est non uniuersaliter omnes, sed quosdam saluos fieri uelle pro omnibus? Ergo quicumque pereunt, contra illius pereunt uoluntatem.... Praesto est ergo cotidie Christi gratia, quae, dum *uult omnes homines saluos fieri et ad agnitionem ueritatis uenire*, cunctos absque ulla exceptione conuocat" (*Ibid.* 13,7, p. 156).

212. "Si autem non omnes uniuersaliter, sed quosdam aduocat, sequitur ut nec omnes sint onerati uel originali uel actuali peccato nec uera sit illa sententia: *omnes enim peccauerunt et egent gloria Dei*" (*Ibid.*).

213. "Praesto est ergo cotidie Christi gratia" (*Ibid.*).

214. "Dominus... nonnumquam perniciosas dispositiones nostras letalesque conatus ab effectu detestabili retardat ac reuocat, ac properantes ad mortem retrahit ad salutem et de inferni faucibus extrahit ignorantes" (*Ibid.* 13,7, p. 157).

215. We should not forget Augustine's idiosyncratic exegesis of 1 Tim 2,4, a text which he eventually interprets from a predestinarian perspective. Cf., for instance: "Ita dictum est: *Omnes homines uult saluos fieri*, ut intelligantur omnes praedestinati quia omne genus hominum in eis est" (Augustine, *De correptione et gratia* 14,44 [CSEL, 92], p. 272). See *infra*, pp. 357ff (Augustine's interpretation) and pp. 376ff (the Massilians' perspective).

216. "Ergo quicumque pereunt, contra illius *[God's]* pereunt uoluntatem" (Cassian, *Conlatio* 13,7 [SC, 54], p. 156); "Et in tantum omnes qui pereunt contra Dei pereunt uoluntatem" (*Ibid.*).

will. Yet, if the latter is normally prompted by God himself (and Cassian had previously spoken of the *initium uoluntatis bonae* as being
inspired by God[217]), it may well be that in some cases the beginning of
good will can be the direct result of man's efforts, because he is naturally endowed with a "spark of good will" (*scintilla bonae uoluntatis*)[218]. This spark can be kindled and brought to life either by God
himself, who strikes it from the "hard flint of man's heart", or by human
efforts[219]. Both possibilities are conceivable. On the one hand, divine
providence, out of a merciful love for man, not only accompanies, but
precedes man's action, and on the other, God leans on his creature with
the only aim of enlightening and strengthening the beginning of good
will (*ortum quendam bonae uoluntatis*)[220] coming from the soul itself.
To illustrate the presence of this double reality, Cassian puts on the lips
of Chaeremon various scriptural quotations[221] which, at first sight, seem

217. *Ibid.* 3,19 (SC, 42), p. 162.
218. "Cuius benignitas cum bonae uoluntatis in nobis quantulamcumque scintillam
emicuisse perspexerit uel quam ipse tamquam de dura silice nostri cordis excuderit, con-
fouet eam et exsuscitat suaque inspiratione confortat" (*Ibid.* 13,7 [SC, 54], p. 155). Cf.
Ibid. 3,19 (SC, 42), p. 162; 13,3 (SC, 54), p. 151. *Scintilla* is a term already used in this
respect by the Stoa which had no little impact on monasticism. According to Colish,
"it was Cassian more than any other single figure who monasticized Stoicism in the
west and who produced one of its most original and durable reformulations in this
period" (COLISH, *The Stoic Tradition from Antiquity to the Early Middle Ages.* Vol. II
[n. 178], pp. 114-115). We should point out, however, that the Stoa was not the only
philosophical school to have influenced Cassian. His thought, either through his mentors
or by a direct access to the sources, shows in fact "un fondo di dottrina eclettica, diffusa
ai suoi tempi, risultante di stoicismo, aristotelismo, neoplatonismo" (TIBILETTI, *Giovanni
Cassiano* [n. 118], p. 356). For the influence of the Stoa on Cassian see *infra*, pp. 272-289
passim.
219. Cassian, *Conlatio* 13,7 (SC, 54), p. 155.
220. "Adest igitur inseparabiliter nobis semper diuina protectio tantaque est erga creaturam suam pietas creatoris, ut non solum comitetur eam, sed etiam praecedat iugiter
prouidentia, quam expertus propheta apertissime confitetur dicens: *Deus meus misericordia eius praeueniet me.* Qui cum in nobis ortum quendam bonae uoluntatis inspexerit,
inluminat eam confestim atque confortat et incitat ad salutem, incrementum tribuens ei
quam uel ipse plantauit uel nostro conatu uiderit emersisse" (*Ibid.* 13,8, p. 158). Cf. *Ibid.*
13,3.7.9, pp. 151.155.160; *Ibid* 3,19 (SC, 42), p. 162.
221. Is 1,19 (*Si uolueritis, et audieritis me, quae bona sunt terrae manducabitis*) and
Rom 9,16 (*Non uolentis neque currentis, sed miserentis sit Dei*); Rom 2,6 (*Reddet* [Deus]
unicuique secundum opera eius) and Phil 2,13 / Eph 2,8-9 (*Deus est qui operatur in uobis
et uelle et perficere, pro bona uoluntate* / *Hoc non ex uobis, sed Dei donum est: non ex
operibus, ut ne quis glorietur*); Jam 4,8 (*Adpropinquate Domino, et adpropinquabit
uobis*) and Jn 6,44 (*Nemo uenit ad me nisi pater qui misit me adtraxerit eum*); Pr 4,26
[LXX] (*Rectos cursus fac pedibus tuis, et uias tuas dirige*) and Pss 5,9 / 16,5 (*Perfice
gressus meos in semitis tuis* / *ut non moueantur uestigia mea*); Ez 18,31 (*Facite uobis cor
nouum, et spiritum nouum*) and Ez 11,19-20 (*Dabo eis cor unum, et spiritum nouum
tribuam in uisceribus eorum: et auferam cor lapideum de carne eorum, et dabo eis cor
carneum: ut in praeceptis meis ambulent, et iudicia mea custodiant*); Jer 4,14 (*Laua a
malitia cor tuum Hierusalem, ut salua fias*) and Ps 50,12.9 (*Cor mundum crea in me Deus*

to be in opposition to one another because of the value attached univo-
cally to either grace or free will. They should be regarded, instead, as
two realities existing side by side. This means that man's free will can,
at times (*interdum*), rise autonomously in desiring a virtuous life by its
own initiative (*suis motibus*), although eventually it always needs the
help of God[222]. However difficult it might be to hold both these precepts,
"les deux bouts de la chaîne"[223], simultaneously, it is beyond all question, in Cassian's eyes, that an operative synergism or co-operation
between the two should remain. This is in line with scriptural revelation
and the common tradition of the Church. Moreover, the beginnings of
good will (*bonarum uoluntatum principia*)[224] are made possible because
of the *naturae bonum* which is connatural to human nature, a primordial
gift from God the creator[225]. It is here, in this optimistic outlook on the
graced status of human nature, that we find the ultimate reason, the key
that enables us to understand why, on some occasions, it is possible that
the will acts alone, independently of God's intervention, although the
accomplishment of what is willed (the *consummatio uirtutum*)[226] always
pertains to God's grace, which fruitfully assists man's will until the end.
Cassian's use of the expression *naturae bonum* reveals, once again, his
theological background. Generally speaking, nature was, for the Church
Fathers of the *pars Orientis*, on whom Cassian heavily depends, a synonym for good and was directly connected to the goodness of creation[227]. Cassian saw the principle of goodness as something inherent in

---

– *Lauabis me, et super niuem dealbabor*); Hos 10,12 [LXX] (*Inluminate uobis lumen
scientiae*) and Pss 93,10. 145,8. 12,4 (*Qui docet hominem scientiam – Dominus inluminat
caecos – Inlumina oculos meos ne umquam obdormiam in mortem*) (*Ibid.* 13,8 [SC, 54],
pp. 159-160).

222. Cf. *Ibid.* 13,9, p. 160.

223. The expression is found in J.B. Bossuet, *Traité sur le libre arbitre* 4, in *Œuvres
complètes.* T. II, Paris, 1856, cc. 715-756, c. 736.

224. "Ut autem euidentius clareat etiam per naturae bonum, quod beneficio creatoris
indultum est, nonnumquam bonarum uoluntatum prodire principia, quae tamen nisi a
domino dirigantur ad consummationem uirtutum peruenire non possunt, apostolus testis
est dicens: *uelle enim adiacet mihi, perficere autem bonum non inuenio*" (Cassian, *Conlatio* 13,9 [SC, 54], p. 160).

225. Cassian employs the term *natura* in relation to the goodness that characterizes
God's creation. Apart from this primordial theological meaning, he did not feel it necessary to develop the concept from a philosophical and autonomous point of view. See
infra, pp. 272-289 *passim*.

226. Cassian, *Conlatio* 13,9 (SC, 54), p. 160. See also, Id., *De institutis coenobiorum*
12,15.19 (SC, 109), pp. 470-478.

227. "Bien rares – writes Hausherr – sont ceux qui admettraient des expressions telles
que 'nature mauvaise', 'nature viciée'. La φύσις est bonne, étant l'œuvre de Dieu. Aucun
mal ne peut venir d'elle, ni avant ni après le peché originel. Dire le contraire, leur paraî-
trait rendre responsable du mal le Créateur lui-même" (I. Hausherr, *L'erreur fondamentale et la logique du Messialinisme*, in *OCP* 1 [1935] 328-360, p. 334).

human nature; something that is connatural, in that it is not an outside influence, but is present in man's soul[228] from the very moment of creation. This inherent goodness allows man to reach out to his creator and ensures that he receives the sustenance of divine grace.

Through the words of Chaeremon, Cassian has thus attempted to define the status of both free will and divine grace and their mutual relationship. It is certainly worth noting that he does not try to tackle the problem from an ontological point of view, by asking whether it is grace or free will that comes first. Such an approach would inevitably jeopardize the mutual interaction existing between the two, by assuming that there is a primacy/priority of one of the two terms over the other[229]. As a matter of fact, grace and human will are so enigmatically interwoven (*permixta atque confusa*) that it is not always clear which comes into operation first[230]. Yet the two realities must be kept together and accepted equally, and in such a way that the value of each is taken into account and recognized by reason and faith alike or, as Cassian says, by the reason of our religion (*pietatis ratio*) and by the rule of the Church's faith (*ecclesiasticae fidei regula*)[231]. Not to accept this harmonious encounter between grace and free will, would mean abandoning the rule of the Church's faith. Holy Scripture itself teaches that in some instances

228. Cassian speaks of the *uirtutum semina* as something that is "inserted" in every soul due to the benevolence of the creator (cf. Cassian, *Conlatio* 13,12 [SC, 54], p. 166). See also: "Id quod per naturam conditionis insertum est" (*Ibid.*, 3,15 [SC, 42], p. 158); "Deus hominem creans omnem naturaliter ei scientiam legis inseruit" (*Ibid.*, 8,23 [SC, 54], p. 31). The same verb *inserere* indicates that the knowledge of good, or virtue, and the capability of following it are inscribed in man's created nature. Once again, Cassian employs the term *natura* in its primordial, pre-Augustinian meaning, indicating the goodness attached to man's original state at the moment of creation, a goodness which was not completely lost after Adam's fall.

229. As it has been rightly noted: "Ce qu'il *[Cassian]* rejette... c'est l'effort théorique qui sous-tend la systématisation augustinienne, c'est-à-dire la scission rationaliste de l'union de la liberté et de la grâce et sa mise en question en termes de primauté absolue. La théorisation de cette union occulte sa nature énigmatique, telle que l'Ecriture nous la révèle dans des textes qui paraissent contradictoires" (M. ZANANIRI, *La controverse sur la prédestination au Vᵉ siècle: Augustin, Cassien et la Tradition*, in P. RANSON [ed.], *Saint Augustin, s. l.*, 1988, p. 260).

230. "Et ita sunt haec quodammodo indiscrete permixta atque confusa, ut quid ex quo pendeat inter multos magna quaestione uoluatur, id est utrum quia initium bonae uoluntatis praebuerimus misereatur nostri Deus, an quia Deus misereatur consequamur bonae uoluntatis initium. Multi enim singula haec credentes ac iusto amplius adserentes uariis sibique contrariis sunt erroribus inuoluti" (Cassian, *Conlatio* 13,11 [SC, 54], p. 162).

231. "Haec ergo duo, id est uel gratia Dei uel liberum arbitrium sibi quidem inuicem uidentur aduersa, sed utraque concordant et utraque nos pariter debere suscipere pietatis ratione colligimus, ne unum horum homini subtrahentes ecclesiasticae fidei regulam excessisse uideamur" (*Ibid.* 13,11, p. 163). Cf. also *Ibid.* 13,13, p. 168; 3,19 (SC, 42), pp. 162-163; 7,8, p. 254.

it is God who takes the initiative, for example the call/conversion of Matthew the tax collector (cf. Mt 9,9) or that of Saul the persecutor of Christians (cf. Ac 9,3ff). In other instances the initiative is ascribed to man, for example Zacchaeus (cf. Lk 19,2) and the robber crucified with Jesus (cf. Lk 23,40ff)[232]. Cassian insists on this "successionist" model, which goes both from God to man and from man to God. Sometimes God's grace intervenes on behalf of man's free will, when man makes the first move; at other times it is grace which not only inspires, but even acts decisively through man's free will[233], allowing him to take the first step on the way to God. Good will, therefore, should not always be attributed either to God's grace or to man's free will[234]. However confusing and inconsistent such an approach may seem from a rationalist point of view, it nevertheless shows Cassian's desire to remain faithful to the apparent contradictions of Scripture, which stress the value and role of both grace and free will, without concern for a rationalist systematization of their mutual relationship in terms of primacy.

As already hinted at, the other important feature of *Conlatio* 13 is the emphasis that Cassian places on the free will, which he regards as a demonstration of the ultimate goodness of human nature (*naturae bonum*). With a certain optimism he reaffirms that man is not only responsible for the evil that he does, but also for the good that is positively willed and chosen by himself (*a semetipso*)[235]. In point of fact, the

232. Cf. *Ibid.* 13,11 (SC, 54), p. 163. The attempt at solving the use of these and other opposed biblical *loci* by explaining them through the distinction between πρακτική (*scientia actualis*) and θεωρητική (*scientia contemplationis*) employed by Cassian in *Conlatio* 14 (*Ibid.* 14,1 (SC, 54), p. 184; see M. SPINELLI, *Teologia e "Teoria" nella* Conlatio De Protectione Dei *di Giovanni Cassiano*, in *Ben* 31 [1984] 23-35) is not wholly convincing. The fact, for instance, that Cassian interprets the *scientia actualis* as the *conditio sine qua non* of the *scientia contemplationis*, viz. as two successive stages where the latter replaces the former on the way to perfection, does not do justice to the "interplay" in human life between God's action and man's agency.

233. "Nam bonarum rerum non tantum suggestor, sed etiam fautor atque inpulsor est Deus, ita ut nonnumquam nos etiam inuitos et ignorantes adtrahat ad salutem" (Cassian, *Conlatio* 7,8 [SC, 42], p. 254).

234. "Nam cum uiderit nos Deus ad bonum uelle deflectere, occurrit, dirigit atque confortat: *ad uocem* enim *clamoris tui statim ut audierit, respondebit tibi*, et *inuoca me*, inquit, *in die tribulationis: et eripiam te, et glorificabis me*. Et rursus si nos nolle uel intepuisse prespexerit, adhortationes salutiferas admouet cordibus nostris, quibus uoluntas bona uel reparetur uel formetur in nobis" (*Ibid.* 13,11 [SC, 54], pp. 163-164). Prosper was convinced rather that Cassian's attempt at keeping in balance the two principles of good was a sign of contradiction (cf. Prosper, *De gratia Dei et libero arbitrio contra Collatorem* 4,2 [PL, 51], c. 224).

235. "Nec enim talem Deus hominem fecisse credendus est, qui nec uelit umquam nec possit bonum. Alioquin nec liberum ei permisit arbitrium, si ei tantummodo malum ut uelit et possit, bonum uero a semetipso nec uelle nec posse concessit" (Cassian, *Conlatio* 13,12 [SC, 54], p. 164).

knowledge of good and the capability of doing it, was not irremediably
lost after Adam's fall, even though man's will has certainly suffered
some weakness and irresolution since then[236]. As a result, mankind has
had to struggle with the problematic presence of evil, with sinfulness
and with the constant lure of the worldly pleasures, always in opposition
to spiritual ideals; a condition that was unknown before Adam's fall[237],
and which makes it now more difficult for man to choose the good[238].
Cassian asserts that one should carefully avoid a unilateral position that
awards God all the good merits of the saints in such a way that nothing
can be ascribed to human nature but evil and obstructiveness to good[239].
In Cassian's eyes, the *naturae bonum*, a goodness not destroyed by
Adam's fall, presupposes a beneficent God who created everything
good, including man, but it is also the *conditio sine qua non* for man's
moral actions which are carried out through the exercise of free will and
are integral to his God given nature[240].

236. This aspect of the infirmity of the will has been treated by Cassian in *Conlatio*
3,12 (SC, 42), pp. 155-157 *passim*.
237. "Concepit ergo Adam post praeuaricationem quam non habuerat scientiam mali,
boni vero quam acceperat scientiam non amisit" (*Ibid.*, 13,12 [SC, 54], p. 164).
238. Cf. *Ibid.*
239. "Vnde cauendum nobis est, ne ita ad Dominum omnia sanctorum merita referamus, ut nihil nisi id quod malum atque peruersum est humanae adscribamus naturae"
(*Ibid.* 13,12, pp. 165-166). To a some extent we find this same anxiety in Jerome: "Et
revera grandis iniustitia Dei, si tantum peccata punire et bona opera non susciperet"
(Jerome, *Aduersus Iouinianum* 2,3 [PL, 23], c. 299). It must be noted that the Jerome who
writes against Jovinian in ca. 392 is not yet the anti-Pelagian Jerome of several years
later, from 414 onwards. By that time it had become clear to Jerome that "the Pelagian
debate was the continuation of both the ascetic and the Origenist controversies" (CLARK,
The Origenist Controversy [n. 128], p. 221). We should not forget that Jerome, an avid
student of Origen, espoused the anti-Origenist cause after 396. He did so, firstly "for personal rather than intellectual reasons, to rescue his own reputation from the taint of hereti-
cal association.... Secondarily, and his central religious concern, Jerome was determined
to preserve the notion of moral hierarchy (based largely on degrees of ascetic renunciation) both in this life and in the next" (*Ibid.*, pp. 121-122).
240. In Eastern theology the potentialities of free will have always been intimately
linked to the goodness of creation. More particularly it is in the tradition of Origenism
that human free will has been emphasized as a basic reality stemming as it does from the
"fundamental nature of the soul as a self moving agent" (G. BOSTOCK, *The Influence of
Origen on Pelagius and Western Monasticism*, in W.A. BIENERT and U. KÜHNEWEG
[eds.], *Origeniana Septima. Origenes in den Auseinandersetzungen des 4. Jahrhunderts*
[BETL, 137], Louvain, 1999, pp. 381-396, p. 387). This same belief was shared by the
Pelagians for whom the goodness of free will was connatural with the goodness of man's
creation and therefore could not possibly perish through the sin of Adam: "Liberum arbitrium in omnibus esse naturaliter nec Adae peccato perire potuisse" (reported by Augustine, *Contra duas epistulas Pelagianorum* 1,29 [CSEL, 60], p. 447). As Pelagius himself
wrote, there is a *naturalis quaedam sanctitas* in our souls which, presiding in the mind's
citadel, judges evil and good: "Est enim, inquam, in animis nostris naturalis quaedam
(ut ita dixerim) sanctitas: quae par velut in arce animi praesidens, exercet mali

Conlatio 13 continues with abba Chaeremon saying that no one should doubt that mankind possesses *naturaliter*, in itself, the *uirtutum semina* that God has placed in every soul and that He "awakens" and brings to perfection by his intervention (*opitulatio*)[241]. Yet man retains always the freedom to neglect or to love the divine grace that comes to his help[242]. Moreover, occasionally (*nonnumquam*) it happens that, instead of forestalling man's will, God's grace first waits for some effort (*conatus*) on the part of man, before bestowing on him his saving protection[243], although we know already that human efforts obviously do not diminish the power and gratuity of grace[244]. To back up all these considerations, abba Chaeremon affirms that there are times when temptations have to be regarded as allowed by God, in order that man's free will be put to the test and activated. More subtly still, God's action

bonique iudicium" (Pelagius, *Ep. ad Demetriadem* 4 [PL, 30], c. 20). As Kelly has remarked, "the keystone of his *[Pelagius]* all system is the idea of unconditional free-will and responsibility" (J.N.D. KELLY, *Early Christian Doctrines*, London, 1958, p. 357).

241. "Dubitari ergo non potest inesse quidem omni animae naturaliter uirtutum semina beneficio creatoris inserta: sed nisi haec opitulatione dei fuerint excitata, ad incrementum perfectionis non poterunt peruenire, quia secundum beatum apostolum *neque qui plantat est aliquid, neque qui rigat, sed qui incrementum dat Deus*" (Cassian, *Conlatio* 13,12 [SC, 54], p. 166). See also the *naturalia uirtutum semina* in *Conlatio* 23,11 (SC, 64), p. 154. The metaphor of the *uirtutum semina* is Stoic (see *infra*, pp. 272-289 *passim*), but its understanding is profoundly modified by Cassian's insight based upon Christian faith and revelation. In fact, although Cassian partly shares the Stoic optimism linked with the concept of *semina* and the goodness of human nature, the latter is not a self-evident and autonomous reality, but depends ultimately upon God and his providence. See TIBILETTI, *Giovanni Cassiano* (n. 118), pp. 360-362; 372-373.

242. "Et idcirco manet in homine liberum semper arbitrium, quod gratiam Dei possit uel neglegere uel amare" (Cassian, *Conlatio* 13,12 [SC, 54], p. 167).

243. "Et ita semper gratia Dei nostro in bonam partem cooperatur arbitrio atque in omnibus illud adiuuat, protegit ac defendit, ut nonnumquam etiam ab eo quosdam conatus bonae uoluntatis uel exigat uel expectet, ne penitus dormienti aut inerti otio dissoluto sua dona conferre uideatur" (*Ibid.* 13,13, p. 168). See also: "*et gratia eius in me uacua non fuit, sed abundantius illis omnibus laboraui: non autem ego, sed gratia Dei mecum.* nam cum dicit *laboraui*, conatum proprii signat arbitrii: cum dicit *non autem ego, sed gratia Dei*, uirtutem diuinae protectionis ostendit: cum dicit *mecum*, non otioso neque securo, sed laboranti ac desudanti eam cooperatam fuisse declarat" (*Ibid.* 13,13, p. 170). The terms *conatus* and *labor* (among others) recur several times in the monastic writings of Cassian, bearing evidence of the importance he attached to human efforts in the cooperation with God's grace. For the use of the term *conatus* see, for instance: Id., *De institutis coenobiorum* 4,26 (SC, 109), p. 158; 12,13-16 *passim*, pp. 466-472; *Conlationes* 1,4-10 *passim* (SC, 42), pp. 81-89; *Ibid.* 2,16, p. 131; 3,15, p. 159; 7,3, p. 247; 10,7 (SC, 54), p. 81; 12,16, p. 145; 13,3-18 *passim*, pp. 149-181; 22,3 (SC, 64), p. 118. As to the term *labor*, see: Id., *De institutis coenobiorum* 3,8,4 and 3,11 (SC, 109), pp. 112 and 116; *Ibid.* 5,22, p. 228; 6,1, p. 262; 12,13, p. 466; *Conlationes* 1,2 and 9 (SC, 42), pp. 80 and 87; *Ibid.* 7,21, p. 262; 11,5 (SC, 54), p. 104; 14,9, p. 193; 24,23, p. 195.

244. "Quantumlibet ergo enisa fuerit humana fragilitas, futurae retributionis par esse non poterit nec ita laboribus suis diuinam inminuet gratiam, ut non semper gratuita perseueret" (*Ibid.* 13,13, p. 169).

should be interpreted as a way of preventing man's will from becoming imprisoned by idleness and laziness (*torpor*)[245]. There are instances in Scripture that seem to illustrate that the testing and proving of man's soul by God are intended to prompt and ultimately benefit his own will power. This is the case, for example, with Job and Abraham. Satan himself recognized that he had been defeated by the endurance of Job[246] who, seemingly, had been deliberately abandoned by God in order to fight temptation[247]. In a similar manner, Abraham's faith and obedience to the divine request to sacrifice his only son, Isaac, were the fruits of his own free will, and were not inspired by God, since it was God who put him to the test[248]. Temptation can, therefore, be seen as a testing ground where God steps back in order that man's free will might be stimulated to make some efforts, rather than merely and passively relying on divine help. Man's ability to endure, and his capacity for withstanding the attacks of the devil, enable him, by the use of his own free will, to take moral responsibility for his action in the midst of trial[249]; though of course God remains vigilant and, like a nursemaid (*nutrix pia atque sollicita*)[250], never ceases to watch over man.

245. "Occasiones quodammodo quaerens quibus humanae segnitiae torpore discusso non inrationabilis munificientiae suae largitas uideatur, dum eam sub colore cuiusdam desiderii ac laboris inpertit" (*Ibid.* 13,13, p. 168). The mention of *torpor* betrays Cassian-the-monk's fear of moral ease or spiritual relaxation and what that might imply for a monastic community. It is easy to see in Cassian's mind a possible connexion between laziness and a wrongly-understood absolute dependence on grace. See also the references to *tepor*: "Tepidum nostrae uoluntatis arbitrium" (*Ibid.*, 4,12 [SC, 42], p. 177); "Essemus itaque penitus absque remedio tepidi, utpote non habentes indicem neglegentiae nostrae..." (*Ibid.*, 4,16, p. 181); "Et ita inuenti in illo tepido statu, qui deterrimus iudicatur" (*Ibid.*, 4,19, p. 183), and the verbal form *intepuisse* (*Ibid.* 13,11 [SC, 54], p. 164).

246. With regard to this Old Testament figure "bleibt Augustinus mit seiner H.*[iob]*interpretation im Rahmen, 'heilspädagogischer' Auslegung" (E. DASSMANN, *Hiob [Job]*, in *RAC* 15 [1989] 366-442).

247. "Non Dei, sed illius se euictum uiribus" (Cassian, *Conlatio* 13,14 [SC, 54], p. 170). See CHADWICK, *John Cassian* (n. 84), p. 125.

248. "Non enim illam fidem quam ei Dominus inspirabat, sed illam quam uocatus semel atque inluminatus a Domino per libertatis arbitrium poterat exhibere, experiri uoluit diuina iustitia" (Cassian, *Conlatio* 13,14 [SC, 54], p. 171).

249. "Et quid eos necesse est uel temptari, quos ita infirmos nouit ac fragiles, ut nequaquam uirtute sua ualeant resistere temptatori? sed utique nec temptari eos iustitia Domini permisisset, nisi parem in eis resistendi scisset inesse uirtutem, qua possent aequitatis iudicio in utroque merito uel rei uel laudabiles iudicari" (*Ibid.* 13,14, p. 172). See also *Ibid.*, p. 173. The experience of being abandoned by God's grace for the sake of testing is also present in the well known episode of Antony's trial: cf. Athanasius, *Vita Antonii* 10 (SC, 400), pp. 162.164. For the full text, see *infra*, ch. III, n. 128.

250. Cassian, *Conlatio* 13,14 (SC, 54), p. 173. A similar metaphor can be found in Pseudo-Macarius, *Homilia* 27,3 (*Coll.* III) (SC, 275), pp. 320-322; *Hom.* 46,3 (*Coll.* II),in *PTS* 4, p. 302. See also Cassian, *Conlatio* 13,17 (SC, 54), p. 179, where divine providence is compared to the tender heart of a mother (*tenerrimis piae matris uisceribus* [cf. Is

Furthermore, there are a variety of ways in which God's intervention occurs: either preceding man's free will (*e.g.*, the vocation of Peter and Andrew [cf. Mt 4,18], and of Paul [cf. Ac 9,3ff]) or confirming and rewarding man's efforts (*e.g.*, Zacchaeus [cf. Lk 19,2ff] and Cornelius [cf. Ac 10]), but always according to the circumstances and the capacities of each man and the degree of his faith[251]. Accordingly, dissociating himself from the opinion of those who believe that the *summa salutis* depends exclusively on man's efforts and that grace is granted as a reward for merits[252], Chaeremon insists that, in some cases, God takes into account man's good will and desire, and bolsters them. In other cases it is He himself who inspires them from the very beginning and brings them to completion[253]. In fact, not only does God exercise a direct saving action through his role as *protector et saluator*, but He also relates to man as *adiutor ac susceptor*, namely by persuading him and by confirming and rewarding his efforts[254]. This is what we deduce from Holy Scripture, where it is evident that, in one way or another, God intervenes in order to draw men to salvation[255], although the precise

49,15]). "Our author – writes Macqueen – sees God everywhere active among sinners, restraining some, pushing others forward in his merciful concern to guide them all from the jaws of hell to the gates of heaven. It is apparently difficult, on the other hand, for Cassian to conceive of sinners who would actually refuse saving grace: this is again another source of tension between his modes of thought and Augustine's" (MACQUEEN, *John Cassian on Grace and Free Will* [n. 179], p. 23, n. 78).

251. "Secundum capacitatem uniuscuiusque" (Cassian, *Conlatio* 13,15 [SC, 54], p. 175). "Secundum capacitatem humanae fidei" (*Ibid.* 13,15, p. 176).

252. Cf. *Ibid.* 13,16, p. 176. Although he does not mention them by name, Cassian is obviously alluding to the Pelagians.

253. "Nunc quidem ut inpleantur ea quae utiliter a nobis desiderata perspexerit adiuuare, nunc uero etiam ipsius sancti desiderii inspirare principia et uel initium boni operis uel perseuerantiam condonare" (*Ibid.* 13,17, p. 178). See also: "Nunc quidem salutis inspirare principia et inserere unicuique bonae uoluntatis ardorem, nunc uero ipsius operationis effectum et consummationem donare uirtutum"; "Et alios quidem uolentes currentesque suscipere, alios uero nolentes resistentesque pertrahere et ad bonam cogere uoluntatem" (*Ibid.* 13,18, p. 180).

254. "Inde est quod orantes non solum protectorem ac saluatorem, sed etiam adiutorem ac susceptorem Dominum proclamamus. In eo enim quod prior aduocat et ignorantes nos atque inuitos adtrahit ad salutem, protector atque saluator est, in eo autem quod adnitentibus nobis opem ferre refugientesque suscipere ac munire consueuit, susceptor ac refugium nominatur" (*Ibid.* 13,17, p. 178). According to Rousseau, "God plays the role of the ideal abbot.... demanding, in other words, the trust of a disciple in the wisdom of his master. God does not call upon his power and prescience to impose straight lines on the graph of human progress, but allows himself to follow the variable curve of individual ambition and ability.... Behind this image of God lay Cassian's firm belief in authority based on persuasion; a belief that demanded the possibility of merit and reward" (ROUSSEAU, *Ascetics, Authority and the Church* [n. 81], pp. 233-234).

255. "Euidenter ostenditur *inscrutabilia esse iudicia Dei et inuestigabiles uias eius*, quibus ad salutem humanum adtrahit genus" (Cassian, *Conlatio* 13,17 [SC, 54], p. 174).

method of this intervention, and the reasons behind it, belong to God's inscrutable decision[256]. No doubt, Cassian underlines, what one must retain as being evident from faith and palpable experience is the fact that the God of the universe works all things evenhandedly in everyone as the most tender of fathers[257].

Abba Chaeremon concludes his conference by appealing to tradition, and by comparing its teaching to what he claims are the definitions of the catholic Fathers on this particular issue of grace and free will (*hoc ab omnibus catholicis patribus definitur*)[258]. These definitions are recalled

---

It is interesting to see the different way the Pauline quotation of Rom 11,33 is used by Cassian and Augustine. Cassian refers to it optimistically to convey the certainty that God's grace acts, although at times mysteriously, to bring all men to salvation (see also *Ibid.* 13,17, p. 178, where he speaks of the *dispensationis Dei multiplex largitas* and of his *interminabilis pietas*). Augustine's use of Rom 11,33 in the treatises he addresses to the monks of Hadrumetum and Marseilles, has, instead, a negative connotation. It is employed to answer the question of why grace is sometimes accorded to the infants of heathen people and not to those of believers (cf. Augustine, *De gratia et libero arbitrio* 22,44 [PL, 44], c. 909); to back up his conviction that perseverance is not given to those who have not been chosen (cf. Id., *De correptione et gratia* 8,17-19 [CSEL, 92], pp. 237-241; *De praedestinatione sanctorum* 6,11 [PL, 44], c. 969); to assert once again, especially in the case of infants, that God delivers whom he wishes and does not help those he does not wish to help (cf. *Ibid.* 8,16, cc. 972-973; *De dono perseuerantiae* 11,25 [PL, 45], c. 1007; *Ibid.* 12,30, c. 1011). Cassian on the contrary states that it would be a grievous blasphemy (*ingens sacrilegium*) to imagine that God wills the salvation of only a few and not all (cf. 1 Tim 2,4; Cassian, *Conlatio* 13,7 [SC, 54], p. 156).

256. "Euacuare conabitur, quisque crediderit illius inaestimabilis abyssi profunditatem humana ratione se posse metiri. Nam qui ad plenum dispensationes Dei, quibus salutem in hominibus operatur, uel mente concipere uel disserere se posse confidit, procul dubio inpugnans apostolicae sententiae ueritatem scrutabilia esse Dei iudicia et uestigabiles uias eius profana pronuntiabit audacia" (*Ibid.* 13,17, p. 179). Cassian is again alluding to Augustine, against whom he employs the Pauline text of Rom 11,33, that same quotation to which the bishop of Hippo referred to on several occasions in order to justify predestination.

257. "Et idcirco fide non dubia et ut ita dicam palpabili experientia conprobatur uniuersitatis Deum uelut piissimum patrem benignissimumque medicum secundum apostolum indifferenter omnia in omnibus operari" (*Ibid.* 13,18, p. 180).

258. *Ibid.* Cassian had already claimed to represent the teaching of the Fathers in his works by using their very words ("ut ipsis quibus tradunt uerbis patrum sententiam proferamus": Id., *De institutis coenobiorum* 12,13 [SC, 109], p. 466); the teaching of the elders ("seniorum sententia": *Ibid.* 12,14, p. 468); the genuine faith of the most ancient Fathers ("haec est antiquissimorum patrum sincera fides": *Ibid.* 12,19, p. 478). Cassian's expression *ab omnibus catholicis patribus* reminds us of his contemporary Vincent of Lérins' criteria for defining the authenticity of a doctrine, namely when it is taught *ubique, semper, ab omnibus*: "In ipsa item catholica ecclesia magnopere curandum est, ut id teneamus quod ubique, quod semper, quod ab omnibus creditum est" (Vincent of Lérins, *Commonitorium* 2,5 [CCL, 64], p. 149). See also: "Necesse est profecto omnibus deinceps catholicis, qui sese ecclesiae matris legitimos filios probare student, ut sanctae sanctorum patrum fidei inhaereant, adglutinentur, inmoriantur, *profanas* uero profanorum *nouitates* detestentur" (*Ibid.* 33,6, pp. 194-195). Two other affirmations of Vincent, the first to a well-known, holy and respected bishop who, at a certain point, started teaching

as follows: 1) it is by God's gift that man is enlightened with the desire
for good, whilst his will in following this path remains entirely free; 2)
it is through grace that man is rendered capable of practising virtue, and
yet his own use of free will is never annihilated; 3) once he has acquired
virtue, man looks to God to receive the grace of perseverance, though
his will is never subject to slavery[259]. It must not be forgotten that
appealing to tradition was not an unusual move, especially in controversies[260]. No doubt Cassian and his followers "regarded themselves as the
conservative representatives of traditional Christian theology against
dangerous innovation"[261]. Augustine's teaching on predestination must,
from the very start, have seemed a novel doctrine in their eyes. Yet, sig-
nificantly, in *Conlatio* 13 Cassian never appeals explicitly to any
authoritative voice of the Church[262]. His only quotations are from Scripture; a clear sign that he never actually "succumbed to treating doctrines
as hard external propositions"[263]. Finally, however difficult or enigmatic
it may seem to understand how everything man does is the result of
God's action working within him, and how, at times, man's achievements may be attributed to the use of his own free will[264], we have
to realize that God operates in everybody by urging, protecting and

---

noxios errores (*Ibid.* 10,8, p. 159), and the second to a great doctor who had deviated
from the common and general teaching of the Church (cf. *Ibid.* 28,8, p. 187), are a possible allusion to Augustine. See L. LONGOBARDO (ed.), *Vincenzo di Lerino, Commonitorio-
Estratti. Tradizione e novità nel cristianesimo*, Rome, 1994, pp. 38-40. Finally, we ought
to remind ourselves that the question of the conciliation of grace and free will had never
posed problems to the Fathers of the Church prior to Augustine. If they ever tackled the
question, it was mainly out of concern for and defence of the autonomy of free will (cf.
infra, pp. 193ff.). It was with Pelagius' stress on the sufficiency of the latter that the problem of its relationship with grace was forced into the open where it broke new ground.
And it is in answering the Pelagian standpoint that Augustine took his teaching to some
extreme consequences.

259. "Diuini esse muneris primum ut accendatur unusquisque ad desiderandum omne
quod bonum est, sed ita ut in alterutram partem plenum sit liberae (*sic!*) uoluntatis arbitrium: itemque etiam secundum diuinae esse gratiae ut effici ualeant exercitia praedicta
uirtutum, sed ita ut possibilitas non extinguatur arbitrii: tertium quoque ad Dei munera
pertinere ut adquisitae uirtutis perseuerantia teneatur, sed ita ut captiuitatem libertas
addicta non sentiat" (Cassian, *Conlatio* 13,18 [SC, 54], p. 181).

260. Augustine himself made use of this claim, especially in his works against Julian
of Aeclanum.

261. CHADWICK, *John Cassian* (n. 84), p. 119.

262. The only exception is a reference to the *Pastor of Hermas* about man's neutral-
ity of choice between the two angels who watch over him, one good and one bad (cf.
Cassian, *Conlatio* 13,12 [SC, 54], pp. 166-157; cf. *Pastor Hermae* 36 [*Praec.* 6,2] [SC,
53], p. 172). Prosper will judge this reference as "nullius auctoritatis testimonium" (Prosper, *De gratia Dei et libero arbitrio contra Collatorem* 13,6 [PL, 51], c. 250).

263. CHADWICK, *John Cassian* (n. 84), p. 120.

264. Cf. Cassian, *Conlatio* 13,18 (SC, 54), p. 181.

confirming, without ever interfering with the freedom He has granted
mankind[265].

At the end of this short exposition of *Conlatio* 13, we could be left
with a feeling of uneasiness regarding Cassian's lack of systematic
thinking and metaphysical strength[266], for his attempt to save human
agency from being annihilated by the power of grace, seems to give way
to some contradiction. In reality, what he wishes to retain, at the expense
of metaphysical clarity, is the inner (and inclusive) coherence of the
dialectical co-operation between grace and free will. For this reason,
Cassian is at pains to state formally, and with a slightly "emphatic
delight"[267], man's absolute dependence on God's grace and his constant
need for God's help and protection[268], while at the same time being
ready to accord a tiny segment of power to the initiative of the human
will in making some small change of heart in the direction of God. As
we have hinted at, Cassian bases this optimistic anthropological outlook
on the concept of *naturae bonum*, the basic goodness and health of
human nature. Unlike Augustine[269], he believes that, despite the consequences of Adam's fall, man's nature is not irreparably perverted and, in

---

265. "Universitatis Deus omnia in omnibus credendus est operari, ut incitet, protegat
atque confirmet, non ut auferat quam semel ipse concessit arbitrii libertatem" (*Ibid.*).

266. The point was already made by A. HOCH, *Lehre des J. Cassianus von Natur und
Gnade. Ein Beitrag zur Geschichte des Gnadenstreites im 5. Jahrhundert*, Freiburg i. Br.,
1895, pp. 109ff; KEMMER, *Charisma Maximum* (n. 196), p. 39. See also: "Telle est cette
fameuse conference XIII, où la multiplicité des détails, la finesse même de certaines
analyses psychologiques, n'arrivent pas à masquer l'incertitude de la pensée métaphysique" (AMANN, *Semi-Pélagiens* [n. 197], c. 1808). "D'une page à l'autre, on voit
l'auteur tenir des positions contradictoires, impuissant à les concilier dans une synthèse
plus vaste.... La synthèse théologique qu'il tente ici manque au moins de vigueur et de
solidité" (E. PICHERY, *Introduction*, in Jean Cassien, *Conférences* [SC, 42], pp. 149 and
151, in the footnote).

267. CHADWICK, *John Cassian* (n. 84), p. 126. And again: "Often it *[the Conlatio 13]*
sounds more like a hymn in praise of God's grace" (*Ibid.* p. 120).

268. Cf., for instance: "Manifeste colligitur non solum actuum, uerum etiam cogita-
tionum bonarum ex Deo esse principium, qui nobis et initia sanctae uoluntatis inspirat et
uirtutem atque oportunitatem eorum quae recte cupimus tribuit peragendi: *omne* enim
datum bonum et omne donum perfectum de sursum est descendens a patre luminum, qui
et incipit quae bona sunt et exsequitur et consummat in nobis" (Cassian, *Conlatio* 13,3
[SC, 54], p. 151). Cf. also *Ibid.* 13,6, pp. 153f.

269. According to Augustine, "natura sana non est" (Augustine, *De natura et gratia*
3,3, [CSEL, 60], p. 235) and needs to be renewed by grace: "Nec sane isto modo naturam siue animae siue corporis, quam Deus creauit et quae tota bona est, accusamus, sed
eam dicimus propria uoluntate uitiatam sine Dei gratia non posse sanari" (Id., *De perfectione iustitiae hominis* 6,12 [CSEL, 42], pp. 11-12). We cannot agree with Macqueen's
statement that the differences between Cassian and Augustine can be reduced to "a clash
of temperaments rather than of doctrine" (MACQUEEN, *John Cassian on Grace and Free
Will* [n. 179], p. 19). On the contrary, they must be read against their differing theological approach to the notion of nature. See *infra*, pp. 272ff.

certain instances, remains capable of good even without the direct help
of grace. It is true, however, that in spite of Cassian's concern to balance
the grace of God and the human action, there remains some uncertainty
as to the theoretical development of this assumption. It seems to us that
there are two reasons for this. First of all, we should not forget that Cassian was anxious to avoid the polarization of Pelagianism and Augustinianism, which the echo of the recent controversy would have pushed to
the foreground[270]. Rejecting the former (whose ascetic thrust he must
have however shared) and feeling uneasy about some of the excesses
and rigidities in the latter, Cassian, under the influence of the Eastern
Christian and monastic tradition in which he was formed, seems to
search for a synergetic solution or for a *uia media*. A solution, that is, in
which some room could be reserved for the power of man's free will,
without the constraint of an appeal to God's prevenient grace, but at the
same time a solution which would preserve the necessity and sovereignty of grace[271]. To keep this balance is exactly what made it difficult
for Cassian to present a clear cut conceptual definition of grace vis-à-vis
free will. When viewed from the perspective of his particular assumptions and goals, however, his attempt to give reasons for the interaction
of grace and (moral) human freedom betrays no lack of "inner" logic[272].
This leads us to the second reason and explanation for Cassian's seemingly unsteady and incoherent thought. The lack of a strong metaphysical thinking in Cassian's *Conlatio* 13 should, in fact, be interpreted
in the light of the "ethical" option and the "practical" nature of his

270. "La controverse Pélage-Augustin est à l'arrière-plan" (DE VOGÜÉ, *Pour comprendre Cassien* [n. 156], p. 261). We can well believe that this same background influenced not only the *Conlationes* (and in particular *Conlatio* 13), but also the *De institutis
coenobiorum*, especially the chapters devoted to the energetic struggle against the eight
principal vices. As it has been noted, "there can be no doubt that a deeply serious preoccupation with the controversy between Augustine and the Pelagians on the subject of the
necessity of divine grace for all human endeavour towards perfection underlies the whole
of the *Institutes* also, and may well have been the principal incentive in the composition
of this work" (CHADWICK, *Poetry and Letters in Early Christian Gaul* [n. 78], p. 221).

271. "What Cassian proposes – writes Colish – is the synergistic interaction between
God and man typical of the Byzantine Church Fathers and the eastern orthodox tradition
as a whole. Stoicism provides him with a way of conceptualizing the human contribution
to this ethical enterprise. But it would be incorrect to suppose that he sees man as ethi-
cally autonomous" (COLISH, *The Stoic Tradition from Antiquity to the Early Middle Ages.*
Vol. II [n. 178], p. 116).

272. "Admittedly, indeed, his discussion of the topic... is deficient in the method and
precision appropriate to a formal treatise on theology. It does, however, exhibit an underlying unity and coherence" (MACQUEEN, *John Cassian on Grace and Free Will* [n. 179],
p. 24).

teaching[273]. In harmony with the monks' severe education, focused
as it was on the merit of the pragmatic virtues of obedience, humility,
vigils, fasting and constant struggle against passions and vices, Cassian
lays emphasis upon the psychological features[274] and the moral responsibility of their religious commitment. The monks' main concern was a
moral one, and had to do with the " know-how" of the journey of the
soul towards perfection, rather than with metaphysical and speculative
questions. The terms themselves that Cassian uses to define the monks
and their combat against passions and vices (*miles [Christi]* or *militia
Christi/spiritalis*[275], *athleta*[276], *agon*[277], *certamen*[278], *conluctatio*[279])
emphasize the strong and masculine *Sitz im Leben* of those for whom his
teaching was intended.

It must not be forgotten that Cassian was also a monk and that any
leanings he might have towards scholarship, although not done away
with, were nevertheless subjugated to the greater vocation of a life dedicated to the quest for God and to the teachings of Holy Scripture and of
the orthodox Christian writers[280]. Cassian's suspicion of intellectual
abstraction, which can be perceived in some of his statements[281], must

273. "The essentially practical nature of his teaching accounts for the underlying
apparent inconsistency of his theory of Free-Will and Grace, and of the absence of logic
in his argument" (CHADWICK, *Poetry and Letters in Early Christian Gaul* [n. 78], p. 237).

274. See OLPHE-GALLIARD, *Cassien (Jean)* (n. 118), cc. 237ff. According to Guy,
Cassian's leanings towards a psychological description is precisely what diminishes the
power of his speculative thought (cf. GUY, *Jean Cassien* [n. 118], p. 58). Tibiletti does not
agree with this conclusion (cf. TIBILETTI, *Giovanni Cassiano* [n. 118], p. 369, n. 108).

275. Cf., for instance, Cassian, *De institutis coenobiorum* 1,11,1 (SC, 109), p. 52;
Ibid., 2,1, p. 58; 2,3,2, p. 62; 5,19,1, p. 222; 5,21,1, p. 224; 7,21, p. 322; 10,3, p. 390;
11,3 and 7, pp. 428 and 434; Id., *Conlationes* 1,1 (SC, 42), p. 78; *Ibid.*, 4,12, p. 178;
7,19, p. 261; 8,18 (SC, 54), p. 26; 24,26 (SC, 64), p. 205.

276. Cf., for instance, Id., *De institutis coenobiorum* 5,17,1 (SC, 109), p. 216; *Ibid.*
5,18,2, p. 220; 5,19,1, p. 222; 8,22, p. 364; 10,5, p. 390; 11,19,1, p. 446; 12,32, p. 498;
Conlationes 7,20 (SC, 42), p. 261; *Ibid.*, 13,14 (SC, 54), p. 170.

277. Cf., for instance, Id., *De institutis coenobiorum* 5,1–5,18,1 *passim* (SC, 109), pp.
190-218; 220; *Ibid.* 6,5, p. 268; 7,20, p. 322; 8,5, p. 344; 11,19,1, p. 446; 12,32, p. 498;
Conlationes 7,21 (SC, 42), p. 262.

278. Cf. Id., *De institutis coenobiorum* 5,3-5,19 *passim* (SC, 109), p. 192-222; *Ibid.*
6,1, p. 262; 6,7,2, p. 270; 8,1,1, p. 336; 9,1 and 2, p. 370; 10,1, p. 384; 11,1, p. 428;
11,7,1, p. 434; 12,1, p. 450; *Conlationes* 5,6-26 *passim* (SC, 42), pp. 193-216; *Ibid.* 7,20,
p. 261; 8,13 (SC, 54), p. 20; 13,14, p. 171; 18,6 (SC, 64), p. 17; 24,8, p. 178.

279. Cf., for instance, Id., *De institutis coenobiorum* 5,12,22–5,19,1 *passim*; pp. 210-
222; *Ibid.*, 6,4,2, p. 268; 7,20, p. 322; 11,17,1, p. 444; *Conlationes* 2,17 (SC, 42), p. 132;
Ibid. 4,18, p. 181; 6,16, p. 240; 7,21, p. 262; 10,10, p. 88; 12,11, p. 138; 19,16, p. 54.

280. Cassian, *Ibid.* 2,24, p. 135.

281. See, for instance: "Inanis philosophia mundi huius ac uanitas saeculi" (*Ibid.*);
"Diaboli perniciosa inlusio" (*Ibid.*); "Nomismata aerea falsaque" (*Ibid.* 1,20 [SC, 42], p.
102). See E.L. FORTIN, *Christianisme et culture philosophique au cinquième siècle. La
querelle de l'âme humaine en Occident* (CEAug.SA, 10), Paris, 1959, pp. 66-67.

be understood from this monastic perspective. The desire for perfection in a God-orientated soul does not depend on man's intellectual abilities, but is thoroughly bound to God. To attain perfection monks are not required to use the weapons of the *uaniloquia disputatio*[282], the *ars dialectica* or the *philosophica disputatio*[283], the *syllogismi dialectici* or the *Tulliana facundia*[284], but the practice of virtue[285]. In that respect, the monks have to look for inspiration and encouragement in those who have already attained perfection and possess an experiential knowledge of the hard struggle that the acquisition of virtue requires. It is precisely against this background that Cassian addresses the monks as an experienced master[286] in the ascetic struggle, and with a clear pedagogical purpose in mind: to offer the monks practical guidelines that can help them reconcile their ascetic efforts with their trust in God's grace. The fact that Cassian, in the last paragraph of *Conlatio* 13, makes reference several times to the priority of experience (*re atque opere*) over an excessive and sometimes vain confidence in intellectual powers (*inani disputatione uerborum*)[287] shows his genuine

282. Cassian, *De institutis coenobiorum* 12,15 (SC, 109), p. 470.
283. Id., *De incarnatione Domini contra Nestorium* 3,15 (CSEL, 17), p. 280.
284. Id., *De institutis coenobiorum* 12,19 (SC, 109), p. 478.
285. See abba Macarius' words paraphrasing 1 Cor 4,20: "Non est in uerbo regnum Dei, sed in uirtute" (Id., *Conlatio* 15,3 [SC, 54], p. 213).
286. Cf. GENNADIUS, *De uiris inlustribus* 62 [ed. RICHARDSON, p. 82]: "Scripsit, experientia magistrante...".
287. "Per quod euidenti ratione colligitur ab his qui non loquacibus uerbis, sed experientia duce uel magnitudinem gratiae uel modulum humani metiuntur arbitrii" (Cassian, *Conlatio* 13,18 [SC, 54], pp. 179ff); "Et idcirco hoc ab omnibus catholicis patribus definitur, qui perfectionem cordis non inani disputatione uerborum, sed re atque opere didicerunt" (*Ibid.*, pp. 180f); "Si quid sane uersutius humana argumentatione ac ratione collectum huic sensui uidetur obsistere, uitandum magis est quam ad destructionem fidei prouocandum" (*Ibid.* 13,18, p. 181). Many times Cassian speaks of experience as a constitutive part of the monastic teaching which, as he states in the preface to the third group of *Conlationes*, comes down from "antiqua traditio et longae experientiae ... industria" (Id., *Praef.* to *Conlationes* 18-24 [SC, 64], p. 9). Thus, about the goal of chastity, he writes: "Haec de castitatis fine, quantum potuimus, non uerbis, sed experientia magistrante digessimus" (*Ibid.* 12,16 [SC, 54], p. 145); about the goal of cenobitic and eremitical life: "Nulli namque dubium est neminem de his uel fidelius posse uel plenius disputare quam illum, qui utramque perfectionem longo usu ac magistra experientia consecutus meritum earum ac finem ueridica potest insinuare doctrina" (*Ibid.* 19,7 [SC, 64], p. 45). Integrity, which is the gift of grace, can only be learned by experience, as from a master ("experientiae magisterio": *Ibid.* 12,4 [SC, 54], p. 125). Prayer can also only be taught by those who have experienced in themselves this reality: "In quantum experti sumus" (*Ibid.* 9,31 [SC, 54], p. 66). Generally speaking, the *experientia cotidiana* plays an instructive role in the life of the monk (*Ibid.* 9,7, p. 48). Finally, there was a strong belief that the spiritual masters did reach a life of perfection "non uaniloqua disputatione somniantes, sed re atque experimentis adprehendentes" (Id., *De institutis coenobiorum* 12,15 [SC, 109], p. 470). See ROUSSEAU, *Ascetics, Authority and the Church* [n. 81], p. 198.

concern[288]. Apart from the fact that God's grace is necessary in man's struggle for perfection, the attainment of which remains ultimately a theandric phenomenon, he deems it more important to stress the role of ceaseless toil in the life of the monk[289]. Stimulation to a patient life-long effort and endeavour is the only alternative to a dangerous state of torpidity. In this sense the general ethical attitude is far more important for a monastic community engaged in the daily practice of virtue, than metaphysical deduction, philosophical logic or polemical dialectic[290]. Religious and ascetic experience appears indeed to be the privileged source for knowing God and divine truths far more than intellectual endeavour, at least in as far as the latter is reduced to sheer speculation[291].

In conclusion, the central place and role accorded to experience emphasizes the underlying spiritual principles of monastic life which Cassian shared. His unsystematic thought processes are a clear manifestation of this, namely that spiritual life draws its inspiration and its first and foremost rationale from God's Word and commandments and from the exemplary life of those who have already made these commandments their own. This practical ethos, with the emphasis on "doing" the words of Scripture and on "imitating" the examples of the elders, reflects no doubt the strong practical orientation of the desert monks[292]

---

288. "Cassian grenzt die der monastischen Erfahrung zugeordnete Theologie von der wissenschaftlich arbeitenden Schultheologie deutlich ab. Der Lebensbezug der *experientia* steht gegen die intellektuelle Abstraktion der *verba*" (H. HOLZE, *Die Bedeutung der* experientia *in der monastischen Theologie Johannes Cassians*, in StPatr 20, Louvain, 1989, pp. 256-263, p. 259).

289. With regard to the emphasis on human initiative and responsibility in this process, a sort of "monasticisation" of Stoic ethics can indeed be detected (see TIBILETTI, *Giovanni Cassiano* [n. 118], pp. 358ff). Cassian, however, was aware of the shortcomings of Stoicism, and did not adopt any aspect of it in an uncritical manner. That is why, for instance, he "eschews the psychic autarchy that is the main thrust of Stoic ethics" (COLISH, *The Stoic Tradition from Antiquity to the Early Middle Ages*. Vol. II [n. 178], pp. 115-116).

290. "His own position owed little to cautious logic or skilful compromise in argument. His great fear was that experience would not play a sufficient part in the formulation of theological positions" (ROUSSEAU, *Ascetics, Authority and the Church* [n. 81], p. 231).

291. It should be clear, in fact, that Cassian was not an anti-intellectualist. The intellect and the reasoning process are not done away with, as Cassian's openness to philosophical influence (*e.g.*, Stoicism) clearly shows. As it has been rightly stated: "Point de préjugés anti-intellectualistes chez Cassien, mais une méfiance pour la spéculation, dont la logique risque de durcir toute la souplesse de l'expérience" (P. MIQUEL, *Un homme d'expérience: Cassien*, in CCist 30 [1968] 131-146, p. 146).

292. "The desert fathers were often reticent to enter into speculative discussion about the meaning of Scripture or even to speak about it at all. They were convinced that the practical ethical demands of their life required their undivided attention. Only by

with whom Cassian had come into contact and with whom he had spent several years. From them he must have certainly learnt that monastic (spiritual) life is a daily stimulus to live out in practice the demands of the Christian faith and, as it were, to "measure" them *sur le terrain*. We should not forget that this was indeed the ground on which Cassian stood and from which, as an "ascetic theologian", he did theology[293]. It is from this same ground that his attempt to provide a more "humanistic" theology of grace, as an echo of Eastern thought and as an alternative to some of Augustine's extreme theories on the doctrine of grace, should be properly understood.

3. AUGUSTINE'S REPLY TO MASSILIANISM:
THE *DE PRAEDESTINATIONE SANCTORUM* AND
THE *DE DONO PERSEUERANTIAE*

The *De praedestinatione sanctorum* and the *De dono perseuerantiae* are Augustine's answer to Prosper and Hilary's letters (*Epp.* 225 and 226)[294]. It was thanks to them that the bishop of Hippo had learned of the Provencal monks criticism of his theology of grace and soteriology[295]. Augustine's answer to the Massilians' objections, however, does

focusing their attention on these primary demands, they believed, the meaning of words – those of Scripture as well as the elders – become clear" (D. BURTON-CHRISTIE, *The Word in the Desert. Scripture and the Quest for Holiness in Early Christian Monasticism* [OECS], New York-Oxford, 1993, p. 151).

293. Cassian "writes as a participant in a process of spiritual growth that is a mysterious interplay of human and divine elements. He describes rather than prescribes, teaches rather than defines" (STEWART, *Cassian the Monk* [n. 115], p. 78).

294. Originally the two books formed one single treatise under the name *De praedestinatione sanctorum*. Augustine's reference in the *De dono perseuerantiae* to the *De praedestinatione sanctorum* as "the former book" (cf., *e.g.*: "in priore libro": Augustine, *De dono perseuerantiae* 1,1 [PL, 45], c. 993) indicates that he wrote the two books as two parts of one single treatise. Prosper too reports that the two books were parts of a single work: "In *libris* beatae memoriae Augustini episcopi, quorum titulus est: *De praedestinatione sanctorum*" (Prosper, *Pro Augustino responsiones ad excerpta Genuensium*, *Praef.* [PL, 51], c. 187). From the 9th century onwards the two books were mentioned separately with a slightly different title for the second one, *De bono perseuerantiae* instead of *De dono perseuerantiae*. Cf., for instance: "Unde et sanctus Augustinus duos libros, alterum de Praedestinatione sanctorum, alterum de Bono perseuerantiae, ad... Prosperum... et Hilarium scripsit" (Hincmarus Rhemensis, *De praedestinatione Dei et libero arbitrio* 1 [PL, 125], c. 72). See also Remigius Lugdunensis, *De tenenda immobiliter Scripturae ueritate* 9 (PL, 121), c. 1107.

295. It should be noted that Augustine speaks of a more detailed piece of information (*scripta prolixiora*: Augustine, *De praedestinatione sanctorum* 3,7 [PL, 44], c. 964) sent to him by Prosper and Hilary. This means that beside the *Epp.* 225 and 226, and a previous letter mentioned by Hilary (cf. Hilary, *Ep.* 226,9 [CSEL, 57], p. 479) that has been lost, a more precise and updated account of the reaction of the monks of Provence must have reached the bishop of Hippo through one or more letters, unfortunately now lost.

not follow the plan suggested by his two correspondents[296]. The bishop of Hippo preferred some freedom in structuring his response, and chose to concentrate his argumentation around two main issues: the *initium fidei* (beginning of faith, or beginning of salvation), on one hand, and the question of final perseverance (viz. the attainment of eternal life) on the other. These two questions are approached respectively in the *De praedestinatione sanctorum* and in the *De dono perseuerantiae*. In each case it is clear to Augustine that man's agency is prompted, sustained and directed by God's gratuitous support. It is against this background that the concept of predestination, both to the life of grace as to eternal glory, is located and reiterated.

296. The fact that in refuting the objections of the Massilians, Augustine does not follow the pattern offered by Prosper and Hilary's *Epp.* 225 and 226, could in itself be a further hint that more material reached Hippo from the two Gallic correspondents, material whose content was probably set up and arranged in a different way. In our view this could also explain why Augustine praises some of the affirmations of the Massilians concerning human will and its relationship to prevenient grace, whereas in the context of the *Epp.* 225 and 226 such affirmations actually have a meaning contrary to Augustine's teaching. Thus, it is difficult to reconcile the following words of the bishop of Hippo: "Pervenerunt etiam, ut praeueniri voluntates hominum Dei gratia fateantur" (Augustine, *De praedestinatione sanctorum* 1,2 [PL, 44], c. 961), with the passage of Prosper: "Nec considerant se gratiam Dei, quam comitem, non praeuiam humanorum uolunt esse meritorum, etiam illis uoluntatibus subdere, quas ab ea secundum suam phantasiam non negant esse praeuentas" (Prosper, *Ep.* 225,5 [CSEL, 57], pp. 461-462). As a matter of fact, Prosper speaks of *phantasia* (imaginatio, or contradiction, as we would put it) because the Massilians seem to understand grace as dependent on human merits! Likewise, the passage that Augustine quotes from Hilary's letter, namely the fact that nobody can begin and accomplish any good work by himself ("Pervenerunt etiam ut [...] ad nullum opus bonum vel incipiendum vel perficiendum sibi quemquam sufficere posse consentiant": Augustine, *De praedestinatione sanctorum* 1,2, c. 961; cf. Hilary, *Ep.* 226,2 [CSEL, 57], p. 469), when compared to the context in which Hilary wrote those words, leaves us in some doubt. In fact, immediately afterwards, Hilary reported that the Massilians did not regard the "fear" produced by illness (*i.e.*, the sinful state), nor the need to beseech God so as to be delivered from it, as being part of those "actions" through which man could win salvation (*uelle sanari*): "Neque enim alicui operi curationis eorum adnumerandum putant exterrita et supplici uoluntate unumquemque aegrotum uelle sanari" (*Ibid.*). It seems as if neither of these "actions" (which rely on God's intervention) actually plays an important role, and that man is able to regain his health through his own will power! Trapè believes that here Augustine is intentionally looking for any hint or opportunity that would provide a common ground for agreement between himself and the monks of Provence (see A. Trapè, *Introduzione a La predestinazione dei santi*, in Id. [ed.], *Sant'Agostino. Grazia e libertà: La grazia e il libero arbitrio, La correzione e la grazia, La predestinazione dei santi, Il dono della perseveranza* [NBA, 20], Rome, 1987, p. 201 and p. 225, n. 5).

a) Augustine's De praedestinatione sanctorum. *The Grace of Faith and Its Beginning*

The fundamental problem that Augustine deals with in the *De praedestinatione sanctorum* is quite different from what the title would lead us to expect. In fact, to be placed in the limelight is not the issue of predestination but that of faith as a gift of God. Augustine states that such a gift is bestowed on man from the beginning and not simply at a second stage, such as an increase (*incrementum*) of a reality that man could initially achieve for himself. In the eyes of the bishop of Hippo, to deny that the beginning of faith (*initium fidei*) is also due to God's power would mean that one was of the opinion that mankind is only gifted with God's grace according to merit[297]. If that were the case, it would then follow that the increase of faith (*augmentum fidei*) and everything that the human being asks of God, is but the response of God to human initiative, which thus maintains an independent role even in the acquisition of faith[298].

To counter this opinion Augustine quotes several scriptural passages, which are then followed by small commentaries underlining the fact that man cannot claim the awakening of faith for himself and then leave God with the responsibility of its completion. God's grace is at work at all stages. In this respect, the most significant quotations Augustine uses are Rom 11,35-36, 2 Cor 3,5 and most importantly 1 Cor 4,7[299]. This last reference is quoted in connection with Cyprian's words: *In*

297. Cf. Augustine, *De praedestinatione sanctorum* 2,3 (PL, 44), c. 961. Augustine is thinking of the proposition condemned at the Council of Diospolis, in Palestine, in 415 (Cf. Id., *De gestis Pelagii* 14,30 [CSEL, 42], p. 84).

298. "Si non pertinet ad Dei gratiam quod credere coepimus, sed illud potius quod propter hoc nobis additur, ut plenius perfectiusque credamus: ac per hoc, initium fidei nostrae priores damus Deo, ut retribuatur nobis et supplementum eius; et si quid aliud fideliter poscimus" (Id., *De praedestinatione sanctorum* 2,3 [PL, 44], c. 962). This conclusion, according to Hilary's report, had been reached also by the monks of Provence (cf. Hilary, *Ep.* 226,2 [CSEL, 57], pp. 469-470).

299. "Quis prior dedit ei, et retribuetur illi? Quoniam ex ipso, et per ipsum, et in ipso sunt omnia *[Rom 11,35-36]*" (Augustine, *De praedestinatione sanctorum* 2,4 [PL, 44], c. 962); "Non quia idonei sumus cogitare aliquid quasi ex nobismetipsis, sed sufficientia nostra ex Deo est *[2 Cor 3,5]*" (*Ibid.* 2,5, c. 962; also in Id., *De gratia et libero arbitrio* 7,16 [PL, 44[, c. 891; *De dono perseuerantiae* 8,19.20; 13,33 [PL, 45], cc. 1003.1004; 1013); "Quid autem habes quod non accepisti? Si autem et accepisti, quid gloriaris quasi non acceperis? *[1 Cor 4,7]*" (Id., *De praedestinatione sanctorum* 3,7, c. 964; cf. *Ibid.* 4,8, c. 966; 5,9, c. 967; also in Id., *De gratia et libero arbitrio* 6,15 [PL, 44], c. 890; *De correptione et gratia* 2,4 and 6,9.10 [CSEL, 92], pp. 222 and 226.228; *De dono perseuerantiae* 17,43 [PL, 45], c. 1020) For Augustine's use of 1 Cor 4,7 see P.-M. HOMBERT, *Gloria gratiae. Se glorifier en Dieu, principe et fin de la théologie augustinienne de la grâce*, Paris, 1996, *passim.*

nullo gloriandum, quando nostrum nihil sit[300], and the two quotations together form as it were a banner under which Augustine defends the omnipresent gratuity of grace at work in the life of the believer *ab initio usque in finem.* Moreover, 1 Cor 4,7 provides an occasion for Augustine to remind his interlocutors that it was precisely this text that led to his understanding of the error he had fallen into before becoming bishop. At that time, in fact, he held the belief that faith was not a gratuitous gift of God but something that human being could procure for himself by his own efforts. To this purpose he quotes *in extenso* a long paragraph of his *Retractationes*[301] in which he affirms that, prompted by the *auctoritas* of various Christian writers[302], he had revised and corrected several ambiguous expressions written in ca. 394, in his first attempt to prepare a commentary on some propositions of Paul's letter to the Romans[303]. Explicitly admitted in his *Retractationes,* this "correction" had already

300. Cyprian, *Ad Quirinum (Testimoniorum l. iii)* 3,4 (CCL, 3), p. 92.
301. The reported passage is from: Augustine, *Retractationes* 1,23,2.4 (CCL, 57), pp. 68-70. Cf. Id., *De praedestinatione sanctorum* 3,7 (PL, 44), cc. 964-965.
302. "Postea, lectis quibusdam diuinorum tractatorum eloquiorum, quorum me moueret auctoritas" (Id., *Retractationes* 1,23,1 [CCL, 57], p. 67). The commentators whose authority influenced Augustine in understanding and interpreting Rom 7, are above all: Cyprian, *De Dominica oratione* 16 (CCL, 3/A), pp. 99-100; and Ambrose, *De paenitentia* 1,3 (SC, 179), pp. 60-66. "Mit seinem Landsmann Cyprian und noch mehr mit seinem geistlichen Vater Ambrosius verbindet Augustinus ein besonderes, auch emotional gefärbtes Vertrauensverhältnis" (E. DASSMANN, *"Tam Ambrosius quam Cyprianus" [c. Iul. imp. 4,112]. Augustins Helfer im pelagianischen Streit*, in D. PAPANDREOU – W.A. BIENERT – K. SCHÄFERDIEK [eds.], *Oecumenica et Patristica. Festschrift für Wilhelm Schneemelcher zum 75. Geburtstag*, Chambésy-Gerf, 1989, pp. 259-268, p. 261). Besides, Augustine was aware of the fact that both Cyprian (a bishop-martyr) and Ambrose were held in great esteem both in the Western as well as in the Eastern Church, and that this esteem was also shared by the Pelagians (cf. Augustine, *Contra duas epistulas Pelagianorum* 4,8,21 [CSEL, 60], c. 543; Id., *Contra Iulianum* 1,7,30 [PL, 44], c. 661). See E. DASSMANN, *Ambrosius*, in *AugL* 1 (1986) 270-285; ID., *Cyprian*, in *AugL* 2 (1996) 196-211. It goes without saying, however, that for Augustine the first unquestionable *eminentissima auctoritas* (Augustine, *De ciuitate Dei* 11,3 [CCL, 48], p. 323) is the *diuina auctoritas*, namely Holy Scripture (cf. *e.g.*: Id., *De correptione et gratia* 1,1 [CSEL, 92], p. 219). As a consequence, the Catholic Fathers, viz. the Christian writers who had drawn inspiration from the Bible and whose writings found in it their pivotal point, are called *diuinorum tractatores eloquiorum* (*e.g.*, Id., *Retractationes* 1,19,8 and 1,23,1 [CCL, 57], pp. 59-60 and 67; *De dono perseuerantiae* 19,48 [PL, 45], c. 1023; *Contra Iulianum* 4,9 [PL, 44], c. 768; *Contra secundam Iuliani responsionem imperfectum opus* 6,39 [PL, 45], c. 1599; *De Trinitate* 12,13,20 [CCL, 50], p. 373) or *diuinarum Scripturarum tractatores* (*e.g.* Id., *De doctrina christiana* 4,4,6 [CCL, 32], p. 119: *De ciuitate Dei* 15,7,18 [CCL, 48], p. 460; *Contra secundam Iuliani responsionem imperfectum opus* 6,40 [PL, 45], c. 1603). See also K.-H. LÜTCKE, *Auctoritas*, in *AugL* 1/4 (1990) 498-510, cc. 507-508.
303. Cf. Augustine, *Expositio quarumdam propositionum ex epistula ad Romanos* 60-64 *passim* (CSEL, 84), pp. 42-45. There his exegesis was particularly concerned with Rom 9,10-29. Cf. Id., *De praedestinatione sanctorum* 3,7 (PL, 44), cc. 964-965. Some of Augustine's former assertions, refuted in his *Retractationes*, are, for instance: "Ut quem sibi crediturum esse praescivit, ipsum elegerit cui Spiritum Sanctum daret, ut bona

been made in Augustine's *De diuersis quaestionibus ad Simpli-cianum*[304], written in 396, soon after Augustine had been ordained bishop[305]. This work contains the necessary adjustment and formulation by which he rejected as wrong his previous belief that both faith[306] and the will[307] to believe were the result of human agency. Also with regard to the power of grace — although at that stage he was still interpreting the *ego carnalis* (cf Rom 7,14) in relation to the man *sub lege*[308] (it was,

operando etiam aeternam vitam consequeretur" (Id., *Expositio quarumdam proposi-tionum ex epistula ad Romanos* 55 [CSEL, 84], p. 40; cf. Id., *Retractationes* 1,23,2 [CCL, 57], p. 68: "Nondum diligentius quaesiveram nec adhuc inveneram, qualis sit electio gra-tiae..."); "Quod ergo credimus nostrum est, quod autem bonum operamur illius est qui credentibus dat Spiritum Sanctum" (Id., *Expositio quarumdam propositionum ex epistula ad Romanos* 60 [CSEL, 84], p. 42; cf. Id., *Retractationes* 1,23,2 [CCL, 57], p. 69: "Pro-fecto non dicerem, si iam scirem etiam ipsam fidem inter Dei munera repperiri, quae dan-tur in eodem Spiritu"). See also Id., *De diuersis quaestionibus lxxxiii*, above all the qq. 66-68 ([CCL, 44/A], pp. 150-183) in which he tackles the interpretation of the Pauline text of Rom 7,7-25 on the law, and that of Rom 9,10-29 on divine election and the gratu-itous gift of faith (cf. Id., *Retractationes* 1,26 [CCL, 57], pp. 83-87). Regarding various passages in Augustine's *Epistulae ad Romanos inchoata expositio* and *Expositio epistulae ad Galatas* cf. respectively Id., *Retractationes* 1,25 (CCL, 57), pp. 73-74 and *Ibid.* 1,24,1-2, pp. 71-73.

304. In the prologue, while mentioning his previous commentaries on Paul's epistles to the Romans and to the Galatians, Augustine openly manifests his dissatisfaction with the insufficient knowledge of Holy Scripture that he had built in the early years of his priesthood: "Et illa quidem quae de Paulo apostolo dissolvenda proposuisti iam a nobis erant utcumque discussa litterisque mandata. Sed tamen eadem ipsa verba apostolica tenoremque sententiarum non contentus inquisitione atque explicatione praeterita, ne quid in ea neglegentius praeterissem, cautius attentiusque rimatus sum" (Id., *De diuersis quaestionibus ad Simplicianum, Praef.* [CCL, 44], p. 7).

305. "In ipso exordio episcopatus mei" (Id., *De praedestinatione sanctorum* 4,8 [PL, 44], c. 966). Cf. also "In mei episcopatus exordio" (Id., *De dono perseuerantia* 20,52 [PL, 45], c. 1026).

306. Cf. for instance: "Quod si eam credendo [*God's mercy*] se meruisse quis iactat, noverit eum sibi praestitisse ut crederet, qui misereretur inspirando fidem cuius misertus est, ut adhuc infideli vocationem impertiret" (Id., *De diuersis quaestionibus ad Simpli-cianum* 1,2,9 [CCL, 44], p. 34). Augustine reminds us in the *De dono perseuerantiae* that his initial views had already been corrected in the *De diuersis quaestionibus ad Simpli-cianum*: "Quod plenius sapere coepi in ea disputatione, quam scripsi ad beatae memoriae Simplicianum episcopum Mediolanensis Ecclesiae, in mei episcopatus exordio, quando et initium fidei donum Dei esse cognovi, et asserui" (Id., *De dono perseuerantiae* 20,52 [PL, 45], c. 1026).

307. Faith is a gift that entails the preparation of the will, for it is the latter that comes to faith. Yet the will is not moved to faith as the result of human agency, but thanks to God's intervention. See *e.g.*: "Quis habet in potestate tali uiso attingi mentem suam, quo eius uoluntas moueatur ad fidem?... Cum ergo nos ea delectant quibus proficiamus ad Deum, inspiratur hoc et praebetur gratia Dei, non nutu nostro et industria aut operum meritis comparatur, quia ut sit nutus uoluntatis... ille *[Deus]* tribuit, ille largitur" (Id., *De diuersis quaestionibus ad Simplicianum* 1,2,21 [CCL, 44], pp. 53-54).

308. Cf. *Ibid.* 1,1,9, pp. 14-15. Cf. also Augustine's conclusion after having com-mented Rom 7,(14)15-23: "Huc usque sunt uerba hominis sub lege constituti nondum sub gratia" (Id., *De diuersis quaestionibus lviii* 66,5 [CCL, 44A], p. 158).

in fact, only later on[309] that he understood it as referring *probabilius*[310] to the *spiritalis homo*, namely to the man already *sub gratia*[311]) — he stressed the general truth about the necessity and the primary role of pre-venient grace[312]. Augustine states that there is nothing good in the human being that does not come from God, and this holds true not only for man's qualities on a moral and spiritual level, but also for the *initium fidei*[313]. Faith can only be said to belong to human nature inasmuch as

309. It was in consequence of the Pelagian controversy that Augustine clearly affirmed that Rom 7 ought to be understood in relation to the man *sub gratia*: cf. Id., *De nuptiis et concupiscentia* 1,27,30-31,36 (CSEL, 42), pp. 242-248; *Contra duas epistulas Pelagianorum* 1,8,13-11,24 (CSEL, 60), pp. 433-445. See A. DE VEER, *Notes complé-mentaires*, BA 23, pp. 770-777.

310. Augustine, *Retractationes* 2,1,1 (CCL, 57), p. 89.

311. *Ibid.*; Cf. Id., *De praedestinatione sanctorum* 4,8, c. 966; *De dono perseueran-tiae* 20,52 and 21,55 (PL, 45), cc. 1026 and 1027. It is evident that from 396, the time of the editing of his letter-treatise to Simplicianus, Augustine had already changed his mind about the *initium fidei*. He no longer considered it an independent initiative of man, but saw it pertaining to the "safe haven" of sovereign grace. As Chéné has noted, in the fol-lowing words of Augustine: "In cuius quaestionis solutione laboratum est quidem pro libero arbitrio voluntatis humanae; sed vicit Dei gratia" (Id., *De praedestinatione sancto-rum* 4,8 [PL, 44], c. 966), we can see his original intention of defending the cause of human free will and initiative in the work of salvation, in line with his commentary on some propositions of Paul's letter to the Romans. Subsequently, however, he received some intuitive enlightenment which convinced him of the primacy and sovereignty of grace (cf. J. CHÉNÉ, *Notes complémentaires* [BA, 24], p. 813). Augustine's intuition, which he compared to a "revelation" ("...quam mihi Deus in hac quaestione solvenda, cum ad episcopum Simplicianum, sicut dixi, scriberem, revelavit": Augustine, *De praedestinatione sanctorum* 4,8 [PL, 44], c. 966), came from the following sentence of Paul's letter to the Corinthians: "Quid autem habes quod non accepisti?" (1 Cor 4,7). These words opened his eyes with regard to the interpretation of difficult passages in Rom 9. It is clear, however, that in 1 Cor 4,7 Paul was not speaking of the gift of faith, although that was the way Augustine understood this sentence. Paul was simply writing about the boasts of the Corinthians and inviting them to be humble. It is precisely this *intentio* of Paul (humility vs boasting) that Augustine takes up and applies to the *initium fidei* (and to perseverance). What the bishop of Hippo says about the *initium fidei* and per-severance is dealt therefore in the light of humility, and it cannot be read "correctement sans l'éclairage de ce qui précède: ce vaste propos sur l'orgueil et l'humilité, où se livre, à travers l'*intentio Apostoli*, l'intention d'Augustin lui-même" (HOMBERT, *Gloria gratiae* [n. 299], p. 298, *et passim*). Likewise, in his work for Simplicianus, Augustine had also stressed the *intentio* of Paul's letter to the Romans: "Nulla igitur intentio tenetur Apos-toli... nisi ut *qui gloriatur in Domino glorietur*" (Id., *De diuersis quaestionibus ad Sim-plicianum* 1,2,21 [CCL, 44], p. 53).

312. "Cum ergo nos ea delectant quibus proficiamus ad Deum, inspiratur hoc et prae-betur gratia Dei, non nutu nostro et industria aut operum meritis comparatur, quia ut sit nutus voluntatis, ut sit industria studii, ut sint opera caritate ferventia, ille tribuit, ille lar-gitur" (*Ibid.* 1,2,21, p. 54).

313. Here Augustine explicitly attacks the standpoint of the Massilians who held the opinion that faith was given to human nature at the moment of creation: "Illud vero quod putant, de hac fide ideo non posse dici, *Quid enim habes quod non accepisti?*, quia in eadem natura remansit, licet vitiata, quae prius sana ac perfecta donata sit" (Id., *De praedestinatione sanctorum* 5,9 [PL, 44], c. 967; it is a quotation from Hilary, *Ep.* 226,4

the possession of it is believed to belong to the believer who has been graced by God's election[314]. Everything must be attributed to God so that man may not be tempted to glorify himself[315]. Commenting on Jesus' speech on the bread of life, particularly on the passage in which the Lord says: "No one can come to me unless the Father who sent me draws him"(Jn 6,44), Augustine asserts that there is a secret presence of God in the act of faith. It is He, in fact, who makes us believe through the sovereignty of his grace, and it is thanks to its efficacious power that our hardened hearts can be converted[316].

Augustine's primary contention that faith, as well as the will to believe, are God's gifts and depend on his inscrutable designs and gratuitous predestination, is substantiated as follows. Firstly, referring to Cyprian[317], the bishop of Hippo argues that the prayers offered by the believers on behalf of non-believers (in order that the latter may be granted the gift of faith) would be nonsensical if such a gift was not given by God, but was something that human beings could procure for

(CSEL, 57), pp. 472-473). See also: "Fides igitur, et inchoata, et perfecta, donum Dei est: et hoc donum quibusdam dari, quibusdam non dari, omnino non dubitet, qui non vult manifestissimis sacris Litteris repugnare" (Augustine, *De praedestinatione sanctorum* 8,16 [PL, 44], c. 972).

314. "Proinde posse habere fidem... naturae est hominum: habere autem fidem... gratiae est fidelium. Illa itaque natura, in qua nobis data est possibilitas habendi fidem, non discernit ab homine hominem; ipsa vero fides discernit ab infideli fidelem. Ac per hoc, ubi dicitur, *Quis enim te discernit? Quid autem habes quod non accepisti?* quisquis audet dicere, Habeo ex me ipso fidem, non ergo accepi; profecto contradicit huic apertissimae veritati: non quia credere vel non credere non est in arbitrio voluntatis humanae, sed in electis praeparatur voluntas a Domino. Ideo ad ipsam quoque fidem, quae in voluntate est, pertinet, *Quis enim te discernit? Quid autem habes quod non accepisti?*" (*Ibid.* 5,10, c. 968). This distinction between nature and grace should not be understood as a distinction between natural and supernatural. Such distinction belongs to later speculation. See Augustine, *De Genesi ad litteram l. xii* 9,17 (CSEL, 28/1), p. 292; Id., *De Trinitate* 14,8,11 (CCL, 50/A), p. 436, where the bishop of Hippo affirms that human nature has in itself a *capacitas* of accepting grace, a sort of *potentia oboedientialis*. He also says that in some people there exists an inner disposition that enables them to receive the gift of faith when they hear words or see miracles that are congruous to their mind: "Ex quo apparet habere quosdam in ipso ingenio divinum naturaliter munus intelligentiae, quo moveantur ad fidem, si congrua suis mentibus, vel audiant verba, vel signa conspiciant" (Id., *De dono perseuerantiae* 14,35 [PL, 45], c. 1014). The idea of congruous grace is also affirmed in Id., *De diuersis quaestionibus ad Simplicianum* 1,2,13 (CCL, 44), p. 38.

315. Speaking of Cornelius' conversion Augustine writes: "Quidquid igitur et antequam in Christum crederet, et cum crederet, et cum credidisset, bene operatus est Cornelius, totum Deo dandum est, ne forte quis extollatur" (Id., *De praedestinatione sanctorum* 7,12 [PL, 44], c. 970). Cf. also Id., *De dono perseuerantiae* 6,12f (PL, 45), cc. 1000-1001.

316. "Ideo quippe tribuitur, ut cordis duritia primitus auferatur" (Id., *De praedestinatione sanctorum* 8,13 [PL, 44], c. 971).

317. Cf. Cyprian, *De dominica oratione* 18 (CCL, 3/A), pp. 101-102.

themselves[318]. As to the question why not all are granted God's grace and his salvation, he refers to God's inscrutable plans, through which he shows not only his mercy but also his just judgement, however hard it might be to understand. The human being cannot explain why God's designs remain hidden and are so impenetrable to his understanding, but he can be certain that there is nothing unjust about them[319]. Secondly, referring to Porphyry's objection concerning the time of the appearance of the Christian religion, an objection dealt with in a previous letter (*Ep.* 102)[320], the bishop of Hippo reminds his readers that on that occasion he simply gave a provisional and partial solution, a solution which, at that time, he judged sufficient to refute this particular pagan objection. Augustine's response as to when Christ appeared on earth was essentially this: Christ came into the world and preached among the people where and when he knew that his Gospel would meet with some acceptance[321]. The Massilians understood this statement to mean that this

318. Cf. Augustine, *De praedestinatione sanctorum* 8,15 (PL, 44), c. 972.
319. *Ibid.* 8,16, c. 973.
320. Cf. *Ibid.* 9,17-18, cc. 973-974; Id., *Ep.* 102,8-15 (q. 2: *De tempore christianae religionis*) (CSEL, 34/2), pp. 551-558. The *Ep.* 102, written to the priest Deogratias, contains the answers to six questions which were submitted to Augustine by a pagan friend of his (cf. Id., *Retractationes* 2,31 [CCL, 57], pp. 115-116). Whereas in the *Ep.* 102 Augustine does not doubt the Porphyrian provenance of the objections to Christian faith (although he does not discuss who this Porphyry actually was), in the *Retractationes* (cf. 2,31 [CCL, 57], p. 115) he explicitly rules out that the objections might come from the Porphyry who was a famous Neoplatonist philosopher (See P.F. BEATRICE, *Porphyrius*, in *TRE* 27 [1997] 54-59), who published Plotinus' *Enneads* and who was a native of Syria (the fact that he was wrongly designated as *Siculum* was probably due to the fact that the philosopher sojourned in Sicily from 268 to 271). We do not know why Augustine ruled out the authorship of the Neoplatonist Porphyry. Either he was not acquainted with the fifteen books of Porphyry's treatise against the Christians (Κατὰ Χριστιανῶν) or he could not believe that the objections he was asked to refute were the product of a philosopher whom he had admired in the past. As Courcelle writes: "Augustin ne peut croire que le Porphyre antichrétien auquel on réfère certaines des objections <que lui transmet le diacre Deogratias> soit le philosophe Porphyre de Sicile dont les théories sur le retour de l'âme l'ont captivé dans sa jeunesse. Mais l'identité des deux Porphyre ne fait aujourd'hui de doute pour personne" (P. COURCELLE, *Les Lettres grecques en Occident, de Macrobe à Cassiodore*, 2nd ed., Paris, 1948, pp. 197-198). On another occasion, however, Augustine did not hide the philosopher's enmity towards Christianity: "Doctissimus philosophorum, quamvis christianorum acerrimus inimicus" (Augustine, *De ciuitate Dei* 19,22 [CCL, 48], p. 690). See also L. VAGANAY, *Porphyre*, in *DTC* 12/II, cc. 2555-2590, especially cc. 2562-2579.
321. "Quid enim est verius, quam praescisse Christum, qui et quando et quibus locis in eum fuerant credituri?" (Augustine, *De praedestinatione sanctorum* 9,18 [PL, 44], c. 974). See Id., *Ep.* 102,14-15 (CSEL, 34/2), pp. 556-558. Augustine believed in and defended God's prescience. In fact he was well aware of the scriptural testimonies to God's foreknowledge of the conditional future (*e.g.*, Mt 11,21: "Woe to you, Chorazin! woe to you Bethsaida! for if the mighty works done in you had been done in Tyre and Sidon, they would have repented long ago in sackcloth and ashes"). In the *Ep.* 102,

great gift of grace was due to Christ's foreknowledge of those who would eventually believe in him, a foreknowledge which would also take into account the merit deriving from their adhesion to faith[322]. Augustine strongly rejected this interpretation as not reflecting the evolution of his thought and the conclusive turn that it eventually took. Yet, what he did not actually address in the *Ep.* 102 was the problem of whether faith was still regarded as a gift of God after the coming of Christ, namely if, in regard to believers, there was also divine predestination besides divine foreknowledge[323]. But of course at that time, and within the context of Porphyry's particular objection, this issue was not taken into account. It was after the condemnation of Pelagianism[324] that Augustine felt it necessary to treat the question in depth, asserting with confidence that Christ came and preached his doctrine where and when he knew people would believe in him, because they had been chosen for belief before the foundation of the world[325]. Salvation, therefore, does not depend on human will, but on grace and divine predestination. The

Augustine affirms explicitly: "His enim temporibus et his locis, quibus euangelium eius non est praedicatum, tales omnes in eius praedicatione futuros esse praesciebat, quales non quidem omnes sed tamen multi in eius corporali praesentia fuerunt, qui in eum nec suscitatis ab eo mortuis credere uoluerunt" (*Ibid.* 14, pp. 556-557). Cf. Id., *De praedestinatione sanctorum* 9,17 (PL, 44), c. 973. In quoting and commenting Wis 4,11 (*Raptus est, ne malitia mutaret intellectum eius:* Cf. *Ibid.*, 14,26, cc. 979-980) Augustine asserts that God knows what would happen if certain conditions were fulfilled (in the particular case of Wis 4,11, the condition was the continuation of the life of the just one). God's prescience is thus to be taken *stricto sensu* as an anticipated foreknowledge of something which is going to happen in the future: "Qui hoc praescivit quod futurum erat, non quod futurum non erat" (*Ibid.*, 14,26, c. 979). Cf. also: "Quid, quod ipsa exinanitur omnino praescientia, si quod praescitur non erit?" (Id., *De natura et origine animae* 1,12 [CSEL, 60], p. 316).

322. Cf. Hilary, *Ep.* 226,3 (CSEL, 57), p. 471.

323. "Sed utrum praedicato sibi Christo a se ipsis habituri essent fidem, an Deo donante sumpturi, id est, utrum tantummodo eos praescierit, an etiam praedestinaverit Deus, quaerere atque disserere tunc necessarium non putavi" (Augustine, *De praedestinatione sanctorum* 9,18 [PL, 44], c. 974).

324. "Nunc ex admonitione Pelagiani erroris necesse est copiosius et laboriosius disputari" (*Ibid.*).

325. "Tunc voluisse hominibus apparere Christum, et apud eos praedicari doctrinam suam, quando sciebat et ubi sciebat esse qui electi fuerant in ipso ante mundi constitutionem" (*Ibid.*). Also in his *Retractationes*, referring to *Ep.* 102,15 ("Salus religionis huius, per quam solam ueram salus uera ueraciterque promittitur, nulli umquam defuit, qui dignus fuit; et cui defuit, dignus non fuit": [CSEL, 34/2], pp. 557-558) in the light of the condemnation of Pelagianism, Augustine felt it necessary to explain that God's salvation is not offered or refused according to the worthiness or unworthiness (merits or demerits) of mankind but only according to God's designs: "Non ita dixi, tamquam ex meritis suis quisque dignus fuerit, sed quemadmodum ait Apostolus: *Non ex operibus sed ex uocante* dictum esse: *Maior seruiet minori*, quam uocationem ad Dei propositum asserit pertinere" (Id., *Retractationes* 2,31 [CCL, 57], pp. 115-116).

only difference between grace and predestination is that whereas predestination is the preparation for the gift of grace (*gratiae praeparatio*), grace is the realization of this gift (*ipsa donatio*)[326]. Besides, predestination cannot exist without prescience, for in order to predestine God must have foreknowledge of his own (future) actions. On the other hand, prescience can exist without predestination, as in the case of God's foreknowledge of men's sins[327]. Moreover, contrary to the interpretation given by the Massilians[328], Augustine reiterates that the Pauline expression *Si credideris, saluus eris* (Rom 10,9) cannot be interpreted to mean that man is able of himself to produce faith. God is the only one who has the power (*potestas*) to bring about faith, together with salvation which is the eventual goal of faith. Both belief and salvation depend on God's will[329].

b) Two Examples of Gratuitous Predestination: The Baptized Infants and Jesus Christ

There are two examples, above all, which illustrate the mystery of predestination: one is the case of infants and the other Christ the Mediator. In both cases, merits play no part: they play no part in the case of baptized infants set apart through no merits of their own (nor in the case of unbaptized infants who are condemned at death, though obviously not because of demerit or actual sins). Neither does it play a part in the case of Christ who, being simultaneously God and man, could not be regarded as Mediator and Saviour of humanity simply on account of his possible merits[330].

---

326. "Inter gratiam porro et praedestinationem hoc tantum interest, quod praedestinatio est gratiae praeparatio, gratia vero iam ipsa donatio" (Id., *De praedestinatione sanctorum* 10,19 [PL, 44], c. 974). See also: "Praedestinatio Dei quae in bono est, gratiae est, ut dixi, praeparatio: gratia vero est ipsius praedestinationis effectus" (*Ibid.* 10,19, c. 975). Cf. Id., *De dono perseuerantiae* 18,47 (PL, 45), cc. 1022-1023.

327. "Praedestinatio est, quae sine praescientia non potest esse: potest autem esse sine praedestinatione praescientia. Praedestinatione quippe Deus ea praescivit, quae fuerat ipse facturus.... Praescire autem potens est etiam quae ipse non facit; sicut quaecumque peccata..." (Id., *De praedestinatione sanctorum* 10,19 [PL, 44], c. 975). Behind the mystery of predestination we should read the promise that God made to Abraham about the eventual faith of the heathen nations: "Promisit autem filios Abrahae; quod esse non possunt, si non habeant fidem: ergo ipse donat et fidem" (*Ibid.*, 10,20, c. 976).

328. "Quod enim dicitur: 'Crede et saluus eris', unum horum exigi adserunt aliud offerri, ut propter id, quod exigitur, si redditum fuerit, id, quod offertur, deinceps tribuatur" (Hilary, *Ep.* 226,2 [CSEL, 57], pp. 469-470). Cf. Augustine, *De praedestinatione sanctorum* 11,22 (PL, 44), c. 976.

329. "Cur non utrumque in [*potestate*] Dei, et quod iubet, et quod offert?... Ideo enim haec et nobis praecipiuntur, et dona Dei esse monstrantur; ut intelligatur quod et nos ea facimus, et Deus facit ut illa faciamus, sicut per prophetam Ezechielem apertissime dicit. Quid enim apertius, quam ubi dicit, *Ego faciam ut faciatis?*" (*Ibid.*).

330. "Ubi venitur ad parvulos, et ad ipsum Mediatorem Dei et hominum, hominem Christum Iesum, omnis deficit praecedentium gratiam Dei humanorum assertio meritorum:

The problem of infants is dealt with in accordance with the doctrine of original sin. If some infants die after baptismal regeneration, this should be attributed exclusively to the merciful grace of God. He it is who has saved them from the eternal damnation. On the other hand, if some infants die without baptismal regeneration and are not saved, this is not due, as the Massilians would hold, to the *futura merita mala*[331], which, of course, would never happen (*futura quae non sunt futura*)[332], but to original sin, the birthright of every human being born into this world, and from which these children have not been delivered[333]. For Augustine it was absolutely clear that the reason for God's just judgement regarding those infants dying before baptism[334] rested on the reality of original sin and not on the *futura merita mala*. Moreover, Augustine could not accept, and found it *absurdum*, that the *futura merita mala* could only be the object of God's punishment and not of his mercy[335]. Thus, it would

quia nec illi ullis bonis praecedentibus meritis discernuntur a caeteris, ut pertineant ad liberatorem hominum; nec ille ullis humanis praecedentibus meritis, cum et ipse sit homo, liberator factus est hominum" (*Ibid.* 12,23, c. 977).

331. Augustine judges as unacceptable the Massilians' theory of the *futura merita mala* as a possible explanation of the destiny of unbaptized infants. He counters their position by quoting the scriptural passage of 2 Cor 5,10: "*Omnes astabimus ante tribunal Christi, ut referat unusquisque secundum ea quae per corpus gessit, sive bonum, sive malum: gessit,* inquit; non adiunxit, Vel gesturus fuit" (*Ibid.* 12,24, c. 977).

332. Augustine finds annoying (*moleste*) the conviction that the opportunity for an infant to be baptized before death was abscribed to his hypothetical future repentance and merits. How such thinking is possible is beyond Augustine's reach: "Ut futura quae non sunt futura, puniantur, aut honorentur merita parvulorum" (*Ibid.*). Cf. also: "Sed quia hominum futura, quae non sunt futura, procul dubio nulla sunt merita, et hoc videre facillimum est" (*Ibid.*, 13,25, c. 979). See Prosper, *Ep.* 225,5 (CSEL, 57), pp. 461-462.

333. Augustine was well aware that if the theory of the *futura merita* (wholly untenable in his eyes) was adopted, it would lead automatically to the suppression of the doctrine of original sin. Cf. Augustine, *De praedestinatione sanctorum* 13,25, *Pl* 44, cc. 978-979. With regard to the Massilians' understanding of baptism, according to Weaver, Augustine argues that by referring "to future (unreal) merit and demerit, it fails to take into account a prior (original) sin that requires remission [*cf. Ibid.* 12,23ff, cc. 977-979]". Their "argument did bypass the doctrine of baptism for the remission of original sin. For them inherited culpability had little import. Moreover, by their subordination of the grace of baptism to merit, they had undercut the gratuitous character of the divine decision to save" (WEAVER, *Divine Grace and Human Agency* [n. 69], p. 56). The position of the Massilians, however, ought to be better nuanced. It is not so much a question of the subordination of baptismal grace to merit as the safeguarding of the place and role of human's (moral) agency.

334. "Ad quod tempus corporis pertinet etiam quod Pelagiani negant, sed Christi Ecclesia confitetur, originale peccatum: quo sive soluto per Dei gratiam, sive per Dei iudicium non soluto, cum moriuntur infantes, aut merito regenerationis transeunt ex malis ad bona, aut merito originis transeunt ex malis ad mala. Hoc catholica fides novit" (Augustine, *De praedestinatione sanctorum* 12,24 [PL, 44], c. 978). Cf. also: "Quae [*gratia*] maxime apparet in parvulis; quorum cum alii baptizati, alii non baptizati vitae huius terminum sumunt, satis indicant misericordiam et iudicium; misericordiam quidem gratuitam, iudicium debitum" (*Ibid.* 14,29, c. 981).

335. "Quicumque enim dicit, puniri tantum posse Deo iudicante futura peccata, dimitti autem Deo miserante non posse, cogitare debet quantam Deo faciat gratiaeque

be really nonsensical to establish, between these two categories of infants (those who die with baptism and those who die without it) a discrimination based on a foreknowledge of future merits that would never happen[336]. Augustine also uses the quotation of Wis 4,11 (*Raptus est, ne malitia mutaret intellectum eius*[337]) to confirm through Scripture (and with the support of Cyprian's interpretation of the same passage[338]) that

eius iniuriam; quasi futurum peccatum praenosci possit, nec possit ignosci. Quod si absurdum est; magis ergo futuris, si diu viverent, peccatoribus, cum in parva aetate moriuntur, lavacro quo peccata diluuntur, debuit subvenire" (*Ibid.*, 12,24, c. 978).

336. Augustine, who had fought to wipe out any discrimination derived from the Neoplatonic opinion of the preexistence of souls, according to which the division between good and evil men depended on deeds done in a previous existence (cf. Id., *Ep.* 166,9,27 [CSEL, 44], pp. 582f; *Ep.* 164,7,20 [CSEL, 44/3], p. 539), is now engaged in contesting a discrimination based on hypothetical merits or demerits which are projected on to a *post mortem* future, or better, merits and demerits that would have existed if the infants had not died.

337. Cf. Id., *De praedestinatione sanctorum* 14,26-29 (PL, 44), cc. 979-981. Augustine stressed that the book of Wisdom was traditionally read in the Church and that its authority had long been accepted (cf. *Ibid.* 14,27, c. 980). The real problem for him was not the canonicity of the book of Wisdom (which he accepted) but the problem of its authorship, viz. the scriptural attribution to Jesus Sirach and not to Solomon (cf. Id., *De doctrina christiana* 2,8,13 [CCL, 32], p. 40). The Massilians, instead, as Hilary had pointed out (cf. Hilary, *Ep.* 226,4 [CSEL, 57], p. 473) did not consider the book of Wisdom a canonical one and rejected its authority. It is likely that they shared the view of the Eastern Fathers according to which some books of Scripture (among which the book of Wisdom) were not considered "canonical" but simply "ecclesiastical", useful for instruction and preaching. Cf., for instance, Athanasius, *Festal Letters* 39,7, in A. ROBERTSON (ed.), *Select Writing and Letters of Athanasius, Bishop of Alexandria* (NPNF, 2nd ser., 4), Edinburgh 1897, repr. Edinburgh-Grand Rapids/MI, 1991, p. 552. Since Cassian had spent a considerable time of his life in the East, especially in Egypt, it is not surprising that he had adopted (and retained also in Marseilles) the eastern division between canonical and ecclesiastical books in Scripture. An analogous case is that of Rufinus of Aquileia, who also spent many years in the East before he returned to Italy. Cf. C. LARCHER, *Études sur le livre de la Sagesse* (Études bibliques), Paris, 1969, pp. 55-57.

338. The scriptural passage of Wis 4,11 is taken into account citing Cyprian's *De mortalitate* 23 ([CSEL, 3/1], pp. 311-312). See A.-M. LA BONNARDIERE, *Biblia Augustiniana A. T. Le livre de la Sagesse*, Paris, 1970, p. 56. Augustine's reference to Cyprian, a sure witness of the Church's tradition, was undoubtedly a move to counter the accusation that his doctrine was a "novelty". "It is apparent – writes Weaver – that his heavy reliance on Cyprian was an attempt to demonstrate the congruence of his views with the accepted teaching of the church. What is not apparent, however, is to what degree Cyprian, the martyr bishop of Carthage whose memory was highly revered in the African church, carried weight outside Africa, particularly among those Gallic monks who had been molded by the fathers of the Eastern church" (WEAVER, *Divine Grace and Human Agency* [n. 69], p. 59; also p. 51). Further on, Augustine explicitly says that since the Fathers of the Church did not face the specific questions he was faced with (for the simple fact that such questions had not yet arisen), he would come to the conclusion that there was no contradiction between him and their writings, nor could his doctrine be considered a "novelty" with regard to positions which in some particular instances had not yet been defined by the Church (cf. Augustine, *De praedestinatione sanctorum* 14,27 [PL, 44], c. 980).

an early death removes the believer from the possibility of sin and that this is ultimately beneficial. In fact Augustine infers that early death would be of little advantage to the believer if God were to judge on the basis of how a life might have been lived, rather than on the performance of a life already lived[339]. In the light of the *futura merita mala*, instead, an early death would be completely useless, because its "prevenient" goal would be lost[340].

In considering the most illustrious instance of predestination and grace (*praeclarissimum lumen praedestinationis et gratiae*[341]), Christ the Saviour, the bishop of Hippo states that it is obviously not because of any precedent merits that his human nature obtained the privilege of being assumed into oneness of person by the Logos, the Word co-eternal with the Father. The man born of the Virgin Mary had been predestined from all eternity by an absolutely gratuitous divine decree to be assumed by the Son of God from the very first moment of his existence. And it was precisely because divinity made the human nature of Jesus Christ (which was the same as ours) its own, that such nature received a perfect and unchangeable sanctity, a sanctity that has become the source and paradigm of human sanctity ever since[342]. Furthermore, Augustine

---

339. *Ibid.* 14,26.28, cc. 979-981.

340. "Sed quid prodest, si etiam futura, quae commissa non sunt, peccata puniuntur?" (*Ibid.* 14,26, c. 979).

341. *Ibid.*, 15,30, c. 981. "Cette idée – writes Plagnieux – de lier orthodoxie christologique et doctrine de la grâce paraît bien être un fruit de la polémique antipélagienne.... De plus il appert que si l'argument est une conquête de sa pensée aux prises avec Pélage, c'en est aussi devenu une constante pour toute cette période, et donc jusqu'à la fin.... Il reste que c'est le chapitre XV du *De praedestinatione sanctorum* qui de cet argument nous offre la forme accomplie" (PLAGNIEUX, *Le grief de complicité entre erreurs nestorienne et pélagienne d'Augustin à Cassien par Prosper d'Aquitaine?* [n. 146], pp. 396.399). Cf., for instance, Augustine, *Enchiridion ad Laurentium* 12,40 (CCL, 46), p. 72; *Ibid.* 11,36, pp. 69-70. The last words of this quotation remind us of those of *De correptione et gratia* 11,30 (CSEL, 92), pp. 254f.

342. "Est etiam praeclarissimum lumen praedestinationis et gratiae, ipse Salvator, ipse Mediator Dei et hominum homo Christus Iesus: qui ut hoc esset, quibus tandem suis vel operum vel fidei praecedentibus meritis natura humana quae in illo est comparavit? Respondeatur, quaeso: ille homo, ut a Verbo Patri coaeterno in unitatem personae assumptus, Filius Dei unigenitus esset, unde hoc meruit? Quod eius bonum qualecumque praecessit? Quid egit ante, quid credidit, quid petivit, ut ad hanc ineffabilem excellentiam perveniret? Nonne faciente ac suscipiente Verbo, ipse homo, ex quo esse coepit, Filius Dei unicus esse coepit?... Nempe ista omnia singulariter admiranda, et alia si qua eius propria verissime dici possunt, singulariter in illo accepit humana, hoc est, nostra natura, nullis suis praecedentibus meritis" (Id., *De praedestinatione sanctorum* 15,30 [PL, 44], cc. 981-982). Augustine insisted on the hypostatic union of Christ as the most sublime example of the gratuity of grace: "Nullum autem est illustrius praedestinationis exemplum quam ipse Iesus: unde et in primo libro iam disputavi, et in huius fine commendare delegi: nullum est, inquam, illustrius praedestinationis exemplum quam ipse Mediator" (Id., *De dono perseuerantiae* 24,67 [PL, 45], cc. 1033-1034). See also: "Qua ergo gratia

continues, the fact that the humanity of Jesus Christ, the head of the body, was predestined to be taken up in the hypostatic union with the Logos is clearly witnessed by Paul (cf. Rom 1,1-4)[343]. And if Christ was gratuitously predestined to be our head, so we too are predestined to be his members without having to gain this position by means of our own merits[344].

This is also proved by God's double *uocatio*: there is a call which remains ineffective and another which leads infallibly to faith and salvation for all who are its object. In this last case God's gifts and his call are irrevocable and cannot be changed (cf. Rom 11,29), and his mercy precedes those who have been elected[345]. The latter, in fact, are not elected because they already possess faith, but in order that they may believe. This is in line with the words that Jesus himself said to his apostles: "You did not choose me, but I chose you" (Jn 15,16). Augustine says

homo ille ab initio factus est bonus, eadem gratia homines, qui sunt membra eius, ex malis fiunt boni" (Id., *Contra secundam Iuliani responsionem imperfectum opus* 1,138 [CSEL, 85/1], p. 154); "Ut intellegant homines per eandem gratiam se iustificari a peccatis, per quam factum est ut homo Christus nullum posset habere peccatum?" (Id., *Enchiridion ad Laurentium* 11,36 [CCL, 46], p. 70).

343. "[*Iesus Christus*]... qui factus est ei ex semine David secundum carnem, qui praedestinatus est Filius Dei in virtute, secundum Spiritum sanctificationis ex resurrectione mortuorum" (Id., *De praedestinatione sanctorum* 15,31 [PL, 44], c. 982; cf. Rom 1,1-4). The actual meaning given by Paul to Rom 1,1-4 was not the same as that given by Augustine. The Apostle meant that Christ, the offspring of David according to the flesh, had been constituted according to the Spirit of holiness in the power of Sonship of God thanks to his resurrection from the dead. "Constituted" is the most probable and accepted meaning of the Greek aorist ὁρισθέντος (= to mark out, to delimit as a boundary [ὅρος], to constitute), a term which in the Latin text used by Augustine has been translated with *praedestinatus*. Thus, Paul does not speak of the man Jesus being predestined to become Son of God by virtue of the assumption of his humanity by the Son of God himself. "Denn wenn nach Paulus das Evangelium Jesus Christus als Sohn Gottes verkündigt, kann dieser nicht erst durch die Auferstehung der Toten zum Sohn Gottes werden, wohl aber zum Sohn Gottes 'in Macht'" (H. SCHLIER, *Der Römerbrief* [HTK, 6], Freiburg-Basel-Wien, 1977, p. 24). Yet, as J. Chéné writes: "Si l'exégèse d'Augustin est inexacte, la pensée qu'il exprime est incontestable: on ne peut douter que l'assomption de la nature humaine de Jésus par le Verbe de Dieu ait été décrétée *ab aeterno,* et donc que l'homme Jésus ait été prédestiné à cette assomption qui le ferait Fils de Dieu: prédestination toute gratuite comme la grâce de l'assomption elle-même" (J. CHÉNÉ, *Notes complémentaires* [BA, 24], p. 822).

344. "Sicut ergo praedestinatus est ille unus, ut caput nostrum esset: ita multi praedestinati sumus, ut membra eius essemus. Humana hic merita conticescant, quae perierunt per Adam: et regnet quae regnat Dei gratia per Iesum Christum Dominum nostrum" (Augustine, *De praedestinatione sanctorum* 15,31 [PL, 44], c. 983). "Moreover – writes Weaver – as the example of Christ demonstrates that the predestinating judgment precedes not only human merit but also human existence, one can infer that the divine decision to save takes place, in the case of those who will receive salvific grace, even before the person's existence. Human agency is entirely irrelevant to the determination of human destiny" (WEAVER, *Divine Grace and Human Agency* [n. 69], p. 56).

345. Cf. Augustine, *De praedestinatione sanctorum* 16,32-33 (PL, 44), cc. 983-985.

that to deny this truth and affirm that one might believe in order to be chosen by Christ, would mean clinging to the misapprehension that one could choose Christ first, rather than be chosen by him. And this is contrary to Scripture[346].

The mystery of the divine call leads Augustine to comment also on the doxology of Paul's letter to the Ephesians (1,3-12) where, according to the bishop of Hippo, it is clearly demonstrated that if God has called us in Christ before the foundation of the world (and therefore before we were born), it would mean that he has chosen us in virtue of his predestination[347]. This scriptural evidence is used, above all, to reinforce his refusal of the theory according to which man's predestination to sanctity and salvation rests upon the foreknowledge that God has of man's works. Augustine reiterates that in reality God does not choose human beings on the basis of his foreknowledge of their future belief and holiness. On the contrary, God calls and elects them by his grace so that they might believe and become holy[348]. Thus the Massilians' opinion, according to which God has foreknowledge of man's faith and that man is therefore predestined on the basis of divine prescience[349], must be rejected. The divine call always precedes human agency, even with regard to faith and its beginning[350]. This same conviction is supported by various biblical quotations which refer to the issue of the *initium fidei*. For instance, Paul's thanksgiving to God for the gift of faith given to both the Ephesians (cf. Eph 1,13-16) and the Thessalonians (cf 1 Thes 2,13) through the preaching of the gospel, is a clear sign that the Apostle considered the result of his preaching, viz. the faith of the newly converted, as being, from its very conception, the gift of God[351].

---

346. Cf. *Ibid.* 17,34, cc. 985-986 *passim*.

347. "Elegit Deus in Christo ante constitutionem mundi membra eius: et quomodo eligeret eos qui nondum erant, nisi praedestinando? Elegit ergo praedestinans nos" (*Ibid.* 18,35, c. 986).

348. "Non ergo quia futuri eramus, sed *ut essemus*. Nempe certum est, nempe manifestum est: ideo quippe tales eramus futuri, quia elegit ipse, praedestinans ut tales per gratiam eius essemus" (*Ibid.*, 18,36, c. 987; see also 18,37, c. 987).

349. Cf. Prosper, *Ep.* 225,3 (CSEL, 57), p. 457. Cf. Augustine, *De praedestinatione sanctorum* 19,38 (PL, 44), c. 988.

350. "Vocationem quippe illam... nec fides ipsa praecedit.... Nec quia credidimus, sed ut credamus vocamur: atque illa vocatione, quae sine poenitentia est, id prorsus agitur et peragitur, ut credamus" (*Ibid.*).

351. Cf. *Ibid.*, 19,39, c. 989. The *initium fidei* is also signified by the image of the *ostii uerbi apertionis* (cf. Col 4,3), once again belonging to God's agency: "Quomodo aperitur ostium verbi, nisi cum sensus aperitur audientis ut credat, et initio fidei facto, ea quae ad aedificandam salubrem doctrinam praedicantur et disputantur admittat?" (*Ibid.*, 20,40, c. 989; also 20,41, c. 990). The example of Lydia, the seller of purple goods (cf. Ac 16,14), who was converted by the preaching of Paul, offers concrete evidence to the

Augustine's main task, in the *De praedestinatione sanctorum*, was to prove that without the grace of God, man is incapable of taking part in the economy of salvation, and consequently of believing, since faith is the first act by which man enters into the divine project of salvation. According to the Massilians, instead, man is able to adhere by himself to the word of God, because the beginning of faith (*initium fidei*) pertains to his willing (the intervention of grace is not needed at this stage), whereas only at a second stage does it belong to God's grace to increase (*augmentum*) and bring to perfection this same faith. According to the divines of Provence, man can begin by himself to believe, to pray, to desire and to hope for his salvation through sincere repentance. Grace would intervene subsequently only to bring man's initial inner dispositions to fruition, and to reward his meritorious commitment. It follows then that predestination to grace can no longer be considered gratuitous, but something based solely on God's foreknowledge of those who, through personal initiative, will adhere to God's call to conversion. Augustine counters this point of view with the same argument put forward in his former works, viz. that grace is the foundation of faith, and that the latter is caused and sustained by the former at each and every stage, from beginning to end. This grace, which is the basis of faith, is completely independent of human merits, since mankind is incapable of gaining merits unless through grace itself.

The position that the bishop of Hippo took, over and against the assumptions of the Massilians, on the question of the *initium fidei,* would eventually become an article of faith[352]. But there were two other assertions, dependent on the centrality of grace, which Augustine considered beyond dispute. First, that the grace of faith, from beginning to end, is dependent on God's election and predestination to grace, which is a gift not given to everybody. Of course, the rationale of this election remains hidden in God himself. Second, the grace accorded by God is by nature infallible and invincible and it brings with it not only the gift of faith, but also the perseverance and the accomplishment of faith itself, viz. eternal life. These assertions, which were not new in Augustine's writings but were the logical consequence of his theological construction

---

truth that the *initium fidei* is a gift of God: "Hoc donum coelestis gratiae in illam purpurariam descenderat, cui, sicut Scriptura dicit in Actibus Apostolorum, *Deus aperuerat sensum eius, et intendebat in ea quae a Paulo dicebantur.* Sic enim vocabatur, ut crederet. Agit quippe Deus quod vult in cordibus hominum, vel adiuvando, vel iudicando, ut etiam per eos impleatur quod manus eius et consilium praedestinavit fieri" (*Ibid.*, 20,41, c. 990).

352. Augustine's position on this point was ratified by the Can. 5 of the 2nd Council of Orange, in 529 (cf. *Concilia Galliae A. 511 – A. 695* [CCL, 148A], pp. 56-57).

on grace, were opposed and criticized in the monastic settlements of Provence.

c) Augustine's De dono perseuerantiae: The Grace of Final Perseverance

As he did in the *De praedestinatione sanctorum*, here too, in the *De dono perseuerantiae*, Augustine declares his theme right from the beginning. The theme that he develops and defends is his conviction that final perseverance is the gift of God[353]. In spite of the lack of systematization and the sinuosity of Augustine's thought which unfolds through many excursions, parentheses and repetitions, this treatise can be divided into two main parts: the first devoted to the question of final perseverance and the second to that of predestination.

That the point at stake for Augustine is not an *ad tempus* perseverance, but the "final" one, is all too evident, because only final perseverance, reaching out to and coinciding with the end of earthly life, can be said to be truly authentic and indisputable[354]. Only man's faithfulness to Christ unto the moment of death is a sure test of final perseverance[355], and such faithfulness could not but be a gift of God. To prove it, Augustine quotes several scriptural passages, including the Pauline text of Phil 1,29: *Vobis donatum est pro Christo, non solum ut credatis in eum, uerum etiam ut patiamini pro eo.* With reliance on this quotation, Augustine points out the starting-point and the supreme end of Christian life: to believe in Christ and to suffer in his name[356]. The bishop of Hippo then turns his thoughts to Christian prayer and above all to the Lord's prayer, discussing each petition (guided and supported by the authority of Cyprian[357]) separately in order to illustrate that in this prayer scarcely anything is requested but perseverance[358].

---

353. "Asserimus ergo donum Dei esse perseverantiam qua usque in finem perseveratur in Christo" (Augustine, *De dono perseuerantiae* 1,1 [PL, 45], c. 993).

354. "Finem autem dico, quo vita ista finitur" (*Ibid.*).

355. Cf. Mt 10,22: *Qui perseuerauerit usque in finem, hic saluus erit.* "Hanc certe de qua nunc agimus perseverantiam, qua in Christo perseveratur usque in finem, nullo modo habuisse dicendus est, qui non perseveraverit usque in finem; potiusque hanc habuit unius anni fidelis, et quantum infra cogitari potest, si donec moreretur fideliter vixit, quam multorum annorum, si exiguum temporis ante mortem a fidei stabilitate defecit" (Id., *De dono perseuerantiae* 1,1 [PL, 45], c. 995).

356. "Quod enim est initium verius christiano, quam credere in Christum? Quis fdinis melior est, quam pati pro Christo?" (*Ibid.* 2,2, c. 995).

357. Cf. *Ibid.* 2,4-5,9, cc. 267-294. The commentary of the bishop of Hippo is based on Cyprian, *De dominica oratione* (CCL, 3/A), pp. 90-113. Augustine had already quoted this work in one of his antipelagian writings (cf. Augustine, *Contra duas epistulas Pelagianorum* 4,9,25 [CSEL, 60], pp. 549ff). He also read and explained it to the monks

At this point follows Augustine's reply to an objection raised by the Massilians. They asserted that the gift of perseverance could actually be gained through prayer or simply lost by man's obstinacy[359]. Augustine agrees with the first assertion, viz. that perseverance may indeed be obtained by prayer[360] (after all that is the meaning of the sixth petition of the Lord's prayer: *Ne nos inferas in temptationem* [Mt 6,13]), but he also reiterates that ultimately, perseverance is the gift of God. It is only if God answers man's petition not to be led into temptation that it is granted, for nothing occurs in the life of man without God allowing it[361]. Once again, the key to so much of Augustine's interpretation is his definition of the "nature" of final perseverance, a definition which excludes the idea that perseverance can be enjoyed in a temporary fashion, and then lost, perhaps by man's obstinacy, as the Massilians asserted. If one receives the gift of final perseverance, one would necessarily persevere to the end because such a gift is sure and not subject to the alternative conditions of winning and/or losing[362]. Augustine concludes this description of final perseverance; a description given on the basis of the petitions contained in the Lord's prayer, by saying that the latter alone would suffice to prove that perseverance is in fact a gift of God, and is

Cresconius and the two Felix's when he instructed them about the Pelagian errors during their stay at Hippo (cf. Id., *Ep.* 215, 3 [CSEL, 57/4], p. 390).

358. "An vero quisquam eorum est, qui non sibi poscat a Deo ut perseveret in eo; cum ipsa oratione quae Dominica nuncupatur, quia eam Dominus docuit, quando oratur a sanctis, nihil pene aliud quam perseverantia posci intelligatur?" (Id., *De dono perseuerantiae* 2,3 [PL, 45], c. 996).

359. "Sed nolunt,… isti fratres, ita hanc perseverantiam praedicari, ut non vel suppliciter emereri, vel amitti contumaciter possit" (*Ibid.* 6,10, c. 999). Cf. Hilary, *Ep.* 226,4 (CSEL, 57), p. 473.

360. "Hoc ergo Dei donum suppliciter emereri potest" (Augustine, *De dono perseuerantiae* 6,10 [PL, 45], c. 999). The gift of perseverance is not granted *nonnisi orantibus* (cf. *Ibid.* 16,39, c. 1017).

361. "Nihil enim fit, nisi quod aut ipse facit, aut fieri ipse permittit" (*Ibid.* 6,12, c. 1000). In stating that the expression "ne nos inferas in temptationem" is the equivalent of "ne nos inferi sinas", Augustine strikes a familiar note concerning his theology of grace and original sin, especially in connection with his concept of concupiscence. It is the latter, and not God, that leads man into temptation. The bishop of Hippo develops this interpretation, with regard to original sin and actual sins, in *Contra secundam Iuliani responsionem imperfectum opus* 4,82 (PL, 45), c. 1385. See J. Lössl, *Mt 6:13 in Augustine's Later Works*, in StPatr 33, Louvain, 1997, pp. 169f.

362. "Perseverantiam vero usque in finem, quoniam non habet quisquam, nisi qui perseverat usque in finem, multi eam possunt habere, nullus amittere. Neque enim metuendum est, ne forte cum perseveraverit homo usque in finem, aliqua in eo mala voluntas oriatur, ne perseveret usque in finem. Hoc ergo Dei donum suppliciter emereri potest: sed cum datum fuerit, amitti contumaciter non potest. Cum enim perseveraverit quisque usque in finem, neque hoc donum potest amittere, nec alia quae poterat ante finem. Quomodo igitur potest amitti, per quod fit ut non amittatur etiam quod posset amitti?" (Augustine, *De dono perseuerantiae* 6,10 [PL, 45], c. 999).

entirely dependent on gratuitous grace[363]. He underscores this contention by referring to the angels and particularly to Adam. Whereas Adam, in his prelapsarian status, enjoyed the ability to choose, by his own free will, to totally adhere to God and never depart from him, since the fall, man is only able to approach God and persevere in his will through his grace[364]. Such grace, Augustine continues, is bestowed on men through Christ, the *Adam nouissimus*[365], in whom we are chosen and predestined to become members of his body, the Church, and to form, together with him as head, the *Christus totus*. Since Christ was predestined never to depart from God, so we, the members of his body, are predestined to remain in God (*permanentes cum Deo*) and persevere in him[366]. To back up this teaching, Augustine reminds his opponents that we are also asked to pray so that we might grow in awareness of him by whom we are benefitted[367]. It has also been part of the Church's practice to pray not only that unbelievers might believe, but that believers too might persevere in faith[368]. This is particularly evident from the regular use made of the petitions in the Lord's prayer, petitions which, in Augustine's mind (in line with Cyprian), all request perseverance. He particularly cites the request not to be led into temptation[369].

The teaching that perseverance is a gift of God's grace, undeserved by man and independent of his merit, could not but lead to the persistent question of the wider mystery of God's merciful wisdom and justice, a mystery to which the doctrine of predestination is strictly related. Taking for granted that in God no unrighteousness exists[370], Augustine affirms that the total gratuity of God's grace (*gratis ab eo datur gratia*)[371], is manifested, above all, in the case of infants who die after baptismal regeneration, and in those adults whose lifelong perseverance is the result of the will of God, which presides over man's thoughts and

363. "Si ergo alia documenta non essent, haec dominica oratio nobis ad causam gratiae, quam defendimus, sola sufficeret: quia nihil nobis reliquit, in quo tanquam in nostro gloriemur" (*Ibid.* 7,13, c. 1001).

364. "Post casum autem hominis, nonnisi ad gratiam suam Deus voluit pertinere, ut homo accedat ad eum; neque nisi ad gratiam suam voluit pertinere, ut homo non recedat ab eo" (*Ibid.*).

365. *Ibid.* 7,14, c. 1001.

366. Cf. *Ibid.*

367. "Oratione nostra nos voluit admoneri, a quo accipiamus haec beneficia" (*Ibid.* 7,15, c. 1002).

368. "Prorsus in hac re non operosas disputationes exspectet Ecclesia: sed attendat quotidianas orationes suas. Orat, ut increduli credant: Deus ergo convertit ad fidem. Orat, ut credentes perseverent: Deus ergo donat perseverantiam usque in finem" (*Ibid.*).

369. Cf. *Ibid.*

370. Cf. *Ibid.* 8,16, c. 1002.

371. *Ibid.*

heart[372]. In light of this, the reason why, of two infants one would be
taken and the other left, or in the case of adults, why one should be chosen over the other, remains a mystery and is hidden in God's design. The
reason why, in the case of two equally pious people, one should be given
the grace of final perseverance and the other not, is even more incomprehensible. This differentiation (*discretio*)[373] is due to God's predestination, since the gift of final perseverance is a privilege granted only to
those who are predestined, namely to those who have been called *secundum Dei propositum*[374].

Augustine takes up again, if somewhat reluctantly (*ut etiam refellere
pudeat*)[375], the Massilians' theory of *the futura merita mala*[376]. If the gift
of remaining in God's grace until the time of death is gratuitous, it is
simply absurd to believe that an infant could be judged after death on
grounds of any possible behaviour that, had he lived, might have been
his. Such a theory not only damages Christian and human good sense
(*sensibus christianis aut prorsus humanis*)[377] but it is also contrary to the
words that Jesus addressed to the people of Tyre and Sidon, who would
have repented if the same miracles performed in Chorazin had been done
in their midst (cf. Mt 11,21)[378]. Augustine claims support for his teaching from a *quidam disputator catholicus*[379] whose exegesis of Mt 11,21
is in agreement with his rebuttal of the absurd opinion that, after death,
one will be judged not only on what one did during his earthly life, but
also on what one might have done in a hypothetical future life[380].

However, it is the problem of infants that gives Augustine the opportunity to begin a long excursus in reply to the Massilians, who maintained that the case of infants could not be used as a paradigm to illustrate the condition of adults[381]. In this regard they opposed several

372. *Ibid.* 8,17-20, cc. 1002-1004. Citing Ambrose's *De fuga saeculi* 1,1 [CSEL,
32/2], p. 163f.) Augustine underlines the fact that, given the limited control that man possesses even over his own thoughts and desires, God's help is definitely necessary to him
in order to entertain that kind of thoughts that nourish and support faith.

373. Cf. Augustine, *De dono perseuerantiae* 9,21 (PL, 45), c. 1004.

374. *Ibid.* 9,21, cc. 1004-1005; cf. also 11,25, cc. 1007-1008.

375. *Ibid.* 9,22, c. 1005; cf. also 10,24, c. 1007.

376. Augustine had already tackled at length this problem (cf. Id., *De praedestinatione sanctorum* 12,24ff [PL, 44], cc. 977ff). He is now taking it up again in connection
with Jesus' words about Tyre and Sidon (cf. Mt 11,21) and with the passage of Wis 4,11,
which the Massilians did not accept as canonical. Cf. also Id., *De correptione et gratia*
8,19 (CSEL, 92), p. 240; *De praedestinatione sanctorum* 14,26 (PL, 44), cc. 979-980; *De
dono perseuerantiae* 10,24 (PL, 45), cc. 1006-1007.

377. *Ibid.* 9,22, c. 1005; cf. also 12,31, c. 1011.

378. Cf. *Ibid.* 9,22-23, cc. 1005-1006.

379. Cf. *Ibid.* 10,24, c. 1006. Who this *disputator catholicus* was, is unknown.

380. Cf. *Ibid.* 10,24, cc. 1006-1007.

381. "Causam parvulorum ad exemplum maiorum non patiuntur afferri" (*Ibid.* 11,26,
c. 1008). Cf. Hilary, *Ep.* 226,8 (CSEL, 57), p. 477.

passages of Augustine's *De libero arbitrio* where he allegedly supported views that were contrary to his current teaching[382]. In his reply, the

382. Cf. Augustine, *De dono perseuerantiae* 11,6 (PL, 45), c. 1008. See Id., *De libero arbitrio* 3,23,66-68 (CCL, 29), pp. 314-315. In his dialogue on free will, Augustine gave his opinion about the eternal destiny of those infants dying before the age of reason. The question he had to face was whether those infants who die without being reborn in baptism are really condemned and punished, and whether those who die after receiving baptism are actually delivered and rewarded ("Si enim quando libros de Libero Arbitrio laicus coepi, presbyter explicavi, adhuc de damnatione infantium non renascentium et de renascentium liberatione dubitarem": Id., *De dono perseuerantiae* 12,30 [PL, 45], c. 1010). Although with a certain reserve, Augustine developed an opinion that seemingly allowed infants who died before the age of understanding the possibility of being taken up, in life after death, into an intermediate state between condemnation/punishment and deliverance/reward. Such an understanding of the destiny of these infants could be regarded as an attempt on the side of Augustine to explain man's naturally infirm state without appealing to the doctrine of original sin, or at least without considering the latter as the decisive explanation (see J. CHÉNÉ, *Notes complémentaires* [BA, 24], p. 828).
It must be remembered that the question of the infants who die before the age of reason is dealt with in a larger context in which Augustine tackles the problem of the double infirmity of *ignorantia et difficultas* (which humanity inherited after the fall of Adam) in connection with the problem of the origin of the soul. The direct causality that ties together the fall of the first man and the state of moral infirmity in humanity is what provided the necessary ground for the Manichaean objection: "Si Adam et Eva peccauerunt, quid nos miseri fecimus, ut cum ignorantiae caecitate, et difficultatis cruciatibus nasceremur?" (Augustine, *De libero arbitrio* 3,19,53 [CCL, 29], p. 306). After having answered that with the help of God man can be delivered from the natural misery into which he is born, Augustine, echoing Plato's formulation (cf. *Timaeus* 41d-e; 42e-43b; *Phaedo* 70c-72a; *ResPublica* 619b-620b), enumerates four different hypotheses about the origin of the soul: traducianism, creationism and the twofold theory of the preexistence of souls according to which the latter are either sent by God to inhabit a body or have descended *sponte* into them (cf. Augustine, *De libero arbitrio* 3,20,55-58 [CCL, 29], pp. 307-309). Augustine argues that in the absence of clear scriptural evidence, none of these four hypotheses imposes itself upon another (cf. *Ibid.* 3,21,59-62, pp. 309-312). For that reason, his discussion on the issue remained inconclusive until the end of his life (cf. Id., *Retractationes* 1,1,3 [CCL, 57], p. 10). A proof of this inconclusiveness was already present in *De libero arbitrio* 3,20,56 [CCL, 29], p. 307), a passage in which, while he admits that traducianism would be the clearest solution to the problem of original sin (see G. O'DALY, *Anima, animus*, in *AugL* 1 [1986-1988] 315-340, cc. 319-322; M. LAMBERIGTS, *Julian and Augustine on the Origin of the Soul*, in *Aug(L)* 46 [1996] 243-260, pp. 249ff.), he also seems to incline towards the hypothesis of creationism. In fact, he affirms that the double state of *ignorantia et difficultas*, seen as a punishment due to the acts of our forefathers, ought to be regarded as the natural state of the soul coming into existence: "ut malum meritum prioris natura sequentis sit" (Augustine, *De libero arbitrio* 3,20,56 [CCL, 29], p. 307). That Augustine really meant that moral infirmity is constitutive of the natural state into which man is born is the opinion of some scholars (cf., for instance, C. BOYER, *Dieu pouvait-il créer l'homme dans l'état d'ignorance et de difficulté?*, in *Greg* 11 [1930] 32-57). Others believe that Augustine never at any time developed his theology independently of the doctrine of original sin, even if he never solved the "how" of its transmission to Adam's descendants (see, for instance, M. LAMBERIGTS, *Augustine, Julian of Aeclanum and E. Pagels'* Adam, Eve and the Serpent, in *Aug(L)* 39 [1989] 393-435, pp. 399-400; ID., *Julian and Augustine on the Origin of the Soul*, p. 251). Besides, both *ignorantia et difficultas* can be interpreted not only as a punishment for Adam's fall, but also and more simply as a "consequence" of it (cf., for instance, Y. DE MONTCHEUIL, *L'hypothèse de l'état originel d'ignorance et de difficulté*

bishop of Hippo explains the method which guided the writing of the *De libero arbitrio*, and the different set of problems he had to face in that work. At that time he was, in fact, reacting against the dualist doctrine of the Manichees who, believing in two coeternal, immutable and mixed principles of good and evil, rejected the doctrine of original sin and denied, as a consequence, that any responsibility should be attached to man's free will vis-à-vis evil — the latter being caused, according to the Manichaean teaching, by the principle of evil itself. Moreover, the Manichaeans rejected the authority of the Old Testament and much of the New Testament, especially the Pauline corpus where the doctrine of original sin is plainly stated[383].

Against such a background, viz. on one hand having to refute the Manichaean denial of human responsibility and being preoccupied on the other with the assertion that there is only one human nature stemming from the one Adam, Augustine chose to develop the theme of man's double infirmity: *ignorantia et difficultas*. It is not at all clear, however, whether he regarded them as being a punishment for Adam's fall or simply aspects of man's natural condition. The possibility of considering both *ignorantia et difficultas* as either a punishment or a natural aspect of the *condition humaine* (an alternative which Augustine seems to have envisaged in the *De libero arbitrio* 3)[384] was definitively abandoned once the threat of Pelagianism appeared on the scene. In point of fact, in his *Retractationes* Augustine makes it clear that he had restricted

---

d'après le "De libero arbitrio" de saint Augustin, in *RScR* 23 [1933] 197-221, above all 217-218; A. TRAPÈ, *Introduzione generale*, in *Sant'Agostino, Dialoghi/II* [NBA, III/2], Rome, 1976, pp. XV-XVII). It is against such a background that Augustine introduces and tackles the problem of the suffering and death of the infants. After stating the general principle that in the order of creation no human being is useless ("Non posse superfluo creari qualemcumque hominem": Augustine, *De libero arbitrio* 3,23,66 [CCL, 29], p. 314) he asserts, with regard to the destiny of those who die in infancy, the possibility of a *uia media*: "Non enim metuendum est ne uita esse potuerit media quaedam inter recte factum atque peccatum, et sententia iudicis media esse non possit inter praemium atque supplicium" (*Ibid.*). Undoubtedly in the *De libero arbitrio* original sin (intended in the meaning of transmission of guilt from Adam to his descendants) is not clearly pictured, and certainly does not play a decisive role with regard to the question of the destiny of the dead infants. Maybe this is what "pouvait faire croire qu'au moment où il écrivait ce traité, Augustin n'avait pas des convictions bien arrêtées sur cette vérité catholique" (J. CHÉNÉ, *Notes complémentaires* [BA, 24], p. 829). Certainly, the supposed intermediate state of those infants, after death, does not correspond to Augustine's standpoint on the same subject during the Pelagian controversy. By then it will be clear to him that infants are baptized for the remission of their "own" sin, viz. for their sharing in the sin of Adam. Cf. Augustine, *Ep.* 98 (CSEL, 34/2), pp. 520-533. See J.M. RIST, *Augustine: Ancient Thought Baptized*, Cambridge, 1994, pp. 48, 121ff., 317-320, 326.

383. Cf. Augustine, *De dono perseuerantiae* 11,26 (PL, 45), c. 1008.

384. See *supra*, n. 382.

the field of his earlier statements to one single option, namely that *igno-rantia et difficultas* do not belong to man's primordial state, but consti-tute the punishment of original sin[385] in which all are born, and in which all automatically partake. The attainment of this position (whose alter-ation was criticized by the Massilians)[386] was a clear reaction against the view held by the Pelagians for whom *ignorantia et difficultas* were sim-ply the expression of human creatureliness, a view corresponding to their denial of original sin[387]. But above all, the "just condemnation" was now understood by Augustine in the light of his defined doctrine of grace and original sin, by which mankind is punished for a sin they too are "guilty" of. All human beings inherit the guilt of Adam's original sin and partake fully of this guilt[388]. After this digression, which begs, as it were, the central question of perseverance, Augustine once again points out the absurdity of the theory of the *futura merita mala*, the out-come of which would be to refuse the gratuitous character of grace for both infants and adults[389]. He then concludes this first part of the book by re-asserting some of his arguments under the banner of omnipotent and gratuitous grace. This grace exercises its lordship over human beings regardless of merits, from the very stirrings of faith until life ends with final perseverance[390].

---

385. Cf. Augustine, *Retractationes* 1,9,6 (CCL, 57), p. 29.

386. This criticism was raised also by the Pelagians. See M. LAMBERIGTS, *Julien d'Éclane et Augustin d'Hippone. Deux conceptions d'Adam*, in *Aug(L)* [*Mélanges T. J. Van Bavel*, T. I] 40 (1990) 373-410, *passim*.

387. Cf. Augustine, *Retractationes* 1,9,2 (CCL, 57), pp. 23-24. Cf. the quotation in *De dono perseuerantiae*: "Ex qua miseria peccantibus iustissime inflicta, liberat Dei gratia: quia homo sponte, id est, libero arbitrio cadere potuit, non etiam surgere: ad quam mise-riam iustae damnationis pertinet ignorantia et difficultas, quam patitur omnis homo ab exordio nativitatis suae; nec ab isto malo liberatur quisquam, nisi Dei gratia: quam mis-eriam nolunt Pelagiani ex iusta damnatione descendere, negantes originale peccatum" (Id., *De dono perseuerantiae* 11,27 [PL, 45], c. 1009). See also: "Ita in tertio libro de Libero Arbitrio secundum utrumque sensum restiti Manichaeis, sive supplicia, sive pri-mordia naturae sint ignorantia et difficultas, sine quibus nullus hominum nascitur; et tamen unum horum teneo, ibi quoque a me satis evidenter expressum: quod non sit ista natura instituti hominis, sed poena damnati" (*Ibid.* 12,29, c. 1010). As Weaver writes: "Augustine was seeking to demonstrate that his recent teaching was, if not latent in the earlier writings, at least not inconsistent with them. He also made the point that even if his position had changed somewhat over the years, surely he was not to be begrudged growth and development in understanding" (WEAVER, *Divine Grace and Human Agency* [n. 69], pp. 64-65).

388. "Because Augustine conceives the moral agent as a co-participant in Adam's fall, the agent bears the full responsibility for his ignorance and difficulty" (M. DJUTH, *The Hermeneutics of* De libero arbitrio III: *Are There Two Augustines?*, in *StPatr* 27, Louvain, 1993, pp. 281-289, p. 287).

389. Augustine, *De dono perseuerantiae* 12,31-13,32 (PL, 45), cc. 1011-1012.

390. Cf. *Ibid.* 13,33, cc. 1012-1013.

d) The Teaching on Predestination

In the second part of the *De dono perseuerantiae* Augustine rebukes
those who hold that his teaching on grace and predestination makes
preaching or exhortation redundant[391], except to fill people with
despair[392]. This was, in fact, the Massilians' argument: that the effect
of preaching predestination would weaken and devalue, possibly even
make superfluous, human will and effort, and that it would ultimately
instill fear. Augustine replies by stating that the Christian doctrine of
predestination and the practice of exhortation are to be found in Scripture as well as in Church tradition, and as such it should be preached
in its entirety. Christ himself taught the concept of predestination when
he spoke of Tyre and Sidon (cf Mt 11,21), as did the apostle Paul in his
letters, teaching predestination and exhorting Christ's followers to obedience[393]. At this point Augustine gives a formal definition of predestination. It is the *praescientia* and the *praeparatio beneficiorum*, on the
part of God, thanks to which those who have been predestined (by his
eternal decree) to be freed from the *massa perditionis* will be infallibly
saved[394]. Furthermore, predestination should be preached together with
faith and perseverance[395]. Vice versa, the preaching of faith and perseverance should not hinder or diminish the teaching of the doctrine of
predestination. Those who live in accordance with faith and persevere
in it obediently should not boast of themselves, but ascribe their perseverance to God's predestination[396], as the teaching of Cyprian also

---

391. "Sed aiunt 'praedestinationis definitionem utilitati praedicationis adversam'"
(*Ibid.* 14,34, c. 1013). Augustine is referring to Hilary's letter: "Nouum et inutile esse
praedicationi, quod quidam secundum propositum eligendi dicantur, ut id nec arripere
ualeant nec tenere nisi credendi uoluntate donata. Excludi putant omnem praedicandi vig-
orem, si nihil, quod per eam excitetur, in hominibus remansisse dicatur" (Hilary, *Ep.*
226,2 [CSEL, 57], p. 469). Cf. also: "Adserunt inutilem exhortandi consuetudinem"
(*Ibid.* 226,5, p. 474); "Praedestinationis definitionem utilitati praedicationis adversam, eo
quod hac audita, nemo possit correptionis stimulis excitari" (Augustine, *De dono
perseuerantiae* 17,43 [PL, 45], c. 1020; cf. *Ibid.* 17,46, c. 1021). See Prosper, *Ep.* 225,3
(CSEL, 57), pp. 457-458. As we know, a similar issue, in relation to the usefulness of
reproof, was dealt with by Augustine in his *De correptione et gratia.*
392. "Ut dicant quandam desperationem hominibus exhiberi" (Hilary, *Ep.* 226,6
[CSEL, 57], p. 475);
393. Augustine, *De dono perseuerantiae* 14,34 (PL, 45), c. 1013.
394. "Haec est praedestinatio sanctorum, nihil aliud: praescientia scilicet, et praeparatio beneficiorum Dei, quibus certissime liberantur, quicumque liberantur" (*Ibid.* 14,35,
c. 1014).
395. *Ibid.* 14,35-36, cc. 1014-1015.
396. "Nec rursus, praedicatione fidei proficientis et usque ad ultimum permanentis,
impedienda est praedicatio praedestinationis, ut qui fideliter et obedienter vivit, non de
ipsa obedientia tanquam de suo non accepto bono extollatur: sed qui gloriatur, in Domino
glorietur" (*Ibid.* 14,36, c. 1015).

confirms[397]. Thus, preaching and exhortation as well as listening and obedience, belong to those who have already received the gift of either exhortation or obedience from God[398]. In point of fact, preaching and exhortation are meant for the benefit of those who have been given "ears to hear" (cf. Lk 8,8) so that they may recognize God's hand upon them and live accordingly, in obedience to what they hear[399]. In this sense those who receive the gift of "ears" and "obedience" are not harmed by preaching and exhortation[400].

Underlining his conviction that, when necessary, predestination should be mentioned, Augustine cites the example of foreknowledge which, as such, is not questioned by the Massilians, but which could lead to wrong and ruinous conclusions being drawn, in exactly the same way as false conclusions could be arrived at from the doctrine of pre-destination. In other words, if, on the ground of divine election and pre-destination, the argument used was that no one should be rebuked for his disobedience, for what he is or is not, does or does not, then the same argument could be used for God's foreknowledge. In fact, if in spite of the doctrine of divine *praescientia* being taught, the necessity of reproof is not done away with, but continues to be upheld, then one should agree

---

397. "Quod vidit fidelissime Cyprianus, et fidentissime definivit *[Ad Quirinum 4]*, per quod utique praedestinationem certissimam pronuntiavit. Nam si 'in nullo gloriandum est, quando nostrum nihil sit': profecto nec de obedientia perseverantissima gloriandum est; nec ita nostra, tanquam non sit nobis desuper donata, dicenda est... His Cypriani verbis procul dubio praedestinatio praedicata est: quae si Cyprianum a praedicatione obe-dientiae non prohibuit, nec nos utique debet prohibere" (*Ibid.*).

398. "Ac per hoc sicut exhortatur et praedicat recte, sed ille qui accepit hoc donum" (*Ibid.* 14,37, c. 1016).

399. Augustine also has in mind "the danger of pride and the necessity of proper attri-bution of glory.... Augustine argued that predestination must be preached for the benefit of the obedient so that they might not begin to feel self-important. They must be allowed to hear that their obedience is not self-derived but is a divine gift, that their boasting is to be in the Lord" (R.H. WEAVER, *Augustine's Use of Scriptural Admonitions Against Boasting in His Final Arguments on Grace*, in *SP* 27, Louvain, 1993, pp. 424-430, p. 429). Cassian too was keenly aware of the dangers of pride, considered as the most deadly among the eight principal faults, and he also recognized the necessity of grace. Yet, he was not led to the conclusion that the dispensation of divine salvation precluded the possibility of a self-generated *initium fidei* (or *salutis*). On the contrary, "for Augus-tine, with his far severer notion of the human condition, the possibility of self-generated merit would seem to have necessarily entailed pride, and it was pride that the divine dis-pensation specifically disallowed" (*Ibid.*, p. 430).

400. "It should be noted that once again Augustine established no direct connection between the action of preaching and the outcome of belief.... The relationship between the human activity of preaching and the human response of belief can be realized only if and when divine action establishes such a relationship.... Thus preaching as an instru-ment for effecting perseverance is a human action of undeniable relevance to the salvific process... although the primary agent does remain the divine one" (WEAVER, *Divine Grace and Human Agency* [n. 69], p. 66).

that even in the case that it is predestination to be taught, the need for
reproof maintains its importance[401]. Similarly, one might state that even
prayer would seem pointless, since, according to Jesus' words, God
knows in advance what we need before we ask him (cf. Mt 6,8). And
yet, Augustine goes on to say that even if some of God's gifts, such as,
for instance, the *initium fidei,* are bestowed without man's petition, there
are other gifts, such as final perseverance, that are granted by God to
those who implore them through prayer. In like manner prayer, since it
plays an important role in the divine plan of predestination, should be
the object of exhortation[402]. Moreover, not to ask people to pray for perseverance would allow those who hear obediently to run the risk of
falling into the trap of pride.

Augustine argues that the same objection about the uselessness of
preaching and exhortation could be used against his dissenters. They
also preach about those virtues reckoned to be gifts of God, such as wisdom, continence, patience or modesty[403]; but they would never consider
the preaching of these virtues a useless thing, nor would they believe
that urging people to practise these same virtues would imply a diminu-
tion or a nullification of the need of exhortation. On the contrary, the
bishop of Hippo contended that the Massilians themselves urged people
to both strive and hope for these qualities. That being so, why, Augustine asks, should the practice of preaching and exhortation be regarded
as useless or held responsible for driving people to despair, simply
because they mention, as gifts of God, the issues of the beginning of
faith and final perseverance?[404]. If the Massilians were not prepared to
consider the beginning of faith and final perseverance gifts of God, then,
consistent with their own conviction, they should only preach and exhort
about these two realities, viz. the beginning of faith and perseverance,
which they believed they could master by their own will power and

---

401. "Ista cum dicuntur, ita nos a confitenda vera Dei gratia, id est, quae non secundum merita nostra datur, et a confitenda secundum eam praedestinatione sanctorum deter-
rere non debent; sicut non deterremur a confitenda praescientia Dei, si quis de illa populo
sic loquatur, ut dicat: 'Sive nunc recte vivatis, sive non recte, tales eritis postea, quales
vos Deus futuros esse praescivit, vel boni si bonos, vel mali si malos'. Numquid enim, si
hoc audito nonnulli in torporem segnitiemque vertantur, et a labore proclives ad libidinem
post concupiscentias suas eant, propterea de praescientia Dei falsum putandum est esse,
quod dictum est? Nonne si Deus illos bonos futuros esse praescivit, boni erunt, in quantalibet nunc malignitate versentur; si autem malos, mali erunt, in quantalibet nunc bonitate cernantur?" (Augustine, *De dono perseuerantiae* 15,38 [PL, 45], cc. 1016-1017). Cf.
Hilary, *Ep.* 226,2 and 5 (CSEL, 57), pp. 469 and 474.
402. Augustine, *De dono perseuerantiae* 16,39 (PL, 45), c. 1017.
403. Cf. *Ibid.* 17,43, c. 1020.
404. Cf. *Ibid.*

effort. Consequently, they should stop preaching about those virtues that they regard as God's gifts, such as continence[405], and concentrate on those autarchic virtues which are in man's power to attain, but whose practice would still require sustainance through exhortation and encouragement.

At this point, Augustine again lingers on the question of predestination and its link with prescience, referring to Paul's usage[406] and to the approach of the *uerbi Dei tractatores*[407]. He affirms that if in the past some commentators have used the term prescience as a synonym of predestination, in explaining Holy Scripture, this was simply due to the fact that the term prescience was more easily understood than that of predestination, and was therefore employed as equivalent to it. Besides, continues Augustine, prescience was defined in full accord with the truth preached about the predestination of grace[408], as it was defended by eminent witnesses like Cyprian, Ambrose[409] and Gregory of Nazianzus. Cyprian's teaching on predestination is summed up in one of his sentences: "We must boast in nothing since nothing is our own"[410]. Ambrose, who taught that our hearts and thoughts are not in our power[411], echoes the words of Pr 8,35 (LXX) about God's preparation of man's will[412] and stresses his freedom in choosing those He desires[413]. Finally, Gregory of Nazianzus speaks (at least according to Augustine's interpretation) of both belief in God and confession of faith in God as being his gifts[414].

405. Cf. *Ibid.* 17,45f, c. 1021.
406. Cf. *Ibid.* 18,47, cc. 1022-1023.
407. "Quid ergo nos prohibet, quando apud aliquos verbi Dei tractatores legimus Dei praescientiam, et agitur de vocatione electorum, eamdem praedestinationem intelligere?" (*Ibid.* 19,48, c. 1023).
408. Cf. *Ibid.*
409. For Augustine's recurse to Cyprian and Ambrose, see *supra*, n. 302.
410. Cyprian, *Ad Quirinum (Testimoniorum l. iii)* 3,4 (CCL, 3), p. 92; cf. Augustine, *De dono perseuerantiae* 19,48-49 (PL, 45), cc. 1023-1024.
411. Ambrose, *De fuga saeculi* 1,2 (CSEL, 32/2), pp. 163f.
412. Id., *Expositio euangelii secundum Lucam* 1,10 (CCL, 14), pp. 11-12; cf. Augustine, *De dono perseuerantiae* 19,49 (PL, 45), c. 1025.
413. Ambrose, *Expositio euangelii secundum Lucam* 7,27 (CCL, 14), pp. 223-224; cf. Augustine, *De dono perseuerantiae* 19,49 (PL, 45), c. 1025.
414. Augustine quotes a passage from an oration addressed by Gregory of Nazianzus to those who denied the full divinity of the Holy Spirit, viz. the Pneumatomachi, to underline his conviction that God's predestination lies at the root of both belief and perseverance. Gregory stressed that what really matters is to confess the Trinity as one Deity or nature. In fact, if anyone acknowledges that the Spirit is one with the Father and the Son he also acknowledges (even if he does not use that term) that the Spirit is "God", and that he will certainly receive the grace of eventually calling him so, that is "God": (Μιᾶς Θεότητος, ὦ οὗτοι, τὴν Τριάδα ὁμολογήσατε, εἰ δὲ βούλεσθε, μιᾶς φύσεως καὶ τὴν 'Θεὸς' φωνὴν παρὰ τοῦ Πνεύματος ὑμῖν αἰτήσομεν. Δώσει γὰρ, εὖ οἶδα, ὁ τὸ

Having underlined that his standpoint on grace, *initium fidei* and predestination was not something new, but that in its essence it dated back to the *De diuersis quaestionibus ad Simplicianum*[415] and to the

πρῶτον δούς, καὶ τὸ δεύτερον: "May you confess, I beg you, the Trinity as one Deity or, if you prefer, as one nature; we shall then ask for you to the Holy Spirit the word 'God' (καὶ τὴν Θεὸς φωνὴν παρὰ τοῦ Πνεύματος ὑμῖν αἰτήσομεν). He who has bestowed on you the first gift *[i.e., that of confessing the Trinity]* will bestow on you, I am sure, also the second one *[that of confessing that the Spirit is 'God']*" (Gregory of Nazianzus, *Oratio* 41 [On Pentecost], in *Grégoire de Nazianze, Discours 38-41* [SC, 358], p. 330). Augustine interprets this passage in a different way, as he explains while quoting Gregory: "*...et Deus uocem dari uobis a sancto Spiritu deprecabitur*; id est, rogabitur Deus, ut permittat vobis dari vocem, qua quod creditis, confiteri possitis. *Dabit enim, certus sum; qui dedit quod primum est, dabit et quod secundum est;* qui dedit credere, dabit et confiteri" (Augustine, *De dono perseuerantiae* 19,49 [PL, 45], cc. 1024-1025). As we can see, Augustine's interpretation no longer refers to the necessity of calling the Holy Spirit "God", but to the need of confessing externally the faith in the Trinity. As to the problem of the different contexts and interpretations (see, for instance, the expression *uocem dari* which in Augustine means the gift of the *voice* by which the faith in the Trinity is confessed, whereas in Gregory the words τὴν Θεὸς φωνήν were intended as an invocation upon the Pneumatomachi of the gift of a 'word' [φωνή], namely that of 'God' [Θεός]), as well as to that of the translation into Latin of the Greek text (*e.g.*, 'deprecabitur' instead of 'deprecabimur: αἰτήσομεν), see J. CHÉNÉ, *Notes complémentaires* (BA, 24), pp. 831-835. See also ID., *Sur un texte du "De dono perseuerantiae" (Cap. XIX, n. 49)*, in *REAug* 6 (1960) 309-313; G. BARTELINK, *Die Beeinflussung Augustins durch die griechischen Patres*, in J. DEN BOEFT - J. VAN OORT (eds.), *Augustiniana Traiectina. Communications présentées au Colloque International d'Utrecht 13-14 novembre 1986*, Paris, 1987, pp. 9-24, p. 20, n. 57.

The argument of "tradition", to which Augustine appeals in order to find support for his teaching on predestination, is undoubtedly dealt with very swiftly and with very few references to the Fathers of the Church. The only two authorities of the Latin Church that Augustine refers to are Cyprian and Ambrose. Gregory of Nazianzus is the only representative, although of impeccable credentials, that the bishop of Hippo quotes to link himself to the Eastern Church tradition. These three witnesses constitute a very scanty choice indeed; all the more so if we think that Gregory was probably quoted by Augustine to show that some proof could also be drawn from the Eastern tradition (upon which the Massilians relied) in support of his doctrine. For Augustine, the first two witnesses, Cyprian and Ambrose, would have been *per se* sufficient: "Sed his duobus, qui sufficere debuerunt, sanctum Gregorium addamus et tertium" (Augustine, *De dono perseuerantiae* 19,49 [PL, 45], c. 1024). As a matter of fact, it looks as if Augustine were satisfied with stating the general principle that the *uerbi Dei tractatores* (*Ibid.* 19,48, c. 1023) have always agreed, in line with Holy Scripture and Church tradition, that faith and final perseverance are the gifts of God, no matter if prescience was intended as having the same meaning as predestination. The very few citations from Church tradition, however, seem to be clear evidence that Augustine could not find other sources which, while supporting his doctrinal standpoint on predestination, could at the same time disprove the charge of novelty brought against him by the Massilians (cf. Prosper, *Ep.* 225,2 [CSEL, 57], p. 455; Hilary, *Ep.* 226,2 [CSEL, 57], p. 469). This is not to say that Augustine did not make use of other sources (in his other works) in order to prove that he was in harmony with tradition. In *Contra Iulianum* 1 and 2 (PL, 44), cc. 641-702 *passim*, for instance, there appear several references to other Church Fathers.

415. Augustine affirms explicitly that at the time of *De diuersis quaestionibus ad Simplicianum* (therefore long before Pelagianism made its appearance, and without being

Confessiones[416] (taking a definitive shape at the time of the Pelagian controversy), Augustine insists on the necessity of preaching such truths, although with discretion and prudence[417]. He gives a few examples in this direction, starting with a Pauline sentence which he uses as a type of heading: *Sic currite, ut comprehendatis* (1 Cor 9,24). The preacher should exhort believers to run, so that they may come to the knowledge of themselves as being foreknown as lawful runners and contenders for the prize[418]. In other words, in leading a good and just way of life, they may expect with humble and trusting hope (though they can never be certain of it), that they belong to those predestined by divine grace[419]. Therefore, preaching, even when truth is at stake, must not be pursued in a crude manner. On the contrary, it should be done in such a way that those hearing it be encouraged to pray and hope for perseverance, thereby trusting that they be numbered among the elect[420]. Prayer too is of great importance with respect to this. It is through prayer, in fact, that believers learn that those who do not seem to be called by God (*e.g.*, the heathens) may in fact be efficaciously called and become part of the elect[421]. Thus, Augustine advises those who are *tardi corde et*

---

aware of it) he had already drawn his conclusions about those questions sorrounding grace that the Pelagians will bring to the fore: "... et antequam Pelagiani apparere coepissent... multis... locis futuram nescientes Pelagianam haeresim caedebamus, praedicando gratiam, qua Deus liberat a malis erroribus et moribus nostris, non praecedentibus bonis meritis nostris, faciens hoc secundum gratuitam misericordiam suam. Quod plenius sapere coepi in ea disputatione, quam scripsi ad beatae memoriae Simplicianum episcopum Mediolanensis ecclesiae, in mei episcopato exordio, quando et initium fidei donum Dei esse cognovi, et asserui" (Augustine, *De dono perseuerantiae* 20,52 [PL, 45], c. 1026). See V.H. DRECOLL, *Die Entstehung der Gnadenlehre Augustins* (BHT, 109), Tübingen, 1999, pp. 218-250.

416. "Cum et ipsos *[the books of the* Confessiones*]* ediderim antequam Pelagiana haeresis exstitisset, in eis certe dixi Deo nostro, et saepe dixi: *Da quod iubes, et iube quod vis*" (Augustine, *De dono perseuerantiae* 20,53 [PL, 45], c. 1026). See DRECOLL, *Die Entstehung der Gnadenlehre Augustins* (n. 415), pp. 251-354 *passim*.

417. Cf. Augustine, *De dono perseuerantiae* 22,57 (PL, 45), cc. 1028-1029.

418. "Atque ut ipso cursu vestro ita vos esse praecognitos noveritis, ut legitime curreretis" (*Ibid.* 22,57, c. 1028). Cf. 2 Tm 2,5.

419. "De ipso autem cursu vestro bono rectoque condiscite vos ad praedestinationem divinae gratiae pertinere" (*Ibid.* 22,59, c. 1029).

420. "Vos itaque etiam ipsam obediendi perseverantiam a Patre luminum, a quo descendit omne datum optimum et omne donum perfectum, sperare debetis, et quotidianis orationibus poscere, atque hoc faciendo confidere, non vos esse a praedestinatione populi eius alienos; quia etiam hoc ut faciatis, ipse largitur. Absit autem a vobis, ideo desperare de vobis, quoniam spem vestram in ipso habere iubemini, non in vobis" (*Ibid.* 22,62, c. 1030).

421. "Cur enim non potius ita dicitur: Et si qui sunt nondum vocati, pro eis ut vocentur oremus? Fortassis enim sic praedestinati sunt, ut nostris orationibus concedantur, et accipiant eamdem gratiam, qua velint atque efficiantur electi. Deus enim qui omnia quae praedestinavit implevit, ideo et pro inimicis fidei orare nos voluit; ut hinc intelligeremus,

infirmi[422] and unable to grasp the meaning of Scripture, not to pay too much heed to the discussions on predestination, because this might result in confusion. Instead, they ought to commit themselves in simplicity of heart to the Church's practice of praying for unbelievers and believers alike[423]. Augustine continued by saying that if the Church believed that the requests conveyed by her prayers were within the capacity and reach of human beings, then she would stop such a practice, since she would look upon it as mere mockery[424]. Moreover, since prayer is a gift of God, strictly connected with the work of the Holy Spirit[425], the prayer of the Church for the conversion of the unbelievers and for the perseverance of the believers is a further proof that the utility of prayer is not, as such, nullified by the teaching on predestination[426]. Finally, reiterating his conviction on the mysterious and impenetrable doctrine of predestination, Augustine concludes his treatise, by reminding his readers once again that in order to understand such a

quod ipse etiam infidelibus donet ut credant, et volentes ex nolentibus faciat" (*Ibid.* 22,60, cc. 1029-1030).

422. Cf. *Ibid.* 23,63, c. 1031.

423. "Quando enim non oratum est in ecclesia pro infidelibus atque inimicis eius ut crederent? Quando fidelis quisquam amicum, proximum, coniugem habuit infidelem, et non ei petivit a Domino mentem obedientem in christianam fidem? Quis autem sibi unquam non oravit, ut in Domino permaneret? Aut quis sacerdotem super fideles Dominum invocantem, si quando dixit, Da illis, Domine, in te perseverare usque in finem; non solum voce ausus est, sed saltem cogitatione reprehendere?" (*Ibid.* 23,63, c. 1031).

424. "Quandoquidem non oraret Ecclesia ut daretur infidelibus fides, nisi Deum crederet et aversas et adversas hominum ad se convertere voluntates: nec oraret Ecclesia ut perseveraret in fide Christi, non decepta vel victa tentationibus mundi, nisi crederet Dominum sic in potestate habere cor nostrum, ut bonum quod non tenemus nisi propria voluntate, non tamen teneamus nisi ipse in nobis operetur et velle. Nam si haec ab ipso quidem poscit Ecclesia, sed a se ipsa sibi dari putat; non veras, sed perfunctorias orationes habet: quod absit a nobis. Quis enim veraciter gemat, desiderans accipere quod orat a Domino, si hoc a se ipso se sumere existimet, non ab illo?" (*Ibid.* 23,63, cc. 1031-1032).

425. Cf. *Ibid.* 23,64, c. 1032.

426. "Quae bona si semper oravit, semper ea Dei dona esse utique credidit: nec ab illo esse praecognita unquam ei negare fas fuit. Ac per hoc praedestinationis huius fidem, quae contra novos haereticos nova sollicitudine nunc defenditur, nunquam Ecclesia Christi non habuit" (*Ibid.* 23,65, cc. 1032-1033). Yet Augustine's appeal to the reality of prayer in order to back up his teaching on perseverance (and predestination), does not seem to work. In fact, if divine grace acts gratuitously, viz. independently of human merit or of man's requests, then the purpose of the very practice of prayer as a demonstration that perseverance is a gift of God, is called into question. As Weaver rightly remarks, the very fact that perseverance is a gift bestowed "by divine determination only shows that whether one prays for it or not has no effect on whether one receives it. Augustine's very appeal to prayer put the point of prayer in doubt" (WEAVER, *Divine Grace and Human Agency* [n. 69], p. 61).

mystery one must set oneself to the contemplation of Jesus Christ, the highest example of predestination[427].

At the end of this short summary of the *De dono perseuerantiae* we are left with the feeling that Augustine's standpoint with regard to the gift of final perseverance and predestination (a standpoint he had already worked out in his *De correptione et gratia*) not only appears to have been strongly restated, but somehow even hardened by developing the "logic" of grace to its extreme consequences. The following considerations may, for the moment, be sufficient to enlighten us as to the meaning of such a development. In his treatise *De gratia et libero arbitrio*, fully dedicated, as the title says, to the relationship between grace and free will, Augustine was at pains to keep a balance between the agency of man and that of grace, although the latter played a prominent role. In the *De dono perseuerantiae*, however, the bishop of Hippo no longer seems preoccupied with keeping such a balance. Free will and human agency, at this stage, seem to have become mere "instruments for expressing the outworking of grace"[428]. One more concrete indication arises from the way in which Augustine answers the objection concerning the meaning of preaching, exhortation and prayer within a rigid predestinarian scheme. As already hinted at, he never manages to clarify the status of preaching and exhortation, and such ambiguity, with regard the place that human initiative and agency occupy in relationship with the agency of prevenient and gratuitous grace acting in a predestinarian perspective, is never fully cleared up. Such ambiguity remains, as it were, palpable. In point of fact, the line of argument taken by the bishop of Hippo clearly emerges as a continual and intransigent insistence on the predestinarian "logic" of his theological construction on grace. So much so that the overriding role of divine agency overshadows, if not *de facto* replaces, a healthy form of libertarianism[429] whose role in the process of the economy of salvation should not be underrated.

---

427. "Nullum autem est illustrius praedestinationis exemplum quam ipse Jesus" (Augustine, *De dono perseuerantiae* 24,67 [PL, 45], c. 1033). Cf. Id., *De praedestinatione sanctorum* 15,30-31 (PL, 44), cc. 981-983.

428. WEAVER, *Divine Grace and Human Agency* (n. 69), p. 68.

429. By "libertarianism" we mean the ability of human beings to act with free will and moral responsibility, with the proviso, however, that such ability is free of any determination caused by anything outside the agent, and with the guarantee that the agent could have acted otherwise. Cf. E. STUMP, *Augustine on Free Will*, in E. STUMP – N. KRETZMANN (eds.), *The Cambridge Companion to Augustine*, Cambridge, 2001, pp. 124-147, pp. 125-126.

CHAPTER THREE

GRACE, FREE WILL AND THE STRUGGLE FOR PERFECTION

To retrace the prehistory and the development of the concept of Christian grace and the role of free will in the works of Christian writers and theologians since the beginning of Christianity would take us too far from the specific purpose of our research. We shall content ourselves with a short and general survey of both the place occupied by the concept of grace in the process of Christian theological thought of the first centuries and the interactive role played in it by the issue of human initiative. More attention shall be paid to the latter, in an attempt to highlight the way the concept of human free will was dealt with, particularly in the Eastern theological construction, before Augustine's systematization of the doctrine of grace. We hope in this way to be able to appropriately assess, within an objective context, alien from later doctrinal definitions, the position of Cassian and of Massilianism on this subject, particularly with regard to the issue of *naturae bonum* and *initium fidei* (which will be dealt with in this chapter) and of *praedestinatio* (to which the following chapter will be devoted). A bird's-eye view on the relationship (or tension) between freedom and (divine/astral) determinism and fatalism in the ancient pagan world, and an equally and necessarily sketchy view on the more harmonized relationship between freedom and divine grace in Scripture, will set the introductory scene to the discussion that, across the theological construction of the first centuries, reached Augustine and the Massilians.

1. The Dilemma of Freedom
versus Determinism and Fatalism in the Ancient Pagan World[1]

The dilemma constituted by freedom and responsibility or libertarianism on one side, and determinism and fatalism or inevitability[2] on the

---

1. See D. AMAND, *Fatalisme et liberté dans l'antiquité grecque. Recherches sur la survivance de l'argumentation morale antifataliste de Carnéade chez les philosophes grecs et les théologiens chrétiens des quatre premiers siècles* (RTHP, 3ème série, 19), Louvain, 1945, pp. 1-28.
2. Although apparently identical, the notion of determinism should be distinguished from that of fatalism. The thesis concerning determinism is in itself very simple: it states that all events in the world, particularly those pertaining to human life, are without

other, was already apparent in the most ancient Greek attempt to describe and understand human being, namely the *Homeric* literature. The two poles are present there and face each other dialectically. Although man's actions are often based on the influence of both the Olympian gods and destiny (μοῖρα), and although the gods themselves appear to be powerless with regard to the sovereignty of destiny, the hero's extraordinary feats of will and intelligence, viz. human power[3], do become apparent in the *Odyssey* in particular, without seeming to be vitiated by either the presence of destiny or the activity of the gods[4]. The historian *Herodotus* also took man's autonomous capabilities into consideration, as is shown by the use of the expression ἐπ' ἡμῖν ἐστι ("it

exception, effects of earlier events or causes. All events, that is, are necessitated by earlier events in a causal chain (cf. R.C. WEATHERFORD, *Determinism*, in T. HONDERICH [ed.], *The Oxford Companion to Philosophy*, Oxford-New York, 1995, pp. 194-195). Fatalism, on the other hand, concerns the belief that the future will be the same, no matter what we do, and that there is no point for man to deliberate, viz. choose and act, because he can in no way affect the future. This belief is illustrated by the famous "lazy argument (ἀργος λόγος)" of antiquity. As Weatherford puts it: "If it is fated for you to recover from this illness, you will recover whether you call in a doctor or not; similarly if it is fated for you not to recover from this illness, you will not recover whether you call in a doctor or not; and either your recovery or your non-recovery is fated; therefore there is no point in calling a doctor" (ID., *Fatalism*, in HONDERICH [ed.], *The Oxford Companion to Philosophy*, p. 270). Determinists reject fatalism on the ground that it may be determined that we can be cured only by calling the doctor. Opposed to determinism are the theories of "libertarianism" and "compatibilism". Libertarianism disrupts the necessity of the causal chain of events and affirms that man, freed from the determination of both the past and the present, can choose and act so as to make the future different (cf. ID., *Libertarianism*, in HONDERICH [ed.], *The Oxford Companion to Philosophy*, p. 485). On the other hand, "compatibilism is a view about determinism and freedom that claims we are sometimes free and morally responsible even though all events are causally determined" (ID., *Compatibilism and Incompatibilism*, in HONDERICH [ed.], *The Oxford Companion to Philosophy*, p. 144).

3. The intellectual effort as the primary feature of man's power will be a distinguishing theme in Greek thought. According to Dihle, "the freedom to choose the ends and means of action which human beings seeem to enjoy is not primarily, in the Greek view, the freedom to direct one's intention wherever one pleases. Free will does not exist in its own right.... It depends on man's alleged potential ability to reach an adequate understanding of reality by his own intellectual effort" (A. DIHLE, *The Theology of Will in Classical Antiquity*, Los Angeles, 1982, p. 45).

4. From the time of the Homeric literature, a fundamental feeling arises that will never completely disappear in Greek thought, namely that the Greek man "vuole foggiare in tutto e per tutto la vita secondo la sua volontà; tale sentimento è così forte da fargli sentire il destino come un Tu, come una presenza nemica, come una barriera contro la quale egli urta nella sua corsa" (M. POHLENZ, *L'uomo greco* [Il pensiero storico, 44], Florence, 1962, p. 37). Moreover, we do not find in Homer any systematic formula for the relationship between destiny and the gods. It is only with the loss of confidence in the latter that fate became increasingly prominent and men "tended more and more to resign themselves to fate" (W. JAEGER, *Paideia. The Ideals of Greek Culture*, Vol. III, New York, 1945, p. 278).

lies in our power")[5]. The *Greek tragedies*, in their turn, although at times retaining a clear theological determinism whereby man is ineluctably submitted to fate (*e.g.* Sophocles' Oedipus king), were also an attempt to harmonize the different forces playing in the world. They made themselves the interpreters of the Greek conviction that man does in fact possess some inner force, which enables him to master, at least to a certain extent, his destiny. We find an example of this in the *Oresteia* trilogy of Aeschylus. Seeking to balance the tyranny of destiny, the power of the Olympian gods and the responsibility of man, Aeschylus concluded his trilogy with the words: "Peace endureth for future time between the citizens of Pallas' burgh and them that have come to dwell therein. Zeus, the all-seeing, and Fate have lent their aid unto this end"[6].

As to the great Greek philosophers, *Socrates* gave a rational justification to the thinking that man can find in his innermost being the source of a decision-making power, a power which it is up to him to use freely and with full responsibility. Besides, man's interiority was also considered the abode of those values that make him happy. In this way, thanks to his inner freedom and his capacity for self-determination, the human being experiences his independence vis-à-vis the supposed dominion of the external world over his own destiny. The view of *Plato*, the disciple of Socrates, is of some interest too. Quoting *en passant* the common opinion that "nobody can escape fate"[7], Plato implicitly and ironically rejected this "womanish belief"[8]. Thus, although in the *Timaeus* he seems to elevate necessity to the status of an overwhelming force[9] and although he quotes in the *Laws* the traditional opinion that not even the gods could oppose necessity[10], he nevertheless attempted to maintain a balance between divine governance, luck (τύχη), timing (καιρός) and skill (τέχνη)[11]. The doctrine of free choice was adumbrated also in

5. Cf. Herodotus, *Historiae* 8,29 (ed. GODLEY), p. 28.

6. Aeschylus, *Eumenides* 1044-1046 (ed. LLOYD-JONES), p. 370, English translation, p. 371. "La tensione tra la volontà dell'uomo e il destino – writes Pohlenz – è il tratto fondamentale della tragedia greca. Ma l'uomo non è consegnato impotente nelle mani del destino, bensì porta nel suo intimo la libertà ed una forza che, attraverso l'azione morale, lo solleva al di sopra del destino fuori di lui.... Il senso morale esige che l'uomo non venga alleggerito in nessun caso della responsabilità connessa alle sue azioni" (POHLENZ, *L'uomo greco* [n. 4], pp. 50-52).

7. These are the words that Hector addressed to Andromache (cf. Homerus, *Iliad* VI, 488 [ed. GOOLD], p. 310).

8. Plato, *Gorgias* 512e.

9. Cf. Id., *Timaeus* 48.

10. Cf. Id., *Leges* 741a.

11. Cf. *Ibid.*, 709b-c. See also: "The blame is his who chooses: God is blameless" (αἰτία ἑλομένου· θεὸς ἀναίτιος) (Id., *ResPublica* 617e).

Aristotle[12] according to whom it is characteristic of intuition to be aware of the fact that man can determine his life autonomously. Yet he did not tackle the fundamental question of whether the act of willing is free or conditioned, a problem which will be taken into consideration during the Hellenistic period.

With regard to philosophical Hellenism it is worth mentioning the *Stoa*[13]. The doctrine of εἱμαρμένη, elaborated by its founder, Zeno, was taken up and defended by his followers Cleanthes of Assos and Chrysippus of Soli[14]. Influenced by Eastern fatalism, this doctrine reduced considerably the importance attributed by Greek thought to man's self-determination. The religious faith of the Stoics and their concept of all-embracing fate reveal in fact a monist and materialist interpretation of reality[15]. However, beside their deterministic conception of the world order, it was their belief that εἱμαρμένη, with its inflexible laws, was not merely the equivalent of a blind destiny, but coincided with divine providence on which the task of regulating everything in the best possible way depends, including individuals. Fate was, as it were, rationalised and identified with the good will of the deity[16]. That is why the wise man will always choose consciously and willingly what εἱμαρμένη orders or even compels him to do, for he knows that to adhere to it is at the same time necessary and salutary (for himself and for the universe) and perfectly rational[17]. After Chrysippus, who recognized the freedom of self-determination and the responsibility of human actions in order to safeguard the moral element[18], the Stoa was led to soften a fatalistic εἱμαρμένη by introducing the element of man's willing and positive co-operation with divine providence. *Neo-Stoicism* was to produce a clearer

---

12. Cf. Aristotle, *Ethica Nicomachea* II,9,4-III,5,2 (1109b30-1113b2).

13. See J.M. RIST, *Stoic Philosophy*, Cambridge-London-New York-Melbourne, 1969, esp. pp. 112-132.

14. See M.L. COLISH, *The Stoic Tradition from Antiquity to the Early Middle Ages*. Vol. I: *Stoicism in Classical Latin Literature*, 2nd impression with addenda and corrigenda, Leiden, 1990, pp. 31-35.

15. Its most articulate critic was Carneades, the founder of the New Academy (2nd century B.C.) whose work was directed explicitly at Chrysippus.

16. See J.B. GOULD, *The Stoic Conception of Fate*, in *JHI* 35 (1974) 17-32. "Lo stoico – writes Pohlenz – non combatte contro il destino, ma vede in esso i clementi decreti della divinità, che vuole il meglio anche per lui, e s'abbandona lieto, mosso da un intimo convincimento, a quella guida" (POHLENZ, *L'uomo greco* [n. 4], p. 57). For the notion of συγκατάθεσις (assent), see ID., *Griechische Freiheit. Wesen und Werden eines Lebensideal*, Heidelberg, 1955, pp. 135-141.

17. See DIHLE, *The Theology of Will* (n. 3), p. 103. Seneca, interpreting a verse of Cleanthes, writes: "Ducunt uolentem fata, nolentem trahunt" (Seneca, *Ad Lucilium epistulae morales*. 107,11 [ed. GUMMERE], p. 228).

18. Cf. AMAND, *Fatalisme et liberté dans l'antiquité grecque* (n. 1), pp. 10-11.

position on this point distinguishing between the things that, belonging to the inner man (τὰ ἐφ' ἡμῖν), are in his power and can be mastered by him, thus escaping any coercion, and those that lie outside of him (τὰ οὐκ ἐφ' ἡμῖν) and keep exercising their influence on him[19]. The importance of man's self-determination was further and seriously challenged by the penetration in the West of the Babylonian *astral* religions with their faith in the power of the planets whose conjunctions were believed to affect and determine the destiny of man from the very moment of his birth and throughout his life. This governing of human destiny by the planets was also called εἱμαρμένη, although with a completely different meaning from that given to it by the Stoics. According to the astral religions, man was seen as defencelessly abandoned to his destiny, whose rationale rested on unforeseeable and mysterious astral powers[20].

The Roman world was also very much impressed with the power of destiny. *Ovidius*, for instance, in his *Metamorphoses*, represented Jupiter as admitting that both he and the other gods were ruled by the Fates[21]. But it was in the period when Neo-Stoicism occupied an important place in the philosophical panorama of the Roman Empire, a period coinciding with the incursion of the Chaldean astrologers, that the consciousness and affirmation of fate grounded on the Stoic doctrine of necessity became predominant. Thus, *Cicero* could affirm that reason compels us to admit that all things take place by fate, namely through the ordered series of causes[22]. By identifying fate with divine will, late Stoicism came to surrender the freedom of human will. In the popular mind, however, rather than the Stoic theories of necessity, the belief that human freedom and responsibility were undercut because of the predetermination of the stars began to take root. A pagan contemporary to the Christian apologists asserted: "Fate has decreed as a law for each person, the

19. Cf. Epictetus, *Diatribae* 1,1; 3,24,2-3 [ed. OLDFATHER] Vols. I and II, pp. 6-14 and 184. See also M. POHLENZ, *La Stoa*, Vol. II, Firenze, 1967, pp. 109-110. As to the discussions on the Stoic τὰ ἐφ' ἡμῖν as the foundation of ethics, see G. GRESHAKE, *Gnade als konkrete Freiheit. Eine Untersuchung zur Gnadenlehre des Pelagius*, Mainz, 1972, p. 169, n. 58.

20. As a reaction to this "fatalistic invasion" there soon appeared on the horizon the magical movements and the Mystery religions, with their rites and sacraments, and their *gnosis*, which offered to the initiated the release from the tragedies and limitations of human existence. After a long process of initiation and purification the initiate was in fact taken up into union with the god of the particular religion he was belonging to, accompanied by the promise of the attainment of immortality.

21. Cf. Ovidius, *Metamorphoses* 9, 433-434 (ed. MILLER), p. 34.

22. "Fieri igitur omnia fato ratio cogit fateri. Fatum autem id appello, quod Graeci εἱμαρμένην, id est ordinem seriemque causarum, cum causae causa nexa rem ex se gignat" (Cicero, *De diuinatione* 1,55,125 [ed. FALCONER], p. 360).

unalterable consequences of his horoscope"[23]. And according to Svetonius, even the emperor Tiberius stopped paying homage to the gods
because of the unwavering confidence that his own destiny (*magna nec
incerta spes futurorum*) had already been written in the stars[24].

2. THE CONCEPT OF GRACE IN SCRIPTURE

The Old Testament presents us with a series of terms which indicate,
on the level of both language and doctrine, the attempt to describe God's
saving activity towards man and the world[25]. Terms such as *ḥēn* (the
benevolence of the powerful one who stoops to those he wishes to
favour gratuitously[26]), *ḥæsæd* (fidelity and love, implying reciprocity),
*raḥ*a*mīm* (compassion and tenderness), *ṣædæq* (justice), correspond by
and large, each with its own particular accentuation, to the meaning that
grace will acquire in the New Testament. These essential features, which
in the Old Testament are often associated with one another so as to
describe a religious and moral ideal comprising both God's and man's
activity, will find their full expression in the gift of God's only-begotten
Son.

If we turn to the New Testament, however, we must not expect to find
in the use of the term χάρις a necessary or a sufficient clue to the doctrine of grace. Its use is, in fact, not univocal; on the contrary, it conveys
complementary, if not synonymous meanings such as beauty, favour,
gift, gratitude and reward, which reveal the various facets of the underlying reality of Christian grace[27]. It is above all in *Paul* (where the term

23. Vettius Valens, *Anthologiarum libri nouem* 5,5,2 (BSGRT, 214), p. 209; F.C.
GRANT (ed.), *Hellenistic Religions: The Age of Syncretism*, New York, 1953, pp. 60ff.
24. See Svetonius, *Tiberius* 14 [ed. ROLFE], T. I, p. 316.
25. For the pre-history of grace in the Old Testament, see W. ZIMMERLI, art. χάρις, *B.
Altes Testament*, in *TWNT* 9 (1969) 366-377.
26. This term, which came from the secular usage, was given a religious connotation
and applied to God. The LXX will translate it by χάρις.
27. For the New Testament understanding of grace, see H. CONZELMANN, art. χάρις,
D. Neues Testament, in *TWNT* 9 (1969) 381-390; F. MUSSNER, *Die Neutestamentliche
Gnadentheologie in Grundzugen*, in *MySal* Bd. IV/2: *Das Heilsgeschehen in der
Gemeinde. Gottes Gnadenhandeln*, Einsiedeln-Zürich-Cologne, 1973, pp. 611-629;
O. KNOCH, *Gnade. B. Christlich*, in *RAC* 11 (1980) 351-359; E. RUCKSTUHL, *Gnade. III.
Neues Testament*, in *TRE* 13 (1984) 467-476; L. SCHEFFCZYK, *Die Heilsverwirklichung in
der Gnade. Gnadenlehre* (Katholische Dogmatik, 6), Aachen, 1998, pp. 99ff; V. GROSSI
– B. SESBOÜÉ, *Grâce et justification: du témoignage de l'Écriture à la fin du Moyen-Âge*,
in B. SESBOÜÉ (ed.), *Histoire des Dogmes*. T. II: *L'homme et son salut*, Paris, 1995,
pp. 276ff. Apart from the Old Testament, and particularly the translation of the LXX (see
H. DITTMANN, *Gnade, A. Nichtchristlich. II. Israelitisch-jüdisch*, in *RAC* 11 [1980] 333-
345; H. GRAF REVENTLOW, *Gnade, I. Altes Testament*, in *TRE* 13 [1984] 459-464), the
New Testament semantics of "grace" (and "justification") was also influenced by

χάρις occurs 109 times, mainly in his letter to the Romans [24 times] and in the second letter to the Corinthians [18 times]), that we find the first attempt to systematize the theology of grace[28]. It was he, in fact, who gave to the expression χάρις (with the exception of a few passages) the central Christian meaning of divine grace, namely the gift of the Son of God whom the Father, in his love, has sent into the world to deliver and save humanity from the bonds of sin and slavery (cf. Rom 4,5; 5,6; Gal 3,22). Yet, whereas the person of Jesus was the source of the grace spoken of in the New Testament, the source of the "language" used to describe such grace was not Jesus but Paul himself. Following his conversion, the determination to build a new life fully possessed by God's grace, made him employ the Greek word which he found ready to hand and which was currently used to denote the gracious favour of the Roman Emperor[29]: χάρις. It was precisely this term that Paul chose to

contemporary wisdom literature (*e.g.*, wisdom as the personification of Christ [cf. Pr 8,22]) and the context of Hellenistic Judaism (DITTMANN, *Gnade*, pp. 345-351; R. GOLD-ENBERG, *Gnade, II. Judentum*, in *TRE* 13 [1984] 465-467). The latter had in Philo of Alexandria the theoretician of anthropological grace. His essential standpoint was the acknowledgement of God's providential presence in the life of the creatures. All is but χάρις that comes to man from God. Man is asked to gratefully recognize that God is the source of every gift, including that of virtue (see Philo of Alexandria, *De sacrificiis Abelis et Caini* 54-56, in *Les œuvres de Philon d'Alexandrie* 4, Paris, 1966, pp. 118-120), which cannot be attained by human effort alone. The latter, in fact, if bereft of God's intervention, cannot lead to any purity or perfection of life (see Id., *De somniis* 2,25, in *Ibid.* 19, Paris, 1962, pp. 142.144).

28. In the gospel of *Luke* the term χάρις (which is not present either in Matthew or in Mark) focuses on both the common meaning of "gratitude" (cf. Lk 6,32.33.34; 17,9) and the idea of God's "favour/benevolence" (cf. Lk 1,30; 2,40; 2,52), but does not come through as the technical theological meaning of grace (see C. BAUMGARTNER, *La Grâce du Christ*, Paris, 1963, p. 12; H. RONDET, *Gratia Christi. Essai d'histoire du dogme et de théologie dogmatique*, Paris, 1948, p. 43, n. 4), most probably for the simple reason that at the centre of the gospel narratives there was Jesus as the central figure, viz. as the epitome of grace. A more technical meaning of grace makes its appearance in the gospel of John and in the Acts of the Apostles. In *John* theological grace is spoken of in connection with the coming of the Word incarnate, from whose fullness all men receive (cf. Jn 1,14. 16. 17; see RONDET, *Gratia Christi*, pp. 44-45) and thanks to which they can all partake of life eternal (cf. Jn 17,3); in *Acts* the transforming power of grace is often expressed by coupling the term χάρις with that of δύναμις (cf. Ac 4,33; 6,8; 11,23; 13,43; 14,3.26; 15,11.40; 18,27; 20,24.32; see BAUMGARTNER, *La Grâce du Christ*, p. 13).

29. In classical and hellenistic Greek, among the several senses it bore, χάρις was used concretely to indicate a favour or boon granted or returned, for example a grant from the Emperor (cf. H. CONZELMANN, art. χάρις, A. *Profangräzität*, in *TWNT* 9 [1969] 363-366). Likewise, the latin term *gratia* was extended from the initial religious sphere (God-man relationship) to the moral, social and political one (man-man relationship). Both during the time of the Republic and of the Empire, Roman law conveyed the idea of grace as benevolence through synonyms such as *abolitio, indulgentia, uenia, restitutio* (see W. GEERLINGS, *Römisches Recht und Gnadentheologie. Eine typologische Skizze*, in C. MAYER [ed.], *Homo Spiritalis. Festage für Luc Verheijen OSA, zu seinem 70. Geburtstag*

underline the gratuity and universality of God's redeeming love, as it was revealed in Christ. The Apostle contended that this Christian perspective of salvation contrasted with a supposed salvation coming from the Jewish system of law (the *Torah*) and merit. Christ fulfils and replaces the *Torah*, superseding its grace with his own grace (cf. Rom 4,16; Gal 2,31), a grace which overrides human works (cf. Rom 4,4; 11,6). Also the election of Israel now finds its accomplishment in the election of the "new people" of God, namely of those who are justified by their faith in Christ the Saviour (cf. Rom 3,22-26; 5,1; 10,4; Gal 2,16). Furthermore, the gratuitous justification bestowed on Jews and Gentiles alike as the result of divine action in man (cf. Rom 3,24; 5,15.19) brings about communion with the Son of God (cf. 1Cor 1,9), so much so that, through the reception of Christ's Spirit and his gifts (cf. Gal 3,2f; 4,6; Rom 5,6), men themselves are adopted as sons of God (cf. Rom 8,14-17; Gal 4,4-7). This is, ultimately, the work of divine grace: the salvation brought about through the divine and spiritual gifts of the new life bestowed on men by Christ the Saviour.

To sum up briefly, the fundamental meaning of $\chi\acute\alpha\rho\iota\varsigma$ in the New Testament points to God's favour, to his gratuitous and merciful benevolence with regard to sinful humanity. Such benevolence, although inseparable from the gifts of new life bestowed on man, can be rightly understood as the gift of Christ the Redeemer himself. In him, the gratuitousness of grace is revealed from both its "redemptive" and "divinising" aspects, the former being prominent in Paul, who stresses the sinforgiving role of the life of grace, the latter more obvious in John. From a temporal and historical point of view, such grace was made manifest in Jesus Christ whose incarnation constituted the definitive and irrevocable *entrée* in history of God's saving grace. From an eschatological point of view, however, grace manifests God's unforeseeable, absolutely free and merciful plan of saving all men by calling them to become his adoptive sons through Jesus Christ the Mediator.

[Cass., 38], Würzburg, 1987, pp. 357-377, pp. 358-360). What Paul (and Christianity after him) seems to have obscured was the meaning of remuneration beside that of gratuity, both included in the notion of *gratia*. In fact, whereas Paul regarded *gratia* as a synonym of disinterested benevolence, Roman law considered gratuity and remuneration as being intimately linked to one another, and not in the least antonyms. "Toutes deux se fondent sur la réciprocité: le don gratuit, comme toute autre prestation, appelle une compensation, un contre-don" (C. MOUSSY, *Gratia et sa famille*, Paris, 1966, p. 476). See also, J. HELLEGOUARC'H, *Le vocabulaire latin des relations et de partis politiques sous la république*, 2nd ed., Paris, 1972, p. 206.

3. The Interaction of Grace and Free Will
in Pre-Augustinian Theology

The evolution in Christian tradition of the relationship of grace and its saving effects with human free will, has been a long drawn-out process. Before Augustine there was probably no compelling need for a synthesis in either the New Testament or in theological construction. Although grace and free will were regarded as co-operating with one another and were not conceived as merely juxtaposed, no comprehensive and coherent theory of their relationship had in fact been thoroughly elaborated in Christian theology before Augustine. It was the bishop of Hippo, in fact, when confronted with Pelagianism, who gave a decisive explanation to the way the interplay between grace and free will should be understood[30], an explanation so conclusive that it will be incorporated almost entirely in the Church's doctrine. For that reason Augustine is rightly considered the dividing line with regard to the understanding and definition of such a relationship.

Thus before the Augustinian doctrine of grace took shape, the term χάρις (and its Latin counterpart *gratia*) continued to be used in Christian theology in such a way that it was not constrained to confronting itself with the place and role of human free will. The term would be generally employed to indicate the unfolding of divine benevolence in the *oeconomia salutis,* and particularly to express the central idea that God's saving activity had finally found its way through the incarnation, death and resurrection of Christ. The internal and external aids granted to men, namely the new life in Christ bestowed on the believers by the outpouring of the Holy Spirit through baptism, faith, individual conversion and renewal, were seen as the immediate result of God's saving presence. These and other varying statements about God's grace working in the life of the faithful were rooted in a fundamental belief that can be described as "non-reflective synergism". Beyond the central truth of the redemption won by Jesus Christ on behalf of mankind, no rationale for divine grace was actually given, nor was the need felt to differentiate between the manifold aspects of God's intervention or between the means by which grace was bestowed upon men. Moreover, the day-to-day-life of the early Christians, their consciousness of being elected as

---

30. By admission of Augustine himself, it was with the rise of Pelagianism that the question of the relationship between grace and free will became urgent, calling for a new theological reinterpretation: "Quid igitur opus est ut eorum *[the Catholic writers]* scrutemur opuscula, qui priusquam ista haeresis *[Pelagianism]* oriretur, non habuerunt necessitatem in hac difficili ad solvendum quaestione versari?" (Augustine, *De praedestinatione sanctorum* 14,27 [PL, 44], c. 980). Cf. Id., *De dono perseuerantiae* 2,4, (PL, 45), c. 996.

well as guided and saved by God's grace, on one hand, and their commitment to coherent Christian conduct on the other, was present without them being aware of the possible tension that such co-operation could imply on a theoretical level[31].

a) Grace and Free Will in the Eastern/Greek Church

At the beginning of Christian theological reflection, the Greek term χάρις (and its Latin counterpart *gratia*) was not immediately favoured as the technical word for expressing the specifically Christian doctrine of grace. The latter was often described by the ancient Christian writers by means of terms such as χάρισμα (and its latin counterpart *donum, munus, dignatio*[32]) which translated God's saving activity in strict connection with the exercise of man's freedom. Far from feeling the need for a formal definition of grace, Greek theology was thus satisfied with qualifying it as the way by which God makes effective his salvation in the world. Accordingly, the term "grace" was applied to the whole of Christian faith, be it conceived either as God's benevolence towards man or as the gifts which flow from him into the life of the faithful, like baptism, the remission of sins, and ecclesiastical life. Creation, providence, redemption, they all fell within the province of grace.

Although, in trying to describe the way in which God's saving process takes place in the life of man and in the world, Eastern theologians trod a variety of semantic paths[33], nevertheless, beyond the various approaches and descriptions they gave of grace, we can find a common denominator in the biblical definition of man made "in the image (κατ' εἰκόνα) of God" (cf. Gn 1,26). It is such a definition that provides the Eastern theologians with a starting point for the comprehension of God's salvific action, whose aim is to restore the divine image man was created

31. This coherent coexistence was lived out especially when Christianity was still a *religio illicita* and the environment alien if not hostile to it. With Constantine's tolerance towards Christianity, and after imperial favour was given to the Christian faith, things changed for the Church and Christian coherence ceased to be the distinctive feature. A nominal and superficial faith would more often replace the endeavour at living a fully engaged Christian life. It is against the background of such environmental and social changes that the striving for the evangelical perfection of both the monastic growth of the 4th century and the Pelagian movement are ultimately to be set.

32. On the evolution of the Christian meaning of grace see MOUSSY, *Gratia et sa famille* (n. 29), pp. 445-473.

33. For an overview of the development of the concept of grace from the Apostolic time up to Augustine, see: O. KNOCH – A. SCHINDLER, *Gnade, B. Christlich*, in *RAC* 11 (1980) 359-416; SCHEFFCZYK, *Die Heilsverwirklichung in der Gnade* (n. 27), pp. 99-122; GROSSI–SESBOÜÉ, *Grâce et justification* (n. 27), pp. 276-286; GRESHAKE, *Gnade als konkrete Freiheit* (n. 19), pp. 173ff.

with, by delivering him from the corruption of sin. It is precisely for this reason, namely in order to restore the image of God in man in the best possible way, that God's saving action was developed through a long pedagogical process, which started with creation (the initial moment in which Adam's likeness with God had not yet been deformed by the fall) and culminated in the redemptive act of Christ, whereby the wounded nature of Adam's stock was newly raised and restored to its intended communion with God. The incarnate Christ represents the apex of such a pedagogical, saving process[34], and man is called to join in and participate in it by answering God's initiative through his own freedom and will. The reinstatement of man in the goodness of creation through the mediation of Christ and the capability of man's freedom to adhere to this project are the two constitutive elements of the one process of salvation.

If the issue of man's free will, compared to that of grace, occupied a privileged position, this was due to the challenge with which the Christian writers of the first centuries were confronted, namely Gnostic determinism and pagan fatalistic outlook on reality. The vocabulary they employed was often the same as that used by Greek-Roman paganism, although a Christian meaning was attached to it in the light of the Christian vision of God, of man and of the world[35]. It is noteworthy, for

---

34. The Christian teaching of the first centuries borrowed the Greek concept of παιδεία (educational process) and applied it to Christian faith. In the pagan world, since Plato, it was believed that man could find his realisation by adhering to a prototype. Along the same line, and convinced of being the true *paideia*, the *paideia Christi*, Christianity proposed to the Christian believer the Son of God Jesus Christ as his prototype. Christ became thus the "neue Paideia mit ihrer Quelle im göttlichen Logos selbst" (W. JAEGER, *Das frühe Christentum und die griechische Bildung*, Berlin, 1963, p. 37). See GRESHAKE, *Gnade als konkrete Freiheit* (n. 19), pp. 158ff. The *paideia Christi* stresses "die Selbsteinordnung des Christentums in ein schon vorgefundenes Kultursystem und Geschichtsbild... und den Anspruch der neuen Religion, eine erzieherische Weltmission zu haben" (W. JAEGER, *Paideia Christi*, in *ZNW* 50 [1959] 1-14, pp. 1f). The manifestation of Christ, however, although the central point in the pedagogical process of salvation, is not the final one. The divine process continues after Christ through the activity of the Holy Spirit and the Church. See W. GEERLINGS, *Christus Exemplum. Studien zur Christologie und Christusverkündigung Augustins* (TTS, 13), Tübingen, 1978, pp. 65-95.

35. "La notion de libre arbitre – writes Baudry – s'est, de fait, trouvée liée avec le développement du christianisme confronté avec le paganisme gréco-romain. La nouvelle conception de Dieu, du monde et de l'homme issue de l'Evangile entraînait une refonte de la morale. Une nouvelle problématique se faisait jour, centrée sur la liberté humaine. La responsabilité du chrétien par rapport à un Dieu d'amour, personnel et créateur, posait violemment la question du libre choix de l'homme, et ceci précisément dans le monde culturel antique dominé par la notion de destin" (G.-H. BAUDRY, *Libre arbitre*, in *Cath* 7 [1975] 707-710, c. 707). The influence of Stoicism, for instance, should not be underrated. Despite the difficulty that the Stoics themselves felt about safeguarding human freedom vis-à-vis cosmic providence, characterised by a fatalistic tendency, they remain the champions of individual liberty (see M. SPANNEUT, *Le stoïcisme des Pères de l'Église*.

instance, to see how during the ante-Nicene and immediate post-Nicene period, the debates concerning the formulation of a Christian anthropology noticeably and positively primed the recognition of human free will and responsibility, considered as a reflection of the freedom of God, in whose image man was created. Relying on the evidence of Holy Scripture, the Christian theologians of the first centuries then faced the confrontation between human free will and the deterministic explanation and inevitability of the human predicament from a theological point of view. Free will being a mark of man's likeness with God, it followed that it was within the power of the will to interact with divine activity, whose notion of providence was employed to counter and replace that of astrological fatalism[36]. Generally speaking we can confidently affirm that the relationship between grace and free will was not a central issue (in the sense of a "debated" one) in Greek theology. Their interplay was rather given for granted and their synergism accepted as part of the daily experience, and even when one of the two poles were highlighted[37], the role of the other remained understood.

With the Apologists of the 2nd and 3rd centuries, who were in harsh polemic with Gnostic and pagan fatalism, great emphasis was laid on the very aim of the Incarnation of Christ and of God's salvific pedagogical process, namely man's adoption as "son of God", his "deification"

De Clement de Rome à Clement d'Alexandrie [PatSor, 1], Paris, 1957, p. 235). For this reason it is not surprising that the Church Fathers who, without any ado, could base their defence of free will on the Bible, where the continuous call to moral responsibility presupposes man's freedom of choice, looked at the Stoa as a suitable philosophical framework through which they could channel the rationale of their belief.

36. See H.O. SCHRÖDER, *Fatum (Heimarmene)*, in *RAC* 7 (1969) 524-636, c. 608.

37. The centrality of Christ, for instance, was clearly indicated by *Clement of Rome*, who says that repentance and conversion are given to the faithful by the grace of Christ's death, whose blood was shed for the salvation of humanity: "Let us fix our gaze on the blood of Christ and realize how precious it is to his Father, seeing that it was poured out for our salvation and brought the grace of conversion to the whole world (μετανοίας χάριν ἐπήνεγκεν)" (Clement of Rome, *Epistula ad Corinthios* 7,4 [SC, 167], p. 110). Also the pagan initiation to the "mysteries", through which a god was believed to be revealing himself and bring about salvation, influenced the theology of the Christian sacraments. Like the cultic action of the pagan mysteries, so the action of the Christian sacraments was regarded as being the *locus mediator* of God's salvation, "materialised" in Christ, through whom and by whom the sacraments are actually performed. A text from a sermon of the 2nd century highlights the significance of the salvation in Christ in the general context of the initiation to the mysteries (cf. [Hippolytus/*Spuria*], *In sanctum Pascha* 53 [SC, 27], pp. 178-180). This category of "mystery" will be taken up by later Church Fathers (*e.g.* Cyril of Jerusalem, John Chrysostom in the East, Ambrose of Milan in the West) in their attempt to convey that only through the "mysteries", viz. the Christian sacraments (especially baptism), was salvation offered to man.

(θείωσις)[38]. Such deification was described as coming about thanks either to the grace or the Spirit or the divine Logos (the real active subject of God's pedagogical saving activity) in co-operation with man's freedom and intelligence. This conviction was to be illustrated by Irenaeus' dictum about God having become man in Christ so that man might share in the divine life itself[39], a dictum which became a sort of classic saying in Christian literature[40]. Along these same lines, and against the background of the fall of Adam and the consequent weakness that humanity as a whole inherited from it, *Justin* developed his anthropological approach to the issue. This is particularly evident in his *First Apology* where Justin argues that, as a result of the fall, human existence must unfold itself through the exercise of freedom. Given the fact that God has created mankind intelligent and capable of acting and freely choosing what is true and good, no reasonable excuse can be offered by human beings for not adhering to truth and goodness themselves[41]. In his *Second Apology* Justin writes: "In the beginning God made angels and men totally free (αὐτεξούσιον), and for that reason they shall be punished with justice in the eternal fire and shall be submitted to the chastisement

38. The concept of "deification" was not new to the religious philosophy of the Hellenistic world which had in fact already spread the Platonic doctrine of man's assimilation to the divine (see Plato, *Theaetetus* 176b-177a; *ResPublica* X,613a). The great Greek theologians of the 4ᵗʰ century, while giving an official status to the θείωσις motif within salvation history, gave also a definitive Christian interpretation of its Platonic provenance. Cf. Athanasius, *Orationes contra Arianos* 4,2 (PG, 26), c. 469; Gregory of Nazianzus, *Oratio* 1,5 (SC, 247), p. 78.

39. "Quemadmodum enim in Novo Testamento ea quae est ad Deum fides hominum aucta est, additamentum accipiens Filium Dei, ut et homo fieret particeps Dei (Ἵνα καὶ ἄνθρωπος γένηται μέτοχος θεοῦ)" (Irenaeus, *Aduersus haereses* 4,28,2 [SC, 100**], p. 757). "Propter hoc enim Verbum Dei homo, et qui Filius Dei est Filius hominis factus est, ut homo, commixtus Verbo Dei et adoptionem percipiens, fiat filius Dei (ἵνα ὁ ἄνθρωπος συγκραθεὶς τῷ Λόγῳ, καὶ τὴν υἱοθεσίαν λαβὼν γένηται υἱὸς τοῦ θεοῦ)" (*Ibid.*, 3,19,1 [SC, 211], p. 374). Cf. also *Ibid.* 4,20,7, pp. 647.649; 4,38,2-4, pp. 949-961.

40. This formula was taken up, often in very similar terms, by other Church Fathers. Cf., for instance, Clement of Alexandria, *Protrepticus* 1,8 (SC, 2), p. 63; Origen, *Contra Celsum* 3,28 (SC, 136), p. 69; Athanasius, *Oratio de incarnatione uerbi* 54,3 (SC, 199), p. 459; Gregory of Nyssa, *Antirrheticus aduersus Apolinarium* 11, *Gregorii Nysseni opera* 3/1, pp. 146f; *Ibid.*, 15, c. 1152; John Chrysostom, *In Iohannem homiliae* 11,1 (PG, 59), c. 79; Augustine, *De trinitate* 4,2,4 (CCL, 50), p. 164.

41. See, for instance: "Καὶ τὴν ἀρχὴν νοερὸν καὶ δυνάμενον αἱρεῖσθαι τἀληθῆ, καὶ εὖ πράττειν, τὸ γένος τὸ ἀνθρώπινον πεποίηκεν, ὥστ᾽ ἀναπολόγητον εἶναι τοῖς πᾶσιν ἀνθρώποις παρὰ τῷ θεῷ" (Justin, *Apologia prima* 28 [PG, 6], c. 372). Cf. *Ibid.* 43, cc. 391.394. See also Id., *Dialogus cum Tryphone Iudaeo* 88 (PG, 6), c. 685; *Ibid.* 102, c. 713. As Amand writes: "Dans la pensée de Justin, la liberté n'est pas une fin en soi, mais simplement la condition *sine qua non* de l'activité morale, du mérite, et que son usage détermine les sanctions d'outre-tombe" (AMAND, *Fatalisme et liberté dans l'antiquité grecque* [n. 1], p. 201).

of the sins they will have committed. The nature of every creature is capable of good and evil. There would be no reason for praising men if they did not possess the faculty and the power (δύναμις) to choose between good and evil"[42]. The power to choose and freedom are thus the gifts bestowed by God upon the human soul, and the means by which man has the possibility of either turning to God and being justified or turning away from him and become liable to condemnation and perdition. Contrary to any fatalistic attitude, Justin's insistence on man's responsibility in the use of his freedom of choice, indicates that there is only one "hypothetical" necessity, viz. that by which man will be either happy or unhappy, rewarded or chastised for all eternity, according to what he has chosen to pursue during his earthly life[43].

In *Irenaeus* the biblical topos of man's likeness to God (ὁμοίωσις θεῷ)[44] comes into the limelight in opposition to the dualistic and rational tendencies of the Gnosis and in connection with the pedagogical goal of Redemption, viz. the restoration of the divine image in man, an image that was obscured and corrupted by sin[45]. Referring to Eph 1,10, Irenaeus calls this restoration ἀνακεφαλαίωσις (recapitulation)[46]. God being the only absolutely perfect being, it follows that the creatures necessarily share a state of imperfection. Such an imperfect condition is made manifest by the fact that man is endowed with the gift-power of

---

42. Justin, *Apologia secunda* 7 (PG, 6), c. 456.

43. Stoic fatalism was energetically opposed by Justin. He writes: "We have learned from the prophets that penalties and punishments and good rewards are given according to the quality of each person's actions. If this were not so, and all things happened according to destiny, nothing would be dependent on ourselves (τὰ ἐφ' ἡμῖν)" (Id., *Apologia prima* 43 [PG, 6], cc. 392-393). See also *Ibid.* 44, cc. 394f, where Justin quotes two scriptural texts (Dt 30,15.19 and Is 1,16-20) which presuppose the existence of free will and the possibility of choosing between good and evil. Although Justin's argument is commonplace, what appears here for the first time is the link established between the doctrine of free choice and Scripture: "Although the arguments are well worn, the claim that free choice is a Christian teaching appears here explicitly for the first time" (R.L. WILKEN, *Free Choice and Divine Will in Greek Christian Commentaries on Paul*, in W.S. BABCOCK [ed.], *Paul and the Legacies of Paul*, Dallas, TX, 1990, pp. 123-140, p. 126). As to the objection based on the fact that the prophecies do predict the future (thus favouring, so it would seem, the fatalist law of εἱμαρμένη which dominates all things and events), Justin explains that God's prescience and providence, although effectively exercised, do not hinder the exercise of human freedom and leave it intact. See Justin, *Dialogus cum Tryphone Iudaeo* 102,4 (PG, 6), c. 713; *Ibid.*, 141, c. 798.

44. Irenaeus distinguishes between the "image" and the "likeness". Whereas the former is said also of the carnal man, the latter concerns only the man inhabited by the Holy Spirit. Cf. Irenaeus, *Aduersus haereses* 5,6,1 (SC, 153), p. 76.

45. "Kristallisationspunkt der frühchristlichen Gnadenlehre ist die (paideutische) Wiederherstellung des durch die Sünde korrumpierten Bildes Gottes im Menschen" (GRESHAKE, *Gnade als konkrete Freiheit* [n. 19], p. 173).

46. Cf., for instance, Irenaeus, *Aduersus haereses* 1,3,4 (SC, 264), p. 57.

free will[47]. Without making distinctions between prelapsarian and infralapsarian freedom, Irenaeus stresses that thanks to this gift of free will, the rational creature can decide, or not, to persevere in the pursuit of goodness, and thus co-operate or not with divine grace. Irenaeus' insistence on free will is particularly strong against a veiled form of εἱμαρμένη, outlined by Valentinian determinism[48]. Seeming to consider free will as a faculty in the full sense of the word, he teaches the traditional Christian doctrine about the "ancient law of liberty" (τὸν ἀρχαῖον νόμον τῆς ἐλευθερίας) which is rooted in Scripture[49]: men are enabled to reach salvation, if they wish, by opting for a responsible decision with regard to good, without any constraint. In the *Aduersus haereses* Irenaeus employs the image of the wheat and the straw to make it clear that becoming either one or the other, namely to be saved or not, depends on man's free will. To be endowed with such a faculty is what constitutes man's main characteristic. Because of this, human being can be said to have been created in the image and likeness of God, with both the freedom to choose goodness, in accordance with divine will, or to oppose God's righteousness[50]. Self-determination in the direction of

47. Cf., for instance: "Igitur erat liber (ἐλεύθερος) et suae potestatis (αὐτεξού-σιος)" (Id., *Demonstratio praedicationis apostolicae [Epideixis]* 11 [SC, 406], p. 98).

48. The Gnostic theologian Valentinus held the *Dreimenschenklassenlehre*, viz. the doctrine according to which humankind is classed by God into three different categories: the spirituals or "pneumatics" (the Valentinians themselves) who alone, through their gnosis, enter the *pleroma* and are necessarily saved; the "psychics" (cf 1 Cor 2,14), namely those Christians who are susceptible to good or evil, to salvation or perdition, and who attain only the middle realm of the Demiurge through their faith and good works; the earthly ones or "hylics" (engrossed in matter), viz. the rest of mankind which are given up to eternal perdition. See A. MAGRIS, *La logica del pensiero gnostico*, Brescia, 1997, pp. 45-46; 153-157; 289-298; 388-401 *et passim*; A.H.B. LOGAN, *Gnostic Truth and Christian Heresy. A Study in the History of Gnosticism*, Edinburgh, 1996, pp. 167ff.

49. Irenaeus' notion of free will (which shall be shared by almost all the Greek Fathers) does not derive from Hellenistic philosophy. It is rather rooted in Scripture, and more precisely in Mt 23,37: "But that which he said: 'How often have I desired to gather your sons and you would not?' demonstrates the ancient law of man's liberty (τὸν ἀρχαῖον νόμον τῆς ἐλευθερίας τοῦ ἀνθρώπου): how God made man free from the beginning, having his own power (ἰδίαν ἐξουσίαν), as he had a soul of his own, to act upon God's will freely and not upon compulsion from God" (Irenaeus, *Aduersus haereses* 4,37,1 [SC, 100**], pp. 919-921). See also *Ibid.* 4,37,2 and 3, pp. 922 and 928.

50. Cf. *Ibid.* 4,4,3, p. 425: "Man being rational, and therefore like God, created free in will and in his power (ἐλεύθερος τὴν γνώμην γεγονὼς καὶ αὐτεξούσιος), is the cause to himself why he should become in one case wheat and in another chaff. From which also he will be justly condemned, because being created rational he has lost true reason, and living irrationaly has opposed the righteousness of God, giving himself over to every earthly spirit, and serving all kinds of pleasures". Further developments in *Ibid.* 4,37,2-5, pp. 922-934. We must also remember that Philo of Alexandria had already seen in freedom a specific feature of man's likeness with God (see Philo of Alexandria, *Quod Deus sit immutabilis* 47-48, in *Les œuvres de Philon d'Alexandrie* 7-8, Paris, 1963, pp. 84-86).

200 CHAPTER THREE

what is good includes the possibility of radically refusing such a choice[51], because although free will is a gift bestowed by God on the human creature, it is in man's power to use it in a responsible manner so as to attain the good and to co-operate with God's salvific designs[52].

According to *Clement of Alexandria* the real gnostic is the believer in Christ, namely the one who has been regenerated and restored in the image of God, as his adoptive son, through baptism and the growth of the Holy Spirit. The Christian is the πνευματικός who yearns for his "deification"[53]. On the basis of Gen 1,26 and 2,7 (and like Irenaeus) Clemens makes a distinction between the "image of God" (κατ' εἰκόνα), in which man is born, and the "likeness of God" (καθ' ὁμοίωσιν)[54], and claims that only Jesus, the Incarnate Logos of God, enjoys both the image and the likeness of the Father[55]. Man is conceived as being created in the image of God, but not in his likeness[56]. The latter has to be acquired by seeking virtue and justice under the power of the Holy Spirit. The question of free will is approached and dealt with positively against the threat of Gnostic determinism[57], that of the Basilians

51. Cf. Irenaeus, *Aduersus haereses* 4,37,1 (SC, 100**), pp. 918.920.
52. *Ibid.* 4,37,4, p. 933.
53. "The view I take is that He himself formed man of the dust and regenerated him by water; and made him grow by his Spirit; and trained him by his word to adoption and salvation, directing him by sacred precepts; in order that, transforming earth-born man into a holy and heavenly being by his advent (ἵνα δὴ τὸν γηγενῆ εἰς ἅγιον καὶ ἐπουράνιον μεταπλάσας ἐκ προσβάσεως ἄνθρωπον) He might fulfil, to the utmost, that divine utterance: *Let us make man in our own image and likeness*" (Clement of Alexandria, *Paedagogus* 1,12,2 [SC, 70], p. 284). Duly christianised by Clement, this participation in the divine nature, that is the assimilation to God or deification, was not conceived as the result of a rational dialectics, of a human ascesis and purification or of magical rites. On the contrary, it was regarded as a gift of God who associates his creatures to himself more intimately through the incarnation of Christ and the work of the Holy Spirit. Besides, Clement compares divine grace to the divine favour (θεία/μοίρα) of the Platonists (cf. PLATO, *Timaeus* 30 b 5), even though he believes that divine grace is an aid given to the faithful by the Holy Spirit. It is the latter, in fact, that allows man to come to the true knowledge of the true being (cf. Clement of Alexandria, *Stromata* 5,13,88,1-3 [SC, 278], p. 88). "Elle *[grace]* – writes Spanneut – entre dans les facultés logiques de l'homme spirituel, comme un perfectionnement qui facilite leur marche vers le bien" (M. SPANNEUT, *Le stoïcisme des Pères de l'Église. De Clément de Rome à Clément d'Alexandrie* [PatSor, 1] Paris, 1957, p. 240). See also P. CASEY, *Clement of Alexandria and the beginnings of Christian Platonism*, in HTR 18 (1925) 39-101, p. 52, where the author affirms that Clement did not conceive grace as a special strength provided by God to repair the weakness caused by sin. God's grace would rather be a natural grace, and its activity part of the normal functioning of the organism of the spiritual man.
54. Cf. Clemens of Alexandria, *Stromata* 2,22,6 (SC, 38), p. 133.
55. Cf. Id., *Paedagogus* 1,11,97 (SC, 70), p. 282.
56. Cf. *Ibid.* 1,12,98, p. 284.
57. See E.A. CLARK, *Clement's use of Aristotle. The Aristotelian Contribution to Clement of Alexandria's Refutation of Gnosticism*, New York-Toronto, 1977, pp. 45 and 129 n. 2.

and particularly that of the Valentinians who had assigned the exercise of free will only to an intermediate category of men called "psychics"[58]. Against such a view Clement advocated that no one is predestined to commit good or bad actions, to be saved or to be damned. The responsibility for his ultimate fate depends on man's freedom and on his decision-making power. More particularly, volition and choice are essential to man's ability in doing what is good and in seeking a virtuous life. Following the path already trodden by both Justin and Irenaeus, who derived the faculty of free choice from man's endowment of reason (the intellectual forces which are at the basis of man's being made in God's image)[59], Clement strictly connects free decision (upon which moral responsibility rests) with man's intellectual perception and intention or disposition (προαίρεσις)[60]. Since man is responsible for his voluntary actions, moral evil depends entirely on his αὐτεξούσιον, on his freedom of choice as well as on his freedom to determine responsibly (morally) his own decision[61]. God, in fact, must be kept free of blame with regard to man's irresponsible (immoral) decisions. It is man's "moral freedom", Clement contended, that must be regarded as the *conditio sine qua non* of a moral life, pursued in accordance with Christian tenets and with the support of divine help, as well as the source and the justification of praise and blame alike. On the basis of the psychological reality and character of free will, Clement can thus affirm that, although free to

58. Cf. Clement of Alexandria, *Excerpta e Theodoto* 56,3 (GCS, 17/2), p. 127. Cf. *supra*, n. 48. Pagels claims that in directing his refutation towards the Valentinians' determinism, Clement has saddled them with a false issue. According to her, the description of the three natures, rather than being set within the framework of a philosophical determinism, should be regarded as an exegetical interpretation of Johannine and Pauline theology of election. See E. PAGELS, *The Johannine Gospel in Gnostic Exegesis. Heraclon's Commentary on John*, Nashville, 1973, pp. 100-104; CLARK, *Clement's use of Aristotle* (n. 57), pp. 46-47.

59. Clement seems to believe in the existence of a special faculty, whose task is that of choosing: "Willing presides over everything, because the logic powers are born to serve the will" (Clement of Alexandria, *Stromata* 2,17 [77,5], [SC, 38], p. 95).

60. Our activities are not judged simply by their results but also by our intention and choice. For Clement the term προαίρεσις does not indicate, as in Aristotelian ethics, the right choice, but simply a choice (either good or bad). Cf. *Ibid.* 1,17 (84,2) (SC, 30), p. 111.

61. Cf. Id., *Paedagogus* 2,8,62ff. (SC, 108), p. 126. "The emphasis on moral action is expressed by the other terms borrowed from Greek philosophy which have been mentioned above together with the αὐτεξούσιον. Thus the ἐφ' ἡμῖν indicates the range of man's moral freedom and coincides with the αὐτεξούσιον. The οὐκ ἐφ' ἡμῖν (not depending on us) on the other hand, expresses the actions beyond our reach" (P. KARAVITES, *Evil, Freedom and the Road to Perfection in Clement of Alexandria* [SVigChr, 43], Leiden-Boston-Cologne, 1999, p. 119).

desire and follow God's commandments or to transgress them[62], man's
"moral freedom" is ultimately intended to help him in choosing goodness
and avoiding evil[63]. In Clement's view, in fact, man's αὐτεξουσιότης is
not merely something arbitrary or indifferent; on the contrary, it is
intended to come to the knowledge of good. In this sense God's grace is
aimed at saving those who choose, and choose what is good[64].

Origen, whose teaching exercised an enormous influence upon the
theological thinking process of the first centuries, also develops the
theme of the divine sonship of the believer[65], maintaining the distinction
(made by Irenaeus and Clement of Alexandria) between "image" and
"likeness"[66]. Whilst the first is received at the moment of creation, the
second has to be acquired through man's industrious efforts. According
to Origen, "the *imago Dei* is an ability (disposition) given at creation
which, however, must be kept and trained through right moral and religious conduct and in this way reach the perfect likeness (cfr. *similitudo*)
with God"[67]. This task to strive for the perfect likeness with God begins
with the grace of baptism, which signals the start of man's religious conversion (μετανοία)[68], and takes its course through the exercise of man's
free will, an indispensable premise in order to bring the task to fulfilment. No wonder then that, within this strongly ascetic perspective, Origen deemed it necessary to deeply analyse the question of free will, an
issue which, besides constituting a *pièce maîtresse* within his religious
and philosophical system[69] and the key to its interpretation[70], became an
inspirational source for later theological thinking on the subject.

62. Cf. Clement of Alexandria, *Stromata* 4,13,94 (SC, 463), pp. 212.214.

63. According to Clement free will is indeed "un principe efficace de vie éthique, et
non un simple postulat *a priori*, sans aucune relation avec notre activité morale" (AMAND,
Fatalisme et liberté dans l'antiquité grecque [n. 1], p. 269).

64. "To save men against their will is an act of force, but to save them when they
choose is an act of grace (Τὸ μὲν γὰρ σώζειν, ἐστὶ βιαζομένου· τὸ δὲ αἱρουμένους,
χαριζομένου)" (Clement of Alexandria, *Quis diues saluetur* 21,2 [GCS, 17/2], p. 173).

65. See Origen, *Commentarii in epistulam ad Romanos* 7,3 (FC, Bd. II/4), pp. 38-42.

66. Cf. Id, *Contra Celsum*, 4,30 (SC, 136), p. 254; *De principiis* 3,6,1 (SC, 268),
pp. 236.238; *Commentarii in Iohannem* 20,22 (SC, 290), pp. 246-248. See A.J. HOBBEL,
The Imago Dei *in the writings of Origen*, in StPatr 21, Louvain, 1989, pp. 301-307,
pp. 304-307.

67. *Ibid.*, p. 305.

68. See Origen, *Commentarii in Iohannem* 6,6,33 (SC, 157), p. 155.

69. "Le libre arbitre constitue une pièce maîtresse dans le système de philosophie
religieuse d'Origène. Dogme religieux et théorie rationnelle, tel est le double aspect sous
lequel notre théologien métaphysicien considère la liberté morale de l'homme" (AMAND,
Fatalisme et liberté dans l'antiquité grecque [n. 1], p. 297). Also Simonetti speaks of Origen's principle of free will as being "il fondamento di tutta la sua cosmologia" (M.
SIMONETTI [ed.], *Introduzione*, in Origene, *I principi*, Turin, 1968, p. 77).

70. "The idea of free-will provided the key to Origen's whole system" (J.N.D.
KELLY, *Early Christian Doctrines*, London, 1958, p. 182). Remarkably enough, Origen's

Origen's elaborated view on free will is to be found in his treatise *De principiis*, and more precisely in the third book. We can easily divide his standpoint into three sections: the first dealing with the question of free will in philosophical terms, the second calling for biblical texts upholding the doctrine of free will, and the third discussing in detail some scriptural passages that seem to deny the agency of free will. In the first section, Origen's philosophical argument in favour of free will rests upon the evidence that only rational creatures (unlike other created beings and things such as animals or stones[71]) possess the privilege of being able to "move" from within themselves and direct their course of action, by choosing freely and responsibly one outlet instead of another, without being compelled or determined by external factors[72]. Freedom is the obvious corollary of reason and in this regard man has to shape his natural constitution and develop his reason by sound doctrine, in order to meet external circumstances in the right way[73]. The following quotation clearly illustrates Origen's standpoint about this binomial reason-free will and the importance that he attached to it: "It belongs to our own task to live a good life. God asks this of us, not as the result of his own work, nor as something that comes to us from someone else, nor (as some think) from destiny, but as our own task (ἀλλ' ὡς ἡμέτερον ἔργον)"[74]. It follows that even when man is faced with temptations, he

discussion on free will has come down to us in one of the main fragments of his works that have survived in Greek. For this reason we might be confident that also his real thought has come down with it, unaltered and untouched by the translator's interpolations or interpretations, although, being a fragment, we cannot be absolutely sure that *all* his thought has survived. "Tout ce que nous possédons du texte grec se limite à quelques fragments dans la *Philocalie* et dans deux édits de l'empereur Justinien Ier. L'ouvrage survit cependant en entier dans une traduction très libre de Rufin. Celui-ci l'a manifestement expurgé en supprimant ici ou là des passages discutables" (J. QUASTEN, *Initiation aux Pères de l'Église*, T. II, Paris, 1957, p. 74). The *Philocalia* is a collection of different texts of Origen taken from a number of his works and compiled by Basil the Great and Gregory of Nazianzus. Cf. also H. CROUZEL – M. SIMONETTI (eds.), *Introduction*, in Origene, *Traité des principes*, T. I (SC, 252), pp. 22-33.

71. Origen, *De principiis* 3,1,2 (SC, 268), pp. 18-22.

72. *Ibid.* 3,1,3-5, pp. 22-32. See also Id., *De oratione* 6 (GCS, 3), pp. 311-315. It must be noted that Origen's discussion "si inserisce nella polemica sul libero arbitrio che dal tempo di Carneade divideva il campo dei filosofi: tutta la parte iniziale della lunga trattazione sul libero arbitrio di III,1 è in perfetta armonia, nei concetti e nella terminologia, con tale problematica" (SIMONETTI [ed.], *Introduzione* [n. 69], p. 77).

73. See H.S. BENJAMINS, *Origen's Concept of Free Will in Relationship to the Fight against Opposing Powers (de Principiis III.2-3)*, in StPatr 26, Louvain, 1993, pp. 217-220, p. 218.

74. Origen, *De principiis* 3,1,6 (SC, 268), pp. 32.34. Concerned, as he was, to stress and demonstrate the existence of man's free will, Origen did not regard it as imperative, at this stage, to mark out the sphere of the agency of grace (although the necessity for the latter was indisputable in the eyes of the great Alexandrian theologian) nor the concept of

possesses the will and the power to counter them through self-discipline[75]. Moral responsibility is thus the outcome of man's capacity to move from within in the decision-making process[76] in such a way that he

---

original sin and the status of sinful man. All this would find a theological systematization with Augustine. Origen was simply concerned to establish the reality of free will over and against the Gnostics' position. Thus, the above straightforward and seemingly onesided statement which gives the impression of excluding divine grace, should be balanced and illuminated by other passages of Origen, like the following: "And it is a proper quality of the goodness of God to conquer the one who is being benefitted while he is benefitting him, taking in advance the one who will be worthy and, before he becomes worthy, adorning him with sufficiency that, after the sufficiency, he might reach the point of being worthy. It is not at all the case that on the basis of his worthiness he should reach the point of being sufficient, anticipating the giver and receiving his gifts in advance" (Id., *Commentarii in Iohannem* 6,36,181; English tr. in R.E. HEINE [ed.], *Origen, Commentary on the Gospel according to John. Books 1-10* [FaCh, 80], Washington, 1989, p. 219. Greek text in SC, 157, p. 264). See also H. CROUZEL, *Theological Construction and Research: Origen on Free Will*, in B. DREWERY – R. BAUCKHAM (eds.), *Scripture, Tradition and Reason. A Study in the Criteria of Christian Doctrine*, Essays in honour of Richard P.C. Hanson, Edinburgh, 1988, pp. 239-265, p. 244.

75. As already stated in the preface to *De principiis* the free will of the rational soul is closely connected with the struggle man has to maintain with the devil and his angels and opposing powers (cf. Origen, *De principiis, Praef.* 5 [SC, 252], p. 83).

76. Although Origen's attitude with regard to the different philosophical schools is fairly complex (for the philosophical background, see H. CHADWICK, *Introduction*, in Origen, *Contra Celsum*, Cambridge, 1953, ix-xxxii, pp. lx-xiii) some influence on Origen, exercised particularly by Middle Platonism and Stoicism, is evident. The concept of man's freedom of choice as the basis for moral responsibility, for instance, comes from Plato (cf. *Phaedrus* 245c; *Leges* X,904c) through Middle Platonism. The latter was, in its turn, influenced by Stoicism, which was going in the same direction, as the following passage of Epictetus shows eloquently: "What says Zeus? Epictetus... we have given you a certain portion of ourself, this faculty of choice and refusal, of desire and aversion, or, in a word, the faculty which makes use of external impressions" (Epictetus, *Diatribae* 1,1,10-12 [ed. OLDFATHER], T. I, pp. 8 and 10; English translation, pp. 9 and 11). Origen too was not immune to the appeal of Stoicism and its essential concern with ethical problems. As he himself tells us (cf. Origen, *Contra Celsum* 6,2 [SC, 147], p. 180), there was an immediate popular appeal about the simple ethical exhortations of Epictetus' discourses. Especially, Origen draws from the Stoics their defence of the doctrine of providence, although he distances himself from their pantheistic metaphysics. Whereas Stoicism considers reason just as a manifestation of the *pneuma* which is immanent in all the elements of the universe, Origen deals with reason against the background of the revelatory datum according to which the human being is the image of God thanks to his participation in the life of the Logos. Furthermore, Stoicism sees the universe as being made up of a unique and perfectly reasonable system where everything is determined by εἱμαρμένη in the best possible way. Nothing can modify what has been determined by destiny, not even human free will. The latter is in fact called to know and adhere harmoniously to the world order. In other words, free will does not act as a determining factor in the sphere of events, but it is transposed entirely to the human consciousness where it is responsible for man's mental and moral status (cf. A. DIHLE, *Liberté et destin dans l'antiquité tardive*, in *RTP* 121 [1989] 129-147, pp. 132f). Unlike Stoicism, the Platonist ontological explanation, based on the opposition between matter and spirit, was able to stress more the imperfection of the empirical world, thus leaving more scope for man's freedom of choice and its concrete consequences.

is detached from any extrinsic necessity. At this point, the modern mind will be surprised at realizing that Origen's philosophical argumentation, especially directed against Gnostic fatalism (physical determinism of good and evil) and astrological fatalism[77], rests on "ecclesiastical preaching" and on the "doctrine of the just judgment of God"[78]. This was not only its starting point, but also its constant framework. As a matter of fact, Origen contends, the conviction that every rational being is endowed with free will, and that his actions are freely chosen and are not subject to determinism, belongs to the rule of the Church's faith and to apostolic preaching. Such allusion, at this stage, betrays the religious direction along which Origen will address his thought, namely the deeper issue of the quality of the relationship with God[79], defined by his understanding of λόγος and νοῦς in a biblical and exegetical perspective, particularly with regard to the Pauline teaching[80]. To pursue a life which ends up by being good or bad, lies within the rational creature's power of self-determination[81]. Nevertheless, whenever human agency is

77. As it has been noted, "Origène vise surtout la triade Basilide-Valentin-Marcion". Even though "les reproches qu'il leur fait et les thèses qu'il leur prête sont en quelque sorte stéréotypés et ne manifestent guère une connaissance poussée et directe" (H. CROUZEL, *Origène*, Paris, 1985, p. 204). See also A. LE BOULLUEC, *La place de la polémique antignostique dans le Peri Archon*, in H. CROUZEL (ed.), *Origeniana*, Bari, 1975, pp. 47-61. H.S. BENJAMINS, *Eingeordnete Freiheit. Freiheit und Vorsehung bei Origenes*, Leiden, 1994, p. 107, n. 112.

78. Origen, *De principiis* 3,1,1 (SC, 268), p. 16. Origen had already pointed out in the preface to the first book of the *De principiis* the strict connection tying together the three essential doctrines by which free will is defined: moral freedom, the necessity of spiritual ascesis in order to deliver the soul from negative, demoniac influences, and the opposition to fatalism: "Est et illud definitum in ecclesiastica praedicatione, omnem animam esse rationabilem liberi arbitrii et uoluntatis; esse quoque ei certamen aduersum diabolum et angelos eius contrariasque uirtutes, ex eo quod illi peccatis eam onerare contendant, nos uero si recte consulteque uiuamus, ab huiuscemodi labe exuere nos conemur. Vnde et consequens est intellegere, non nos necessitati esse subiectos, ut omni modo, etiamsi nolimus, uel mala uel bona agere cogamur. Si enim nostri arbitrii sumus, inpugnare nos fortasse possint aliquae uirtutes ad peccatum et aliae iuuare ad salutem, non tamen necessitate cogimur uel recte agere uel male; quod fieri arbitrantur hi, qui stellarum cursum et motus causam dicunt humanorum esse gestorum, non solum eorum, quae extra arbitrii accidunt libertatem, sed et eorum, quae in nostra sunt posita potestate" (Id., *Praef.* 5 to *De principiis* 1 [SC, 252], pp. 82-84).

79. That Origen's "whole attitude was fundamentally religious is no doubt true. This explains why in the preface of the *contra Celsum* he feels it necessary to apologize to his readers for undertaking such a rational defence at all.... The *contra Celsum*, in fact, brings into prominence one side of Origen's work and shows him diverted from his central task of Biblical exegesis and textual criticism into the line of apologetic" (CHADWICK, *Introduction* [n. 76], p. xiii).

80. E. SCHOCKENHOFF, *Zum Fest der Freiheit. Theologie des christlichen Handelns bei Origenes* (TTS, 33), Mainz, 1990, pp. 23-94.

81. Cf. Origen, *De principiis* 3,1,1 (SC, 252), and 3,1,6 (SC, 268), p. 16 and pp. 32-34. Origen's polemic against astrological and cosmic determinism can be found in his

involved in choosing good, divine action is also present. Living well is our responsibility, it is our "task" (ἡμέτερον ἔργον), and yet such a task must not be understood as depending solely on human capabilities. In Origen's mind, the "pedagogical" character of divine agency is exercised through a "providential governance" which does not impose itself upon human freedom and will. Although the human soul needs God's grace to overcome the enticements of evil, divine help remains ineffectual if the rational creature does not co-operate with it[82]. The last choice

commentaries on the O.T. (*e.g.*, Id., *In librum Iudicum homiliae* 2,3 [SC, 389], p. 84; *In Iesu Naue homiliae* 7, 4 [SC, 71], p. 4) and in the discussions that have come down to us in the *Philocalia* (*Ibid.* 23 [SC, 226], pp. 130-210) and which were probably based on his lost commentary on Genesis. Against the Gnostics (so far as he understood them) Origen wanted to prove that God cannot be held responsible for evil and injustice in the world (cf., for instance, Id., *In Iesu Naue homiliae* 10,2; 12,3 [SC, 71], pp. 274, 300; *De principiis* 3,1,9 [SC, 268], pp. 52-56). With this aim he interprets some difficult biblical passages in such a way that any deterministic explanation is excluded. Thus, in the light of the divergent fates of Esau and Jacob, the defects, errors and sufferings that men endure have to be understood either in the light of one's demerits accumulated in a previous existence (the hypothesis of the "preexistence of souls", inspired by Greek philosophy, will be condemned in the 5th ecumenical council, the second of Constantinople, in 553) or against the background of the present life or by the theory that some souls of high merit opt to assist the process of salvation by showing solidarity and suffering in this life along with imperfect souls: cf. *e.g.* the texts of Gen 25,25-26; Mal 1,2-3; Rom 9,10-13 and Origen's exegesis (cf. Id., *De principiis* 2,9,7 [SC, 252], pp. 369ff.; 3,1,22 [SC, 268], pp. 136-140; 2,9,5 [SC, 252], pp. 361ff, and Rom 9,18-21 and Origen's explanation (cf. *Ibid.* 3,1,21 [SC, 268], pp. 128-136; 2,9,8 [SC, 252], pp. 371ff). Likewise, Pharaoh's "hardening" is the result of his own evil and must not be attributed to God's creation of a "lost nature": cf. Ex 7,3; Rom 9,17-18, and Origen's understanding (cf. *Ibid.* 3,1,7-10 [SC, 268], pp. 40-60). Yet, even in the midst of human errors God works to heal and bring all back to their original blessed condition. See E. CLARK, *The Origenist Controversy. The Cultural Construction of an Early Christian Debate*, Princeton, 1992, pp. 195-196.

82. The real good of a rational being is attainable as the result of human freedom on one side and of divine power on the other, the latter coming to the help of a virtuous man (cf. Origen, *Fragmenta in diuersos psalmos* 4 [PG, 12], c. 1161). Once again, beside clearly affirming that free will is a necessary requirement for choosing and living a moral life (cf. also Id., *Contra Celsum* 4,3 [SC, 136], p. 193), Origen is likewise stressing the need that man has of divine grace in order to direct his will towards the good and thus obtain salvation. See the several scriptural passages he refers to and which are crucial in the context of Origen's understanding of free will: cf. Id., *De principiis* 3,1,19 (SC, 268), pp. 114-124. Simonetti writes: "L'insistenza con cui Origene rileva in senso antignostico il libero arbitrio come fondamento di vita morale e la sua responsabilità nella scelta fra il bene e il male possono a volte dare l'idea che Origene abbia concepito Dio soltanto come chi, avendo fornito l'uomo della capacità di conquistare liberamente il bene, assista poi indifferente e impassibile alla vicenda con cui questo liberamente decide la sua sorte. Ma nulla potrebbe essere più falso: in più punti dei *Principi* (III,1,19.24; III,2,5) e altrove (cf., p. es., *Ho. Luc.*, 39,7) Origene chiaramente fa dipendere la nostra salvezza dalla cooperazione fra la nostra volontà e l'aiuto della grazia divina; ed è ben consapevole che in questa cooperazione la parte maggiore è svolta da Dio... Basta rileggere la parte finale di I,3 dove si profila la partecipazione dell'uomo alla vita del logos a diversi livelli mercé

between good and evil, and the amount of responsibility that goes with it, depends entirely on the decision of the human soul which, possessing the *possibilitas utriusque partis* as its essential property, is *laudis et culpae capax*[83].

In the second section, Origen deals with the problem of free will by rationally demonstrating it through the observation of nature, psychology, moral philosophy and the appeal to daily inner experience whereby man can personally detect his compliance with, or his resistance to external impulses and events. Origen supports his previous philosophical argumentation with a number of scriptural references[84] out of his conviction that the ecclesiastical faith and preaching which, as we have seen, are the precondition of any philosophical argumentation about free will, strictly depend on Scripture. Four passages from the Old Testament are quoted. The most explicit is undoubtedly Dt 30,19 (and 15): "See, I have set before you this day life and good, death and evil ... choose life, that you and your descendants may live". It deals with the problem of choosing good or evil, life or death, a problem man is always confronted with. The other three texts (Mic 6,8; Is 1,19f; Ps 80,14f), while being exhortations to obey God, imply at the same time the possibility of disobeying him. Then Origen quotes three precepts from the Sermon of the

---

la grazia dello spirito santo, e II,1,3 dove il logos è concepito come *anima mundi*, perciò sempre operante in noi, per escludere che la cooperazione dell'uomo e di Dio nella salvezza sia stata concepita da Origene come meramente esterna e non come compenetrazione totale dell'essere e dell'agire dell'uomo da parte di Dio" (SIMONETTI [ed.], *Introduzione* [n. 69], p. 78).

83. "Est ergo omnis creatura rationabilis laudis et culpae capax; laudis, si secundum rationem, quam in se habet, ad meliora proficiat, culpae, si rationem recti tenoremque declinet; propter quod recte etiam poenis ac suppliciis subiacet" (Origen, *De principiis* 1,5,2 [SC, 252], p. 176). "Reason – writes Crouzel – appears here as the power of distinguishing good and evil, and hence of giving its verdict on the ensuing action as worthy of praise or blame: its purpose is ethical" (CROUZEL, *Theological Construction and Research* [n. 74], p. 242).

84. It is useful to be reminded of the nature of theological research as Origen himself understood it, namely as an *exercitium* (γυμνασία: Origen, *De principiis* 1, Praef. 3 [SC, 252], p. 80). In point of fact, when neither Scripture nor rational endeavour (the latter meaning the sound reasoning as well as the knowledge derived from experience) lead to well-grounded affirmations whose certainty is undisputed, then Origen proceeds in his enquiries with modesty and speaks his thought γυμναστικός (cf. *Ibid.* 1-3, pp. 76-81). We might as well be reminded of what Lonergan wrote with regard to the theological speculation of the first Christian centuries which was groping towards the discovery of its proper method and technique: "*Non affirmando sed coniectando* is a fairly frequent phrase in the old writers: it is a signal that they are not enunciating their faith but trying to elaborate its speculative coherence. At any time such work is difficult enough, but it was particularly so in its initial phases when essential theorems were still in process of finding formulation" (B. LONERGAN, *Grace and Freedom: Operative Grace in the Thought of St. Thomas Aquinas*, London-New York, 1971, pp. 1-2).

Mount to show that it lies in man's power (δύναμις) to observe the divine commandments and that he shall with good reason be condemned to the judgement if he ever transgresses them[85]. To these texts he adds the parable of the house built on a rock and that built on sand (cf. Mt 7,24-26) and the scene of the Last Judgement (cf. Mt 25,34ff). Finally, although many other biblical passages could be added in order to endorse the existence of free will, Origen concludes this short collection of scriptural references with a quotation from Rom 2,4-10.

The third section[86], besides being the longest, is the most important and the most difficult one. Here Origen acknowledges that beside many scriptural passages that prove the existence of free choice with utmost clarity there are some others that incline us to opposite conclusions, in the direction of a denial and suppression of free will[87]. With an allegorical interpretation of those biblical passages Origen intends to come to the help of the many (πολλοί) who, being simple-minded, do not possess a spiritual understanding. But above all he aims at countering the misinterpretation upheld by the Valentinian gnostics and by the Marcionites: the first ones because (in Origen's understanding) they deny free will[88] to two of their three categories of "natures", the πνευματικοί (those who are sure to attain salvation) and the earthly ones, the χοϊκοί (those who will no doubt be condemned)[89]; the second ones because of the distinction they made between the "just" God (or the harsh creator) of the Old Testament and the "good" God (or the loving redeemer) of the New Testament[90].

---

85. Origen, *De principiis* 3,1,6 (SC, 268), p. 32.

86. *Ibid.* 3,1,7-24, pp. 40-151. See also CROUZEL, *Theological Construction and Research* (n. 74), pp. 245-265; J.W. TRIGG, *Origen. The Bible and Philosophy in the Third-century Church*, Atlanta, 1983, pp. 118-120; BENJAMINS, *Eingeordnete Freiheit* (n. 77), pp. 64ff.

87. It is interesting to note that the texts Origen used became, with regard to the discussions on the issue of free will, the standard ones in Christian tradition for several centuries, although Augustine's different interpretation of them have dominated the scene ever since.

88. Although the Gnostic systems were "an attempt to honor the priority of God in defining the causes of the human dilemma in a material and corruptible world", it seems "that Gnostic thought as a whole exhibited a clear notion of a cosmic history from creation to eschaton in which the myth of redemption was subjected to linear and contingent history of unfolding dependent to some degree on real free will in humankind" (J.P. GORDAY, Paulus Origenianus: *The Economic Interpretation of Paul in Origen and Gregory of Nyssa*, in BABCOCK [ed.], *Paul and the Legacies of Paul* (n. 43), 141-163, pp. 143, 144-145).

89. Cf. Origen, *De principiis* 3,1,8 (SC, 268), p. 48. Even though the ψυχικοί occupy in the Valentinian system an intermediary position where moral responsibility and life play a certain role, such attitudes, at the end of the day, are not really meaningful in that they are not efficacious as to the attainment of salvation.

90. Cf. *Ibid.* 3,1,9, pp. 52-54.

The first biblical text that Origen takes into consideration is that of the hardening of Pharaoh's heart (cf Ex 7–10, especially 9,12)[91], a passage which represented a crux for the Alexandrian Father in that it seems to support a Gnostic deterministic view. The objection raised by Ex 7–10 is obvious and soon stated: if Pharaoh's heart was repeatedly hardened by God so that he would not be moved by miracles, nor would he let the Hebrews go, then he was not free. The first, provisional answer that Origen offers is the following: "(God) needed Pharaoh's repeated disobedience in order to display his mighty works for the salvation of many"[92]. In the context of his divine designs God allowed Pharaoh's hardening to happen because it was bearer of an "economic" purpose with regard to the Hebrews. "God – writes Babcock – provides the evil as well as the good that will ultimately conduce to the redemption of all. In this sense God is, for Origen, an accomplice in evil, the hardener of Pharaoh's heart (although not, of course, the author of Pharaoh's – or anyone's – specific evil acts). God is the designer of the setting and the director of the events in which the economy of salvation is realized; and this means that God, without overriding free will, orchestrates the evil as well as the good intermixed in that setting and in those events"[93]. On a more personal level, however, the hardening of the heart is a figurative way of describing the effects of God's grace on a soul which was already weakened in itself and, as it were, already condemned by its own obstinate pursuit of evil. In this case, a further hardening of God's action would be superfluous indeed. Yet, God, as a wise physician who at times allows

91. This question is tackled also in other writings of Origen: cf. Id., *Philocalia* 27 (SC, 226), pp. 268-315; *In Exodum homiliae* 3,3; 4,1-7; 6,3-4.9 (SC, 321), pp. 98-114; 116-138; 176-182.190-196; *Commentarii in epistulam ad Romanos* 7,16, FC, Bd. II/4, pp. 148ff. See E. JUNOD, *Introduction*, in Origen, *Philocalia* 21-27 (SC, 226), pp. 103-120; CROUZEL, *Theological Construction and Research* (n. 74), pp. 246ff; W.J.P. BOYD, *Origen on Pharaoh's hardened heart. A study on Justification and election in St. Paul and Origen*, in StPatr VII (TU, 92), Berlin, 1966, pp. 434-442; M. HARL, *La mort salutaire du Pharaon selon Origène*, in *Studi in onore di Alberto Pincherle* (SMSR, 38/I), Rome, 1967, pp. 260-268; L. PERRONE (ed.), *Il cuore indurito del Faraone. Origene e il problema del libero arbitrio*, Genua, 1992.

92. Origen, *De principiis* 3,1,8 (SC, 268), p. 50.

93. W.S. BABCOCK, *Introduction*, in ID. (ed.), *Paul and the Legacies of Paul* (n. 43), pp. xiii-xxviii, p. xxi. "This line of thought leads Origen to the conclusion that he felt he must maintain: that God is indeed providentially good in supplying the resources from which both good and evil will come and that much will depend on the free response of the finite subject.... The Gnostic postulate of the two gods is avoided, and instead, the unity and goodness of the one God are upheld. Origen had no intention of suggesting that what appears to be evil really is not so in the long run; rather, he believed that in a rational universe, evil itself can be seen to have served some purpose consistent with the nature of God" (GORDAY, *Paulus Origenianus* [n. 88], pp. 146 and 147).

the disease to reach a crisis before alleviating it, may allow sinners to reach the full extent of their wickedness in order that, once utterly satiated with evil-doing and its consequences, they may repent, turn to God and live[94]. It does not matter if the time allotted to a soul on earth is not enough to reach full repentance. Because of the soul's immortality, God deals with them "not in view of the fifty years, so to speak, of our life here, but in view of the endless world"[95]. That is why, continues Origen, Pharaoh was not destroyed when he drowned in the Red Sea[96]. His soul went on for further purgation prepared by God for him so that he might eventually be saved.

If the scriptural passages concerning the hardening of Pharaoh's heart seemed to imply that it was God who actually made him sin, there are other passages which, if taken literally, seem to imply that only God can help man in doing good and that human efforts do not play any significant part in it. One of these texts, examined by Origen, is Ez 11,19-20: "I will remove the heart of stone from their flesh and give them a heart of flesh, so that they may follow my statutes and keep my ordinances and obey them"[97]. He argues that the need of being healed of our stony heart does not suppress our free will, or detract from our moral responsibility. We can ask God to heal our hearts in the same way an unlearned person asks a teacher to be enlightened over things he does not know. He is certainly not less free or responsible in seeking the help he needs[98].

Other problematic texts come from Rom 9. Here Origen's concern focuses upon the nature and implications of divine election, in connection with the "famous problem concerning Jacob and Esau"[99]. To Origen, such a problem demanded cogent solutions (as it will to the Greek Christian commentators as a whole[100]) in order to counter what appeared to be a devastating attack to human freedom. Besides, the seriousness of this attack was all the more disturbing because it was not coming only from pagan philosophical determinism and blind fate, but also from the Bible itself, from the Christian God[101], a God who seems to relate

---

94. Origen, *De principiis* 3,1,13 (SC, 268), pp. 68-80; 3,1,17, pp. 100f.

95. *Ibid.* 3,1,13, p. 80.

96. *Ibid.* 3,1,14, p. 86.

97. Cf. *Ibid.* 3,1,15-17, pp. 88-110. See CROUZEL, *Theological Construction and Research* (n. 74), pp. 252ff.

98. Cf. Origen, *De principiis* 3,1,15 (SC, 268), pp. 88ff.

99. Id., *Commentarii in Iohannem* 2,191 (SC, 120), p. 336.

100. The defence of free choice vis-à-vis Ex 7-10 and Rom 9 was a recurrent theme in Greek Christian commentators. See WILKEN, *Free Choice and Divine Will* (n. 43), pp. 123-140.

101. In the first quarter of the 3rd century, this difficulty was put forward by Minucius Felix in a dialogue held with two friends, the Catholic Octavius and the pagan Caecilius.

himself to human affairs in a way that would empty the responsibility of human agents and eviscerate the very meaning of virtue. The first text which attracted Origen's attention was Rom 9,16: "It does not depend on him who wills or him who runs, but on God who has mercy"[102]. His interpretation is somewhere in the middle. Developing a synergetic model, he stresses that there is not a mutual exclusiveness but rather a complementary relationship between man's efforts in doing good and God's gracious assistance. Even if God's help exceeds our own work, in that it is infinitely greater than that of our free will[103], it does not entail that the latter is suppressed[104]. Origen draws an example from the case of the κυβερνήτης/*gubernator* of a ship who, although quite aware of his own indispensable skill in bringing the ship to dock, does not doubt in ascribing to God's providence the favourable winds and the good weather and the shining of the stars that have guided him in completing his role[105]. Our efforts, therefore, must begin with us and whenever we do what is in our power to do in order to achieve what is good, then God's help will certainly assist us. Free will is in fact the power, given to man by God, to will and act by choosing personally and responsibly what is good (which, paradoxically, includes also the possibility of refusing it)[106].

The other passage about which Origen was concerned, particularly because it seems to suggest that man is without free will, is Rom 9,18-

---

The latter addresses to the Christians the same critique that the former addresses to the pagans, viz. the attribution of their actions to fate. In fact, in Caecilius' eyes, the Christians affirm, in a similar way, that human actions belong to God. Thus, concludes Caecilius, those who join Christianity do so not of their own free will, but because they have been chosen (*electos*), whereas other human beings are injustly punished not for their intention (*uoluntatem*) but for their lot in life (cf. Minucius Felix, *Octauius* 11,6 [CSEL, 2], p. 15). The evidence from Minucius Felix, although only confirming what we know from Galen and Celsus, is paradigmatic of a way of thinking according to which the Christian concept of divine providence and election could be open to criticism just in the same way as pagan determinism and fatalism was.

102. Cf. Origen, *De principiis* 3,1,18 (SC, 268), pp. 112ff. See CROUZEL, *Theological Construction and Research* (n. 74), pp. 256f.

103. Cf. Origen, *De principiis* 3,1,19 (SC, 268), p. 122.

104. "Come appare anche dalla quarta *quaestio* del Trattato, su Rm 9,16 (*Prin* 3,1,18-19), O*[rigene]*. sviluppa un modello 'sinergistico', per cui l'iniziativa di Dio non sopprime la responsabilità dell'uomo bensì la sollecita; d'altra parte deve restare viva la coscienza del rapporto gerarchico: la volontà dell'uomo non basta insomma da sola per giungere alla meta e alla grazia divina spetta il primato quanto ai risultati raggiunti. Guardando al modo con cui s'esprime concretamente il libero arbitrio, si dovrà ammettere un reciproco condizionamento dell'iniziativa divina e della responsabilità dell'uomo" (L. PERRONE, *Libero arbitrio*, in A. MONACI CASTAGNO [ed.], *Origene. Dizionario, la cultura, il pensiero, le opere*, Rome, 2000, pp. 237-243, p. 242).

105. Origen, *De principiis* 3,1,19 (SC, 268), p. 122.

106. Cf. *Ibid.* 3,1,20, pp. 126-128.

21 about the vessels for honour and those for dishonour[107]. Origen clearly affirms that there cannot possibly be such a thing as an unmerited election and that Rom 9,18-21 must not be understood in a deterministic way. In fact, to strip human agency of its moral responsibility would mean to misunderstand and contradict the standpoint that Paul has taken up throughout his letters on the matter. Rather, the fact that God has made some vessels of honour and other ones of dishonour (as the case of Jacob and Esau, who inherited unequal situations in the world, shows[108]) must be ascribed to antecedent causes regarding the pre-existence of the souls and their pre-mundane fall, by which some souls have merited an earthly life far less happy than others[109]. In this way Origen explains how the human condition, rather than depending upon God's arbitrary will or favouritism, is the consequence of merits and demerits that the souls have gained previously to their embodiment[110].

---

107. "Ergo cui uult miseretur, et quem uult indurat. Dices ergo mihi: Quid adhuc queritur? Voluntati enim eius quis resistet? Enim uero, o homo, tu quis es, qui contra respondeas deo? Numquid dicit figmentum ei qui se finxit: Quid me fecisti sic? Aut non habet potestatem figulus luti ex eadem massa facere aliud quidem in honorem uas, aliud autem in contumeliam?" (Rom 9,18-21). The beginning of this passage had already been quoted by Origen in *De principiis* 3,1,8 in a paragraph concerning Ex 4,21 (cf. SC, 268, pp. 46-52). Here he is concerned especially with the last part of the quotation, regarding the potter and the vessels, whose relationship can be easily interpreted in a deterministic sense. See also CROUZEL, *Theological Construction and Research* (n. 74), pp. 259ff.

108. This case is often evoked by Origen in order to support, with the help of Scripture, the doctrine of existing merits and demerits before birth: cf., *e.g.*, Origen, *De principiis* 1,7,4 (SC, 252), pp. 214-216; *Ibid.*, 2,8,3, pp. 342-348; 2,9,7, pp. 366-370; *Commentarii in epistulam ad Romanos* 7,17, FC, Bd. II/4, pp. 158ff. The distinction between the two kinds of vessels was also assumed by the Valentinians as indicating the spirituals/*pneumatikoi* beings and the earthly/*hylics* ones.

109. Cf. Id., *De principiis* 3,1,22 (SC, 268), pp. 136f. See H. CROUZEL – M. SIMONETTI, *Notes*, in Origen, *Traité des Principes* (Livres III et IV) (SC, 269), pp. 44-47.

110. "God – writes Gorday – is the perfectly good creator who makes all souls from one lump, loving them all equally and yet bound by the possibility that free will may lead them astray, until a fall occurs in which each soul (except that of Jesus!) is enfleshed, relative to the degree of its sin, in a divinely foreseen earthly state, there to struggle with good and evil in order to be purified for a return to the spiritual world at the restoration of all things" (GORDAY, Paulus Origenianus [n. 88], p. 148). This implies, however, a sort of transcendent "inevitability" inherited by the "embodied" souls. "Origen – continues Gorday – was perfectly aware that the *actual* situation of any particular person is a product of a chain of causation, which at some point precedes his own willing – the willing of his earthly self, that is – and that there are antecedents which determine his lot, but – and *this is the catch that makes Origen akin to the Gnostics* – these antecedents are premundane, belonging to a transcendent realm where both evil and the form of enfleshment taken by any particular soul originate. The implication is that sin is rendered inevitable and necessary – not any particular sin (free will is responsible for *that*), but some kind of sin – since otherwise corporeality could not exact its price on the soul and providence could not proceed with its purification" (*Ibid.*).

God's initiative and human co-operative response must therefore be harmonized into one perfect affirmation (ἕνα λόγον [...] τέλειον)[111]. "Our own action – concludes Origen – is nothing without God's knowledge (grace), and the latter cannot force us to progress if we ourselves do not do anything in the direction of the good. In fact, free will without God's knowledge (grace) and the capability of using one's freedom in a worthy manner cannot lead anybody to honour or dishonour. Likewise, God's action alone cannot destine anybody to honour or dishonour without the human will being itself orientated towards good or evil"[112]. In this way, Origen keeps free will and God's helping grace in a constant interaction: the ultimate human moral responsibility on one side and the manifold operation of grace on the other.

After Origen, the issue of free will, will be influenced by the philosophical and theological framework provided by the great Alexandrian master[113], although some will prefer to limit themselves to stressing a more biblical or pragmatic approach[114]. *Athanasius* speaks of the process of divinisation, which occurs thanks to man's participation in the divine sonship of the Logos, the one perfect image of God the Father. As λογικός man is capable of partaking of the knowledge that the Logos has of the Father, although, unlike the Logos, he does not possess divine sonship by nature but receives it as a gift from God's grace[115]. Athanasius

---

111. Origen, *De principiis* 3,1,24 (SC, 268), p. 148.

112. *Ibid.* 3,1,24, pp. 148-150. See also his commentary on Psalm 4 where Origen says that the real good of a rational creature is the result of human freedom and divine power that comes to its aid: "Sic bonum rationabilis creaturae mixtum est ex voluntate ipsius, et conspirante divina virtute in eo qui honestissima suscipit" (Id., *Fragmenta in diversos psalmos* 4 [PG, 12], c. 1159).

113. Eusebius of Caesarea, for instance, while insisting on free will as the condition of his theology of sin and salvation in Christ, repeats almost in a servile way what Origen had expounded on the subject (cf. Eusebius of Caesarea, *Demonstratio euangelica* 4,1,4 and 4,6,7-8 [GCS, 23], pp. 150 and 160. The passage quoted in 4,1,4 echoes Origen's *De principiis* 1,5.8; 2,9,6 and 3,1). See AMAND, *Fatalisme et liberté dans l'antiquité grecque* (n. 1), pp. 355f.

114. Thus, Methodius of Olympus, rather than the Origenian explanation of human free will as a freedom of indifference (viz. as the power of choosing between good and evil), comes closer to the position of Irenaeus and considers human free will as a divine gift through which man (if he so wishes) can orient himself to God and obey him (cf. Methodius of Olympus, *De libero arbitrio* [Περὶ τοῦ αὐτεξουσίου], PO 22, pp. 795-799). Against astrological fatalism, Methodius insists on the freedom of man also in his *Conuiuium decem uirginum* 8,16-17 passim (SC, 95), pp. 246-260. See AMAND, *Fatalisme et liberté dans l'antiquité grecque* (n. 1), pp. 333ff.

115. Cf., for instance: "... καὶ ἄνθρωποι τυγχάνοντες ἀπὸ γῆς θεοὶ χρηματίζομεν οὐχ ὡς ὁ ἀληθινὸς θεὸς ἢ ὁ τούτου λόγος, ἀλλ' ὡς ἠθέλησεν ὁ τοῦτο χαρισάμενος θεός, οὕτως καὶ ὡς ὁ θεὸς οἰκτίρμονες γινόμεθα οὐκ ἐξισούμενοι τῷ θεῷ, οὐδὲ φύσει καὶ ἀληθινοὶ εὐεργέται γινόμενοι· οὐ γὰρ ἡμῶν εὕρεμα τὸ εὐεργετεῖν, ἀλλὰ τοῦ θεοῦ" (Athanasius, *Orationes contra Arianos* 3,19, *Athanasius Werke*, Bd. I/1, 3. Lieferung, p. 329). See also Id., *De decretis Nicaenae synodi* 24, *Athanasius Werke*, Bd. II/1, p. 20.

insists on our becoming sons of God thanks to our participation in the incarnate Son who has come among us so that we too, through him, may be united to God[116]. To this aim God has sent his Holy Spirit, the Spirit of the Son, which works in us as the Spirit of sonship. He is in fact the seal (σφραγίς) of the Son and conforms us to him[117]. As to the place and role of man's agency, Athanasius gives us some indication in his *Festal Letters* and in his *Vita Antonii*. In his *Festal Letters*, he considers the mystery of Easter as a microcosm of Christian life. The observance of what the Paschal mystery entails becomes the type of a Christian disciplined life on its way to the heavenly feast. Christ's death and resurrection have in fact made accessible the "way up" (ἄνοδος) to heaven by defeating death and Satan. Now it is up to the believer to cultivate that grace by which Christ has made accessible the way to heaven, and to commit himself to it through his own effort, viz. through the use of his free will. Grace and human striving call for each other, and even though the *Festal Letters* lay emphasis on divine initiative and grace, we do not find – as it has been noted – "any corresponding de-emphasis on human striving, volition, moral progress, attainment of virtue"[118]. Man's need to strive is aimed at responding fittingly to the gift of grace. There is reciprocity and complementarity between divine grace and human will and it is in this light that Athanasius highlights man's responsibility. "Our will – he writes – ought to keep pace with the grace of God, and not fall short, lest while our will remains idle, the grace given us should begin to depart, and the enemy finding us empty and naked, should enter *[into us]*"[119]. Human beings are seen as free and captains of their own destiny: "We float on this sea *[the world]*, as with the wind, through our own free will, for every one directs his course according to his will, and either, under the pilotage of the Word, he enters into rest, or, laid hold on by pleasure, he suffers shipwreck, and is in peril by storm"[120]. Thanks to the incarnation of the Word, all human beings are free to accept the grace that has been bestowed on them, and the believers are

116. Cf. Id., *Oratio de incarnatione Verbi* 3, 5, 7-8, 11, 17, 54 (SC, 199), pp. 268-274; 278-282; 286-294; 302-306; 324-328; 456-460; *Orationes contra Arianos* 1, 9, 16, 34, 45-46, 49, *Athanasius Werke*, Bd. I/1, 2. Lieferung, pp. 117-118, 125-126, 143-144, 154-156, 159, et *passim*.
117. Cf. Id., *Epistulae ad Serapionem* 1,23 and 25 (PG, 26), cc. 584-589.
118. K. ANATOLIOS, *Athanasius. The coherence of his thought*, London-New York, 1998, p. 173.
119. Athanasius, *Epistulae festales* 3,3. English translation by A. ROBERTSON (ed.), *Select Writing and Letters of Athanasius, Bishop of Alexandria* (NPNF, 2nd ser., 4), Edinburgh 1897, repr. Edinburgh-Grand Rapids/MI, 1991, p. 513.
120. *Ibid.* 19,7 (English tr. p. 547).

precisely those who consciously and thankfully receive it and cultivate it diligently in pursuit of a virtuous life[121]. The reciprocity between the divine bestowal of grace and human response to it, however, should not be understood in merely dialectical terms, as if both divine and human action enjoyed an absolutely independent action. If this is certainly true of divine agency, it does not hold in the case of human "response" which, in fact, as the term itself suggests, is strictly derivative of the divine initiative. Thus, whereas to strive responsibly for virtue is to act in accordance with God's grace, not to strive for virtue amounts to despising grace[122]. To consent to the gift of grace (virtue) or to refuse it (vice) remains, however, an act of human self-determination, a choice of man's free will. "Athanasius himself – writes Anatolios – does not seem to see any contradiction in conceiving of human life as both directed by the will and under the pilotage of the Word. The will continues to be free and can still be said to be directing the course of one's life"[123].

In the *Vita Antonii*, a manifesto of ascetic/monastic life[124], the themes of divine grace and free will are so much interwoven that it provides us with both an ideal representation of Athanasius' concept of the life of grace and with the epitome of his practical and theoretical ascetic program. Antony is so succesful in his ascetic undertaking because Christ has become his co-worker and he has become a co-worker of Christ. Their relation appears indeed to be characterized by "co-working" (συνεργία): "Verily the Lord worked with this man (Συνήργει γὰρ ὁ Κύριος)"[125]. In this co-working (although asymmetrical)[126] Antony's success in his struggle for perfection is thus simultaneously the result of the Saviour's success and of his practising asceticism in earnest (συντόνως ἐκέχρητο τῇ ἀσκήσει)[127]. Another example in which the emphasis is laid on both divine aid and Antony as the very model of

---

121. "Athanasius thus shared the standard pre-Augustinian view that grace or providence provided the context in which human beings made free choices and proved beneficent or punitive depending on those choices" (D. BRAKKE, *Athanasius and the Politics of Asceticism*, Oxford, 1995, p. 156).

122. Athanasius, *Epistulae festales* 3,3; 5,3; 6,1; 6,4; 7,9 (in ROBERTSON [ed.], *Select Writing and Letters of Athanasius* [n. 119], pp. 518, 519f, 520, 526-527).

123. ANATOLIOS, *Athanasius* (n. 118), p. 176.

124. See *supra*, p. 50, n. 122.

125. Athanasius, *Vita Antonii* 5,7 (SC, 400), p. 248 (English translation by R.T. MEYER [ed.], *St. Athanasius. The Life of Saint Antony* [ACW, 10], Westminster, MD, 1950, p. 23).

126. Anatolios reminds us that "such co-working is an asymmetrical relationship in which Antony's work derives from that of Christ" (ANATOLIOS, *Athanasius* [n. 118], p. 181).

127. Cf. Athanasius, *Vita Antonii* 7,3 *et passim* (SC, 400), pp. 150f.

ascetic striving occurs in a famous key passage of the *Vita Antonii*,
where the ascetic is described as being confronted with a fierce attack by
the demons: "And here again the Lord was not forgetful of Antony's
struggle, but came to help him. (…) Antony, perceiving that help had
come, breathed more freely and felt relieved of his pains. And he asked
the vision: 'Where were you? Why did you not appear at the beginning
to stop my pains?'. And a voice came to him: 'Antony, I was right here,
but I waited to see you in action (ἰδεῖν τὸν σὸν ἀγωνισμόν). And now
because you held out and did not surrender, I will ever be your helper
(…)'. Hearing this, he arose and prayed; and he was so strengthened that
he felt his body more vigorous than before"[128]. This principle of complementarity in the divine-human "co-working" comes to the fore also
in one of Antony's pastoral discourses to his fellow monks: "Therefore,
children, let us persevere in the practice of asceticism and not be care-
less. For in this also we have the Lord with us to help us (Ἔχομεν οὖν
[…] τῆς ἀσκήσεως), as Scripture says: 'God co-operates (συνεργόν)
unto good' with everyone who chooses the good"[129]. For our purpose, it
is sufficient at this point to establish, in the light of what we can infer
from both the *Festal Letters* and the *Vita Antonii*, that the element of
volition and human striving appears to be integral to that of divine aid,
viz. grace, and that (although in an asymmetrical way) Athanasius conceived of the interaction of divine and human in an harmonious fashion.

Among the *Cappadocian* Fathers, *Basil of Caesarea* affirms that
human freedom possesses in itself an element of "command" because of
the fact that each person is made in God's image (κατ' εἰκόνα). Human
beings, that is, have the power to begin action within themselves and
around themselves, because they have been equipped with the means
which are necessary to safeguard their own salvation (τῆς οἰκείας
αὐτῶν σωτηρίας)[130]. However, to counter the assumption that may
attribute to man a degree of perfection which is characteristic of God,
Basil too recurs to the distinction between image (εἰκών) of God, which
everybody receives from the Creator, and likeness (ὁμοίωσις) to God,
which has yet to be striven for and fulfilled. In this way he makes clear
that likeness to God comes only through the aid of grace and its prior

---

128. *Ibid.* 10, pp. 162.164 (English translation by MEYER [ed.], *St. Athanasius*
[n. 125], pp. 28-29).

129. *Ibid.* 19,1, p. 184 (English translation p. 36).

130. Basil of Caesarea, *Homiliae in Exaemeron* 9,4, eds. AMAND DE MENDIETA –
RUDBERG (GCS, NS 2), p. 153. "The conjunction of this point with references to
'unlearned' nature makes it clear that Basil was arguing chiefly against a sense of dependence on fate or necessity" (P. ROUSSEAU, *Basil of Caesarea*, Berkeley-Los Angeles-
Oxford, 1994, p. 340, n. 130).

influence. In fact, although controlling human potential and development, human freedom, left to itself, lacks persistence with regard to the choice of good, and it is unable to actually guarantee the final achievement and participation in the good[131]. This view, which gives a "theological" character to man's striving for perfection and union with God, is forcefully stated in Basil's *De Spiritu sancto*. There is no likeness with God without knowledge, declares Basil[132], that is to say without a process of recognition and return which is made possible by the ἐνέργεια of the Spirit at work in human lives. It is the powerful agency of the Spirit that brings to men the boon of salvation[133], by introducing them into communion with the grace of Christ and by fortifying them with the power of the divine glory, reflected in everyday life[134]. Reaffirming Origen's essential tenets on moral freedom, Basil emphasizes the historical implications (rather than the philosophical ones) of the tie existing between man's free will and his likeness with God[135]. One condition, essential to the enlightening activity of the Spirit in man's life, is that each Christian should commit himself, through zeal and sound choices, to ascesis and moral progress[136], even in the midst of hindrances and tribulations. As Basil wrote to some monks who were persecuted by the Arians, urging them not to grow faint-hearted but to add to their zeal (σπουδή), "it is not names that save us, but the choices (αἱ προαιρέσεις) we make"[137].

Also *Gregory of Nazianzus* is confident in attributing some power to man's free will in the process of salvation. Man, he says, is not saved

131. Basil of Caesarea, *Homiliae in exaemeron* 9,6, eds. AMAND DE MENDIETA – RUDBERG (GCS, NS 2), pp. 158ff.

132. Id., *De Spiritu sancto* 1,2 (SC, 17bis), p. 252.

133. *Ibid.* 12,28, p. 346.

134. "Through the Holy Spirit comes our restoration to paradise, our ascension into the kingdom of heaven, our return to the adoption of sons, our liberty to call God our Father, our being made partakers of the grace of Christ (κοινωνὸν γενέσθαι τῆς χάριτος τοῦ Χριστοῦ), our being called children of light, our sharing in eternal glory" (*Ibid.* 15,36, pp. 370.372).

135. "Διὰ τί δὲ ὅλως δεκτικὴ τοῦ κακοῦ; Διὰ τὴν αὐτεξούσιον ὁρμήν, μάλιστα πρέπουσαν λογικῇ φύσει. Λελυμένη γὰρ πάσης ἀνάγκης, καὶ αὐθαίρετον ζωὴν λαβοῦσα παρὰ τοῦ κτίσαντος, διὰ τὸ κατ' εἰκόνα γεγενῆσθαι θεοῦ, νοεῖ μὲν τὸ ἀγαθὸν, καὶ οἶδεν αὐτοῦ τὴν ἀπόλαυσιν, καὶ ἔχει ἐξουσίαν καὶ δύναμιν, ἐπιμένουσα τῇ τοῦ καλοῦ θεωρίᾳ καὶ τῇ ἀπολαύσει τῶν νοητῶν, διαφυλάσσειν αὐτῆς τὴν κατὰ φύσιν ζωήν· ἔχει δὲ ἐξουσίαν καὶ ἀπονεῦσαί ποτε τοῦ καλοῦ" (Id., *Quod Deus non est auctor malorum* 6 [PG, 31], c. 344). Cf. also Id., *Homiliae super psalmos* 48,8 (PG, 29), c. 449. See AMAND, *Fatalisme et liberté dans l'antiquité grecque* (n. 1), pp. 390ff.

136. See ROUSSEAU, *Basil of Caesarea* (n. 130), pp. 344-345.

137. Basil of Caesarea, *Ep.* 257,2, in *Saint Basile, Lettres*, T. III (ed. COURTONNE), p. 99.

only on account of God's gift of grace, but also thanks to his own
efforts[138]. It is, however, in *Gregory of Nyssa* that the freedom of choice
is highly emphasized. He sees history as a process of deification within
which man is called to become a full image of God. From the level of
the order of grace he underscores the gratuity of such a process; the
divine image in man, in fact, is not the result of human ability and effort,
but of God's benevolence. It is God who created man's nature in his
own image[139]. Nevertheless, grace, despite being a reality far above
human nature[140], calls upon the co-operation of human freedom. According to Gregory the freedom of choice (τὸ αὐτεξούσιον) is the most precious gift bestowed by God on human nature[141], the royal character that
distinguishes him from other creatures. Thanks to the freedom of choice
the process of recovering the divine image, which has been effaced but
which has never ceased to abide in human beings, is made possible[142].
For this reason man is not enslaved by outward necessity; his feelings
towards what pleases him depend on his own private judgement through
which he exercises his power to choose what he wishes[143]. In other

138. Cf. Gregory of Nazianzus, *Oratio* 40,27 (SC, 358), pp. 258f.
139. "Οὐ γὰρ ἡμέτερον ἔργον οὐδὲ δυνάμεως ἀνθρωπίνης ἐστὶ κατόρθωμα ἡ
πρὸς τὸ θεῖον ὁμοίωσις, ἀλλὰ τοῦτο μὲν τῆς τοῦ θεοῦ μεγαλοδωρεᾶς ἐστιν" (Gregory of Nyssa, *De uirginitate* 12,2 [SC, 119], pp. 408-410). Soon afterwards, however,
Gregory allows the interplay with free will and initiative to come to the fore as well (cf.
Ibid. 12,3, p. 410).
140. "Ὑπὲρ τὴν φύσιν ἡ χάρις" (Id., *De beatitudinibus* or. 7, *Gregorii Nysseni
opera* 7/2, p. 149). See J. ZACHHUBER, *Human Nature in Gregory of Nyssa. Philosophical
Background and Theological Significance* (SVigChr, 46), Leiden-Boston-Cologne, 2000,
pp. 125-186.
141. "He who made man for the participation of his own peculiar good... would
never have deprived him of that most excellent and precious of all goods, I mean the gift
implied in being his own master, and having a free will (τῆς κατὰ τὸ ἀδέσποτον καὶ
αὐτεξούσιον χάριψος). For if necessity in any way was the master of the life of man,
the 'image' would have been falsified in that particular part.... Was it not, then, most
right that that which is in every detail made like the divine should possess in its nature a
self-ruling and independent principle, such as to enable the participation of good to be the
reward of its virtue?" (Gregory of Nyssa, *Oratio catechetica* 24, *Gregorii Nysseni opera*
3/4, pp. 19-20 (English translation by W. MOORE, *The Great Catechism* 5 [NPNF, 2nd ser.,
5], Edinburgh-Grand Rapids/MI, repr. 1994, p. 479])).
142. "Return again to the same thing from which you have fallen away, since the
power of freely allotting to themselves whatever they wish, whether the good or the bad,
lies in the power of human choice (προαίρεσις)" (Gregory of Nyssa, *In inscriptione
Psalmorum*, *Gregorii Nysseni opera* 5, pp. 46-47). Cf. Id., *De opificio hominis* 4 (ed.
FORBES), T. I, p. 126. See R. LEYS, *L'image de Dieu chez saint Grégoire de Nysse*, Brussels-Paris, 1951, pp. 72-75.
143. Cf. Gregory of Nyssa, *De uirginitate* 12 (SC, 119), p. 402. See also Id., *De opificio hominis* 17,11 (ed. FORBES), T. I, p. 202; *Dialogus de anima et resurrectione* (PG,
46), c. 101; *Contra fatum*, *Gregorii Nysseni opera* 3/2, pp. 29-63. In this last work Gregory refutes fatalist arguments and underlines the importance of establishing the reality of

words, his freedom of choice[144] enables him to govern his own life and to shape his moral character as if he were lord of his own destiny[145]. Yet, man's freedom becomes a free choice supported by the will (προαίρεσις)[146] – which in its turn includes a moral or religious evaluation –, only when it is governed by the cognition of good and evil, of virtue and vice[147]. In this respect, divine grace operates primarily by strengthening and enlightening the human intellect so that the believer may rightly choose according to knowledge rather than ignorance[148]. By enlightening man's intellect, which is made in the image of God, grace orientates man's προαίρεσις towards the good. This means that there exists a basic correspondence between the constitution of man's mind and the choice of the good. Man is authentically free (in his intellect) when he chooses the good in which and for which he was created. However, since free will is bereft of any coercion or necessity, such orientation towards the good does not rule out that free will may choose evil as an alternative. This possibility is, as it were, a sort of "guarantee" by which the nature of προαίρεσις is safeguarded, for "it is through our freedom that we are brought closest to God and through our freedom that we betray him"[149].

freedom. He explicitly stresses the sovereignty of man's free choice as being governed autonomously by its own individual volitions.

144. In itself freedom, for Gregory of Nyssa, seems to be a matter of choice between two possibilities, a free movement or impulse directed either towards good or evil: "Πᾶσα δὲ προαίρεσις ὁρμητικὴ ἤτοι κατὰ τὸ ἀγαθὸν ἐνεργεῖται πάντως ἢ πρὸς τὸ ἀντικείμενον φέρεται" (Id., *Contra Eunomium* 3,9, *Gregorii Nysseni opera* 2, p. 266).

145. Id., *De opificio hominis* 4 (ed. FORBES), T. I, p. 126.

146. For an analysis of Gregory of Nyssa's concept of man's προαίρεσις see G. DAL TOSO, *La nozione di* proairesis *in Gregorio di Nissa. Analisi semiotico-linguistica e prospettive antropologiche* (Patrologia, Beiträge zum Studium der Kirchenväter, 5), Frankfurt am Main-Berlin-Bern-New York-Paris-Vienna, 1998, pp. 244-302.

147. Cf. Gregory of Nyssa, *De uita Moysis* 2,1 (SC, 1bis), p. 32. Gregory counters the belief that virtue and vice are lorded over by necessity (cf. Id., *Contra fatum*, *Gregorii Nysseni opera* 3/2 *passim*).

148. It must be said, however, that the failure to choose the good is not simply a problem of knowledge or will. It is after all "a problem endemic to this life where passions interfere with proper decision making" (J.J. O'KEEFE, *Sin*, ἀπάθεια *and Freedom of the Will in Gregory of Nyssa*, in StPatr 23, Louvain, 1989, pp. 52-59, p. 57). In this regard Gregory is quite clear: "What takes hold of the will (προαίρεσις) and twists it toward evil and away from virtue is, in reality, πάθος" (Gregory of Nyssa, *Oratio catechetica* 49, *Gregorii Nysseni opera* 3/4, pp. 45-46). As a consequence, since it bears no moral culpability, the will should not be blamed for sin. Its responsibility, in fact, depends on correct functioning which comes about only when the proper information has been received. In this framework grace, no doubt, appears as a kind of reward for the effort endured by man in his struggle for perfection.

149. A. MEREDITH, *Gregory of Nyssa*, London-New York, 1999, p. 24.

Furthermore, we must note that in Gregory's understanding the desire
for good, by which the προαίρεσις is nourished and kept in motion[150],
is never entirely fulfilled. Man's freedom finds itself in a process of endless growth, particularly with regard to the attainment of the good. To
explain this Gregory recurs to the concept of ἐπέκτασις. Derived from
Paul's words ("Forgetting what lies behind and straining forward [ἐπεκ-
τεινόμενος] to what lies ahead, I press on towards the goal for the prize
of the heavenly call of God in Christ Jesus": Phil 3,13b-14), this concept describes the attitude of the soul which participates in the good, viz.
God. Once the experience of the good is tasted, the desire for it is not
quenched but rather increased in a never ending process[151]. Of paramount importance in this context is not only the presence of the Holy
Spirit, which supports the process of man's deification, but above all the
significance of the person of Christ. His incarnation, in fact, has offered
to human beings the paradigm of a sinless individual being, entirely oriented to God and participating by nature in his divine life. It is Christ,
the Logos made flesh, the perfect image of God, that Christians are
called to imitate in order to restore in themselves their original image-
character. This restoration comes about through imitation, and is clearly
illustrated in one of Gregory's ascetic writings, the *De perfectione*.
There he affirms optimistically that men should learn perfection by imitating the perfect example of the virtuous life that Christ set before
them. Like a pupil who does his best to imitate a model of a well-drawn
picture that has been put before him, so the Christians should imitate
the perfect image of God in Christ to the best of their ability[152]. The

---

150. "Our free will (προαίρεσις) tends towards a goal set, as it is, in motion (εἰς
κίνησιν) by its natural desire (ἐπιθυμίας) for good" (Gregory of Nyssa, *Oratio catechetica* 96, *Gregorii Nysseni opera* 3/4, p. 56).

151. "The fruition *[of the good]* on the part of the soul becomes an impulse to an even
greater desire, for it is precisely through participation in the good that the desire is
extended ever more forward" (Id., *In Canticum canticorum* hom. 6, *Gregorii Nysseni
opera* 6, p. 174). "Since, then, those who know what is good by nature desire participation in it, and since this good has no limit, the participant's desire itself necessarily has
no stopping place (στάσιν οὐκ ἔχει) but stretches out with the limitless" (Id., *De uita
Moysis*, Praef. 7 [SC, 1bis], p. 50).

152. "Accordingly, this Person *[the Second Person of the Trinity]*, the ineffable and
the 'unspeakable' *[1 Pt 1,8]* and the 'inexpressible' *[2 Cor 9,15]* in order that he might
again make you an 'image of God', because of his love for man, became himself an
'image of the invisible God' *[Col 1,15]* so that he by his own form which he assumed be
formed inside you and you through himself be again made like the beauty of the arche-
type, as you have been from the beginning. Therefore, if we also are to become an 'image
of the invisible God', it is fitting that the form of our life be struck according to the
'example' *[Jn 13,15]* of the life set before us.... Therefore, just as when we are learning
the art of painting, the teacher puts before us on a panel a beautifully executed model, and

restoration of the divine image in man comes about "by fellowship with Jesus". "It seems evident that Gregory embraces the 'humanistic' paradigm. It is by imitation, by following the path of virtue, that human beings will retain their original state"[153].

At this point, despite the redactional problems which are still a debated issue, it is worth mentioning another work of Gregory of Nyssa, the *De instituto christiano*[154]. Addressed to a monastic community, it contains explicit passages about grace and human agency. One of them consists of an exhortation to the monks to pursue a virtuous life, whose acquisition is presented as being part of man's process of deification[155]. In this quest for perfection, the monks' human freedom, supported by reason, plays an important role while positively co-operating with God's grace. The latter, in fact, does not force itself upon man; on the contrary it is "measured by the labours of the receiver"[156], since grace "does not

---

it is necessary for each student to imitate in every way the beauty of that model on his own panel, so that panels of all will be adorned in accordance with the example of the beauty set before them; in the same way, since every person is the painter of his own life, and choice is the craftsman of the work, and the virtues are the paints for executing the image, there is no small danger that the imitation may change the prototype.... But, since it is possible, one must prepare the pure colours of the virtues,... so that we become an image of the image, having achieved the beauty of the prototype through activity as a kind of imitation, as did Paul, who became an 'imitator of Christ' [*1 Cor 4,16*] through his life of virtue" (Id., *De perfectione, Gregorii Nysseni opera* 8/1, pp. 194-196 [English translation by V. Woods-Callahan (ed.), *Saint Gregory of Nyssa. Ascetical Works* (FaCh, 58), Washington/D.C., 1967, pp. 110-111]).

153. Zachhuber, *Human Nature in Gregory of Nyssa* (n. 140), pp. 194-195.

154. The problem lies with the intricate phenomenon (unique in Early Christian literature) of the intimate intertwining of two texts, viz. Gregory's *De instituto christiano* and the so-called *Great Letter* of Ps.-Macarius. In the synoptic edition of Staats is possible to compare the great deal of sentences, words, scriptural quotations that the two works have in common (see R. Staats, *Makarios-Symeon, Epistola Magna. Eine messialianische Mönchsregel und ihre Unschrift in Gregors von Nyssa "De instituto christiano"* [AAWG.PH, 3. Folge, 134], Göttingen, 1984). As to the precedence of one writing over the other, the opinions are discordant. The priority of Gregory' *De instituto christiano* is defended by Jaeger (see W. Jaeger, *Two Rediscovered Works of Ancient Christian Literature: Gregory of Nyssa and Macarius*, Leiden, 1954, pp. 37-47; 174-230). Other scholars believe that the Ps.-Macarius' *Great Letter* is the source from which *De instituto christiano* has drawn (see R. Staats, *Gregor von Nyssa und die Messalianer: die Frage der Priorität zweier altkirchlicher Schriften* [PTS, 8], Berlin, 1968; M. Canévet, *Le 'De instituto christiano' est-il de Grégoire de Nysse?*, in *REG* 82 [1969] 404-423; J. Daniélou, *Orientations actuelles de la recherche sur Grégoire de Nysse*, Leiden, 1971, pp. 4-17). Due to this state of affairs the weight of the content of the *De instituto christiano* with regard to our enquiry remains subject to this proviso. See also V. Harrison, *Grace and Human Freedom According to St. Gregory of Nyssa* (SBEC, 30), Lewiston (N.Y.), 1992, pp. 8-9.

155. Undoubtedly, the concept of Greek *paideia*, revisited from a Christian perspective, exercised a considerable influence in the understanding of this process.

156. "Τοῖς τοῦ δεχομένου πόνοις ἡ δωρεὰ μετρεῖται τῆς χάριτος" (Gregory of Nyssa, *De instituto christiano, Gregorii Nysseni opera* 8/1, p. 46). And again: "The

naturally frequent souls which are fleeing from salvation"[157]. Great
emphasis is laid on the fact that human beings are endowed with a natural ability or impulse whereby they can reach out to God and experience his beauty through reason, the latter being the seal of the image of
God in man. It is by reason that human beings relieve themselves from
emotions and passions and ascend to God, although reason can only lead
up to a certain point where the knowledge of truth, which is grace, is
needed. But, again, grace is bestowed upon and becomes operative only
in those who accept it eagerly, even though to refuse it would represent
an "unnatural" state. In fact, if the image of God is made manifest in
man through reason, then the responsible use of such reason should
"naturally" bring forth the enactment of one's personal capabilities for
virtue[158].

With the proviso of the redactional problems mentioned above[159], it is
worth spending a few words also on *Ps.-Macarius*. Referred to as such
because his homilies had been handed down under the name of Macarius, his real name was *Symeon of Mesopotamia*, and he was a monk and
leader of the so-called Messalian movement[160]. Besides laying great
stress on the co-operation of divine grace with human efforts, he

growth of the soul depends, unlike that of the body, on man's own free will; the Spirit
makes this growth possible in accordance with the zeal/effort (σπουδή) of him who
receives it; the farther we extend the efforts of our works the more the soul grows through
our efforts" (*Ibid.*).

157. *Ibid.*, p. 47.

158. "Human freedom is a necessity for salvation. If a person chooses not to turn
towards God, grace is not accorded to him or her, and there is no salvation. Moreover,
this is an unnatural state. The gift of reason is the image of God in human beings, and the
power to choose wisely and responsibly is the operation of this gift" (V. LIM-
BERIS, The Concept of 'freedom' in Gregory of Nyssa's De instituto christiano, in StPatr
27, Louvain, 1993, pp. 39-41, p. 41). "The tradition of Greek ethical philosophy and its
ideal of *aretè* is very much alive in this Christian Platonist", writes Jaeger, who continues: "From the point of view of the Pelagian controversy, which his treatise foreshadows,
Gregory must be defined as a Semipelagian" (JAEGER, Two Rediscovered Works of
Ancient Christian Literature [n. 154], p. 12).

159. See *supra*, n. 154.

160. The Messalian movement originated in Mesopotamia in the middle of the 4th
century and spread quickly, particularly to Syria and Asia Minor. The name "Messalians"
was derived from a Syriac word which, like its corresponding Greek Εὐχῖται, means
"praying people". In fact, it was their characteristic to lay a strong emphasis on ceaseless
prayer, the aim of which was to eliminate all passions and desires. The followers of this
movement, already attacked at several local synods, were finally condemned as heretics
at the Council of Ephesus of 431 where their spiritual manifesto, the so-called *Ascetikon*,
was anathematized. See H. DÖRRIES, *Die Theologie des Makarios/Symeon* (AGWG.PH, 3.
Folge, 103), Göttingen, 1978; C. STEWART, *Working the Earth of the Heart: the Messalian Controversy in History, Texts and Language to AD 431* (OTM), Oxford, 1991;
K. FITSCHEN, *Messalianismus und Antimessalianismus: ein Beispiel ostkirchlicher
Ketzergeschichte* (FKDG, 71), Göttingen, 1998.

emphasized the efficacy of ascetic practice brought about by man's free will and action[161]. He even upheld the conviction that human will is, as it were, the *conditio sine qua non* for God to intervene and act efficaciously in the life of man[162]. Symeon's starting point is the concrete situation of man. Since, due to Adam's fall, the human soul was stripped of its divine qualities, it now finds itself between the two contending parties: God and his angels on one side, and Satan and his satellites on the other. It is as if man were now confronted with two antithetical powers, grace and evil, both acting within the soul, even after baptism[163]. It is up to man's free will to decide which of the two to choose. Grace and evil are not constraining; on the contrary they are both "protreptic" with regard to the role that human freedom has to play, a freedom that was not destroyed by original sin, and that could not be hindered or obliterated by actual sins either. It follows that as for good as for evil, the responsibility of the choice falls entirely upon man[164].

John Chrysostom, whose approach was not so much speculative as pastoral and parenetical, defines divine grace as a powerful gift of God[165] bestowed from above[166], from the fullness of the Holy Spirit, which is what enables man to perform virtuous actions and reach out to heaven[167]. Yet, he likewise insists that the contribution of man's free will and moral responsibility must be sought as necessary. Not everything is God's, and even though divine grace is of paramount importance in human straining after perfection[168], it does not retain, in Chrysostom's eyes, an absolute sovereignty on man. Certainly it does not act regardless of the latter's zeal and efforts. If in fact man's zeal has

---

161. "Sie *[Gnade]* wirkt in erster Linie da, wo der Mensch sich anstrengt und Fortschritte macht, vor allem wirkt sie in Entsprechung zum Glauben des Menschen und in Korrespondenz zu seinem freien Willen. Gott antwortet mit seiner Gnadenwirkung auf die Gegenleistung des Menschen, wobei der freie Wille seinerseits schon auf Gottes Wohltaten reagiert" (K. FITSCHEN, *Einleitung* to PSEUDO-MAKARIOS, *Reden und Briefe* [BGrL, 52], Stuttgart, 2000, p. 24). See also Ps.-Macarius/Symeon, *Homiliae spirituales (Typus III-Collectio C)* 26,3,1 (SC, 275), pp. 297-299.

162. "Τὸ οὖν θέλημα τοῦ ἀνθρώπου ὡς παράστασις ὑποστατική· μὴ παρόντος δὲ τοῦ θελήματος οὐδὲ αὐτὸς ποιεῖ, καίπερ δυνάμενος ὡς θεός· ἀλλὰ διὰ τὸ αὐτεξούσιον" (Id., *Sermones* 36,5,1 [Typus I-Collectio B] [GCS, 55/2], p. 50).

163. This doctrine was condemned as Messalian. Cf. John of Damascus, *De haeresibus* 80,2-3 (PG, 94), c. 729.

164. Cf. Ps.-Macarius/Symeon, *Sermones* 6,5 (GCS, 55/1), p. 88.

165. John Chrysostom, *In epistulam ad Romanos homiliae* 1,4 (PG, 60), c. 400.

166. Id., *In Genesim homiliae* 54,1 (PG, 54), c. 471; *In Matthaeum homiliae* 22,3 (PG, 57), c. 303.

167. John Chrysostom also uses the metaphor of the wings of the Spirit which are needed in order to be able to fly to heaven (cf. *Ibid*. 2,5, c. 29).

168. Id., *In epistulam ad Romanos homiliae* 16,9 (PG, 60), c. 561.

no sufficiency by itself unless it is helped from above, similarly the
influence of heavenly grace is of no benefit to man, unless his zeal is
present also. The Christian life of perfection is woven out of these two
together[169]. One aspect on which Chrysostom insists vigorously is that
despite the fact that Adam's misuse of his own freedom caused his fall,
the latter has not undermined the freedom of future mankind; on the
contrary the freedom of Adam's offspring has remained undamaged and
fully operative. Freedom, in fact, is a gift bestowed by God to man as
part of the very essence of his nature, and as such this gift has never
ceased to be efficacious in the infralapsarian man, who has always
enjoyed the capability of choosing his course of action with responsibility. Consequently, the person's free will continues to be at the basis of
his moral activity. For this reason, conscious of the need to urge the
believers to make efforts in the direction of an efficacious and personal
involvement in Christian faith and life (in the sense of an evangelical
morality), Chrysostom never fails to stress the power that human freedom is able to enjoy[170]. In point of fact, he expounds this view so confidently that his position can indeed be regarded as standing poles apart
from Augustine's rather sombre view on the same subject. He does not
do away with grace of course, nor does he consider the relationship
grace-free will in antithetical terms. His emphasis on freedom and autonomy goes together with the recognition of the necessity of grace as a
conditio sine qua non for attaining the good that has been desired and
chosen by the will. Grace, that is, intervenes in such a way as to support
human freedom, acting in its regard as an auxiliary reality[171] and not as
the first reason for man's movement towards the good. "What then? –
writes John Chrysostom – Does nothing depend on God? All indeed
depends on God, but not so that our free will is hindered (...). It depends
then on us (ἐφ' ἡμῖν ἐστιν), and on Him. For we must first choose the

---

169. "Ἐντεῦθεν μανθάνομεν δόγμα μέγα, ὡς οὐκ ἀρκεῖ προθυμία ἀνθρώπου,
ἂν μὴ τῆς ἄνωθέν τις ἀπολαύσῃ ῥοπῆς· καὶ ὅτι πάλιν οὐδὲν κερδανοῦμεν ἀπὸ τῆς
ἄνωθεν ῥοπῆς, προθυμίας οὐκ οὔσης" (Id., *In Matthaeum homiliae* 82,4 [PG, 58], c.
742). "So – writes Scheffczyk – nimmt die Gnade den Charakter einer geistig-sittlichen
Gabe und einer Kraft zur Tugendübung an" (SCHEFFCZYK, *Die Heilsverwirklichung in der
Gnade* [n. 27], p. 116).
170. "Οὐκ εὔδηλον, ὅτι διὰ τὸ ἕκαστον οἰκείᾳ προαιρέσει ἢ τὴν ἀρετὴν
αἱρεῖσθαι; Εἰ γὰρ μὴ τοῦτο ἦν, μηδὲ ἐν τῇ φύσει τῇ ἡμετέρᾳ τὰ τῆς ἐξουσίας
ἔκειτο, οὔτε ἐκείνους κολάζεσθαι ἔδει, οὔτε τούτους ἀμοιβὰς λαμβάνειν τῆς
ἀρετῆς· ἀλλ' ἐπειδὴ ἐν τῇ προαιρέσει τῇ ἡμετέρᾳ κατέλιπε μετὰ τὴν ἄνωθεν
χάριν τὸ πᾶν, διὰ τοῦτο καὶ τοῖς ἁμαρτάνουσι κολάσεις ἀπόκεινται, καὶ τοῖς
κατορθοῦσιν ἀντιδόσεις καὶ ἀμοιβαί" (John Chrysostom, *In Genesim homiliae* 22,1
[PG, 53], c. 187).
171. See G. BARDY, *Jean Chrysostome (Saint)*, in DTC 8/1 (1924) 660-690, c. 678;
AMAND, *Fatalisme et liberté dans l'antiquité grecque* (n. 1), p. 497ff.

good; and then He leads us to his own. He does not anticipate our choice, lest our free will should be outraged. But when we have chosen, then great is the assistance He brings to us"[172]. No doubt, his conviction about the power of free will (whose necessity he stressed also against astrological fatalism and the risk of a paralysis of moral action) led him to lay more emphasis on human agency, but the importance of grace was certainly not neglected[173].

This brief overview on the approach of the Eastern Fathers to the concept of grace and free will shows us, beyond the particular emphasis of the one or the other, an attempt at keeping the two realities positively and fruitfully interwoven, an attempt that in some cases is clearly synergetic. The Greek theologians were convinced that the co-operational model was in line with both Scripture and the teaching of the Church, and for that reason they did not deem it necessary to consider the problem of their relationship in theoretical terms only, or in terms of precedence. Moreover, their anthropological presupposition that man is vertically oriented[174] towards his true goal, God, and the "paideutical" framework within which such goal is sought, have led them to integrate the "divine" aspect of grace and its mystical and eschatological dynamics into the daily and concrete experience of man. Thus, concepts such as adoption as God's sons, rebirth through the Holy spirit, new creation through Christ or deification (all implying a participation in the divine nature) shaped their optimistic theological anthropology in symbiosis with man's natural freedom, and in the light of their daily experience of such interaction.

b) Grace and Free Will in the Latin Church

As to the Latin Church, there is little explicit allusion to an absolute divine "predominance" of grace, at least before Augustine[175]. It may suffice to simply hint at some essential information about the position of some Latin Fathers: Tertullian, Cyprian, Ambrose and Jerome. Pelagius and Julian of Aeclanum will be taken in consideration vis-à-vis Augustine's views.

172. John Chrysostom, *In epistulam ad Hebraeos argumentum et homiliae* 12,3 (PG, 63), c. 99. Cf. also Id., *In Iohannem homiliae* 10,1 (PG, 59), c. 73.
173. See, *e.g.*, Id., *Homilia habita postquam presbyter Gothus* 8,6 (PG, 63), c. 509.
174. See P. FRANSEN, *Dogmengeschichtliche Entfaltung der Gnadenlehre*, in *MySal* Bd. IV/2: *Das Heilsgeschehen in der Gemeinde. Gottes Gnadenhandeln*, Einsiedeln-Zürich-Cologne, 1973, pp. 636-641.
175. See KNOCH–SCHINDLER, *Gnade, B. Christlich* (n. 33), pp. 389ff., 412ff; SCHEFFCZYK, *Die Heilsverwirklichung in der Gnade* (n. 27), pp. 118-121.

226 CHAPTER THREE

Aside from *Tertullian*'s individual perspective, whereby free will is regarded as a particular gift of grace, the "mark" of the soul in fact, derived to man from his being made in the image and likeness of God[176], we also find, in the African Church, meaningful elements in connection with the reflection on the Church and her sacraments (above all baptism), both understood as realities conveying the grace of salvation. *Cyprian*, for instance, borrowing from the Roman cultural milieu, where the value of institutions was duly stressed, applies the category of *salus* to all the life of the Church seen as the *uia salutaris*[177]. The sacraments are the *instituta salutaria*: through baptism the heavenly water bestows the *gratiam salutaris*[178], the Eucharist is the *cibus salutis*[179] and the sacrament of penance is the *indulgentia salutaris*[180]. Also the ministers of the Church, above all the bishops, are the mediators of salvation in that they administer the sacraments. Christ is of course the author of (and therefore the ultimate way to) salvation[181]. Grace is thus regarded as the manifold gift of Christ's salvation bestowed on all men, first

176. "Liberum et sui arbitrii et suae potestatis inuenio hominem a Deo institutum, nullam magis imaginem et similitudinem Dei in illo animaduertens quam eiusmodi status formam. Neque enim facie et corporalibus lineis, tam uariis in genere humano, ad uniformem Deum expressus est, sed in ea substantia, quam ab ipso Deo traxit, id est anima, ad formam Dei spondentis et arbitrii sui libertate et potestate, signatus est. Hunc statum eius confirmauit etiam ipsa lex tunc a Deo posita. Non enim poneretur lex ei, qui non haberet obsequium debitum legi in sua potestate, nec rursus comminatio mortis transgressioni adscriberetur, si non et contemptus legis in arbitrii libertatem homini deputaretur" (Tertullian, *Aduersus Marcionem* 2,5 [SC, 368], pp. 44.46). See also Id., *De anima* 20,5; 22,1-2; 38,6 (CCL, 2), pp. 812. 814.842.
177. "Nec ambulando proficiet ad salutem, qui salutaris uiae non tenet ueritatem" (Cyprian, *De catholicae ecclesiae unitate* 2 [CCL, 3], p. 250).
178. Cf. Id., *Epistula* 73,10 (CCL, 3c), pp. 540-541. Aligned with the African Church's practice, first clearly reported by Tertullian (cf. Tertullian, *De baptismo* 18,4 [CCL, 1)], p. 293), baptism was intended by Cyprian for both adults and infants. In a letter addressed to Fidus (who had asked him whether infants could be baptized before their eigth day of life) Cyprian argued that baptism could be legitimately conferred on infants at any time after their birth. The reason is clearly stated: "Porro autem si etiam grauissimis delictoribus et in Deum multum ante peccantibus, cum postea crediderint, remissa peccatorum datur et a baptismo atque gratia nemo prohibeutr, quanto magis prohiberi non debet infans qui recens natus nihil peccauit, nisi quod secundum Adam carnaliter natus contagium mortis antiquae prima natiuitate contraxit, qui ad remissam peccatorum accipiendam hoc ipso facilius accedit quod illi remittuntur non propria sed aliena peccata" (Cyprian, *Ep.* 64,5 [CCL, 3c], pp. 424-425).
179. Cf. Id., *De dominica oratione* 18 (CSEL, 3/1), p. 280.
180. Cf. Id., *Ad Demetrianum* 25 (CSEL, 3/1), p. 370.
181. Cf. Id., *De bono patientiae* 9 (SC, 291), p. 203. Echoeing Irenaeus, Cyprian states that the ultimate purpose of men's salvation is that they may become sons of God: "... quod conseruandis ac uiuificandis nobis pater filium misit ut reparare nos posset quodque filius, missus, esse et hominis filius uoluit ut nos Dei filios faceret" (Id., *De opere et eleemosynis* 1 [CCL, 3A], p. 55).

through his incarnation and then through the *instituta salutaria* of the Church[182]. In the fluctuating thought-process of the time, Cyprian seems to be quite at ease with a plain synergism between the work of saving grace and man's co-operation. If on one hand the divine gifts are limitless, on the other the extent of man's access to the abundance of such grace depends on the degree of his faith[183], whereas to be saved or to be damned rests upon his free will[184]. Moreover, in a letter in which he discusses the reward awaiting those who suffer on behalf of Christ, he clearly says that God looks from on high upon those who strive for him and comes to their help crowning their victory and lavishly rewarding them, like an affectionate father, for having done what He himself had wanted to accomplish through their own agency[185].

Ambrose of Milan, whose dependence on Eastern theology is well established[186], maintains the assumption that man's free will and its efforts are sustained by divine help in a way which is interactive and co-operative. At times, however, he forcefully emphasizes man's will[187] without describing the exact place of God's intervention and

182. Cf. Id., *Ad Quirinum* 2,7 (CSEL, 3/1), p. 71.

183. "Quantum illuc fidei capacis adferimus, tantum gratiae inundantis haurimus" (Id. *Ad Donatum* 5 [CCL, 3A], p. 5).

184. "Seruans scilicet legem qua homo libertati suae relictus et in arbitrio proprio constitutus sibimet ipse uel mortem adpetit uel salutem" (Id., *Ep.* 59,7,2 [CCL, 3C], p. 348); Id., *De catholicae ecclesiae unitate* 10 (CCL, 3), p. 256.

185. "Quis non pretiosam in conspectu Dei mortem fortiter et constanter excipiat placiturus eius oculis qui nos in congressione nominis sui desuper spectans uolentes conprobat, adiuuat dimicantes, uincentes coronat, retributione bonitatis ac pietatis paternae remunerans in nobis quicquid ipse praestitit et honorans quod ipse perfecit?" (Id., *Ep.* 76,4 [CCL, 3C], p. 613).

186. Ambrose was deeply influenced by the Greek theological tradition, especially by Origen, Eusebius of Caesarea, Basil the Great, Didymus the Blind, and, to a lesser extent, by Athanasius, Cyril of Jerusalem and Gregory of Nazianzus. See E. DASSMANN, *Ambrosius von Mailand*, in *TRE* 2 (1978) 362-386, p. 374. Ambrose acted also as a go-between: "Neben Hilarius von Poitiers… ist Ambrosius damit der wichtigste Vermittler griechischer Theologie für das Abendland geworden" (*Ibid.*).

187. "Ebenso bleiben zustimmung und Mitwirken des menschen von der Hilfe Gottes getragen, wenngleich Ambrosius nicht versucht, die Art und Weise der Einwirkung Gottes auf den Willen des Menschen näher zu erklären, und die Fähigkeit des menschlichen Willens bisweilen stark hervorhebt" (ID., *Die Frömmigkeit des Kirchenvaters Ambrosius von Mailand. Quellen und Entfaltung* [MBT, 29], Münster Westfalen, 1965, p. 284). This is mainly due to the fact that the ethical aspect of the truth (rather than the speculative one) plays an important part in his teaching, often expressed in a context of preaching: "Der voluntarische Charakter seiner Ethik bestimmt auch seine Gnadenlehre. Der Grund dafür liegt zum Teil in der Art der ambrosianischen Darstellung. Wird doch die populäre Sittenpredigt, wenn man sie nüchtern auf ihre theologischen Konsequenzen untersucht, semipelagianische Tendenzen kaum vermeiden, weil sie pointiert und verkürzt ihre Anliegen ohne Hinzufügung des theologischen Hintergrundes aussprechen muß" (*Ibid.*, p. 291).

viceversa[188], so that it looks as though one pole is highlighted at the expense of the other. For instance, whereas in some passages he states that free will gives us either a propensity to virtue or an inclination to sin[189], and that the Lord's grace of salvation only comes to and co-operates with those who make some efforts[190], in other passages he stresses the gratuity of God's grace saying that it is not bestowed on man to reward his merits, but according to the will of God alone[191]. Moreover, considering the Old Testament law as *annuntiatrix Christi,* he lays such a strong emphasis on human action vis-à-vis law and grace that the latter seems to be a mere help to man's moral struggle[192]. Somewhere else, instead, Ambrose states that justification takes place only through grace[193] and in a context of faith, thanks to which man opens up to the reality of God. Again, it is the action of grace that delivers man from sin[194] and makes him holy through the renewal of his innermost being. Important in this regard is the tie that exists between the action of the Holy Spirit and the understanding of grace[195], calling attention to the

188. Cf., for instance: "Qui uult igitur manu Christi leuari ante ipse euolet, habeat pennas suas – qui fugit saeculum pennas habet – et si suas non habet – ne forte ille solus habeat suas qui potestatem habet uolandi – si suas inquam non habet, ab eo qui habet accipiat" (Ambrose, *De fuga saeculi* 5,30 [CSEL, 32/2], pp. 187-188).

189. "Voluntate arbitra, siue ad uirtutem propendimus, siue ad culpam inclinamur" (Id., *De Iacob et uita beata* 1,1 [CSEL, 32/2], p. 3).

190. Cf., for instance: "Domini uirtus studiis cooperatur humanis" (Id., *Expositio euangelii secundum Lucam* 2,84 [CCL, 14], p. 68). See also Id., *Expositio de psalmo* 118, litt. 12,13 (CSEL, 62), pp. 258-259; *De Abraham* 2,74 (CSEL, 32/1), p. 628.

191. "Sic gratia Domini non quasi ex mercedis merito, sed quasi ex uoluntate defertur" (Id., *Exhortatio uirginitatis* 7,43, *Opera omnia di Sant'Ambrogio* [ed. GORI] 14/2, p. 232).

192. Commenting on the healing of the woman who had been ill for eighteen years, Ambrose interprets the number "eighteen" (10+8) as an indication of both the perfection of the law and the fullness of grace brought about by baptism: "Nec aliter curari potuisset haec mulier nisi quia legem inpleuit et gratiam, legem in praeceptis, in lauacro gratiam, per quam mortui saeculo resurgimus Christo; nam in decem uerbis legis perfectio est, in octauo numero resurrectionis est plenitudo" (Id., *Expositio euuangelii secundum Lucam* 7,173 [CCL, 14], p. 274).

193. "Venit ad Abraham, uenit ad Moysen, uenit ad Mariam, hoc est uenit in signaculo, uenit in lege, uenit in corpore. Aduentum eius ex beneficiis recognoscimus: alibi purificatio, alibi sanctificatio, alibi iustificatio est. Circumcisio purificauit, sanctificauit lex, iustificauit gratia" (*Ibid.,* 7,166, p. 271).

194. In this regard, Ambrose calls the redemptive action of baptism the grace of the initial conversion which he explains by the scriptural words: *A Deo praeparatur uoluntas hominum* (Pr. 8,35, LXX): cf. *Ibid.,* 1,10, p. 12.

195. Cf., for instance: "Non ergo sanctus spiritus de substantia corporalium; hic enim corporalibus incoream infundit gratiam. Sed nec de substantia invisibilium creaturarum est; nam et illae sanctificationem huius accipiunt et per hunc reliquis mundi operibus antecellunt" (Id., *De Spiritu sancto* 1,5,62 [CSEL, 79], p. 41); "An non bonus spiritus, qui bonos de pessimis facit, peccatum abolet, malum delet, crimen excludit, bonum munus infundit, de persecutoribus apostolos fecit, de peccatoribus sacerdotes?" (*Ibid.* 1,5,71, p. 45).

sealing of the soul by the Holy Spirit and the indwelling of the Triune God as the highest goals of Christian life[196].

Jerome, although not so much inclined to speculative theology, was involved in the discussion around the reality of grace during the first part of the Pelagian controversy. As a biblical theologian he takes up the distinction made by Paul between the justice of the law and the grace of the gospel[197], and highlighting the power of divine mercy, he points out that man's justice and virtue are not something earned by human power but are God's gift[198]. Having assessed the necessity of grace in the process of salvation, Jerome speaks also of man's free will and his meritorious works in relation to and in co-operation with grace. Upholding the traditional belief that man was indeed created by God endowed with free will, he maintains the view that man has the power to act freely, and that he does not lie under the dominion of necessity[199]. The way he formulates such a relationship between grace and free will seems to point to grace as a help offered to man in his daily struggle for the good, and not necessarily as the source or the inspiration that lies at the basis of the struggle itself[200].

A renewed emphasis on the place and role of human free will, its ethical responsibility and its relevance vis-à-vis the agency of divine grace, was strongly advocated by Pelagianism. In the next paragraph we shall briefly examine the way Pelagius and Julian of Aeclanum considered the question, and the challenge that their view raised with regard to Augustine's doctrine. Within the framework of this chapter, we deem it sufficient to recall their position by presenting it in a systematic way, rather than in a historical and chronological one[201].

196. Cf. *Ibid.*, 1,6,76-80, pp. 47-48.

197. "Legis iustitia ad comparationem Euangelicae gratiae non uideatur esse iustitia" (Jerome, *Dialogi contra Pelagianos* 1,16 [CCL, 80], pp. 20-21).

198. Referring to Tit 3,5-6, Jerome writes: "Bonitas enim et misericordia Saluatoris nostri non ex operibus iustitiae quae fecimus, sed secundum misericordiam suam saluos fecit nos, ut, iustificati illius gratia, haeredes simus iuxta fidem uitae aeternae" (*Ibid.*, 2,10, p. 67).

199. "Deus autem aequali cunctos sorte generauit et dedit arbitrii libertatem, ut faciat unusquisque, quod uult, siue bonum siue malum" (Id., *Ep.* 120,10 [CSEL, 55], p. 503). "Liberi arbitrii nos condidit Deus, nec ad virtutes, nec ad vitia necessitate trahimur. Alioquin ubi necessitas, nec corona est" (Id., *Aduersus Iouinianum* 2,3 [PL, 23], c. 299).

200. "Vbi autem misericordia et gratia est, liberum ex parte cessat arbitrium, quod in eo tantum est, ut uelimus atque cupiamus et placitis tribuamus assensum; iam in Domini potestate est, ut quod cupimus, laboramus ac nitimur, illius ope et auxilio implere ualeamus" (Id., *Dialogi contra Pelagianos* 3,10 [CCL, 80], p. 111).

201. For the historical context and the course of Pelagianism, see O. WERMELINGER, *Rom und Pelagius. Die theologische Position der römischen Bischöfe im pelagianischen Streit in der Jahren 411-432* (PuP, 7), Stuttgart, 1975, *passim*; G. BONNER, *St Augustine*

4. PELAGIANISM VERSUS AUGUSTINIANISM

Modern scholars have become increasingly sensitive, and rightly so, about the over-simplification which considers Pelagius the "eponymous founder"[202] of both an ascetic movement and a heresy. In point of fact, Pelagianism involved various persons[203] at different times and at different levels, and such persons – like Rufinus the Syrian[204], Caelestius[205] and Julian of Aeclanum[206] – often held more definite views than Pelagius himself[207]. As it has been pointed out, whereas Pelagius' chief concern, based on an optimistic notion of free choice and human nature, was with Christian practice, "the others took a more speculative interest in the *consequences* and the *preconditions* of free choice", making of Pelagianism "a symbiosis of these two distinct sets of concerns"[208].

The main intuition of Pelagianism as a whole is undoubtedly the emphasis laid on the goodness and strength of human nature, on free will and on the quality of man's personal commitment and responsibility in

of Hippo. Life and controversies, London, 1963, 2nd ed., Norwich, 1986, pp. 312-351; ID., *Pelagius/Pelagianischer Streit*, in *TRE* 26 (1996) 176-185; E. TESELLE, *Pelagius, Pelagianism*, in A.D. FITZGERALD (ed.), *Augustine through the Ages. An Encyclopedia*, Grand Rapids, MI – Cambridge, 1999, pp. 633-640.

202. "Since Jerome and Augustine in the fifth century, theologians have lumped both heresy and movement under the same name and treated Pelagius as the eponymous founder of both. From the early fifth to the late twentieth century he has fallen victim to over-simplification and culpable misinterpretation" (B. REES, *Pelagius. A Reluctant Heretic*, Woodbridge, 1988, p. xi).

203. See F.G. NUVOLONE, *Pélage et Pélagianisme. I: Les écrivains*, in *DSp* 12/2 (1986) 2889-2923; O. WERMELINGER, *Neuere Forschungskontroversen um Augustinus und Pelagius*, in C. MAYER – K.H. CHELIUS (eds.), *Internationales Symposion über den Stand der Augustinus-Forschung. Vom 12. bis 16. April 1987 im Schloß Rauischholzhausen der Justus-Liebig-Universität Gießen* (Cass., 39/1), Würzburg, 1989, pp. 204-216.

204. See E. TESELLE, *Rufinus the Syrian, Caelestius, Pelagius: Explorations in the Prehistory of the Pelagian Controversy*, in *AugSt* 3 (1972) 61-95; NUVOLONE, *Pélage et Pélagianisme. I: Les écrivains* (n. 203), cc. 2890-2891.

205. See *Ibid.*, cc. 2891-2895; G. BONNER, *Caelestius*, in *AugL* 1 (1986) 693-698; G. HONNAY, *Caelestius, discipulus Pelagii*, in *Aug(L)* 44 (1994) 271-302; M. LAMBERIGTS, *Caelestius*, in FITZGERALD (ed.), *Augustine through the Ages* (n. 201), pp. 114-115; C. and L. PIETRI (eds.), *Caelestius*, in *Prosopographie chrétienne du Bas-Empire. 2. Prosopographie de l'Italie chrétienne (313-604)*, Vol. I: *A-K*, Rome, 1999, pp. 357-375.

206. See NUVOLONE, *Pélage et Pélagianisme. I: Les écrivains* (n. 203), cc. 2902-2908; M. LAMBERIGTS, *Julian of Eclanum*, in FITZGERALD (ed.), *Augustine through the Ages* (n. 201), pp. 478-479; C. and L. PIETRI (eds.), *Iulianus 9*, in *Prosopographie chrétienne du Bas-Empire. 2. Prosopographie de l'Italie chrétienne* (n. 205), pp. 1175-1186.

207. As Bonner rightly affirms, the Pelagians were not "a party with a rigidly defined doctrinal system; they were a mixed group, united by certain theological principles which nevertheless left the individual free to develop his own opinions upon particular topics" (G. BONNER, *'Rufinus of Syria and African Pelagianism'*, in *AugSt* 1 [1970] 31-47, p. 31).

208. TESELLE, *Pelagius, Pelagianism* (n. 201), pp. 633-640.

his striving for perfection[209]. This is well summed up in Pelagius' following words: "God is with us for so long as we are with Him"[210], and: "God would never have commanded something which is impossible"[211], expressions that can be understood as a strong appeal to moral perfectionism. After all, Christ himself, in the Sermon of the Mount (cf. Mt 5,48), had commanded to his disciples nothing less than sanctity and perfection[212], "an injunction –Pelagius' fervent disciple Caelestius would contend – He would not have issued if He had known that what He commanded was not possible to achieve"[213]. The ordering of a commandment implies that it can be obeyed or disobeyed, and whatever attitude man assumes, it is always the outcome of his free choice. Pelagius and Caelestius even envisage the possibility that human beings can live without sin (posse non peccare) thanks to the power that the will has to avoid it[214]. To affirm that they are not able to avoid sin, would be like blaspheming God himself[215].

What really matters in Pelagianism is that man, by virtue of the goodness of his nature[216], made in the image and likeness of God the

209. "Set in the context of human freedom, the Pelagian controversy asked the perennially radical question of the quality of human behaviour" (R. HAIGHT, The Experience and Language of Grace, Dublin, 1979, p. 32).
210. "Deus enim nobiscum est quam diu fuerimus cum illo" (Pelagius, Expositiones XIII epistularum Pauli [in 1 Cor 6,13] [PLS, 1], c. 1197).
211. "Numquam Deus aliquid inpossibile praecepisset" (Id., Ep. de possibilitate non peccandi 4,2 [PLS, 1], c. 1461).
212. "Sed, ut, praeceptum esse, manifestum sit, sanctae legis utamur exemplis. Scriptum est enim: Sancti estote.... Estote perfecti..." (Ibid.).
213. "At enim ait Dominus: estote perfecti, sicut pater uester caelestis perfectus est; quod non praeciperet si sciret fieri non posse quod praecipit" (quoted in Augustine, De peccatorum meritis et remissione et de baptismo paruulorum 2,15,22 [CSEL, 60], p. 94).
214. "Cum autem tam forte, tam firmum ad non peccandum liberum in nobis habeamus arbitrium, quod generaliter naturae humanae creator inseruit, rursus pro inaestimabili eius benignitate cotidiano ipsius munimur auxilio" (Pelagius, De libero arbitrio, quoted in Augustine, De gratia Christi et de peccato originali 1,28,29 [CSEL, 42], p. 148). Cf. also Pelagius, De natura, quoted in Augustine, De natura et gratia 8; 11; 51; 69 (CSEL, 60), pp. 237-238; 239-240; 271; 285. "Iterum quaerendum est peccatum uoluntatis an necessitatis est. Si necessitatis est, peccatum non est; si uoluntatis est, uitari potest" (Caelestius, Definitiones, quoted in Augustine, De perfectione iustitiae hominis 2,2, [CSEL, 42], p. 4). See also Augustine, De peccatorum meritis et remissione et de baptismo paruulorum 2,6,7 (CSEL, 60), p. 77.
215. "Peccatores ideo sumus. Non quia non possumus sed quia nolumus vitare peccatum per neglegentiam nostram. Si enim dixero quia non possum [vitare peccatum] Deum blasphemabo" (Expositio fidei catholicae [PLS, 1], c. 1685). "Expositio haec, quam conscripsit Pelagianus ignotus, Libelli fidei Juliano Aeclanensi adscripti valde similis est" (A. HAMMAN [ed.], PLS, 1, c. 1680). Cf. also Pelagius, Ep. ad Adolescentem 2 (PLS, 1), cc. 1375-1376.
216. This fundamental principle of Pelagian doctrine, based on the biblical doctrine of man created in the image of God, is one of the key concepts of Pelagius' letter to Deme-

Creator[217], can indeed tend "naturally" to the good and can choose, responsibly and through the exercise of his freedom (which is not merely a neutral datum), the right course of action. In the Pelagian view the goodness of human nature, its faculties and possibilities (the *posse*), is what actually constitutes God's first grace to man[218], a grace which, based upon an optimistic theology of man's creation, can be described as a "natural" grace[219]. Any disparagement of human nature would be simultaneously regarded as a disparagement of grace. The possibilities inherent in human nature (the *posse*) constitute, in fact, an "ontological datum": they are a gift of God the creator. Any other (external) intervention of God, has a role of mere incitement[220], for grace is primarily attached to the goodness of man's nature (*naturae bonum*). Endowed with a free will as well as with a *sanitas*[221], the human being is able to discern what is good and what is evil. This characteristic of man's nature is what constitutes the fundamental form of grace[222].

Obviously Pelagius did not deny that the natural faculties of man (more specifically his freedom and his capability of doing good) were somehow damaged by the fall, but he ruled out that they were compromised to the point of being deprived of their creational qualities. Since

---

trias: "Quoties mihi de institutione morum et sanctae vitae conversatione dicendum est, soleo prius *humanae naturae vim qualitatemque* [*Italic mine*] monstrare et quid efficere possit, ostendere: ac iam inde audientis animum ad species incitare virtutum: ne nihil prosit ad ea vocari quae forte sibi impossibilia esse praesumpserit... Primum itaque debes naturae humanae bonum de eius auctore metiri, Deo scilicet, qui cum universa mundi, et quae intra mundum sunt, opera bona, et valde bona fecisse referatur: quanto, putas, praestantiorem ipsum hominem fecit: propter quem omnia etiam intelligitur illa condidisse! Quem dum *ad imaginem et similitudinem suam* facere disposuit, antequam faciat, qualem esset facturus ostendit" (Id., *Ep. ad Demetriadem* 2 [PL, 30], cc. 16-17). See GRESHAKE, *Gnade als konkrete Freiheit* (n. 19), pp. 54-80.

217. Cf. Augustine, *De gestis Pelagii* 31,56 (CSEL, 42), p. 110.

218. Cf. Id., *De gratia Christi et de peccato originali* 1,35,38 (CSEL, 42), p. 154.

219. "Pélage – writes Lancel – était positivement 'naturaliste'; il pensait que Dieu avait crée en l'homme une nature bonne, exempte de péché, dotée d'un libre arbitre qui permettait à la créature humaine de choisir entre le bien et le mal" (S. LANCEL, *Saint Augustin*, Paris, 1999, pp. 470-471).

220. "Venire *[ad Christum]* posse in natura ponit Pelagius uel etiam,..., in gratia,..., 'qua ipsa', ut dicit, 'possibilitas' adiuuatur" (Pelagius, *De libero arbitrio*, quoted in Augustine, *De gratia Christi et de peccato originali* 1,14,15 [CSEL, 42], p. 138).

221. Pelagius refused the idea of a permanent *aegritudo animi* which would point to the inability of doing anything good without the intervention of divine grace (cf. Pelagius, *De natura*, in Augustine, *De natura et gratia* 19,21-21,23 [CSEL, 60], pp. 246-248 *passim*). See J.B. VALERO, *Las bases antropologicas de Pelagio en su tratado de las Expositiones* (Estudios, 18), Madrid, 1980, pp. 198-201; 244ff.

222. See J. LÖSSL, *Intellectus gratiae. Die erkenntnistheoretische und hermeneutische Dimension der Gnadenlehre Augustins von Hippo* (SVigChr, 38), Leiden-New York-Cologne, 1997, pp. 245ff.

man was created in the image of God, it was his presupposition that human nature could not be utterly compromised, and that despite the fall it remained *capax Dei*. For that reason God never ceases to come to the help of man through the manifold events of the history of salvation, whose apex is represented by the life, teaching and example of Jesus Christ. All these events are aimed at revitalising man's wounded liberty by challenging it in an even deeper involvement in the universal process of salvation. In other words, where there is man there too is grace, because human nature itself is a manifestation of grace[223].

Besides the ontological capabilities of human nature, as the fundamental form of grace, there follows a grace which can be identified with the *adiutorium* (or *auxilium/cura*)[224] which divine benevolence gives to man in order to accomplish good works more easily (*facilius*). According to Pelagius there are several features which illustrate concretely the agency of such grace. It is, for instance, identified with both the Mosaic law and the new Law of Jesus Christ, viz. with the Old Testament and the New testament. The saving value of the Mosaic law is affirmed by Pelagius several times in his *Expositiones*. Interpreting the passage of Rom 7,6-25 as speaking of the man *sub lege*, Pelagius affirms that the Mosaic law is holy[225], although he admits that the Law of Christ is superior because the life and teaching of Jesus have unveiled what was hidden in the Mosaic law[226]. Both Testaments, however, constitute a grace of salvation in that the divine revelation that they transmit helps man to know God's will and to observe his commandments[227]. Another feature

223. See GRESHAKE, *Gnade als konkrete Freiheit* (n. 19), pp. 245ff.

224. "Pro inaestimabili eius benignitate cotidiano ipsius munimur auxilio.... Quod per liberum homines facere iubentur arbitrium, faciliunt possint implere per gratiam" (Pelagius, *De libero arbitrio*, quoted in Augustine, *De gratia Christi et de peccato originali* 1,28,29 [CSEL, 42], pp. 148-149). Bohlin speaks of these two aspects of grace by referring to them respectively as "Gnade I A und B" (T. BOHLIN, *Die Theologie des Pelagius und ihre Genesis* [AUU, 9], Upsala, 1957, p. 19).

225. "Contra impugnatores legis et contra eos qui iustitiam a bonitate secernunt, lex [et] bona et sancta dicitur et gratia iusta" (Pelagius, *Expositiones XIII epistularum Pauli* [in Rom 7,12] [SPL, 1], c. 1143).

226. *Ibid.* (in Rom 3,21) (SPL, 1), c. 1128; see also Id., *Ep. ad Demetriadem* 5-7, (PL, 30), cc. 19-22; GRESHAKE, *Gnade als konkrete Freiheit* (n. 19), pp. 93-100. Bohlin speaks here of Grace II A (Mosaic law) and II B (Law of Christ) (cf. BOHLIN, *Die Theologie des Pelagius und ihre Genesis* [n. 224], pp. 26-28).

227. The *praecepta* of the two Laws/Testaments must not be regarded as merely the object of a notional knowledge, as Augustine seems to have understood Pelagius' position in that regard (cf. *e.g.* Augustine, *De spiritu et littera* 2,4-3,5 [CSEL, 60], p. 157). The two Laws do not simply offer an external doctrine. They are also meant to instruct and stimulate the inner man and to push him, with the help of concrete examples, to adhere to virtues, especially to charity. See GRESHAKE, *Gnade als konkrete Freiheit* (n. 19), pp. 115-125; A. SOLIGNAC, *Pélage et Pélagianisme. II. Le mouvement et sa doctrine*, in

assumed by grace is that of baptism, by which adult men are delivered from the *acts* of past sins[228]. Against the background of the ontological goodness of human nature, that cannot be taken away, sin is but an *act*, affirms Pelagius, and as such it does not have any substance[229]. If sin, including the sin of Adam, is but an act, it means that it is an "accident", and as such it cannot engender other sins, nor vitiate human nature to the point of jeopardizing the will's possibilities of choosing the good. It follows that it is only on the level of his acts that man needs reconciling with God[230]. Thus, in baptism man dies to the *consuetudo* of the sins whose effects are destroyed, and is enabled to lead a new life in that the baptismal grace restores him to his original capacity for good. If under the ancient law Abraham obtained the remission of sins because of his faith, now baptism gives access into a new life and a perfect justice[231]. Moreover, he who receives baptism worthily and lets himself be taken by its significance through a real and personal conversion (by which he nails his vices to the cross), will not experience fleshy concupiscence any longer[232]. Finally, there are other ways through which grace can operate, as, for instance, through the example and teaching of Jesus as well as of the saints who lived in a just and sinless manner[233]; through

DSp 12/2 (1986) 2923-2936, c. 2928. According to Pelagius the rational knowledge must go hand in hand with the concrete adhesion of life. This is confirmed by the following passage concerning the *lectio diuina*: "Ita Scripturas sacras lege, ut semper memineris Dei illa verba esse, qui legem suam non solum sciri, sed etiam impleri iubet. Nihil enim prodest facienda didicisse, et non facere" (Pelagius, *Ep. ad Demetriadem* 23, [PL, 30], c. 37).

228. In the case of infants, baptism was regarded as a sanctification, in the sense that they were believed to be aggregated to the new people of God. See GRESHAKE, *Gnade als konkrete Freiheit* (n. 19), pp. 81-92.

229. "Unde ante omnia quaerendum puto quid sit peccatum: substantia aliqua an omnino substantia carens nomen, quo non res, non existentia, non corpus aliquod, sed perperam facti actus exprimitur" (Pelagius, *De natura*, quoted in Augustine, *De natura et gratia* 19,21 [CSEL, 60], p. 246).

230. "Inimici ergo actibus non natura: reconciliati autem [ideo] quia conciliati naturaliter fueramus" (Pelagius, *Expositiones XIII epistularum Pauli* [in Rom 5,10] [PLS, 1], cc. 1135-1136). Sin is to man as a guest or a stranger; it is something accidental, not natural: "Habitat quasi hospes et quasi aliut *(sic!)* in alio, non quasi unum, ut accidens scilicet, non naturale" (*Ibid.* [in Rom 7,17], c. 1144). "En bref, – writes Solignac – pour Pélage, la *nature*, prise comme une essence immuable, reste indépendante de *l'histoire* de la personne" (A. SOLIGNAC, *Autour du De Natura de Pélage*, in M. SOETARD [ed.], *Valeurs dans le stoïcisme. Du Portique à nos jours* [Textes rassemblés en hommage à Michel Spanneut], Lille, 1993, pp. 181-192, p. 184).

231. According to Bohlin we have here respectively Grace III A and Grace III B (cf. BOHLIN, *Die Theologie des Pelagius und ihre Genesis* [n. 224], pp. 32-33).

232. "Si omnia simul uitia cruci fixa sunt, et caro, quasi pendens in ligno, non concupiscit" (Pelagius, *Expositiones XIII epistularum Pauli* [in Gal 5,24] [SPL, 1], c. 1286).

233. From fragments of the *De natura* and the *De libero arbitrio* Pelagius appears to be cautious about the existence *de facto* of sinless people. He limits himself to admit the

the bestowal of the Holy Spirit upon those who seek God's commandments with purity of heart; through the justification of heathen people through faith[234].

Another interesting feature of Pelagius' teaching is his allusion to the action of divine grace as being needed in any individual human act (*ad singulos actus*)[235], a belief of which Pelagius, through common friends[236], had informed Augustine even after his condemnation in 418[237]. Although he does not fully explain what he really means by this expression, we may infer that Pelagius was simply thinking of an *adiutorium* offered by God to man's freedom of choice. Such inferring seems to be corroborated by a subtle and noteworthy distinction that he makes between the *possibilitas* (or *posse*) and both the *uoluntas* (or *uelle*) and the *actio* (or *esse*)[238]. Whereas the *uoluntas* and the *actio* are existential developments of man's freedom, the *possibilitas*, as we have already underlined, is an ontological datum, resting on the fact that human nature is endowed with goodness by God's act of creation[239]. Thus, the

---

possibility of human beings living in a holy, just and sinless way (cf. Augustine, *De natura et gratia* 35,41 [CSEL, 60], p. 263). Nonetheless Pelagius names several people, *e.g.* Abel, Enoch, Joseph [the husband of the Virgin Mary] among men; and Deborah, Ann, Elizabeth and the Virgin Mary herself among women. These people, according to him, have *de facto* lived sinlessly and justly ("Qui non modo non peccasse, uerum etiam iuste uixisse referuntur": *Ibid.* 36,42, p. 263).

234. See GRESHAKE, *Gnade als konkrete Freiheit* (n. 19), pp. 143-147; 247-252; BOHLIN, *Die Theologie des Pelagius und ihre Genesis* (n. 224), pp. 10-45.

235. "Nunc uero cum *[Pelagius]* anathematizat eos qui gratiam Dei et adiutorium non ad singulos actus dicunt dari, sed in libero arbitrio esse uel in lege atque doctrina, satis euidenter apparet eam illum dicere gratiam, quae in Christi Ecclesia praedicatur, quae subministratione sancti Spiritus datur, ut ad nostros actus singulos adiuuemur.... Ecce anathematizat qui hoc sentiunt, ecce nec naturam liberi arbitrii nec legem atque doctrinam uult intellegi gratiam, qua per actus singulos adiuuamur" (Augustine, *De gestis Pelagii* 14,31 [CSEL, 42], p. 85). Cf. also Id., *Ep.* 217,6,18 (CSEL, 57), p. 417.

236. Albina, Melania the Younger and Pinianus.

237. See Pelagius' words reported to Augustine by Albina, Melania and Pinianus, and recorded by the bishop of Hippo in his *De gratia Christi et de peccato originali*: "Anathemo qui uel sentit uel dicit gratiam Dei, qua Christus uenit in hunc mundum peccatores saluos facere, non solum per singulas horas aut per singula momenta, sed etiam per singulos actus nostros non esse necessariam et qui hanc conantur auferre poenas sortiantur aeternas" (Id., *De gratia Christi et de peccato originali* 1,2,2 [CSEL, 42], p. 125).

238. "Denique gratia Dei non ista duo, quae nostra omnino uult esse, id est uoluntatem et actionem, sed illam, quae in potestate nostra non est et nobis ex Deo est, id est possibilitatem, perhibet adiuuari, tamquam illa quae nostra sunt, hoc est uoluntas et actio, tam sint ualentia ad declinandum a malo et faciendum bonum, ut diuino adiutorio non indigeant, illud uero, quod nobis ex Deo est, hoc sit inualidum, id est possibilitas, ut semper gratiae adiuuetur auxilio" (Pelagius, *De libero arbitrio*, quoted in Augustine, *De gratia Christi et de peccato originali* 1,3,4 [CSEL, 42], p. 127).

239. "Posse in natura, uelle in arbitrio, esse in effectu locamus. Primum illud, id est posse, ad Deum proprie pertinet, qui illud creaturae suae contulit; duo uero reliqua, hoc

possibilitas, or man's natural capability, remains unaltered, even when it does not issue in *uoluntas* and *actio*, namely in a "voluntary action". In such a distinction, we perceive again Pelagius' understanding of grace as being primarily a "fundamental" grace inherent in human nature and not extrinsically added to it. Bestowed by God through the creation of man, this grace is an integral part of the latter's nature, and as such it cannot be thought to affect, from without, the autonomous exercise of human free will, viz. the crucial principle upon which Pelagius' "theological anthropology" depends.

Pelagius underlines vigorously that also the freedom of man to will and act upon his own decisions is a fundamental value belonging to human nature. Man was created with such intelligence and spiritual strength (*intellectum uigoremque mentis*) that he is enabled to exercise his sovereignty over animals, to know his Creator and to serve him willingly and without constraint[240]. According to Pelagius, human freedom is rooted in a "voluntary nature", namely on the will's natural constitution as a created entity, endowed at the moment of creation with a "natural" (created) openness to either good or evil[241]. In accordance with this principle, Pelagius quotes, with preference, scriptural passages which emphasize the freedom and responsibility of man, such as the following: *Deus ab initio constituit hominem et reliquit eum in manu consilii sui (...) Apposuit tibi aquam et ignem; ad quod uis, porrige manum tuam* (Eccl 15,14.17). Moreover, beside man's *posse*, viz. his capability of being what he wishes to be[242], Pelagius insists on the *possibilitas boni*

est uelle et esse ad hominem referenda sunt, quia de arbitrii fonte descendunt. Ergo in uoluntate et opere bono laus hominis est, immo et hominis et Dei, qui ipsius uoluntatis et operis possibilitatem dedit, quique ipsam possibilitatem gratiae suae adiuuat semper auxilio" (*Ibid.*, 1,4,5, p. 128).

240. "Quem inermem extrinsecus fecerat, melius intus armavit: ratione scilicet atque prudentia, ut per intellectum vigoremque mentis, quo caeteris praestabat animalibus, factorem omnium solus agnosceret: et inde serviret Deo, unde aliis dominabatur. Quem tamen iustitiae exsecutorem Dominus voluntarium esse voluit, non coactum. Et ideo reliquit eum in manu consilii sui. Posuitque ante eum vitam et mortem, bonum et malum" (Pelagius, *Ep. ad Demetriadem* 2 [PL, 30], c. 17).

241. "De qua possibilitate Pelagius in libro primo pro libero arbitrio ita loquitur: 'habemus autem', inquit, 'possibilitatem utriusque partis a Deo insitam uelut quandam, ut ita dicam, radicem fructiferam atque fecundam, quae ex uoluntate hominis diuersa gignat et pariat et quae possit ad proprii cultoris arbitrium uel nitere flore uirtutum uel sentibus horrere uitiorum" (Id., *De libero arbitrio*, quoted in Augustine, *De gratia Christi et de peccato originali* 1,18,19 [CSEL, 42], p. 140).

242. "Volens namque Deus rationabilem creaturam voluntarii boni munere et liberi arbitrii potestate donare: utriusque partis possibilitatem homini inserendo, proprium eius fecit esse quod velit, ut boni ac mali capax, naturaliter utrumque posset: et ad alterutrum voluntatem deflecteret.... Licet... nobis eligere, refutare, probare, respuere" (Pelagius, *Ep. ad Demetriadem* 3 [PL, 30], cc. 17-18). See GRESHAKE, *Gnade als konkrete Freiheit*

that God has bestowed on human nature as a constitutive aspect of its essence[243]. Such possibility points to the fact that an equal option for goodness or evil is not merely an arbitrary or indifferent choice, as if the will could somehow be located *in medio*, viz. in a neutral position. The ambivalence, which is there before a choice is made, is in fact overcome by the "perception" of an original inclination towards what is good and holy. Such an inclination is part of man's nature, and makes itself manifest through the discernment of the effects felt after a particular choice has been made. According to Pelagius it is as though a "natural sanctity" (*naturalis quaedam sanctitas*), presiding in the mind's citadel, judges the good and the evil[244]. In today's language we could speak of man's conscience acting as a sort of psychological "detector" thanks to which the outcome of a choice that has been made is judged upon: a sense of assuring endurance in the case of a good choice or a sense of remorse, fear and sadness in the case of an evil choice.

Finally, we must underline that a very close link exists between Pelagius' doctrine of free will and the approach of the Eastern theologians,

---

(n. 19), pp. 58ff. That everyone is capable, by nature, of making moral choices, is also witnessed by the moral life of pagans, whose conduct could be at times an example even for the Christian believers: "Cuius bonum ita generaliter cunctis institutum est, ut in gentilibus quoque hominibus, qui sine ullo cultu Dei sunt, se nonnumquam ostendat, ac proferat. Quam multos enim philosophorum et audivimus et legimus, et ipsi vidimus castos, patientes, modestos, liberales, abstinentes, benignos, et honores mundi simul, et delicias respuentes, et amatores iustitiae non minus quam scientiae! Unde, quaeso, hominibus alienis a Deo placent? Unde autem illis bona nisi de naturae bono? Et cum ista, quae dixi, vel omnia in uno, vel singula in singulis haberi videamus, cum omnium natura una sit, exemplo suo invicem sibi ostendunt, omnia in omnibus esse posse, quae vel omnia in omnibus, vel singula in singulis inveniantur. Quod si etiam sine Deo homines ostendunt, quales a Deo facti sunt: vide quid Christiani facere possunt, quorum in melius per Christum natura et vita instructa est: et qui divinae quoque gratiae iuvantur auxilio" (Pelagius, *Ep. ad Demetriadem* 3 [PL, 30], c. 18).

243. See Augustine, *De gratia Christi et de peccato originali* 1,3,4 (CSEL, 42), p. 127. In Pelagius' view, this argument counteracts Augustine's doctrine of original sin, which Pelagius considered destructive of the natural capability of the will's goodness. Pelagius held the belief that free will could not possibly have perished because of Adam's sin (see Augustine, *Contra duas epistulas Pelagianorum* 1,15,29 [CSEL, 60], p. 447). Augustine strongly objected to the Pelagian use of the expression *possibilitas boni* conceived as a natural endowment bestowed upon man at the moment of creation. This *possibilitas*, argues Augustine, perished with Adam's fall, and Christ's redemption alone could give it back to the fallen moral agent. Only then could the latter, delivered from evil tendencies, again choose goodness effectively. Cf. Id., *De natura et gratia* 2,2-3,3 (CSEL, 60), pp. 234-235; *De correptione et gratia* 12,37-38 (CSEL 92), pp. 264ff.

244. "Est enim... in animis nostris naturalis quaedam (ut ita dixerim) sanctitas: quae par velut in arce animi praesidens, exercet mali bonique iudicium: et ut honestis rectisque actibus favet: ita sinistra opera condemnat, atque ad conscientiae testimonium diversas partes domestica quadam lege diiudicat" (Pelagius, *Ep. ad Demetriadem* 4 (PL, 30), c. 19).

above all that of Origen[245]. A parallel can even be drawn between Origen's defence of free will vis-à-vis the theories of both Stoic fatalism[246] and Gnostic determinism, on one side, and on the other Pelagius' emphatic reassertion of human freedom in the face of Manichaean fatalism[247] and the Augustinian concept of sovereign grace that seemed to

245. What Kelly has said about Origen (see *supra* n. 70) holds also for Pelagius: "The keystone of his *[Pelagius']* whole system is the idea of unconditional free-will and responsibility" (KELLY, *Early Christian Doctrines* [n. 70], p. 357). In his turn Bostock affirms: "The doctrine of free-will, so clearly formulated by Origen, evoked a ready response from the monastic movement and from Pelagius in particular, seen as a moral reformer within the monastic tradition, but aroused controversy because of its radical implications as these were articulated by Origen and developed by Pelagius. The history of the attack on Pelagianism is effectively the history of the attack on the implications of Origen's core-doctrine of human free-will" (G. BOSTOCK, *The Influence of Origen on Pelagius and Western Monasticism*, in W.A. BIENERT – U. KÜHNEWEG [eds.], *Origeniana Septima. Origenes in den Auseinandersetzungen des 4. Jahrhunderts* [BETL, 137], Louvain, 1999, 381-396, p. 381). We believe that such a "conceptual link" was not merely accidental or unconscious, since we gather that Pelagius was able to have access to some of Origen's works thanks to the translation provided by Rufinus of Aquileia. This represented, in fact, the "material link" in the line that, starting with Origen, reached down to Pelagius. "Of especial significance were the links between Pelagius and Rufinus, when the latter came to Rome in 398. It was through Rufinus of course that Pelagius read Origen's work the *De principiis* and such writings as Origen's commentary on Romans which greatly influenced his own commentary" (*Ibid.* p. 383). See H.-I. MARROU, *Les attaches orientales du Pélagianisme*, in *Patristique et Humanisme* [PatSor, 9], Paris, 1976, pp. 341-344 *passim*; P. BROWN, *Pelagius and his Supporters: Aims and Environments*, and *The Patrons of Pelagius: The Roman Aristocracy between East and West*, in ID., *Religion and Society in the Age of St. Augustine*, London, 1972, pp. 183-207; 208-226 *passim*.

246. With regard to Stoicism, however, it must be said that even Pelagius was not outside the reach of its influence on more than one point, particularly on the ethical level. For instance, the idea that human nature is part of a universal nature brought the Stoics to the conclusion that man's destiny is to live according to nature, namely according to the common law or right reason or divine law – all expressions with which nature is identified. For points of contact between Pelagius and Stoicism, see J.B. VALERO, *El estoicismo de Pelagio*, in *EE* 57 (1982) 39-63; A. SOLIGNAC, *Autour du* De Natura de Pélage (n. 230), pp. 188-192. There were also, underlines Solignac, ecclesiological and sociological aspects which encouraged Pelagius' adaptation of some Stoic notions: "Le premier projet de Pélage était celui d'un *réformateur ascétique*; il visait à assurer la qualité de vie chrétienne des membres de l'aristocratie romaine qui se convertissaient alors au christianisme.... Le stoïcisme étant l'idéologie dominante de cette aristocratie, Pélage n'avai pas tort de faire siennes ses exigences morales, après leur avoir donné un solide fondement dans la théologie de la création" (*Ibid.*, p. 192).

247. "Il considerait le déterminisme manichéen comme un danger pour une éthique chrétienne véritable qui, selon lui, ne pouvait seulement exister que dans des composantes pures telles la liberté et la responsabilité garanties" (M. LAMBERIGTS, *Le mal et le péché. Pélage: la réhabilitation d'un hérétique*, in *RHE* 95 [2000] 97-111, p. 102). "Ironically it may have been his reading of the early anti-Manichaean writings of Augustine in the library of Paulinus which first alerted Pelagius to the dangers of Manichaeanism" (BOSTOCK, *The Influence of Origen on Pelagius and Western Monasticism* [n. 245], p. 384, n. 32). See BROWN, *Pelagius and his Supporters* (n. 245), p. 212. Moreover,

annihilate man's free will. Pelagius' teaching on human nature and its countless possibilities supports his conviction that the attainment of virtue and perfection concerns ultimately the free will of man. Ensuing from a "graced" nature, human free will is quite capable (at least in principle) of avoiding sin, fighting against temptations and persevering in a just life. However, the biggest unsolved problem with Pelagius' view, as Augustine had sharply underlined[248], remains how to account for the ultimate significance, the place and role, of Christ's "redemptive" act.

The background of *Julian of Aeclanum*'s theology of grace is also constituted by the goodness of God's creation, the *naturae bonum*. Basing himself on the assumption that Christ too (as the second person of the Trinity) was responsible for creation, Julian would regard Christ's redeeming activity as consisting in the renewal and adoption of men. In fact, He who had made them good (*fecerat bonos*) at the moment of creation, makes them now better (*facit meliores*)[249]. In this context, man's *libertas arbitrii* plays a fundamental role[250]. This is first of all because free will is a *gratia creationis*, viz. the result of God's creating activity whereby man is *a Deo emancipatus* and is given the possibility of abstaining from sinning and of doing good[251]. In fact far from being an

Augustine himself at first "regarded Pelagius as an ally in his championing of the responsibility of the human will against the determinism of Manichean doctrine" (R.A. MARKUS, *Life, Culture, and Controversies of Augustine*, in FITZGERALD [ed.], *Augustine through the Ages* [n. 201], pp. 498-504, p. 504).

248. Cf., for instance, Augustine, *De natura et gratia* 1,1 and 2,2 (CSEL, 60), pp. 233-235. The same problem, however, comes back in Augustine himself. The unique significance of Christ's redemption, although reiterated over and over again, is in fact jeopardized by the bishop of Hippo's theory of predestination (see *infra*, pp. 353-357).

249. "Christus enim, qui est sui operis redemptor, auget circa imaginem suam continua largitate beneficia; et quos fecerat condendo bonos, facit innouando adoptandoque meliores" (Julian of Aeclanum, *Ad Turbantium*, Frag. 16 [CCL, 88], p. 345). Cf. M. LAMBERIGTS, *Julian of Aeclanum on Grace: Some Considerations*, in StPatr 27, Louvain, 1993, pp. 341-349, pp. 342-343; J. Mc W. DEWART, *The Christology of the Pelagian Controversy*, in StPatr 17/3, Oxford, 1982, pp. 1221-1244, pp. 1236-1237.

250. For an overview of Julian's vision on free will, see M. LAMBERIGTS, *De polemiek tussen Julianus van Aeclanum en Augustinus van Hippo. Een bijdrage tot de theologiegeschiedenis van de tweede pelagiaanse controverse (418-430)*, Deel I-Vol. I: *Iulianus van Aeclanum* (unpublished doctoral dissertation, Faculty of Theology, K.U.Leuven), Louvain, 1988, pp. 104ff; J. LÖSSL, *Julian von Aeclanum. Studien zu seinem Leben, seinem Werk, seiner Lehre und ihrer Überlieferung* (SVigChr, 60), Leiden-Boston-Cologne, 2001, pp. 140-146.

251. "Libertas arbitrii, qua a Deo emancipatus homo est, in amittendi peccati et abstinendi a peccato possibilitate consistit" (Julian of Aeclanum, *Ad Florum*, quoted in Augustine, *Contra secundam Iuliani responsionem imperfectum opus* 1,78 [CSEL, 85/1], p. 93).

estrangement *from* God, man's emancipation ought to be regarded as
something brought about *by* divine initiative itself[252]. That man be
endowed with free will is thus the result of the goodness of God's creation. It is a gift of God who, rather than compelling, invites human
nature to obedience and partnership with him. As such, free will will
never be taken away from man[253]. It is an irremovable part of his substance, a *bonum necessarium*[254], in the sense that it cannot be done away
with and that its use remains unaltered, independently of the choices that
are made. The ideal aim of such a gift of free will would of course be that
man might choose good instead of evil. Yet, God does not apply any pressure, nor does He compel man to take this course of action, although He
is always ready to help him and to reward him whenever his choice goes
in the direction of the good. After all the admission of both possibilities of
choice, good or evil, would be the proof that free will really works[255].

At this point, Julian makes a very important distinction between
libertas arbitrii and *uoluntas*. Whereas the former, as we have seen, is
not accidental but belongs to human nature from an ontological point of
view, the latter, being the fruition of the freedom of choice, belongs to
the ethical level. In other words, whereas the *liberum arbitrium* is connected with the *necessitas* (*i.e.* the way God has created man, viz. in his
image and likeness), the *uoluntas* is linked with the *possibilitas*. This
means that the essence of the *libertas arbitrii* remains intact and free
from any pressure (*nullo cogente*)[256], and that only the *uoluntas*, and not
God, must be held responsible for the choices that are made, even in the
case of sin. This, in fact, has to be counted among the various possibilities of the actual fruition of man's own free will. It is precisely because
sin is a "possibility" that its choice and performance on the part of man
cannot cause the good nature of his free will to be stained and blamed[257].

252. "*A Deo* must be translated as by God, not as from God" (LAMBERIGTS, *Julian of Aeclanum on Grace* [n. 249], p. 349). Augustine, on the contrary, had interpreted Julian's use of the word *emancipatio* according to the classical and juridical meaning of it, namely as an estrangement "from" the *patria potestas*. Cf. Augustine, *Contra secundam Iuliani responsionem imperfectum opus* 1,78 (CSEL, 85/1), p. 93.
253. "Confitemur datam a Deo libertatem arbitrii in hominum permanere natura" (Julian of Aeclanum, *Ad Florum* 1,76 [CSEL, 85/1], p. 92).
254. Augustine, *Contra secundam Iuliani responsionem imperfectum opus* 5,59 (PL, 45), c. 1492.
255. "Ut ergo constaret ius boni, admissa est possibilitas mali" (*Ibid.* 5,61, c. 1496). Cf. also *Ibid.* 1,81 (CSEL, 85/1), p. 95.
256. *Ibid.* 5,41 (PL, 45), c. 1477.
257. Cf. *Ibid.* 5,63 (PL, 45), cc. 1500-1501; 1,108 (CSEL, 85/1), p. 127. See LAM-BERIGTS, *De polemiek tussen Julianus van Aeclanus en Augustinus van Hippo* (n. 250), p. 107; J.M. RIST, *Augustine: Ancient Thought Baptized*, Cambridge, 1994, pp. 130ff.

From the above, one can spontaneously infer that there cannot be any place for the doctrine of original sin as it was proposed by Augustine. To agree with his own terms would entail, according to Julian, admitting the destruction of free will, and consequently denying the possibility of leading a moral life. Despite the fall of Adam, continues the Italian divine, the *liberum arbitrium* has not undergone any change, nor does it whenever it leads to sin by choosing evil, because its integrity cannot be undermined[258]. Besides, even after sinning, the *liberum arbitrium* retains the power of shrinking from evil and searching for good instead. Thus to add a *malum congenitum* in human nature, because of Adam's fall, would leave room for man's despair, for he would have to face the sombre awareness of an incapability of meeting the demands of Jesus Christ, together with the grace of liberation attached to Him[259].

What kind of grace, we might ask ourselves at this point, does Julian foresee? Certainly not the sovereign grace supported by Augustine and which "creates", viz. "determines" man's free will. Once again, such grace, according to Julian, would in fact destroy the very existence and meaning of *liberum arbitrium*. Resting on the assumption that free will is the real mark of the goodness of man's nature, a mark of an unrestricted freedom which never fails, Julian tries to relate in a very consistent and rational way the notion of a naturally free man with the notion of divine grace. The latter is described as a *multiplex gratia*[260] which, through countless benefits, shows to man God's benevolence towards him. The principal facets of such divine benevolence are man's creation *ex nihilo*, his being endowed with the rational soul (by which he is made similar to God), his free will, the Law with its deterrent and pedagogical function, and above all the coming of Jesus Christ who takes away the sins of men through the medicinal help of his merciful love. Such manifold grace always remains operative and helps all those who seek the good, but it will never act by stealing the task belonging to free will. On the contrary, it co-operates with it[261].

It follows that Christ's redemptive grace must not be regarded as a "correction" of man's nature, which was in fact created good, but as a help and inspiration to man's moral life[262]. The *gratia Christi* received in baptism, for instance, is, according to Julian, an *auxilium abundantis*

---

258. Cf. Julianus of Aeclanum, *Ad Florum* 1,96 (CSEL, 85/1), p. 111. See M. LAMBERIGTS, *Iulianus IV (Iulianus von Aeclanum)*, in *RAC* 19 (1999) 483-505, cc. 500ff.
259. Cf. Julianus of Aeclanum, *Ad Florum* 1,110 (CSEL, 85/1), p. 129.
260. *Ibid.* 1,94, p. 109.
261. Cf. *Ibid.* 1,95, p. 110.
262. Cf. *Ibid.* 3,154, pp. 457-458.

misericordiae[263]. In the case of adults, this help consists mainly in the remission of personal sins (Julian denied deleterious consequences for humanity because of Adam's fall[264]), whereas in the case of children, who are incapable of sinning, this help has only a positive connotation: it brings about the *illuminatio spiritalis*, the *adoptio filiorum Dei*, the *muncipatus Hierusalem caelestis*, the *sanctificatio atque in Christi membra translatio et possessio regni caelorum*[265]. Moreover, the *gratia Christi* comes to the help of adults in many other ways, supporting their free will and their good will which, rather than being irreparably compromised, had simply lost the knowledge of justice (*conscientia iustitiae*)[266]. Thus, although man remains responsible for his moral activity, God's helping grace is also at work co-operating with him whenever something good is achieved[267].

5. The Constant Elements and the Developing Factors in Augustine's Concept of Grace and Free Will: A Bio-Bibliographical Sketch

If Augustine's thought on the relationship between grace and free will differs from that of Pelagius and Julian of Aeclanum, it is because the perspective from which he tackles this issue is different from the view adopted by his opponents. The basic difference in approach resides in both the concept of the "sin of origin" (or "original sin") and in the model of all-encompassing grace that goes with it, already cultivated by Augustine before the Pelagian controversy broke out. In fact, when he wrote the *De diuersis quaestionibus ad Simplicianum* (396), where the expression *peccatum originale*[268] appears for the first time, he already possessed the doctrines of original sin and of grace[269], the latter reaching

263. *Ibid.* 2,222, p. 335.
264. Cf. M. LAMBERIGTS, *Julien d'Éclane et Augustin d'Hippone. Deux conceptions d'Adam*, in *Aug(L)* [*Mélanges T. J. Van Bavel*, T. I] 40 [1990] 373-410, pp. 373-382.
265. Julianus of Aeclanum, *Ad Florum* 1,53 (CSEL, 85/1), p. 49.
266. *Ibid.* 1,91, p. 104.
267. *Ibid.* 5,48 (PL, 45), c. 1484.
268. Coined by Augustine, such expression appears under his pen while commenting on Rom 7,18 (cf. Id., *De diuersis quaestionibus ad Simplicianum* 1,1,10 [CCL, 44], p. 15). See V.H. DRECOLL, *Die Entstehung der Gnadenlehre Augustins* (BHT, 109), Tübingen, 1999, p. 204.
269. Cf. G. BARDY, *Notes complémentaires*, BA 12, Paris, 1950, p. 576; A. SAGE, *Péché originel. Naissance d'un dogme*, in *REAug* 13 (1967) 211-248, pp. 218ff. Rigby suggests that Augustine's concept of original sin was defined in its essential tenets in the *Confessiones* (cf. P. RIGBY, *Original Sin in Augustine's Confessions*, Ottawa, 1987, p. 7; ID., *Original Sin*, in FITZGERALD [ed.], *Augustine through the Ages* [n. 201], pp. 607-614, p. 608). These two sister doctrines, of original sin and of grace, represent the two faces of the same medal, and it is around them that Augustine's theological system hinges.

out to embrace the *initium fidei* and the *electio/praedestinatio* theory[270]. The Pelagian controversy did have the effect of radicalizing and bringing to a full and definitive formulation the doctrine of the absolute sovereignty of grace, in close connection with the doctrine of original sin.

It may be sufficient, in order better to understand their intertwining, to hint at the development of Augustine's concept of original sin. Three major steps or stages can be roughly detected[271]. The first covers the time between Augustine's conversion and the writing of the *De diuersis quaestionibus ad Simplicianum* (396), a time in which Augustine still shared the traditional viewpoint[272] that Adam's fall had provoked the mortality of the body. Such mortality, weighing heavily on the soul, brings upon it the eternal damnation that the personal sins have earned. Only the intervention of Christ could save the soul from being doomed for ever. The second stage, opened by the *De diuersis quaestionibus ad Simplicianum* and reaching out until the beginning of the Pelagian controversy (412), represents a change in attitude on the part of the bishop of Hippo. He detaches himself from the *communis opinio* about Adam's sin and its repercussions on humanity, affirming that every man comes into the world taking upon himself the punishment (*poena*) of Adam's sin. Such punishment does not concern the body alone (destined to death), but also the soul. And since this is the nest of concupiscence, Augustine thought that it must share not only in the punishment but also in the guilt of Adam, in his culpability (*reatus*)[273]. Finally, at the third

270. Cf. Augustine, *De diuersis quaestionibus ad Simplicianum* 1,2 (CCL, 44), pp. 24ff. In our opinion the affirmation that "nicht die Sündenlehre, sondern die Gnadenlehre ist der eigentliche Gegenstand von *Simpl.* I,2" (DRECOLL, *Die Entstehung der Gnadenlehre Augustins* [n. 268], p. 234) should be nuanced. Even if in *Ad Simplicianum* 1,2 Augustine's primary intention was to "emphasize" the doctrine of the absolute necessity of grace in all domains, the doctrine of original sin remained as a backdrop. The teaching on grace could not be propounded without its essential relation to the doctrine of original sin, even though the latter was only present in an incipient way. Also the fact that the *peccatum originale* of *Ad Simplicianum* 1,1 becomes the *originalis reatus* in *Ad Simplicianum* 1,2 (cf. Augustine, *De diuersis quaestionibus ad Simplicianum* 1,2,20 [CCL, 44], p. 52) is indicative, according to us, of Augustine's attempt always to keep in (or at the back of) his mind the intertwining of grace and original sin.

271. For the different views concerning the development of Augustine's doctrine of original sin, see RIGBY, *Original Sin* (n. 269), pp. 607-614.

272. See H. RONDET, *Le péché originel dans la tradition patristique et théologique*, Paris, 1966, pp. 35-143; J. LIÉBAERT, *La tradition patristique jusqu'au Vᵉ siècle*, in P. GUILLUY (ed.), *La culpabilité fondamentale. Péché originel et anthropologie moderne* (RSSR.M, 11), Gembloux-Lille *[1975]*, pp. 34-55.

273. See *supra*, n. 270. Augustine, writes Trapè, "vede sempre insieme le due tristi conseguenze del primo peccato: la pena e la colpa"' (A. TRAPÈ, *Introduzione generale* a *Natura e grazia. Sant'Agostino, Il castigo e il perdono dei peccati ed il battesimo dei bambini – Lo Spirito e la lettera – La natura e la grazia – La perfezione della giustizia dell'uomo* [NBA, 17/1], Rome, 1981, p. CVIII).

stage, compelled by his harsh confrontation with the Pelagians, Augustine arrived at the definition of "original sin" as a "sin" properly so called: a sin that affects human nature by way of transmission or biological propagation. As such, original sin loses its exemplary characteristic and acquires a "causal" one instead. In the light of this interpretation, original sin designates now both the sin of Adam and the sinful state in which, because of the fall, all human beings are born[274]. The theory of the seminal identity of mankind with Adam was thus firmly established. Original sin alone is sufficient to cause the soul to be eternally

274. Augustine finds a scriptural proof above all in Rom 5,12 (cf. Augustine, *De peccatorum meritis et remissione et de baptismo paruulorum* 1,10,11 [CSEL, 60], pp. 12-13) and Jn 3,3-5 (*Ibid.* 1,20,26, pp. 25f). The Old Latin version used by Ambrosiaster in his commentary on Paul's letters (and followed also by Augustine), had a faulty translation of the expression ἐφ' ᾧ of Rom 5,12, which was rendered into a relative clause: "in whom (*in quo*) all sinned". In Paul, however, the Greek text runs: "Καὶ οὕτως εἰς πάντας ἀνθρώπους ὁ θάνατος διῆλθεν, ἐφ' ᾧ πάντες ἥμαρτον: So death passed to all men *in as much as/because* (ἐφ' ᾧ) all sinned". In fact, "ist ἐφ' ᾧ Wahrscheinlichkeit nach nicht relativisch, sondern konjunktional im Sinn von ἐπὶ τούτῳ ὅτι, 'daraufhin, daß alle sündigten', also '*weil* alle sündigten', zu verstehen, so wie es im übrigen auch sonst gebraucht wird, z. B. 2 Kor 5,4; Phil. 3,12 (4,10)" (H. SCHLIER, *Der Römerbrief* [HTK, 6], Freiburg-Basel-Wien, 1977, p. 162). The Greek Fathers never understood ἐφ' ᾧ in the sense of "in whom", nor did they ever think that ἥμαρτον indicated a sin committed by all men "in Adam". They interpreted it as referring to personal sin only (cf., *e.g.*, Cyril of Alexandria, *Explanatio in epistulam ad Romanos* [in Rom 5,12-14] [PG, 74], cc. 784-785 *passim*). See also, S. LYONNET, *Péché. IV. Dans le Nouveau Testament*, in *DBS* 7 (1966) 486-567, c. 531. Despite the faulty translation of ἐφ' ᾧ, Ambrosiaster interpreted the sin of Adam as a sin of idolatry whose consequences on humanity are the corruption of the flesh and the physical death (cf. Ambrosiaster, *Commentarius in xiii epistulas Paulinas [ad Romanos]* 5,14 [CSEL, 81/1], pp. 171f). In Ambrosiaster, however, there is no evidence of a causal "direct" influence of Adam's sin on humanity. It is only a matter of a negative example set by our forefather through the fall. Beside bringing about physical death this can also be the cause of spiritual death in so far as we imitate Adam's sin of idolatry. In opposition to the anthropological determinism of the dualistic movements, Ambrosiaster is at pains to emphasize individual freedom and responsibility in guilt. Unlike Ambrosiaster, the mistaken reading of Rom 5,12 became of crucial significance to Augustine's theology, for it represented the sealing of his theory of seminal identity of mankind with Adam, and the consequent share in the latter's culpability. "It seems likely – Rist affirms – that Augustine's concept ot the oneness of man in Adam is influenced by the Stoic and Neoplatonic doctrine of the σπερματικοὶ λόγοι, which are themselves all contained within the Divine Logos of the world" (J.M. RIST, *Augustine on Free Will and Predestination*, in *JTS* 20 [1969] 420-447, p. 431). We might as well add that Augustine reads the second part of Rom 5,12 (*per omnes homines mors pertransisse credatur*) omitting the term *mors*, in such a way that the subject becomes *peccatum*, with the relative consequences for his doctrine of original sin. By contrast, Cassian and the Massilians read the passage without omissions (cf. C. TIBILETTI, *Giovanni Cassiano. Formazione e dottrina*, in *Aug* 17 [1977] 355-380, p. 377, n. 153). For the crucial role played by Rom 5,12 see G. BONNER, *Augustine on Romans 5,12*, in *StEv* 5 (1968) 242-247. According to Rigby, however, rather than Rom 5,12, the major influence came from Rom 7 and 9 and 1 Cor 15 (Cf. RIGBY, *Original Sin* [n. 269], p. 607). See also LIÉBAERT, *La tradition patristique jusqu'au V* siècle* (n. 272), p. 34, n. 2.

doomed, unless the grace of Jesus Christ intervenes to remit it through baptism. In Augustine's view, the proof that his view is correct rests on the Church custom of baptising infants in order to deliver them from the bonds of both physical and spiritual death.

It was therefore Augustine's conviction that man's nature had been fundamentally *uitiata*[275] by Adam's fall, and that in consequence of this mankind cannot follow God's commandments by the agency of free will alone. Man needs help by divine grace in order to reach salvation. Of course, Augustine does not question the grace that has been at work in the creation of man, but he concentrates his interest on the redemptive grace by which man is saved[276]. Man, left to himself, is but a sinner, and cannot but turn down the offer of grace, because his sinful state inclines him towards evil and deprives him of the ability to choose good as an alternative[277]. In other words, Augustine believes that man can be justified only by Christ's redemption, and that only in the light of this saving intervention can he experience true *libertas*. This, however, does not imply the annihilation of human freedom, and it is precisely with the aim of doing away with such an objection that Augustine eventually comes to the formulation of grace as acting irresistibly (*indeclinabiliter et insuperabiliter*)[278], through the will of man. The context of such a formulation is the presupposition that man's will is attracted by what gives pleasure and that it loves that which gives delight[279]. The acting grace adapts itself to such spontaneous and natural movement of the will, and it does it gradually, taking as it were the will by the hand: from its initial openness, through its growth until it becomes *magna,* namely capable of bringing to effect what is desired[280]. The love for the good (*inspiratio caritatis*) is so deeply instilled by the Holy Spirit[281] in the heart of man, that the will lets itself be guided by him and, while it experiences

275. *Vitiata, uulnerata, sauciata, uexata, perdita* are terms belonging to the technical vocabulary which speaks of the human nature inherited by Adam. Cf. Augustine, *De natura et gratia* 53,62 (CSEL, 60), p. 279.

276. "Non tunc de illa gratia quaestio est, qua est homo conditus, sed de ista, qua fit saluus per Iesum Christum Dominum nostrum" (*Ibid.*, p. 278).

277. "Non enim est in nostra potestate cor nostrum" (Id., *De dono perseuerantiae* 13,33 [PL, 45], c. 1013).

278. Id., *De correptione et gratia* 12,38 (CSEL, 92), p. 266.

279. "Non enim amatur nisi quod delectat" (Id., *Sermo* 159,3 [PL, 38], c. 869). Cf. also Id., *De spiritu et littera* 35,63 (CSEL, 60), p. 223; *De peccatorum meritis et remissione et de baptismo paruulorum* 2,19,32 (CSEL, 60), p. 103.

280. "Gratia vero Dei semper est bona, et per hanc fit ut sit homo bonae voluntatis, qui prius fuit voluntatis malae. Per hanc etiam fit ut ipsa bona voluntas, quae iam esse coepit, augeatur, et tam magna fiat, ut possit implere divina mandata quae voluerit, cum valde perfecteque voluerit" (Id., *De gratia et libero arbitrio* 15,31 [PL, 44], cc. 899-900).

281. Cf. Id., *De gratia Christi et de peccato originali* 1,39,43 (CSEL, 42), p. 157.

246

delight, it is inclined steadily and infallibly towards God. Augustine tries to show that grace can cause the will to act irresistibly and infallibly, without being constrained to do so[282]. Since man, of himself, could reject God's mercy and thus jeopardize his action, there must be, argues Augustine, a conquering delight of the will (*delectatio uictrix*)[283]. This is precisely the work of God's grace that moves the innermost part of man and calls forth through love and delight the free operation of his will (*inspiratio dilectionis, ut cognita sancto amore faciamus*)[284]. Thus, if the will is the motivating force in man, the motivating force of the will or its natural *pondus* is love/delight, *caritas/delectatio*: "The law of love is the law of liberty" (*Lex itaque libertatis lex caritatis est*)[285], bestowed upon man as a gift of the Holy Spirit[286]. In fact, since man's will is always goal-directed and acts according to what gives it delight, only

282. To illustrate the distinction between infallible and necessary, and to show that something which is infallible can also be free, Chéné has suggested the following example: "Un fils qui aime profondément sa mère, s'il apprend qu'elle va mourir, ira infailliblement vers elle: dirons-nous pour cela qu'il n'y va librement?" (J. CHÉNÉ, *Notes complémentaires* [BA, 24], p. 783).

283. This expression occurs only once in the Augustinian corpus: "Nos, quantum concessum est, sapiamus et intelligamus, si possumus, Dominum Deum bonum ideo etiam sanctis suis alicuius operis iusti aliquando non tribuere uel certam scientiam uel uictricem delectationem, ut cognoscant non a se ipsis, sed ab illo sibi esse lucem, qua inluminentur tenebrae eorum, et suauitatem, qua det fructum suum terra eorum" (Augustine, *De peccatorum meritis et remissione et de baptismo paruulorum* 2,19,32, [CSEL, 60], p. 103). Cf. also: "Tanto enim quidque uehementius uolumus, quanto certius quam bonum sit nouimus eoque delectamur ardentius.... Ut autem innotescat quod latebat et suaue fiat quod non delectabat, gratiae Dei est, qua hominum adiuuat uoluntates" (*Ibid.* 2,17,26, p. 99). See C. HARRISON, *Delectatio Victrix: Grace and Freedom in Saint Augustine*, in *StPatr* 27, Louvain, 1993, pp. 298-302, pp. 300ff).

284. Augustine, *Contra duas epistulas Pelagianorum* 4,5,11 (CSEL, 60), p. 532.

285. "Lex itaque libertatis lex caritatis est" (Id., *Ep.* 167,19 [CSEL, 44], p. 606). Cf. also: "Pondus meum amor meus" (Id., *Confessiones* 13,9,10 [CCL, 27], p. 246); "Animus quippe uelut pondere amore fertur quocumque fertur" (Id., *Ep.* 157,9 [CSEL, 44], pp. 454-455); "Delectatio quippe quasi pondus est animae" (Id., *De musica* 6,29 [PL, 32], c. 1179); "Quod enim amplius nos delectat, secundum id operemur necesse est" (Id., *Epistulae ad Galatas expositio* 49 [CSEL, 84], p. 126); "Porro si poetae *[Virgilius, Ecloga* 2, v. 65] dicere licuit: Trahit sua quemque uoluptas, non necessitas, sed uoluptas; non obligatio, sed delectatio, quanto fortius nos dicere debemus, trahi hominem ad Christum, qui delectatur ueritate, delectatur beatitudine, delectatur iustitia, delectatur sempiterna uita, quod totum Christum est?" (Id., *Tractatus in Euangelium Ioannis* 26,4 [CCL, 36], p. 261).

286. Augustine had already emphasized this view at the beginning of his pastoral ministry, when Paul's passage of Rom 5,5 had attracted his attention: "Propterea, ergo intellegendum est opera bona per dilectionem fieri, dilectionem autem esse in nobis per donum Spiritus sancti, sicut idem dicit apostolus: *Caritas Dei diffusa est in cordibus nostris per Spiritum sanctum qui datus est nobis*" (Id, *Expositio quarumdam propositionum ex epistula ad Romanos* 52 [60] [CSEL, 84], p. 34). See A.M. LA BONNARDIERE, *Le verset paulinien Rom 5,5 dans l'oeuvre de saint Augustin*, in *AugMag*, T. II, Paris, 1954, pp. 657-665.

grace, whose effectiveness is made to depend upon its attraction, can change man's *delectatio* from being a *delectatio iniquitatis*[287] to being a *delectatio iustitiae*[288], and make him experience the delight and sweetness of what is good and true[289]. This "blessing of sweetness" (*benedictio dulcedinis*), as Augustine calls it, is the result of grace acting in man in such a way as to make him taste and desire and love God's commandments[290]. Since grace is understood as *delectatio/caritas*, viz. as the inmost disposition or movement of man's will, the action of grace, as actually causing the decision of the will, cannot be questioned. God's action remains predominant, whereas the action of man is ultimately limited to that of a passive recipient of divine grace. Although there is no sense of constraint with regard to man's will, all he needs to do is to "respond" to the delight of love and attraction stirred up within him[291].

Although Augustine's theological construction gives unequivocal emphasis to the predominant role of grace, he had never questioned the importance and the agency of free will. On the contrary, he had always defended its existence and necessity, basing his conviction on both existential experience and the authority of the Scriptures, where divine commands entail the concept of human freedom and responsibility[292]. In

287. Augustine, *Contra duas epistulas Pelagianorum* 1,3,7 (CSEL, 60), p. 428.
288. *Ibid.* 1,13,27, p. 446.
289. The good begins to be desired when it begins to be sweet: "Tunc enim bonum concupisci incipit, quando dulcescere coeperit" (*Ibid.* 2,9,21, p. 483).
290. "Ergo benedictio dulcedinis est gratia Dei, qua fit in nobis, ut nos delectet et cupiamus, hoc est amemus, quod praecipit nobis" (*Ibid.*).
291. Of course, if the sovereignty of grace is unquestionable, one must then ask himself why salvation, in Augustine's view, is not universal. The problem of predestination comes here to the fore for the first time in all its crudity, challenging Augustine's *intellectus fidei* (see *infra*, ch. IV *passim*).
292. See for instance: "Revelavit autem nobis per Scripturas suas sanctas, esse in homine liberum voluntatis arbitrium... Primum, quia ipsa divina praecepta homini non prodessent, nisi haberet liberum voluntatis arbitrium, quo ea faciens ad promissa praemia perveniret" (Augustine, *De gratia et libero arbitrio* 2,2 [PL, 44], c. 882); "Quomodo iubet [Deus], si non est liberum arbitrium?" (*Ibid.* 2,4, c. 883). Augustine says explicitly that the *liberum arbitrium* is created by God (cf., *e.g.*: "Nos autem dicimus humanam voluntatem sic divinitus adiuvari ad faciendam iustitiam, ut praeter quod creatus est homo cum libero arbitrio voluntatis, praeterque doctrinam qua ei praecipitur quemadmodum vivere debeat, accipiat Spiritum Sanctum, quo fiat in animo eius delectatio" [Id., *De spiritu et littera* 3,5 (CSEL, 60), p. 157]), and that it has remained operative even after the fall (cf., *e.g.*: "Nam liberum arbitrium usque adeo in peccatore non periit" [Id., *Contra duas epistulas Pelagianorum* 1,2,5, (CSEL, 60), 426]). Only once Augustine affirms the opposite, viz. that the *liberum arbitrium* was indeed lost after the fall (cf. Id., *Enchiridion ad Laurentium* 9,30 [CCL, 46], p. 65), but it is a hyperbole which is comfortably corrected by the context in which it is found (see N.W. DEN BOK, *Freedom of the Will. A Systematic and Biographical Sounding of Augustine's Thoughts on Human Willing*, in *Aug[L]* 44 [1994] 237-270, pp. 262-263, n. 79).

point of fact, even if prompted by new insights and marked by further elucidation during both the Manichaean and the Pelagian controversy, the essential tenets of Augustine's understanding of free will vis-à-vis grace can be traced back to the years 395-398.

Before tackling the original answer given by Augustine to the problem of free will, however, it is necessary to draw the distinction he makes between the concept of *liberum arbitrium* and that of *libertas*[293]. The *liberum arbitrium* is the power of choosing which every man is born with and which cannot be lost. It is at the root of a particular option whereby the will either decides for the good, when it is aided by grace, or it inclines to evil, when it relies on itself. Without the help of grace, in fact, fallen man's freedom is merely the freedom or power to sin. He is *liber*, in that his will and choice are free, but he is not *liberatus*[294]. True *libertas* is the synergetic combination of divine grace and human agency, whereby what is good is both willed and accomplished. It is the freedom from the slavery of vice, from the necessity of sin[295] to which fallen man, bereft of grace, is subjected[296]. This unified and harmonized state was naturally possessed by Adam before the fall, when the first man had the *potestas* to do the good and resist evil (*posse non peccare* or *prima libertas*). Properly speaking, the *libertas* is not the power of choosing but the love for the good. It is the state of the will orientated towards the Good, viz. God. Such *libertas* cannot exist but through

293. "Tout s'éclaire, pensons-nous, et tout s'explique quand on discerne à travers ses textes *[of Augustine]* une distinction capitale, qui passe trop souvent inaperçue: il ne faut pas confondre libre arbitre et liberté" (J. BALL, *Les développements de la doctrine de la liberté chez saint Augustin*, in *RPL*, 55 [1957] 404-413, p. 375). "Il faut donc introduire une distinction – qu'Augustin n'explicite pas toujours – entre libre arbitre et liberté" (I. BOCHET, *Saint Augustin et le désir de Dieu*, Paris, 1982, p. 112). Such a distinction is the *Leitmotiv* in M. HUFTIER, *Libre arbitre, liberté et péché chez saint Augustin*, in *RTAM* 33 (1966) 187-281. See also F.J. WEISMANN, *The problematic of freedom in St. Augustine: Towards a new hermeneutics*, in *REAug* 35 (1989) 104-119, pp. 104-107. A certain ambiguity derives also from the fact that in Latin only the attribute *liber* is available to indicate both those who make use of their *liberum arbitrium* and those who enjoy the *libertas*. See, for instance: "Semper est autem in nobis voluntas libera, sed non semper est bona. Aut enim a iustitia libera est, quando servit peccato, et tunc est mala; aut a peccato libera est, quando servit iustitiae, et tunc est bona" (Augustine, *De gratia et libero arbitrio* 15,31 [PL, 44], c. 899).

294. Cf. Id., *Contra secundam Iuliani responsionem imperfectum opus* 1,94 (CSEL, 85/1), pp. 107-108; *Contra duas epistulas Pelagianorum* 1,2,5 (CSEL, 60), p. 426. See also *Ep.* 157,2,8-10 (CSEL, 44), pp. 454-457.

295. "We are brought to the view that, although our 'wills' and our 'choices' are free, in the sense that we alone are responsible for them, yet without the intervention of God we are bound to an evil which we cannot escape" (RIST, *Augustine on Free Will and Predestination* [n. 274], p. 424).

296. Cf., for instance, Augustine, *De natura et gratia* 66,79 (CSEL, 60), p. 293; Id., *De libero arbitrio* 2,13,37 (CCL, 29), p. 262.

grace. In Augustine's eyes the distinction between *libertas* and *liberum arbitrium* (a distinction, however, which implies a close connection between the two elements[297]) was perfectly clear[298]. Acting on the will, grace does not rule out man's *liberum arbitrium*, but it grants it true *libertas*. In other words, in Augustine's thought *libertas* constitutes the correct use of the *liberum arbitrium*. The will remains always free: it happens nonetheless that it may not always consent to what is true and good. The will is always free as to the use of the *liberum arbitrium* but not always free in the sense of *libertas*. An independent free will detached from divine agency cannot enjoy, in Augustine's eyes, true freedom. He makes clear that *libertas* and *liberum arbitrium*, although interwoven, are not two elements situated on the same level, like two horses drawing the same cart. Only within the first element, informed by grace, can the second one find its correct status and aim. *Stantibus sic rebus*, the will's self-control and possession is no mere psychological experience. It is a "theological" experience[299], the result of that *libertas* which perfects man and leads him to the possession of wisdom, justice, truth, and participation in the divine and eternal laws. Authentic *libertas* is a perfect gift related to grace, it is a "theological freedom", the plenitude of the person and at the same time the basis for the possibility of free choice. It is against this background that some of Augustine's formulae, which at first appear to be paradoxical, reflect the exact meaning

297. Cf. Id., *De spiritu et littera* 30,52 (CSEL, 60), pp. 208-209, where Augustine observes a close connection between *liberum arbitrium* and *libertas*.

298. See, for instance: "Item ne quisquam etsi non de operibus, de ipso glorietur *libero uoluntatis arbitrio*, tanquam ab ipso incipiat meritum, cui tanquam debitum reddatur praemium bene operandi ipsa *libertas*" (Id., *Enchiridion ad Laurentium* 32 [CCL, 46], p. 66); "Redimuntur autem *[homines]* in *libertatem* beatitudinis sempiternam, ubi iam peccato servire non possunt. Nam si, ut dicis, boni malique voluntarii possibilitas sola *libertas* est; non habet *libertatem* Deus, in quo peccandi possibilitas non est. Hominis vero *liberum arbitrium* congenitum et omnino inamissibile si quaerimus, illud est quo beati omnes esse volunt, etiam hi qui ea nolunt quae ad beatitudinem ducunt" (Id., *Contra secundam Iuliani responsionem imperfectum opus* 6,11 [PL, 45], c. 1521).

299. It should be noted that, with regard to the relationship *libertas-uoluntas*, we have in Augustine the same close association as for *liberum arbitrium-uoluntas* (see *supra*, pp. 62f, n. 163). Since he does not make a perfectly clear distinction between the two terms, such an association may seem at times obscure or even confusing, and for this reason each term should be seen and understood in its particular context. See, for instance, the following formula: "In tantum enim libera est, in quantum liberata est, et in tantum appellatur *uoluntas*; alioquin tota cupiditas quam *uoluntas* proprie nuncupanda est, quae non est, sicut Manichaei desipiunt, alienae naturae additamentum, sed nostrae uitium a quo non sanamur nisi gratia Saluatoris" (Id., *Retractationes* 1,15,4 [CCL, 57], pp. 47-48). It is evident that here Augustine uses the term *uoluntas* in a flexible way. In fact it indicates both the *will* that has been *delivered* (and which enjoys the *libertas*) and the *cupiditas*, to which the *uoluntas* is also connected.

of his notion of *libertas*, namely of freedom that, through grace, orientates the *liberum arbitrium* towards goodness and the Good. As a consequence, the agency of free will is *par excellence* the consent of a will that has been converted by Christian grace. Its precise role is that of actively welcoming the divine initiative that reaches man thanks to the Redemption effected by Christ[300]. The more the will is submitted to grace, the healthier (*sanior*)[301] and the freer it is: *Eris liber, si fueris seruus: liber peccati, seruus iustitiae*[302].

a) From Anti-Manichaeism to Anti-Pelagianism

If this is the position acquired by the mature theologian, we must concede that in his early works, at the beginning of his ecclesiastical career, Augustine had not yet embraced the fully metaphysical and theological notion of Christian *libertas* inspired and nourished by grace[303], a notion that will characterize his later understanding of the issue. At the time of the *De libero arbitrio*[304], for instance, there are some formulae, touching on the inner reality of the *liberum arbitrium*[305], which show that Augustine did not then consider free will within a theological perspective, viz. from the point of view of faith, but according to the common vision given by reason. He had in mind the ability of an agent to act freely and to be morally responsible for his act in the absence of causal determinism. The Massilians (like the Pelagians before them) appealed precisely to this view in order to make their point against Augustine's change of mind. In favouring these early statements, in which the concept of operative grace was not yet fully developed, they made clear their choice for

---

300. "Redemtus sum et ipsa redemtione liber effectus sum" (Id., *Tractatus in Euangelium Ioannis* 41,8 [CCL, 36], p. 362).

301. "Haec enim uoluntas libera tanto erit liberior quanto sanior, tanto autem sanior quanto diuinae misericordiae gratiaeque subiectior" (Id., *Ep.* 167,2,8 [CSEL, 44], p. 454).

302. Id., *Tractatus in Euangelium Ioannis* 41,8 (CCL, 36), p. 362 (cf. Rom 6,20-22). See also Id., *De gratia et libero arbitrio* 15,31 (PL, 44), cc. 899-900. Remarkably enough, already in one of his earliest works, written after his conversion, Augustine affirmed that the total submission to God is the maximum of freedom: "Illo solo dominante, liberrimus" (Id., *De moribus ecclesiae catholicae* 1,12,21 [CSEL, 90], p. 25).

303. Cf. E. GILSON, *Introduction à l'étude de saint Augustin*, 3rd ed., Paris, 1949, pp. 205-210.

304. It is generally accepted that books I and II of the *De libero arbitrio* were written some years before book III; in 388 the former, and in 395 the latter.

305. See, for instance: "Nihil tam in nostra potestate quam ipsa uoluntas est" (Augustine, *De libero arbitrio* 3,3,7 [CCL, 29], p. 279); "Nec est cui recte inputetur peccatum nisi peccanti. Non ergo est cui recte inputetur nisi uolenti" (*Ibid.* 3,17,49, p. 304). Cf. also *Ibid.* 3,18,50, p. 304. Augustine will recall all these formulae in his *Retractationes* 1,9 (CCL, 57), pp. 23-29.

a "successionist" model. According to this model, human freedom retains its full exercise in the process of conversion, without having to appeal to a necessary interior grace that would empower the will to move in the direction of the good. This "successionist" model was still used by Cassian, as we have seen[306], as one of the ways in which God effects the process of conversion. But Augustine will make it clear that at the time of his *De libero arbitrio* he had mistakenly held that faith could arise out of a "natural" desire for God, and that only upon the consent of the human will were the divine gifts bestowed upon the moral agent, who is thus enabled to live righteously[307]. Likewise, in his study of Paul's letter to the Romans, in order to safeguard human free will from what could jeopardize it, Augustine had clearly stressed that man retains the power of desiring, willing, and performing the good[308]. Even about this initiative Augustine was ready to admit that he was mistaken[309], although we should understand this recognition in the sense "that his views of grace were undeveloped, not that his views of free will were wrong"[310].

We should not forget, however, that in the *De libero arbitrio* Augustine was opposing Manichaeism and its fatalistic outlook on reality, on account of which the *liberum arbitrium* was annihilated. His preoccupation with free will as the faculty of choice was, at that time, motivated by his concern with the problem of evil, more specifically with the question: *unde malum*? Once God was ruled out as the possible author of evil, then the only alternative was man, more specifically man's will. The latter, and the latter alone, was held responsible for sin and its consequences. This entails that the intelligent human creature be endowed with the precious gift of directing himself towards that which is good and true by his own efforts, but at the same time, and without any constraint[311], it entails that man is free to choose evil as well. Man's *liberum arbitrium* can thus incline him towards both the higher and the lower realities, that is towards justice (and this reveals the perfection inherent in the person's essence) or towards evil (and this reveals man's imperfection and

306. Cf. *supra*, pp. 133-153 *passim*.
307. Cf. Augustine, *De praedestinatione sanctorum* 3,7–4,8 (PL, 44), cc. 964-966.
308. Cf. Id., *Expositio quarumdam propositionum ex epistula ad Romanos* 44 (CSEL, 84), pp. 24-25.
309. Cf. Id., *De praedestinatione sanctorum* 3,7 (PL, 44), cc. 964-965.
310. E. STUMP, *Augustine on Free Will*, in E. STUMP – N. KRETZMANN (eds.), *The Cambridge Companion to Augustine*, Cambridge, 2001, pp. 124-147, p. 130.
311. Cf. Augustine, *De libero arbitrio* 1,10,20-21 (CCL, 29), pp. 224-225; *Ibid.* 3,1,2, p. 275.

indigence)[312]. This possibility of opting for one or the other means that man is "basically" or "constitutionally" free[313]. It is within this framework that Augustine speaks of a *naturale iudicium*, a natural capability of discerning what is wise and peace bearing, against error and difficulty[314].

In the *De libero arbitrio* Augustine limited himself to underlining the will's power as such, his intention being simply to establish the natural constitution of free will as a created entity, namely that the will is free because it is constitutive of the agent's power[315]. The cause of evil in the world has thus to be attributed solely to a disordered will, and not to a superhuman power acting upon man from without (as the Manichees believed), for the capacity to will rightly as well as wrongly lies fully within man's power. It is therefore important to underline the anti-Manichean polemic which guided Augustine in his *De libero arbitrio*, for this helps us to avoid interpreting it according to the Pelagian exaltation of free will, to the detriment of grace. Revising this early work towards the end of his life, Augustine stated clearly that he had not tackled the question of grace at the time of his *De libero arbitrio*, whose main concern was with the problem of evil, and to counteract Manichean fatalism[316].

Furthermore, Augustine did not deem it necessary, on that occasion, to focus on the origin of a "good" will. The lack of such a distinction (*i.e.* that Augustine did not take into account the will's role in the acquisition of moral virtue), explains the misunderstanding of Pelagius and the Massilians who equated the will's natural constitution with the

312. Cf. *Ibid.* 3,1,2-3 (CCL, 29), p. 274. Cf. also: "Liberum... arbitrium et ad malum et ad bonum faciendum confitendum est nos habere" (Id., *De correptione et gratia* 1,2 [CSEL, 92], p. 220).

313. Cf. *Ibid.*

314. "Non enim ante omne meritum boni operis parum est accepisse naturale iudicium quo sapientiam praeponat errori et quietem difficultati" (Id., *De libero arbitrio* 3,20,56 [CCL, 29], p. 308).

315. "Nihil tam in nostra potestate quam ipsa uoluntas est" (*Ibid.* 3,3,7, p. 279); "Non enim negare possumus habere nos potestatem, nisi dum nobis non adest quod uolumus; dum autem uolumus, si uoluntas ipsa deest nobis, non utique uolumus. Quod si fieri non potest ut dum uolumus non uelimus, adest utique uoluntas uolentibus nec aliud quicquam est in potestate nisi quod uolentibus adest. Voluntas igitur nostra nec uoluntas esset nisi esset in nostra potestate. Porro, quia est in potestate, libera est nobis" (*Ibid.* 3,3,8, p. 280).

316. "De gratia uero Dei,..., nihil in his libris disputatum est propter hanc propositam quaestionem" (Id., *Retractationes* 1,9,2 [CCL, 57], pp. 23-24); "Quapropter noui heretici Pelagiani, qui liberum sic asserunt uoluntatis arbitrium, ut gratiae Dei non relinquant locum..., non se extollant, quasi eorum egerim causam, quia multa in his libris dixi pro libero arbitrio, quae illius disputationis causa poscebat" (*Ibid.* 1,9,3, p. 24). Cf. *Ibid.* 1,9,4, p. 26.

assumed existence of the *possibilitas boni*, conceived as a natural endowment of a created being. On this presupposition they thought they had the necessary ground for reproaching Augustine with a change of mind on the subject[317]. It is fair, however, to assert that in his *De libero arbitrio* Augustine's view on the human being was already sketched within the sombre Christian framework of the fall of Adam whose mis-use of freedom had caused the whole of humanity to fall *et in errorem, et in erumnam et in mortem*[318]. Without having to wait for the anti-Pela-gian Augustine, his references to Adam's fall and to humanity's need for divine grace do somehow implicitly anticipate the distinction between the will's natural constitution and its role in the acquisition of moral virtue. Although not yet explicitly and radically expressed as in his later anti-Pelagian works, the status of man handicapped by ignorance and concupiscence, and the necessity of his being saved by the redemptive grace of Christ, are indeed hinted at[319].

Augustine's emphasis on free will was reiterated several times in his anti-Manichaean works. Fighting the sect's concept of co-eternal souls/principles of light and darkness from which the realms of goodness and evil derive respectively[320], and both of which abide in the life of man, Augustine opposes strenuously the "psychological determinism" rooted in such a *biceps, uel potius praeceps animarum uarietas*[321]. It is a destructive dualism, Augustine rightly thought, because it deprives man of his freedom and his personal responsibility in acting and, more par-ticularly, in sinning. Bereft of his responsible freedom man is reduced, as it were, to a passive automaton, to a sort of battlefield where the strife between good and evil takes place independently of his assent. Augustine

---

317. As a matter of fact, nowhere in the *De libero arbitrio* does Augustine ever men-tion the notion of the *possibilitas boni*. Cf. M. DJUTH, *The Hermeneutics of* De libero arbitrio III: *Are There Two Augustines?*, in *StPatr* 27, Louvain, 1993, pp. 281-289, pp. 285-286.

318. Augustine, *De libero arbitrio* 3,20,55 (CCL, 29), p. 307. According to De Plin-val, "c'est déjà la théorie des *poenalia peccata* qu'il *[Augustine]* reprendra à nouveau, *De natura* 24 et surtout *De Civ. Dei*, 14,15-16" (G. DE PLINVAL, *Notes complémentaires* [BA, 21], p. 626).

319. This is clearly indicated, for instance, in Augustine's decisive affirmation that, in the *De libero arbitrio*, he never intended to do away with grace: "Gratiam Dei non euacuaui" (Augustine, *De natura et gratia* 67,81 [CSEL, 60], p. 296).

320. Cf. Id., *Retractationes* 1,51,1 (CCL, 57), p. 45; *De haeresibus* 4,196 (CCL, 46), p. 319. See J. VAN OORT, *Jerusalem and Babylon. A Study into Augustine's* City of God *and the Sources of his Doctrine of the Two* Cities (SvigChr, 14), Leiden-NewYork-Copenhagen-Cologne, 1991, pp. 212-222; ID., *Mani, Manichaeism and Augustine. The Rediscovery of Manichaeism and Its Influence on Western Christianity*, Tbilisi/Georgia, 1998, pp. 16-20.

321. Augustine, *De duabus animabus* 22 (CSEL, 25/1), p. 79.

was at pains to make clear that the clash taking place within man between the flesh and the spirit does not have ontological causes, but theological and anthropological ones. It is a matter of a defective will which, as a result of Adam's fall, has to find its way between a tendency towards evil and the desire for good. A fundamental step towards this certainty must undoubtedly be Augustine's personal experience, in his search for the truth and in his conversion, which so evidently clashed with those Manichaean tenets to which he had assented for about ten years, even though such assent, after some time, would not be given full-heartedly any more[322]. He started to realize in an ever clearer way that he, and nobody or nothing else, was to be held responsible for any assent or refusal of his, and it became evident to him that the cause of sin was to be looked for in the human will[323]. The conviction that the cause of personal sin does not reside in an ontological *necessitas*, but in the *liberum arbitrium* (or in the *uoluntas*)[324] which is in our power (*in nostra positus potestate*)[325] was reiterated very frequently by Augustine in his anti-Manichaean works[326].

The emphasis on man's *liberum arbitrium*, dictated by his need to counteract Manichaean determinism, never completely overshadowed Augustine's strong belief that free will would be really free only when informed by grace. If a late allusion to that (made in the *Retractationes*) with regard to one of his anti-Manichaean works[327], might engender a suspicion that Augustine read and interpreted his earlier polemic works through the spectacles of his later staunch anti-Pelagianism, there is other evidence to be found in these works themselves. There, the sovereignty

322. "Ex quo accidebat, ut quidquid dicerent, miris quibusdam modis, non quia sciebam, sed quia optabam uerum esse, pro uero adprobarem" (*Ibid.* 11, p. 66).

323. "Itaque cum aliquid uellem aut nollem, non alium quam me uelle ac nolle certissimus eram et ibi esse causa peccati mei iam iamque animaduertebam" (Id., *Confessiones* 7,3,5 [CCL, 27], pp. 94-95); "Cum libero arbitrio me creauit Deus; si peccaui, ego peccaui" (Id., *Enarrationes in psalmos* 31,2,16 [CCL, 38], p. 237); "Ego peccaui; non fortuna, non fatum, non gens tenebrarum" (*Ibid.* 140,11 [CCL, 40], p. 2034).

324. As already mentioned, Augustine fails to draw a clear distinction between the *liberum arbitrium* (as the *conditio sine qua non* of the activity of the will) and the *uoluntas*. See *supra* n. 299.

325. Augustine, *De libero arbitrio* 3,1,3 (CCL, 29), p. 276.

326. See, for instance, *Ibid.* 1,1,1, p. 211; 3,1,3, p. 276; 3,3,7-8, pp. 279-280; Id., *De haeresibus* 46,19 (CCL, 46), p. 319; *De duabus animabus* 12.14-18 *passim* (CSEL, 25/1), pp. 68-75; *Contra Fortunatum Manichaeum* 15 (CSEL, 25/1), pp. 91-92; *Ibid.* 20-22 *passim*, pp. 97-107; *Contra Faustum Manichaeum* 22,22 (CSEL, 25/1), pp. 614-617; *Contra Felicem Manichaeum* 2,3-5 *passim* (CSEL, 25/2), pp. 830-833; *Ibid.* 8.16.18, pp. 836.845.847; *Contra Secundinum Manichaeum*18 (CSEL, 25/2), pp. 931-932.

327. Cf. Id., *Retractationes* 2,8 (CCL, 57), p. 97. The work Augustine is referring to is the *Contra Felicem Manichaeum*.

of grace and its ultimate saving character is more than occasionally brought to the foreground in a vivid way. That can be seen, for instance, when Augustine employs the Pauline distinction *sub lege* and *sub gratia* to underline his conviction that the law alone merely points to the *uirtus peccati*, and above all that the *lex sine gratia iubet, non iuuat*[328]. Only the spiritual, merciful and gratuitous grace of Christ, to which man adheres by faith, can justify him and deliver his life from the bite of sin and death[329]. Augustine's theological framework is consistent. It hinges around that primordial cause which has undermined the direction of man's life: original sin. That initial *auersio a Deo* has prevented man from rejoicing in divine truth and justice ever since, unless his heart is turned every time again to God[330]. Only by a *conuersio ad Deum*, through the exercise of one's personal freedom (whose role remains decisive against any form of determinism) and by the acknowledgment of the need of his guidance, can man make his way effectively towards his own fulfilment.

It is in 396, with the *De diuersis quaestionibus ad Simplicianum*, that Augustine develops the new insight (never abandoned thereafter)[331] that grace operates on the level of faith from the very start. In answering the Milanese priest, Augustine gave himself the opportunity to linger more attentively (*cautius adtentiusque*)[332] on the Pauline passages of Rom 7,7-25 and 9,10-29. Not only did this allow him to write what can possibly be considered the first treatise on grace, but it represented above all a point of no return in the elaboration of his doctrine of grace: so much so that the conclusions drawn in this work would never be abandoned[333].

---

328. Id., *Contra Faustum Manichaeum* 15,8 (CSEL, 25/1), pp. 432-433.

329. *Ibid.* 19 *passim*, pp. 496ff; 22 *passim*, pp. 591ff.; Id., *Contra Fortunatum Manichaeum* 22 (CSEL, 25/1), p. 106; *Contra Secundinum Manichaeum* 5 (CSEL, 25/2), p. 913; *Ep.* 140,48.64 (CSEL, 44), pp. 195.211; *Ibid.* 70-72 *passim*, pp. 217ff.

330. "Ab ea ergo ueritate quisquis auersus est, et ad seipsum conuersus, et non de rectore atque illustratore Deo, sed de suis motibus quasi liberis exsultat, tenebratur mendacio" (Id., *De Genesi contra Manichaeos* 2,16,24 [CSEL, 91], p. 146).

331. The work written for Simplicianus already contains the issues that will become central during the Pelagian controversy. It was indeed much more than "only a promise of Augustine's final insight" (J. WETZEL, *Pelagius anticipated: Grace and election in Augustine's Ad Simplicianum*, in J. MC WILLIAMS [ed.], *The Making of Orthodoxy. Essay in honour of Henry Chadwick*, Cambridge, 1989, pp. 200-213, p. 130).

332. Augustine, *De diuersis quaestionibus ad Simplicianum*, Praef. (CCL, 44), p. 7.

333. It may be useful to be reminded that the basic points of Augustine's concept of grace had already been developed before the Pelagian controversy broke out. At the end of the last century, F. Loofs took position against those who spoke of a tightening of Augustine's position on the question of grace after the Pelagian controversy broke out. Loofs referred to the *De diuersis quaestionibus ad Simplicianum* to show that "Man kann die spezifisch 'augustinische' Gnadenlehre, die A. gegenüber den Pelagianern und

Augustine's pivotal idea that grace is "gratuitous", and therefore precedes any good work, is reinforced by the interpretation of Rom 9,12: *Non ex operibus, sed ex uocante*[334]. Against this background, even the initiative of faith (the *initium fidei*) that opens up to desiring, willing and doing the good, does not come from man, but pertains only to God[335]. The *liberum arbitrium* is now exercised in the form of consent or dissent. From now onwards, the shift that occurred in the *De diuersis quaestionibus ad Simplicianum*, particularly after the "revelation" of 1 Cor 4,7, which so powerfully affected Augustine's thought, will be kept fundamentally the same in its content, and as such it will be revived by the aging bishop of Hippo towards the end of his life[336].

gegenüber den Massiliensern vertreten hat schon mit Zitaten aus den *Libri de quaestion. ad Simpl.* darstellen" (F. LOOFS, *Augustinus*, in *RE* 1 [1897] 257-285, p. 279). He then continued by saying that since the Augustinian system had already acquired a definitive form in 397, one ought to conclude that "der Augustinismus war nicht eine Reaction gegen den Pelagianismus; vielmehr war unmgekehrt der Pelagianismus eine Reaction gegen A.s Anschauungen" (*Ibid.*, p. 278). Loofs' position is generally shared by Augustinian scholars. See, for instance: "L'*Ad Simplicianum* marquait pour Augustin un renversement des rapports entre la grâce et le libre arbitre. L'absolue priorité de la grâce sur le libre arbitre est une acquisition définitive qu'il ne se lassera pas de rappeler" (A. SAGE, *Péché originel: naissance d'une dogme*, in *REAug* 13 [1967] 211-248, p. 221). "Rien ne permet de parler de changements substantiels dans la théologie augustinienne de la grâce entre 395-396 et 430. Il y a certes des exégèses nouvelles (Rm. 7), des approfondissements, des insistances plus grandes.... Mais en son fond la théologie d'Augustin est mue par les mêmes convictions durant toute cette période" (P.-M. HOMBERT, *Gloria gratiae. Se glorifier en Dieu, principe et fin de la théologie augustinienne de la grâce*, Paris, 1996, p. 571). See also, G. BARDY, *Introduction* to *De diuersis quaestionibus ad Simplicianum*, *BA* 10, pp. 389-404; J. CHÉNÉ, *Notes complémentaires* (BA, 24), p. 812; G. MARTINETTO, *Les premières réactions antiaugustiniennes de Pélage*, in *REAug* 17 (1071) 83-117; A. SCHINDLER, *Augustin/Augustinismus I*, in *TRE* 4 (1979) 646-698, c. 673; D. MARAFIOTI, *L'uomo tra legge e grazia. Analisi teologica del* De spiritu et littera *di S. Agostino*, Brescia, 1983, pp. 216-220; ID., *Il problema dell' "Initium Fidei" in sant'Agostino fino al 397*, in *Aug* 21 (1981) 541-565; T.G. RING, *"An Simplicianum zwei Bücher über verschiedene Fragen"*, *Aurelius Augustinus, Schriften gegen die Pelagianer. Prolegomena*, Bd. III, Würzburg, 1991, pp. 289-300; 313-315. We can hardly share the opinion of Patout Burns, according to which the ecclesial and social context, rather than the reflection on Paul, would have determined the change of Augustine's thought on this point (cf. J.P. BURNS, *The Development of Augustine's Doctrine of Operative Grace*, Paris, 1980, p. 87).

334. "Vocantis est ergo gratia, percipientis uero gratiam consequenter sunt opera bona, non quae gratiam pariant, sed quae gratia pariantur.... Sic nemo propterea bene operatur ut accipiat gratiam sed quia accepit.... Prima est igitur gratia, secunda opera bona" (Augustine, *De diuersis quaestionibus ad Simplicianum* 1,2,3 [CCL, 44], p. 27).

335. "Liberum uoluntatis arbitrium plurimum ualet; *immo uero est quidem*, sed in uenundatis sub peccato *[Rom 7,14]* quid *ualet*?... Quis habet in potestate tali uiso attingi mentem suam, quo eius uoluntas moueatur ad fidem?... uoluntas ipsa, nisi aliquid occurrerit quod delectet atque inuitet animum, moueri nullo modo potest. Hoc autem ut occurrat, non est in hominis *potestate*" (*Ibid.* 1,2,21-22, pp. 53.55). See *infra*, pp. 298-302.

336. See the reference to the *De diuersis quaestionibus ad Simplicianum* in Augustine, *De praedestinatione sanctorum* 4,8 (PL, 44), c. 966, where the bishop of Hippo

Thus, before the Pelagian controversy broke out and reached its climax, Augustine had settled on his insight about the relationship between grace and free will in lucid terms. This conviction is reiterated, for instance, in the *De spiritu et littera*, written in ca. 412. There, it is said that divine grace acts in many human domains without first calling for human agency, and that this is anticipated by God's mercy whenever any good action is performed. Although to the question: "Are we then doing away with free choice through grace?", he answers vehemently: "God forbid! (*absit*)", yet he is convinced that the *liberum arbitrium*, if naided by the Holy Spirit, is in fact of no avail[337]. Moreover, the human *uoluntas* is itself a gift of God because it proceeds from the *liberum arbitrium* that man has received at the moment of creation (*quod nobis naturaliter concreatum est*)[338]. Accordingly, there is no human consent to God's call without God's action in man. Such action operates by persuading man about what is right, and by attracting him through pleasure to desire and will the good by means of exhortations that come both from without (*e.g.* commandments) and from within (*suasio* or *uocatio*). Yet, argues Augustine, the freedom of choice does not become void because of grace. Even if an individual acted under compulsion, he would still, no doubt, act through his own will[339].

In the *Contra duas epistulas Pelagianorum* (420-421) which, as it were, opens the second period of Augustine's anti-Pelagian campaign, characterised by the long and tiring debate with Julian of Aeclanum, Augustine begins his work by opposing Julian's claim that he had

---

quotes the judgement he had expressed in *Retractationes* 2,2,1. See also Id., *De dono perseuerantiae* 20,52 and 21,55 (PL, 45), cc. 1026 and 1027.

337. Id., *De spiritu et littera* 3,5 (CSEL, 60), p. 157.

338. *Ibid.* 34,60, p. 220. Here the term *uoluntas* ought to be understood as the (will of the) *arbitrium* (see DEN BOK, *Freedom of the Will* [n. 292], p. 260, n. 69).

339. "Hoc quisque in potestate habere dicitur, quod, si uult, facit, si non uult, non facit" (Augustine, *De spiritu et littera* 31,53 [CSEL, 60], p. 210). "Siue extrinsecus... siue intrinsecus..., sed consentire uel dissentire propriae uoluntatis est. His ergo modis quando Deus agit cum anima rationali, ut ei credat; neque enim credere potest quodlibet libero arbitrio, si nulla sit suasio uel uocatio cui credat; profecto et ipsum uelle credere Deus operatur in homine, et in omnibus misericordia eius praeuenit nos: consentire autem uocationi Dei, uel ab ea dissentire, sicut dixi, propriae uoluntatis est.... Accipere quippe et habere anima non potest dona, de quibus hoc audit, nisi consentiendo: ac per hoc quid habeat, et quid accipiat, Dei est: accipere autem et habere utique accipientis et habentis est" (*Ibid.* 34,60, p. 220). The aspect of *suasio* or *delectatio* is an essential element that runs all through Augustine's thought and which, more specifically, is linked to his concept of grace. *Suasio*, however, is not yet the act of adhering to God's will. This happens when *suasio* becomes *persuasio*. In fact, whereas the latter is infallible, in that it determines man into believing, the former simply spurs him to believe without any compulsion. How that transition takes place is a mystery (cf. *Ibid.*)

destroyed the *liberum arbitrium* and clung to his Manichaean past. The bishop of Hippo's reply is absolutely clear: "But which one of us says that *liberum arbitrium* has vanished from the human race by the sin of the first man?"[340]. In reality what concerned Augustine most was the Pelagians' overemphasis on the "independence" of the *liberum arbitrium* (claimed especially by Julian): its supposed autarchy with regard to doing good and living well[341].

It is on these very grounds that Augustine will argue that the *possibilitas boni*, attributed by the Pelagians and (partly) by the Massilians to man's *liberum arbitrium*, actually perished in the fall. To deny that the upright will (which depends upon that possibility) perished with the *possibilitas boni* is to deny the doctrine of original sin and the need for Christ's redemption[342]. Although corrupted and diminished in strength (due to the lack of the *possibilitas boni*), the will remains in the power of man for it is inseparable from human nature. Moreover, Augustine argues, the exercise of free will will be more or less perfect depending upon how far God restores the *possibilitas boni* in human nature[343]; for the divine restoration of the *possibilitas boni* does not destroy, but strengthens and brings to perfection the exercise of free choice, which has always remained in the agent's power.

Augustine had the difficult task of steering a middle path, a *uia regia*, between the extremes of Manichaeism and Pelagianism: trying to defend a conception of free choice that would be compatible with fallen nature. Undoubtedly, Augustine's own personal conversion played an important role in this task, for it was experienced as the emergence and liberation of his *liberum arbitrium*, which until then had been dominated by his passions[344]. Only under God's motions could he find the "centre"

---

340. "Quis autem nostrum dicat quod primi hominis peccato perierit liberum arbitrium de humano genere?" (Id., *Contra duas epistulas Pelagianorum* 1,2,5 [CSEL, 60], p. 425).

341. "quid est quod iste libero arbitrio uult bene uiuendi tribuere *potestatem*, cum haec *potestas* non detur nisi gratia Dei per Iesum Christum...?" (*Ibid.*, p. 426). "Il ne reproche pas à Julien de revendiquer le pouvoir de choisir; sans celui-ci, bien sûr, il n'y a plus ni responsabilité, ni mérite, ni démérite. Mais il lui reproche d'exagérer ce pouvoir" (BALL, *Les développements de la doctrine de la liberté chez saint Augustin* [n. 293], p. 412).

342. Cf. Augustine, *De natura et gratia* 2,2-3,3 (CSEL, 60), pp. 234-235; Id., *De correptione et gratia* 12,37-38 (CSEL, 92), pp. 265-266.

343. The *arbitrium* is there, but by itself "non sufficit": "Quamuis esse non dubitetur arbitrium uoluntatis, tamen eius potestas non sufficiat, nisi adiuuetur infirmitas" (Id., *Ep.* 177,4 [CSEL, 44], p. 673). See also: Id., *De peccatorum meritis et remissione et de baptismo paruulorum* 2,15,22 (CSEL, 60), pp. 94-96; 2,17,26-27, pp. 98-100; *De spiritu et littera* 31,53 (CSEL, 60), pp. 209-210; *De dono perseuerantiae* 8,20 (PL, 45), c. 1004.

344. Cf. Id., *Confessiones* 9,1 (CCL, 27), p. 133. According to Gilson, "ce qui domine toute l'histoire de la controverse *[pélagienne]*, c'est que le pélagianisme était le négation radicale de l'expérience personnelle d'Augustin ou, si l'on préfère, l'expérience personnelle

(*unum*) of his willing, and eventually choose for the eternal goods *tota uoluntate*[345]. By the time he began to write the *Confessiones,* some ten years after becoming a Christian, Augustine had grown rather pessimistic, and certainly far less confident both of the freedom of the will and its unaided power to choose the good and adhere to it. Starting with the story of his conversion, Augustine had come to underscore all the more the fallibility of man and the mutability and inconstancy of his will. Moreover, his encounter with Paul's epistles had made him more aware that the soul is beset by competing desires and inner conflicts that at times prevent man from doing what he wants, immobilising or frustrating his good intentions. The old Augustine will fully espouse this insight during the Pelagian controversy, when he will decisively teach that man's free will is capable of virtue and good only as it is freed and sustained by divine grace. Finally, highly indicative of his growing pessimism about human powers is also the fact that "his nomination of obedience as the mother of virtues in the *City of God*[346], rather than Stoic prudence, Aristotelian justice, or Ambrosian temperance, reflects the deep misgivings of the later Augustine about man's ability to function as a moral agent *sui iuris*"[347].

b) Augustine's Struggle for Coherence in His Non-Polemic Works

The radicalism Augustine had arrived at with regard to his concept of grace vis-à-vis free will can be followed not only in his more elaborate works, but also in those sermons and letters which are bereft of a *uis polemica.* Yet, in spite of his struggle to be coherent, we can detect here and there little holes in the net of his thought, which witness how Augustine himself (at least before the Pelagian controversy took shape) was aware of the difficulty in giving the reasons for his theological approach to the sovereignty of grace. Even though his doctrine of grace was substantially, albeit non entirely, formulated in the *De diuersis quaestionibus ad Simplicianum,* there remained in Augustine what Hombert has called a *sensibilité*[348] towards the undeniable role played

---

d'Augustin était dans son essence et jusqu'en ses particularités les plus intimes, la négation même du pélagianisme" (GILSON, *Introduction à l'étude de saint Augustin* [n. 303] p. 206).

345. "Donec eligatur unum, quo feratur tota uoluntas una, quae in plures diuidebatur" (Augustine, *Confessiones* 8,24 [CCL, 27], p. 128).

346. Cf. Id., *De ciuitate Dei* 14,12 (CCL, 48), p. 434.

347. M.L. COLISH, *The Stoic Tradition from Antiquity to the Early Middle Ages.* Vol. II: *Stoicism in Christian Latin Thought through the Sixth Century,* Leiden, 1990, p. 227.

348. P.-M. HOMBERT, *Augustin prédicateur de la grâce au début de son épiscopat,* in G. MADEC (ed.), *Augustin prédicateur (395-411).* Actes du Colloque International de Chantilly, 5-7 septembre 1996 (CEAug.SA, 159), Paris, 1998, 217-245, p. 227.

by free will in Christian life and daily experience. A *sensibilité* which, once again, discloses Augustine's awareness of the difficulty of integrating, within his concept of grace, the indispensable place that free will occupies in human existence both at the level of language and experience. During the Pelagian controversy, such uneasiness will be fully absorbed into the concept of the overwhelming sovereignty of grace.

A few examples may illustrate this point. In his commentary on the first letter of St. John, written in *ca.* 406-407, there is passage in which Augustine says that to be reborn of water and the Holy Spirit, and also to grow or regress in the life of faith, belongs to the will[349]. Likewise, commenting on different psalms, the bishop of Hippo shows a surprising optimism with regard to the possibilities which are still inherent in the human will, despite its defective status, and through which man can conform to the divine will. Thus, in 403, explaining Psalm 32, Augustine said something the Pelagians too would have been keen to subscribe to. He affirmed that, during his agony in Gethsemane (cf. Mt 26,39), Jesus Christ personified the way in which any human will should conform with God's will. In fact, continues Augustine, although the human will is in possession of man, who may even will to go astray from God's path (*Pater, si fieri potest, transeat a me calix iste*), such human will is ultimately called to resemble God's will (*Verum non quod ego uolo, sed quod tu uis, Pater*)[350]. Commenting again on the same psalm, a few days later, Augustine reiterates his conviction that God requires man's full responsibility in the use of his free will. Through the distinction *non posse* and *nolle*, he asserts that there might be circumstances in which, by necessity, man's will is not able to receive God's gifts, whereas at other times it may be that it does not even want to receive them. In the second instance, there is a *reatus uoluntatis*[351]. Likewise, explaining Psalm 102, in *ca.* 412, the bishop of Hippo affirmed that God is always

---

349. "Ubi nativitas in voluntate est, et crementum in voluntate est. Nemo ex aqua et Spiritu nascitur nisi volens. Ergo si vult, crescit: si vult, decrescit" (Augustine, *In Ioannis epistulam ad Parthos* 3,1 [PL, 35], cc. 1997-1998). For this and the following examples, see HOMBERT, *Augustin prédicateur de la grâce au début de son épiscopat* [n. 348], *passim*.

350. Quia potes aliquid proprium uelle, ut aliud Deus uelit, conceditur hoc humanae fragilitati, conceditur humanae infirmitati; aliquid proprium uelle, difficile est ut non tibi contigat; sed statim cogita qui sit supra te.... *[Christus]* corrigens te, subiungensque uoluntati eius, ac dicens: *Verum non quod ego uolo, sed quod tu uis, Pater.* Quomodo disiunctus es a Deo, qui iam hoc uis quod Deus?" (Augustine, *Enarrationes in psalmos* 32,II, s. 1,2 [CCL, 38], p. 248).

351. "Idipsum enim exigitur, quia noluit accipere cum daretur. Aliud est enim non posse accipere, aliud nolle; illic excusatio necessitatis est, hic reatus voluntatis" (*Ibid.* 32,II, s. 2,2, p. 258).

ready to heal men, as long as "they want" to be healed. It sounds as though healing depended on man's will or self-determination, as if he himself could bring this healing about[352].

A certain ambivalence, due to some uncertainty of the language, can also be detected in a letter written by Augustine to Deogratias in ca. 409. There we read that the good or bad result of a choice depends on the inclination (*affectus*) of the will, which is, as it were, the *mensura* of every action and merit[353]. In *Sermo* 193, preached on Christmas day in 410, we find again a certain fluidity in Augustine's language. Before stating unequivocally that good can only be willed and performed under the power of grace, he writes a sentence in which the *bona uoluntas* appears to be self-sufficient in willing and performing something good even before the grace of God is implored[354]. And already well into the second decade of the 5th century, in *Ep.* 157, addressed to the Sicilian Hilary in ca. 414-415, Augustine seems to attach a "functional initiative" to man's free will. This, affirms Augustine, is not given to man so that he may oppose God's help by a *superba uoluntas*, but so that he may be able to invoke him by means of a *pia uoluntas*[355]. It seems indeed that the bishop of Hippo leaves some room for the independent agency of the will, at a stage in which it asks for the intervention of divine grace. The latter, of course, remains necessary in order to bring to fulfilment the desires of the will[356].

Apart from these examples, from which we infer Augustine's difficulty in describing both the sovereignty of grace and the place and role that free will retains in human life, the primacy of the former remains at the core of Augustine's theological construction, even before the definitive systematization prompted by the Pelagian controversy. Whether implicitly hinted at, or whether formulated in a discrete or discontinuous manner, the basic tenets of Augustine's doctrine of sovereign grace were thus also present, by and large, in those sermons and letters which precede the confrontation between the bishop of Hippo and the Pelagians.

---

352. Cf. *Ibid.* 102,6 (CCL, 40), p. 1455.

353. "Quoniam, ubi quisque bonus est, cum bene uult, ibi etiam malus, cum male uult. Ac per hoc ibi etiam fit uel beatus uel miser, hoc est in ipso suae uoluntatis affectu, quae omnium factorum meritorumque mensura est" (Id., *Ep.* 102,26 [CSEL, 34/2], p. 567).

354. "Persistat igitur bona uoluntas aduersus concupiscentias malas, et persistens imploret auxilium gratiae Dei" (Id., *Sermo* 193,2 [PL, 38], c. 1014).

355. Cf. Id., *Ep.* 157,2,8 (CSEL, 44), pp. 453-454.

356. Cf. *Ibid.* 157,2,10, p. 456.

c) Is Augustine an "Innovator" ?

Undoubtedly, the clash between Augustinianism and Pelagianism brought about the sea change that Augustine was pioneering in Western theological thinking. Such a confrontation would display more clearly the differences that were growing wider between the Eastern approach (upon which even the Occidental Pelagians still relied) and the Western one (of which Augustine would become the coryphaeus). Whereas the former would always consider God's *oeconomia salutis* as taking place in a cosmic, unitarian and harmonic process, and as having a universal pedagogical goal, the παιδεία, the latter (via Augustine) would operate a significant shift by giving priority to the individual and his needs[357]. In stressing, with a noticeably pessimistic outlook, God's mystery rather than God's loving justice, divine determination rather than human responsibility, human sinfulness rather than human potentiality, Augustine detached himself from the cosmological model of salvation in which man was a constitutive element of the salvific process itself. Now, being placed outside this process, man begins to ask himself how he can obtain salvation, viz. how he can become really free from sin and reach his full potential. The answer is apparently the same as before, that is: with the help of grace. With the proviso, however, that now grace has acquired an exclusive significance; it is the invincible, irresistible divine power bestowed on man by God, through Christ the Redeemer. Man can be delivered from sin and enabled to pursue his true goal only thanks to the *gratia per Iesum Christum*. We can no longer say that "all" is grace, because this is now described as an "inner" reality working in man and coming directly from God through the mediation of Christ. Whereas the Greek Fathers continued to see grace as a "theological" quality of God's saving activity, viz. his "divine benevolence", acting in the world in harmonious co-operation with man's freedom[358], Augustine developed the doctrine of grace in strict connection with his doctrine of original sin and the anthropological quest for salvation, centred on human individuality and more and more detached from a holistic process.

Furthermore, the Fathers of the Church of the first four centuries, basing themselves on Scripture, shared the assumption that all humanity

---

357. See GRESHAKE, *Gnade als konkrete Freiheit* (n. 19), pp. 266ff; ID., *Geschenkte Freiheit. Einführung in die Gnadenlehre*, Freiburg i. Br.-Basel-Wien, 1992, pp. 37-40.

358. The Greek Fathers, contemporary or even posterior to Augustine had practically remained untouched by the issues that had nourished the Pelagian controversy. Cyril of Alexandria, for instance, who died in 444 (fourteen years after Augustine) did not mention any of those discussions at all. See LIÉBAERT, *La tradition patristique jusqu'au Ve siècle* (n. 272), pp. 34-35.

partakes in the sin of Adam in view of the universal salvation to which all men are called. The meta-historical and symbolic parable of Adam's fall was meaningful as understood in terms of the salvation offered in the New Adam, Jesus Christ. The unity and solidarity among men, with regard to the consequences of Adam's sin as well as to the redeeming activity of Christ in their life, was firmly rooted in the universal perspective of salvation history, in the divine pedagogy that brings unity to all cosmic realities, and in a fundamental optimism about the possibilities inherent in human nature to co-operate with God's plan of salvation. For Augustine, on the other hand, the two Adams (and the unity and solidarity of humanity with them) were not to be regarded as different stages of the one cosmic process of salvation, but as two realities opposed to one another. What prevails in the bishop of Hippo's viewpoint now is the new interpretation of original sin, according to which humanity also shares in the guilt, *i.e.*, in the culpability (*reatus*) of Adam's sin, and not merely in the punishment (*poena*). Whereas the tradition of the Church had always considered guilt as something personal, resting on man's responsibility, Augustine introduced the notion of hereditary guilt, according to which all men are born in a sinful state and share in it. Adam's *peccatum originale* is no longer the symbol of human mortality and personal sin, but is regarded as an *originalis reatus*, a sin/guilt which is inherited. Confirmed by the presence of the *concupiscentia carnis*, it is a mark by which every man who comes into the world is affected[359], and which can only be expiated through baptism in Christ, the new Adam. As a result of this, great emphasis is laid on the individual person who thus becomes the privileged recipient of both the concrete consequences of Adam's original sin and the offer of grace. Salvation or damnation will be decided by either God's gratuitous bestowal of grace or by its imponderable restraining[360]. Prisoner of his own interpretation of original sin, a radical shift in the concept of grace was but the consequential, logical step. Grace does not reflect primarily the superabundant generosity and mercy of God's heart, but appears to be the divine invincible tool whose main purpose (not without exaggeration)

---

359. Reactions against this view of a *peccatum originale* that affects all infants coming into the world, were not voiced only by Pelagianism. See also pope Zosimus' reluctance to use, in his *Tractoria*, the word *peccatum* in relation to infants: *supra*, p. 22, n. 7.

360. As Chéné rightly writes: "Ce qu'on peut appeler la "rigueur" du système augustinien touchant la dispensation de la grâce, dérive entièrement de la chute primitive" (J. CHÉNÉ, *La théologie de saint Augustin. Grâce et prédestination*, Le Puy-Lyon, [1962], p. 52).

is to repair the damage caused by Adam's sin, and to restore the *natura uitiata* to its original destiny[361].

The two different approaches (the Greek and the Latin), rather than meeting in what could have become a fruitful dialogue, came into conflict in the controversy that broke out between Pelagius and his followers, on one side, and Augustine on the other. Such conflict caused a violent collision that produced a hardening of the extreme positions of both parties. The Pelagians were still attached to the Greek cosmological model according to which grace was communicated and concretely experienced within a pedagogical process through which man, the *imago Dei*, was led towards his prototype. In the eyes of the Pelagians this was made possible because the experience of grace was strictly correlated with human freedom and the historic-salvific situations with which it is confronted, particularly the Christ event. These situations are produced by God from outside, in order to create the possibilities for human freedom to be exercised, while developing and guiding it to its goal: God. Augustine, on the other hand, detached himself from this cosmological model and built up a theological construction where the doctrine of grace goes hand in hand with that of original sin. In this sense, because of the radical changes of perspective he introduced, Augustine can be regarded as an "innovator"[362]. No doubt, his personal experience of

---

361. "Prisonnier de sa propre problématique, Augustin fait plus large la place du péché que celle de la grâce" (RONDET, *Le péché originel dans la tradition patristique et théologique* [n. 272], p. 142).

362. The charge of innovation was rejected by Augustine himself during the debate with Julian of Aeclanum. If Augustine claimed his "traditional" position ("Non ego finxi originale peccatum quod catholica fides credit antiquitus": Augustine, *De nuptiis et concupiscentia* 2,12,25 [CSEL, 42], p. 278), Julian literally challenged such a claim ("Non est haec fides antiquitus tradita atque fundata, nisi in conciliis malignantium, inspirata a diabolo, prolata a Manichaeo, celebrata a Marcione, Fausto, Adimanto, omnibusque eorum satellitibus et nunc a te in Italiam, quod graviter gemimus, eructata": Julian of Aeclanum, *Ad Florum* 1,59 [CSEL, 85/1], pp. 55-56). Cf. also *Ibid.* 3,29 (CSEL, 85/1), pp. 367-368; Augustine, *Contra Iulianum* 1,5,20-6-28 (PL, 44), cc. 654-660. Among modern scholars, Gross is deeply convinced that Augustine is by all means the father of the concept of the original sin and the architect of the theology of original sin: "Der Bischof von Hippo ist nicht nur der Vater der Erbsündenidee, sondern auch dr Architekt der Erbsündentheologie"; and again: "Augustinus ist somit im Vollsinn des Wortes der Vater des Erbsündendogmas" (J. GROSS, *Entstehungsgeschichte des Erbsündendogmas. Von der Bibel bis Augustinus* [Geschichte des Erbsündendogmas, Bd. I], München-Basel, 1960, pp. 368 and 375). Other scholars, however, believe that Augustine's elaboration of original sin was rooted in African, Italian and, somehow, also in Greek milieu (cf. F. REFOULÉ, *Datation du premier concile de Carthage contre les Pélagiens et du 'Libellus fidei' de Rufin*, in *REAug* 9 [1963] 41-49; G. BONNER, *Les origines africaines de la doctrine augustinienne sur la chute et le peché originel*, in *Augustinus* 12 [1967] 97-116; ID., *Augustine on Romans 5,12* (n. 274); RONDET, *Le péché originel dans la tradition patristique et théologique* (n. 272); P.F. BEATRICE, *Tradux peccati. Alle fonti della*

divine grace as an "inner" and "secret" reality[363] coming directly from God, bursting upon his life and radically changing it regardless of the freedom of the will, affected his thought. Grace was no longer to be experienced at the level of a cosmic process of salvation (as it unfolds in the world) and within a "paideutic" framework. Its *locus* had now become the human subjectivity, man's knowledge and will. And this was the domain of grace's unquestioned sovereignty.

Cassian and the Massilians, still strongly connected with the Eastern theological thought to which they were deeply indebted, tried to keep a dialogue open between the two antagonistic approaches by attempting to safeguard the capability of man's free will to initiate the process of conversion (the *initium fidei*). It soon became clear that the Massilians were not able to follow the thought of Augustine to the point of giving to divine grace the role that they believed man had always fulfilled in making at least the first step towards God. The Massilians' opposition to Augustine's view about the absolute ruling of grace and their position on the question of the *initium fidei*, was indeed rooted in different convictions about Christian "protology", particularly the understanding of the concept of *naturae bonum*, and the actual role of man in the process of salvation. We shall attempt in the next paragraphs to find the reasons why the Massilians were eager to hold to such convictions.

6. THE STRUGGLE FOR PERFECTION: CASSIAN'S "HUMANISTIC" THEOLOGY VIS-À-VIS AUGUSTINE'S THEOLOGY OF GRACE

The Christian Platonism of the school of Alexandria, which reached its climax through Origen, its unrivalled genius, exercised an enormous influence on Egyptian monasticism. Origen can in fact be considered the first to have laid down the basis for an ascetic theology and to have

---

dottrina agostiniana del peccato originale [SPMed, 8], Milan, 1978, pp. 29-38). Against a straight line from North African doctrine in matter of original sin and *concupiscentia* (despite some affinities, especially with Tertullian), and in favour of Augustine's ultilmately independent elaboration, see J.P. YATES, *Was there "Augustinian" concupiscence in pre-Augustinian North Africa?*, in *Aug(L)* 51 (2001) 39-56. For a *status quaestionis* of the different opinions with regard to Augustine's position vis-à-vis the doctrine of original sin, see BEATRICE, *Tradux peccati*, pp. 29-38. There is no good reason, however, to doubt the sincerity of Augustine's conviction that he was simply taking the potentialities present in the Pauline doctrine of the two Adams to their full development. See BONNER, *Augustine on Romans 5,12* (n. 274), p. 244.

363. "Legant ergo et intellegant... interna et occulta, mirabili ac ineffabili potestate operari Deum in cordibus hominum" (Augustine, *De gratia Christi et de peccato originali* 1,24,25 [CSEL, 42], p. 145).

fomulated it with the help of Platonism. As O. Chadwick writes: "He took the Platonist language and tried to harmonize it with Christian doctrine. He took the Platonist ethic and began to apply its ideas to the journey of the Christian soul"[364]. Above all, an important feature of Origen's theology became very appealing to, and had a great impact on, the monks populating the Egyptian desert, namely the interaction of grace and free will which he regarded as the commonly held "rule" of the Church[365]. In fact, the place and role of free will which Christian tradition before Augustine had always defended and enhanced in synergy with God's grace, found in Origen its most elaborated philosophical and theological articulation[366]. In highlighting to human autonomy and responsibility, Origen had provided a framework within which the ascetic/monastic ideal could find the means to seek perfection in obedience to God's commands.

The influence of Origenism on the monk Cassian is due to the latter's long stay with the monastic colonies of Egypt and above all to his connection with Evagrius Ponticus (345-399)[367], undoubtedly the greatest among the sophisticated and intellectual monks of the Egyptian desert[368], as well as the first to systematize monastic spirituality[369] through his interpretation of Origen's ascetic theology. Evagrius was

364. O. CHADWICK, *John Cassian. A Study in Primitive Monasticism*, 2nd ed., Cambridge, 1968, p. 84.

365. Cf. Origen, *De principiis* 1, *Praef.* 2 (SC, 252), p. 78.

366. See *supra*, pp. 202-213.

367. "La spiritualità di Cassiano ripete quella di Origene ed Evagrio Pontico" (TIBILETTI, *Giovanni Cassiano* [n. 274], p. 356). See also M. OLPHE-GALLIARD, *Cassien (Jean)*, in *DSp* 2 (1953) 214-276, p. 229; M. CAPPUYNS, *Cassien (Jean)*, in *DHGE* 11 (1949) 1319-1348, c. 1335.

368. "Évagre était des moines d'Égypte la personnalité la plus marquante" (M. VILLER, *Aux sources de la spiritualité de saint Maxime. Les oeuvres d'Évagre le Pontique*, in *RAM* 11 [1930] 156-184; 239-268; 331-336, p. 264). Imbued with Hellenistic culture, once become a monk Evagrius did not cease to be a διαλεκτικώτατος (cf. C. BUTLER, *The Lausiac History of Palladius* [TaS, 6/1-2], Cambridge, 1898-1904, p. 200). We know, however, that such an intellectual presence in the Egyptian desert was not positively accepted by the majority of the unlearned monks. Without any doubt, the disgrace which fell on the "Tall Brothers", when the so-called Origenist controversy reached its climax in 400, and on those monks who had been under Evagrius' direction, would not have spared the latter, had he lived longer.

369. "It was Evagrius who developed the Origenist ideas into the first system of monastic spirituality known to the Christian Church" (CHADWICK, *John Cassian* [n. 364], p. 86). See also L. BOYER, *The Spirituality of the New Testament and the Fathers* (A History of Christian Spirituality, 1), New York, 1982, p. 381. Evagrius can rightly be considered as the "ideologue" of late Antique monasticism (cf. S. OTTO, *"Esoterik und individualistische Gnosis: Der mönchische Platonismus des Euagrios Pontikos"*, in ID., *Die Antieke im Umbruch* [List Taschenbücher der Wissenschaft; Geschichte des politischen Denkens, 1513], Munich, 1974, p. 70).

thus the central figure in the formation of Cassian's understanding of the nature of monastic life and its quest for perfection[370]. *De institutis coenobiorum* and the *Conlationes* are to a great extent indebted to Evagrian speculations and there are few leading ideas which cannot find parallels in Evagrius[371]. The Origenist distinction, for instance, between πρακτική and θεωρητική[372] (active/ascetic life and contemplative life)

370. "Evagrius Ponticus was the single greatest inspiration for Cassian's spiritual theology" (C. STEWART, *Cassian the Monk* [OSHT], New York-Oxford, 1998, p. 36). And Marsili writes: "La dottrina che il monaco erudito di Scete aveva vissuto e insegnato, è diventata l'eredità spirituale che Cassiano ha riportato dall'Egitto.... Noi in Cassiano rileggiamo Evagrio" (S. MARSILI, *Giovanni Cassiano ed Evagrio Pontico. Dottrina sulla carità e contemplazione* [StAns, 5], Rome, 1936, p. 161). This strict dependence was already pointed out by Reitzenstein: "Zwischen Cassian und Euagrius bestehen Beziehungen welche näherer Untersuchung wert wären" (R. REITZENSTEIN [ed.], *Historia Monachorum und Historia Lausiaca*, Göttingen, 1916, p. 125, n. 1). Cf. also CHADWICK, *John Cassian* [n. 364], p. 92. A direct influence of Origen on Cassian must however be supposed as well. As Courcelle points out: "Tout en évitant de le nommer, Cassien fait de fréquents emprunts à Origène dont il a lu au moins le *De principiis*, le *Commentaire sur le Cantique* et les homélies sur la Genèse et l'Exode" (P. COURCELLE, *Les Lettres grecques en Occident, de Macrobe à Cassiodore*, 2nd ed., Paris, 1948, p. 214). See also the textual parallels established in MARSILI, *Giovanni Cassiano ed Evagrio Pontico*, pp. 150-158. Another source of Cassian's writings are the *Apophtegmata Patrum* (see H.-O. WEBER, *Die Stellung des Johannes Cassianus zur ausserpachomianischen Mönchstradition. Eine Quellenuntersuchung*, Münster i. W., 1961).

371. The influence of Evagrius on the works of Cassian has been studied by MARSILI, *Giovanni Cassiano ed Evagrio Pontico* (n. 370). By approaching and comparing a large number of texts, the author shows first Cassian's literary dependence upon Evagrius (cf. *Ibid.*, pp. 87-103) and then the influence exercised by the latter upon the former on the doctrinal level, more precisely with regard to the different stages of the spiritual life, the degrees of contemplation (ἀπάθεια/*puritas cordis*) and the theory of prayer (cf. *Ibid.*, pp. 103-144). See also CHADWICK, *John Cassian* [n. 364], pp. 93ff.

372. Already Plato had used the couple πρακτική–γνωστική (cf. Plato, *Politicus* 258e-259c) when, in his attempt at defining sciences as a whole, he divided them into two parts, assigning the manual activities to the first one (πρακτική) and the spiritual activity to the second one (γνωστική). See also Id., *ResPublica* V,476a-b. The opposition πρακτικός–θεωρητικός (where γνωστικός is substituted by θεωρητικός) belongs to Aristotle. He distinguished between the practical intellect whose goal is action, and the theoretical intellect, which finds its goal within its own activity. Similarly, whereas the goal of practical philosophy is action and efficacity, the aim of theoretical philosophy is the quest for truth (cf. Aristotle, *Metaphysica* I,1). This same division is applied by Aristotle to the different forms of life, the βίος πρακτικός and the βίος θεωρητικός (cf. Id., *Ethica Nicomachea* 1095b,15-20): the first does not apply only to manual activities, but to whatever leads to action, including politics; the second indicates pure contemplation. The Pythagoreans were actually the first to lead this type of "contemplative" life (βίος θεωρητικός) which was based on the search for truth and goodness by means of knowledge, considered the highest form of both purification and communion with the divine. The Stoics affirmed that practical activity concerns human things and aims at acquiring happiness in life especially through politics and social action, whereas things divine and theoretical happiness are the object of the theoretical activity (cf. A. GUILLAUMONT, *Étude historique et doctrinale*, in *Évagre le Pontique, Practicus* [SC, 170], pp. 42f). Like Plato and Aristotle, the other Greek philosophers made use of the term πρακτικός to refer to a

that Evagrius had developed, unlike Origen[373], as two distinct and successive stages[374], is taken up by Cassian who names the first stage *scientia actualis* and the second one *scientia contemplationis*[375], pointing out that the latter can only be apprehended when the former, the active virtue, is already possessed[376]. In Evagrius, the distinction between

profane activity. It is with Philo that for the first time (so it seems) the term acquires a moral and religious meaning (cf. Philo of Alexandria, *De praemiis et poenis* 51 [ed. BECKAERT], p. 66). The Christian writers made use of the term πρακτικός by stressing its meaning either in the Aristotelian/Stoic sense or in the way it was intended by Philo, and to which Evagrius felt akin. According to the Cappadocian Fathers, both πρακτική and θεορητική bear a religious meaning. The first defines all activities that aim at applying and spreading Christian truths (the clerical and episcopal active life), whereas the second refers to contemplative life, identified with the monastic vocation (cf. *e.g.*, Gregory of Nazianzus, *In laudem funebrem s. Basilii [Oratio 43]* 62 [SC, 384], pp. 258-260). Both point to a state of life which is independent and self-sufficient.

373. In Origen the two terms did not indicate two rigidly successive stages, the active life as coming first and the contemplative one as following. These two aspects of the spiritual life are overlapping and complementary. There is no antithesis between them but a gradualness and a reciprocal predisposition, to the extent that one cannot stand without the other. Thus, if it is true that contemplation constitutes the higher degree of human life, it is likewise true that that degree cannot be reached unless the experience of practical life is lived in close connection with the contemplative one. In other words, the more the soul becomes proficient in the ascetic struggle against vices and in the consequent practical acquisition of moral virtues (active life), the more it is turned towards the assimilation of truth (contemplative life). Cf. Origen, *Commentarii in Iohannem* 1,1 and 1,39 (SC, 120), pp. 56-60 and 282f; Id., *In Lucam homiliae*, Frag. 72 (SC, 87), pp. 520-522.

374. Evagrius' Origenism ought not to be identified in all its aspects with the thought of Origen himself. As O. Chadwick writes: "The first great difference between Origen and Evagrius lay in the distinction between the active life, *practice*, and the contemplative life, *theoretice*. Both writers agreed that the one led to the other. But in Origen they seem to overlap more than they do in Evagrius. For Origen a man does good and so approaches the vision of God; and conversely he approaches the vision of God and so comes to do good. Mary and Martha were complementary. In Evagrius the two lives were distinct and successive" (CHADWICK, *John Cassian* [n. 364], p. 88). It must be kept in mind that "practical/active life" means the "practice of virtue" which aims at purifying the soul from its passions. As Evagrius himself writes: "The πρακτική is that spiritual method which purifies the passionate part of the soul" (Evagrius Ponticus, *Practicus* 78 [SC, 171], p. 666). Indirectly the πρακτική purifies also the intellect freeing it from its susceptibility to imaginations and passions (cf. Id., *Gnosticus* 11 [SC, 356], p. 105). See A. GUILLAUMONT, *Étude historique et doctrinale* (n. 372), pp. 38-63; H. CROUZEL, *Origène*, Paris, 1985, pp. 231-232. On the problem of Evagrius' Origenism, see A. GUILLAUMONT, *Les 'Képhalaia gnostica' d'Évagre le Pontique et l'histoire de l'Origénisme chez les Grecs et chez les Syriens* (PatSor, 5), Paris, 1962, pp. 40-43 *et passim*.

375. "quidem duplex scientia est: prima πρακτική, id est actualis, quae emendatione morum ei uitiorum purgatione perficitur: altera θεωρητική, quae in contemplatione diuinarum rerum et sacratissimorum sensuum cognitione consistit" (Cassian, *Conlatio* 14,1 [SC, 54], p. 184).

376. "Quisquis igitur ad θεωρητικήν uoluerit peruenire, necesse est ut omni studio atque uirtute actualem primum scientiam consequatur. Nam haec πρακτική absque theoretica possideri potest, theoretica uero sine actuali omnimodis non potest adprehendi. Gradus enim quidam ita ordinati atque distincti sunt, ut humana humilitas possit ad

πρακτική and θεωρητική corresponds roughly to his two works, the *Practicus* (organized around the struggle against the λογισμοί, the evil thoughts[377], in view of the cleansing of the soul) and the *De oratione*. Similarly, in Cassian, the distinction between *scientia actualis* and *scientia contemplationis* corresponds to his two monastic writings, the *De institutis coenobiorum* and the *Conlationes*. The first, which describes the organization and the discipline (chs. 1-4), as well as the causes of and remedies to the eight principal faults (chs. 5-12), provides a framework within which the contemplative/spiritual ideals of the second find the place to develop freely[378]. Besides, whereas the *De institutis coenobiorum* were intended to focus on cenobitic life, viewed primarily from the perspective of the "outer person"[379] and his way of life (to which the emendation of faults is attached), the *Conlationes* are permeated with an "anchoritic flavour"[380] and are mainly concerned with the "inner person" that strives for perfection[381].

The peculiarity of Evagrius in maintaining the distinction between πρακτική and θεωρητική as two successive stages, rests on the fact that in speaking of the πρακτικός he has in mind the monk of the desert, more specifically the anchorite or semi-anchorite. Applied to this kind of monk, the πρακτική was essentially viewed as a struggle against the

---

sublime conscendere: qui si inuicem sibi ea qua diximus ratione succedant, potest ad altitudinem perueniri, ad quam sublato primo gradu non potest transuolari" (*Ibid.* 14,2, p. 184). Cf. *Ibid.* 15,2, pp. 211-212; Id., *De institutis* 5,33 (SC, 109), p. 243.

377. The scheme of the λογισμοί, inherited from Origen, was also adopted by Cassian through Evagrius. Cf. I. HAUSHERR, *L'origine de la théorie orientale des huit péchés capitaux*, in *OCP* 86 (1933) 164-175.

378. However, as Chadwick rightly warns us, "here, as in Evagrius, the distinction is in part made for clarity. In Cassian's ideas the two lives are entangled beyond hope of unravelling. He wrote the *Institutes* for those in the active life, the *Conferences* for those who are reaching "higher". Yet the *Conferences*, more often than not, are as engaged with the "life of virtue" as the *Institutes*" (CHADWICK, *John Cassian* [n. 364], p. 93). Moreover, the converse is also true: "The *Institutes* are a foundational work designed to guide and instruct and thus are more than simply a collection of customs and rules.... The teaching of the *Conferences* is often to be found in germ among the *Institutes*" (STEWART, *Cassian the Monk* [n. 370], p. 29). See also K.S. FRANK, *Johannes Cassian, De institutis coenobiorum. Normativer Erzähltext, präskriptiver Regeltext und appellative Du-Anrede*, in T. KÜHN – U. SCHAEFER (eds.), *Dialogische Strukturen. Dialogic Structures. Festschrift für Willi Erzgräber*, Tubingen, 1996, pp. 7-16; P. ROUSSEAU, *Cassian, Contemplation and the Coenobitic Life*, in *JHE* 26 (1975) 113-126, p. 126.

379. "Exterior ac uisibilis monachorum cultus" (Cf. Cassian, *Praef.* to *Conlationes* 1-10 [SC, 42], p. 75).

380. "Anachoretarum instituta sublimia" (*Ibid.*, p. 74).

381. "Inuisibilis interioris hominis habitus" (*Ibid.*, p. 75). It should be noted, however, that Cassian's terminological distinction between "anchorite" and "cenobite" is not to be taken rigidly, as it is not so much a taxonomy of forms of monastic life as the description of the common ideal of monastic perfection pursued in different ways.

λογισμοί, indispensable to the attainment of the γνοστική. Evagrius gives the term πρακτική an ascetic meaning that fits in well with the anchoritic/semi-anchoritic life of the Egyptian desert and defines it in its relation to the doctrine of ἀπάθεια (impassibility[382]). This, viewed as the gateway to ἀγάπη, which is the spontaneous fruit of ἀπάθεια, is in its turn the portal to the knowledge of God (γνῶσις)[383]. Thus ἀγάπη represents the condition for attaining the higher stage of contemplation or final goal consisting in the spiritual science (γνωστική), or the science of God (θεολογική), which invites man into eternal bliss (ἐσχάτη μακαριότης)[384].

382. Evagrius defines ἀπάθεια also as the "health of the soul (ὑγεία ψυχῆς)" (Evagrius Ponticus, *Practicus* 56 [SC, 170/2], p. 630). See GUILLAUMONT, *Étude historique et doctrinale* (n. 372), pp. 98-112. The ideal of ἀπάθεια was already known in the ancient Stoa (cf. *Stoicorum Veterum Fragmenta* [ed. HARNIM], Vol. III: *Chrysippi Fragmenta moralia, Fragmenta successorum Chrysippi*, Lipsia, 1903, n. 201, p. 48,30; n. 448, p. 109,12) but spread especially with the neo-Stoa in the Roman Empire (see, for instance, Seneca, *De tranquillitate animi* 2,4 [ed. BASORE], T. II, p. 214; Cicero, *Tusculanae* 4,17,37 [ed. KING], pp. 366-367). The first to transpose the ideal of ἀπάθεια into Christian asceticism was Clement of Alexandria (see GUILLAUMONT, *Étude historique et doctrinale* [n. 372], p. 101). It was Evagrius, however, who greatly developed this doctrine, introducing the term as well as the notion into monastic literature. Guillaumont writes that Evagrius' *Practicus* "pourrait aussi bien s'intituler περὶ ἀπαθείας" (*Ibid.*, p. 98). See also TIBILETTI, *Giovanni Cassiano* (n. 274), pp. 365-368; G. BUNGE, *Evagrios Pontikos: Briefe aus der Wüste* (Sophia, 24), Trier, 1986, pp. 118-125; ID., *Evagrios Pontikos: Praktikos oder der Mönch, Hundert Kapitel über das geistliche Leben*, Köln, 1989, pp. 189-213. Even though Evagrius' use of ἀπάθεια is generally linked with that of Clement of Alexandria, it must not be forgotten that Origen also had proposed several times the ideal of the complete suppression of passions. Although Origen very seldom uses the term ἀπάθεια and its derivates – which is why some scholars believe that "Origène incline davantage vers la métriopathie aristotelicienne que vers l'apathie stoïcienne" (H. CROUZEL – M. SIMONETTI, *Notes* to *De principiis [Books III and IV]* [SC, 269], p. 60) – the Evagrian concept of impassibility should be seen also in close relationship with Origen's ethical doctrine, more than it is generally thought (see R. SOMOS, *Origen, Evagrius Ponticus and the Ideal of Impassibility*, in W.A. BIENERT – U. KÜHNEWEG [eds.], *Origeniana Septima. Origenes in den Auseinandersetzungen des 4. Jahrhunderts*, Louvain, 1999, pp. 365-373). See also, M. SHERIDAN, *The Controversy over* ἀπάθεια: *Cassian's sources and his use of them*, in StMon 39 (1997) 287-310. A brief summary about both the meaning and the sources of Cassian's use of ἀπάθεια (and its combination with εὐπάθεια) can be found in COLISH, *The Stoic Tradition from Antiquity to the Early Middle Ages*. Vol. II (n. 347), pp. 118-120.

383. Cf. Evagrius Ponticus, *Practicus* 81 (SC, 171), p. 670. On the role of ἀγάπη, cf. *Ibid.* 38 and 84 (pp. 586 and 674); Id., *Gnosticus* 47 (SC, 356), p. 184; *Kephalaia gnostica* (versio syriaca) 3,35, *PO* 28, p. 111; *Ad monachos* 3, *TU* 39, p. 45. See GUILLAUMONT, *Étude historique et doctrinale* (n. 372), p. 49.

384. Cf. Evagrius Ponticus, *Practicus*, Prol. 8 (SC, 171), p. 492. See GUILLAUMONT, *Étude historique et doctrinale* (n. 372), pp. 103, 109-112. The relationship between love and knowledge in Evagrius' thought is somewhat ambiguous. In fact, in positing the knowledge of God as the ultimate goal, he seems to be suggesting that love is simply a means towards that goal. Bunge has argued, however, that Evagrius does not exalt

Cassian depends heavily on Evagrius' description of the ascetic struggle. In fact, for Cassian also, such a struggle aims at *caritas,* the spontaneous fruit of the achieved *puritas cordis*[385], usually viewed as an intermediate goal leading to something greater in strict connection with the enjoyment of the kingdom of God[386]. For both Evagrius and Cassian, the acquisition of ἀγάπη and access to the realm of contemplation is thus described as the positive result of a struggle waged by human effort and man's self-control against the subtle attacks of the λογισμοί. This is not to say that the place and role of divine assistance were neglected. Evagrius was well aware (as was Cassian) that without God's grace the ascetic combat would be ineffective, and that human effort needed the support of divine grace[387]. The fact is that for Evagrius (and Cassian) the matter at stake was not a choice between grace and man's will and efforts, but acknowledgement that the search for perfection needed both. Monastic life would provide the *locus* for their co-habitation and interaction, standing out as the evident day-to-day demonstration that human

γνῶσις over ἀγάπη, and that the latter should be seen as the organizing principle for all the stages of spiritual life. See BUNGE, *Evagrios Pontikos: Briefe aus der Wüste* (n. 382), pp. 129-139; C. JOEST, *Die Bedeutung von Akedia und Apatheia bei Evagrios Pontikos,* in *StMon* 35 (1993) 7-53, pp. 41-45.

385. Cf. Cassian, *De institutis coenobiorum* 4,43 (SC, 109), p. 184. The Cassianic expression *puritas cordis* replaces the Evagrian term ἀπάθεια. As Stewart writes: "Cassian's complete avoidance of the word *apatheia* – despite borrowings of other Evagrian terminology – signifies more than prudence about controversial aspects of his mentor's theology. Evagrius' term *apatheia* was prone to misinterpretation. Jerome, for example, caricatured *apatheia* as sinlessness and condemned the audacity of such a claim. Cassian's choice of "purity of heart" also avoids the awkwardness of an obviously technical and philosophical term. The biblical anchor for Cassian's doctrine of purity of heart is "blessed are the pure in heart, for they shall see God" (Matt. 5:8). By linking purity of heart to the vision of God, the beatitude connects "goal" to "end".... Cassian tends to simplify Evagrius' schemata and to avoid his highly technical vocabulary" (STEWART, *Cassian the Monk* [n. 370], p. 43).

Moreover, besides *caritas,* the "purity of heart" makes possible other experiences, such as "contemplation" (cf. Cassian, *De institutis coenobiorum* 2,12,2 and 5,32,1 [SC, 109], pp. 80 and 240; Id., *Conlatio* 1,10.15 [SC, 42], pp. 89 and 97; *Ibid.,* 9,15 [SC, 54], pp. 52f); spiritual knowledge (cf. *De institutis coenobiorum* 1,11 and 5,33 [SC, 109], pp. 52f and pp. 242f; *Conlationes* 1,14 and 14,9.15 [SC, 42], pp. 93ff and [SC, 54], pp. 192ff); prayer (cf. *Ibid.* 9,8 [SC, 54], pp. 48f); chastity (cf. *Ibid.* 12,7.8 [SC, 54], pp. 131ff); union with God (cf. *Ibid.* 2,2 [SC, 42], p112ff); beatitude (cf. *Ibid.* 22,6 [SC, 64], pp. 121ff).

386. Cf. *Ibid.* 1,4-7.11-13 (SC, 42), pp. 81 and 89-93. At times, however, Cassian emphasizes purity of heart as a goal in itself. See, for example: Id., *De institutis coenobiorum* 4,43 (SC, 109), p. 184; 5,7, p. 200; 5,22, p. 228; 8,22, p. 366; 12,15.24, pp. 470.484; *Conlatio* 1,7 (SC, 42), p. 84; 2,26, p. 136; 4,12, p. 176; 5,27, p. 217; 10,14 (SC, 54), p. 95; 12,5-8, pp. 126-135; 14,4, p. 185; 17,14, p. 259; 19,14 (SC, 64), p. 53; 21,36, p. 112; 22,3, p. 118.

387. Cf. *e.g.* Evagrius Ponticus, *Practicus* 43 (SC, 170), p. 600.

striving and divine grace are not to be seen and experienced as mutually exclusive, nor as if the former were to be totally subordinated to the latter. There is a touch of "humanism" (in the monastic theology of the desert as well as in Cassian's ascetic theology), which is at the basis of an optimistic outlook with regard to the possibilities of the human being to search for God and give him the adhesion of his own will and faith, possibilities that are rooted in the notion of the goodness of nature.

a) Free Will and the naturae bonum

A passage of Athanasius' *Vita Antonii* makes the best introduction to the present discussion on the *naturae bonum*, not only for the value attached to the goodness of human nature, but also because it is emblematic of the reaction of the Fathers of the Eastern Church to a pessimistic view of man and the world. Athanasius writes: "Virtue has need only of our will, since it is within us and springs from us. Virtue exists when the soul keeps in its natural state. It is kept in its natural state when it remains as it came into being. Now it came into being fair and perfectly straight"[388]. The emphasis on virtue as the "natural" state of the soul goes together with the certainty that this state can be brought forward by means of the human will, whose potentialities are rooted in the *naturae bonum*. It is Athanasius' assumption that if we abide in the state of goodness in which we have been made, we are in a state of virtue too.

Cassian's standpoint with regard to the co-operation of grace and free will rests on this same optimistic assumption: the *naturae bonum* is constitutive of man's nature as the result of the goodness of God's creative action, a goodness which, to some degree, has survived the fall of Adam. The same example given by Cassian about pagans who possess only a partial (μερικήν) chastity[389] is indicative of the fact that original sin did not completely choke the image of God in man, nor did it deprive him entirely of the knowledge of what is good and virtuous. In sharing this vision, Cassian places himself in direct contradiction with Augustine's sombre depiction of the mystery of man's sinful state inherited from Adam. Since the human being, continues the divine of Marseille, was created in order to seek the good and to enjoy the knowledge of it[390], one

---

388. "Οὐκοῦν ἡ ἀρετὴ τοῦ θέλειν ἡμῶν μόνου χρείαν ἔχει, ἐπειδήπερ ἐν ἡμῖν ἐστι καὶ ἐξ ἡμῶν συνίσταται. Τῆς γὰρ ψυχῆς τὸ νοερὸν κατὰ φύσιν ἐχούσης ἡ ἀρετὴ συνίσταται. Κατὰ φύσιν δὲ ἔχει, ὅταν ὡς γέγονε μένῃ· γέγονε δὲ καλὴ καὶ εὐθὴς λίαν" (Athanasius, *Vita Antonii* 20,5-6 [SC, 400], pp. 188.190 [English translation by MEYER [ed.], *St. Athanasius* [n. 125], p. 37).

389. Cf. Cassian, *Conlatio* 13,5 (SC, 54), p. 152.

390. "fecit Deus hominem rectum, id est, ut tantummodo boni scientia iugiter frueretur" (*Ibid.* 13,12, p. 164).

could not possibly admit that, after the fall, man was deprived of the power of the will to attain virtue/good[391]. This conviction was reinforced through the option for the doctrine of creationism (as a solution to the problem of the origin of the soul[392]) that Cassian had espoused in line with the majority of the Fathers of the Church and Christian writers[393] who had also embraced this theory. According to it, God creates a new soul for each individual at the moment of its infusion in the foetus or in the body of the newly born child. Not only is this soul spiritual, due to the fact that it is created directly by God who is a spiritual being[394], but it is also made in God's image. For this reason, the soul is endowed with knowledge and free will, so that it may be able to comply with God's demands and have part in his communion.

In the light of the creationist theory, Cassian did not feel the need to deepen and give a clear-cut explanation of the problem of the relationship between Adam's sin (*Ursünde*) and its transmission to Adam's stock (*Erbsünde*)[395]. Once the co-operation of grace and free will was safeguarded, together with the insistence that man's free will remains operative after the fall, and that the cause of actual sin must be looked for in the assent of the will to the fascination of evil[396], there was no room left for a "tragic" doctrine of an inherited original sin, as Augustine

391. "Nec enim talem Deus hominem fecisse credendus est, qui nec uelit umquam nec possit bonum" (*Ibid.*).

392. Unlike Augustine who, in this respect, had never really made up his mind. See *supra*, p. 173, n. 382.

393. "Cette... doctrine finira par demeurer à peu près la seule soutenue dans l'Église" (G. ROTUREAU, *Âme [Théologie]*, in *Cath* 1 [1948] 430-434, c. 432). See also J. TURMEL, *Histoire des dogmes. I. Le péché originel. La rédemption*, Paris, 1931, p. 146; BEATRICE, *Tradux peccati* (n. 362), p. 100.

394. Such a conviction is also expressed by Cassian in the following terms: "Ut enim paulo ante diximus spiritus spiritum non generat, sicut ne animam quidem potest anima procreare, licet concretionem carnis non dubitemus humano semine coalescere, ita de utraque substantia, id est carnis et animae, quae cui adscribatur auctori, apostolo manifestius distinguente: *deinde patres*, inquit, *carnis nostrae habuimus eruditores et reuerebamur: non multo magis subiciemur patri spirituum et uiuemus?* Quid hac diuisione clarius potuit definire, ut carnis quidem nostrae patres homines pronuntiaret, animarum uero Deum solum esse patrem constanter exprimeret?" (Cassian, *Conlatio* 8,25 [SC, 54], p. 35).

395. "Die Möglichkeit einer Sündenvererbung scheint dadurch gänzlich ausgeschlossen zu sein. Um so mehr, als Cassian den Generatianismus ausdrücklich ablehnt und sich zum Kreatianismus bekennt" (J. GROSS, *Entwicklungsgeschichte des Erbsündendogmas im nachaugustinischen Altertum und in der Vorscholastik (5.-11. Jahrhundert)* [Geschichte des Erbsündendogmas, Bd. II], München-Basel, 1963, p. 30).

396. According to Cassian, the evil of sin (*malum peccati*) can take possession of the soul only if the latter gives its assent. But this happens only when the heart is coward and the will corrupt: "Nec enim potuit aliquando cuiquam nolenti ac resistenti malum peccati alter inferre nisi illi soli, qui illud in sese cordis ignauia et corrupta uoluntate suscepit" (Cassian, *Conlationes* 6,4 [SC, 42], p. 224).

would teach. As a consequence, Cassian did not deem it necessary to give the original sin that central place that the bishop of Hippo had accorded to it in his theological system[397]. Without indulging in theological speculations[398], and as a perfect disciple of the East, Cassian shared the optimistic outlook of the Greek theologians and (most probably under the influence of John Chrysostom) considered original sin as a simple "punishment" and not as a "sin", even less as an "inherited debt/guilt"[399]. The same expression *peccatum originale*, which appears only once in Cassian's works, retains the traditional pre-Augustinian meaning, viz. that of the (original/first) sin of Adam (*Ursünde*) which caused him and his stock the loss of incorruption and immortality as well as that of supernatural knowledge and eternal bliss, and the consequent enslavement to the devil.

Moreover, Cassian did not mention the *peccatum originale* in an attempt to describe its "ins" and "outs", but in relation to the question of God's call to universal salvation, which he defended in opposition to the Augustinian view that only a number of people would be saved. Relying on two scriptural quotations: *Per omnes homines mors pertransisse* (Rom 5,12), concerning the entrance and the consequences of death into man's life, caused by Adam's sin; and: *Omnes enim peccauerunt et egent gloria Dei* (Rom 3,23), alluding to personal/actual sins, Cassian argues that Christ died indeed for the salvation of all men, without

---

397. "Cassian hat die Erbsünde lediglich dem Worte, nicht aber der Sache nach" (J. GROSS, *Entwicklungsgeschichte des Erbsündendogmas* [n. 395], p. 31).

398. "Man hat zwar immer gesehen, daß das griechische Denken (im Gegensatz zu dem der Lateiner) weniger von der anthropologischen Problemstellung betroffen war und deshalb auch an den Fragen nach Ur- und "Erbsünde" ein geringeres Interesse bezeigte" (L. SCHEFFCZYK, *Urstand, Fall und Erbsünde von der Schrift bis Augustinus*, in M. SCHMAUS *et al.* [eds.], *Handbuch der Dogmengeschichte*, Bd. II, 3a [1.Teil], Freiburg-Basel-Wien, 1981, pp. 123-124).

399. "Il ne nie point le péché originel, sauf toutefois, à l'exemple de saint Chrysostome…, à le tenir pour une simple pain, non pour un péché ni même une dette héréditaire" (P. GODET, *Cassien Jean*, in *DTC* 2 [1910] 1823-1829, c. 1827). Cf., for instance, John Chrysostom's interpretation of Rom 5,19 ("So just as by the one man's disobedience the many were made sinners, so by the one man's obedience the many will be made righteous"): "What then is the question? It is the saying that through the offence of one many were made sinners. For the fact that when he had sinned and become mortal, those who were of him should be so also, is nothing unlikely. But how would it follow that from his disobedience another would become a sinner? For at this rate a man of this sort will not even deserve punishment, if, that is, it was not from his own self that he became a sinner. What then does the word 'sinners' mean here? To me it seems to mean liable to punishment and condemned to death" (John Chrysostom, *In epistulam ad Romanos homiliae* 10,2.3 [PG, 60], cc. 476-478 [English translation by J.B. MORRIS – W.H. SIMCOX (eds.), *The Homilies of St. John Chrysostom on the Epistle of St. Paul the Apostle to the Romans* (NPNF, first series, 11), s.l., s.d., repr. Grand Rapids, MI, 1979, p. 403]).

exception, and that God comes to the help of all those (*i.e.* all men) who are under the yoke of death and lie open to actual sinning. Conversely, the belief that only a limited number of men will be saved, would entail that not all have been reached by Adam's sin (viz. death and its consequences) and that, therefore, not all are liable to actual sins[400]. Cassian, in other words, focuses on the fact that since all men are reached by the consequences (*ruina et mors*) of Adam's sin, they are all called as well to *resurrectio et uita* by the second Adam, Christ[401]. The condemnation brought about by the first man must be viewed, as it were, as a *felix culpa* which calls for Christ's mediation, thanks to which Adam's descent is delivered from its ancient fetters[402].

Apart from the above isolated use of the expression *peccatum originale*, the term Cassian generally uses to describe the sin of Adam is *praeuaricatio*[403], a common term which also has the advantage of immediately suggesting the ascetic framework in which he set his teaching and within which Adam's fall should be approached and understood. The ideal of pure contemplation, which ought to enable the monk to see and possess God (*Deus uel uidetur uel tenetur*)[404], comes into conflict with those evil thoughts and vices that wage war against man's desire for God and that try to hinder his union with him. Man, as it were, is always in danger of *praeuaricatio*. In the words of abbot Moses, the monk experiences in himself the opposition between the kingdom of God and the kingdom of the devil, between Christ's lordship over his own heart and that of the devil[405]. The monk is thus led to the awareness that the contemplation and possession of the kingdom of God, which represents his ultimate goal (*finis*), cannot be achieved without the pursuit of the intermediate goal (*scopos*), viz. the *puritas cordis*[406], which, in its turn, can be obtained through the practice of virtues such as solitude, austerity, poverty, fasting and meditation on the Scriptures[407].

---

400. "Si autem non omnes uniuersaliter, sed quosdam aduocat, sequitur ut nec omnes sint onerati uel originali uel actuali peccato nec uera sit illa sententia: *omnes enim peccauerunt et egent gloria Dei*, nec *per omnes homines mors pertransisse* credatur" (Cassian, *Conlatio* 13,7 [SC, 54], p. 156).

401. "Ille *[Adam]* primus ad ruinam et mortem, hic *[Christ]* primus ad resurrectionem et uitam. Per illum omne genus hominum condemnatur, per istum omne genus hominum liberatur" (*Ibid.* 5,6 [SC, 42], p. 193).

402. Cf. *Ibid.* 23,12 (SC, 64), p. 155.

403. See, for instance, *Ibid.* 5,6 (SC, 42), pp. 193-194; 5,24, p. 215; 13,12 (SC, 54), p. 164; 23,12 (SC, 64), p. 154.

404. *Ibid.* 1,15 (SC, 42), p. 97.

405. *Ibid.* 1,13, p. 91.

406. Cf. *Ibid.* 1,7, p. 85.

407. *Ibid.* 1,7, pp. 84-85.

Beside triggering and keeping the monk's strong commitment alive, the
need of the *puritas cordis* reminds him of the real status of man, namely
his being created by God in his own image and likeness. The aim of the
ascetic efforts of the monk is therefore to recover the truth and the
beauty of God's image and likeness imprinted in man, but violated and
perverted by the devil when he tempted Adam and caused his *praeuaricatio*[408].

Allusion to the devil (or serpent) and emphasis on his role in the fall
of Adam was commonplace in the Christian writers of the first centuries[409]. In the case of Cassian, it is possible that he was under the influence of Irenaeus, via the latter's connection with the school of Lérins,
where an echo of the great bishop of Lyon can be retraced in some sermons of Hilary and Honoratus and in the works of Vincent[410]. Irenaeus
had clearly stated that the first man had been created by God in order to
possess life (*i.e.* immortality), but that he had lost it and had procured
himself mortality because of the fall, prompted by the devil. Yet, to
acknowledge man's exclusion from eternal life would have meant God
having to admit that his will had been defeated by the malice of the
devil, an admission which would be unthinkable. In God's *oeconomia
salutis*, in fact, the devil was going to be overwhelmed by Christ, the
second Adam. He would destroy death and give life back to the first
Adam (= man) who, in the meantime, had become the slave of death and
the property of the devil to whose lordship he was subdued[411]. Emphasis
(such as that of Irenaeus) on the devil allowed the theologians of the first
centuries to regard man's fallen nature not as a nature that was *per se*
bad, (for this would question the goodness of God's creation), but as a
nature that had fallen and become prisoner of the devil for having freely
yielded to his instigations. In this *negotiatio damnosa fraudulentumque
commercium* – as Cassian writes[412] – Adam had opted for the kingdom of
the devil, rather than for that of God, and had sold himself and his

---

408. Cf. *Ibid.* 5,6 (SC, 42), pp. 193-194, where Adam's *praeuaricatio* is depicted as a
subjugation to the fascinations of the devil (*deceptus incelebris diaboli*) which caused
him to lose his image and likeness with God.
409. Cf. L. BOUYER, *La vie de S. Antoine. Essai sur la spiritualité du monachisme
primitif* (SpOr, 22), Bégrolles en Mauges, 1977, pp. 215-216.
410. See F.R. MONTGOMERY HITCHCOCK, *Irenaeus of Lugdunum. A Study of his
Teaching*, Cambridge, 1914, p. 348.
411. Cf. Irenaeus, *Aduersus haereses* 3,23,1 (SC, 211), pp. 445, and 447. See also
Ibid. 5,21,1-3 (SC, 153), pp. 261-279 *passim*. See M. HAUKE, *Heilsverlust in Adam. Stationen griechischer Erbsündenlehre: Irenäus-Origenes-Kappadozier* (KKTS, 58), Paderborn, 1993, pp. 247ff.
412. Cassian, *Conlatio* 23,12 (SC, 64), p. 154.

descendants to the *lex peccati*[413] and to the perpetual bondage (*perpetua seruitus*) of the devil[414]. In spite of Adam's fall, however, the deep-seated goodness of human nature was not done away with. God, continues Cassian, did not totally lose the right of property over fallen man, since the devil was not allowed to take hold of God's treasure (*peculium Dei*) entirely[415]. The fall has indeed caused the corruption of the *lex natu-ralis*[416] and has indeed brought about the acquisition of the *scientia mali*[417] and man's *uoluntaria caecitas*[418], but it would be unjust to attribute to fallen human nature only that which pertains to evil. In point of fact, the human being did not completely lose the *scientia boni*[419], viz. the capacity, stemming from the goodness at the core of human nature, of discerning good[420].

According to Cassian (and in this respect he shares the Pelagians' thought[421]) sin, whether the sin of the first man or personal sin, is always something adventitious and extraneous to the substance of human nature, something that does not belong to it "naturally", something that tries to take hold of human nature (although it does not have any right to it) in order to dominate it, precisely as an invader would do[422]. Here Cassian shows once again his dependence upon the Eastern theological tradition, most probably via two of his masters, Origen and Evagrius. According to Origen, in fact, God did not plant an evil tree in man, which produces wicked fruits. If wicked fruits are produced, then they must not be regarded as the product of human nature (which is in itself good and cannot be the source of evil), but as the result of sin, which attacks human nature from without, and tries to subdue it[423]. Every time

413. *Ibid.* 23,11, p. 153.
414. Cf. *Ibid.* 23,12, pp. 154f.
415. *Ibid.*, p. 155.
416. *Ibid.* 8,24 (SC, 54), p. 33.
417. "Concepit ergo Adam post praeuaricationem quam non habuerat scientiam mali"; "... facti enim sunt ... scientes bonum et malum" (*Ibid.* 13,12, p. 164).
418. *Ibid.*, p. 165.
419. "...boni uero quam acceperat scientiam non amisit" (*Ibid.*, p. 164).
420. "Nobis ne quid boni umquam sapere aut cogitare possimus, naturaliter denegatur" (*Ibid.*, p. 166).
421. See *supra*, nn. 229 and 230.
422. "Nam uoluntas Domini possessionem cordis nostri non uitiis, sed uirtutibus naturaliter deputauit. Quae post praeuaricationem Adae insolescentibus uitiis, id est populis Chananaeis a propria regione depulsae cum ei rursum per Dei gratiam diligentia nostra ac labore fuerint restitutae, non tam alienas occupasse terras quam proprias credendae sunt recepisse" (Cassian, *Conlatio* 5,24 [SC, 42], p. 215). Cf. *Ibid.* 23,11 (SC, 64), p. 154; Id., *De institutis coenobiorum* 12,5 (SC, 109), p. 456. See also V. CODINA, *El aspecto cristo-logico en la espiritualidad de Juan Casiano* (OCA, 175), Rome, 1966, pp. 45-47.
423. Cf. Origen, *Commentarii in epistulam ad Romanos* 6,5, *FC*, Bd. II/3, pp. 216-226.

that man lets himself be enslaved by sin, the image of God in him is
defaced and is replaced by the image of the devil[424]. Also according to
Evagrius, evil thoughts could not possibly be begotten by human
nature[425], because men were not created wicked (πονεροὶ). God has
sown good seeds in his field (cf. Mt 13,24), the *uirtutum semina* that
cannot be destroyed[426].

From the Eastern theological tradition, therefore, Cassian draws the
generally accepted teaching that evil as such does not belong to human
nature. It comes from outside[427], and it is the work of the devil who tries
to win over the compliance of man's free will. It is as if nature were considered to be almost a synonym of good[428], so that whatever does not
belong to the goodness of man's nature, like the vices, can indeed be
cancelled out, counteracted and uprooted[429]. Sin and nature are regarded
as contradictory concepts[430]. We can then understand why, whereas the
Latin theologians speak of *natura lapsa* or *uitiata*, the Greek theologians

424. Cf. Id., *In Lucam homiliae* 8,3 (SC, 87), pp. 166.168. See also, H. CROUZEL,
Théologie de l'image de Dieu chez Origène (Théol [P], 34), Paris, 1956, pp. 190-191.

425. "Ἐκ δὲ τῆς φύσεως οὐδεὶς ἐξέρχεται λογισμὸς πονηρός" (Evagrius Ponticus, *De malignis cogitationibus* 31 [PG, 40], c. 1240).

426. "Ἀνεξάλειπτα γὰρ τὰ σπέρματα τῆς ἀρητῆς" (*Ibid.*). We may as well quote
another representative of the ancient monastic tradition, Marcianus (Pseudo-Nylus), who
strikes the same note when he affirms that the sinful powers are not innate (σύμφυτα),
but adventitious because they are brought from outside (ἐπείσακτα) (cf. Marcianus
[Ps.-Nylus], *Tractatus moralis et multifarius* 2 [PG, 79], c. 1281).

427. "Das Übel kommt von aussen und bleibt der Natur immer freund" (A. KEMMER,
*Charisma Maximum. Untersuchung zu Cassians Vollkommenheitslehre und seiner Stel-
lung zum Messalianismus*, Louvain, 1938, p. 30).

428. "Bien rares – writes Hausherr – sont ceux qui admettraient des expressions telles
que 'nature mauvaise', 'nature viciée'. La φύσις est bonne, étant l'oeuvre de Dieu. Aucun
mal ne peut venir d'elle, ni avant ni après le peché originel. Dire le contraire, leur paraî-
trait rendre responsable du mal le Créateur lui-même.... Κατὰ φύσιν est synonyme de
vertu; παρὰ φύσιν synonime de vice" (I. HAUSHERR, *L'erreur fondamentale et la logique
du Messialinisme*, in *OCP* 1 [1935] 328-360, p. 334). Cf. also: "Τῷ δὲ ἀγαθῷ λογισμῷ
δύο μόνον ἀντίκεινται λογισμοί, ὅ τε δαιμονιώδης, καὶ ὁ ἐκ τῆς ἡμετέρας
προαιρέσεως ἀποκλινούσης ἐπὶ τὸ χεῖρον. Ἐκ δὲ τῆς φύσεως οὐδεὶς ἐξέρχεται
λογισμὸς πονηρός. Οὐ γὰρ ἀπαρχῆς γεγόναμεν πονηροί, εἴπερ καλὸν σπέρμα
ἔσπειρεν ὁ Κύριος ἐν τῷ ἰδίῳ ἀγρῷ" (Evagrius Ponticus, *De malignis cogitationibus*
31 [PG, 40], c. 1240). We must be reminded that chapters 63-71 of the *Practicus*, in the
Migne edition, do actually belong to Evagrius' treatise *De malignis cogitationibus*. See A.
and C. GUILLAUMONT (eds.), *Évagre le Pontique, Traité pratique ou le moine*, T. I (SC,
170), pp. 193,418-419,425; J. MUYLDERMANS, *À travers la tradition manuscrite d'Evagre
le Pontique. Essai sur les manuscrits grecs conservés à la bibliothèque nationale de Paris*
(BMus, 3), Louvain, 1932, p. 53.

429. The fire of libido, for instance, is not natural, and therefore can be quenched (cf.
Cassian, *Conlatio* 12,12 [SC, 54], p. 140).

430. Cf. KEMMER, *Charisma Maximum* (n. 427), pp. 29-30.

prefer to speak of "evil habit (ἕξις τοῦ κακοῦ)"[431], which is the result of man turning away from God. This habit takes, as it were, the form of second nature, and can be fought only by an ascetic life through which man can strenuously and efficaciously wage war against those vices upon which the habit rests. We can thus comprehend Cassian's relative optimism, as opposed to Augustine's sombre and pessimistic approach. Despite Adam's fall, Cassian believed that because of the ultimate goodness of man's nature, the latter has remained in possession of his intelligence and free will, and even the image and likeness of God in him are not utterly compromised, but merely defaced[432].

The goodness of human nature having survived the fall, it follows that God, in his bounty, continues to offer man several occasions whereby he can experience salvation[433]. Because of that natural principle of virtue (*uirtutum semina*) implanted by God in man's soul, man, with the help of divine grace, must do what he can to respond positively to God's merciful condescension and fight against those vices that, like thorns (*aculei*), try to suffocate this process[434]. This image of the *uirtutum semina* echoes the Stoic interpretation of the virtuous nature of man, on one side, and of the hindrances caused by the vices that come from outside, on the other[435]. According to Stoicism, in fact, vices may obscure those natural faculties/virtues (*uirtutum semina*) human nature has been endowed with, but they are not able to overwhelm or extinguish them[436].

---

431. Cf. I. HAUSHERR, *Les orientaux connaissent-ils les "nuits" de Saint Jean de la Croix?*, in *OCP* 12 (1946) 5-46.

432. We cannot but register a striking similarity with Julian of Aeclanum's thought in his treatment of the *peccatum originale*. Cassian, the practical theologian, and Julian, the speculative one, seem to meet on this particular point. Rather than an influence of one upon the other, it is most likely that this agreement is due to the common Eastern sources on which they both rely, and to the undoubted influence of Stoicism on their thought.

433. "Sicut occasiones salutis diuersis modis Deum cognoscimus operari, ita nostrum est occasionibus a diuinitate concessis uel enixius uel remissius famulari" (Cassian, *Conlatio* 3,12 [SC, 42], p. 155). Cf. also *Ibid.* 3,19, p. 162; Id., *De institutis coenobiorum* 12,14,2 [SC, 109], p. 468.

434. "...aculeis naturalia uirtutum semina praefocantur" (Id., *Conlatio* 23,11 [SC, 64], p. 154).

435. "Erras enim si existimas nobiscum vitia nasci; superuenerunt, ingesta sunt... Nulli nos vitio natura conciliat; illa integros ac liberos genuit" (Seneca, *Ad Lucilium epistulae morales* 94,55-56 [ed. GUMERRE], T. III, p. 46).

436. There is a natural good, says Seneca, which only at a second stage is attacked, polluted and obscured by the evil that allures the life of man: "Falsum est; peiores morimur quam nascimur. Nostrum istud, non naturae vitium est" (Seneca, *Ep.* 22,15, *Ibid.*, T. I, p. 156); "Non enim extincta in illo indoles naturalis est, sed obscurata et oppressa" (Id., *Ep.* 94,31, *Ibid.*, T. III, p. 32). Likewise, Cicero writes that it is the task of man to bring to light these primordial elements, called by the Stoics not only *semina* but also *igniculi* or *scintillae*: "Nunc parvulos nobis dedit [*natura*] igniculos, quos celeriter malis moribus opinionibusque depravati sic restinguimus, ut nusquam naturae lumen

We find a similar (although Christianized) assumption in Cassian: the principle of virtue and good, abiding in the nature of man, is innate to his being[437]. It is a *bonum naturale*[438], inserted into man's soul at the very moment of creation as a sure pathway along which the human being can reach out to the Creator and be prevented from falling away from him[439]. There is something concretely positive within the soul, viz. a "principle of good", which God, in creating man in his own image and likeness, had destined for him as an essential property of his nature. It is not something occasional, a mere inclination or a simple attitude, but an ontological good, a primordial and positive nucleus constituted by the *uirtutum semina*. Such a property, however, precisely because it concerns the "seeds" of virtues, is not accomplished in itself once and for all. It needs developing so that it may achieve perfection, and this can only come about through the help of divine enlightenment[440]. Moreover, since God's action takes place in different and inscrutable ways[441], it

---

appareat. Sunt enim ingeniis nostris semina innata virtutum" (Cicero, *Tusculanae* 3,1,2 [ed. KING] pp. 224.226); "Est enim natura sic generata vis hominis, ut ad omnem virtutem percipiendam facta videatur, ob eamque causam parvi virtutum simulacris, quarum in se habent semina, sine doctrina moventur;... non sine causa eas quas dixi in pueris virtutum quasi scintillas videmus" (Id., *De finibus* 5,15,43, [ed. RACKHAM], p. 442). See also Seneca: "Omnium honestarum rerum semina animi gerunt, quae admonitione excitantur.... Erigitur virtus, cum tacta est et inpulsa" (Seneca, *Ep.* 94,29 [ed. GUMMERE], p. 30). The term *uirtutum semina*, used by Cassian, points undoubtedly to the influence that Stoic literature exercised on his thinking.

437. Julian of Aeclanum too speaks of virtues as *congenitae*: "Homo per omnia probus congenitis dicitur florere virtutibus" (Julian of Aeclanum, *Ad Florum* 4,129 [PL, 45], c. 1426). Virtues are thus imprinted in the goodness of the human nature and wait to be brought to fulfilment by man's agency. This explains the great emphasis laid on human voluntary commitment and responsibility.

438. Cassian, *Conlatio* 14,3 (SC, 54), p. 184.

439. "Id quod per naturam conditionis insertum est" (*Ibid.* 3,15 [SC, 42], p. 158); "Deus hominem creans omnem naturaliter ei scientiam legis inseruit" (*Ibid.* 8,23 [SC, 54], p. 31). Also man's *motus carnales*, whose aim is procreation, "utiliter sunt corpori nostro prouidentia Creatoris inserti" (Id., *De institutis coenobiorum* 7,3,2 [SC, 109], p. 294). The same is true for other movements such as anger or sadness, which are "a Creatore nobis insertos" (*Ibid.* 7,4, p. 296) in order that they may be usefully employed for one's own salvation. The verb *inserere* shows that the knowledge of good and the capability of following it are inscribed in man's creation. Cf. also Id., *Conlatio* 5,8 (SC, 42), pp. 196-197; *Ibid.* 14,3 (SC, 54), p. 185.

440. "Sciens nequaquam sibimet sufficere posse id quod per naturam conditionis insertum est, nisi cotidiana Domini inluminatione... sensus ipsius ab eodem fuerit inlustratus" (*Ibid.* 3,15 [SC, 42], p.158). "Dubitari ergo non potest inesse quidem omni animae naturaliter uirtutum semina beneficio creatoris inserta: sed nisi haec opitulatione Dei fuerint excitata, ad incrementum perfectionis non poterunt peruenire, quia secundum beatum apostolum *neque qui plantat est aliquid, neque qui rigat, sed qui incrementum dat Deus*" (*Ibid.* 13,12 [SC, 54], p. 166).

441. "Multiformis illa sapientia Dei salutem hominum multiplici atque inscrutabili pietate dispensat" (*Ibid.* 13,15, p. 175); "Euidentissime poterimus aduertere diuersis

may sometimes happen that a divine intervention follows the initiative of the human will. When this is the case, then the intervention of enlightening grace is aimed at helping man's will to bring its good thoughts and desires to fulfilment. At other times, though, it is God himself who directly inspires the pursuit of the good[442], and on some occasions He even seems to abandon a soul in order to put it to the test and help it to grow towards perfection[443]. It is clear, however, that when it is man who, thanks to the *uirtutum semina*, takes the initiative and pursues the good, this happens in accordance with God's designs and never independently of them. Cassian's expression *utiliter quodammodo subsistentem*[444] seems to indicate that God's providence never departs from man but it is always at work for his well-being and salvation. Thus, even when good is first sought by human initiative, this does not happen without divine providence allowing and confirming it[445].

The constant reference to God's creation and to the activity of his providence in the life of man clearly indicates that Cassian's doctrine of the *uirtutum semina* must be understood against the background of Christian faith and revelation. In fact, although he shares the Stoic terminology, and partly also its optimism, Cassian is aware that man cannot accomplish any good work nor save himself by his own efforts alone. Human nature, considered by Stoicism as an independent and autarchic reality, is, in Christianity, essentially connected with and dependent upon God the Creator and his providence. In sharing the Stoic optimism about human nature, therefore, Cassian views it from a different perspective. His approach is imbued with Christian revelation, with

atque innumeris modis et inscrutabilibus uiis Deum salutem humani generis procurare" (*Ibid.* 13,17, p. 178).

442. "Et quorundam quidem uolentium ac sitientium cursum ad maiorem incitare flagrantiam, quosdam uero etiam nolentes inuitosque conpellere, et nunc quidem ut inpleantur ea quae utiliter a nobis desiderata perspexerit adiuuare, nunc uero etiam ipsius sancti desiderii inspirare principia et uel initium boni operis uel perseuerantiam condonare" (*Ibid.*). Cf. also *Ibid.* 13,18, p. 180.

443. "Utiliter a Domino subrelictus" (*Ibid.* 12,6, p. 130). As to God who abandons the soul for a while in order to make it feel the need of grace more urgently, see the following quotation: "Necesse est ut superno illo praesidio paululum denudati tamdiu illis quas diuina uirtus extinxerat passionibus opprimantur, quamdiu experientia docente cognoscant, se uiribus atque industria sua puritatis bonum obtinere non posse" (*Ibid.* 12,16, p. 145).

444. *Ibid.* 12,6, p. 130.

445. "Adest igitur inseparabiliter nobis semper diuina protectio tantaque est erga creaturam suam pietas creatoris, ut non solum comitetur eam, sed etiam praecedat iugiter prouidentia... Qui cum in nobis ortum quendam bonae uoluntatis inspexerit, inluminat eam confestim atque confortat et incitat ad salutem, incrementum tribuens ei quam uel ipse plantauit uel nostro conatu uiderit emersisse" (*Ibid.* 13,8, p. 158).

the theological reflection of the Fathers of the Church and with the teaching of the monastic writers[446]. He agrees that nature is in itself good and that the role it has to play ought not to be underrated, as happens when one lends oneself to the temptation of attributing all good to grace alone[447]. He also shares the Stoic conviction that vices are not a product of man but come from outside, and that they can be fought effectively and expelled from the soul, which, once it has been purified and has regained its natural faculties[448] and its healthy natural state (*naturalis sanitas*), can truly contemplate the mysteries of Holy Scripture[449]. The insight and wisdom of the natural faculties with which human nature

---

446. As Tibiletti puts it, "non è il caso di pensare a due fonti distinte dell'ascetica di Cassiano: stoicismo e teologia monastica di Origene, Basilio, Gregorio Nisseno, Evagrio Pontico ed altri. Il rigore ascetico del monachesimo doveva quasi inevitabilmente incontrarsi con l'ascesi stoica, e raccoglierne, con la terminologia, gli accenti vitali" (TIBILETTI, *Giovanni Cassiano* [n. 274], p. 377).

447. "Vnde cauendum nobis est, ne ita ad dominum omnia sanctorum merita referamus, ut nihil nisi id quod malum atque peruersum est humanae adscribamus naturae" (Cassian, *Conlatio* 13,12 [SC, 54], pp. 165-166).

448. "Curemus mentem ab omnibus terrenis uitiis expurgatam cunctisque mundatam faecibus passionum ad subtilitatem perducere naturalem" (*Ibid.*, 9,4, p. 43). See also *Ibid.* 1,14 (SC, 42), p. 96. The same concept can be found in Evagrius Ponticus, *Sermo siue dogmatica epistula de sanctissima Trinitate* (Ps.-Basilius, *Epistula* 8) 12, in *S. Basile, Lettres* (ed. COURTONNE), T. I, pp. 36-37; cf. MARSILI, *Giovanni Cassiano ed Evagrio Pontico* (n. 370), p. 89.

449. "Quibus expulsis *[the vices]* confestim cordis oculi sublato uelamine passionum sacramenta scripturarum naturaliter contemplarentur…; quibus rursum naturali redditis sanitati ipsa scripturarum sanctarum lectio ad contemplationem uerae scientiae abunde etiam sola sufficiat" (Cassian, *De institutis coenobiorum* 5,34 [SC, 109], p. 244). The *naturalis sanitas* Cassian speaks of has a precedent in Tertullian: "*[Anima]* … sanitatem suam patitur" (Tertullian, *Apologeticum* 17,5 [CSEL, 69], p. 45). This doctrine of the *bonum animae proprie naturale* (cf. Id., *De anima* 41 [CSEL, 20], p. 368) betrays traces of Stoic speculation. In the soul, affirms Tertullian, there exists a *bonum naturale* which God has given at the moment of creation. It is something innate (*insit*). But there exists also a *malum* which, besides that which is caused by the operations of the devil, is derived primarily from original sin. This *malum*, which is inherent in the soul from the very beginning, is "somewhat" a natural one (*naturale quodammodo*). The corruption of nature is in fact like a second nature, although the *bonum animae*, the original good which is derived from God, lives on and remains fundamental, divine, fully itself and "really" natural (*proprie naturale*). The original good may thus be obscured, in that it is not the goodness of God himself, but it cannot be destroyed because it proceeds from him (cf. *Ibid.*). Tertullian reiterates the thesis he had already discussed in his *De testimonio animae* and that had found a clear expression in the *Apologeticum*. Because of its capacity of preserving under any circumstance the original goodness received by the Creator, the soul is defined as *naturaliter christiana*: "O testimonium animae naturaliter Christianae" (Id., *Apologeticum* 17,6 [CSEL, 69], p. 45). See C. TIBILETTI, *Tertulliano, La testimonianza dell'anima*, Firenze, 1984, pp. 14ff. Thus, despite the vices that besiege it, the soul can experience the original healthy condition (*sanitas*: a variation of *bonum*) received by God the Creator. Moreover, the responsibility of the soul is emphasized on account of the fact that it possesses the *semen boni* (See J.H. WASZINK [ed.], *Tertullianus, De anima*, Amsterdam, 1947, p. 453). See also *infra*, n. 463 (Pelagius).

was endowed by God the Creator[450], together with the revelation of Holy Scripture, constitute one of the ways by which man can acquire the knowledge of divine realities and experience a virtuous life[451].

To avoid possible misinterpretation, we should note at this point that Cassian did not make any distinction between natural and supernatural, for the simple reason that such a distinction was foreign to him. It did not belong to the theological speculation of the first third of the 5th century[452]. Cassian used the term *natura* in the original meaning derived from *nasci* and connected to creation[453]. Likewise, when the term is employed in relation to man, it points to his original state at the moment of creation, and to the goodness attached to such a state. Augustine never considered *natura* as an abstract power either, nor as a concept

450. "Deus hominem creans omnem naturaliter ei scientiam legis inseruit" (Cassian, *Conlatio* 8,23 [SC, 54], p. 31).

451. "Verum haec omnia uobis uel pro sapientia naturali uel pro indefesso sacrarum studio litterarum... cognita esse non ambigo" (*Ibid.*, 20,4 [SC, 64], p. 61). See also *Ibid.*, 23,2, p. 140; 13,9 (SC, 54), p. 160.

452. The temptation of reproaching Cassian with the lack of the distinction natural-supernatural, within a perspective neither Cassian nor Augustine were familiar with, is not avoided by some modern commentators. See for instance: "L'erreur fondamentale du présent chapitre [*Conlatio* 13,12] est de ne pas distinguer entre le deux ordres, naturel er surnaturel. Dieu a créé l'homme libre, il l'a constitué en grâce, et enrichi de dons préter-naturels. Mais l'homme, en péchant, a perdu tout ce qui n'était pas dû à la nature humaine, c'est-à-dire et la grâce et les dons préternaturels. De ce chef, il se rendait inca-pable des oeuvres du salut. Il a gardé, certes, avec la liberté, le pouvoir de produire des actes moralement bons; mais ceux-ci ne mènent pas à la vie. La grâce seule lui restitue la possibilité de faire le bien dans l'ordre du salut" (E. PICHERY [ed.], *Jean Cassien, Con-férences* VIII-XVII [SC, 54], p. 164, n. 1). "Es wird unbestimmt gelassen, ob es sich um das natürlich oder übernatürlich Gute handle" (L. WRZOL, *Die Psychologie des Johannes Cassianus*, in *DT* 7 [1920] 70-96, p. 94); "Cassian schreibt der Menschennatur gewisse Güter welcher Ordnung es sich handelt" (KEMMER, *Charisma Maximum* [n. 427], p. 29). See also GODET, *Cassien Jean* (n. 399), c. 1827.

453. We must be reminded that the meaning of the term "nature" (*natura*/φύσις) is primarily that of "origin" or "birth" – the word *natura* coming from *nasci*. Only at a sec-ondary stage, and by derivation, the meaning of "originating power" was extended to the word "nature", considered as the intrinsic principle and the cause of any movement and development. Thus, Aristotle could write that any human being possesses in itself by nature, and *not* accidentally, any movement and development (cf. Aristotle, *Physica* II,1,192b). See also: "Nature is said of the generation of what grows: φύσις λέγεται ἡ τῶν φυομένων γένεσις" (Id., *Metaphysica* V,4, 1014b). The Christian doctrine of cre-ation and providence has indeed deeply transformed the Greek philosophical concept of nature whose fundamental meaning, according to the Aristotelic vision, was "l'idée d'une existence qui se produit ou du moins se détermine elle-même, en tout ou en partie, sans avoir besoin d'une cause étrangère" (J. LACHELIER, *[Note on] Nature*, in A. LALANDE [ed.], *Vocabulaire technique et critique de la philosophie*, 6th ed. revue et augmentée, Paris, 1951). This concept of nature was taken up by Christian thought and placed within the framework of creation and salvation history. As De Lubac puts it: "Pour tout dire d'un mot, l'antique nature est devenue en climat chrétien la création" (H. DE LUBAC, *Le mystère du surnaturel* [Théol(P), 64], Paris, 1965, p. 42).

regarded as antagonistic to the "non–natural". Like Cassian, he never made a distinction between a natural order and a supernatural one (in the sense we are used to nowadays), nor did he ever say that grace belongs to the latter's realm[454]. Rather than elaborating a philosophical notion of it, both Cassian and Augustine appear to be more concerned with the existential context of *natura*. As aptly described, for the Fathers of the 4th and 5th century, the problem of human nature "was one of history rather than analysis. They sought to explain man's present situation, and also to throw light on his hope or redemption, by expounding the story... of his creation and fall"[455].

Both Cassian and Augustine, therefore, never approached and viewed human nature *in abstracto*, but from the experiential point of view, always keeping in mind the historic, concrete man. Augustine, however, arrived at a different conclusion. First of all, he took it for granted that only God possesses an immutable nature, since the nature of creatures reflects only a certain degree of being and perfection, given by God himself at the moment of their creation (here the link *natura–nasci* is evident). The insistence on the total dependence of creatures upon God the Creator led Augustine to emphasize that even though the *natura humana* was created upright, and in this sense it was obviously good[456], it became radically *uitiata* after Adam's fall, in the sense of having become incapable of anything good by itself. The true human nature, properly speaking, was only that of the first man created without sin. Since the "innocence" Gn 2 speaks of and which was possessed by Adam no longer exists, having been lost in his original sin[457], the expression

454. Cf. CHÉNÉ, *La théologie de saint Augustin* (n. 360), pp. 11ff.
455. KELLY, *Early Christian Doctrines* (n. 70), p. 344.
456. "A Deo bona est instituta natura: sed per malam voluntatem a serpente vitiata est" (Augustine, *Sermo* 294,13,14 [PL, 38], c. 1344); "Quod in eis Deus fecit, quia fecit Deus hominem ad imaginem et similitudinem suam, bonum est" (Id., *Sermo* 23A,1 *[Sermo Mai 16]* [CCL, 41], p. 321); "...esse autem natura, in quo nullum bonum sit, non potest" (Id., *De ciuitate Dei* 19,13 [CCL, 48], p. 679); "Natura humana, etsi mala est, quia uitiata est, non tamen malum est, quia natura est. Nulla enim natura, in quantum natura est, malum est, sed prorsus bonum" (Id., *Contra secundam Iuliani responsionem imperfectum opus* 3,206 [CSEL, 85/1], p. 501).
457. To assert that human nature was seriously damaged by the fall, Augustine even suggested that it was "dead": "...qui *[Christus]* profecto nisi natura humana magnum esset bonum, non pro illa homo fieret, cum Deus esset; nisi magno peccati malo mortua esset, non pro illa moreretur, cum sine peccato ipse venisset et mansisset" (*Ibid.* 5,23 [PL, 45], c. 1459). Cf. also *Ibid.* 5,9, c. 1439. Even in his first commentary on Genesis Augustine had written that Adam had "lost" the image of God (cf. Id., *De Genesi ad litteram* 6,27 [CSEL, 28/1], p. 199), but he later corrected himself during the revision of this work: "In sexto libro quod dixi *Adam imaginem Dei, secundum quam factus est, perdidisse peccato*, non sic accipiendum est, tamquam in eo nulla remanserit, sed quod tam

"human nature", according to the bishop of Hippo, is but a metaphor employed for all men that come into the world, despite the fact that they are born with a vitiated nature[458]. And that is why Christ himself came into the world: to "repair" what had been damaged, namely the vitiated condition in which human nature lay *post peccatum*[459]. Augustine argues that an anthropological approach that presumes to start from the "original/innocent", prelapsarian state which characterized human nature at the very beginning of creation, and that does not take into account the actual historical situation of humanity after the fall, falls short of its aim. The distinction between "upright" and "fallen" nature[460] is fundamental in Augustine. He will always view it in the light of Adam's fall, namely as a nature that needs healing by the redemptive sacrifice of Christ[461]. In the eyes of the bishop of Hippo, the essential role of Christ's grace with regard to human nature is precisely to restore what had been damaged.

We do not believe, as suggested by some, that Cassian made the mistake of having underestimated the development that the original meaning of *natura* had undergone in Augustine's thinking, particularly during

---

deformis, ut reformatione opus haberet" (Id., *Retractationes* 2,24,2 [CCL, 57], p. 110). Thus, affirmations such as those reported above, in which Augustine says that, because of Adam's fall, human nature had died and the image of God lost, should be regarded as hyperboles. Augustine's aim, in fact, was to point out the gravity of the wound inflicted by Adam's sin on human nature and the conviction that the latter cannot be healed of its own accord, that it would die if left unaided and that it needs a life-giving act of grace in order to be revived. A more precise view of the bishop of Hippo is that human nature is half-dead (*semidefuncta* or, more positively said, *semiuiua*), like the traveller to Jericho in the so-called parable of the good Samaritan (cf. Id., *De natura et gratia* 43,50 [CSEL, 60], p. 270) and in need of a doctor (*Ibid.* 64,76, p. 291). According to Augustine's thought, therefore, the image of God in man was not completely extinct after Adam's fall. Nevertheless, only grace can rehabilitate it.

458. "... hoc dictum ad naturam talem referatur, qualis sine uitio primitus condita est; ipsa enim uere ac proprie natura hominis dicitur. Translato autem uerbo utimur, ut naturam dicamus etiam qualis nascitur homo..." (Id., *Retractationes* 1,10,3 [CSEL, 57], pp. 32-33).

459. "Quod fuit in Adam culpae, non naturae, nobis propagatis factum est iam naturae. Ab hoc vitio naturae, cum quo nascitur homo, non liberat nisi qui natus est sine vitio" (Id., *Sermo* 294,13,14 [PL, 38], c. 1344). See also: "Natura per Adam perdita, per illum reparatur, qui dixit venire '*se quaerere et salvare quod perierat' [Lk 19,10]*" (Id., *De gratia et libero arbitrio* 13,25 [PL, 44], c. 896).

460. "Etiam ipsam naturam aliter dicimus cum proprie loquimur naturam hominis in qua primum in suo genere inculpabilis factus est, aliter istam in qua ex illius damnati poena et mortales et ignari et carni subditi nascimur" (Id., *De libero arbitrio* 3,19,54 [CCL, 29], p. 307). This passage is taken up and reproduced in Id., *De natura et gratia* 67,81 (CSEL, 60), p. 296.

461. See F.-J. THONNARD, *La notion de nature chez saint Augustin. Ses progrès dans la polémique antipélagienne*, in *REAug* 11 (1965) 239-265.

the Pelagian controversy[462]. The Pelagian position, in fact, provoked Augustine's rethinking of the content of the word *natura* and caused his firm reaction against what, in his eyes, had deprived the notion of grace of its salvific meaning. Cassian was certainly acquainted with the fact that Pelagius had assumed the *naturae bonum* as a capital tenet of his ascetic theology[463], and he was aware of the optimistic and overwhelming emphasis that Pelagianism had laid on the term *natura* as the first recipient of grace. For this reason Cassian opposed the Pelagians' view about the possibilities of man's natural faculties and the "gracious" status they would seemingly enjoy and recovered (surely *optima fide*) the primitive use of the word *natura*. In contrast to Augustine's innovative teaching on the absolute sovereignty and power of grace, and without conceding to Pelagius's over-optimistic "gracious naturalism"[464], such recovery of the concept of nature must have looked to Cassian as the only feasible way of saving the place and autonomous role of free will in "certain" instances of human life without having to come into conflict with the sovereign activity of grace.

Furthermore, it seems that Cassian felt a certain uneasiness with regard to a rigid distinction between the "natural" grace (bestowed on man through creation) and the "redemptive" grace of Christ[465], or with

462. "Cassians Fehler besteht darin, dass er entgegen der genauen Bestimmung des Ausdrucks fortfuhr, ihn im früheren Sinn zu gebrauchen" (KEMMER, *Charisma Maximum* [n. 427], p. 32).

463. In Pelagius' letter to Demetrias, for instance, the *naturae bonum* is often pointed to as the reason upon which any ascetic effort hinges and is made possible (cf. Pelagius, *Ep. ad Demetriadem* 2-8 *passim* [PL, 30], cc. 16-23). Pelagius too must have been acquainted with the Eastern theological thought and must have cultivated some conceptual ties with it, as in the specific case of the *naturae bonum*. See, once again, the assertion about the *naturalis sanctitas* (the equivalent of the *naturae bonum*) upheld by Pelagius: "Est enim, inquam, in animis nostris naturalis quaedam (ut ita dixerim) sanctitas: quae velut in arce animi praesidens, exercet mali bonique iudicium" (*Ibid.* 4 [PL, 30], c. 19). As to a possible "historical link" between Pelagius and Cassian, Chadwick suggests that Cassian might have encountered Pelagius on the occasion of his stay in Rome (cf. CHADWICK, *John Cassian* [n. 364], p. 32, n. 4). Julian of Aeclanum moved along the same line, holding the same belief in the fundamental goodness of creation. Cf. M. LAMBERIGTS, *Julian of Aeclanum. A Plea for a Good Creator*, in *Aug(L)* 38 (1988) 5-24, pp. 9-10.

464. The term "naturalism", in relation to Pelagianism, may be used provided it is not detached from its theological connotation. As Kelly has wrightly written, "Pelagius's teaching is often described as a species of naturalism, but this label scarcely does justice to its profoundly religious spirit. Defective though it is in its recognition of man's weakness, it radiates an intense awareness of God's majesty, of the wonderful privileges and high destiny He has vouchsafed to men, and of the claims of the moral law and of Christ's example" (KELLY, *Early Christian Doctrines* [n. 70], pp. 360-361). We believe that the expression "gracious naturalism" does Justice to Pelagius' position.

465. This distinction, on the other hand, is clearly formulated by Augustine, who writes about the grace "qua est homo conditus" and the grace "qua fit saluus per Iesum

regard to the subordination of nature to a spiritual/inner grace. His theological formation would encourage him to interweave these different
types of grace, rather than make a sharp distinction between them. As a
matter of fact, what is often believed to be Cassian's search for a compromise between the "gracious naturalism" of Pelagianism and Augustine's doctrine of God's absolute and prevenient grace, is rather an
attempt to retain the traditional position held by the Eastern Fathers of
the Church that the capabilities inherent in the *naturae bonum* remain
active even after Adam's fall. That could not possibly destroy what was
primarily intended in the act of God's creation.

If that is so, we are then led to the conclusion that divine grace, viz.
the "redemptive grace of Christ", does not add anything substantially
new to what is already inherent in human nature, in that it would be
regarded as a "renewing principle", a *Wiederherstellung*[466], viz. as a
reality that brings into effectiveness the goodness and the quest for perfection which are already present in the "natural/original" condition and
faculties of man. From this point of view, then, grace and human nature
would not be radically distinct and foreign to one another. On the contrary, they would stand out as two realities that are intimately and syner-
getically interrelated. Once again, Cassian could rely on the reflection of
Eastern theologians according to whom the two concepts were not considered to be antithetic[467]. Although man needs helping by the intervention

---

Christum Dominum nostrum" (cf. Augustine, *De natura et gratia* 53,62 [CSEL, 60],
p. 278). See also: "Ipse est autem creator eius qui saluator eius. Non ergo debemus sic
laudare creatorem, ut cogamur, immo uere conuincamur dicere superfluum saluatorem"
(*Ibid.* 34,39, pp. 261-262).

466. "Auch Cassian sieht in der Vervollkommnung des Menschen nur die Wiederherstellung des natürlichen Zustandes im Menschen" (KEMMER, *Charisma Maximum*
[n. 427], p. 31).

467. Gregory of Nyssa, for instance, basing his anthropological doctrine on Gn 1,26
(viz. that God created man in his own image and likeness) affirms that the desire of what is
good and beautiful is consubstantial (συνουσιωμένη) and connatural (συμπεφυκυῖα) to
man. Likewise, man's love for the intellectual image of which he is himself an imitation, is
strictly tied to nature: "Εὑρήσει γὰρ τοῦτον τὸν τρόπον ἐπισκοπῶν συνουσιωμένην τε
καὶ συμπεφυκυῖαν τῷ ἀνθρώπῳ τὴν ἐπὶ τὸ καλόν τε καὶ ἄριστον τῆς ἐπιθυμίας
ὁρμὴν καὶ τῆς νοητῆς ἐκείνης καὶ μακαρίας εἰκόνος, ἧς ὁ ἄνθρωπος μίμημα, τὸν
ἀγαθῆ καὶ μακάριον ἔρωτα συνημμένον τῇ φύσει" (Gregory of Nyssa, *De instituto
christiano, Gregorii Nysseni opera* 8/1, p. 40). See ZACHHUBER, *Human Nature in Gregory
of Nyssa* (n. 140), pp. 125-186. According to Gregory, man's nature (in the soul) is as it
was created by God. It is in the soul where man's likeness with God resides, his being created in his image, namely his intellectual and supernatural life – the "animal" life being
something added to man's essential nature. As Daniélou has pointed out, rather than a
sense of inferiority with regard to the superior reality of which it is a reflection, the divine
"image" which is in man implies a sense of participation in this same reality, a true
"communauté de 'nature' " (J. DANIÉLOU, *Platonisme et théologie mystique. Essai sur la
doctrine spirituelle de saint Grégoire de Nysse* (Théol[P], 2), 2nd ed., Paris, 1954, p. 48).

of divine grace, the task of this is not so much (as Augustine would argue) the *reformatio*[468], in the sense of a substantial transformation or restoration of human nature, as its reinforcement, its sustenance and "cleansing"[469]. Cassian shared this traditional view, convinced that human beings retain some vestige of their created goodness thanks to which they can learn how to walk again as God had always intended them to do. The monks' strong commitment (*propositum*) goes precisely in this direction[470]. In this respect, we should not forget that Cassian's conviction about divine-human interaction was not only the fruit of his acquaintance with Eastern theological thinking, particularly with the ascetic theology of Evagrius and Origen, but also of his personal experience. Cassian was himself a monk and knew first-hand how significant human efforts were for the education and development of Christian life[471] and what an important role they played in the monastic pursuit of perfection. That is why he certainly agreed that without divine grace man could do nothing good, but he would not uphold the conviction that such a grace was monolithic and irresistible at any stage. On the contrary, the necessity of grace which Cassian taught has to be intended as a "liberal" grace pervading a creation still rich in possibility, a possibility that Christ has brought to fulfilment[472]. Above all, although he believed that anything good that is done by human beings is the work of God, who "stirs" it up, protects and strengthens it (but not in such a way as to nullify human action), the initiative of the will, however small, to

---

468. Cf. *supra*, n. 457.

469. In the context of Gregory of Nyssa's view concerning man's salvation through the imitation of Christ, Zachhuber writes: "That this result can possibly be reached is expressly stated and employed as a means of exhortation. This optimism is, I think, not primarily a result of Gregory's belief in human free will, but reveals the assumption of an undestroyed core of godlike human nature as underlying this argument: no 'substantial' change needs to be made to this nature; rather the 'mud', to use the language of *De virginitate*, covering the nature and obscuring its image-character has to be cleansed" (ZACHHUBER, *Human Nature in Gregory of Nyssa* [n. 140], pp. 191-192). According to Augustine, instead, "natura sana non est" (Augustine, *De natura et gratia* 3,3 [CSEL, 60], p. 235) and needs to be restored by grace: "Nec sane isto modo naturam siue animae siue corporis, quam Deus creauit et quae tota bona est, accusamus, sed eam dicimus propria uoluntate uitiatam sine Dei gratia non posse sanari" (Id., *De perfectione iustitiae hominis* 6,12 [CSEL, 42], pp. 11-12).

470. In Cassian's view, "monasticism, like the Christianity of which it is a trope, educates and develops the human person called forth by God from sin into freedom" (STEWART, *Cassian the Monk* [n. 370], p. 22).

471. As to Cassian's optimism with regard to this, see A. HOCH, *Lehre des J. Cassianus von Natur und Gnade. Ein Beitrag zur Geschichte des Gnadenstreites im 5. Jahrhundert*, Freiburg i. Br., 1895, pp. 50-69; WRZOL, *Die Psychologie des Johannes Cassianus* (n. 452), pp. 81-96.

472. For the redemptive and exemplary role of Christ, see *infra*, pp. 379ff.

turn to God by its own inclination and desire (*initium fidei*) has to be regarded as feasible.

b) The initium fidei in Context

If it is in the framework of the *naturae bonum* that free will acquires a positive and active status, the same is true for the question of the *initium fidei* (or *salutis*). In condemning Pelagianism in 418, the Church did not pronounce itself explicitly on the subject[473] and the doctrinal uncertainty on this particular issue left room for Cassian and the Massilians to develop their own view. The problem at stake ran as follows: can conversion and adhesion to faith be brought about autonomously by man, or does the action of grace forestall such a process, inducing man's will to believe? In other words, who is at the beginning of conversion to faith: man or God?

Before tackling the problem, however, we must point to a terminological peculiarity. Despite the fact that both Augustine and the Massilians addressed the same issue, they employed a different terminology. To begin with, the expression *initium fidei*, used several times in the course of our enquiry, was not, as such, used by the Massilians, nor is it to be found in Prosper and Hilary's letters reporting to Augustine on their position[474]. Cassian has only one reference to this expression, and in the passage in which it occurs it is employed in consonance with Augustine's view on the subject, viz. to say that even the beginning of belief is a gift of God's prevenient grace[475]. Elsewhere Cassian turns to other terms or equivalent expressions such as *credulitas*[476], *initium uoluntatis bonae*[477], *initia sanctae uoluntatis*[478], *scintilla bonae uoluntatis*[479], *ortum quendam bonae uoluntatis*[480], *bonarum uoluntatum principia*[481], *salutis principia*[482] and *bonae uoluntatis ardor*[483].

473. See CHÉNÉ, *La théologie de saint Augustin* (n. 360), pp. 28-29.

474. Prosper speaks of the *initium salutis* (cf. Prosper, *Ep.* 225,6 [CSEL, 57], p. 464), whereas Hilary speaks of *fidei augmentum* (cf. Hilary, *Ep.* 226,2 [CSEL, 57], p. 469) with regard to the one who has started willing ("ut iuuetur, qui coeperit uelle": *Ibid.*, p. 470).

475. "Hic quoque et initium conuersionis ac fidei nostrae et passionum tolerantiam donari nobis a Domino declarauit" (Cassian, *Conlatio* 3,15 [SC, 42], p. 158).

476. *Ibid.* 1,14, p. 96; 3,19, p. 163; 7,5, p. 251; 8,4 (SC, 54), p. 13.

477. *Ibid.* 3,19 (SC, 42), p. 162.

478. *Ibid.* 13,3 (SC, 54), p. 151.

479. *Ibid.* 13,7, p. 155.

480. *Ibid.* 13,8, p. 158.

481. *Ibid.* 13,9, p. 160.

482. *Ibid.* 13,18, p. 180.

483. *Ibid.*

The bishop of Hippo, by contrast, uses the expression *initium fidei* explicitly. Quoting the latin translation of Ct 4,8 (LXX): *Veni de Libano, sponsa mea, ueni de Libano, uenies et pertransies ab initio fidei*[484], Augustine reads and interprets this passage as an invitation of Christ to his bride, the Church, to join him through faith (*ab initio fidei*), from which the good works follow. The stress is laid on the priority of the act of faith in which good works have their source. Thus, generally speaking, for Augustine, *initium fidei* means the beginning of salvation in as much as life, through faith, is turned towards God[485], but it also points to faith itself that needs strengthening in times of trials and temptations[486], or to the faith of the catechumens not yet born into a life divine[487]. A new focus in Augustine's interpretation of Ct 4,8 comes to light after the Pelagian controversy broke out. That would give the bishop of Hippo occasion to speak not merely of the priority of man's act of faith over his good works, but also of the precedence of divine action with regard to the act of faith itself. The emphasis is now on the *initium fidei* as God's gift[488]. In the works Augustine addressed to the Massilians, the expression *initium fidei* recurs several times with an already well-defined meaning derived from his doctrine of prevenient grace, viz. that the beginning of faith is itself the gift of God[489].

The expression *initium fidei* was finally taken up as a technical formulation in can. 5 of the 2nd Council of Orange (529)[490], where a condemnation

484. According to the original Hebrew text, instead of "from the beginning of faith", we should read: "From the peak of Amana". The translation "ἀπὸ ἀρχῆς πίστεως: *ab initio fidei*" follows the LXX interpretation of the term Amana as pointing to faith.
485. Cf., for instance, Augustine, *Enarrationes in psalmos* 33, s. 1, 10 (CCL, 38), p. 281; *Ibid.* 67,41 (CCL, 39), p. 698; *Ibid.* 134,18 (CCL, 40), p. 1950; *Tractatus in Euangelium Ioannis* 15,24 (CCL, 36), p. 160; Id., *Enchiridion ad Laurentium* 5 (CCL, 46), p. 50.
486. Cf., for instance, Id., *Enarrationes in psalmos* 35,1 (CCL, 38), p. 322; *Epistulae ad Galatas expositio* 38 (CSEL, 84), p. 107.
487. Cf., for instance, Id., *De diuersis quaestionibus ad Simplicianum* 1,2,2 (CCL, 44), pp. 24-25. See J. CHÉNÉ, *Que signifiaient "initium fidei" et "affectum credulitatis" pour les Semipélagiens?*, in *RSR* 35 (1948) 566-588, pp. 571ff.
488. Cf. Augustine, *De perfectione iustitiae hominis* 19,41 (CSEL, 42), p. 44; Id., *De gestis Pelagii* 14,34 (CSEL, 42), p. 90; *Ep.* 194,9, (CSEL, 57), p. 183.
489. Cf. Id., *De praedestinatione sanctorum* 2,3-4 (PL, 44), cc. 961-962; *Ibid.* 4,8, c. 966, and 19,39-21,43, cc. 989-992 *passim* (where Augustine reiterates the thesis strongly defended in 2,3-4); Id., *De dono perseuerantiae* 20,52 and 21,54-55 (PL, 45), cc. 1026 and 1027. Augustine refers explicitly to the issues raised in the second part of the first book of the *De diuersis quaestionibus ad Simplicianum*. The agency of divine grace precedes not only human works and merits, but also the will (cf. especially Id., *De diuersis quaestionibus ad Simplicianum* 1,2,10.12 (CCL, 44), pp. 34-35 and 36-37; *Ibid.* 1,2,21-22, pp. 53-56).
490. Cf. *Concilia Galliae A. 511 – A. 695* (CCL, 148A), p. 56.

was pronounced against all those who upheld the belief that the *initium fidei* (and its *augmentum*) was not caused by grace but was inherent in the capabilities of human nature itself[491]. It is in this sense that can. 5 of the 2nd Council of Orange can also be seen as a reaction to the Cassianic *ortum quendam bonae uoluntatis* and to other similar expressions considered the equivalent of the *initium fidei*. In fact, speaking of the beginning of belief in terms of "beginning/spark of good will", Cassian assumed that free will maintains and plays an important role in its relationship with grace not only on a *co*-operative level, but also on a *pre*-operative level. This means that free will must not be regarded as a mere subordinated *potentia oboedientiae passiua*, but, on the contrary, as a reality retaining all the marks of a *potentia actiua*. In other words, it is Cassian's conviction that man can indeed be considered as the active subject of the *initium fidei,* namely as the owner of a positive attitude by which he can take the necessary step towards receiving the gift of faith and adhering to it through prayer and penitence.

Cassian's position about the *initium fidei*, however, was not something new. Firstly, we find some biblical references which indicate that Holy Scripture lends itself to more than one single clear-cut interpretation with regard to free will. In fact, if there are scriptural passages in which the emphasis seems to fall on the powerlessness of man who needs the help of divine grace in order to come to faith (cf., *e.g.*, Jn 6,44 and 65: "No one can come to me unless drawn by the Father who sent me"; Eph 2,8: "For by grace you have been saved through faith, and this is not your own doing; it is the gift of God"), there are also other references where it looks as if God were waiting for man to make the first move, the *initium fidei*, before bestowing his grace. This is the case, for instance, of Pr 16,1 (LXX): *Hominis est praeparare animam*; Ps 80,11: *Dilata cor tuum et implebo illud*; Zech 1,3: *Conuertimini ad me et conuertar ad uos*; and of the New Testament narratives about the conversion of Zacchaeus (cf. Lk 19,1-10) and the centurion Cornelius (cf. Ac 10,4), and Jesus' words to his disciples: "Ask, and it will be given you; seek, and you will find; knock, and it will be opened to you" (Lk 11,9; cf. Mt 7,7). As well as Holy Scripture, Cassian relies upon a favourable and dynamic interpretation of the autonomy of man's free will, such as had been put forward by some of the Fathers of the Church who had occupied an important place in the theological construction of Christian doctrine, and whose solid reputation within ecclesiastical

---

491. "Si quis, sicut augmentum, ita etiam *initium fidei* ipsumque credulitatis affectum... non per gratiae donum... sed naturaliter nobis inesse dicit..." (*DS* 375).

tradition was universally recognised. They had spoken of grace leaving
the possibility open, or even expressing themselves clearly on that point,
that man may indeed take the "initiative" of bringing about the work of
salvation, even though it was clear to them that it was up to God to continue it, and bring it to fulfilment.

Among the Greek Fathers we find as witnesses to this Clement of
Alexandria and Origen, representatives of the school of Alexandria, and
John Chrysostom, representative of the school of Antioch and one of
Cassian's mentors. *Clement of Alexandria* maintains that since man is a
free being, it is up to him to desire and choose to be saved, whereas the
gift or the accomplishment of what has been chosen is God's alone, who
comes to the help of those who yearn and search: "God breathes his
own power into souls when they desire"[492]. The human initiative
appears to be evident[493]. To *Origen*'s general standpoint on this question[494], we can add a quotation from his commentary on Psalm 120
where he says that God is ready to hold out his hand to man when He
sees his efforts in following the way of the divine commandments[495],
that is, when He realizes that man has taken some initiative in the direction of salvation. *John Chrysostom*, who was mainly preoccupied in
encouraging his audience to personal efforts, is also at pains to stress
that divine grace, although necessary for the accomplishment of good
works and for salvation, is not really necessary at the stage when one
desires and wishes to follow God's commandments[496]. Chrysostom's
general thinking indicates that desiring and leaning towards what is good
pertains to man, whereas it belongs to God to increase and strengthen
such yearning[497]. Thus, commenting on Rom 9,16 (*Non uolentis, neque
currentis sed miserentis est Dei*), a passage which in itself seems to
emphasize God's agency at the expense of human agency, Chrysostom
highlights the role that man's freedom is called to play. It is up to man,
he affirms, to start the work of salvation, for the beginning of faith and

492. "Βουλομέναις μὲν γὰρ ταῖς ψυχαῖς ὁ Θεὸς συνεπιπνεῖ" (Clement of
Alexandria, *Quis diues saluetur* 21 [GCS, 17/2], p. 173).
    493. "'Ἐπὶ τῷ ἀνθρώπῳ γὰρ ἦν ἡ αἵρεσις ὡς ἐλευθέρῳ, ἐπὶ θεῷ δὲ ἡ δόσις ὡς
κυρίῳ. δίδωσι δὲ βουλομένοις καὶ ὑπερεσπουδακόσι καὶ δεομένοις, ἵν' οὕτως
ἴδιον αὐτῶν ἡ σωτηρία γένηται. οὐ γὰρ ἀναγκάζει ὁ Θεός, βία γὰρ ἐχθρὸν θεῷ,
ἀλλὰ τοῖς ζητοῦσι πορίζει καὶ τοῖς αἰτοῦσι παρέχει καὶ τοῖς κρούουσιν ἀνοίγει"
(*Ibid.* 10, pp. 165-166).
    494. See *supra*, pp. 202-213.
    495. "Ὥστε παρ' ἡμῶν δεῖ εἶναι τὰς ἀρχάς, καὶ ὁ Θεὸς τοῦ ὀρέξαι χεῖρα
ἕτοιμος" (Origen, *Fragmenta in diuersos Psalmos* 120 [PG, 12], c. 1632).
    496. See A. KENNY, *Was St. John Chrysostom a semi-Pelagian?*, in *ITQ* 27 (1960)
16-29, pp. 17-22.
    497. Cf. John Chrysostom, *In epistulam ad Philippenses* 8,1 (PG, 62), p. 240.

the desire to choose what pertains to it comes from man's good will. God's grace does not forestall man's initial move, but intervenes only at a second stage. Once man has made his first choice (τὸ προελέσθαι), then God bestows the necessary help that leads that choice to completion (εἰς τέλος ἀγαγεῖν)⁴⁹⁸, because the most relevant part (τὸ πλέον) of the saving action and its fulfilment or totality (τὸ πᾶν) belongs to God⁴⁹⁹. In other words, God shows his mercy to man if he first (πρότερον) shows himself worthy of it⁵⁰⁰. In fact, "if grace did not demand our initiative first (τὰ παρ' ἡμῶν πρότερον) it would be bestowed abundantly on everybody's soul, for it does not make preferences of persons. Since it encourages our agency (τὰ παρ' ἡμῶν ζητεῖ), however, it follows some people's actions and remains there (ἕπεται καὶ παραμένει), from other people it flies away (ἀφίπταται), and it does not even reach some others in an incipient form (οὐδὲ τὴν ἀρχὴν καθικνεῖται)"⁵⁰¹.

Similarly, the Cappadocian Fathers attributed the first step towards salvation and the forgiveness of sins (which are the work of God) to the initiative of man. *Basil of Caesarea* speaks of man's loving desire for God as being ἀδίδακτος. It is not apprehended through discipline as something coming from outside (ἔξωθέν), for it is an inner (οἴκοθεν) tendency, a sort of natural istinct, a σπερματικὸς λόγος with which God has endowed human beings. This tendency to love God, abiding in

---

498. "Ἡμῶν γὰρ τὸ προελέσθαι καὶ βουληθῆναι, θεοῦ δὲ τὸ ἀνύσαι καὶ εἰς τέλος ἀγαγεῖν" (Id., *In Epistulam ad Hebraeos argumentum et homiliae* 12,3 [PG, 63], c. 99).

499. *Ibid*. See also: "The beginning of belief (τὸ παρὰ τὴν ἀρχὴν πιστεῦσαι) comes from our good will or disposition (προαίρεσις) and from our obedience to the call; but after the foundation of faith has been laid, then we need the help (βοήθεια) of the Spirit, if faith is to remain in us unshakeable and unassailable. For neither God, nor the grace (χάρις) of the Spirit precedes our own resolution (προαίρεσις). Though He calls us, He waits for us to approach him spontaneously and of our own will. Then only, when we have approached, does He confer all his help" (Id., *De uerbis apostolis: Habentes autem eumdem spiritum...* 1,5 [PG, 51], c. 276).

500. "Ἀπὸ τούτου τοίνυν μανθάνομεν, ὅτι κἂν ἐλεεῖσθαι μέλλωμεν, ἀξίους τοῦ ἐλέου πρότερον παρέχειν ἡμᾶς ἑαυτοὺς χρή" (Id., *In Epistulam II ad Corinthios argumentum et homiliae* 2,4 [PG, 61], c. 397). "Τοῦτον οὖν, παρακαλῶ, τὸν δίκαιον καὶ ἡμεῖς μιμώμεθα, καὶ τὰ παρ' ἑαυτῶν σπουδάζωμεν εἰσφέρειν, ἵνα ἀξίους ἑαυτοὺς κατασκευάσωμεν τῶν παρὰ τοῦ Θεοῦ δωρεῶν. Διὰ τοῦτο γὰρ ἀναμένει τὰς παρ' ἡμῶν ἀφορμὰς, ἵνα πολλὴν ἐπιδείξηται τὴν φιλοτιμίαν" (Id., *In Genesim homiliae* 25,7 [PG, 53], c. 228). See also *Ibid*. 42,1 (PG, 54), c. 385. Against the background of the necessity of God's grace, such statements, according to Farrelly, "show not a definite Semipelagian doctrine, but that lack of accuracy that is common before a heresy has made the Church aware of a particular difficulty.... Hence a certain ambivalence or inexactness of expression appears from time to time" (M.J. FARRELLY, *Predestination, Grace and Free Will*, Westminster, MD, 1964, p. 75.

501. John Chrysostom, *Ad Demetrium de compunctione* 1,9 (PG, 47), c. 408.

man as a primordial reality since creation, is then taken to fulfilment by divine grace (εἰς τελείωσιν ἄγειν Θεοῦ χάριτι πέφυκεν)[502]. The same ideas can be found in *Gregory of Nazianzus*[503] and *Gregory of Nyssa*. The latter is particularly confident on the subject. He seems to require the necessity of grace only in order to bring the virtuous act to fulfilment and make it effective, but not as a reality that precedes the virtuous act and inclines towards it[504]. A synergism exists there, a strict co-operation between the pursuit of virtue by man's free will, and its achievement brought about by operative grace. The first step seems undeniably to belong to man. If he contemplates his soul, once it has been delivered from passions, he will find that the yearning (τῆς ἐπιθυμίας ὁρμήν) for what is good and beautiful is consubstantial and connatural (συνουσιουμένην τε καὶ συμπεφυκυῖαν) to himself[505]. For that reason, Gregory asserts, the grace/gift of freedom of choice (αὐτεξούσιος χάρις) attests that the good that man can reach may be regarded as the fruit of his willing[506].

Very conversant with the efforts demanded by the monastic ideal of perfection, the conviction of *Ps.-Macarius* about the possibility that man himself takes the first step in the process of salvation, rests on the writer's optimistic outlook on the fall. Since original sin did not destroy human freedom, man can always decide to turn towards God and call out for help. In order to illustrate the feasibility of such a process, the Ps.-Macarius draws some examples from Scripture: Zacchaeus (who took the initiative of going up the tree to see Jesus: cf. Lc 19,1-10), blind

---

502. Basil of Caesarea, *Asceticon magnum* sive *Quaestiones (Regulae fusius tractatae)* 2,1 (PG, 31), c. 908 *passim*.

503. Cf., for instance: "Μᾶλλον δὲ αὐτὸ τὸ προαιρεῖσθαι τὰ δέοντα θεῖόν τι καὶ ἐκ Θεοῦ δῶρον φιλανθρωπίας· δεῖ γὰρ καὶ τὸ ἐφ' ἡμῖν εἶναι, καὶ τὸ ἐκ Θεοῦ σώεζεσθαι" (Gregory of Nazianzus, *Oratio* 37,13 [SC, 318], p. 300). The presence of terms which belong to the Stoic vocabulary ought to be noted, as, for instance, προαιρεῖσθαι which indicates the choice of the free will (τὸ ἐφ' ἡμῖν).

504. "Εἰ δὲ πρὸς τὸ κρεῖττον γένοιτο ἡ ῥοπή, τοῦ θεοῦ χρεία τοῦ τὴν ἐπιθυμίαν εἰς ἔργον ἄγοντος" (Gregory of Nyssa, *De oratione dominica* 4, *Gregorii Nysseni opera* 7/2, p. 48). "Τῷ γὰρ τοῖς τῆς ἀρετῆς προσκαρτεροῦντι πόνοις ἀκολουθεῖ ταχέως ἡ τοῦ πνεύματος χάρις" (Id., *De instituto christiano*, *Gregorii Nysseni opera* 8/1, p. 57). In another place, Gregory defines virtue as the rectitude of the free will: "ἀρετὴ προαιρέσεως ἐστὶ κατόρθωμα" (Id., *Antirrheticus aduersus Apolinarium* 64, *Gregorii Nysseni opera* 3/1, p. 197). The term κατόρθωμα (the "right action") is again a term derived from the Stoic vocabulary.

505. Cf. Id., *De instituto christiano*, *Gregorii Nysseni* opera 8/1, p. 40.

506. Cf. Id., *In Canticum canticorum*, Or. 2, *Gregorii Nysseni opera* 6, p. 55. See also the description of the Holy Spirit as the interior co-operator: συνεργὸν καὶ σύνοικον (Id., *De instituto christiano*, *Gregorii Nysseni opera* 8/1, p. 44). It is possible that Cassian knew Gregory's *De instituto christiano* through Evagrius Ponticus, and that he made use of it in the redaction of his *Conlationes*.

Bartimaeus (who called out to Jesus, who was passing by: cf. Mc 10,46-52) and especially the woman with the issue of blood (who made her way through the crowd in the hope of touching Jesus and being healed: cf. Lc 8,43-48). Taking the initiative, calling out, getting ready, is what man can and must do in order to create an opportunity (πρόφασις)[507] for God's saving intervention. Once the opportunity is brought about, the Holy Spirit will do the rest.

Other examples can be drawn from the Fathers of the Latin Church. *Hilary of Poitiers*, much influenced by Eastern theology, commenting on Ps 118,124: *Fac cum seruo tuo secundum misericordiam tuam*, writes that man can desire to serve God and even start doing so, but on account of his weakness he needs the help and strength of God. The initiative, once again, belongs to man, whereas the achievement of what is desired belongs to God[508]. The so-called *Ambrosiaster* does not leave any doubt about attributing the act of believing to man's will, whereas the accomplishing belongs to God[509]. *Optatus of Mileuis*, while disagreeing with the Donatists' claim of being the only true and holy Church of Christ, also affirmed that it pertains to the faithful to desire the good, and to God to bring it to fulfilment[510]. Likewise, *Jerome*, who

---

507. Cf. Ps.-Macarius, *Homiliae spiritales* 26,3,1 (Typus III, Collectio C) (SC, 275), p. 298.

508. "Nam in eo ipso, quod dixit: *Fac,* adiecit: *Cum seruo tuo.* Et quia *seruitus* nostra ad id ipsum, ut in *seruitutis* fide maneat, *misericordia Domini* indiget, superaddidit: *Secundum misericordiam tuam*: quia miseratione eius opus est, ut in hac *seruitutis* nostrae professione maneamus. Imbecilla enim est per se aliquid obtinendi humana infirmitas, et hoc tantum naturae suae officium est, ut adgregare se in familiam Dei et uelit et coeperit. *Diuinae* uero *misericordiae* est, ut uolentes adiuuet, incipientes confirmet, adeuntes recipiat; ex nobis autem initium est, ut illa perficiat" (Hilary of Poitiers, *Tractatus super psalmos* 118, litt. 16,10 [SC, 347], p. 188). "Et licet a Deo *intellegentia* perfecta sit, tamen a nobis incipiendum est, ut possimus perfectam *intellegentiam* promereri. His enim qui non hoc per se inchoant, clausa a Deo omnia sunt" (*Ibid.*, litt. 13,12 p. 116). "Est quidem in fide manendi a Deo munus, sed incipiendi a nobis origo est. Et uoluntas nostra hoc proprium ex se debet, ut uelit. Deus incipienti incrementum dabit, quia consummationem per se infirmitas nostra non obtinet, meritum tamen adipiscendae consummationis est ex initio uoluntatis" (*Ibid.*, litt. 14,20, pp. 150.152). "A nobis est ergo, cum oramus, exordium" (*Ibid.*, litt. 5,12 [SC, 344], p. 214).

509. "Credere autem aut non credere uoluntatis est" (Ambrosiaster, *Commentarius in xiii epistulas Paulinas [ad Romanos]* 4,4 [CSEL, 81/1], p. 128); "Omnem enim gratiam semper reportat ad Deum, ut nostrum sit uelle, perficere uero Dei" (*Ibid. [ad Philippenses]* 2,13 [CSEL, 81/3], p. 146).

510. "Est enim christiani hominis, quod bonum est, uelle et in eo, quod bene uoluerit, currere; sed homini non est datum perficere, ut post spatia, quae debet homo inplere, restet aliquid Deo, ubi deficienti succurrat; quia ipse solus est perfectio et perfectus solus Dei filius Christus. Ceteri omnes semiperfecti sumus, quia nostrum est uelle, nostrum est currere, Dei perficere" (Optatus of Milevi, *Contra Parmenianum Donatistam* 2,20 [CSEL, 26], p. 55). This text, of eastern derivation, is evidence of the close relationship that existed between African and Eastern Christianity. See W. TELFER, *The Origins of Christianity in Africa*, in StPatr 4 (TU, 73), Berlin, 1961, 512-517, pp. 513-514.

spent the last and most meaningful part of his life in the East, shows a similar conviction. While refuting some of the most controversial tenets of Pelagianism (against which he strove bitterly), he expressed his opinion by pointing out that the *initium fidei* belongs to man. It is up to the latter to pray, whereas God bestows what has been prayed for. Man begins and offers and God brings to fulfilment what man cannot accomplish[511].

It must be noticed that all these witnesses, with the exception of Jerome, precede the advent of Pelagianism and the controversy with Augustine. This shows that before the new elaboration of the theology of grace by the bishop of Hippo, the synergetic context in which the *initium fidei* was understood reflected the commonly held and professed doctrine of the Church in general, and that of the Eastern Fathers and theologians in particular.

As to the position of Cassian and the Massilians on this issue, we should firstly make it clear that the *initium fidei* was not interpreted by them as the *fidei rudimenta* or *praeambula*, viz. as the external and internal dispositions that precede and prepare the act of faith[512]. They claimed that once challenged by the Word of God, man is capable of opening up and rising to faith by himself (*naturaliter*), actually "starting" the process of believing (*initium fidei*) through attitudes such as feeling attracted towards a new life, repentance for the former one, desire and hope of being saved, and the prayer that ensues from this desire. The capability to will and to believe belongs to the goodness of human nature, and in this sense both willing and believing are something "natural", something that cannot be corrupted to the point of excluding for ever even the desire to be healed and the will to look for the doctor[513]. Such an ability to will and to believe shows also that what is under consideration is not a

511. "Et tamen hoc scito, baptismum praeterita donare peccata non futuram seruare iustitiam, quae labore et industria, ac diligentia, et semper super omnia Dei clementia custoditur: ut nostrum sit rogare, illius tribuere quod rogatur; nostrum incipere, illius perficere; nostrum offerre quod possumus, illius implere quod non possumus" (JEROME, *Dialogi contra Pelagianos* 3,1 [CCL, 80], p. 98). Cf. also: "Oro te, non legisti: 'Non enim uolentis neque currentis, sed miserentis est Dei'? Ex quibus intelligimus nostrum quidem esse uelle et currere; sed ut uoluntas nostra compleatur et cursus, ad Dei misericordiam pertinere, atque ita fieri, ut et in uoluntate nostra, et in cursu, liberum seruetur arbitrium, et in consummatione uoluntatis et cursus, Dei cuncta potentiae relinquantur" (*Ibid.* 1,5, p. 9); "Haec autem uniuersa dicuntur, ut liberum hominis monstraretur arbitrium. Dei enim uocare est, et nostrum credere" (Id., *Commentarii in Esaiam* 13,49 [CCL, 73A], p. 535).
512. See J. CHÉNÉ, *Notes complémentaires* (BA, 24), pp. 809-810; ID., *Que signifiaient "initium fidei" et "affectum credulitatis" pour les Semipélagiens?* (n. 487), pp. 567ff.
513. Cf. Hilary, *Ep.* 226,2 (CSEL, 57), pp. 469-470.

reality abstracted from divine action, since its cause, viz. the *naturae bonum*, comes ultimately from God himself; it is his "inheritance" present in creation. When interpreted in this way, the *initium fidei* can indeed be understood, in a broader sense, as being synonymous with the *initium salutis*, viz. as being a first step that can be taken by man towards salvation, independently of an external intervention of divine grace. In fact, if man is able, through faith and prayer, to open himself to the gift of justification, then he can also obtain, through a continued effort in faith and prayer, the gift of perseverance that leads to salvation.

Furthermore, it is important to be aware of the fact that by such an interpretation of the *initium fidei* the Massilians did not consider it "the" condition for being saved, but regarded it as "a" possibility that ought not to be read as exclusive. In Cassian's practical approach, the persuasion that the *initium fidei* could occasionally be attributed to God, served as a safeguard for human self-initiative, particularly in connection with his aim of fostering the monks' striving for perfection[514]. Cassian points to such a possibility as found in Scripture. There, besides examples of direct intervention of divine grace, he finds some instances where human initiative takes the lead in the process of conversion to God. Since both ways lead to God, Cassian, like most of the Fathers of the Church, both East and West, upheld the synergetic vision of the co-operation of grace and free will. Undoubtedly, on the central point about man's dependence on God's grace (whose importance he recognizes at the very beginning of *Conlatio* 13[515]) Cassian aligns himself with Augustine. It might even surprise us to read a statement in the divine of Marseilles which sounds very much Augustinian in content, and which is probably influenced by the bishop of Hippo's theology. This statement says that true and perfect freedom can only be found in true submission to God. He who becomes truly free, becomes prisoner of the Lord[516]. Left to himself, and caught

---

514. "This self-initiation was fundamental to his view of the monastic life as a genuine interaction of divine initiative and human initiative. Through the training and discipline that the monastic context made available, the self was formed to God" (R.H. WEAVER, *Divine Grace and Human Agency. A Study of the Semi-Pelagian Controversy* [PatMS, 15, Macon, GA, 1996, p. 114).

515. Cf. Cassian, *Conlatio* 13,3 (SC, 54), p. 151. The need for man's dependence on grace is shown in other passages. Cf., for instance: "Nam bonarum rerum non tantum suggestor, sed etiam fautor atque inpulsor est Deus" (*Ibid.* 7,8 [SC, 42], p. 254). *Ibid.* 3,10-19, pp. 153-163; 4,5, p. 170; 5,14-15, pp. 204-207; Id., *De institutis coenobiorum* 12,4-18 (SC, 109), pp. 455-478; *De incarnatione Domini contra Nestorium* 2,5 (CSEL, 17), pp. 256-258. Also the importance attached to prayer is indicative of the need of God's grace: cf. Id., *Conlationes* 9-10 (SC, 54), pp. 38-96.

516. "Ille uere liber fit qui coeperit tibi esse captiuus" (Id., *De incarnatione Domini contra Nestorium* 7,1 [CSEL, 17], p. 352). Cf. Augustine's similar expression: "Eris liber, si fueris seruus: liber peccati, seruus iustitiae" (Augustine, *Tractatus in Euangelium*

up as he is in the struggle between worldly and spiritual desires, man
does not possess a full and perfect freedom of choice. On the other hand,
apart from the general conviction that man needs God's help and protection, Cassian also firmly believes that man's capacity for taking the first
step in the process of faith and conversion is already foreseen by God's
benevolence. Besides, we should not forget that when he speaks of the
anteriority of human efforts, he has "concrete" examples from Scripture
in mind that he believed could be suitable for encouraging the monks to
a deeper commitment in their *propositum*. It is because of this "practical" aim, for which he relied continually on scriptural data of revelation,
that Cassian did not feel the need to allude to prevenient grace *stricto
sensu*, viz. as the only, exclusive way to salvation. He contents himself
with speaking in general terms of a divine protection or merciful providence whereby God looks upon the life and agency of his creatures[517].

As for Augustine, the concept of the *initium fidei* was revisited and
brought into focus over and against the aspect of *meritum*[518]. Addressing
the problem directly in a passage of the *De praedestinatione sanctorum*
he reiterated very strongly that there is nothing that man possesses,
including faith, that he has not received from God. This is not because to
believe or not to believe has nothing to do with the choice of the human
will (*arbitrio uoluntatis humanae*), but because the will to believe is
itself a gift that God bestows on the elect[519]. The main reasoning underlying this conviction was the following: if man is able to do something
by his own powers, be it even the mere willing the good or the desire of
God, then God would find himself in the position of owing something to
man. The latter, that is, would stand on meritorious ground with regard
to God. This ground, which was named *uoluntas* by the Pelagians, and
ortum quendam bonae uoluntatis (and other similar expressions) by the
Massilians, could not possibly have status in Augustine's eyes.

It is however true that before becoming a bishop (ca. 395/396) Augustine himself had believed that the initiative of willing to believe pertains

---

Ioannis 41,8 [CCL, 36], p. 362). In this respect, Cassian's consideration of humility as the
magistra uirtutum, is also very meaningful (Cassian, *Conlatio* 15,7 [SC, 54], p. 217).

517. *Ibid.* 13,3, p. 151.

518. See MARAFIOTI, *Il problema dell' "Initium Fidei" in sant'Agostino fino al 397*
(n. 333), pp. 541-565.

519. "Ac per hoc, ubi dicitur: *Quis enim te discernit? Quid autem habes quod non
accepisti?* Quisquis audet dicere: Habeo ex me ipso fidem, non ergo accepi; profecto
contradicit huic apertissimae veritati: non quia credere vel non credere non est in arbitrio
voluntatis humanae, sed in electis praeparatur voluntas a Domino. Ideo, ad ipsam quoque
fidem, quae in voluntate est, pertinet: *Quis enim te discernit? Quid autem habes quod
non accepisti?*" (Augustine, *De praedestinatione sanctorum* 5,10 [PL, 44], c. 968).

to man[520]. Thus, in his *Expositio quarumdam propositionum ex epistula ad Romanos*, while reflecting on Rom 9,11-13, where the Apostle quotes Mal 1,2-3 about God's love for Jacob and his hate for Esau, Augustine asks himself why this is so. He comes to the conclusion that the "future faith" of Jacob, foreseen by God, must be the reason for such discrimination. It follows that man can reach out to faith autonomously and freely: *nostrum enim est credere et uelle*[521]. Divine grace would only add to such initiative the capability needed by man to do good and merit eternal life. Augustine was convinced at that time that there was an element present in man, previous to the action of grace. He identified this element as "faith", which, in his eyes, constituted man's *meritum,* or the beginning of that merit through which he can obtain the grace necessary to accomplish what is good[522]. It is true that Augustine had also underlined that God's call (*uocatio*) was behind man's decision for faith, and that this decision was therefore dependent on God's gracious initiative[523]. Augustine, however, had not yet worked out[524] the nature and paramount importance of such a call and its consequences for mankind. At that time he still considered God's *uocatio* to faith a grace in the sense that, within a successionist framework, it offered man and his capacity to will and respond positively, the chance to convert and to adhere to the preaching of the Gospel[525].

---

520. Augustine later recanted this view as erroneous. See: "Quo praecipue testimonio etiam ipse convictus sum, cum similiter errarem, putans fidem qua in Deum credimus, non esse donum Dei, sed a nobis esse in nobis, et per illam nos impetrare Dei dona quibus *temperanter et iuste et pie vivamus in hoc saeculo.* Neque enim fidem putabam Dei gratia praeveniri, ut per illam nobis daretur quod posceremus utiliter; nisi quia credere non possemus, si non praecederet praeconium veritatis: ut autem praedicato nobis Evangelio consentiremus, nostrum esse proprium, et nobis ex nobis esse arbitrar. Quem meum errorem nonnulla opuscula mea satis indicant, ante episcopatum meum scripta" (*Ibid.* 3,7 [PL, 44], c. 964). See *supra,* pp. 156f.

521. Augustine, *Expositio quarumdam propositionum ex epistula ad Romanos* 53 (61), (CSEL, 84), p. 36. Cf. DRECOLL, *Die Entstehung der Gnadenlehre Augustins* (n. 268), pp. 167-168. It should not be forgotten that Augustine's *De libero arbitrio* belongs to the same period in which the *Expositio* was written. We may thus infer that the focus on man's freedom, present in the *De libero arbitrio,* must have influenced the bishop of Hippo's other contemporary writings.

522. "Non opera sed fides inchoat meritum, ut per munus Dei bene operentur" (Augustine, *Expositio quarumdam propositionum ex epistula ad Romanos* 54 [62], [CSEL, 84], p. 37).

523. See, for instance: "Quia neque uelle possumus nisi uocemur" (*Ibid.* 54 [62], p. 36); "Misericordia Dei uocamur, ut credamus" (*Ibid.* 56 [64], p. 40).

524. "Nondum diligentius quaesiueram nec adhuc inueneram, qualis sit electio gratiae" (Id., *Retractationes* 1,23,2 [CCL, 57], p. 68).

525. Analogously, in the *De libero arbitrio,* Augustine had employed the image of God's right hand (the divine call) extended to humanity through Jesus Christ, and man's hand of faith extended to God in a plea for divine assistance (cf. Id., *De libero arbitrio*

A similar solution is present also in Augustine's *De diuersis quaestionibus lxxxiii*. After having introduced the notion of *massa peccati* in which all men equally partake after Adam's fall[526], he asks himself why some men are justified and others not, why some become *uasa misericordiae* and others *uasa irae*[527]. What is it that makes the former "worthy" of being such? It is, says Augustine, the will to accept God's call and the desire to know him and believe in him[528]. This *uoluntas credendi* is precisely what enables man to adhere to the *uocatio* of God and to become the recipient of his mercy. The rising of this faith, Augustine thought, is the *meritum* of man[529]. In fact, God's *uocatio* itself, although it belongs to the gratuitous initiative of God, and cannot be attributed to man (who remains a *uocatus*)[530], is an opportunity given to man (either in the form of preaching or miracles or in some other way) so that he may come to a resolution favouring his conversion and faith. God's *uocatio* is, as it were, a grace before which man has to make a decision. It is his responsibility to believe and adhere to it. A grace, therefore, which should not be confused with the grace "necessary" to man in order to accomplish what is good and thus be saved, given to him by God after his adhesion to faith. The *meritum* of faith (or the *uoluntas credendi*) occupies, as it were, a middle position: it is an answer to the *uocatio* of God, on the one hand, and it precedes God's *gratia* and *misericordia* needed to pursue effectively the good, on the other[531]. Moreover, Augustine's brief allusion to God's *uocatio* not acting merely from without, but as something somehow present *intrinsecus, ubi nullus*

2,20,54 [CCL, 29], p. 273). Also the expression *gratia fidei*, used in the commentary to Paul's epistle to the Galatians (cf. Id., *Epistulae ad Galatas expositio* 1 [CSEL, 84], p. 55), does not mean that faith is the work of grace, but that grace is the condition for salvation, salvation which reaches out to man through faith (cf. DRECOLL, *Die Entstehung der Gnadenlehre Augustins* [n. 268], p. 173).

526. "Ex quo ergo in paradiso natura nostra peccauit, ab eadem diuina prouidentia non secundum caelum sed secundum terram, id est non secundum spiritum sed secundum carnem, mortali generatione formamur, et omnes una massa luti facti sumus, quod est massa peccati" (Augustine, *De diuersis quaestionibus lxxxiii* 68,3 [CCL, 44A], p. 177).

527. "Ex eadem ergo massa, id est peccatorum, et uasa misericordiae protulit quibus subueniret, cum eum deprecarentur filii Israel, et uasa irae quorum supplicio illos erudiret" (*Ibid.* 68,4, p. 179).

528. The Pauline text on which Augustine relies is Rom 1,28: "Quoniam non probaverunt Deum habere in notitia, dedit illos Deus in reprobum sensum".

529. "Credendo... meritum comparatur" (Augustine, *De diuersis quaestionibus lxxxiii* 68,3 [CCL, 44A], p. 177).

530. "Et si quisquam sibi tribuit quod uenit uocatus, non sibi potest tribuere quod uocatus est" (*Ibid.* 68,5, p. 181).

531. "Deus non miseretur... nisi uoluntas praecesserit" (*Ibid.*). At this stage "der Begriff *misericordia* bietet gegenüber *gratia* den Vorteil, nicht zu betonen, daß das Erbarmen ohne vorangehende *merita* geschieht" (DRECOLL, *Die Entstehung der Gnadenlehre Augustins* [n. 268], p. 217).

hominum uidet[532], does not imply as yet the direct intervention of God upon the will of man from the very moment of the *uocatio*.

It is in the *De diuersis quaestionibus ad Simplicianum* that Augustine makes a definitive step forward. Abandoning the idea of Jacob being loved by God because the latter had foreseen his future faith[533], he begins to speak explicitly of the *gratia fidei*[534] in an inclusive way, asserting that nothing good happens outside the grace of God[535]. Faith itself depends upon the *gratia [fidei]* which, in turn, depends upon the divine *uocatio*[536] (or *gratia uocationis*[537]). The *meritum fidei* he had spoken of previously as the determinant element for being justified and saved, is now done away with. The *gratia uocationis* does not require any previous merit any more[538]. Following the "revelation" of 1 Cor 4,7[539], in Augustine's eyes there is only a "causal relation"[540] between God's *uocatio* and man's *uoluntas credendi* (or *initium fidei*), and not a temporal succession. These two elements are no longer distinct[541]. Now the second one, the will of man to believe, is the work of God and is totally dependent upon his gracious call. There, and only there, in the inscrutable *uocatio* of God, resides the source and the beginning of faith and of any good will.

That the *initium fidei*, or the beginning of a good will[542], is a *munus Dei* will also be reiterated by Augustine in his works addressed to the

532. Augustine, *De diuersis quaestionibus lxxxiii* 68,5 (CCL, 44A), p. 181.

533. The weak point of such affirmation is that the same thing could be appropriately said of good works: God loved Jacob because he foresaw his future good works! Cf. Id., *De diuersis quaestionibus ad Simplicianum* 1,2,5 (CCL, 44), p. 30.

534. *Ibid.* 1,2,2, pp. 24 and 25.

535. "Nihil tamen horum sine gratia misericordiae Dei" (*Ibid.* 1,2,2, p. 25).

536. "Nemo enim credit qui non uocatur. Misericors autem Deus uocat nullis hoc uel fidei meritis largiens, quia merita fidei sequuntur uocationem potius quam praecedunt.... Nisi ergo uocando praecedat misericordia Dei, nec credere quisquam potest, ut ex hoc incipiat iustificari et accipere facultatem bene operandi" (*Ibid.* 1,2,7, pp. 31-32).

537. This terminology is explicitely used by Augustine. Cf. *Ibid.* 1,2,3, p. 26.

538. DRECOLL, *Die Entstehung der Gnadenlehre Augustins* (n. 268), pp. 218ff.

539. Cf. Augustine, *De diuersis quaestionibus ad Simplicianum* 1,2,9 (CCL, 44), p. 34.

540. The following words (among many others) do illustrate this point perfectly: "*[Gratia]* praevenit hominis uoluntatem bonam, nec eam cuiusquam inuenit in corde, sed facit" (Id., *Ep.* 217,2,5 [CSEL, 57], p. 406).

541. As Marafioti writes: "Prima, la chiamata di Dio e la decisione della volontà erano due cose distinte e separate, tanto separate che avevano origine diversa, l'una da Dio l'altra dall'uomo. L'unico punto di contatto era l'illuminazione dell'intelligenza che avveniva esteriormente.... Il tutto non andava al di là di una proposta a cui la volontà aderiva o meno, in maniera completamente autonoma. Ma ora Agostino... si rende conto che nulla può essere lasciato all'uomo di cui poi questi si possa 'vantare'" (MARAFIOTI, *Il problema dell' 'Initium Fidei' in sant'Agostino fino al 397* [n. 333], p. 559).

542. In Augustine's eyes the *initium fidei* and the *initium bonae/piae uoluntatis* are equivalent. See: "Tu autem..., initium fidei, ubi est etiam initium bonae, hoc est piae

Massilians, where he will carry out his demonstration on a threefold
level: biblical, liturgical and theological. On the biblical level, Augustine gathered some quotations (*e.g.*: Rom 11,35-36; 2 Cor 3,5; 1 Cor
4,7; Jn 6,44; Ez 11,19) from which it could be inferred that the *initium
fidei* is God's gift, the result of the direct and generous intervention of
his grace, bestowed on human hearts in the first place (*primitus*) to take
away their hardness (*duritia*) (cf. Ez 36,26-27)[543] and allow them to
believe. Since *totum Deo dandum est*[544], the movement of a heart that
begins to turn to God also belongs to God. Secondly, the liturgical argument is brought in to support this view. Augustine refers to the explicit
custom of the Church of praying for heathens and for her enemies, so
that they may convert[545]. What would be the point of doing so unless the
Church was convinced that the will (to believe) is prepared by God?[546]
Thirdly and finally, from the strictly theological point of view Augustine's constant reference is a christological one. The incarnation of the
Word of God, viz. the gratuitous assumption of humanity by the Godhead in Christ (the *summum exemplum gratiae*) remains at the centre of
Augustine's doctrine of grace and of his manifold expressions, including
the *initium fidei*[547].

To extend God's grace to the entire will of man was the only way, in
Augustine's eyes, to save the gratuitousness of grace and its very existence and necessity. However, his defence of the gratuitousness of grace
before any human merit, and the attribution to God of man's *initium
fidei*, and not only of his (final) perseverance, could not remain an isolated conviction. In point of fact it pushed Augustine's thought to move
forward even more, towards a view of a restricted dispensation of grace
and towards a deeper reflection on the mystery of predestination. In
Augustine's mind, this mystery became the theoretical justification and
the natural theological solution for giving man's volitions and contingencies their right place in God's eternal, inscrutable and just designs.
We shall devote the next chapter to these problems.

---

uoluntatis, non uis esse donum Dei, sed ex nobis nos habere contendis, ut credere incipiamus" (Augustine, *Ep.* 217,7,29 [CSEL, 57], p. 424).
    543. "Ideo quippe tribuitur, ut cordis duritia primitus auferatur" (Id., *De praedesti-
natione sanctorum* 8,13 [PL, 44], c. 971). See also, Id., *De gratia et libero arbitrio* 14,29
(PL, 44), c. 898.
    544. Id., *De praedestinatione sanctorum* 7,12 (PL, 44), c. 970.
    545. Cf. *Ibid.* 8,15, c. 972; Id., *De dono perseuerantiae* 23,63 (PL, 45), c. 1031; *De
gratia et libero arbitrio* 14,29 (PL, 44), c. 898; *Ep.* 217,1,2.2,6 (CSEL, 57), pp. 404.407-
408.
    546. Cf. Id., *Contra duas epistulas Pelagianorum* 4,9,26 (CSEL, 60), p. 553.
    547. Cf. Id., *De praedestinatione sanctorum* 15,30-31 (PL, 44), cc. 981-983.

CHAPTER FOUR

THE *VEXATA QUAESTIO* OF PREDESTINATION

If we turn to Holy Scripture[1], the theme that in the Old Testament comes closest to the theological problem of predestination, is that of election which, to be properly understood, must be set against the background of the covenant between Yahweh and Israel. Through the election of Israel the gratuity of God's covenant is not restricted to a particular human group, but it becomes the reference point for the fulfilment of God's historical designs regarding humanity as a whole. In fact, although Israel was set apart by God in a special way, and had become the object of his numerous gifts and benefits, it is precisely thanks to this "chosen" people that the other nations are included in God's blessing (cf. Gen 12,2-3). In the divine plan of salvation, Israel has a precise mission to accomplish: "I will give you as a light to the nations, that my salvation may reach to the ends of the earth" (Is 49,6b; see also Ps 96,1-3). The conversion of Niniveh, as the book of Jonah makes clear, is a demonstration of how the love of God is bestowed on all peoples. None of the things that exist and that He has made is excluded from it (cf. Wis 11,24). Even in the case of misbehaviour or refusal on the part of man, God takes no pleasure in the death of the wicked but would rather that he turn from his wicked ways and live (cf. Ez 33,11).

As for the New Testament, the coming of Jesus, the Messiah, and his preaching about the kingdom of God, bring the divine universality of salvation to the foreground. Jesus, the Word of God, has come into the world to save it (cf. Jn 3,17b), to be "the true light that enlightens every man" (Jn 1,9), "the Lamb of God who takes away the sin of the world" (Jn 1,29; cf. 1 Jn 2,2). Paul approaches the problem of universal salvation underlying the parallel between the old Adam (whose fall led to the condemnation of all humanity) and the new Adam, Jesus Christ, who has brought acquittal and salvation to sinful humanity (cf. Rom 5,15.18-19). The goal of Christ's incarnation was indeed the deliverance of men from all their sins (cf. 1 Tim 1,15; Rom 4,25), and their justification and

---

1. See A. LEMONNYER, *Prédestination*. I: *La prédestination dans la sainte Écriture*, in *DTC* 12/2 (1935) 2809-2815; F. FERRIER, *Prédestination*, in *Cath* 11 (1988) 764-781, cc. 764-766; E. FASCHER, *Erwählung*, in *RAC* 6 (1966) 409-436, cc. 411-419.

salvation by his blood (cf. Rom 5,9; Col 1,14.19-20; Eph 1,9-10). The effects of Christ's mission are extended to all men without exception, because it is God's will that all men be saved (cf. 1 Tim 2,4; see also Rom 5,9; 8,32; 2 Cor 5,15).

The notion of predestination is found exclusively in the New Testament. With the exception of Acts 4,28, the verb προορίζειν appears only in the Pauline and deutero-Pauline letters (cf. Rom 8,29.30; 1 Cor 2,7; Eph 1,5.11) to suggest a purpose/design or eternal election. The *loci classici* are Rom 8,28-30 and Eph 1,13-14, from which it can be inferred that the object of eternal predestination is a salvific order which God has prepared for men. They are all called to be justified and glorified by way of Jesus Christ the Mediator and the Church, which depends on him (cf. Eph 1,14f; 2,10; 3,9-11).

Problems begin to arise, however, when we attempt to work out how salvation really comes about for all humanity. Does the efficacy of such salvation depend exclusively on the will of God? Indeed, if we turn to Scripture, we shall find out that passages asserting the universality of God's salvation, such as 1 Tim 2,4, are put in question by other scriptural quotations in which the will of God about men's salvation appears to depend on specific conditions, such as faith in the Lord, in whom man is justified (cf. Rom 5,1f; Eph 1,13), love (cf. Rom 8,28), and the necessity of being baptized in Christ, by whom man is regenerated (cf. Jn 3,5). Moreover, in spite of the universality of God's call to salvation, there are New Testament passages which point out that the opposite, viz. damnation, is also a real possibility. We infer this, for instance, from the depiction of the last judgement (cf. Mt 25), or from Paul's lists where some categories of people are doomed not to possess the kingdom of God (cf. 1 Cor 6,9-10; Gal 5,19-21). It is clear, therefore, that there is also room, on the part of man, for refusal and defection with regard to God's call; refusal and defection which seem to contradict the divine call to universal salvation, and which render more acute the question of the real significance of such a call.

The problem of predestination which, as it has been noted, has never ceased to test theologians[2], is thus essentially a problem concerning the way in which salvation is intended and brought about from the point of

---

2. The doctrine of predestination has been defined the "casse-tête des débutants et tourment des vieux maîtres" (A.D. SERTILLANGES, *"Agnosticisme et anthropomorphisme" [Réponse à M. Gardair]*, in RevPhil 5 [1906] 158-181, p. 162); "Le mot de prédestination a le don d'énerver les théologiens" (M.A. SMALBRUGGE, *La prédestination entre subjectivité et language. Le premier dogme moderne*, in RTP 127 [1995] 43-54, p. 43).

view of God in relation to humanity. Besides, it will become clear that in order to be properly tackled and understood, the problem of predestination must not be detached from the central issues of Christian faith with which it is so closely interwoven: grace and its attributes, the nature of divine election, God's foreknowledge and providence, final perseverance and the place and role of human free will vis-à-vis God's gifts. Augustine was the first to lay the basis in Christian tradition[3] for a full and systematic doctrine of predestination, which he discussed in connection with the above implications. By so doing, he profoundly marked the theological reflection of the West[4], even though the solutions he propounded have never lacked criticism, right up to the present day[5], and have never been accepted by the Church in their entirety. But how did Augustine develop his thinking? And how much did his thinking develop in the light of previously accepted Christian doctrine? A brief enquiry will suffice to set the background against which the relevance of Augustine's contribution may be better grasped.

1. THE CONCEPT OF PREDESTINATION IN CHRISTIAN TRADITION

The Greek tradition, with its cosmic vision of salvation and its defence of human freedom against the different forms of gnosticism and fatalism[6], was rather homogeneous in offering an optimistic solution with regard to the problem of election/predestination[7]. A peaceful coexistence of the belief in the universal salvation, and the seemingly impelling demands laid on man in order to partake of it, was taken for granted. If God, the Greek theologians would argue, has really saved the world in Christ, and if man, despite the fall, has really maintained the efficiency of his freedom in accord with the activity of grace, then

---

3. "Die Theologie vor Augustin kennt keine Prädestinationslehre" (E. BRUNNER, *Dogmatik*, Bd. I: *Die christliche Lehre von Gott*, Zürich, 1946, p. 369). "Vogliamo rivendicare a S. Agostino la paternità esclusiva della sua dottrina sulla predestinazione" (V. BOUBLÍK, *La predestinazione. S. Paolo e S. Agostino* [CorLat, 3], Rome, 1961, p. 166).

4. "Senza S. Agostino non vi sarebbe la teologia occidentale della predestinazione e della riprovazione" (BOUBLÍK, *La predestinazione* [n. 3], p. 166). "Die Linien dieser in den verschiedensten theologischen Lagern aktuellen Prädestinationsproblematik kann man zeitlich rückwärts verfolgen zu einem einzigen Punkt, von dem sie alle ausstrahlen: Augustin" (G. NYGREN, *Das Prädestinationsproblem in der Theologie Augustins* [StTL, 12], Lund, 1956, p. 8).

5. See, for instance, A. TRAPÈ, *A proposito di predestinazione: S. Agostino ed i suoi critici moderni*, in *Div* 7 (1963) 243-284, pp. 243ff.

6. See *supra*, pp. 194-224 *passim*.

7. For the Greek tradition, see FASCHER, *Erwählung* (n. 1), cc. 422-426; FERRIER, *Prédestination* (n. 1), cc. 766-767.

salvation must depend on God and man alike. Damnation, by contrast, depends only on man's refusal of the offer of salvation.

From the point of view of the Eastern theological tradition, the problem at stake hinges essentially upon a twofold possibility: the decision of co-operating with God's saving activity, on one side, or the attachment to evil and the choice of siding with it, on the other. What stands out as an ultimately decisive element, is the role of man's free will. In fact, although in his bounty God has given to everybody the means to choose the good and obtain salvation, at the same time He has not deprived man of the possibility of choosing evil and becoming liable to punishment by his own accord. Rather than speculating about God's inscrutable intentions and decrees, the Greek theologians considered divine justice on the basis of its effects[8], or put another way, in strict connection with the *divine foreknowledge* of man's behaviour. Their thought on this point shows great coherence and unity of doctrine. Their preoccupation to defend both the justice of God and the freedom of man brought them to an implicit agreement about the "conditional" character of predestination and grace as well as about the universality of God's salvific will[9]. A few examples, however incomplete, will suffice to illustrate their general trend.

According to *Justin*, God would reward men on the basis of their good and virtuous lives which are foreseen by his prescience[10]. *Irenaeus* echoes this view, affirming that through his foreknowledge, God is able to judge justly every man's future choices, abandoning to their unbelief all those He foreknows will not believe in him[11]. *Clement of Alexandria* also speaks of those who are predestined as people whose justice has been foreknown by God since the beginning of the world[12]. Likewise, commenting on Rom 8,28-30, *Origen* affirms that God predestines all those whom He foresees will lead a religious and pious existence (εὐσέβεια), giving themselves entirely to a life of virtue, to share in the

---

8. "Les Grecs s'accordent à considérer toujours l'action divine à partir de ses effects" (H.-D. SIMONIN, *Prédestination. II. La prédestination d'après les Pères grecs*, in *DTC* 12/2 [1935] 2815-2832, c. 2832).

9. See *Ibid.*, cc. 2818ff.

10. "Ὁ ἀριθμὸς τῶν προεγνωσμένων αὐτῷ ἀγαθῶν γινομένων καὶ ἐναρέτων" (Justin, *Apologia* 1,45 [PG, 6], c. 396).

11. "Εἰ οὖν καὶ νῦν ὅσους οἶδε μὴ πιστεύσειν Θεὸς ὁ τῶν ἁπάντων προγνώστης παραδίδωσι τῇ ἀπιστίᾳ αὐτῶν" (Irenaeus, *Aduersus haereses* 4,29,2 [SC, 100**], p. 769).

12. "Οὓς προώρισεν ὁ Θεός, δικαίους ἐσομένους πρὸ καταβολῆς κόσμου ἐγνωκώς" (Clement of Alexandria, *Stromata* 7,17,107,5 [GCS, 17], p. 76).

image of his Son[13] and in his knowledge[14]. Divine predestination is, as it were, the effect of divine foreknowledge[15], whereas the latter is, in its turn, caused by man's freedom of behaviour[16]. Similarly, in *John Chrysostom*'s commentary on the same passage (Rom 8,28-30), the gift of divine sonship (and man's predestination to it) is understood to depend upon God's foreknowledge of man's obedience. Even more boldly, Chrysostom interprets the expression *secundum propositum* (κατὰ πρόθεσιν) of Rom 8,28 as relating not only to God's decree but also to man's will[17]. Finally, while asking himself why not everyone will be saved, despite the fact that it is God's wish that all men be saved, he answers by pointing to man's personal responsibility. Since God does not impose his will on man, the latter can also decide, if he wishes, not to conform to it[18]. God offers to all the necessary means to obtain salvation, and if some are not saved it is because they have not made proper use of such means. Worth noting also is Chrysostom's introduction of the twofold notion of God's "preceding" and "successive" will: whereas his preceding or first (πρῶτον) will is concerned with the salvation of all men, his successive or second (δεύτερον) will deals with those who have become bad and deserve death[19].

13. "Προενατενίσας οὖν ὁ Θεὸς τῷ εἰρμῷ τῶν ἐσομένων, καὶ κατανοήσας ῥοπὴν τοῦ ἐφ᾽ ἡμῖν τῶνδέ τινων ἐπὶ εὐσέβειαν καὶ ὁρμὴν ἐπὶ ταύτην μετὰ τὴν ῥοπήν, καὶ ὡς ὅλοι ἑαυτοὺς ἐπιδώσουσι τῷ κατ᾽ ἀρετὴν ζῆν, προέγνω αὐτούς, γινώσκων μὲν τὰ ἐνιστάμενα προγινώσκων δὲ τὰ μέλλοντα· καὶ οὓς οὕτω προέγνω, προώρισεν συμμόρφους ἐσομένους τῆς εἰκόνος τοῦ υἱοῦ αὐτοῦ" (Origen, *Fragmenta* [In Rom 1], *Philocalia* 25,2 [SC, 226], pp. 216-218).

14. Cf. Id., *Contra Celsum* 7,44 (SC, 150), pp. 116.118. See also, Id., *Commentarii in epistulam ad Romanos* 7,8, *FC*, Bd. II/4, pp. 92-102; Id., *De oratione* 29,19 (GCS, 3), p. 393.

15. "Ἀνωτέρω δέ ἐστι τοῦ προορισμοῦ ἡ πρόγνωσις" (Id., *Fragmenta* [In Rom 1], *Philocalia* 25,2 [SC, 226], p. 216).

16. Cf. *Ibid.* 25,3, p. 224.

17. "Εἰ γὰρ ἡ κλῆσις ἤρκει μόνον, τίνος ἕνεκεν οὐ πάντες ἐσώθησαν; Διὰ τοῦτό φησιν, ὅτι οὐχ ἡ κλῆσις μόνον, ἀλλὰ καὶ ἡ πρόθεσις τῶν καλουμένων τὴν σωτηρίαν εἰργάσατο· οὐ γὰρ ἠναγκασμένη γέγονεν ἡ κλῆσις οὐδὲ βεβιασμένη. Πάντες γοῦν ἐκλήθησαν, ἀλλ᾽ οὐ πάντες ὑπήκουσαν" (John Chrysostom, *In epistulam ad Romanos*, Hom. 15,1 [PG, 60], c. 541).

18. "Πῶς οὖν οὐχ ἅπαντες σώζονται, εἰ θέλει πάντας σωθῆναι; Ἐπειδὴ οὐχ ἁπάντων τὸ θέλημα τῷ θελήματι αὐτοῦ ἕπεται, αὐτὸς δὲ οὐδένα βιάζεται" (Id., *De mutatione nominum* hom. 3,6 [PG, 51], c. 144).

19. "Πανταχοῦ γὰρ εὐδοκία τὸ θέλημά ἐστι τὸ προηγούμενον. Ἔστι γὰρ καὶ ἄλλο θέλημα· οἷον, θέλημα πρῶτον, τὸ μὴ ἀπολέσθαι ἡμαρτηκότας· θέλημα δεύτερον, τὸ γενομένους κακοὺς ἀπολέσθαι" (Id., *In Epistulam ad Ephesios argumentum et homiliae* 1,2 [PG, 62], c. 13). This distinction will be taken up by *John of Damascus* who will also speak of two successive wills being present in God. The first one, God's "antecedent" will, is the will that all men be saved; the second one, God's "consequent" will (which originates in man and is permitted by God), is the will that all those who live sinfully shall perish: "Λέγεται οὖν τὸ μὲν πρῶτον προηγούμενον

There are some instances of this optimistic view being shared also in the Latin Church before Augustine[20]. *Hilary of Poitiers*, for example, commenting on Ps 64,5 (*Beatus quem elegisti et assumpsisti*) affirms that, according to the gospel, the elect are not chosen arbitrarily, but upon the discernment of their merits[21]. *Ambrose*, in his turn, while commenting on Mt 20,23 (*Sedere autem ad dexteram meam uel sinistram non est meum dare uobis, sed quibus paratum est a Patre meo*) asserts that God does not choose some people in preference to others, but simply rewards all men according to the foreknowledge of their merits[22]. *Ambrosiaster* speaks of two groups of people, respectively foreknown for their faith and for their unbelief or temporary belief[23]. *Jerome*, opposing the *uasa irae* (Israel) to the *uasa misericordiae* (the new Israel, the Christians, issued from both the Jews and the Gentiles) says that the latter are saved on account of antecedent causes, viz. their having welcomed the Son of God, whereas the former, who have refused to recognize him, are destined to perish[24]. Finally, *Pelagius* insists that God will

θέλημα καὶ εὐδοκία ἐξ αὐτοῦ ὄν, τὸ δὲ δεύτερον ἑπόμενον θέλημα καὶ παραχώρ-ησις ἐξ ἡμετέρας αἰτίας. Καὶ αὕτη διττή· ἡ μὲν οἰκονομικὴ καὶ παιδευτικὴ πρὸς σωτηρίαν, ἡ δὲ ἀπογνωστικὴ πρὸς τελείαν κόλασιν, ὡς εἰρήκαμεν. Ταῦτα δὲ ἐπὶ τῶν οὐκ ἐφ᾽ ἡμῖν" (John of Damascus, *Expositio fidei* [43] 2,29, *PTS* 12, pp. 102-103). John of Damascus had already explained in another work what he meant by "antecedent" and "consequent" will: whereas the former is one's natural possession, the latter is the result of external events: "Προηγούμενον μέν ἐστι θέλημα ὅπερ τις ἀφ᾽ ἑαυτοῦ θέλει· ἑπόμενον δὲ, ὅπερ ἐκ τῆς τῶν γινομένων αἰτίας" (Id., *Dialogus contra Manichaeos* 79 [PG, 94], c. 1577).
  20. See FASCHER, *Erwählung* (n. 1), c. 767; T.G. RING, *"Electio" in der Gnadenlehre Augustins*, in A. ZUMKELLER – A. KRUEMMEL (eds.), *Traditio Augustiniana: Studien über Augustinus und seine Rezeption. Festgabe für Willigis Eckermann OSA zum 60. Geburtstag* (Cass., 46), Würzburg, 1994, pp. 39-79, pp. 44-47.
  21. "Itaque non res indiscreti iudicii electio est, sed ex meriti electu facta discretio est. Beatus ergo, quem elegit Deus: beatus ob id, quia electione sit dignus" (Hilary of Poitiers, *Tractatus super psalmos* 64,5 [CSEL, 22], p. 236).
  22. "Apostolus ait: *Quos praescivit et praedestinavit*. Non enim ante praedestinavit quam praesciret, sed quorum merita praescivit, eorum praemia praedestinavit" (Ambrose, *De fide* 5,6,83 [CSEL, 78], p. 247).
  23. "Hi ergo secundum propositum vocantur, quos credentes praesciit Deus futuros sibi idoneos, ut, antequam crederent, scirentur... Istos quos praescivit futuros devotos sibi, ipsos elegit ad promissa praemia capessenda... De ceteris, quos non praesciit Deus, non est illi cura in hac gratia, quia non praesciit illos futuros idoneos. Acsi credentes eligantur ad tempus,..., non permanent" (Ambrosiaster, *Commentarius in xiii epistulas Paulinas, Ad Romanos* 8,28-30 [CSEL, 81/1], pp. 289-293 [rec. g] *passim*). See also: "Unum elegit praescientia et alterum sprevit.... non personarum acceptor *[Deus]*, nam neminem damnat, antequam peccet, et nullum coronat, antequam vincat" (*Ibid.* 9,13, p. 313).
  24. "Vasa autem misericordiae, quae praeparauit in gloriam, quae et uocauit, hoc est nos,... non saluat inrationabiliter et absque iudicii ueritate, sed causis praecedentibus, quia alii non susceperunt filium Dei, alii recipere sua sponte uoluerunt" (Jerome, *Ep.* 120,10 [CSEL, 60], pp. 500f).

never hinder the salvation of every person, because salvation is precisely what He himself wills for everybody[25]. He clearly affirms that predestination is the same as foreknowledge, in that God already knows those who will believe and from whom his call will elicit a free and positive answer[26]. In this sense, God does not make any distinction with regard to persons, and He offers his salvation to everybody. If there is a difference at all, it is only in the time in which the encounter between God's will and man's will happens[27].

Rather than looking for a solution to the problem of salvation in the sphere of divine decrees, the Greek and Latin theologians did not hesitate to express their conviction that the election or non-election of men is subordinated to God's foreknowledge with regard to either their meritorious act of faith, or their demerit. In other words, for both the Greek and Latin theologians, divine foreknowledge constituted the *Grundlage* of God's predestination, the key to interpret it, and the way to explain the scriptural evidences that speak of both life and death, salvation and damnation in relation to God's agency as well as man's.

---

25. Cf. Pelagius, *Expositiones xiii epistularum Pauli (ad Timotheum I)* [2,4] (PLS, 1), c. 1348.

26. "Praedestinare idem est quod praescire. Ergo quos praeuidit conformes futuros in uita, uoluit ut fierent conformes in gloria…. Quos praesciit credituros, hos uocauit, uocatio autem uolentes colligit, non inuitos" (Id., *Expositiones xiii epistularum Pauli [ad Romanos]* [8,29-30] [PLS, 1], cc. 1149-1150). "Iacob et Esau…, ante quam nascerentur, aput *(sic!)* Deum fidei [futurae] sunt merito separati, ut propositum Dei de elegendis bonis et refutandis malis etiam in praescientia iam maneret. Ita ergo et nunc quos praesciit de gentibus credituros, elegit, et ex Istrahel *(sic!)* reiecit incredulos" (*Ibid.* [9,10], c. 1153). See also: "Hoc praedestinauit, ut habere[n]t potestatem filius Dei fieri omnis qui credere uoluisse[n]t, sicut scriptum est: 'loquebantur uerbum Dei cum fiducia omni uolenti credere' [Ac 4,31]" (Id., *Expositiones xiii epistularum Pauli [ad Ephesios]* [1,5] [PLS, 1], c. 1289). "Ante destinati per fidem. Sive: Praecogniti" (*Ibid.*, c. 1290).

"So wahrt Pelagius mit seiner 'Prädestinations'-Lehre das Grundanliegen seiner Theologie, daß nämlich der Mensch für sein Heil verantwortlich ist, da Gott sein Heil will und ihm alles zum Heil Notwendige geschenkt hat…. Für das pelagische Denken hat das Problem der 'Prädestination' nur insofern Bedeutung, als er durch seine Interpretation der betreffenden biblischen Stellen die Verantwortlichkeit des Menschen aufrechterhalten und jede Form eines Fatalismus abwehren will" (G. GRESHAKE, *Gnade als konkrete Freiheit. Eine Untersuchung zur Gnadenlehre des Pelagius*, Mainz, 1972, p. 150).

27. "Aut certe discretio non in personis, sed in tempore est" (Pelagius, *Expositiones xiii epistularum Pauli [ad Romanos]* [8,30] [PLS, 1], c. 1150). For Pelagius' understanding of divine election in connection with God's prescience, see also J.B. VALERO, *Las bases antropologicas de Pelagio en su tratado de las Expositiones* (Estudios, 18), Madrid, 1980, pp. 332-337.

2. The Development of Augustine's Doctrine of
Predestination and Its Formal Definition

Augustine did not develop his theological construction on predestination by basing himself on the exegetical results of his Christian predecessors. Rather he relied on his own, independent interpretation of the Pauline letters, the emphasis being on the letter to the Romans. It is in fact by turning to the Apostle with growing interest[28], and by leaning upon those passages in which Paul speaks of election and predestination in connection with God's designs, concerning either Christ[29] or the salvation of men[30], that the bishop of Hippo will arrive at his controversial conclusions on the doctrine of predestination.

In the first years of his theological career, however, Augustine had embraced the loose solution that his predecessors (especially in the East) had found with regard to the question of divine election or predestination[31]. In point of fact, the perspective through which Augustine tackled

28. Although, in a way, "son maître par excellence fut saint Paul" (J. Saint-Martin, *Prédestination. III. La prédestination d'après les Pères latins, particulièrment d'après saint Augustin*, in *DTC* 12/2 [1935] 2832-2896, c. 2834), his approach to the writing of the Apostle was very personal. Souter comes to the point of writing that "where St. Paul was concerned, he may have felt he could do best service to his generation by personal thinking out of the problems involved" (A. Souter, *The Earliest Latin Commentaries on the Epistles of St. Paul: a Study*, Oxford, 1927, anastatic reprint 1999, p. 199). Along the same line, Brown writes: "Paul had spoken; Augustine had understood. That should be enough" (P. Brown, *Augustine of Hippo. A Biography*, London 1967, p. 359).

29. Cf. Rom 1,4: "*... qui [Iesus Christus] praedestinatus est Filius Dei in uirtute secundum Spiritum sanctificationis ex resurrectione mortuorum*". About the interpretation of this verse, following the reading of ὁρισθέντος as "constituted" rather than "predestined", see *supra*, p. 166, n. 343.

30. Cf. Rom 8,28-30: "*Scimus quoniam diligentibus Deum omnia coopera(n)tur in bonum, his qui secundum propositum uocati sunt: quoniam quos ante praesciuit, et* praedestinavit *conformes imaginis Filii sui, ut sit ipse primogenitus in multis fratribus: quos autem* praedestinavit, *illos et uocauit; quos autem uocauit, ipsos et iustificauit; quos autem iustificauit, ipsos et glorificauit*; 1 Cor 2,7: "*... sed loquimur Dei sapientiam in mysterio, quae abscondita est, quam* praedestinavit *Deus ante saecula in gloriam nostram*"; Eph 1,5.11: "*... praedestinans [Deus] nos in adoptionem filiorum per Iesum Christum in ipsum, secundum placitum uoluntatis suae... in quo [Christo] etiam et sortem consecuti sumus, praedestinati secundum propositum, qui uniuersa operatur secundum consilium uoluntatis suae*"; Rom 9,10-29: about the election of Jacob and the reprobation of Esau. With regard to Rom 8,28, we must be reminded that the majority of the critical editions of Augustine's works have retained the reading of the Vulgate "cooperantur", "alors qu'Augustin citait ce verset dès 395 avec le verbe *cooperari* au singulier, calquant de près le texte grec Θεὸς πάντα συνεργεῖ, et faisant du mot *Deus*, sous-entendu, le sujet de *cooperatur*" (G. Folliet, '(Deus) omnia cooperatur in bonum', *Rom. 8,28. Les citations du verset chez Augustin*, in *SE* 37 [1997] 33-55, p. 33).

31. In Augustine's view, election and predestination should be understood and used as synonyms: "Dafür spricht u. a., daß er mitunter electio/eligere und praedestinatio/praedestinare so gut wie synonym gebraucht, jedenfalls ohne wesentlichen Bedeutungs-

the problem fell initially under the category of God's foreknowledge of man's future merits (or demerits) and did not point to a particular doctrine whereby predestination was commanded by God's gratuitous grace alone. In the *De libero arbitrio*, for instance, where the relationship between God's agency and man's freedom is not fully worked out (Augustine being more interested in reacting against Manichaean fatalism by emphasizing man's free will[32]), God's judgement with regard to salvation is dealt with from the viewpoint of *praescientia*. As such, there is no contradiction here with man's inclination to sin, because God, although foreseeing the sins that men will commit wilfully, does not compel man to commit them[33].

Augustine was directly confronted with the problem of election and predestination in his *Expositio quarumdam propositionum ex epistula ad Romanos*, where he set out to explain Rom 8,28-30 (*Quos uocauit, ipsos et iustificauit*). Faced with the problem of reconciling this text, in which it is said that those who have been called by God are also justified, with Mt 22,14 (*Multi uocati, pauci autem electi*)[34], where being called and being elect do not appear to be equivalent terms, Augustine resolved this tension by introducing a distinction which will become central to his concept of predestination: a distinction between God's ordinary *uocatio* and God's *uocatio secundum propositum*[35]. Yet election and predestination are still envisaged in the light of prescience; it rests on God's foreknowledge of man's faith and of his will to co-operate by following his call[36]. This same vision reappears in a commentary on Rom 9,10-29, the text concerning the election of Jacob and the rejection of Esau: *Jacob dilexi, Esau autem odio habui* (Rom 9,13 [quotation of Mal 1,3][37]).

---

unterschied, wenn er z. B. in praed. Sanct. 35 PL 44, 986 festellt: 'Elegit ergo pradestinans nos.' Dies verdeutlicht er dann ebd. 36 PL 44, 987: '...tales eramus futuri, quia elegit ipse, praedestinans ut tales per gratiam eius essemus'. Erwählung ist demnach nichts anderes als Vorherbestimmung und deren zeitliche Umsetzung durch Gnade" (RING, *"Electio" in der Gnadenlehre Augustins* [n. 20], p. 78).

32. See *supra*, pp. 251f.

33. Cf. Augustine, *De libero arbitrio* 3,4,10 (CCL, 29), p. 281.

34. Cf. Id., *Expositio quarumdam propositionum ex epistula ad Romanos* 47 (55) (CSEL, 84), p. 30.

35. "Non enim omnes, qui vocati sunt, secundum propositum vocati sunt, hoc enim propositum ad praescientiam et ad praedestinationem Dei pertinet" (*Ibid.*).

36. "Nec praedestinavit aliquem, nisi quem praescivit crediturum et secuturum vocationem suam" (*Ibid.*).

37. In Malachi "the context is one of God's freely preferring one group over another and of his steadfast perseverance in his original choice" (A. CODY, *Haggai, Zechariah, Malachi*, in R.E. BROWN – J.A. FITZMYER – R.E. MURPHY [eds.], *The New Jerome Biblical Commentary*, Englewood Cliffs/NJ, 1990, pp. 349-361, p. 360). "Le prophète ne s'est pas posé de problème métaphysique à ce sujet.... Il est tout aussi excessif de lire dans ce

Firstly, Augustine states that we should not believe it is purely because of God's election that human free will is taken away[38]; secondly, and more importantly, he confirms that man's *meritum* is a sort of pre-condition for God's election[39] and a guarantee that this does not happen in an arbitrary or whimsical way. However, such *meritum*, which is already known by God and provides the basis for God's election of man, does not come from the moral character of human actions. When God in his foreknowledge elects or rejects somebody (as in the case of Jacob and Esau) He does not choose or reject one's future works, but chooses or rejects one's future *fides* or one's *infidelitas/impietas*[40]. Thus, the merits of works, which are carefully excluded by Augustine, are replaced with the merits of belief or unbelief (*prima merita fidei et impietatis*)[41]. In other words, election rests on God's foreknowledge (*praescientia*) of man's future merits, namely his good will and faith, from which his commitment to the divine call is engendered. That there can be no help of God without the will responding to his call, is illustrated by the hardening of Pharaoh's heart, "merited" on account of his lack of good will and faith (*prior infidelitas*)[42], viz. the refusal of God's appeal, and of his hidden preceding impiety (*occulta superioris impietas*)[43]. It is clear that, at this stage, Augustine's concept of predestination is still inchoative. What is envisaged – no doubt also in the light of Augustine's opposition to Manichaean determinism – is a real and dynamic interplay between

passage une preuve théologique de la prédestination et du rejet définitif d'une partie de l'humanité" (T. CHARY, *Aggée-Zacharie-Malachie*, Paris, 1969, p. 236).

38. Cf. Augustine, *Expositio quarumdam propositionum ex epistula ad Romanos* 52 (60) and 54 (62), (CSEL, 84), pp. 33-35 and 36-39. See also, *Ibid.* 12 (13-18) and 37 (44), pp. 6-9 and p. 19.

39. "Si enim nullo merito non est electio; aequales enim omnes sunt ante meritum, nec potest in rebus omnino aequalibus electio nominari" (*Ibid.* 52 [60], p. 34).

40. "Non ergo elegit Deus opera cuiusquam in praescientia, quae ipse daturus est, sed fidem elegit in praescientia, ut quem sibi crediturum esse praescivit ipsum elegerit" (*Ibid.* 52 [60], pp. 34-35); "Sicut enim in his, quos elegit Deus, non opera sed fides inchoat meritum, ut per munus Dei bene operentur, sic in his, quos damnat, infidelitas et impietas inchoat poenae meritum" (*Ibid.* 54 [62], p. 37); "...quomodo Deus praescius eligat credituros et damnet incredulos" (*Ibid.*, p. 38). Augustine will later recant these statements as the result of his faulty interpretation: cf. Id., *De praedestinatione sanctorum* 3,7 (PL, 44), c. 964.

41. Id., *Expositio quarumdam propositionum ex epistula ad Romanos* 54 (62) (CSEL, 84), p. 38.

42. *Ibid.* 54 (62), p. 37.

43. *Ibid.* 55 (63), p. 40. This biblical motif was already dealt with by Origen. Intrigued by the fact that God must not be held responsible for unworthy things, and determined to defend human free will against the Gnostic views, Origen explained the hardening of Pharaoh's heart as the just reward of his present faults or, in the light of his theory of the pre-existence of the souls, of his antecedent ones. See *supra*, pp. 202-213 *passim*.

human faith and divine election, human merit and divine grace, human will and divine mercy[44].

The *De diuersis quaestionibus lxxxiii* represents a progress, for Augustine, towards a mature and unconditioned doctrine of grace and election. The background is given by Augustine's attempt to grasp Paul's words: *O homo, tu quis es, qui respondeas Deo?* (Rom 9,20)[45]. To begin with, the bishop of Hippo appeals to the most hidden merits of the souls (*animarum occultissima merita*)[46] in order to establish a principle according to which God's mercy comes (or not) to the help of the believer, and in order to prevent God's action from being criticized as arbitrary. Although hidden, there is therefore a form of human merit (and demerit), which is the human positive (or negative) response to the divine call, according to which God's grace is bestowed or withheld[47]. The hardening of Pharaoh's heart is an example of God withholding his mercy because of Pharaoh's demerits, caused by his prior misdeeds towards Israel[48]. But when it comes to love for Jacob and rejection of Esau (dealt with *en passant* at the very end of question 68), the election of the former and rejection of the latter are ascribed by Augustine to God's hidden designs[49]. The belief that God's judgement of man depends on the latter's *occultissima merita* begins to waver. Now the bishop of Hippo is asking himself whether good will, which is still needed in order to answer God's call, and to merit his mercy[50], is really sufficient on its own, or whether the will itself that chooses and acts out the good, is somehow the work of God[51]. Although Augustine does not yet take a decisive step in that direction, a new understanding is nevertheless clearly being shaped, an understanding that would call into question the previously accepted sequence of divine call, human response and divine mercy. The bishop of Hippo's solution, whereby a correlation was maintained between God's action and man's response, as a safeguard against the hint of God's arbitrariness in electing or rejecting people, was now growing thin and beginning to collapse. In saying that

---

44. Cf. Augustine, *Expositio quarumdam propositionum ex epistula ad Romanos* 52 (60) (CSEL, 84), p. 34.

45. Cf. Id., *De diuersis quaestionibus lxxxiii* 68 (CCL, 44A), pp. 174-183 *passim*.

46. *Ibid.* 68,3, p. 179.

47. Cf. *Ibid.* 68,5, pp. 181-182.

48. Cf. *Ibid.* 68,4, pp. 179-180.

49. Cf. *Ibid.* 68,6, pp. 182-183.

50. "Deus non miseretur... nisi uoluntas praecesserit" (*Ibid.* 68,5, p. 181).

51. "Et quoniam nec uelle quisquam potest nisi admonitus et uocatus, siue intrinsecus ubi nullus hominum uidet, siue extrinsecus per sermonem sonantem aut aliqua signa uisibilia, efficitur ut etiam ipsum uelle Deus operetur in nobis" (*Ibid.*).

man's good will "may" also be ascribed to God, Augustine starts depicting God's increasing involvement in human willing[52].

The *De diuersis quaestionibus ad Simplicianum*[53] constitutes a radicalization in Augustine's thinking on sovereign grace, his concept of predestination included. It marks a definitive change (as to its essential content) from Augustine's earlier view on the correlation between God's foreknowledge, election and man's response. The picture which now emerges in his mind about *electio* and *praedestinatio*[54], is poles apart from that which could be inferred from the *Expositio quarumdam propositionum ex epistula ad Romanos* and from the *De diuersis quaestionibus lxxxiii*[55]. The turning point rests precisely on the decisive interpretation of Rom 9,10-29, about the election of Jacob and the rejection of Esau[56]. The second question in the first book of *De diuersis quaestionibus ad Simplicianum* is a commentary on this pericope, which acquires a key role in the development of Augustine's thought[57]. As a result of his

---

52. In his *Retractationes*, Augustine takes for granted that this involvement had already fully occurred: "Nam est misericordia Dei etiam ipsam praeueniens uoluntatem, quae si non esset, non praeparetur uoluntas a Domino" (Id., *Retractationes* 1,26 [CCL, 57], p. 85).

53. Augustine's insights about grace and predestination, worked out in the *De diuersis quaestionibus ad Simplicianum*, will not undergo any change in the subsequent years, except in emphasis and radicalization. "Er bleibt dem Aufriss der Probleme von Ad Simplicianum sein ganzes Leben getreu, obwohl die Prädestinationslehre später aus äusseren Gründen immer stärker bei ihm hervortritt, bedeutet das nichts prinzipiell Neues" (NYGREN, *Das Prädestinationsproblem in der Theologie Augustins* [n. 4], p. 48). To assert, therefore, that the obscure and severe features of Augustine's theology are the work of an old "man whose energy had burnt itself out, whose love had grown cold" (J. BURNABY, *Amor Dei. A Study of the Religion of Saint Augustine*, London, 1938, p. 231), is to go wide of the mark and fall into a sterile psychologism.

54. It must be noted that only the verbal form *praedestinauit* recurs (twice) in this work to Simplicianus, and in both cases with a very general meaning (cf. Augustine, *De diuersis quaestionibus ad Simplicianum* 1,2,8 [CCL, 44], p. 32). The term *praedestinatio*, instead, is substituted with preference by the term *propositum (Dei)*, although the conceptual content remains the same. See A. ZUMKELLER, *<Propositum> in seinem spezifisch christlichen und theologischen Verständnis bei Augustinus*, in C. MAYER (ed.), *Homo Spiritalis. Festgabe für L. Verheijen zu seinem 70. Geburtstag*, Würzburg, 1987, pp. 295-310, pp. 304-310.

55. See RING, *"Electio" in der Gnadenlehre Augustins* [n. 20], pp. 50-56. ID., *Electio*, in *AugL* 2 (2001) 741-752, cc. 744-746.

56. See V.H. DRECOLL, *Die Entstehung der Gnadenlehre Augustins* (BHT, 109), Tübingen, 1999, pp. 218-222.

57. See T.G. RING (ed.), *Aurelius Augustinus. Schriften über die Gnade. An Simplicianum zwei Bücher über verschiedene Fragen* (Aurelius Augustinus. Schriften gegen die Pelagianer. Prolegomena, Bd. III), Würzburg, 1991, pp. 254-263; P.-M. HOMBERT, *Gloria gratiae. Se glorifier en Dieu, principe et fin de la théologie augustinienne de la grâce*, Paris, 1996, pp. 93-99; J. LÖSSL, *Intellectus gratiae. Die erkenntnistheoretische und hermeneutische Dimension der Gnadenlehre Augustins von Hippo* (SVigChr, 38), Leiden-New York-Cologne, 1997, pp. 82-90.

enquiry, he is led to abandon the concept of *praescientia*[58] which had been employed up to then by Christian exegesis to explain God's different attitude (election or rejection) towards the two brothers, a concept he too found useful in his previous works. The same distinction between foreknowledge of works, and foreknowledge of faith, appears now too shaky to Augustine, who abandons it. "If election" – he argues – "is by foreknowledge, and God foreknew Jacob's faith, how do you prove that He did not elect him for his works?"[59]. Thus, if the call to election is not a function of divine foreknowledge nor does it rest on man's merits deriving either from his works or from his faith (for faith itself is a gift of God's mercy[60]), then it means that election pertains to something completely gratuitous whose source must be found in God's impenetrable decrees[61]. Election and inscrutable grace are indissolubly linked together. In fact, as Paul had written, God had made his choice about Jacob and Esau "even before they had been born or had done anything good or bad, so that God's purpose of election might continue, not by works but by his call" (Rom 9,11-12). Yet, if this call highlights the gratuity of Jacob's election, it makes the exclusion of Esau from God's mercy even more dramatic[62]. How can the election of Jacob be just if, apart from God's direct intervention of grace, there is no moral difference between the two brothers?

The dilemma Augustine was faced with was as follows: either Esau was not called or, if he was called, he was not called with the same effectiveness as Jacob. Of course Augustine chooses the second alternative as the only plausible answer. It is at this point that he adopts a predestinarian view, drawing a clear line of demarcation between *uocatio* and *electio*, to demonstrate that they are not exactly the same. If all the elect are also called, not all those who are called are also elected. The grace of election, he asserts, is not given indiscriminately to all those

58. Cf. Augustine, *De diuersis quaestionibus ad Simplicianum* 1,2,5 (CCL, 44), pp. 29-30.
59. "Si igitur electio per praescientiam, praesciuit autem Deus fidem Iacob, unde probas quia non etiam ex operibus elegit eum?" (*Ibid.*, p. 29).
60. Cf. *Ibid.* 1,2,9, p. 34.
61. "In Simpl. radikalisierte Augustin seinen Gnadenbegriff, si daß er nun den Ratschluß Gottes nicht mehr an der vorhergewußten menschlichen Entscheidung orientiert sah, sondern auf dessen allmächtigen, unergründlichen Willen zurückführte.... Das Vorherwissen Gottes vom künftigen Verhalten des Menschen bedarf keiner eigenen Erwähnung mehr, wenn es selbst aus der Vorherbestimmung folgt und sich primär auf das künftige göttliche Tun bezieht" (RING, *"Electio" in der Gnadenlehre Augustins* [n. 20], pp. 74 and 78). See DRECOLL, *Die Entstehung der Gnadenlehre Augustins* (n. 56), pp. 240-245.
62. "Cur haec misericordia subtracta est ab Esau?" (Augustine, *De diuersis quaestionibus ad Simplicianum* 1,2,10 [CCL, 44], p. 34).

who are called by God, but only to those among them who are truly
"affected" (*adfecti*) by this call and are truly "fitted" (*idonei*) to receive
it[63]. In other words, election is only for those who are called "efficaciously" (*congruenter*)[64]. Augustine stresses that, if He wanted, God
could give everybody the necessary means for believing and being
saved, and he reiterates that divine mercy could not be conditioned or
put in jeopardy by human acts or decisions (cf. Rom 9,16: *Non uolentis,
neque currentis, sed miserentis est Dei*). Hence, he explains the rejection
of Esau as the result of divine punishment (*diuina poena*)[65], which hard-
ens the heart of some people, abandoning them to their doomed destiny.
Here, the core of Augustine's "theorem"[66] of predestination appears in
its full light, and from now on much of his efforts will be spent in trying
to justify how the *diuina poena* that falls on the non-elect can be considered as not unjust. He suggests that the best solution is to appeal to
the presupposition that in God there is "a certain hidden equity" (*aliqua
occultas aequitas*)[67] or a "most hidden equity" (*aequitas occultissima*)[68]
that cannot be understood by any human standard of measurement. The
shift that occurs at this stage in Augustine's thought is of paramount
importance: it is the hidden equity on God's part which is now brought
into the limelight and which replaces the earlier appeal to the "most hidden merits of the souls (*animarum occultissima merita*)"[69]. In other
words, the difference is no longer about those who believe (Jacob) and

---

63. "*Multi uocati, pauci electi [Mt 20,16]*, ut quamuis multi uno modo uocati sint,
tamen quia non omnes uno modo adfecti sunt, illi soli sequantur uocationem qui ei capi-
endae repperiuntur idonei" (*Ibid.* 1,2,13, p. 37). Referring to Mt 20,16 Augustine does not
wish to focus on the contrasting pair *multi-pauci*, but on the antithesis *uocati-electi*.
64. *Ibid.*, p. 38. "Diese Konzeption der *vocatio congrua* verdeutlicht, wie Gottes
Berufung nicht nur zeitlich dem Wollen des Menschen vorangeht, sondern den wil-
lentlichen Glaubensentscheid selbst bewirkt" (DRECOLL, *Die Entstehung der Gnadenlehre
Augustins* [n. 56], p. 231).
65. "Quaeritur, utrum de diuina poena sit ipsa duritia, cum eum Deus deserit non sic
uocando, quomodo ad fidem moueri potest. Quis enim dicat modum quo ei persuaderetur
ut crederet etiam omnipotenti defuisse?" (Augustine, *De diuersis quaestionibus ad Simplicianum* 1,2,14 [CCL, 44], p. 39).
66. Cf. D. MARAFIOTI, *Alle origini del teorema della predestinazione (Simpl. 1,2,13-
22)*, in *Congresso Internazionale su S. Agostino nel XVI Centenario della Conversione,
Roma 15-20 settembre 1986*, Vol. II (SEAug, 25), Rome, 1987, pp. 257-277, p. 257.
67. "Alicuius occultae atque ab humano modulo inuestigabilis aequitatis" (Augustine,
De diuersis quaestionibus ad Simplicianum 1,2,16 [CCL, 44], p. 41).
68. "Eorum autem non miseretur, quibus misericordiam non esse praebendam aequi-
tate occultissima et ab humanis sensibus remotissima iudicat" (*Ibid.*, p. 42).
69. Id., *De diuersis quaestionibus lxxxiii* 68,3 [CCL, 44A], p. 179. "This shift in the
locus of 'hiddenness' speaks volumes.... All is engulfed in the impenetrable darkness of
the 'hidden equity' with which God elects some and rejects others" (W.S. BABCOCK,
Augustine's interpretation of Romans [A. D. 394-396], in *AugSt* 10 [1979] 55-74, p. 67).

those who do not (Esau), but about the way God relates to human beings, calling them *congruenter* or not, choosing them as his elect, or not. The difference lies now entirely in God himself[70]. For that reason there are no better words to explain the divine attitude than those of Paul, to which Augustine turns once again with regard to the hardening of Pharaoh's heart: *Ergo cuius uult miseretur et quem uult obdurat* (Rom 9,18)[71]. God, that is, intervenes "directly" to help those He has decided to elect, whereas He abandons those He does not want to save. With regard to the latter, that means that He does not intervene with his mercy to prevent them from sinning and falling away from him[72]. The path towards the concept of the *massa peccatorum*, as the justifying background against which God's election and rejection stand out, is thus laid[73].

So, while undermining the decisiveness of man's commitment and co-operation in the process of salvation, Augustine's exegesis of Rom 9,10-29 brings to light those elements that will become the kernel of his doctrine of election and predestination. From now on God's decision to save men does not rest any longer on his foreknowledge of human merits, but is rooted in his eternal, mysterious, unquestionable, and always just decrees. In shifting from the level of knowledge (*praescientia*) to that of effective intentionality (*propositum*), the concept of predestination acquires (under the bishop of Hippo's pen) an "absolute" and "exclusive" character. Salvation rests solely upon God's eternal and timeless decrees[74]. To make this point even clearer, Augustine introduces a subtle but important distinction between two terms, *electio* and *praedestinatio*, hitherto equivalent[75]. As he puts it: *Non ergo secundum electionem*

70. It is as if Augustine were no longer in the position of delineating "a God who is gracious but not arbitrary. Under the impact of Paul's text, he has ended by sacrificing the comprehensibility of God's justice to the gratuity of God's grace" (Id., *Augustine and Paul: the Case of Romans IX*, in *StPatr* 16 [TU, 129], Berlin, 1985, pp. 473-479, p. 479).

71. Augustine, *De diuersis quaestionibus ad Simplicianum* 1,2,15 (CCL, 44), pp. 39-40.

72. "Ut obduratio Dei sit nolle misereri" (*Ibid.*, p. 40).

73. Cf. *Ibid.* 1,2,16, pp. 41-42.

74. As will become more clear in the development of the exposition, Augustine was aware that the term *propositum* includes an act of positive willing on the part of God and that its use, with regard to evil, would be unthinkable. For this reason he uses the term *propositum* only to indicate those who are predestined to life eternal. For the non-predestined Augustine employs the term *iudicium* and the verb *iudicare*. Cf., for instance, Id., *Contra secundam Iuliani responsionem imperfectum opus* 1,48 (CSEL, 85/1), p. 41; Id., *De correptione et gratia* 13,42 (CSEL, 92), p. 271. See F.-J. THONNARD, *La prédestination augustinienne et l'interpretation de O. Rottmanner*, in *REAug* 9 (1963) 259-287, pp. 261f.

75. Of course, we cannot think of God as acting in a temporal sequence, according to the way we are accustomed: He first decides (*propositum*) and then carries out his decision (*electio*). The two in God happen simultaneously. Augustine's verbal distinction, however, is intended to stress the immutability of God's purpose.

propositum Dei manet, sed ex proposito electio[76]. God's decision alone
is decisive with regard to man's election and salvation. Bereft of, and
with seemingly little interest in the co-operation of man's will and
merits, the divine decrees appear as the only (infallible) judging power,
aloof from the concrete, historical human setting. The balance leans irrevocably towards God's overwhelming agency. In the words of Rottmanner,
a rigorous *unbedingte Prädestination*[77] makes its appearance.

The conclusions reached in the *De diuersis quaestionibus ad Simplicianum* about the concept of election and predestination, in connection
with Augustine's radical understanding of grace, will be reiterated in
subsequent works. Thus, for instance, his standpoint reappears without
substantial change at the time of the Pelagian controversy, when the
necessity and the unlimited sovereignty of grace was put into question.
One of the first problems Augustine was confronted with during the controversy was the destiny of unbaptized children. Set against the background of the doctrine of original sin, the objection of his adversaries
was: why does it happen that of two children one is baptized and saved
whereas the other is left unbaptized and perishes? For the bishop of
Hippo it would make no sense to speak of God's foreknowledge of their
future faith and merits, particularly if one thinks that even from among
the baptized children there grow impious men. Augustine's answer is
based (as the only feasible solution) on God's mysterious election,
which cannot be grasped by the human mind[78]. This same accentuation
is present in a letter written to Paulinus of Nola. After having drawn the
distinction between an ordinary call and a call *secundum propositum*[79],
the bishop of Hippo speaks of the mystery of God's election and predestination in connection with the problem of those children who have
died without baptism over against those children who, without any merit
on their part, are baptized[80]. In another letter to Paulinus the conviction,

76. Augustine, *De diuersis quaestionibus ad Simplicianum* 1,2,6 (CCL, 44), p. 31. He
then continues: "Id est non quia invenit Deus opera bona in hominibus quae eligat, ideo
manet propositum iustificationis ipsius, sed quia illud manet ut iustificet credentes, ideo
invenit opera quae iam eligat ad regnum caelorum" (*Ibid.*).

77. O. ROTTMANNER, *Der Augustinismus. Ein dogmengeschichtliche Studie*, Munich,
1892, p. 5. Cf. G. KRAUS, *Vorherbestimmung. Traditionelle Prädestinationslehre im Licht
gegenwärtiger Theologie* (ÖFS, 5), Freiburg i.Br., 1977, p. 31.

78. "Haec gratia cur ad illum ueniat, ad illum non ueniat, occulta esse causa potest,
iniusta non potest.... Cur alius rapitur, ne malitia mutet intellectum eius, et alius uiuit,
impius futurus?... Unde ista tanta diuersitas, nisi quia inscrutabilia sunt iudicia eius et
inuestigabiles uiae eius?" (Augustine, *De peccatorum meritis et remissione et de baptismo paruulorum* 1,21,29 and 30 [CSEL, 60], pp. 27 and 29). See also, Id., *Sermo*
294,7,7 (PL, 38), c. 1339; *De spiritu et littera* 5,7 (CSEL, 60), p. 159.

79. Cf. Id., *Ep.* 149,2,19 (CSEL, 44), p. 365.

80. Cf. *Ibid.* 149,2,22, p. 368.

stemming from Augustine's doctrine of original sin, that all humanity is a *massa damnata*, comes to the surface together with a strong defence of divine gratuitous grace. God, in his foreknowledge, chooses with absolute certainty those who, being *secundum propositum uocati*, are going to be numbered among his elect[81].

References to the doctrine of election and predestination are also present in several pages of Augustine's *Tractatus in Euangelium Ioannis*. At times it is only a matter of allusion, where the term predestination does not even appear[82], but at other times the doctrine is clearly stated. Commenting on the parable of the good shepherd (cf. Jn 10), Augustine is faced with a paradox. It may well be, he says, that some believers (*oues*), who are now ranked among those who listen to God's commandments and behave accordingly, might turn into rebels, and perhaps only some will come back whereas the rest will go astray for ever. On the other hand, some sinners or unbelievers (*lupi*), who are now excluding themselves (or are excluded) from God's company, might one day, by God's decision, turn into good christians[83]. Backed up by the biblical quotation of 2 Tim 2,19 (*Nouit Dominus qui sunt eius*) and Rom 8,29-33 (*...his qui secundum propositum uocati sunt: quoniam quos ante praesciuit, et praedestinauit conformes imaginis Filii sui*), Augustine suggests that only the mystery of predestination could help us to solve this paradox. In fact, God has chosen his own and set them apart since before the world was made[84]. The same holds true for the final perseverance of Christians. It might well be that believers go astray, but for some of them it will only be a temporary experience because in God's

81. "Certus est ergo et in Dei praescientia praefinitus numerus ac multitudo sanctorum, quibus *diligentibus Deum... omnia cooperantur in bonum....* Sunt enim et alii uocati sed non electi ac per hoc non *secundum propositum uocati*" (ID., *Ep.* 186,7,25 [CSEL, 57], p. 65).

82. Cf., for instance, the following passage where, were it not for the mention of a *populus distinctus* (the certain number of elect) we would be inclined to believe that Augustine still insists on God's (fore)knowledge: "Qui sint enim credituri, et qui non sint credituri, nouit Deus; qui sint perseueraturi in eo quod crediderunt, et qui sint lapsuri, nouit Deus, et numerati sunt Deo omnes futuri in uitam aeternam; et nouit iam illum populum distinctum" (Id., *Tractatus in Euangelium Ioannis* 14,8 [CCL, 36], p. 146).

83. Cf. *Ibid.* 45,11, p. 394.

84. "Nouit praescitos, nouit praedestinatos...; ipsae sunt oves. Aliquando se ipsae nesciunt, sed pastor nouit eas, secundum istam praedestinationem, secundum istam Dei praescientiam, secundum electionem ouium, ante constitutionem mundi.... Secundam istam ergo praescientiam Dei et praedestinationem, quam multae oves foris, quam multi lupi intus; et quam multae oves intus, et quam multi lupi foris!" (*Ibid.* 45,12, pp. 394-395). As Rondet wrightly notes: "On notera que les mots: prescience, prédestination, sont encore pratiquement confondus.... Une plus grand précision devrait inverser l'ordre des termes" (H. RONDET, *La prédestination augustinienne. Genèse d'une doctrine*, in *ScEc* 18 [1966] 229-251, p. 238, n. 62).

plan they have been predestined to eternal salvation[85]. It is in this sense
that Mt 10,22 (*Quis perseuerauerit usque in finem, hic saluus erit*) must
be understood. None of those who have been predestined will ever be
lost; their names have been written in heaven[86]. Basing himself on the
philosophical principle according to which there is no past or future in
God, but only an "eternal present"[87], Augustine identifies an important
dichotomy between reality and appearance, the real sheep, viz. the elect,
and the real wolves, viz. the non elect. Relying on Is 45,11 (*Qui fecit quae
futura sunt*) the bishop of Hippo does not apply the principle of God's
"eternal present" only to divine foreknowledge (and providence)[88], but
also to divine predestination[89]. The latter is "real" for it belongs to "eternity", that is to God's eternal and immutable decrees, whereas "appearance" is a feature of "time", which remains subject to mutability, that
same mutability that causes some sheep to turn into wolves and vice versa.

In the *Enchiridion ad Laurentium* Augustine's concept of predestination is summarized in close connection with the doctrine of gratuitous
grace. Humanity is bleakly depicted as a *massa damnata* in which all
men are rightly enclosed as a result of their solidarity with the sin of
Adam. Although their share in the consequences of such a sin corresponds to the just will of God, the latter's gratuitous mercy (*indebita
misericordia*)[90] is offered to those whom God wishes to deliver from the

85. "Si praedestinatus est, ad tempus errauit, in aeternum non periit" (Augustine,
Tractatus in Euangelium Ioannis 45,13 [CCL, 36], p. 395).
86. "Quis enim alius oues proprias uocat nominatim, et educit eas hinc ad uitam aeternam, nisi qui nouit nomina praedestinatorum?" (*Ibid.* 45,14, p. 396).
87. This notion was already embraced by the newly converted Augustin: "Omne
praeteritum iam non est, omne futurum nondum est; omne igitur et praeteritum et futurum
deest. Apud Deum autem nihil deest, nec praeteritum igitur nec futurum, sed omne prae-
sens est apud Deum" (Id., *De diuersis quaestionibus lxxxiii* 17 [CCL, 44A], p. 22). This
same concept is taken up several times in other works. See, for instance: "In eo autem
quod sempiternum est, sine initio et sine fine, cuiuslibet temporis uerbum ponatur, siue
praeteriti, siue praesentis, siue futuri, non mendaciter ponitur.... Fuit, in praeteritis saeculis, est in praesentibus, erit in futuris. Fuit, quia numquam defuit; erit, quia numquam
deerit; est, quia semper est. Neque enim, uelut qui iam non sit, cum praeteritis occidit;
aut cum praesentibus, uelut qui non maneat, labitur; aut cum futuris, uelut qui non fuerat,
orietur" (Id., *Tractatus in Euangelium Ioannis* 99,5 [CCL, 36], p. 585). See also Id.,
Enarrationes in psalmos 2,6 (CCL, 38), p. 5.
88. See *infra*, pp. 330-334.
89. "Non enim ait: Qui facturus est quae futura sunt, sed: *Qui fecit quae futura sunt*.
Ergo et fecit ea, et facturus est ea. Nam neque facta sunt, si ipse non fecit; neque futura
sunt, si ipse non fecerit. Fecit ergo ea praedestinando, facturus est operando" (ID., *Tractatus in Euangelium Ioannis* 68,1 [CCL, 36], p. 497). "Qui enim certis et immutabilibus
causis omnia futura praedestinauit, quidquid facturus est fecit; nam et per prophetam dictum de illo est: *Qui fecit quae futura sunt*" (*Ibid.* 105,4, p. 605).
90. Cf. Id., *Enchiridion ad Laurentium* 8,27 (CCL, 46), p. 64. See also: "Nisi per
indebitam misericordiam nemo liberatur, et nisi per debitum iudicium nemo damnatur"

massa damnata. The case of Jacob and Esau, here briefly reconsidered, is but an example of God's gratuitous and mysterious dealings with men. It is useless, therefore, to try to understand why He chooses to save only some people and does not help others[91]. The same stark concept is present in the *Contra duas epistulas Pelagianorum*, where Jacob's election is explained through God's absolutely gratuitous predestination[92].

This hardening of Augustine's thought with regard to his doctrine of predestination is detectable also in his *opus magnum*, the *De ciuitate Dei*, where the problem of predestination is discussed in several books and from different angles. Thus, after having stated that humanity (exactly like the society of angels) can be divided historically and concretely into two groups/cities, one loving God, the other hating him, he asks himself why it is so. His answer is that, as in the case of angels, where God is the efficient cause of the good will of those angels who have not fallen away from him[93], but is not the cause of the perversion of the fallen angels[94], so, in the case of mankind, God is not the cause of Adam's fall and of man's perverse will. Consequently it cannot be said that there is injustice in God. It is God's positive decision to intervene and help some men (and angels) to be love-bound to him, while He simply abandons others to perish in their sinful state[95]. With regard to humanity, the sin of Adam gives Augustine occasion to speak of the *certus numerus* of those who are predestined[96] to reign with God, as opposed to those whose destiny is eternal punishment with the devil[97]. These two cities, the *ciuitas Dei* and the *ciuitas saeculi*, are represented respectively by Abel and Cain, the former being predestined, elected and glorified by grace[98] as a *uas misericordiae*, the latter being treated

---

(*Ibid.* 24,94, p. 99); "Cum facit, per misericordiam facit; cum autem non facit, per iudicium non facit, Quoniam *cuius uult miseretur, et quem uult obdurat*" (*Ibid.* 25,98, pp. 100-101).

91. Cf. *Ibid.*

92. Cf. Id., *Contra duas epistulas Pelagianorum* 2,7,15 (CSEL, 60), pp. 475-478.

93. Cf. Id., *De ciuitate Dei* 12,9 (CCL, 48), p. 363.

94. In that case is a question of a *causa deficiens* (cf. *Ibid.* 12,7, p. 362).

95. Cf. *Ibid.* 12,28, p. 385.

96. "Verum tamen omnipotenti Deo,... non defuit utique consilium, quo certum numerum ciuium in sua sapientia praedestinatum etiam ex damnato genere humano suae ciuitatis impleret, non eos iam meritis, quando quidem uniuersa massa tamquam in uitiata radice damnata est, sed gratia discernens et liberatis non solum de ipsis, uerum etiam de non liberatis, quid eis largiatur, ostendens" (*Ibid.* 14,26, p. 450).

97. "ciuitates duas, hoc est duas societates hominum, quarum est una quae praedestinata est in aeternum regnare cum Deo, altera aeternum supplicium subire cum diabolo" (*Ibid.* 15,1, p. 453).

98. "Gratia praedestinatus gratia electus, gratia peregrinus deorsum gratia ciuis sursum" (*Ibid.*, p. 454).

instead as a *uas irae* and left to perish in the *massa damnata*[99]. This antithesis will be suggested again by Augustine under the names of the two brothers Esau and Jacob[100].

We shall not linger on those works written by Augustine towards the end of his life and addressed to the monks of Hadrumetum and Marseilles. We have already given a summary above[101]. We simply wish to recall the main points concerning the problem of predestination. In the *De correptione et gratia*, for instance, the quotation from Ac 13,48 (*Crediderunt quotquot erant ordinati ad uitam aeternam*) appears for the first time in connection with Mt 10,22 (*Qui perseuerauerit usque in finem, hic saluus erit*). The framework is given by the problem of perseverance[102] and non-perseverance, a problem which is tackled in strict relation to that of predestination[103]. Also Rom 8,28-30 is introduced to stress the absolute certainty that those who have been chosen and elected by God *secundum propositum*[104] will be saved. In fact, if any of them were to perish, then the reliability of God's unfailing omnipotence would be called into question, and that is unacceptable[105]. Although no one can know in advance whether he is going to be counted among the elect or not, the number of those who have been chosen by God is certain and cannot be increased nor diminished[106]. Those who are not included in that number, are those who have not received God's gift of perseverance (*non accepto perseuerantiae dono*). They will perish because of their sins, and will be abandoned by God for having abandoned him (*deserunt et deseruntur*)[107]. It is in the light of this dreary picture that Augustine set himself to work trying to give some reason for God's salvific will[108] and for the necessity of rebuke and prayer[109]. It is, however, in the *De*

---

99. Cf. *Ibid.*
100. Cf. *Ibid.* 16,35, pp. 539-540.
101. See *supra*, pp. 57-89 and pp. 153-183.
102. Cf. Augustine, *De correptione et gratia* 6,10 (CSEL, 92), p. 230.
103. Cf. *Ibid.* 8,17ff, pp. 237ff.
104. This distinction appears with a certain insistence also in the following paragraphs.
105. "Illi ergo electi... qui secundum propositum vocati, qui etiam praedestinati atque praesciti. Horum si quisquam perit, fallitur Deus: sed nemo eorum perit, quia non fallitur Deus" (*Ibid.* 7,14, pp. 234-235). See also: "...omnino perire non possunt" (*Ibid.* 9,23, p. 246).
106. "Haec de his loquor qui praedestinati sunt in regnum Dei, quorum ita certus est numerus, ut nec addatur eis quisquam, nec minuatur ex eis" (*Ibid.* 13,39, p. 267). Augustine speaks of a *certissimus et felicissimus numerus* (*Ibid.* 13,42, p. 271). See *infra*, pp. 348-352.
107. Cf. Augustine, *De correptione et gratia* 13,42 (CSEL, 92), p. 271.
108. Cf. *Ibid.* 14,44f, pp. 272f.
109. Cf. *Ibid.* 15,46ff, p. 275ff.

praedestinatione sanctorum where the bishop of Hippo first gives a formal definition of predestination. It consists, he suggests, in the preparation of grace, this being the effect or outcome of predestination: *Praedestinatio Dei quae in bono est, gratiae est, ut dixi, praeparatio; gratia uero est ipsius praedestinationis effectus*[110]. But it is in the *De dono perseuerantiae* that Augustine's mature formulation of predestination is presented: *Haec est praedestinatio sanctorum, nihil aliud: praescientia scilicet, et praeparatio beneficiorum Dei, quibus certissime liberantur, quicumque liberantur. Caeteri autem ubi nisi in massa perditionis iusto diuino iudicio relinquuntur?*[111].

Augustine speaks his mind very clearly, without leaving any doubt as to the actual meaning that must be given to his doctrine of predestination. First of all, predestination is not the result of God's foreknowledge about future choices (good or bad) that each individual is going to make – a view that was held in the Greek and Latin tradition before Augustine. For the bishop of Hippo predestination is rather the foreknowledge and the preparation, by divine decree, of those beneficial acts of God thanks to which those who have been predestined to be saved, will be infallibly saved. Augustine presents two aspects of this mystery: a *positive* one, viz. God's preparation of the gifts of grace that will surely deliver the elect (*liberantur*) from their state of perdition, and a *negative* one, namely the just judgement of God about the non-elect who are abandoned (*relinquuntur*) to the destiny of the *massa damnata*. We realize immediately that Augustine's dealing with the doctrine of predestination, which finds its definitive formulation here, is innovative on both a terminological and a doctrinal level. Firstly, when compared with the way the ancient Fathers of the Church understood it, the bishop of Hippo's emphasis on predestination *to grace*, rather than on predestination *to glory*[112], becomes very relevant. It entails, in fact, a shift from an eschatological orientation (where God leads the life of man with his unwavering mercy) to a meta-historical and meta-temporal orientation, where the divine decrees about human beings, their historical development and their eschatological goal, are already fixed *ab aeternitate*. Of course, God's grace and its efficacy constitute the *conditio sine qua non* for man to share at all in the divine glory, which is and remains the final goal. And yet Augustine prefers to speak of predestination in relation to God's eternally spoken decrees rather than to God's eschatological

110. Id., *De praedestinatione sanctorum* 10,19 (PL, 44), c. 975.
111. Id., *De dono perseuerantiae* 14,35 (PL, 45), c. 1014.
112. Cf. J.-M. DALMAU, *"Praedestinatio, Electio" en el libro "De praedestinatione sanctorum"*, in *AugMag*, T. I, Paris, 1955, pp. 127-136, p. 129.

future[113]. Moreover, the bishop of Hippo's understanding of predestination brings into question the ultimate significance of God's *oeconomia salutis*. If predestination, rather than being considered from an eschatological perspective, is firmly established in God's eternal decrees, then an unbridgeable dichotomy would be discovered between God's and man's agency. In other words, if the concept of predestination does not take into account the concrete arena of human existence wherein man makes choices and strives for salvation, if it is primarily viewed as an *immobilis ueritas*[114], stemming from a transcendent (pre-)-disposition of God[115], located in his eternal decrees, then the problem to be accounted for would indeed be that of the compatibility of God's transcendence with his commitment in history and the way their interplay is envisaged.

3. SOME CONSIDERATIONS ON AUGUSTINE'S APPROACH TO THE DOCTRINE OF PREDESTINATION

Before tackling the most complex and controversial points of Augustine's doctrine of predestination, we would like to hint at some general considerations that will highlight the problems in their proper context. To begin with, we must confidently claim what is undisputable in Augustine's theological thought, namely that his doctrine of predestination is an aspect or, as it were, the clearest example of the far-reaching implications of the absolute gratuity and necessity of grace. It follows that the bishop of Hippo's doctrine of predestination cannot be approached and regarded as a reality that stands alone. It is a "theological theorem"[116], a "corollary" of the central doctrine of the absolute

---

113. If in dealing with Augustine's doctrine of predestination – as has been noted – "attention has often been exclusively focused on the issue of determinism", with the result that "this focus overlooks the doctrine's eschatological context" (cf. K.-L.E. LEE, *Augustine, Manichaeism, and the Good* [Patristic Studies, 2], New York, 1999, p. 61), this is the consequence of Augustine's presuppositions. In fact, even though – more often implicitly than explicitly – Augustine is concerned not only in the *how* an individual is chosen, but also in the *for what* one is chosen, viz. God's cosmic and universal order and the eschatological framework of salvation, the emphasis in his concept of predestination is unequivocally laid on the *terminus a quo*, viz. God's eternal and immutable decrees.

114. Augustine, *De praedestinatione sanctorum* 17,34 (PL, 44), c. 985.

115. "Secundum illam uero uoluntatem suam, quae cum eius praescientia sempiterna est, profecto in caelo et in terra omnia quaecumque uoluit non solum praeterita uel praesentia, sed etiam futura iam fecit" (Id., *De ciuitate Dei* 22,2 [CCL, 48], p. 808).

116. Marafioti uses this expression in order to point out that "si tratta di una dimostrazione a difesa della teologia della gratuità della grazia, da cui dipende strettamente; e non invece di una 'teologia' o 'dottrina' autonoma che possa vivere di vita propria e separata" (MARAFIOTI, *Alle origini del teorema della predestinazione* [n. 66], p. 257, n. 1). And again: "*[Il teorema della predestinazione]* vive di luce riflessa e non

sovereignty of grace[117]. As Augustine himself pointed out, it must be regarded as an *insuperabilis munitio*[118] whose goal is to defend the gratuitousness of God's grace, particularly with reference to the poles of Christian life, the *initium fidei* and the final *perseuerantia*. The remarks of some scholars about the centrality of the doctrine of predestination within the Augustinian theological system[119] should therefore, in our

può pretendere a una esistenza indipendente staccata dalla teologia della gratuità della grazia" (*Ibid.*, p. 274).

117. "En somme – writes Jacquin – sa théorie *[of Augustine]* de la prédestination n'est, à son jugement, rien d'autre que l'application particulière d'un principe général...: l'absolue gratuité de tout don divin" (A.M. JACQUIN, *La prédestination d'après saint Augustin*, in *MA*, Vol. II, Rome, 1931, pp. 853-878, p. 875). " La prédestination n'est... qu'un aspect de la doctrine de la grâce: elle est destinée à prouver la gratuité" (F. CAYRÉ, *La Prédestination dans Saint Augustin. Notes générales*, in *AthA* 2 [1941] 42-63, p. 57). "Toda su preocupación, repetidamente expresada, en la predicación de la predestinación, es la gratuitad de la gracia" (DALMAU, *"Praedestinatio, Electio" en el libro "De praedestinatione sanctorum"* [n. 112], p. 129). "...présenter la divine prédestination en fonction de la grâce est constante dans les derniers traités" (THONNARD, *La prédestination augustinienne et l'interpretation de O. Rottmanner* [n. 74], p. 277). "La verità dunque che stava a cuore ad Agostino e che difendeva con tutta l'energia dello spirito,..., non era la predestinazione ma un'altra, anche se connessa con essa; era la gratuità assoluta della grazia" (A. TRAPÈ, *Introduzione generale*, in ID. [ed.], *Sant'Agostino. Grazia e libertà: La grazia e il libero arbitrio, La correzione e la grazia, La predestinazione dei santi, Il dono della perseveranza* [NBA, 20], Rome, 1987, pp. CXXVIff). "La predestinazione, pur avendo una importanza rilevante, non è una tesi di fondo. La tesi che sta a cuore a S.A. è un'altra;... è, in una parola, la gratuità della grazia e della salvezza" (ID., *A proposito di predestinazione* [n. 5], p. 250). "Anche la dottrina sulla predestinazione è considerata come uno degli argomenti per la difesa della gratuità della grazia" (BOUBLÍK, *La predestinazione* [n. 3], p. 109). "La doctrine de la prédestination est une clé de voûte, non une pierre de fondation.... Au point de départ, Augustin pose le dogme de l'absolue gratuité de la grâce" (A. SAGE, *La prédestination chez saint Augustin d'après une thèse récente*, in *REAug* 6 [1960] 31-40, p. 34). See also Greshake's remark: "Daß die Prädestinationslehre nicht 'in sich' steht, sondern, wie di ganze Gnadenlehre, die Konsequenz einer fundamentalen Erfahrung ist: die der radikalen Ohnmacht und Unfreiheit des sündigen Geschöpfes, das allein durch Gottes souveräne Gnade und unbezwingbare Macht, Freiheit, Heil und Hoffnung empfängt. In der Prädestinationslehre wird diese Grunderfahrung gleichsam 'von oben', von Gott her, betrachtet und in Gottes ewigem Ratschluß verankert" (GRESHAKE, *Gnade als konkrete Freiheit* [n. 26], p. 246).

118. "Praedestinatio praedicanda est, ut possit vera Dei gratia, hoc est, quae non secundum merita nostra datur, insuperabili munitione defendi" (Augustine, *De dono perseuerantiae* 20,53 and 21,54 [PL, 45], cc. 1026 and 1027). See also *Ibid.* 16,41, c. 1018.

119. See, for instance, Rottmanner's definition of Augustinianism: "Unter "Augustinismus" verstehe ich hier die Lehre von der unbedingten Prädestination und vom particularen Heilswillen" (ROTTMANNER, *Der Augustinismus* [n. 77], p. 5). See also: "Augustins theologische Entwicklung führte ihn immer mehr dahin, die Quintessenz der Theologie in dem Problemkreis um die Prädestination zu sehen.... mit dem Prädestinationsproblem lenken wir in die Hauptverkehrsader der augustinischen Theologie ein" (NYGREN, *Das Prädestinationsproblem in der Theologie Augustins* [n. 4], pp. 8-9). "In den letzten zwanzig Jahren seines Lebens *[of Augustine]* steht das problem der

opinion, be revisited and partially corrected. Although it represents the
most complex aspect of Augustine's theology of grace, the doctrine of
predestination is but a corollary of it. What it finally highlights is the
polarization of God's grace and man's agency, whereby the overwhelming compass of the first pole is shown in all its might. It is within this
perspective alone that the Augustinian concept of predestination constitutes, as it were, the climax, the furthest extension of the sovereign gratuity of grace, this remaining the focal point of the bishop of Hippo's
theological construction.

a) Between God's Mystery and Pastoral Necessity

No doubt Augustine's concept of predestination stands as a stark
reminder that the final redemption of humanity's vitiated nature rests
with God alone and with his mysterious intervention. Already in the *De
diuersis quaestionibus ad Simplicianum*, Augustine had stated that all
men have been irretrievably touched by the curse of the fall, and that in
consequence of that they all form a *massa peccati* or a *massa peccatorum et impiorum*[120]. This conviction of the bishop of Hippo was set
against the background of a Pauline passage which became a constant
point of reference for Augustine: *Quid autem habes quod non accepisti?*
(1 Cor 4,7). In the light of this passage, Augustine examined Rom 9,10-
29 and let himself be confronted with the mystery of God's election. The
solution he reached is very emblematic: grace is not offered to all, a
solution dramatically encapsulated in the famous biblical formula that
Paul had quoted from the prophet Malachi: *Jacob dilexi, Esau autem
odio habui* (Rom 9,13). Trying to understand why the benevolent mercy
of God, independently of any human merit, delivers some people from
the *massa peccati* they belong to and not others is a presumption –
asserts Augustine – that melts like snow in the sun before God's incomprehensible but always just decrees. For in God there is no injustice[121].

Vorherbestimmung im Mittelpunkt seines Denkens, wobei er dazu gelangt, "die Quintessenz der Theologie in dem Problemkreis um die Prädestination zu sehen" (KRAUS,
Vorherbestimmung [n. 77], p. 27).

120. Cf. Augustine, *De diuersis quaestionibus ad Simplicianum* 1,2,16 and 19 (CCL,
44), pp. 42 and 48.

121. Cf., for instance, *Ibid.* 1,2,16-17, pp. 41-44; 1,2,22, pp. 55-56; Id., *De peccatorum meritis et remissione et de baptismo paruulorum* 1,21,29 (CSEL, 60), pp. 27-28; *De
spiritu et littera* 34,60 (CSEL, 60), p. 221; *Contra duas epistulas Pelagianorum* 4,6,16
(CSEL, 60), p. 539; *De gratia et libero arbitrio* 21,43 (PL, 44), c. 909; *De correptione et
gratia* 8,17 (CSEL, 92), p. 237; *De praedestinatione sanctorum* 14,27 (PL, 44), c. 980;
De dono perseuerantiae 8,18; 9,21; 11,25 (PL, 45), cc. 1003; 1004; 1007.

It is characteristic of Augustine's method that he insists on the inter-play of the two words predestination-mystery, which emerged in the *De diuersis quaestionibus ad Simplicianum* and which will come back con-sistently in Augustine's later works. Such insistence is usually supported by the quotation from Rom 11,33: *O altitudo diuitiarum sapientiae et scientiae Dei! Quam inscrutabilia sunt iudicia eius, et inuestigabiles uiae eius!* There is no reason to doubt Augustine's sincere belief that the problem of predestination demands the category of mystery as an ulti-mately necessary reference[122]. It is however also true that, beyond due reverence to God's mysterious designs, the use of the category of mys-tery in a theological discussion (as in any other discussion) may turn into a two edged argument. Too frequent a use of it may in fact be seen merely as a rhetorical device used to contradict views which differ from one's own. Too much repetition of the argument might backfire. How can one be so sure that one's own viewpoint is the most suitable to safe-guard God's mysteries? And how could one prove that a statement on God's inscrutable designs is not just clutching at straws in the absence of cogent arguments[123]?

The incomprehensibility of God's mysterious decrees was no doubt emphasized by Augustine also for practical and pastoral reasons. According to the bishop of Hippo, citing the inscrutability of God's pre-destination should help man remain humble and trusting before the mys-tery of his salvation. This would entail unceasing prayer, a docile accep-tance of rebuke[124], a renunciation of the *temeraria scientia*[125] and a

---

122. Thus, for instance, preaching on the problem of the *massa perditionis* in one of his sermons, Augustine recalls the passage of Rom 11,33 insisting more on the verbs *mirare* and *expauescere*, rather than on those of *scrutare* and *disputare*: "Disputare uis mecum? Immo mirare mecum, et exclama mecum: *O altitudo diuitiarum!* Ambo expauescamus, ambo clamemus: *O altitudo diuitiarum!* Ambo in pauore concordemur, ne in errore pereamus.... *Quam inscrutabilia sunt iudicia eius...!* Scrutare inscrutabilia, fac impossibilia, corrumpe incorruptibilia, uide inuisibilia" (Id., *Sermo* 23,13 [CCL, 41], pp. 357-358). See also: "Expavesco altitudinem" (*Ibid.* 27,7, p. 366); "Expavesco, non scrutor" (*Ibid.* 165,7,9 [PL, 38], c. 907).

123. As Rahner writes with regard to Augustine: "Es liegen wohl über seiner eigenen Lehre Dunkelheiten, die nicht Dunkelheiten Gottes und Zeichen seines Geheimnisses sind, sondern Spuren menschlicher Endlichkeit, der auch ein großer Geist unterworfen ist" (K. RAHNER, *Augustin und der Semipelagianismus*, in *ZKT* 62 [1938] 171-196, p. 196). We must, however, give credit to Augustine for being aware of his possible errors or mistaken judgements. He gave voice to such awareness also at the end of his theological career in one of his last polemic works: "Quandoquidem arrogantius loquor quam verius, si vel nunc dico me ad perfectionem sine ullo errore scribendi iam in ista aetate venisse" (Augustine, *De dono perseuerantiae* 21,55 [PL, 45], c. 1028).

124. Id., *De correptione et gratia* 15,46ff (CSEL, 92), pp. 275ff.

125. "Melior est ergo fidelis ignorantia quam temeraria scientia" (Id., *Sermo* 27,4 [CCL, 41], p. 362).

strong conviction that all honour and glory must be given to God alone[126]. That Augustine attached a pedagogical aim to his doctrine of predestination is no doubt legitimate within the context of the pastoral dimension (*wesentlich Gnadenpastoral*)[127] into which the doctrine of grace must be translated in one way or another. He saw it as a means by which to encourage confidence in God, to extinguish the pride that may be triggered by one's own merits, and to urge humility[128]. But to contend that this pedagogical aim constituted "the" aim of Augustine's doctrine of election and reprobation, as somebody has argued[129], seems to us quite tendencious and farfetched. We believe rather that Augustine's pastoral aim should be regarded as a sort of "correction", introduced against those interpretations that might possibly hold his doctrine of predestination responsible for the nullification of human commitment. In point of fact, vis-à-vis the temptation of slackening and moral laxity, a deterministic-like approach to the problem of predestination would inevitably provoke the withdrawal of any voluntary effort.

Furthermore, although Augustine was convinced (unlike the Pelagians and the Massilians[130]) that the issue of predestination and final perseverance ought to be preached to the faithful[131], he also admitted that it would be better at times not to talk too openly about it[132]. Was this admission, perhaps, a sign of his awareness that writing about predestination on a doctrinal level was one thing, whereas discussing the problem in the concrete context of the daily life of the Christian faithful was quite another? Some scholars think precisely that, and believe that Augustine's systematic theory of predestination was indeed corrected by

---

126. "Totum Deo dandum est, ne forte quis extollatur" (Id., *De praedestinatione sanctorum* 7,12 [PL, 44], c. 970); "Tutiores igitur vivimus, si totum Deo damus" (Id., *De dono perseuerantiae* 6,12 [PL, 45], c. 1000).

127. RING (ed.), *Aurelius Augustinus. Schriften über die Gnade* (n. 57), p. 256.

128. "Videant... impediri potius atque subverti hac praedestinationis praedicatione illum tantummodo perniciosissimum errorem, quo dicitur, gratiam Dei secundum merita nostra dari: ut qui gloriqtur, non in Domino, sed in se ipso glorietur" (Augustine, *De dono perseuerantiae* 17,42 [PL, 45], c. 1019).

129. "Augustin sieht demnach in der Verwerfung der Bösen ein heilspädagogisches Mittel der Vorsehung, um die zu Erlösenden zur Demut und damit zur Offenheit gegenüber der Gnade zu bewegen" (RING [ed.], *Aurelius Augustinus. Schriften über die Gnade* [n. 57], pp. 345-346). See also: "Augustin va redire que la doctrine de la prédestination est d'abord une doctrine à visée pastorale, destinée à déraciner la confiance en soi, si dangereuse" (HOMBERT, *Gloria gratiae* [n. 57], p. 336). And again: "Augustin n'élabore donc pas une 'théorie'. Il ne prêche pas une doctrine abstraite" (*Ibid.* p. 335).

130. Cf. Augustine, *De dono perseuerantiae* 17,43 (PL, 45), cc. 1019-1020; Hilary, *Ep.* 226,8 (CSEL, 57), p. 477.

131. Cf. Augustine, *De dono perseuerantiae* 14,36 (PL, 45), c. 1015. See also, *Ibid.* 16,41f, cc. 1018-1019.

132. Cf. *Ibid.* 16,40, cc. 1017-1018.

his pastoral practice[133]. His preference for caution at times rather than speculating on such a difficult subject[134], should be regarded as indicating awareness of the danger that his definition of predestination could cause fear and discontent.

There are also those who believe that Augustine made a distinction between the speculative/theoretical level and the level of (ortho)praxis, and that this distinction would correspond to the distinction that should be made between his dogmatic treatises, on one side, and his speeches and sermons to the people, on the other[135]. Although we must acknowledge that speculative and practical theology are situated on different levels, we do not believe that so sharp a distinction can be made between the two realms. We should rather emphasize their fruitful interplay, and the evidence is there to prove that Augustine did not confine himself to discussing predestination in the field of theological speculation alone. Traces of the importance he attached to translating his theological thought into a pastoral language for the benefit of the faithful can be found in speeches and homilies[136]. This shows clearly that the bishop of Hippo did not recoil from preaching openly to his people on issues such as the exclusion of unbaptized children from the kingdom of heaven, God's gratuitous deliverance through baptism from the *massa perditionis* and the *numerus certus* of the elect[137]. We might perhaps agree that,

---

133. "La doctrine augustinienne de la prédestination... a été corrigée dans la pratique par une pastorale de la conversion et de la persévérance" (RONDET, *La prédestination augustinienne* [n. 84], p. 250).

134. Cf. Augustine, *De dono perseuerantiae* 16,40 (PL, 45), cc. 1017-1018.

135. It is the conviction, for instance, of Rottmanner who points to an "Unterschied zwischen seiner Theorie und Praxis". With regard to predestination, he says: "Man kann sagen: Für Augustinus waren in der Theorie nur wenige, in der Praxis alle prädestiniert" (ROTTMANNER, *Der Augustinismus* [n. 77], p. 30). Likewise, Pontet affirms: "Il reste une différence entre la manière dont saint Augustin parle de la prédestination dans ses sermons et dans ses traités sur la grâce" (M. PONTET, *L'exégèse de S. Augustin prédicateur* [Theol(P), 7], Paris, 1945, p. 512). See also BOUBLÍK, *La predestinazione* (n. 3), p. 162.

136. Unlike those who think that Augustine shrank from engaging the Christian communities in difficult discussions, Kunzelmann has suggested the contrary. It seems, for example, that during the council of Carthage in 418, the bishop of Hippo had kept the people informed about the discussions that were going on in the bishops' assembly, and the decisions that were going to be taken. And he did so precisely by preaching on the disputed questions (cf. A. KUNZELMANN, *Die Chronologie der Sermones des Hl. Augustinus*, in *MA*, Vol. II, pp. 417-520, p. 457). See also Augustine, *Epp.* 175-179 *passim* (CSEL, 44), pp. 652-697.

137. See, for instance: Id., *Sermo* 26,13-15 (CCL, 41), pp. 357-359; *Ibid.* 27,7, pp. 365-366; 47,15, p. 585; *Ibid.* 158 (PL, 38), cc. 862-867; *Ibid.* 251,2,2, c. 1168; *Ibid.* 294,7,7-8, c. 1339-1340; Id., *Enarrationes in psalmos* 64,2 (CCL, 39), p. 824; *Ibid.* 134,8-9 (CCL, 40), pp. 1943-1944; *Ibid.* 150,3, pp. 2193-2194; Id., *Tractatus in Euangelium Ioannis* 12,12 (CCL, 36), p. 127; *Ibid.* 45,12, pp. 394-395; *Ibid.* 53,5-10, pp. 454-456; *Ibid.* 68,1, pp. 497-498; *Ibid.* 86,2, p. 542; *Ibid.* 87,3, p. 545.

in comparison with his theological treatises, Augustine would soften the
tone in his sermons and speeches, but even then it does not seem that
that was always the case[138].

b) The Relationship between praescientia and praedestinatio

In the light of his doctrine of unconditional grace, Augustine was led
to reshape the relationship between prescience and predestination. To
concede that God's foreknowledge of man's future faith and merits constitutes the ultimate cause of predestination to salvation, would be like
admitting that election, justification and glorification are ultimately
man's own responsibility. If that were so, then predestination would
cease to be a mystery, and only God's foreknowledge would still maintain its mysterious character (although limited to the level of mere
knowledge) and remain the key to understanding predestination.

Augustine, therefore, introduces a significant change, while maintaining the close knit relationship between prescience and predestination.
This occurs in the light of his theory of sovereign grace, whose all-
embracing agency extends to man from initial faith, through perseverance, to the attainment of eternal life (*praeuenit, cooperat, perficit*), and
also in the related doctrine of original sin. In fact, if we carefully consider the way Augustine deals with the doctrine of predestination we are
led to infer that it is an "infralapsarian doctrine"[139], in that it is only
applicable in the framework of fallen humanity[140]. The first man, had he

138. See, for instance, what Augustine tells the faithful in a homily about the abandonment of the non-elect: "Sic enim excaecat, sic obdurat Deus, deserendo et non adiu-
uando; quod occulto iudicio facere potest, inique non potest" (*Ibid.* 53,6, p. 454).

139. "Die augustinische Prädestinationslehre infralapsarisch ist, d. h. auf der Voraus-
setzung des Sündenfalles und der Erbschuld beruht" (ROTTMANNER, *Der Augustinismus*
[n. 77], pp. 7-8). It has been argued (cf. *e.g.*, THONNARD, *La prédestination augustinienne
et l'interpretation de O. Rottmanner* [n. 74], pp. 269ff) that the horizon of predestination
should not be restricted to infralapsarian humanity, for in Augustine's view the angels too
are associated with men in God's providential plans (cf. Augustine, *De ciuitate Dei*
14,26-27 [CCL, 47], pp. 449-451). However, beyond this loose association, which is
brought in as part of the general plan of salvation, the primary meaning of predestination remains the efficacity of God's grace *in tempore*, that is with regard to "fallen"
humanity. Augustine's concept of *massa damnata*, in connection with which his doctrine of election and predestination must be understood, should be clear evidence of this
assumption.

140. From the point of view of God's transcendence, however, viz. from a point of
view where only "God's *propositum*" is taken into account, predestination can indeed be
regarded as "supralapsarian" in that the divine decrees are eternal. Cf. H. DIEM,
Augustins Interesse in der Prädestinationslehre, in *Theologische Aufsätze Karl Barth zum
50. Geburtstag*, München, 1936, pp. 362-381, p. 368; E. KÄHLER, *Prädestination*, in *RGG*
5 (1961) 483-487, p. 484.

so wanted, could have persevered, and if that had been the case, God's predestination would have been subordinated to his foreknowledge about Adam's meritorious perseverance[141]. Now, in the new framework in which Augustine's theological thinking is set, the prime subject of the binomial prescience-predestination is God and only God. For him, to predestine is not so much a matter of foreknowing how man will be acting, as of what He himself, God, would do[142]. And since only God foreknows in an absolutely gratuitous way what man will be doing, the exclusive dependence of predestination on divine agency, and its inscrutable and immutable character, stand untouched.

That being the case, Augustine's remark that his view is compatible with the ancient commentators (*uerbi Dei tractatores*)[143], who regarded prescience and predestination as synonyms, is misleading, at least in so far as the exact meaning of the pre-Augustinian theologians is concerned. Whereas according to them God's prescience must be understood in the light of *God's foreknowledge of man's merits or demerits* (that will actually become real in the future), according to Augustine, God's prescience should instead be understood in the light of *God's gratuitous acts or gifts*[144]. The substantial shift by which Augustine makes God the sole, absolute subject of predestination, independently of any possible future behaviour of man (*ante praeuisa merita*), is in itself sufficient to rule out any convergence between Augustine's understanding

141. "Dans l'état d'intégrité, cette loi, qui nous régit, n'existait pas. L'homme eût donc eu, s'il avait persévéré, le mérite de sa persévérance, un mérite dont Dieu n'aurait pas été l'auteur, au moins immédiat. Et par suite, la prédestination à la vie éternelle n'eût pas dépendu totalement du libre vouloir divin: elle eût été *subordonnée* à la prescience du mérite de l'homme, d'un mérite qui n'eut pas été, comme est le nôtre, un pur don de Dieu" (J. CHÉNÉ, *Notes complémentaires* 11, *BA* 24, p. 797).

142. "Hoc est ergo praedestinavit: sine dubio enim praescivit, si praedestinavit: sed praedestinasse, est hoc praescisse quod fuerat ipse facturus" (Augustine, *De dono perseuerantiae* 18,47 [PL, 45], c. 1023).

143. "Quid ergo nos prohibet, quando apud aliquos verbi Dei tractatores legimus Dei praescientiam, et agitur de vocatione electorum, eamdem praedestinationem intelligere? Magis enim fortasse voluerunt hoc verbo in ea re uti, quod et facilius intelligitur, et non repugnat, immo et congruit veritati quae de praedestinatione gratiae praedicatur" (*Ibid.* 19,48, c. 1023).

144. "Namque in sua quae falli mutarique non potest praescientia, opera sua futura disponere, id omnino, nec aliud quidquam est praedestinare" (*Ibid.* 17,41, c. 1019). Augustine, as Cayré affirms, "a moins en vue la prévision des mérites que la prescience des *dons* qu'il *[God]* a décidé d'accorder aux hommes pour leur salut" (F. CAYRÉ, *Précis de patrologie et d'histoire de la théologie*, T. I, 2nd ed., Paris-Tournais-Rome, 1931, p. 671). See also, J. RIVIÈRE, *Notes complémentaires* 47, *BA* 9, p. 405. Bavaud's following affirmation is, therefore, incorrect and cannot be applied to Augustine: "Dieu ne réfuse la grâce de la persévérance finale qu'après la prévision de nombreux démérites" (G. BAVAUD, *La doctrine de la prédestination et de la réprobation d'après saint Augustin et Calvin*, in *REAug* 5 [1959] 431-438, p.431).

of the relationship between prescience and predestination and that of the
ancient Greek and Latin Christian theologians. According to Augustine,
whereas prescience is God's foreknowledge of man's acting and destiny,
predestination is the direct exercise of God's intentions, will and agency
upon the elect[145]. Only in this way are God's chosen ones enabled to
receive the grace of election prepared for them from all eternity[146].

Augustine's statement that prescience can exist without predestination, whereas predestination cannot exist without prescience[147], also
needs some clarification. Such a statement would be obvious if we interpreted it in a temporal sense. In that case prescience would be regarded
as being prior to God's predestination, viz. his decision to act. After all,
if the works or effects of predestination are going to be accomplished in
the future, then we would gather that there is also a temporal aspect
inherent in it. But if that is true from our point of view, it needs correct-
ing when applied to God, at least if we wish to save his transcendence.
Augustine was aware of this aporia. For this reason, borrowing from the
Stoic notion, according to which time can be reduced to the category of
the "present/actual"[148], he made it clear that God is not in time. In him
everything happens in an "eternal present", because everything is
known by him in an utterly instantaneous manner. God's decision to
make something happen coincides with the very moment in which He
foreknows what He will do[149]. According to Augustine's doctrine, therefore, the priority of God's prescience must not be considered as a priority *in tempore*, but as a priority which can only be understood in the
light of the *nunc stans*, where God's timeless and eternal decrees find
their proper setting[150]. It follows that predestination to salvation of individual men relies exclusively on God's will[151], which is at one with his

---

145. Cf. Augustine, *De praedestinatione sanctorum* 10,19 (PL, 44), c. 975.

146. Cf. *Ibid.* 18,35, c. 986.

147. "Praedestinatio... sine praescientia non potest esse: potest autem esse sine
praedestinatione praescientia" (*Ibid.* 10,19, c. 975).

148. Cf. M.L. COLISH, *The Stoic Tradition from Antiquity to the Early Middle Ages.*
Vol. II: *Stoicism in Christian Latin Thought through the Sixth Century*, Leiden, 1990,
pp. 228ff.

149. As Rist writes: "This priority is simply on the analogy of the temporal priority
of a thought that such and such will happen to a decision to make it happen now"
(J.M. RIST, *Augustine on Free Will and Predestination*, in *JTS* 20 [1969] 420-447,
p. 438).

150. See, for instance: "...tamquam praeterita narrantur, quae futura prophetabantur;
quoniam, quae uentura erant, iam in praedestinatione et praescientia Dei uelut facta erant,
<quia certa erant>" (Augustine, *De ciuitate Dei* 17,18 [CCL, 48], pp. 583-584).

151. "It is vain to argue from this kind of priority that the salvation of any individual
fallen man is any less totally the act of God's will and God's will alone" (RIST, *Augustine on Free Will and Predestination* [n. 149], p. 438).

prescience. Such a solution cannot but leave us with the suspicion that in this way time loses any "economic" possibility with regard to human history, and that God's gratuitous initiative in the predestination of people ends up in an apartheid-like form of salvation, reserved to the happy few whom God has decided to endow with the invincible strength of his grace.

On the other hand, when it comes to evil doing, recurring to logical modality[152], Augustine would utterly exclude a view of prescience and predestination as equivalents of causation and necessity. God can foresee those whom He is going to save and on whom He is going to bestow his efficient grace so that they may use their free will rightly. But this does not entail that He is also going to constrain the will of those He does not want to save, as if He were coercing those inclined to evil to sin[153]. This was unacceptable to the bishop of Hippo who, already in his *De libero arbitrio*, was at pains to maintain (against Manichaean psychic determinism) that God's foreknowledge and man's freedom to sin can coexist[154]. However, aware of the difficulty of finding rational criteria upon which to base this claim, Augustine justifies it by appealing to religious experience, piety and fidelity[155]. Thus, in an attempt to show the compatibility of God's foreknowledge with man's freedom to do evil, the bishop of Hippo makes use of an analogy drawn from daily experience. It may well happen, he argues, that we may know exactly what another person is going to do the next day, without having to ascribe to ourselves the responsibility for his behaviour[156]. On the strength of this analogy Augustine concludes that even if God foresees all the things that He is going to be the cause of, it does not follow that He is necessarily the cause of all the things that He foresees. Maintaining the distinction between foreknowledge and cause, Augustine tries to show that man's free agency cannot be regarded as directly caused by God's foreknowledge – at least as far as man's inclination to evil and his performance of sin are concerned[157]. The reality of original sin, above all, and the need

152. See T.G. BUCHER, *Zur formalen Logik bei Augustinus*, in *FZPT* 29 (1982) 3-45.

153. "Quia neque ipsos ideo coegit peccare quia fecit quibus potestatem utrum uellent dedit" (Augustine, *De libero arbitrio* 3,5,14 [CCL, 29], p. 283). See also: "Dominum praescium futurorum, per prophetam praedixisse infidelitatem Iudaeorum; praedixisse tamen, non fecisse" (ID., *Tractatus in Euangelium Ioannis* 53,4 [CCL, 36], p. 453).

154. Cf. Id., *De libero arbitrio* 3,2,4 and 3,2,6 (CCL, 29), pp. 276 and 277-279; *De ciuitate Dei* 5,9,3 (CCL, 47), p. 138.

155. "Religiosus autem animus utrumque elegit, utrumque confitetur et fide pietatis utrumque confirmat" (*Ibid.*, p. 137).

156. Id., *De libero arbitrio* 3,4,10 (CCL, 29), p. 281.

157. "Et sicut tu quaedam quae fecisti meministi nec tamen quae meministi omnia fecisti, ita Deus omnia quorum ipse auctor est praescit, nec tamen omnium quae praescit

for baptismal regeneration are incompatible with God taking part in some way or another in the choice for evil[158].

The way Augustine relates prescience to predestination and roots them in God's acting cannot but leave us sceptical about the actual outcome for human history. As a spontaneous reaction we would be inclined to think that the bishop of Hippo has done no more than christianize the pagan idea of *fatum* – intended as a synonym for the ordering of the world by God as well as for his agency in the world with regard to the elect and the rejected alike. When, for instance, in the *De ciuitate Dei* Augustine places a strong emphasis on God's universal causation[159], the key distinction between (fore)knowledge and causality is blurred. The two terms are confused, rather than being kept apart in a legitimate coexistence, and consequently man's free will and choice are seriously undermined[160]. Wanting to stress God's control over the world, Augustine replaces, as it were, the term providence with those of *praescientia* and *praedestinatio* whose point of reference is ultimately God and God alone. The suspicion is aroused that the bishop of Hippo's view may indeed be thought to resemble a deterministic God, whose unfathomable lordship in history chooses between prosperity and adversity, between salvation and damnation. To this decisive question we shall turn our attention, but not before having sketched Augustine's use of Paul in connection with the problem of predestination.

c) Augustine's Interpretation of Paul

Turning to Paul's letters was certainly not unusual in the Latin Church of "the last decades of the fourth century", which – in the words of Brown – "could well be called 'the generation of St. Paul'"[161]. As a

---

ipse auctor est. Quorum autem non est malus auctor, iustus est ultor" (*Ibid.* 3,4,11, p. 281). "Praescientia quippe Dei... peccatores praenoscit, non facit. Nam si eas animas liberat a peccato, quas innocentes et mundas inplicuit ipse peccato, uulnus sanat quod intulit nobis, non quod inuenit in nobis" (Id., *De natura et origine animae* 1,7,7 [CSEL, 60], p. 308).

158. "Avertat autem Deus et omnino absit, ut dicamus, quando lauacro regenerationis Deus mundat animas paruulorum, tunc eum mala sua corrigere, quae illis ipse fecit" (*Ibid.*).

159. Cf. Id., *De ciuitate Dei* 5 *passim* (CCL, 47), pp. 128-163. "The God with Whom Augustine is treating in this part of the *City of God*, then, is the God Who is the Lord of history and the anti-Pelagian predestinarian God Who has chosen and guided the members of the heavenly city from all eternity" (COLISH, *The Stoic Tradition from Antiquity to the Early Middle Ages*. Vol. II [n. 148], p. 232).

160. See W. RORDORF, *Saint Augustin et la tradition philosophique antifataliste: à propos de* De civitate Dei *5,1-11*, in *VC* 28 (1974) 190-202.

161. BROWN, *Augustine of Hippo* (n. 28), p. 151.

matter of fact, the Apostle's letters had aroused growing interest within the Church of that time. Christian writers like Marius Victorinus, Ambrosiaster, Jerome and Pelagius all wrote commentaries, either wholly or in part, on the Pauline corpus. Augustine was no exception[162]. Having devoted some study to the letters of Paul during the years of his priesthood (a study which resulted in some incomplete commentaries), he continued to go back to the Apostle when looking for answers to the various problems he was confronted with in both his theological and pastoral life. By the time of the Pelagian controversy and up to the confrontation with the Massilians, for instance, the Pauline expression *propositum (Dei)* had become one of Augustine's favourite terms to designate the significance of grace and predestination[163].

One of the Pauline passages he turned to in order to draw support for his doctrine of predestination is Rom 8,28-30[164]. Firstly he insisted that the term *propositum* must not be attributed to man, but to God: *propositum scilicet uocantis, non uocatorum*[165]. Moreover, not all the *uocati* are *electi*, but only those who are *secundum propositum uocati*[166]. In affirming that the *electi* are the *pauci* among the *uocati*, Augustine adopts and maintains, in his exegetical approach to the Pauline pericope, the Matthean distinction of the *Multi uocati, pauci electi* (Mt 20,16)[167], a distinction which, in reality, does not correspond to Paul's semantic world. In fact, by the term *uocati* the Apostle meant all those who effectively respond to the divine call[168], whereas the interpretation of the

162. See B. DELAROCHE, *Saint Augustin lecteur et interprète de saint Paul dans le* De peccatorum meritis et remissione *(hiver 411-412)* (CEAug.SA, 146), Paris, 1996, pp. 92-101; M.G. MARA, *Agostino interprete di Paolo* (LCPM, 16), Milan, 1993, pp. 9-80;

163. See ZUMKELLER, *<Propositum> in seinem spezifisch christlichen und theologischen Verständnis bei Augustinus* (n. 54), p. 304ff.

164. "Scimus quoniam diligentibus Deum omnia cooperantur in bonum, his qui secundum propositum vocati sunt: quoniam quos ante praescivit, et praedestinavit conformes imaginis Filii sui, ut sit ipse primogenitus in multis fratribus: quos autem praedestinavit, illos et vocavit; quos autem vocavit, ipsos et iustificavit; quos autem iustificavit, ipsos et glorificavit" (Rom 8,28-30).

165. Augustine, *Tractatus in Euangelium Ioannis* 115,4 (CCL, 36), p. 645. Already in his *Expositio* on Paul's letter to the Romans Augustine had stated that "propositum autem Dei accipiendum est, non ipsorum *[the elect]*" (Id., *Expositio quarumdam propositionum ex epistula ad Romanos* 47 [55] [CSEL, 84], p. 30). A conviction that will be reiterated several times, *e.g.*: "De hoc proposito Dei dictum est" (Id., *Contra duas epistulas Pelagianorum* 2,10,22 [CSEL, 60], p. 484); "Propositum autem non suum *[of the elect]*, sed Dei" (Id., *De correptione et gratia* 7,14 [CSEL, 92], p. 234); "*Praedestinati secundum propositum*, non nostrum, sed eius" (Id., *De praedestinatione sanctorum* 18,37 [PL, 44], c. 988).

166. Cf., for instance, Id., *Contra duas epistulas Pelagianorum* 2,10,22 (CSEL, 60), p. 484; *Contra Iulianum* 5,4,14 (PL, 44), c. 792.

167. Cf., for instance, Id., *De correptione et gratia* 7,14 (CSEL, 92), p. 234.

168. P. PLATZ, *Der Römerbrief in der Gnadenlehre Augustins*, Würzburg, 1938, p. 206.

bishop of Hippo, restricting the Pauline meaning of the term, attaches the effectiveness of the divine call to God's *propositum*, that is to God's predestination. In this way Augustine's exegesis, in accordance with his own theological presuppositions, posits the effectiveness of man's call (and therefore of his salvation) in God alone.

However, the scriptural passage in which Augustine clearly abandons the traditional exegetical line[169], forcing upon it his personal interpretation, is the famous passage of Rom 9,10-29[170]. Dealing with it, Augustine moves from a biblical approach to a speculative one[171]. Despite his claim of having adhered to the Apostle's *intentio*[172], the main objection that must be raised against his approach here is his misunderstanding and betrayal of Paul's "primary" aim, which can be inferred from the broader context which extends from ch. 9 to ch. 11 of the letter to the Romans[173]. In fact, the context in which Rom 9,10-29 is framed suggests that Paul's focus is upon the salvation promised to corporate Israel, rather than on the grace of faith and on the necessity of not boasting about one's own merits deriving from works. The pre-disposition of God's election concerns the history and destiny of Israel as a "people"[174], and the passage on Jacob and Esau refers to the historical and temporal destiny of the two peoples, represented by the two brothers (cf.

---

169. The Massilians will reproach Augustine for reading the letter to the Romans (and particularly ch. 9) in a way that nobody in ecclesiastical circles had ever read it before: "...quae de epistula apostoli Pauli romanis scribentis ad manifestationem diuinae gratiae praeuenientis electorum merita proferuntur, a nullo umquam ecclesiasticorum ita esse intellecta, ut nunc sentiuntur, adfirmant" (Prosper, *Ep.* 225,3 [CSEL, 57], p. 459).

170. See DRECOLL, *Die Entstehung der Gnadenlehre Augustins* (n. 56), pp. 227-235.

171. Nygren clearly states that Augustine approached Rom 9 from a different perspective than that of biblical theology: "Die biblische Theologie und die augustinische in völlig *verschiedenen Kategorien* arbeiten" (NYGREN, *Das Prädestinationsproblem in der Theologie Augustins* [n. 4], p. 295).

172. Cf. Augustine, *De diuersis quaestionibus ad Simplicianum* 1,2,2.21 (CCL, 44), pp. 24 and 53. It has also been suggested that when Augustine tackled the pericope of Rom 9,10-29 in the *De diuersis quaestionibus ad Simplicianum* he did it in an anti-Manichaean fashion. Against the Manichaeans' interpolation of Rom 9, he was determined to defend the sovereign justice of God and to dismiss their belief that he was also the author of evil. Cf. A. MUTZENBECHER, *Einleitung*, in Augustine, *De diuersis quaestionibus ad Simplicianum* (CCL, 44), pp. IX-LXXIV, pp. XIV-XV and XVII. "Cette préoccupation antimanichéenne est en toile de fond de l'*Ad Simplicianum*" (HOMBERT, *Gloria gratiae* [n. 57], p. 98).

173. Platz reproaches Augustine for having taken and interpreted separately the verses of this pericope: "Er *atomistisch exegetisiert*" (Cf. PLATZ, *Der Römerbrief in der Gnadenlehre Augustins* [n. 168], p. 215). Similar position in BOUBLÍK, *La predestinazione* (n. 3), p. 134.

174. "Alle Geschichte Israels beruht auf der Zusage Gottes, die in sich der erwählende und bestimmende Vor-Satz Gottes ist" (H. SCHLIER, *Der Römerbrief* [HTK, 6], Freiburg-Basel-Wien, 1977, p. 293).

Gen 25,23). The election of the former and rejection of the latter there-fore must not be read as about Jacob and Esau as "individuals", but in the light of a "corporate" reality of which they are symbols[175]. Paul was trying to find a reason why Israel, God's first chosen people, had been replaced by the call to the Gentiles. Here, the analogy with Jacob and Esau is a useful one, and helps him, by way of illustration, to point out that the election of the Gentiles (as well as that of Jacob) must be inter-preted as part of God's plan of salvation. Their election ought to be understood in relation to this plan; it has nothing to do with a divine and eternal decree according to which individuals are predestined or rejected, as Augustine will contend[176]. The same thing must be said about Augustine's exegesis of Rom 9,21 about the potter and the clay. Whereas Paul wanted to underscore the total dependence of man on his Creator, the potter in whom man's destiny ultimately lies, Augustine instead interprets it as an allegory of predestination, speculating about the *uasa misericordiae* (the elect) who have been set apart for election, and the *uasa irae* (the reprobates) who will make up the *massa damna-torum*. Although such a distinction between "individuals" was not con-templated by Paul, Augustine adopted it as *the* sole interpretation of Rom 9,10-29, thus discarding the Apostle's primary intention. This sug-gests once again that Augustine's exegesis was influenced by his theo-logical premises about the supremacy of prevenient grace. In the light of

175. "There is no hint here of predestination to "grace" or "glory" of an individual; it is an expression of the choice of corporate Israel over corporate Edom" (J.A. FITZMYER, *Romans. A New Translation with Introduction and Commentary*, New York, 1993, p. 563). Cf. *Ibid.* p. 542. See also L. MORRIS, *The Epistle to the Romans*, Grand Rapids, 1988, p. 356; J.A. ZIESLER, *Paul's Letter to the Romans*, Philadelphia, 1989, p. 241. We must also admit, however, that individual election – as a secondary meaning – cannot be in principle eliminated, in that groups are in fact composed by individuals. Cf., for instance: T.R. SCHREINER, *Romans* (BECNT, 6), Grand Rapids, 1998, pp. 497f; J. PIPER, *The Justification of God: An Exegetical and Theological Study of Romans 9:1-23*, Grand Rapids, 1993, pp. 68-70; D. J. MOO, *The Theology of Romans 9-11*, in D.M. HAY – E.E. JOHNSON (eds.), *Pauline Theology*, Vol. III: *Romans*, Minneapolis, 1995, p. 252.

176. "Dans le contexte, il ne s'agit pas,…, de la grâce intérieure et de la sanctifi-cation, et a fortiori du salut ou de la damnation éternelle de Jacob et d'Esaü en tant qu'individus. Le prophète parle seulement des *peuples*" (S. LYONNET, *Prédestination et réprobation selon Rom 9*, in ID., *Études sur l'Épître aux Romains* [AnBib, 120], Rome, 1989, pp. 274-297, p. 276). "Le passage indu de l'élection d'Israël et des Gentiles à l'élection éternelle de tel homme, opéré par Augustin, n'est possible qu'au prix d'une lec-ture qui détache les affirmations scripturaires de leur contexte" (HOMBERT, *Gloria gratiae* [n. 57], p. 98). "C'était une erreur d'exégèse – writes Pontet –, et de grande consequence par ses suites" (PONTET, *L'exégèse de S. Augustin prédicateur* [n. 135], p. 484, n. 169). Cf. also PLATZ, *Der Römerbrief in der Gnadenlehre Augustins* [n. 168], p. 242; BOUBLÍK, *La predestinazione* (n. 3), pp. 148f and 164; RING (ed.), *Aurelius Augustinus. Schriften über die Gnade* (n. 57), pp. 263-266; A.F.N. LEKKERKERKER, *Römer 7 und Römer 9 bei Augustin*, Amsterdam, 1942, pp. 109-110.

this, what he saw adumbrated in the election of Jacob and the rejection of Esau would fit well with his view about the salvation and the damnation of "individuals". There is no doubt that the bishop of Hippo was somehow forced to cling to this interpretation – however extraneous to the original intention of Rom 9,10-29 – by his postulating of God's sovereign grace, embracing all the life of the elect, from the *initium fidei* to final perseverance.

Thus, determined to safeguard his conclusion that any activity on man's part to procure grace must be excluded, Augustine bypasses Paul's intention, which was indeed very different. The Apostle wanted to emphasize that human activity, in relation to God, is always a matter of receiving and cherishing that which comes from him, without excluding the part which man has to play[177]. Moreover, for Paul predestination had to be understood in strict connection with Christ's activity. In the Son of God, who is the utmost revelation of divine grace and benevolence, God's universal plan of salvation is made manifest, and only in Christ and through him can the predestination of man be posited and comprehended[178]. Finally, whereas for Paul the concept of predestination envisaged the possibility of all men being saved, Augustine introduces a sort of dualism. Replacing Paul's unitary and soteriologically oriented view, he defines the concept as God's bestowal (or not) of *uera gratia*, resulting either in predestination to grace and glory of the *pauci* (the elect) or rejection of the *multi* (the reprobates)[179]. And so, while depending in many respects on Paul's thought on issues such as God's absolute and free initiative, the gratuity of predestination, the importance of permission to sin, Augustine's "theological" exegesis of Rom 9,10-29 cannot be justified. Rather than drawing enlightenment from Paul's primary intention, as expressed in those passages from which he claims to derive his doctrine of predestination[180], the bishop of Hippo falls, perhaps *malgré soi*, into the unhappy perspective of reading (and looking for sustenance in) the Pauline pericope through the spectacles of his own viewpoint on absolute grace.

177. See NYGREN, *Das Prädestinationsproblem in der Theologie Augustins* (n. 4), pp. 291f.
178. Cf. *Ibid.*, pp. 136-137.
179. See BOUBLÍK, *La predestinazione* (n. 3), pp. 134ff.
180. If we may agree with Hombert about the importance of trying to understand "*pourquoi* il *[Augustin]* a parlé comme il l'a fait, non en function de tel ou tel 'présupposé métaphysique', mais en vertu d'une *intention*, d'une logique *chrétienne et spirituelle* profonde" (HOMBERT, *Gloria gratiae* [n. 57], p. 314, n. 187), we do not follow him any more in his sophistical attempt at persuading us that "une lecture faite au second degré, par-delà la lettre du texte" (as is the case with Rom 9,10-29) could be interpreted as "*l'envers* d'un propos sur la miséricorde" (*Ibid.*, p. 320).

4. DID AUGUSTINE DEVELOP AN ASYMMETRICAL THEOLOGICAL DETERMINISM? AN ASSESSMENT OF HIS DOCTRINE OF PREDESTINATION

Since predestination involves a positive intervention on the part of God, who wills and at the same time performs what He wills, we cannot fail to conclude that the natural aim of divine predestination is the good and the salvation offered to men. Augustine had made it clear that it would be utterly outrageous to even think that a negative, driving force could proceed from the Godhead to man and be eventually the cause of his reprobation[181]. In affirming that predestination is the preparation for grace (whereas grace, in its turn, is the effect of predestination), he actually subscribes to the conviction that the ultimate aim of predestination is the attainment of salvation[182], and that this comes about only through Christ the Mediator[183]. Also in the formal definition that Augustine gives of it, predestination is described as a "predestination *of the saints*" (*praedestinatio sanctorum*), and God's foreknowledge is said to be the preparation of those gifts (*praeparatio beneficiorum* or *quae danda essent*[184]), particularly the gift of final perseverance, that will be bestowed on those who are going to be saved with absolute certainty (*certissime liberantur*)[185]. As a logical conclusion, those who, in God's mind, are not going to be saved, cannot be called predestined.

If God were responsible for predestining man not only to salvation but also to damnation, it would follow that God's influence is efficacious only in the moral success of the saints. Sinners, whose life is marked by moral failings, are obviously left untouched by it. Since there cannot be predestination to sinfulness and damnation, as that would require a direct and positive intervention on God's part[186], the only feasible conclusion is that sin is merely foreseen by God. Thus, asserts Augustine, in the case of those whom God has not predestined to salvation but whose sinful life has been foreseen by him, divine intervention is

---

181. "Elegit ergo praedestinans nos *[cf. Eph 1,3-4]*. Numquid eligeret impios et immundos?" (Augustine, *De praedestinatione sanctorum* 18,35 [PL, 44], c. 986).

182. "Quocirca praedestinatio Dei quae in bono est, gratiae est, ut dixi, praeparatio: gratia vero est ipsius praedestinationis effectus" (*Ibid.* 10,19, c. 975). In the light of expressions such as this, the *capitulum* attributed to Augustine by the Massilians ("Quod per potentiam Deus homines ad peccata compellat": Prosper, *Pro Augustino responsiones ad capitula obiectionum Gallorum calumniantium* 11 [PL, 51], c. 166) is unjust.

183. Augustine, *De praedestinatione sanctorum* 15,30–16,32 (PL, 44), cc. 981-983.

184. God's foreknowledge does not concern only "quibus danda essent", but also "quae danda essent" (Id., *De dono perseuerantiae* 17,43 [PL, 45], c. 1020).

185. Cf. *Ibid.* 14,35, c. 1014.

186. "Saint Augustin refuse toujours de dire que Dieu meut positivement sa créature au péché" (BAVAUD, *La doctrine de la prédestination et de la réprobation* [n. 144], p. 433).

simply withheld. That means that the non-predestined are left to themselves. They are not helped, nor delivered from their attachment to sin,
which may indeed deepen[187], because the only freeedom of choice left to
them is the freedom *ad peccandum*[188]. They have abandoned God and so
they are, in their turn, abandoned by him (*deserunt et deseruntur*)[189].
This divine abandonment, however, continues the bishop of Hippo, takes
nothing away from the sanctity and justice of God. It is the mere consequence of him not bestowing his benefits and final perseverance on
those who freely turn from him. He abandons them to the destiny they
deserve, that which, since the beginning, is the only outcome for all men
born in the sin of Adam and belonging to the *massa perditionis*[190]. This
concept of *massa*, with its different qualifications, is the objective background against which Augustine's view of God's just punishment for the
majority of men must be understood. But it is also the framework within
which is highlighted the manifestation of divine mercy granted to those
whom God wills to help, deliver, elect and predestine[191].

a) Massa peccati/massa damnata *and* massa sanctorum

With the metaphor of the *massa* (or *consparsio*[192]) we reach the core
of Augustine's doctrine of grace and predestination. *Massa* is the latin

187. See the following dismal and pessimistic description: "Iacebat in malis, uel
etiam uoluebatur, et de malis in mala praecipitabatur totius humani generis massa
damnata" (Augustine, *Enchiridion ad Laurentium* 8,27 [CCL, 46], p. 64).
188. Cf. *Ibid.* 9,30, pp. 63f. See also Augustine's *dura necessitas peccati* (Id., *De perfectione iustitiae hominis* 4,9 [CSEL, 42], pp. 8f). Thus, as Greshake writes, a human
being is certainly not prevented from choosing, "aber seine Wahl bleibt im Kreis des
Bösen.... Er kann nur noch sündigen, aber dies gerade nicht gegen, sondern Kraft seines
freien Willens, mit Freude, Lust, Spontaneität" (GRESHAKE, *Gnade als konkrete Freiheit*
[n. 26],
p. 196).
189. Augustine, *De correptione et gratia* 13,42 (CSEL, 92), p. 271. The abandonment
of a creature on the part of God is the equivalent of non-election or non-predestination.
Cf. Id., *De dono perseuerantiae* 9,21 (PL, 45), c. 1004-1005.
190. "Caeteri autem ubi nisi in massa perditionis iusto divino iudicio relinquuntur?"
(*Ibid.* 14,35, c. 1014).
191. "Hoc oportebat, ut damnatis non omnibus, quid omnibus deberetur ostenderet,
atque ita gratius suam gratiam vasis misericordiae commendaret" (*Ibid.* 8,18, c. 1003).
Yet, such an explanation remains clumsy. As it has been rightly observed, it is as though
"la manifestazione della misericordia ha bisogno dell'inferno" (BOUBLÍK, *La predestinazione* [n. 3], p. 120).
192. Augustine uses the two terms as interchangeable synonyms. Although the passage of Rom 9,21 contained in the codex he used, would read *ex eadem consparsione*
(*consparsio* = paste/dough, referring to the clay = *lutum*) instead of *ex eadem massa*, he
eventually preferred the use of the term *massa* on account of its being utilized in many
codices ("in plerisque codicibus legitur": Augustine, *Ep.* 186,6,19 [CSEL, 57], pp. 60-
61). The term *consparsio*, however, will still appear here and there, employed by Augustine as a synonym of *massa*. It may happen, for instance, that while Augustine maintains

translation of the greek word φύραμα (mixture, clay matter, paste, lump of dough) which Paul employed in Rom 9,20-21: *O homo tu quis es, qui respondeas Deo? Numquid dicit figmentum ei qui se finxit: 'Quare sic me fecisti?'. An non habet potestatem figulus luti ex eadem massa facere aliud quidem uas in honorem, aliud uero in contumeliam?* (ἢ οὐκ ἔχει ἐξουσίαν ὁ κεραμεὺς τοῦ πηλοῦ ἐκ τοῦ αὐτοῦ φυράματος ποιῆσαι ὃ μὲν εἰς τιμὴν σκεῦος ὃ δὲ εἰς ἀτιμίαν). Interpreting this passage in the light of the preceding verses (Rom 9,1-20), Augustine rules out a neutral understanding of the term *massa*. In his eyes it mostly assumes a negative connotation in that it points to the whole of humanity, nobody excepted, as being corrupt in consequence of Adam's sin[193]. In fact, if *massa* were to be interpreted as neutral, then the destiny of the *uasa irae*, over and against that of the *uasa misericordiae*, should indeed be regarded as an unbearable injustice on God's part[194]. Augustine's interpretation, however, removes the Pauline passage in question from its broader context, viz. from the issue of the law, and of the relationship between Jews and Gentiles in the Church. He seems to be more concerned to emphasize how the term *massa* ought to be comprehended, namely the situation in which humanity found itself after Adam's fall. It is to this fallen lineage that the term *massa* is applied. Those passages in which the term seems to establish an identification with prelapsarian mankind (Adam)[195], or at least seems to allude to it[196], should also be

the term *consparsio* in the Pauline quotation of Rom 9,21, in the commentary that follows he employs the term *massa* (cf. Id., *Expositio quarumdam propositionum ex epistula ad Romanos* 54 [62] [CSEL, 84], p. 39; *De diuersis quaestionibus lxxxiii* 68,3 and 4 [CCL, 44A], pp. 177 and 178; *Contra duas epistulas Pelagianorum* 2,7,15 [CSEL, 60], p. 476) or both *consparsio* and *massa* indifferently (cf. Id., *De diuersis quaestionibus ad Simplicianum* 1,2,17-22 [CCL, 44], pp. 43-56 *passim*; *Enchiridion ad Laurentium* 25,99 [CCL, 46], pp. 102-103). See also Id., *Contra aduersarium Legis et Prophetarum* 2,4,17 [CCL, 49], p. 105; *Enarrationes in psalmos* 81,2 [CCL, 39], p. 1137; *Contra epistulam Parmeniani* 3,2,5 (CSEL, 51), p. 105; *De Genesi ad litteram* 6,9 (CSEL, 28), p. 182; *De correptione et gratia* 7,12 (CSEL, 92), p. 232. We do not believe, however, as Folliet argues, that "cette synonimie corrige... l'aspect négatif que l'on donne habituellement au mot *massa*" (G. FOLLIET, *"Massa damnata". "Massa sanctorum" chez saint Augustin*, in *RevAg* 33 [1992] 95-109, pp. 98-105).

193. As to a possible influence deriving from the Manichaean concept of βῶλος, see *infra*, pp. 396f.

194. In a letter addressed to Paulinus of Nola, after having quoted Rom 9,20-21, Augustine writes: "Haec massa si esset ita media, ut quem ad modum nihil boni ita nec mali aliquid mereretur, non frustra uideretur iniquitas, ut ex ea fierent uasa in contumeliam" (Augustine, *Ep.* 186,6,19 [CSEL, 57], p. 60).

195. Cf., for instance: "Illa massa primi hominis, cui merito mors debetur" (*Ibid.* 186,6,16, pp. 58-59).

196. Cf., for instance: "Massa in radice vitiata" (Id., *Sermo* 96,6 [PL, 38], c. 587). "Massa quae tota in Adam periit" (Id., *Tractatus in Euangelium Ioannis* 87,3 [CCL, 36], p. 545). "In uno homine tota est massa uitiata et tota damnata" (Id., *Contra secundum Iuliani responsionem imperfectum opus* 2,142 [CSEL, 85/1], pp. 265-266).

interpreted from an infralapsarian perspective. The reason for this is the assumption of solidarity in sin which Augustine improperly inferred from an erroneous latin translation of the Greek words ἐφ' ᾧ: "inasmuch as/because", which were rendered by "in whom" (*in quo* [Adam] *omnes peccauerunt*: Rom 5,12)[197]. It seems likely that besides a wrong translation, Augustine also relied on a commentary on Romans by an anonymous Roman author called Ambrosiaster[198]. Taking up his interpretation, the bishop of Hippo introduced a sort of ontological identification between Adam and his issue, with the result that their solidarity is not simply in the consequences of the sin of their forefather, but also in his *peccatum* itself. According to Augustine, Adam's *peccatum*, namely the disruption of his essential unity with God, and the consequent punishment (*poena peccati*) inflicted on the first man, are shared fully by his descendants. This viewpoint is consonant with the bishop of Hippo'

---

197. See *supra*, p. 244, n. 274. Since the meaning given by Augustine was not that intended by Paul, it would be misleading both to regard the former's doctrine of the *massa damnata* as "une conclusion théologique certaine", and to affirm that Augustine "au fond, n'a de personnel sur ce point que le relief de l'expression" (A. GAUDEL, *Notes complémentaires* 13 [BA, 9], pp. 345-346).

198. In his *Commentary on the Pauline epistles* (a work written in ca. 375), while commenting on Rom 5,12, Ambrosiaster writes: "*Propterea sicut per unum hominem peccatum in hunc mundum intrauit et per peccatum mors et sic in omnes homines petransiit, in quo omnes peccauerunt.... In quo*, id est in Adam, *omnes peccauerunt ....* Manifestum est itaque omnes in Adam peccasse *quasi in massa*, ipse enim per peccatum corruptus quos genuit, omnes nati sunt sub peccato" (Ambrosiaster, *Commentarius in XIII Epistulas Paulinas [Ad Romanos 5,12]* [CSEL, 81/1], pp. 163 and 165 *passim* [rec. g]). Cf. also his interpretation of Rom 9,21: "Cum omnes ex una atque eadem massa simus in substantia et cuncti peccatores" (*Ibid.* 9,21, pp. 327-329 *passim*). Ambrosiaster's interpretation of Rom 9,12 will be reproduced *uerbatim* by the bishop of Hippo (cf. Augustine, *Contra duas epistulas Pelagianorum* 4,4 [CSEL, 60], p. 528) who attributed it mistakenly to *sanctus Hilarius*. However, that Hilary of Poitiers did have a similar vision can be inferred from another quotation, this time indeed from Hilary's *Tractatus in psalmos* 118, litt. Tau 6 (cf. Augustine, *Contra secundam Iuliani responsionem imperfectum opus* 1,52 [CSEL, 85/1], p. 47). Ambrosiaster's influence on Augustine seems to be certain. "Den Kommentar des Ambrosiaster zum Römerbrief hat Augustin sicher gekannt" (A. MUTZENBECHER, *Einleitung*, in Augustine, *De diuersis quaestionibus ad Simplicianum* [CCL, 44], p. XXV). "Agostino era in possesso di un'ottima conoscenza dell'opera dell'Ambrosiaster" (N. CIPRIANI, *Un'altra traccia dell'Ambrosiaster in Agostino [De pecc. mer. et rem. 2,36,58-59]*, in Aug 24 [1984] 515-525, p. 524). See also A.A.R. BASTIAENSEN, *Augustin et ses prédécesseurs latins chrétiens*, in J. DEN BOEFT – J. VAN OORT (eds.), *Augustiniana Traiectina. Communications présentées au Colloque International d'Utrecht 13-14 novembre 1986*, Paris, 1987, 25-57, pp. 27-30. Beatrice shows through a few examples that, besides Ambrosiaster (who, together with Augustine, was the only western witness of this use), the metaphor of φύραμα – *massa* was present in the doctrinal and liturgical language of the East to indicate both Adam and his descendants. Cf., for instance: "Τὸ τοῦ Ἀδὰμ φύραμα" (Basil of Caesarea, *Ep.* 262,1 [ed. Courtonne, III], p. 120). See P.F. BEATRICE, *Tradux peccati. Alle fonti della dottrina agostiniana del peccato originale* (SPMed, 8), Milan, 1978, pp. 80-83.

interpretation of Rom 5,12: all men sinned in Adam and share in his guilt as well as in his punishment.

So for Augustine, the term *massa* becomes a forceful tool to describe the powerless, sinful situation in which humanity finds itself (*massa peccati*), together with the damnation that goes with it (*massa damnata*), and from which only those whom God's decree has predestined will be delivered. To describe this twofold reality in which humanity partakes since the fall of Adam, Augustine coined several expressions in combination with the term *massa*: *massa peccati*[199] or *peccatorum*[200], *massa luti, quod est massa peccati*[201], *massa offensionis*[202], *massa (originalis) iniquitatis*[203], *massa captiuitatis*[204], *massa irae*[205], *massa mortis*[206], *massa alienata*[207], *massa (tota) uitiata*[208], *massa perditionis*[209] or

---

199. "Sunt igitur omnes homines – quando quidem, ut apostolus ait, *in Adam omnes moriuntur*, a quo in uniuersum genus humanum origo ducitur offensionis Dei – una quaedam massa peccati supplicium debens diuinae summaeque iustitiae, quod siue exigatur siue donetur, nulla est iniquitas" (Augustine, *De diuersis quaestionibus ad Simplicianum* 1,2,16 [CCL, 44], pp. 41-42); "Tunc facta est una massa omnium, ueniens de traduce peccati et de poena mortalitatis" (*Ibid.* 1,2,20, p. 51); "Enim Adam peccauerat et omnis illa massa et propago peccati maledicta erat" (Id., *Contra Felicem manichaeum* 2,11 [CSEL, 25/2], p. 841); "... et traducem mortalitatis de parentibus duximus, et massa peccati, massa irae facti sumus" (Id., *Sermo* 22,9 [CCL, 41], p. 299); "Omnes in umbra mortis fuimus, omnes in massa peccati de Adam ueniente colligati tenebamur" (Id., *Sermo* 10,1 [Guelferbitanus], in *MA*, Vol. I, p. 472). See also, Id., *Sermo* 301,4 (PL, 38), c. 1383; *Enarrationes in psalmos* 101,1,11 (CCL, 40), p. 1435.

200. "Una est enim ex Adam massa peccatorum et impiorum, in qua et Iudaei et gentes remota gratia Dei ad unam pertinent consparsionem. Si enim figulus luti ex eadem consparsione facit aliud uas in honorem aliud in contumeliam,... sequitur ut ad unam consparsionem omnes pertinere intellegantur" (Id., *De diuersis quaestionibus ad Simplicianum* 1,2,19 [CCL, 44], p. 48). See also *Ibid.* 1,2,17, p. 43; Id., *De diuersis quaestionibus lxxxiii* 68,4 (CCL, 44A), p. 180; *Enarrationes in psalmos* 70, s.1,15 (CCL, 39), p. 952; *Ep.* 186,4,12 (CSEL, 57), pp. 54-55.

201. "Ex quo ergo in paradiso natura nostra peccauit..., et omnes una massa luti facti sumus, quod est massa peccati" (Id., *De diuersis quaestionibus lxxxiii* 68,3 [CCL, 44A], p. 177). See also Id., *Expositio quarumdam propositionum ex epistula ad Romanos* 54 (62 (CSEL, 84), p. 39; *De diuersis quaestionibus ad Simplicianum* 1,2,20 (CCL, 44), p. 51.

202. Cf. Id., *Ep.* 194,2,4 (CSEL, 57), p. 178.

203. Cf. *Ibid.* 194,8,38, p. 206; ID., *Enarrationes in psalmos* 70, s. 1,15 (CCL, 39), p. 952.

204. Cf. *Ibid.* 70, s. 2,10, p. 968.

205. Cf. Id., *Sermo* 22,9 (CCL, 41), p. 299; *Ibid.* 293,8 (PL, 38), c. 1333.

206. Cf. Id., *Enarrationes in psalmos* 70, s. 2,10 (CCL, 39), p. 968; *Ep.* 186,6,19 (CSEL, 57), p. 61; *Ibid.* 188,2,7, p. 125.

207. Cf. Id., *Sermo* 293,8, (PL, 38), c. 1333.

208. "Omnis massa in radice vitiata est" (*Ibid.* 96,6, c. 587). "Ubi dixit apostolus: *Ex uno omnes in condemnationem*, ipsam massam demonstrauit, quae tota vitiata ex Adam fluxit" (Id., *Contra secundam Iuliani responsionem imperfectum opus* 1,136 [CSEL, 85/1], p. 152). Cf. *Ibid.* 2,142, p. 266; *Ibid.* 4,40 (PL, 45), c. 1360.

209. Augustine makes up the expression by taking the two terms respectively from Rom 9,21 (*massa*) and from Rom 9,23 (*perditio*). The reading of *perditio* (*uasa irae quae*

perdita[210], *massa (iustae) damnationis*[211], *massa damnabilis*[212], *massa (tota) damnata*[213], *massa maledicta*[214].

Original sin, to which all men are bound (*obstricti*)[215], and the resulting universal damnation[216], thus form the background for the exercise of divine predestination and its counterpart, viz. reprobation. God's predestination, in fact, presupposes a primordial idea of "origin" (in this case Adam's "original" sin) in which all men share and from which they are excluded by God's election. It is as though this "origin" were an amor-

---

perfecta sunt in perditionem) instead of the Vulgata *interitus* (*uasa irae apta in* interitum) is already present in Augustine's early works (cf. Id., *Expositio quarumdam propositionum ex epistula ad Romanos* 55 [63] (CSEL, 84), p. 40; *De diuersis quaestionibus ad Simplicianum* 1,2,18 [CCL, 44], p. 46). With regard to the expression *massa perditionis*, see: "... a damnatione totius massae perditionis, quae per unum hominem facta est" (Id., *Tractatus in Euangelium Ioannis* 109,2 [CCL, 36], p. 620); "Vna erat massa perditionis ex Adam, cui non nisi supplicium debebatur" (Id., *Sermo* 23,13 [CCL, 41], p. 357). With regard to Jacob and Esau, Augustine writes: "Duo paruuli nati sunt. Si debitum quaeras, ambo tenet massa perditionis" (*Ibid.*). See also: Id., *Sermo* 71,1,3, in *RBen* 75 (1965) 65-108, p. 67; *Sermo* 18,2 [Guelferbitanus], in *MA*, Vol. I, p. 501; *De gratia Christi et de peccato originali* 2,29,34 (CSEL, 42), p. 194; 2,31,36, p. 195; *Contra duas epistulas Pelagianorum* 2,7,13 (CSEL, 60), p. 474; *Ibid.* 2,7,15, p. 477; *Ibid.* 4,6,16, p. 540; *Contra Iulianum* 3,4,10 (PL, 44), c. 707; *Ibid.* 5,4,14, c. 792; *Enchiridion ad Laurentium* 23,92 (CCL, 46), p. 98; *Ibid.* 25,99, p. 102; *Ibid.* 28,107, p. 107; *De correptione et gratia* 7,12 (CSEL, 92), p. 232; *Ibid.* 7,16, p. 236; *Ibid.* 9,25, p. 249; *Ibid.* 10,26, p. 250; *De dono perseuerantiae* 14,35 (PL, 45), c. 1014; *Contra secundam Iuliani responsionem imperfectum opus* 4,123 (PL, 45), c. 1421; *Ibid.* 4,131, c. 1428; *Ep.* 186,2,4 (CSEL, 57), p. 48; *Ibid.* 188,2,7, p. 125; *Ibid.* 214,3, p. 382.

210. Id., *Contra secundam Iuliani responsionem imperfectum opus* 3,16 (CSEL, 85/1), p. 467; *Ibid.* 4,2 (PL, 45), c. 1339.

211. Cf. Id., *Contra aduersarium Legis et Prophetarum* 1,51 (CCL, 49), p. 84; *Contra Iulianum* 5,4,14 (PL, 44), c. 793; *Ep.* 190,3,12 (CSEL, 57), p. 147; *Ibid.* 194,2,4, p. 178.

212. Cf. Id., *Sermo* 165,7,9 (PL, 38), c. 907; *Ep.* 194,6,30 (CSEL, 57), p. 199.

213. Cf., for instance: "Massa primae praeuaricationis merito damnata" (Id., *Contra aduersarium Legis et Prophetarum* 1,9 [CCL, 49], p. 42). "Vniuersa massa tamquam in uitiata radice damnata est" (Id., *De ciuitate Dei* 14,26 [CCL, 48], p. 450); *Ibid.* 15,1, p. 454; 21,12, p. 778; *Contra Iulianum* 6,1,2 (PL, 44), c. 821; *Enchiridion ad Laurentium* 8,27 (CCL, 46), p. 64; *Contra secundam Iuliani responsionem imperfectum opus* 1,141 (CSEL, 85/1), p. 160; *Ibid.* 2,142, p. 265; *Ibid.* 4,40 (PL, 45), c. 1360; *Ep.* 190,3,9 (CSEL, 57), p. 144; *Ibid.* 194,2,5, p. 179; 194,3,14, p. 187; 194,6,23, p. 194; 194,10,39, p. 207; *Sermo* 301,4 (PL, 38), c. 1383;

214. Id., *Contra Felicem Manichaeum* 2,11 (CSEL, 25/2), p. 840.

215. Before being an example of divine predestination, Jacob and Esau are an example of the universal inclusion in Adam's sin: "Ambo itaque gemini natura irae filii nascebantur, nullis quidem operibus propriis sed originaliter ex Adam uinculo damnationis obstricti" (Id., *Enchiridion ad Laurentium* 25,98 [CCL, 46], p. 101). "Sola enim gratia redemptos discernit a perditis, quos in unam perditionis concreauerat massam ab origine ducta causa communis" (*Ibid.* 25,99, p. 102).

216. In Augustine's vision the *massa damnata* "n'est qu'un corollaire du dogme du péché originel" (GAUDEL, *Notes complémentaires* 13 [BA, 9], p. 346).

phous sinful substance (a sort of *ur*-qualifying element) constituting the physical and moral structure of human beings[217]. Man has no right whatsoever to ask God the reason for this primordial sinful state, precisely as the vessel is not expected to ask the potter, who is shaping it, why it is being given that particular form rather than another one (cf. Rom 9,20-21)[218]. God chooses his elect from the *massa damnata* and predestines them to glory through his mysterious designs, so that if some vessels become recipients of mercy, it is only because of God's gratuitous grace[219]. This becomes all the more evident in the case of the *paruuli*: they are delivered from the *massae damnatio* thanks to the grace of Christ alone[220]. Thus, if some are saved (and the case of baptized infants who die shows this point clearly) it is not because they deserve salvation, nor because of some presumed merits, but only because God wants them to be saved, and bestows on them his gratuitous grace! On the other hand, if other people are going to be condemned, this does not depend on a presumed partiality (*acceptio*) on the side of God. No one could be singled out on the grounds of his own merits[221], for nobody is without sin. Thus, even if God decided to call nobody to salvation, their damnation would not be unjust[222], because, being a *massa damnata*, nobody can claim the right to be saved. So all men, without exception, deserve death and punishment. Their eventual salvation depends

217. "L'azione predestinatrice di Dio, in altri termini, presuppone, nel pensiero agostiniano, che vi sia come una sostanza amorfa peccaminosa nella quale l'uomo viene formato fin dalla nascita e che viene a costituire l'elemento connaturato e qualificante della sua struttura fisica e morale" (BEATRICE, *Tradux peccati* [n. 198], p. 76).

218. "Cum ergo meritum peccando amiserimus, et misericordia Dei remota nihil aliud peccantibus nisi aeterna damnatio debeatur, quid sibi uult homo de hac massa, ut Deo respondeat et dicat: 'Quare sic me fecisti?'. Si uis ista cognoscere, noli esse lutum, sed efficere filius Dei" (Augustine, *De diuersis quaestionibus lxxxiii* 68,3 [CCL, 44A], p. 177).

219. "La 'massa damnata' fonde... la pleine gratuité de la grâce et, par suite, de la prédestination" (THONNARD, *La prédestination augustinienne et l'interpretation de O. Rottmanner* [n. 74], p. 276).

220. Cf., for instance, Augustine, *Ep.* 190,3,10-12 (CSEL, 57), pp.145-147.

221. In one of his early commentaries on Paul, Augustine had proposed in a very radical way the principle that God does not make any exception (*acceptio*) with men, because He does not accept (*accipit*) any human person (face), *i e.*, his state of sinfulness: "Quales aliquando fuerint, id est, quia et ipsi peccatores fuerunt, nihil sua dicit interesse, quia Deus hominis personam non *accipit*, id est sine personarum *acceptione* omnes ad salutem vocavit non reputans illis delicta eorum" (Id., *Epistulae ad Galatas expositio* 12 [CSEL, 84], p. 66). See M.A. SMALBRUGGE, *La prédestination entre subjectivité et language. Le premier dogme moderne*, in *RTP* 127 (1995) 43-54, p. 48.

222. "Vnde etiamsi nullus liberaretur, iustum Dei iudicium nemo iuste reprehenderet" (Augustine, *De correptione et gratia* 10,28 [CSEL, 92], p. 253); "Tam multos liberat misericors Deus de tam debita perditione, ut si inde neminem liberaret, non esset iniustus" (Id., *De dono perseuerantiae* 8,16 [PL, 45], c. 1002).

exclusively on God's will[223]. The truth concerning decayed humanity, a truth that lies against the background of God's gratuitous election and salvation[224], was taken up by Augustine over and over again in his works. It became a sort of *Leitmotiv* which was not simply useful for the concept of liberating grace, but was also the expression of the sombre anthropology by which Augustine was eventually overcome.

It would be deeply unfair, however, to maintain that Augustine's term *massa* bears only a pejorative meaning[225]. On the contrary, more than once he uses *massa* positively, in a soteriological sense. Since Augustine's references in this respect are few, they are often undervalued in comparison with the negative application to which the word *massa* is generally attached, but it would be really unfair to neglect this complementary development[226]. Preaching on the Sunday of the Easter octave about the new life of the blessed (of which the *octavus dies* is a symbol) Augustine speaks in equivalent terms of the *massa purgata* and the *massa sanctorum*. He affirms that once the separation between the saints (wheat) and the reprobates (chaff) is accomplished, the multitude of saints (*massa sanctorum*) – which by now will have been turned into a *massa purgata* – will be gathered in the barn of heaven[227]. Likewise, in a sermon preached to the Christian community at Carthage in an anti-Donatist context, Augustine urges the faithful not to be demoralized with their present minority status. On the contrary, he encourages them to look ahead and nourish themselves with the thought of the eschatological times, when, after having purged the threshing-floor with his

---

223. See, for instance: "Quando autem Deus nulla merita nostra inuenit, sorte uoluntatis suae nos saluos fecit, quia uoluit, non quia digni fuimus" (Id., *Enarrationes in psalmos* 30,II, s. 2,2,13 [CCL, 38], p. 211).

224. It is most likely that the Platonic category of the world as prison, from which men are gratuitously delivered by grace, has influenced Augustine's thought.

225. This was, for example, Rottmanner's conviction: "...hat Augustinus als der erste das paulinische φύραμα = *conspersio, massa* (Rom. 9,21) nicht mehr in neutraler Bedeutung, sondern ausschliesslich im schlimmen Sinne der durch Adam verderbten und von Gott mit Recht verworfenen Menschheit aufgefasst und diese Auffassung constant festgehalten" (ROTTMANNER, *Der Augustinismus* [n. 77], p. 9).

226. See M.-G. MARA, *Agostino d'Ippona: "massa peccatorum", "massa sanctorum"*, in EAD., *Paolo di Tarso e il suo epistolario. Ricerche storico-esegetiche*, L'Aquila, 1983, pp. 130-147, pp. 134-146.

227. "Octavus ergo iste dies in fine saeculi novam vitam significat: septimus quietem futuram sanctorum in hac terra.... Iniqui ergo non ibi erunt: iam enim separabuntur. Tunc, tanquam massa purgata apparebit, veluti in area, multitudo sanctorum, et sic mittetur in horreum coeleste immortalitatis. Sicut enim frumentum prius ubi trituratur, ibi purgatur; et locus ubi frumenta pertulerunt trituram, ut a palea mundarentur, decoratur dignitate massae purgatae.... Sic ergo post ventilationem diei iudicii apparebit massa sanctorum, fulgens dignitate, praepotens meritis, et misericordiam liberatoris sui prae se gerens" (Augustine, *Sermo* 259,2 [PL, 38], c. 1197).

winnowing-fan, God will gather them as a multitude of saints so great that it will be impossible to number (cf. Rev 7,9). This multitude of the elect shall make up the *magna massa*, the *massa sanctorum*, the *massa purgata stans ad dexteram*[228]. The concept of *massa purgata* comes back in *Sermo* 259[229], in *Contra litteras Petiliani*[230] and in *Contra epistulam Parmeniani* – although here Augustine applies the expressions *massa purgata/purgatissima* and *massa purgati tritici*[231] ironically and polemically to the Donatists who considered themselves to be the Church of the pure. The same concept of purification, whose final aim is participation in the kingdom of heaven, is present in another of Augustine's sermons in which he reassures the faithful that at the last judgement the multitude of the chosen ones will be separated from the reprobates and gathered in the heavenly barn[232].

Furthermore, on the anniversary of the martyrs of Utica, called *Massa Candida*, Augustine comments on the true life which the martyrs have entered, viz. eternal life, and explains the meaning of the name *Massa Candida*: *massa* has to do with the multitude of the martyrs that on that occasion died for Christ, whereas *candida* indicates the splendour of their witness[233]. Moreover, the martyrs themselves are a further indication of how in the Church the good and the bad live together, side by side, and that even when the field seems to be covered only with chaff, an attentive eye can indeed also discover the presence of the multitude of wheat (*latet granorum massa*[234]). Its presence will be made manifest

228. "Aream video, grana quaero. Et vix videntur grana, quando area trituratur, sed futurum est ut ventiletur. Pauci ergo qui salvantur in comparatione multorum perditorum. Nam ipsi pauci magnam massam facturi sunt... Tanta massa processura est de hac area, ut impleat horreum caeli..... Haec est massa sanctorum. Quanta clariore voce dictura est area ventilata a turba naufragata malorum falsorumque christianorum, segregata a paleis ad ignem aeternum separatis... segregatis ergo omnibus damnandis, massa purgata stans ad dexteram..." (ID., *Sermo* 111,1 [ed. Lambot], in *RevBen* 57 [1947] 109-116, p. 115).

229. "Tunc tanquam massa purgata apparebit, veluti in area, multitudo sanctorum" (Id., *Sermo* 259,2 [PL, 38], c. 1197).

230. "Quasi uero uos iam sitis massa purgata et mel sincerum et eliquatum oleum et aurum purum uel ipsa species dealbati parietis" (Id., *Contra litteras Petiliani* 2,39,93 [CSEL, 52], p. 76).

231. Cf. Id., *Contra epistulam Parmeniani* 3,3,18 (CSEL, 51), pp. 122-123. See also the *grana purgatissima* (*Ibid.* 3,3,17, p. 121), and the following quotation: "Numquid, frater,..., in massa tritici purgata invenies stercus?" (ID. *Sermo* 254 [ed. Lambot], in *RB* 79, pp. 63-69, p. 64).

232. "in novissima ventilatione massa horreis debita declarabitur" (*Ibid.* 214,11 [PL, 38], c. 1071).

233. "si causa candida, et massa candida. Massa enim dicta est, de numeri multitudine; candida, de causae fulgore" (*Ibid.* 306,2). See also Id., *Enarrationes in psalmos* 49,9 (CCL, 38), p. 583; *Ibid.* 144,17 (CCL, 40), p. 1880.

234. Id., *Sermo* 311,10 (PL, 38), c. 1417.

thanks to persecutions, when the threshing-floor will be purged clean and the wheat revealed[235]. The same consideration, about appearance and reality, is applied to the Church that, like wheat in the midst of chaff, suffers all sorts of tribulations. However, from what seems to be chaff alone, a *magna massa* is going to be purified and made manifest[236]. The faithful must, therefore, be patient, because only at the end of time will the threshing-floor show clearly the multitude (*massa*) of the saints who are going to fill the barns of heaven[237]. Those who live faithfully and who are sustained by the grace of God, although many, are hidden among the reprobates, who are also many. Whereas the latter are going to perish, the *plenitudo massae* of the saints will one day be seated at the right hand of God[238].

Finally, a positive use of the term *massa*, combined with *societas*, can be found in a letter written by Augustine to count Bonifatius on the validity of baptism conferred by heretics. Augustine makes it clear that, even if one is baptized by heretics (*per stipulae ministerium*), it is the duty of the Church (*area*) to help the baptized (*frumenta*), so that, once they have been purified, they too may become part of the multitude of saints (*ad massae societatem perducantur*)[239]. Moreover, in Augustine's positive understanding of the term *massa* we also find the application of this expression to the whole of humanity. That same humanity that Adam had alienated from God is now reconciled to him through the mediation of Christ[240].

b) Certus numerus electorum

The theme of *massa damnata*, complemented by *massa purgata* and *massa sanctorum*, brings to our attention the problem of the mystery of God's inscrutable election. We have already seen above that if on the

235. "floruit Uticensis Massa Candida" (*Ibid.*).

236. "et ex hoc quod totum palea putatur, inde magna massa purgabitur" (Id., *Enarrationes in psalmos* 30,II, s. 2,3 [CCL, 38], p. 204).

237. "ipsam aream unde massa quae implebit horreum, processura est" (*Ibid.* 34, s. 1,10, p. 307). It is interesting to note that in the second commentary on this same psalm 34 the term *massa* is employed with a negative meaning.

238. "Multi sunt et illi qui stabunt ad dexteram. Non solum illi multi erunt qui stabunt ad sinistram, sed et ibi erit plenitudo massae ad dexteram constitutae" (*Ibid.* 47,10, p. 547). See also: "Nec una arista paleae transeat ad massam in horreo recondendam" (*Ibid.* 47,11, p. 547).

239. "Quanto potius in catholica Ecclesia etiam per stipulae ministerium frumenta purganda portantur, ut ad massae societatem mediante area perducantur" (Id., *Ep.* 98,5, [CSEL, 34/2], p. 527).

240. "Hac medietate reconciliatur Deo omnis generis humani massa ab illo per Adam alienata" (Id., *Sermo* 293,8 [PL, 38], c. 1333).

one hand God wishes all men to be saved, on the other, Augustine would argue, only some are "efficaciously" *(congruenter)*[241] called to share in the election of the predestined. As the evangelical words run: *Multi enim uocati, pauci uero electi* (Mt 20,16)[242]. Of course, there must be a reason, continues Augustine, "a certain hidden equity that cannot be searched out by any human standards of measurement"[243] but which, nevertheless, corresponds to God's just purpose and decree *(secundum propositum)*[244]. The election of Jacob (in contrast to the rejection of Esau) is a clear example of God's gratuitous choice, which is due exclusively to the liberality of his *propositum*[245] and to the riches of his wisdom[246]. Through the immutable decrees of his *praedestinatio per gratiam*[247], displayed according to his gratuitous mercy[248], God delivers those He wishes from the *massa originalis iniquitatis*[249], and sets them apart *ab illa originali damnatione*[250]. In fact, it is ultimately because of this original iniquity and damnation, on account of which all men are indebted to God, that mercy is withheld from Esau[251]. In this perspective

241. Cf. Id., *De diuersis quaestionibus ad Simplicianum* 1,2,13 (CCL, 44), pp. 37-38. In point of fact the *"vocatio congrua...* viene a identificarse con la *vocatio secundum propositum"* (J. OROZ RETA, *Predestinación, vocación y conversión según san Agustín*, in J.C. SCHNAUBELT – F. VAN FLETEREN [eds.], *Augustine: Second Founder of the Faith* [CollAug, 1], New York-Bern-Frankfurt a. M.-Paris, 1990, pp. 29-43, p. 33).

242. Augustine makes reference several times to this quotation. See, for instance: Augustine, *Ep.* 149,2,21 (CSEL, 44), p. 367; Id., *Sermo* 90,4 (PL, 38), c. 561; *Ibid.* 95,6, c. 583; Id., *Enarrationes in psalmos* 61,10 (CCL, 39), p. 780; *Ibid.* 77,21, p. 1083; Id., *De ciuitate Dei* 18,45 and 48 (CCL, 48), pp. 641 and 647; *De gestis Pelagii* 3,11 (CSEL, 42), p. 62; *Contra duas epistulas Pelagianorum* 2,10,22 (CSEL, 60), p. 483; *De correptione et gratia* 7,14 and 16 (CSEL, 92), pp. 234 and 237; *De praedestinatione sanctorum* 16,33 (PL, 44), c. 985.

243. "Alicuius occultae atque ab humano modulo inuestigabilis aequitatis" (Id., *De diuersis quaestionibus ad Simplicianum* 2,16 [CCL, 44], p. 41).

244. Id., *De correptione et gratia* 7,13-14 (CSEL, 92), pp. 233f.

245. "Electi sunt autem, quia secundum propositum vocati sunt: propositum autem, non suum, sed Dei" (*Ibid.* 7,14, p. 234).

246. Cf. Id., *Ep.* 194,2,5 (CSEL, 57), pp. 179-180.

247. *Ibid.* 194,8,34, p. 203. Worth noting is the past tense of the verb, referring to Jacob before his birth, and underlying God's eternal and immutable decrees: *"...erat in Dei praedestinatione per gratiam"* (*Ibid.*).

248. "Quid enim diligebat Iacob, antequam natus fecisset aliquid boni, nisi gratuitum misericordiae suae donum?" (*Ibid.*). See M.J. FARRELLY, *Predestination, Grace and Free will*, Westminster, Maryland, 1964, pp. 83ff.

249. "Intellegat Iacob ex illa massa originalis iniquitatis, ubi fratrem, cum quo habuit communem causam, uidet per iustitiam meruisse damnari, nonnisi per gratiam se potuisse discerni" (Augustine, *Ep.* 194,8,38 [CSEL, 57], p. 206).

250. "Quicumque ergo ab illa originali damnatione ista diuinae gratiae largitate discreti sunt" (Id., *De correptione et gratia* 7,13 [CSEL, 92], p. 233).

251. "Et quid oderat in Esau, antequam natus fecisset aliquid mali, nisi originale peccatum?" (Id., *Ep.* 194,8,34 [CSEL, 57], p. 203).

the attitude taken by God does not detract at all from his justice. The grace that He bestows on people does not always necessarily manifest itself as a *uera gratia*, namely as a grace of perseverance. The latter is reserved to the lucky few[252], to those who have been chosen by God to be the recipients of the gratuitousness of his gifts. Here Augustine introduces a typical conviction of his[253], that only a fixed number of people will be allowed to benefit by God's *uera gratia*. In further restricting the whole idea of election (even from a semantic point of view), Augustine makes a meaningful shift in emphasis. Rather than an open, future oriented call, marked by the gift of perseverance which sustains the elect, Augustine insists on a more static and limited meaning. The focus is on God's eternal decrees about the fixed number of the elect.

The formula *certus numerus* appears for the first time in 401, in a writing against the Donatists, viz. *De baptismo contra Donatistas*. Commenting on the words *hortus conclusus*, he applies the expression to those who have been predestined before the foundation of the world to be included in the fixed number (*certus numerus*) of the saints, viz. those who have been elected *secundum propositum*[254]. The formula reappears in the following years in some other works, where the same meaning is maintained, although against a different background. It is applied, for instance, to the good Christians who fear God and are faithful to his precepts, and who are still mingled here on earth with the bad ones, despite their already belonging to the heavenly Jerusalem[255]. It returns in Augustine's commentary on the miraculous catch, where the 153 fish are seen as the symbolic number of the elect[256]. It is employed again, in a letter

---

252. "Dando enim quibusdam quod non merentur, profecto gratuitam, et per hoc veram suam gratiam esse voluit: non omnibus dando, quid omnes merentur ostendit" (Id., *De dono perseuerantiae* 12,28 [PL, 45], cc. 1009-1010). Nothing prevents us from thinking that Augustine's conviction about the *pauci* who are going to obtain God's salvation is not only based on the logion of Mt 20,16, but is also the expression of his realistic approach to the life of the Christian communities, an approach corroborated by his pastoral experiences. Cf. A. ZUMKELLER, *Augustinus über die Zahl der Guten bzw. Auserwählten*, in *Aug* 10 (1970) 421-457, pp. 429ff.

253. "La expresión 'número fijo de elegidos'... no figura en ningún autor anterior a Agustín" (G. FOLLIET, *Certus est numerus electorum: de Agustín a Tomás de Aquino*, in *Augustinus* 43 [1998] 215-227, p. 221).

254. "in illis... iustis... in quibus est numerus certus sanctorum praedestinatus *ante mundi constitutionem* ... Numerus ergo ille iustorum qui *secundum propositum* uocati sunt" (Augustine, *De baptismo contra Donatistas* 5,27,38 [CSEL, 51], p. 294).

255. "Numerus certus est, pertinens ad illam caelestem Ierusalem.... christianos timentes, christianos fideles...; ipsi ad numerum pertinent" (Id., *Enarrationes in psalmos* 39,10 [CCL, 38], p. 433).

256. Cf., for instance: "In prima piscatione numerus piscium nullus dicitur; in ista post resurrectionem numerus piscium certus dicitur.... Ipsa est ecclesia sancta... ipsa erit in certo illo numero et definito, ubi iam nullus inuenitur peccator" (Id., *Sermo* 229, in

written to Paulinus of Nola[257], either to indicate the multitude of saints, or to indicate the elect God chooses in the light of his providential designs[258]. In the *De correptione et gratia*, after having used the generic expression *praedestinatorum numerus*[259], Augustine moves on to a more specific phrase which he formulates three times in a very apodictic manner, without leaving any doubts as to its meaning. The number of the elect/predestined, he states, is certain (*certus*) and fixed, and it excludes any addition or subtraction (*neque augendum, neque minuendum*)[260]. To further explain the radical content of this formula, viz. to reassert that the number of the elect is, in God's eyes, unchangeably fixed, Augustine employs the adjectives in the superlative form, thus speaking of *integerrimus/beatissimus*[261] and *certissimus et felicissimus numerus*[262]. A last mention of the *certus numerus* is made in the *De dono perseuerantiae*, where the elect are said to be purposely intermingled, according to God's inscrutable designs, with those who shall not persevere[263]. Finally, although aware that it is not given to us to know the exact number of those who have been predestined (a number which ultimately includes both angels and men[264]), Augustine believes that the figure is smaller than that of the *abundantia malorum*[265] and of the *filii*

MA, Vol. I, p. 489); "Miserunt *[retia]*, coeperunt: certus est numerus.... Certus numerus erit.... *Centum quinquaginta et tres pisces*, numerus est significans millia millium sanctorum atque fidelium" (*Ibid*. 248,3-4 [PL, 38], c. 1160); "Missa sunt retia in dexteram, nec poterant ea levare prae *multitudine piscium*. Et ibi dicta est multitudo: sed hic certus numerus, et multitudo et magnitudo.... Numerus ad sanctos pertinet, qui sunt regnaturi cum Christo" (*Ibid*. 251,2,2 c. 1168). See also, Id., *Tractatus in Euangelium Ioannis* 122,7 (CCL, 36), p. 672.

257. "Certus est ergo et in Dei praescientia praefinitus numerus ac multitudo sanctorum" (Id., *Ep*. 186,7,25 [CSEL, 57], p. 65).

258. "Omnipotenti Deo... non defuit utique consilium, quo certum numerum ciuium in sua sapientia praedestinatum etiam ex damnato genere humano suae ciuitatis impleret" (Id., *De ciuitate Dei* 14,26 [CCL, 48], p. 450).

259. Id., *De correptione et gratia* 12,36 (CSEL, 92), p. 263.

260. "Haec de his loquor, qui predestinati sunt in regnum Dei, quorum ita certus est numerus, ut nec addatur eis quisquam, nec minuatur ex eis.... Certum uero esse numerum electorum neque augendum neque minuendum. ... Certus est numerus" (*Ibid*. 13,39, p. 267).

261. "Numerus ergo sanctorum per Dei gratiam Dei regno praedestinatus, donata sibi etiam usque in finem perseuerantia, illuc *integer* perducetur, et illic *integerrimus* iam sine fine beatissimus seruabitur" (*Ibid*. 13,40, p. 269).

262. *Ibid*. 13,42, p. 271. Augustine makes it clear that belonging to the number of the elect is the guarantee of a great happiness.

263. "Deus autem melius esse iudicavit, miscere quosdam non perseveraturos certo numero sanctorum suorum" (Id., *De dono perseuerantiae* 8,19 [PL, 45], c. 1003). See also *Ibid*. 12,28 and 14,35, cc. 1009-1010 and 1014.

264. Cf. Id., *Enchiridion ad Laurentium* 9,28-29 (CCL, 46), pp. 64-65; *De ciuitate Dei* 14,26 (CCL, 48), p. 450.

265. Id., *Sermo* 26,13 (CCL, 41), p. 357.

perditionis[266], but equal to or even more than the number of the fallen angels (a number, however, which remains hidden to us too)[267]. All the same, the elect/predestined, who are fewer in comparison with those who shall perish, will make up a great mass (*magnam massam facturi sunt*)[268].

At the end of this short presentation, we cannot avoid a feeling of uneasiness about the way Augustine elaborates the concept of the *certus numerus electorum* in connection with his doctrine of predestination. We are somehow disturbed by what looks like a dualism; a fatalistic approach that divides humanity into two camps[269]. On one side the *certus numerus* of the elect, who are certainly going to be saved, and on the other the non-elect, who are certainly going to perish. They too make up (by subtraction) a *certus numerus*, in that, indirectly, also the number of the reprobates can be said to be decreed by God's immutable will, alongside the number of the elect. The latter, thanks to the *dona Dei* which are *sine mutatione stabiliter fixa*[270], receive the gift of perseverance, and even if they sin or turn away from God temporarily or rebel against him, it is certain that sooner or later they will return to him. The non-elect, on the contrary, even if they obey God temporarily, are not given the perseverance to obey until the end, for it is the judgement of God's will (*definita sententia uoluntatis Dei*) that they shall not be saved[271].

---

266. "Fuerunt ergo isti *[filii perditionis]* ex multitudine uocatorum; ex electorum autem paucitate non fuerunt" (Id., *De correptione et gratia* 9,21 [CSEL, 92], p. 243). See also "Tam multos autem creando nasci uoluit, quos ad suam gratiam non pertinere praesciuit, ut multitudine incomparabili plures sint eis, quos in sui regni gloriam filios promissionis praedestinare dignatus est" (Id., *Ep.* 190,3,12 [CSEL, 57], p. 146).

267. Cf. Id., *Enchiridion ad Laurentium* 9,29 (CCL, 46), p. 65; *De ciuitate Dei* 22,1 (CCL, 48), p. 807.

268. "Pauci ergo qui salvantur in comparatione multorum perditorum. Nam ipsi pauci magnam massam facturi sunt" (Id., *Sermo* 111,1 [ed. Lambot], in *RevBen* 57 [1947] 109-116, p. 115). "In comparatione namque pereuntium pauci sunt, qui salvantur; sine comparatione autem pereuntium et ipsi multi sunt" (Id., *Contra secundam Iuliani responsionem opus imperfectum* 2,142 [CSEL, 85/1], p. 265). See also, Id., *Contra Cresconium* 3,66,75 (CSEL, 52), p. 480; *Ep. ad Catholicos de secta Donatistarum* (seu *De unitate Ecclesiae*) 14,36 (CSEL, 52), pp. 278f.; *Sermo* 88,19,22 (PL, 38), c. 551.

269. See *infra*, pp. 388f.

270. Augustine, *De praedestinatione sanctorum* 16,33 (PL, 44), c. 985.

271. "Quamvis ergo ita se habeat de praedestinatione definita sententia voluntatis Dei, ut alii ex infidelitate, accepta voluntate obediendi, convertantur ad fidem, vel perseverent in fide; caeteri vero qui in peccatorum damnabilium delectatione remorantur, si et ipsi praedestinati sunt, ideo nondum surrexerunt, quia nondum eos adiutorium gratiae miserantis erexit: si qui enim nondum sunt vocati, quos gratia sua praedestinavit eligendos, accipient eamdem gratiam, qua electi esse velint et sint; si qui autem obediunt, sed in regnum eius et gloriam praedestinati non sunt, temporales sunt, nec usque in finem in eadem obedientia permanebunt" (Id., *De dono perseuerantiae* 22,58 [PL, 45], c. 1029).

*c) The Mediation of Christ and the Church in the Light of Predesti-
nation*

Although Augustine voiced his conviction that individual predestination and election should be understood within a christological (Christ is
the "accomplished" example of predestination[272]), as well as a corporate
perspective (the *massa sanctorum*, the *numerus certus electorum*), he
also introduced an insoluble tension between his concept of eternal predestination, and the place and role of the mediation of Christ and the
Church. The tension has its roots in his belief that predestination has
ultimately to do with believers who are set apart "individually" by
God's merciful decree, over against those who, also on an individual
basis, are destined to be damned for eternity. It is precisely this individ-
ualistic principle, lying at the heart of Augustine's doctrine of predestination and election, that makes it difficult for us to understand how it
can be related to the corporate mystery of the Church as the mystical
body of Christ or, to use one of Augustine's central ideas, to the notion
of the *totus Christus*[273].

Because of this apparent contradiction within the Augustinian theological system, at the end of the 19th century Augustine's concept of predestination became the target of harsh criticism. It is sufficient to recall,
for instance, the words of the great scholar A. von Harnack who, emphasizing this irreconcilability, affirms that the Augustinian idea of predestination, and its related concept of the *numerus electorum*, destroys any
notion of the Church as an institution of salvation and transforms her
into a useless thing[274]. And indeed, if predestination has to do with
God's decree electing his chosen ones on an individual basis, then
belonging to the Church of Christ does not seem to be decisive. There
are scholars, however (especially Catholics) who believe that the Augustinian doctrine of predestination does not undermine the significance of
the Church as the body of Christ and sacrament of salvation for the
world, since it is through her that predestination comes eventually into

---

272. See *supra*, pp. 165ff.

273. See T.J. VAN BAVEL – B. BRUNING, *Die Einheit des "Totus Christus" bei
Augustinus*, in C.P. MAYER – W. ECKERMANN (eds.), *Scientia Augustiniana. Festschrift P.
Dr. theol. Dr. phil. Adolar Zumkeller OSA zum 60. Geburtstag* (Cass., 30), Würzburg,
1975, pp. 43-75; G. TEJERINA ARIAS, *La eclesiología agustiniana del* Christus Totus, in
Agustiniana 42 (2001) 1139-1179.

274. "Somit sprengt der Gedanke der Prädestination jeden Kirchenbegriff... und
entwertet alle Veranstaltungen Gottes, das Heilsinstitut und die Heilsmittel: der *numerus
electorum* ist keine Kirche" (A. VON HARNACK, *Lehrbuch der Dogmengeschichte*, Bd. III,
4th ed., Tübingen, 1920 [Anastatischer Neudruck], p. 150).

effect[275]. However, it is precisely Augustine's restricted notion of pre-destination that causes the problem.

If we turn to the bishop of Hippo himself, we must note, first of all, that he never seems to feel the need to define the coexistence of his the-ory of predestination with the centrality of Christ's mediation and the need for the Church. Obviously, the fact that he did not deepen *ex pro-fesso* the relationship between predestination and the Church, is an indi-cation that he did not believe them to be incompatible. What is certain is that Augustine would never conceive of predestination apart from the doctrine of the Church, and apart from the sacrament of baptism, through which one is incorporated into Christ and the Church[276]. If only those who have been predestined to salvation by divine grace are admit-ted into the eternal kingdom of God, the bishop of Hippo also held that the same grace works through baptism to allow men to share in the redemption of Christ. Augustine, however, is not always consistent on this point. At times, he even teaches that the grace of Christ the Media-tor can reach and save people even without baptism and outside the cor-porate reality of the mystical body of Christ, which is the Church. This is the case, for instance, with the just of the Old Testament who (although outside the New Covenant) lived a righteous life before the coming of Christ. Augustine numbers them among the inhabitants of the heavenly Jerusalem because they took part in the Son who is (with the Father) immutable and co-eternal Wisdom[277]. What is of great interest

275. Cf., for instance: "Diese Prädestinationslehre hing auf engste zusammen mit der Kirchenlehre. Denn die Kirche was ja das Kommen des Gottesreiches, und die Erwählung geschah durch die Kirche und ihre Sakramente, die Bewahrung der Erwählung vollzog sich in der Kirche" (P. Simon, *Aurelius Augustinus. Sein geistiges Profil*, Paderborn, 1954, p. 114). See also, G. de Plinval, *Aspects du déterminisme et de la liberté dans la doctrine de saint Augustin*, in *REAug* 1 (1955) 345-378, pp. 367-369; S.J. Grabowski, *The Church. An Introduction to the Theology of St. Augustine*, St. Louis, MO – London, 1957, pp. 622-640; R. Bernard, *La prédestination du Christ total selon saint Augustin*, in *RechAug* 3 (1965) 1-58.

276. "It is true that the Bishop does not synthesize the doctrine of predestination and the Church in their mutual relationship, but his doctrine presumes that the predestined on earth are incorporated into the Church, the body of Christ" (Grabowski, *The Church* [n. 275], pp. 626-627).

277. Cf., for instance: "Idem ipse est Filius Dei Patri coaeternus et incommutabilis sapientia, per quam creata est uniuersa natura et cuius participatione omnis rationalis anima fit beata. Itaque ab exordio generis humani quicumque in eum crediderunt eumque utcumque intellexerunt et secundum eius praecepta pie iusteque uixerunt, quando libet et ubi libet fuerint, per eum procul dubio salui facti sunt" (Augustine, *Ep.* 102,2,11-12 [CSEL, 34/2], p. 554); "Ante aduentum Domini nostri Iesu Christi, quo humilis uenit in carne, praecesserunt iusti, sic in eum credentes uenturum, quomodo nos credimus in eum qui uenit. Tempora uariata sunt, non fides" (Id., *Tractatus in Euangelium Ioannis* 45,9 [CCL, 36], p. 392); "Vel ante diluuium, uel inde usque ad legem datam, uel ipsius legis tempore non solum in filiis Israel, sicut fuerunt prophetae, sed etiam extra eundem

here is that Augustine, besides the objective aspect, viz. Christ the Mediator, underlines as well the importance of the subjective dispositions of
faith, viz. the righteousness of the ancient just. Unfortunately he did not
fully work out these intuitions. For Augustine, the Incarnation of Christ
constitutes a dividing line. Only those who have lived justly before the
coming of Christ could enjoy his "complementary" mediation (the participation in his wisdom). After the Incarnation of Christ, however, baptism becomes the *conditio sine qua non* for the attainment of salvation.
Consequently, the emphasis on the necessity of the sacrament of regeneration was further absorbed into Augustine's theological system, even
to excluding from salvation those infants, born of Christian parents, who
die before baptism[278]. Moreover, the fact that he presents Christ as the
praeclarissimum lumen praedestinationis[279] and the most luminous
praedestinationis exemplum[280], viz. as the key to the mystery of predestination, is undoubtedly of paramount importance, but once again
restricted in purpose. For Augustine it means that the predestined Christ,
viz. the Incarnate Christ[281], is associated with all the members of his

populum, sicut fuit Job" (Id., *De gratia Christi et de peccato originali* 2,24,28 [CSEL,
42], p. 187). The following passage, written by Augustine in one of his last works, is also
of great interest: "Nam res ipsa, quae nunc christiana religio nuncupatur, erat et apud
antiquos nec defuit ab initio generis humani, quousque ipse Christus ueniret in carne,
unde uera religio, quae iam erat, coepit appellari christiana" (Id., *Retractationes* 1,13,3
[CCL, 57], p. 37). Cf. also: Id., *De catechizandis rudibus* 19,33 (CCL, 46), pp. 157-158;
De peccatorum meritis et remissione et de baptismo paruulorum 1,11,13 and 2,29,47
(CSEL, 60), pp. 14 and 118; *Ep.* 102,12 and 15 (CSEL, 34/2), pp. 554 and 557-558; *Ibid.*
190,6 (CSEL, 57), p. 141; *De ciuitate Dei* 18,47 (CCL, 48), p. 645; *Contra duas epistulas Pelagianorum* 1,21,39 and 3,4,8.11 (CSEL, 60), pp. 456-457 and 494.497-498; *Sermo*
4,11 (CCL, 41), p. 28; *Contra secundam Iuliani responsionem imperfectum opus* 1,124
(CSEL, 85/1), p. 138. See A. SOLIGNAC, *Le salut des païens d'après la prédication
d'Augustin*, in G. MADEC (ed.), *Augustin prédicateur (395-411). Actes du Colloque International de Chantilly (5-7 septembre 1996)* (CEAug.SA, 159), Paris, 1998, pp. 419-428;
J. WANG TCH'ANG-TCHE, *Saint Augustin et les vertus des païens*, Paris, 1938.

278. The fact that Augustine, who had worked out a solution for the pre-Christian just
Jews and heathens alike, did not fully work out this intuition about the possibility of being
saved also on the part of those who remain outside the Church once the Incarnation of
Christ occurred, is commented on by Sage as follows: "Il émet des principes, il n'en tire
pas les conséquences; il en était plus ou moins dissuadé par la controverse pélagienne"
(A. SAGE, *La volonté salvifique universelle de Dieu dans la pensée de saint Augustin*, in
RechAug 3 [1965] 107-131, p. 125).

279. Augustine, *De praedestinatione sanctorum* 15,30 (PL, 44), c. 981.

280. Id., *De dono perseuerantiae* 24,67 (PL, 45), c. 1033. See E. BRAEM, *Christus als
model en genadebron van onze predestinatie volgens Sint Augustinus*, in *Aug(L)* 4 (1954)
353-361.

281. It should be clear that the object of predestination is not the divine Logos, but the
Son of God made flesh: "Recte quippe dicitur non praedestinatus secundum id quod est
Verbum Dei, Deus apud Deum. Vtquid enim praedestinaretur, cum iam esset quod erat,
sine initio, sine termino sempiternus? Illud autem praedestinandum erat, quod nondum

body (the Church) who have been predestined in him and through him[282]. He saves and incorporates into himself all those (and *only* those) who have been elected to belong to him before the world was created[283]. They are inseparable, because the same grace works in both the head and the body[284]. It is quite clear that according to the bishop of Hippo, Christ's mediation does not ultimately reach out to humanity as a whole (witness the fate of unbaptized children as well as of heathens who will never hear of Christ), or even to the Church as a whole. The elect are the only predestined ones. If belonging to the Church is a necessary condition for enjoying Christ's redemption, the effectiveness of this gift is thus restricted to those who have been predestined, on an individual basis and within the corporate framework of the *totus Christus*[285], to share infallibly in the grace of salvation that God's inscrutable decree has prepared for them.

It is unfortunate that, although the notion of the mediation of Christ and the Church occupies a central place in Augustine's theology of grace[286], he did not further deepen the significance of his doctrine of predestination in close connection with and in the light of the existing relationship between Christ and the Church. Such connection remains obscure and as such leaves us with a fundamental question that Augustine did not answer: how is it that God predestines only some people to be saved through the mediation of Christ's redemptive action and his

erat, ut sic suo tempore fieret, quemadmodum ante omnia tempora praedestinatum erat ut fieret. Quisquis igitur Dei Filium praedestinatum negat, hunc eumdem filium hominis negat" (Augustine, *Tractatus in Euangelium Ioannis* 105,8 [CCL, 36], p. 607).

282. "Sicut ergo praedestinatus est ille unus, ut caput nostrum esset: ita multi praedestinati sumus, ut membra eius essemus" (Id., *De praedestinatione sanctorum* 15,31 [PL, 44], c. 983). "Et illum ergo et nos praedestinavit *[Deus]*; quia et in illo ut esset caput nostri, et in nobis ut eius corpus essemus" (Id., *De dono perseuerantiae* 24,67 [PL, 45], c. 1034). "Aliter enim est in nobis tamquam in templo suo, aliter autem quia et nos ipse sumus, cum secundum id quod ut caput nostrum esset, homo factus est, corpus eius sumus" (Id., *Tractatus in Euangelium Ioannis* 111,6 [CCL, 36], pp. 632-633).

283. "Elegit Deus in Christo ante constitutionem mundi membra eius: et quomodo eligeret eos, qui nondum erant, nisi praedestinando?" (Id., *De praedestinatione sanctorum* 18,35 [PL, 44], c. 986). "Neminem tamen venire ad Christum, nisi cui fuerit datum, et eis dari qui in illo electi sunt ante constitutionem mundi" (Id., *De dono perseuerantiae* 14,35 [PL, 45], c. 1014). See also *Ibid.* 24,67, cc. 1033-1034.

284. "C'est, en effet, la *même grâce* qui fait du Christ le Saint, qui fera de nous des saints. Des saints *en lui*.... C'est la même grâce qui, de la tête, se répand dans les membres pour les sanctifier et les diviniser" (HOMBERT, *Gloria gratiae* [n. 57], p. 497).

285. "C'est donc le Christ total qui est le premier sujet de la prédestination divine. La prédestination individuelle n'existe qu'à l'intérieur de la prédestination communautaire des élus, solidaires entre eux comme les membres d'un même corps, et liés au Christ comme à la tête de ce corps" (*Ibid.*, p. 490).

286. See G. REMY, *Le Christ médiateur dans l'œuvre de saint Augustin*, T. I, Lille-Paris, 1979, pp. 737-780.

Church? Why is it that He allows a conspicuous part of humanity to be left outside the reach of this saving mediation? Furthermore, we cannot help but be unfavourably struck by the fact that the place and role of Christ as Mediator and Saviour of mankind and, as a consequence, that of the Church (his mystical body and "sacrament" of salvation) do not appear to be decisive, as if they were "preempted" by God's eternal decrees. A precious chance was missed, whereby Augustine could have attempted to "explain" divine agency, with regard to humanity, by focussing on the crucified and risen Christ (and his Church) as the "meeting point" where the encounter between God's universal salvific will and man's response is made possible.

d) The Problem of Universal Salvation: The Interpretation of 1 Tim 2,4

Augustine's belief that man's merits and adhesion to God are themselves the result of God's operative grace called for a new insight into the *mode* by which divine grace is dispensed to humanity, and about the actual extent of man's commitment. The depiction of God's sovereign and absolute grace, acting at the core of Christian faith and life[287], drove Augustine to a stern but (within his theological system) logical conclusion about a restricted dispensation of grace. In his eyes, this was supported by the undeniable fact that a portion of humanity was not reached by the benefits of divine grace; for instance, the heathens who have not heard the preaching of the Gospel, or have refused it, and the infants who die before receiving the baptismal regeneration[288]. Besides,

---

287. We might as well recall that the centrality of the gratuitousness of God's grace was expounded by the bishop of Hippo by means of two other truths which, beside pointing to the sovereignty of gratuitous mercy, can also be regarded as fundamental. These two truths are original sin and the necessity for every man, even when already justified through baptism, to ask forgiveness for his own actual/personal sins. Up to one of his last works, the *De dono perseuerantiae*, Augustine does not cease to point out the fundamental place occupied by this threefold truth. "Nam tria sunt, ut scitis, quae maxime adversus eos catholica defendit ecclesia: quorum est unum, gratiam Dei non secundum merita nostra dari; quoniam Dei dona sunt, et Dei gratia conferuntur etiam merita universa iustorum: alterum est, in quantacumque iustitia, sine qualibuscumque peccatis in hoc corruptibili corpore neminem vivere: tertium est, obnoxium nasci hominem peccato primi hominis, et vinculo damnationis obstrictum, nisi reatus, qui generatione contrahitur, regeneratione solvatur" (Id., *De dono perseuerantiae* 2,4 [PL, 45], c. 996). See also, Id., *Contra duas epistulas Pelagianorum* 3,8,24 and 4,7,19 (CSEL, 60), pp. 516 and 542; *Contra Iulianum* 3,1,2 [PL, 44], c. 702.

288. See for instance: "Hi qui non per illam *[grace]* liberantur, siue quia audire nondum potuerunt siue quia oboedire noluerunt siue etiam, cum per aetatem audire non possent, lauacrum regenerationis quod accipere possent, per quod salui fierent, non acceperunt, iuste utique damnantur, quia sine peccato non sunt, uel quod originaliter traxerunt uel quod malis moribus addiderunt" (Id., *De natura et gratia* 4,4 [CSEL, 60], pp. 235-

concepts such as *massa damnata* and *certus numerus electorum* makes it
even more difficult to imagine how Augustine could still believe in a
divine will oriented towards the salvation of all mankind. If God has
sent his only Son into the world, so that the world might find salvation
through him (cf. Jn 3,17), how is it that He allows so many to perish by
witholding the means (the gift of faith and final perseverance) by which
they would find salvation and glory?[289] Does not such a restriction do
away with the doctrine of universal salvation?[290] Since the soteriological
perspective is all-embracing, it is obvious that such questions are not
peripheral to Christian faith and theology, and it is therefore important to
see how the bishop of Hippo faced the resulting challenges, and what
solutions he suggested.

To begin with, we may look at a biblical passage which Augustine
used quite often, particularly during the Pelagian controversy: *Si unus
pro omnibus mortuus est, ergo omnes mortui sunt* (2 Cor 5,14)[291]. As it
appears from the context, this passage was not only quoted to support
his theological argument about the physical and spiritual "death" caused
by original sin (a death which all those who come into the world experience), but also to stress the universality of Christ's redemption, intrinsically related to the universality of original sin. In harmony with this
Pauline quotation, Augustine assumes that it is precisely on account of
the universality of redemption that the universality of original sin must
be posited[292]. The Son of God came into the world and took up human

236). Cf. also *Ep.* 194,2,4 (CSEL, 57), pp. 178-179; *Enchiridion ad Laurentium* 24,97-
27,103 (CCL, 46), pp. 100-105 *passim*; *Contra Iulianum* 4,8 (PL, 44), cc. 758-760.
   289. Cf. Id., *Enchiridion ad Laurentium* 24,95 (CCL, 46), p. 99.
   290. Rahner, for instance, is convinced that this is the ultimate outcome: "Der späte
Augustinus... kennt in der theologischen Theorie für die *massa damnata* der Erbsünde
keinen allgemeinen Heilswillen Gottes mehr" (K. RAHNER, *Heilswille Gottes, Allgemeiner H.G.*, in *LTK* 5 [1960] 165-168, p. 166). See also: "S'il *[Augustine]* affirme
que le Rédempteur doit juger tout l'univers, parce qu'il a donné son sang pour tout
l'univers, nous ne devons, nous ne pouvons pas entendre cette dernière formule sans une
restriction désolante" (PONTET, *L'exégèse de S. Augustin prédicateur* [n. 135], p. 495).
   291. See, for instance: Augustine, *De peccatorum meritis et remissione et de baptismo paruulorum* 1,27,44 (CSEL, 60), p. 43; Id., *Contra Iulianum* 6,4,8; 15,48; 26,83
(PL, 44), cc. 825; 850; 874; *De ciuitate Dei* 20,6 (CCL, 48), p.707; *Contra secundam
Iuliani responsionem imperfectum opus* 1,117 and 2,30.133.134.163.175 (CSEL, 85/1),
pp. 134 and 184, 259, 260, 284, 295; *Ibid.* 5,9; 6,21 (PL, 45), cc. 1439; 1548. Cf. also
the passages with the quotation of Mt 1,21: "...et vocavit nomen eius Iesum; ipse enim
salvum faciet populum suum a peccatis eorum" (cf. Id., *De nuptiis et concupiscentia*
2,35,60 [CSEL, 42], p. 319; *Sermo* 174,7,9 [PL, 38], c. 944; *Ibid.* 293,11, c. 1334).
   292. Sul piano dell'argomentazione teologica il passaggio va... dall'universalità della
redenzione all'universalità del peccato" (A. TRAPÈ, *S. Agostino*, in A. DI BERARDINO
[ed.], *Patrologia*, Vol. III: *Dal Concilio di Nicea [325] al Concilio di Calcedonia [451].
I Padri latini*, Turin, 1978, p. 410). See also: "S'il a permis le péché originel et l'uni-

flesh with no other goal than that of enlightening, delivering and saving all men who are under the shadow of death (cf. Lc 1,79). That is why he died on the cross for all, no one excluded[293]. Yet, even though Augustine would have wished to dwell without reserve on the concept of universal salvation[294], his mind eventually took him elsewhere. It is no doubt true that Christ shed his blood for everybody but, would affirm Augustine, *super alios perdendos, super alios mundandos: super perdendos iustus, super mundandos misericors*[295]. Overwhelmed by the task of defending his doctrine of sovereign and gratuitous grace, he failed to integrate the concept that, for God, there are no boundaries or limits to the salvation of humanity. This is evident from the different amount of consideration that the two issues of Christ's Redemption and Adam's fall receive respectively[296], and above all from Augustine's peculiar interpretation of a classical scriptural *locus* in which the claim of God's universal salvation is clearly stated: *Deus omnes homines uult saluos fieri* (1 Tim 2,4)[297].

verselle damnation qui en est la conséquence *de jure*, c'est que, d'abord et dès lors, il avait en fait décidé de tout restaurer dans le second Adam" (A. GAUDEL, *Notes complémentaires* 13 [BA, 9], p. 346).

293. "quibus appareat Dominum Iesum Christum non aliam ob causam in carne uenisse ac forma serui accepta factum oboedientem usque ad mortem crucis, nisi ut hac dispensatione misericordiosissimae gratiae omnes, quibus tamquam membris in suo corpore constitutis caput est ad capessendum regnum caelorum, uiuificaret, saluos faceret, liberaret, redimeret, inluminaret, qui prius fuissent in peccatorum morte" (Augustine, *De peccatorum meritis et remissione et de baptismo paruulorum* 1,26,39 [CSEL, 60], p. 37). Augustine goes as far as speaking of a redemption in which even Judas was envisaged: "...nec agnouit pretium quo ipse a Domino redemtus erat" (ID., *Enarrationes in psalmos* 68, s. 2,11 [CCL, 39], p. 925).

294. In a letter to Evodius, for instance, Augustine showed his uneasiness that there might be people who are going to be damned, and he expressed the wish that he would be happy if he could prove that Christ descended to hell to save all those he would find there. But in saying this he eventually avowed that, in point of fact, because of a mysterious divine disposition, a portion of humanity is destined to be damned (cf. ID., *Ep.* 164,2,4 [CSEL, 44], pp. 524-525).

295. Id., *Sermo guelferb.* 10, in *MA*, p. 472. Schwager is very severe towards Augustine's position: "Nie... lehrt er *[Augustine]* eine alle einzelnen Menschen umfassende Heilswirkung des Kreuzes" (R. SCHWAGER, *Der wunderbare Tausch. Zur Geschichte und Deutung der Erlösungslehre*, München, 1986, p. 126).

296. See, for instance, the few paragraphs that, in his *Enchiridion*, Augustine devoted to Redemption (cf. Id., *Enchiridion ad Laurentium* 9,30-32 [CCL, 46], pp. 65-67), compared to those devoted to the Fall and its consequences (cf. *Ibid.* 24,94-26,100, pp. 99-103).

297. See L. DOUCET, *L'exégèse augustinienne de I Tim. 2,4: "Dieu veut que tous les hommes soient sauvés"*, in *BFCL* 73 (1984) 43-61; REMY, *Le Christ médiateur dans l'œuvre de saint Augustin* [n. 286], pp. 675-682; SAGE, *La volonté salvifique universelle de Dieu dans la pensée de saint Augustin* [n. 278], pp. 107-131; J. TURMEL, *Histoire de l'interprétation de I Tim. II,4*, in *RHLR* 5 (1900) 385-415.

If we turn to the context of this affirmation, we shall realize that Paul is talking about the duty of Christians to pray for all men, since all men are the object of God's salvific will. Proclaimed over against the Gnostic claim that salvation can only be reached through gnosis[298], this principle strongly indicates that salvation depends rather on God's salvific will, that will which has become effective through the incarnation of Christ "who gave himself as a ransom for all" (1 Tim 2,6). Believers are called to proclaim this universal salvific will of God, and freely to co-operate with it, making salvation the motive of their life and actions. The Greek Fathers were of course in a position to understand Paul correctly. Reading 1 Tim 2,4 ([Θεὸς], ὃς πάντας ἀνϑπώπους ϑέλει σωϑῆναι) literally, they would interpret it instinctively in a nuanced way, made possible by the flexibility of the Greek language. There are in fact two Greek verbs to indicate the action of willing. The first, ϑέλω, points to a firm desire, whereas the second, βούλομαι, expresses the decision to bring to effect that which has been desired. The application of this nuance to God's universal salvific will makes it possible to posit in God an "antecedent" will (viz. that all men be saved), as well as a "consequent" will, by which He brings into effect his decision, taking account of man's own will, choices and actions[299]. God wants all men to be saved, but this will of his shall not become effective if they refuse to respond positively and co-operate with him. The same interpretation, resting on the possibility for man to refuse salvation, can be found also in some Latin Christian writers[300].

Augustine, by contrast, interpreted the Latin verb *uelle* as referring exclusively to God's absolute will (cf. Ps 113,11: *Omnia quaecumque uoluit, fecit*), and opted for a univocal solution. Rather than trying to understand the meaning of Paul's statement about God's universal salvific will, he was at pains to reconcile the Apostle's words with his

298. Cf. L. OBERLINNER, *Die Pastoralbriefe. 1: Kommentar zum ersten Timotheus brief* (HTK, 11/2/1/), Freiburg-Basel-Wien, 1994, pp. 13ff.

299. See *supra*, p. 307 n. 19.

300. See, for instance: "Vult enim Deus omnes homines salvos fieri, sed si accedant ad eum. Non enim sic vult, ut nolentes salventur, sed vult illos salvari, si et ipsi velint" (Ambrosiaster, *Commentarius in xiii epistulas Paulinas [Ad Timotheum 2,4]* 9 [CSEL, 81/3], p. 260). "Videbat *[Redemptor]* enim laborantes non posse sine remedio saluari et ideo medicinam tribuebat aegris, ideo omnibus opem sanitatis detulit, ut quicumque perierit mortis suae causas sibi adscribat, qui curari noluit, cum remedium haberet quo posset euadere, Christi autem manifesta in omnes praedicetur misericordia, eo quod ii qui pereunt sua pereant neglegentia, qui autem saluantur secundum Christi sententiam liberentur, qui omnes homines uult saluos fieri" (Ambrose, *De Cain et Abel* 2,3,11 [CSEL, 32/1], p. 338). "Vult salvari omnes.... Sed quia nullus absque propria voluntate salvatur (liberi enim arbitrii sumus), vult nos bonum velle" (Jerome, *Commentarii in iv epistulas Paulinas [ad Ephesios]* 1,vers.11 [PL, 26], c. 485).

conviction that the salvation brought about by Jesus Christ does not reach all humanity, as is proved by infants and heathens/pagans who die without baptismal regeneration. This standpoint of the bishop of Hippo does not take us by surprise, of course, for it was the logical outcome of his doctrine of the absolute sovereignty and gratuity of divine grace. Once the extreme consequences were applied (viz. the concept of a restricted predestination and election) and regarded as decisive in order to save God's justice and the gratuitousness of his gifts, Augustine found himself in the awkward predicament of being forced to modify the literal interpretation of 1 Tim 2,4 so that it could fit in with his predestinarian view. So he sacrificed the more traditional exegesis of 1 Tim 2,4 and chose to interpret it quite flexibly in order to accomodate it to his view of a restricted dispensation of grace[301].

Once again, the watershed in Augustine's approach to the issue of universal salvation is the personal "revelation" experienced in dealing with God's grace and election in his *De diuersis quaestionibus ad Simplicianum*, when he was enlightened over the meaning of 1 Cor 4,7. Before this work, 1 Tim 2,4 did not present any difficulty. As to its interpretation Augustine aligned himself with the traditional understanding. Thus, in his *Expositio quarumdam propositionum ex epistula ad Romanos*, where he points to the necessity for Christians to be conscientiously subject to legal authority (cf. Rom 13,5) by referring to the words of 1 Tim 2,4, he states that God wants all men to be saved, even those who hold authority or are in a high position, and who may act against the interests of the Christians[302]. What Augustine ultimately stresses is that God's salvific will might not always be efficacious because of a deficit in man's co-operation. God wishes, as it were, to save man

---

301. "Il *[Augustin]* acquit la conviction qu'entre l'interprétation reçue et la doctrine de la gratuité de l'élection divine, il y avait une opposition irréductible, et qu'il fallait sacrifier l'une à l'autre. Ce fut l'interprétation du texte qui fut sacrifiée" (TURMEL, *Histoire de l'interpretation de I Tim. II,4* [n. 297], p. 393). "On peut dire que le théologien sacrifie à sa thèse doctrinale le sens obvie du texte paulinien" (REMY, *Le Christ médiateur dans l'œuvre de saint Augustin* [n. 286], p. 675). "I *Tim.*, II,4 est parole d'Écriture. Quand Augustin l'évoque..., il la plie, avec parfois une déconcertante subtilité" (SAGE, *La volonté salvifique universelle de Dieu dans la pensée de saint Augustin* [n. 278], p. 109). Pontet defines Augustine's exegesis of 1 Tim 2,4 as "rétrécissante" (PONTET, *L'exégèse de S. Augustin prédicateur* [n. 135], p. 494, n. 197), whereas Rist, with regard to Augustine's interpretation of the same passage, speaks of a "perverse reading" (cf. RIST, *Augustine on Free Will and Predestination* [n. 149], p. 438).

302. Cf. Augustine, *Expositio quarumdam propositionum ex epistula ad Romanos* 66 (74) (CSEL, 84), p. 46; Id., *Epistulae ad Galatas expositio* 28 (CSEL, 84), pp. 93-94.

303. See BOUBLÍK, *La predestinazione* (n. 3), pp. 124f; K. FLASCH, *Logik des Schreckens. Augustinus von Hippo De diversis quaestionibus ad Simplicianus I 2* (Excerpta classica, Bd. VIII), Mainz, 1990, p. 79.

through man. But the ill will or the bad conscience of the latter may jeopardize God's wish to save everybody.

Augustine's exegesis of 1 Tim 2,4 underwent a significant change in his works written after the *De diuersis quaestionibus ad Simplicianum*, namely after the bishop of Hippo had made up his mind about a *de facto* non-universal salvific will on the part of God[303]. In the *De spiritu et littera* (412), for instance, the Pauline quotation is recalled against the background of the origin of the *uoluntas credendi*. If, argues Augustine, this originates from human nature (of which God is the creator), how is it that not everybody is endowed with it? And if it is a gift of God, why is it not offered to all, since He wants all men to be saved? Although the immediate aim of the bishop of Hippo is to counteract the Pelagian emphasis on *liberum arbitrium*, his reference to 1 Tim 2,4 is introduced to ask if God's will to save all men does not eliminate human free will. The emphasis is on the efficacy of grace, on which God's salvific will ultimately depends.

A letter to Paulinus of Nola (ca. 414) shows a further shift in the interpretation of 1 Tim 2,4. There Augustine was confronted with a precise question from his fellow bishop: if God wants to save all men, why – asks Paulinus – according to Rom 11,28, was the enmity of the Jews towards the gospel of Jesus responsible for the Gentiles' coming to faith? Did not God have the power to bring to faith both Jews and Gentiles?[304] In answering this question Augustine introduces an important distinction. By a rhetorical device he affirms that God's call to become members of Christ is addressed to people *ex omni genere hominum*, viz. to people "representing" *all human races*. The fact that such call is not addressed to all men (*omnibus hominibus*) is indicative of his conviction that not all men are called to become members of Christ, and that not all are saved through him, although no one is excluded from this initial perspective[305]. It is clear that, rather than the universality of salvation, it is the role of Christ's mediation that he emphasizes[306], a mediation which reaches out to *some* people from all races, but not to *all* people from all races.

304. Cf. Paulinus of Nola, *Ep.* 121,2,11 (among the Augustinian letters) (CSEL, 34/2), pp. 731-732.

305. Cf. Augustine, *Ep.* 149,2,17 (CSEL, 44), p. 364. This same interpretation, stressing the *genus hominum*, can be found also in Id., *Sermo* 304,3,2 (PL, 38), c. 1396.

306. "Pour Augustin, le salut est universel en ce sens qu'il n'est tributaire d'aucune considération ethnique et charnelle, tout en étant éminemment électif et mystérieux dans son principe divin" (REMY, *Le Christ médiateur dans l'œuvre de saint Augustin* [n. 286], p. 372).

In the *Contra Iulianum* (420/421), 1 Tim 2,4 is referred to in the context of the initiative of salvation which, according to Julian, must be ascribed to man, whereas according to Augustine it belongs to God. In order to counter Julian's viewpoint the bishop of Hippo emphasizes the expression *Deus uult*, rather than the word *omnes*. Since God's will is absolute and does not depend on man's initiative (which is in fact forestalled by divine grace), the word *omnes* must be understood as meaning *multi*, namely *all those* who are going to be actually saved by God's mercy[307]. The *omnes* of 1 Tim 2,4 as well as the *omnes* of Rom 5,18 (*Per unius iustificationem in omnes homines ad iustificationem uitae*) are thus understood in a restricted manner[308]. The point at stake is that any initiative in the direction of salvation belongs to God's absolute will, whose fulfilment, for Augustine, is certain, and cannot be frustrated by man's free will. Once again, this change of exegesis was supported by Augustine's conviction that not all men are saved, a conviction which was corroborated by the specific case of heathens/pagans who do not embrace Christian faith, and of infants who die before being baptized. It is evident, however, that, rather than trying to interpret 1 Tim 2,4 objectively, Augustine was preoccupied by opposing Julian's view with his own staunch belief about the absolute gratuity of grace[309].

The explanation developed in the *Enchiridion ad Laurentium* (421/422) deserves special attention because it represents Augustine's mature solution to the problem of God's universal salvific will. Here too, rather than explaining 1 Tim 2,4 according to Paul's intention, he is more preoccupied by saving the absolute transcendence and infallibility of God's plans within the framework of sovereign grace. The fact that not all men are actually saved cannot simply be ascribed to the ill will of those who refuse to be saved. If it were so, it would mean that God's will were deficient, and that it could be easily jeopardized by man's free will. God's will, on the contrary, is *certa et immutabilis et efficacissima*[310].

---

307. Cf. Augustine, *Contra Iulianum* 4,8,42-44 (PL, 44), cc. 759-760.

308. "Quod apostolicum testimonium si eo modo intelligendum putas, ut dicas *omnes* positos esse pro *multis*, qui iustificantur in Christo (multi quippe alii non vivificantur in Christo): respondebitur tibi, sic etiam illic ubi dictum est, *Omnes homines vult salvos fieri, et in agnitionem veritatis venire; omnes* positos esse pro *multis*, quos ad istam gratiam vult venire. Quod multo convenientius propter hoc intelligitur dictum, quia nemo venit, nisi quem venire ipse voluerit" (*Ibid.* 4,8,44, c. 760).

309. "La réponse est pertinente, s'il s'agit de l'objection de Julien; elle l'est moins, s'il s'agit de l'interpretation de I Tim. II,4.... Fidèle à lui-meme, Augustin interprète I Tim. II,4 en référence avec l'absolue gratuité de la grâce du Christ" (SAGE, *La volonté salvifique universelle de Dieu dans la pensée de saint Augustin* [n. 278], p. 114).

310. Augustine, *Enchiridion ad Laurentium* 24,95 (CCL, 46), p. 99. See also: "...dum tamen credere non cogamur aliquid omnipotentem uoluisse fieri, factumque non

Thus, argues Augustine, salvation depends exclusively on God, both with regard to children (who, lacking the use of free will, could not possibly choose salvation) and to adults (whose will to be saved is prepared by God himself: *Praeparatur uoluntas a Deo*: Pr 8,35, LXX). Against the traditional understanding that God wants to save all men if they, in their turn, want to be saved, Augustine interprets 1 Tim 2,4 in two ways. Firstly, he emphasizes the verb *uult*, in connection with the necessity for prayer[311], in order to affirm that God saves those *He wants* to save[312]. This does not mean, continues Augustine subtly, that there is nobody whom God does not want to save, but that there are no men who could possibly be saved other than those whom God wants to save[313]. Secondly, he stresses the term *omnes*, interpreting it, once again, according to the restricted meaning of *omne hominum genus*[314], by which he meant that God chooses his elect among all races and from different conditions of life.

As in the above works, so also in the *De correptione et gratia* Augustine keeps himself at a distance from the natural and obvious sense of 1 Tim 2,4, and interprets the term *omnes* as all those who have been predestined, and who, as such, represent all mankind[315]. The same idea is taken up in the *De praedestinatione sanctorum* where, once again, Augustine does not deny the principle of God's universal salvific will, but restricts it in its actual realization. Remembering Jn 6,45 (*Omnis qui audiuit a Patre et didicit, uenit ad me*), he gives the following example: "Just as, then, we speak correctly when we say of some teacher of

esse" (*Ibid.* 27,103, p. 105). "Voluntas Dei semper inuicta est" (Id., *De spiritu et littera* 33,58 [CSEL, 60], p. 216).

311. The necessity of praying that all men may be saved is also a proof, in Augustine's eyes, that salvation depends on God rather than on man's free will. Cf. Id., *De ciuitate Dei* 22,2 (CCL, 48), p. 808.

312. "Tanquam diceretur nullum hominem fieri saluum nisi quem fieri ipse uoluerit" (Id., *Enchiridion ad Laurentium* 27,103 [CCL, 46], p. 104).

313. "Non quod nullus sit hominum nisi quem saluum fieri uelit, sed quod nullus fiat nisi quem uelit" (*Ibid.*).

314. "Omnes homines *omne hominum genus* intellegere possumus" (*Ibid.* 27,103, p. 105).

315. "Ita dictum est: *Omnes homines uult saluos fieri*, ut intelligantur omnes praedestinati quia omne genus hominum in eis est" (Id., *De correptione et gratia* 14,44 [CSEL, 92], p. 272). It is interesting to note that Ianuarianus' letter to the monastic community of Hadrumetum reflects the Augustinian view about a restricted form of salvation. Commenting on 1 Cor 15,21-22 (*Sicut enim in Adam omnes moriuntur, sic et in Christo omnes uiuificabuntur*), he writes: "... hoc iam non ad omnes homines pertinet, sed ad illos omnes qui per eius gratiam salvabuntur: multi sunt enim qui sine fide Christi moriuntur" (*Ep. Ianuariani* [ed. Morin], in *RevBen* 18 [1901] 243-255, p. 236). A similar restricted explanation of 1 Tim 2,4 in Prosper shows also the latter's dependence on his heros, Augustine. Cf. Prosper, *Ep. ad Rufinum* 13,14 (PL, 51), c. 85.

literature who is the only one in a city, 'This person teaches literature to everyone here', not because everyone learns, but because no one of those who learn literature learns it except from him, so we say correctly, 'God teaches everyone to come to Christ', not because everyone comes to him, but because no one comes to him in any other way (*non quia omnes ueniunt, sed quia nemo aliter uenit*)"[316]. Finally, in the *De dono perseuerantiae* the issue of God's universal salvation is not tackled by an exegesis of 1 Tim 2,4, but it takes the form (*sub contrario*) of the following question: *Cur non omnibus detur Dei gratia*[317]?

There is no doubt that this variety of restricted interpretations given to 1 Tim 2,4[318], which are unacceptable from an exegetical point of view, respond to the theologian's (and not the exegete's) preoccupation of safeguarding the omnipotence of God in the framework of the doctrine of absolute grace and predestination[319]. Only from this perspective can we fully understand (but not justify) Augustine's position. The lack of one definitive interpretation remains, in fact, an indication of his uneasiness to reconcile the traditional (literal) meaning of 1 Tim 2,4 with his own theological doctrine of sovereign grace and predestination[320]. It was, above all, an attempt to lay the foundation of his belief that 1 Tim 2,4 could not possibly contain the affirmation that God wants all men to be saved by an absolute will. If that were the case, then all men would be certainly saved, but since in reality many find themselves otherwise (*e.g.*, the unbaptized children and the heathens), Augustine concludes, it means that *de facto* God's grace of salvation is not offered to all. The chief methodological fault in Augustine's approach is that he moves from the level of a general, metaphysical principle, viz. God's universal salvific will, to the pragmatic level of its realization in history[321], at least

---

316. Augustine, *De praedestinatione sanctorum* 8,14 (PL, 44), c. 971.
317. Cf. Id., *De dono perseuerantiae* 8,16 (PL, 45), c. 1002.
318. "1 Tim 2,4 wird zwar auf verschiedene Weise, immer aber restriktiv erklärt" (GRESHAKE, *Gnade als konkrete Freiheit* [n. 26], p. 222).
319. As Saint-Martin rightly points out, "ayant à faire non oeuvre d'exégète, mais de théologien, le saint docteur était préoccupé de ne pas infirmer par telle interprétation, tel autre point, non moins acquis, de sa doctrine, en particulier, la gratuité absolue de la prédestination" (J. SAINT-MARTIN, *Prédestination. III. La prédestination d'après les Pères latins, particulièrment d'après saint Augustin*, in *DTC* 12/1 [1935] 2832-2896, c. 2889). Augustine approaches the question "non pas en exégète,..., mais en apologiste des droits de Dieu" (CAYRÉ, *La Prédestination dans Saint Augustin* [n. 117], p. 56). "Se remettre avec lui *[Augustine]* dans cette perspective théocentrique est le seul moyen de le comprendre exactement" (J. RIVIÈRE, *Notes complémentaires* n. 48, *BA* 9, pp. 409-411, p. 410).
320. "Ce verset gêne sa pensée théologique; il se débat contre lui sans parvenir à en avoir raison" (PONTET, *L'exégèse de S. Augustin prédicateur* [n. 135], p. 144).
321. "Saint Augustin n'écarte pas la volonté salvifique universelle, il l'interprète à sa manière éminemment réaliste" (SAGE, *La volonté salvifique universelle de Dieu dans la*

in the way he "imagines" that God's salvific will happens concretely. For Augustine, in fact, it is a *perspicua ueritas*[322] that only the predestined are saved.

5. DOES AUGUSTINE'S CONCEPT OF PREDESTINATION ENTAIL A PRAEDESTINATIO GEMINA?

If Augustine's dependence on Paul for issues such as God's absolutely free initiative, and the gratuity and necessity of grace is not a problem, his dualistic approach to God's plans, based on the *certus numerus praedestinatorum* (and *damnatorum*), is. Such a dualism, which juxtaposes God's mercy and God's justice, predestination and abandonment, not only jeopardizes the biblical intuition of the universality of salvation (viz. a salvation offered to all) but it undermines the notion of the universal mediation of Christ, the significance of the gospel as an instrument of the universal call to salvation, and the place and role of the Church as a *sacramentum* of this call.

Augustine, as we have seen, posits a strained relationship between divine mercy and divine justice; between a God who positively predestines some people to salvation but allows others to perish. This is based on the assumption that God's will is shown either in doing something (*faciendo*) or in allowing something to happen (*sinendo*)[323]. Nothing happens without God's will allowing it (*praeter eius uoluntatem*), even if some things go against his will (*contra eius uoluntatem*)[324], such as sin. Even then, God leaves man free, making it clear that the responsibility for the course of action he has chosen, viz. to commit sins, lies in him alone. Man's sinfulness is always a result of voluntary action. It is in this light that Augustine understands the hardening of Pharaoh's heart (cf. Es 7,3: *Ego indurabo cor Pharaonis*). The *obduratio* is not so much the outcome of God's intervention as of Pharaoh's voluntary choice, of

---

pensée de saint Augustin [n. 278], p. 119). What is problematic, however, is precisely "la manière dont il a essayé de se représenter sa réalisation dans l'histoire en pensant 'sauver' la grâce en affirmant: la preuve qu'elle est vraiment telle, c'est que Dieu ne la donne pas à tous" (DOUCET, *L'exégèse augustinienne de I Tim. 2,4* [n. 297], p. 51). See also, V. GROSSI, *La predestinazione in S. Agostino*, in *DSBP* 15: *Elezione-Vocazione-Predestinazione*, Rome, 1997, pp. 341-347, p. 350.

322. Augustine, *Ep.* 217,6,19 (CSEL, 57), p. 417.

323. "Non ergo fit aliquid nisi omnipotens fieri uelit, uel sinendo ut fiat, uel ipse faciendo" (Id., *Enchiridion ad Laurentium* 24,95 [CCL, 46], p. 99).

324. "Propterea namque magna opera Domini exquisita sunt in omnes uoluntates eius, ut miro et ineffabili modo non fiat praeter eius uoluntatem quod etiam contra eius fit uoluntatem, quia non fieret si non sineret, nec utique nolens sinit sed uolens" (*Ibid.* 26,100 [CCL, 46], p. 103).

his previous demerits and *infidelitas*[325], to which God responds by with-holding his mercy[326]. The example of Pharaoh is used by Augustine to show that God does not stop men choosing a sinful life, if they wish, but, according to his mysterious designs, He precludes many of them from receiving his help, once they have chosen evil. In other words, God does not always arrange the circumstances of the sinful man's life in such a way that, after he has freely chosen to sin, he may repent of his evil doing and choose the good instead. Free to sin (*necessitas peccandi*), but left helpless with regard to a possible conversion, these people are destined to be reprobates. Only when God predestines a man to be saved, is his will irresistibly attracted to the good, and his salvation assured[327].

This view, however, seems to be lacking coherence. First of all, at the level of wording, Augustine is not consistent in applying the term *praedestinatio* to the elect. In some places, in fact, he speaks also of the "predestination of the damned" as if it were something positively willed by God. In this we find several expressions which are used either in an active sense (when they are referred to God's agency), such as *praedestinauit ad poenam*[328], *praedestinauit ad aeternam mortem*[329]; or in a passive way (when man is referred to as the object of God's action), such as

325. "Nam de Pharaone facile respondetur prioribus meritis quibus adflixit in regno suo peregrinos, dignum effectum cui obduraretur cor" (Id., *De diuersis quaestionibus lxxxiii* 68,4 [CCL, 44A], p. 179); "Non autem quisquam potest dicere obdurationem illam cordis immerito accidisse Pharaoni, sed iudicio Dei retribuentis incredulitati eius debitam poenam.... sed quia dignum se praebuit, cui cor obduraretur priore infidelitate" (Id., *Expositio quarumdam propositionum ex epistula ad Romanos* 54 [62] [CSEL, 84], p. 37); "Vt ergo tale cor haberet Pharao, quod patientia Dei non moueretur ad pietatem, sed potius ad inpietatem, uitii proprii fuit" (Id., *Quaestionum in Heptateuchum* 2,18 [CCL, 33], p. 76); "Ac per hoc et Deus induravit per iustum iudicium, et ipse Pharao per liberum arbitrium" (Id., *De gratia et libero arbitrio* 23,45 [PL, 44], c. 911); "*[Deus]* obdurat, digna retribuens" (Id., *De praedestinatione sanctorum* 8,14 [PL, 44], c. 971).

326. "Nec obdurat Deus impertiendo malitiam, sed non impertiendo misericordiam" (Id., *Ep.* 194,3,14 [CSEL, 57], p. 187).

327. God's grace transforms and activates the human will in those who are predestined: "Intelligant si filii Dei sunt, spiritu Dei se agi, ut quod agendum est agant; et cum egerint, illi a quo aguntur gratias agant; aguntur enim ut agant, non ut ipsi nihil agant" (Id., *De correptione et gratia* 2,4 [CSEL, 92], p. 221). "The conclusion is unavoidable – writes O'Daly – that, for Augustine, divine grace is irresistible, in the sense that it is not within our power, if we are predestined, to reject it" (G. O'DALY, *Predestination and Freedom in Augustine's Ethics*, in G. VESEY [ed.], *The Philosophy in Christianity*, Cambridge, 1989, pp. 85-97, p. 92).

328. "Ut... impleret ipse *[Deus]* quod uoluit, bene utens et malis tanquam summe bonus, ad eorum damnationem quos iuste praedestinauit ad poenam, et ad eorum salutem quos benigne praedestinauit ad gratiam" (Augustine, *Enchiridion ad Laurentium* 26,100 [CCL, 46], p. 103).

329. Id., *De natura et origine animae* 4,11,16 (CSEL, 60), p. 396.

praedestinati ad mortem[330], *praedestinati in aeternum ignem*[331], *praedestinata (...) aeternum supplicium subire*[332]. Though rare, these expressions should not be regarded as a slip of Augustine's pen, for they are clear evidence that he employed the same term *praedestinatio* to indicate both the predestined to salvation and the "predestined to damnation". In that case God is not merely a *relictor* but also a *damnator*[333].

This confusing use of the term *praedestinatio*, applied to election and reprobation alike, may give rise to the conviction that Augustine thought of and taught about a *praedestinatio gemina*[334], but it may also be taken, more simply (in our opinion), as an implicit proof of the *cul de sac* he found himself in because of his theory of predestination, and as an indication of his inability to give an acceptable justification for it. His preoccupation with continually stressing the antithesis between the two destinies[335], has eventually induced him to ignore their (implicit) interplay. We must, however, admit that the context in which the above expressions are employed, and the consistency of Augustine's thought on the subject, do not leave any doubt about Augustine's refusal to think that God may positively and actually lead a creature to commit sin. Moreover, the "levels" (in logical modality) on which he discusses predestination/election and reprobation/non-election are different[336]. Whereas predestination to grace or to life eternal is located in God's "merciful" omnipotence, which positively causes the salvation of the elect, reprobation or

---

330. Id., *De ciuitate Dei* 22,24 (CCL, 48), pp. 851-852.

331. *Ibid.* 21,24, p. 789.

332. Speaking about humanity as being divided in *dua genera*, Augustine continues: "...quas etiam mystice appellamus ciuitates duas, hoc est duas societates hominum, quarum est una quae praedestinata est in aeternum regnare cum Deo, altera aeternum supplicium subire cum diabolo" (*Ibid.* 15,1, p. 453).

333. "Verum tamen omnipotenti Deo..., uoluntatum autem bonarum adiutori et remuneratori, malarum autem relictori et damnatori, utrarumque ordinatori, non defuit utique consilium..." (*Ibid.* 14,26, p. 450).

334. This was, for instance, Calvin's view: "La prédestination *ad damnationem* qu'a professée Calvin est un cancer qui s'est développé à partir des textes augustiniens, mais aucunement la pensée de l'évêque d'Hippone" (HOMBERT, *Gloria gratiae* [n. 57], p. 314).

335. It is the opinion of Thonnard, who writes: "Peut-être est-ce le souci de l'antithèse qui l'a poussé à employer le même mot 'praedestinavit'.... Ce que Dieu, en sa justice insondable, veut positivement ('praedestinavit') c'est la sanction du péché; mais ce péché, il le permet et le punit sans le vouloir positivement ni le prédestiner" (F.-J. THONNARD, *Notes complémentaires* 52 [BA, 22], pp. 829-830).

336. It should be clear by now that in the eyes of Augustine, reprobation was in fact the result of non-election: "Es handelt sich streng genommen nicht um eine *reprobatio*, sondern um eine *non-electio*,... um ein *deseri*, um ein Sich-selbst-überlassen-werden, d. h. aber ein Belassenwerden in der Situation, die unser Sündersein gerechterweise verdient" (DIEM, *Augustins Interesse in der Prädestinationslehre* [n. 140], p. 367).

predestination to death is placed in "divine" justice[337]. The latter is activated by man's sinful behaviour (the actual sins committed by the believer's free and perverse will) as well as by unforgiven original sin (as in the case of unbaptized children and heathens/pagans)[338]. On the one hand, therefore, God is the *misericordiosissimus gratiae largitor* towards those He has "predestined to eternal life", whilst on the other He is the *iustissimus supplicii retributor* of those who are "predestined to eternal death" on account of their sinfulness[339]. Augustine would certainly contend that the ultimate cause of "predestination to death" must be located in the sinners themselves and in their deliberate choice for evil[340]. God's punishment is but the demonstration (*documentum*) of his infallible righteousness and justice towards those not predestined to salvation, as well as, *in negativo*, the demonstration of the gratuitous election of those who have instead been predestined to salvation[341].

If we may agree that damnation is the just punishment of those who have freely chosen to adhere to sin, and that God cannot be named as its direct cause[342], we must however concede that in another sense God too

337. "Es ist darum ungenau, bei Augustin von einer, 'doppelten Prädestination' zu sprechen, weil er die Erwählung und die Nicht-Erwählung gar nicht auf der gleichen Ebene erörtert. Während dort Gottes Ehre allein das Thema sein kann, muß hier des Menschen Verantwortlichkeit notwendigerweise zum Thema werden" (*Ibid.*, p. 369).

338. Those who are condemned to perish are normally identified with these categories of people. Cf., for instance, the siding of those "qui originali peccato multa addunt malae uoluntatis arbitrio" with the "multi paruuli, qui tantum modo uinculo peccati originalis obstricti sine gratia mediatoris ex hac luce rapiuntur" (Augustine, *Ep.* 190,3,12 [CSEL, 57], p. 147).

339. "quos praedestinauit ad aeternam uitam misericordiosissimus gratiae largitor, qui est et illis quos praedestinauit ad aeternam mortem iustissimus supplicii retributor" (Id., *De natura et origine animae* 4,11,16 [CSEL, 60], p. 396).

340. "God punishes those 'predestined to death' because they are sinners, but he does not help them to sin in order to punish them" (RIST, *Augustine on Free Will and Predestination* [n. 149], p. 428).

341. "Hoc est gratiae Dei non solum adiutorium, uerum etiam documentum, adiutorium scilicet in uasis misericordiae, in uasis autem irae documentum; in eis enim ostendit iram et demonstrat potentiam suam, quia tam potens est bonitas eius, ut bene utatur etiam malis, et in eis notas facit diuitias gloriae suae in uasa misericordiae, quoniam quod ab irae uasis exigit iustitia punientis, hoc uasis misericordiae dimittit gratia liberantis. Nec beneficium, quod quibusdam gratis tribuitur, appareret, nisi Deus aliis ex eadem massa pariter reis iusto supplicio condemnatis quid utrisque deberetur ostenderet" (Augustine, *Contra duas epistulas Pelagianorum* 2,7,15 [CSEL, 60], p. 476). See also: "Haec sunt magna opera Domini, exquisita in omnes uoluntates eius, et tam sapienter exquisita ut cum angelica et humana creatura peccasset, id est, non quod ille sed quod uoluit ipsa fecisset, etiam per eandem creaturae uoluntatem qua factum est quod creator noluit, impleret ipse quod uoluit, bene utens et malis tamquam summe bonus, ad eorum damnationem quos iuste praedestinauit ad poenam, et ad eorum salutem quos benigne praedestinauit ad gratiam" (Id., *Enchiridion ad Laurentium* 26,100 [CCL, 46], p. 103).

342. "Numquid *[Deus]* eligeret impios et immundos?" (Id., *De praedestinatione sanctorum* 18,35 [PL, 44], c. 986).

is inevitably called into question, in that, ultimately, He is the one who "allows" evil to thrive and to attract so many[343]. The only possible option left to Augustine was to try to integrate the concept of predestination in the general doctrine of divine providence. It was his persuasion that beside allowing evil to exist (for that would not exist at all if God did not allow it) and sinners to sin, God, in his merciful designs, can also draw something good out of evil[344]. Augustine states this general principle several times, painstakingly distinguishing between the will through which God allows sinful actions to come about, and the will through which God applies his justice by punishing those who have attached themselves to evil. Yet, such an explanation is not entirely convincing, especially because (in our opinion) it fails to take into account the "dark" side of the whole question, namely: why the possibility of expiation is not offered to the reprobates? Why is such an inescapable doom allotted to them, without any further chance to win salvation being offered them?

The non-predestined stand out, as it were, as a challenge to God's power to draw good out of evil, for such a power seems to be ultimately "restricted" to the elect, whereas it remains a sort of "aesthetical" operation with regard to the individual non-elect. As far as their actual status is concerned, in fact, they are bypassed by this operation, which remains extrinsic and ineffective. They are simply not touched by it. And if their loss is to any avail, it is as a demonstration of the mercy accorded to the *electi*[345]. Subordinated to the exaltation of the elect, the reprobation of

---

343. See, for instance: "Nullus daemonum aut hominum agat inique, nisi diuino eodemque iustissimo iudicio permittatur" (Id., *De ciuitate Dei* 20,1 [CCL, 48], p. 700); "Nihil enim fit, nisi quod aut ipse facit, aut fieri ipse permittit" (Id., *De dono perseuerantiae* 6,12 [PL, 45], c. 1000); "Nihil enim prorsus fit, nisi quod aut ipse facit aut fieri ipse permittit" (Id., *Ep.* 2,8 [ed. Divjak] [CSEL, 88], p. 16); "Omnino ista *[peccata]* non fierent, nisi ab omnipotente permitterentur,... ita tu confitere facienda non esse, quae a iusto puniantur; ut non faciendo quae punit mereamur ab eo discere cur permittit esse quae puniat " (Id., *De continentia* 6,15 [CSEL, 61], p. 158).

344. "Nec sineret bonus *[Deus]* fieri male, nisi omnipotens et de malo facere possit bene" (Id., *Enchiridion ad Laurentium* 26,100 [CCL, 46], p. 103); "Melius enim iudicauit de malis bene facere quam mala nulla esse permittere" (*Ibid.* 8,27, p. 64); "Potentius et melius esse iudicans etiam de malis bene facere quam mala esse non sinere" (Id., *De ciuitate Dei* 22,1 [CCL, 48], p. 806); "Deus vero tam bonus est, ut malis quoque utatur bene, quae Omnipotens esse non sineret, si eis bene uti summa sua bonitate non posset: et hinc potius impotens appareret et minus bonus, non valendo bene uti etiam malo" (Id., *Contra secundam responsionem Iuliani imperfectum opus* 5,60 [PL, 45], c. 1495).

345. "Videte poenas eorum... et gaudete" (Id., *Enarrationes in psalmos* 57,21 [CCL, 39], p. 727). "Quantum circa me habuit misericordiam, in illis mihi demonstrauit circa quos non habuit" (*Ibid.* 58,1,20, p. 743).

the non-predestined is merely the *äußere Seite* of the elect's call[346], a sad witness to the sovereignty of divine grace that justifies the elect[347]. Even the assertion, as somebody suggested[348], that divine passivity towards the non-predestined should be interpreted as a sign that God leaves man's freedom intact, is not convincing. Not only because it would not add any relief to the situation of the damned, but above all because it would leave us with man as an active and responsible actor only with regard to moral evil. If that were so, it would then follow that, with regard to good, human beings act merely as puppets[349], moved by the strings of God's eternal decrees and bereft of freedom in any acceptable sense of the term. Augustine is therefore right (and we cannot but agree with him) when he says that God could not predestine men *ad peccatum*[350], because He cannot be the cause of sin. Yet, we cannot avoid thinking that this very God is also the same one who witholds his saving grace from those people He allows to be damned. In other words, if God cannot be held responsible for the sin of those He has not predestined to salvation, by standing back (namely by "withholding" his grace and leaving those who have abandoned him to their own destiny of perdition), He nevertheless ratifies in an indirect way (or *per consequentiam*[351]) the *reprobatio* the sinners have incurred[352].

346. RING (ed.), *Aurelius Augustinus. Schriften über die Gnade* (n. 57), pp. 345-346.

347. "La *potentia* divina è capace di convertire il male stesso a strumento di esaltazione del bene; eppure, questa conversione risulta soltanto estrinseca e non intrinseca, conversione apparente dunque, superficiale e meramente estetica, ove il destino del singolo è del tutto tragicamente subordinato e sacrificato all'utilità dell'eletto, ma soprattutto all'esaltazione della *potentia* assoluta, la cui grazia risplende proprio attraverso la manifestazione della nullità della creatura abbandonata a se stessa, dunque 'vanificata' e eternamente strumentalizzata, alienata" (G. LETTIERI, *Fato e predestinazione in* De civ. Dei *V,1-11 e* C. duas ep. Pelag. *II,5,9-7,16, in Aug* 35 [1995] 457-496). Marrou speaks in a colourful way of "les hurlements des damnés" who "entrent à titre de dissonance expressive dans le concert qui fait le bonheur des Élus" (H.-I. MARROU, *Saint Augustin et l'augustinisme*, Paris, [1955], p. 55).

348. Cf., for instance, THONNARD, *La prédestination augustinienne et l'interpretation de O. Rottmanner* (n. 74), p. 261.

349. Cf. RIST, *Augustine on Free Will and Predestination* (n. 149), p. 440. This pessimistic image of "puppet" or "plaything" in relation to God's agency was already used by Plato. Cf., for instance: PLATO, *Leges* 1,13,644d; 7,10,803c.

350. Cf., for instance, the principle already expressed in the *Confessiones*: "Deus ordinator et creator rerum omnium naturalium, peccatorum autem tantum ordinator" (Augustine, *Confessiones* 1,10,16 [CCL, 27], p. 9).

351. We believe that Rottmanner's intuition is correct: "Wahrhaft prädestinirt sind nur die Sancti; streng genommen gibt es keine eigene (directe) *reprobatio*, und am allerwenigsten eine *praedestinatio ad peccatum*. Andrerseits weiss und anerkennt der scharfe Denker Augustinus, dass alle nicht zum ewigen Leben Prädestinirten *per consequentiam* (indirect) zum ewigen Tode und Verderben verurtheilt sind oder vielmehr bleiben" (ROTTMANNER, *Der Augustinismus* [n. 77], p. 17). And again: "Die nicht zum Heile

Augustine tried to soften the severity of this interpretation by arguing that the perversity of the non-elect does not rule out the possibility of being saved. He thinks, for instance, of the inhabitants of Tyre and Sidon. Had they known the miracles performed by Jesus at Chorazin and Bethsaida (cf. Mt 11,21), they certainly would have repented and done penance for their sins. Yet, although God could have saved them (had He wanted to), his decision to let them perish was not unjust[353], because they were not predestined to be delivered from the *massa perditionis*[354]. As it was noted, "the problem, as Augustine would rephrase it (…), is not, 'Why does God not save everyone'?, but 'Why does God save anyone'?; for we are all justly condemned. The problem would not be God's justice, but God's mercy which would seem unjust, or at least at the expense of Justice"[355]. We must admit that, even though Augustine tried to reduce the brutality of a mechanical and infallible non-predestination of the non-elect, such mitigation was in fact posited only on a hypothetical level, and it was little more than a theoretical exercise. To taste the real extent of Augustine's conviction, and its *unerträgliche Schärfe*[356], it suffices to read the very sharp (not to say shocking) remark in which he affirms that it is of no importance (*nullius momenti*) to God whether the mass of the damned is conspicuous or not. He would not really care about the vastness of the numbers involved, since their reprobation and loss are justly deserved[357].

Prädestinirten werden einfach ihrem (im Grunde von Allen verdienten) Schicksal überlassen; ihnen gegenüber verhält sich Gott passiv, dagenen den Prädestinirten gegenüber activ" (*Ibid.*, p. 18). As Magris puts it: "La 'negatività' della predestinazione al negativo è di natura dialettica" (A. MAGRIS, *L'idea di destino nel pensiero antico,* Vol. II: *Da Platone a S. Agostino,* Udine, 1985, p. 881).

352. "La prédestination étant la préparation d'une grâce que Dieu ne donne pas à tous, la non-prédestination risque d'apparaître comme un "refus" de cette grâce, et ce refus impliquerait une sorte de "prédestination au mal" (A. SOLIGNAC, *Les excès de l' "intellectus fidei" dans la doctrine d'Augustin sur la grâce,* in *NRT* 110 [1998] 825-849, pp. 843-844).

353. "Nec utique Deus iniuste noluit saluos fieri, cum possent salui esse si uellent" (Augustine, *Enchiridion ad Laurentium* 24,95 [CCL, 46], p. 99). See also Id., *De dono perseuerantiae* 14,35 (PL, 45), c. 1014.

354. "Sed nec illis profuit quod poterant credere, quia praedestinati non erant ab eo" (*Ibid.*).

355. J.M. RIST, *Augustine: Ancient Thought Baptized,* Cambridge, 1994, p. 273.

356. NYGREN, *Das Prädestinationsproblem in der Theologie Augustins* (n. 4), p. 99.

357. "Tam multos autem creando nasci uoluit, quos ad suam gratiam non pertinere praesciuit, ut multitudine incomparabili plures sint eis, quos in sui regni gloriam filios promissionis praedestinare dignatus est, ut etiam ipsa reiectorum multitudine ostenderetur, quam nullius momenti sit apud Deum iustum quantalibet numerositas iustissime damnatorum" (Augustine, *Ep.* 190,3,12 [CSEL, 57], p. 146).

Of course, such a conclusion raises the central question of the very meaning of God's mercy and love. Augustine has solved the problem by seemingly contenting himself that God's mercy on the one side, and his justice on the other, constitute the general answer to the aporia of the contradictory coexistence of *electio secundum propositum* and *reprobatio*[358]. But as to the actual and particular application of this principle, viz. why God elects some people and not others, Augustine himself believes there is no answer, and would take refuge behind God's inscrutable designs[359]. It really surprises us that Augustine did not realise how the "just" punishment deserved by the sinners could not be contemplated without at the same time encroaching upon the meaning of God's love, and of God himself. In point of fact, predestination is not merely an *anthropo*-logical but also a *theo*-logical problem, and it seems to us that a geometrical justice, bereft of the light and power of love, ultimately impairs the very image of the Christian God, introducing (anthropomorphically speaking) elements such as indifference or even revenge[360] in a God who is essentially a God of love.

Similarly, with regard to the efficacy of prayers raised to God for the conversion of people (prayers which were vigorously defended in connection with the problem of predestination[361]), Augustine was faced with the difficulty of harmonizing them within such a perspective. He acknowledged that some kind of interplay was necessary, lest the intercessory character of prayer were to be reduced to a useless charade[362]. And yet his effort to harmonize prayer and predestination appears to be very clumsy, from a rational point of view, and falls definitively short of the mark. The prayer of the Church, although useful, *de facto* does not affect anything of what has already been (*ab aeterno*) decided by God's decrees. How could the Church be sure that her prayers are going to be

358. "Agostino confessa... una provvidenza divina del tutto paradossale e contraddittoria in se stessa, scissa tra terribile giudizio e misericordioso amore, tra vanificante punizione e eternizzante redenzione, tra l'abbandono alla disperante casualità (almeno *sub specie hominis*) dell'esistenza lapsa e il dono salvifico della necessità della grazia" (LETTIERI, *Fato e predestinazione in* De civ. Dei *V,1-11 e* C. duas ep. Pelag. *II,5,9-7,16* [n. 347], p. 495).

359. Cf., for instance, Augustine, *Ep.* 194,2 (CSEL, 57), pp. 179-180; Id., *De dono perseuerantiae* 8,16-18 (PL, 44), cc. 1002-1003.

360. "Si omnes a tenebris transferrentur in lucem, in nullo appareret ueritas ultionis" (Id., *De ciuitate Dei* 21,12 [CCL, 48], p. 778).

361. See, for instance: Id., *Ep.* 217,2 and 7 (CSEL, 57), pp. 405ff. and 421ff; *Enchiridion ad Laurentium* 27,103 (CCL, 46), pp. 104f; *De gratia et libero arbitrio* 14,29 (PL, 44), c. 898; *De correptione et gratia* 14,45 (CSEL, 92), pp. 273ff.

362. "Inaniter igitur et perfunctorie potius quam ueraciter... Labia dolosa si in hominum quibuscumque sermonibus sunt, saltem in orationibus non sint" (Id., *Ep.* 217,2,6-7 [CSEL, 57], pp. 407-408).

influential with regard to somebody's conversion and salvation? And even if her intercessory prayer had some power, it would necessarily follow that such power could not possibly be regarded as an autarchic one, but as a power which ultimately ensues from God's predestination, viz. from the foreknowledge and the preparation of his beneficial and saving grace deriving from his immutable decrees[363]. Thus, the effectiveness of prayer is not so much ascribable to the "pressure" or influence of the intercessory Church as to God's predestination whose decrees are eternally foreseen and actualised.

In the light of the above remarks, we come to the conclusion that although Augustine never speaks of a *praedestinatio gemina*, his doctrine of predestination contains implicitely and unintentionally a *de facto* indication of it[364]. We maintain that it is an "implicit" and "unintentional" form of double predestination, because we are convinced that an explicit, clear-cut doctrine of double predestination cannot be found in Augustine's works, nor was it deliberately formulated and proposed by him[365]. More simply, we believe that once predestination was presented as the most obvious consequence of his doctrine of sovereign and gratuitous grace, Augustine could no longer free himself from the trap of an asymmetrical determinism: on one side God's positive intervention in the order of good, directed to those He has predestined *secundum propositum* to life eternal, and on the other, his passive non-intervention with regard to those who have not been elected and who will be eternally lost. The fact that Augustine ultimately bowed before the unfathomable mystery of God's designs – as if he really wished to leave the last word to him – is a further indication that he could not give an adequate or satisfying answer to the problem of God's attitude and of his way of acting on the two different levels of election and reprobation. Nor would it be

---

363. "Fortassis enim sic praedestinati sunt, ut nostris orationibus concedantur, et accipiant eamdem gratiam, qua velint atque efficiantur electi. Deus enim qui omnia quae praedestinavit implevit, ideo et pro inimicis fidei orare nos voluit; ut hinc intelligeremus, quod ipse etiam infidelibus donet ut credant, et volentes ex nolentibus faciat" (ID., *De dono perseuerantiae* 22,60 [PL, 45], cc. 1029-1030).

364. "Der Begriff – states Adam – einer 'doppelten Prädestination', zum Heil und zur Verdammnis, findet sich bei Augustin nicht; wohl aber ist die Sache selbst gegeben und nur unter den kunstenvolle Wendungen des Systems versteckt geblieben" (A. ADAM, *Lehrbuch der Dogmengeschichte*, Bd. I: *Die Zeit der Alten Kirche*, Gütersloh, 5th ed., Gütersloh, 1985, pp. 271-272).

365. As a consequence, we cannot accept the opinion claiming that a double predestination represents the last word of Augustine's theology, as Nygren believes instead: "Die Lehre von der doppelten Prädestination, zum Himmel und zur Hölle, hat somit – obwohl sich der positive Sinn der geschichte im gedanken an Christus und die Heiligen erschöpft – das letzte Wort in der augustinischen Theologie" (NYGREN, *Das Prädestinationsproblem in der Theologie Augustins* [n. 4], pp. 265-266).

sufficient, to legitimise Augustine's doctrine of predestination, to claim that it ought to be understood on a "functional" level only[366]. That would mean, in our opinion, devaluing the serious challenge that the bishop of Hippo's view on predestination raises, especially with regard to soteriology, to which grace is intimately connected[367]. If it is true that the doctrine of predestination is but a corollary of the central question of gratuitous and sovereign grace, it is nevertheless of paramount importance that the offer of so gratuitous a grace, concretely translated into God's *oeconomia salutis*, be not detached from the life of man as it unfolds in history. The way Augustine elaborated his doctrine of predestination, namely from the viewpoint of God, made him able to talk about salvation with absolute certainty. But it also led him to a unilateral approach, which resulted in a theoretical impasse. The view that God's omnipotent intervention alone can assure salvation in the face of man's powerlessness[368] and in the midst of historical contingencies would be ultimately detrimental to man's freedom (which would be underestimated) and to man's history (which would be devalued through a "subjectivization" of the significance of grace itself)[369]. In Augustine's view, man's freedom and history would then disappear, as it were, beyond time and space, and would be absorbed in (not to say pre-empted by) God's meta-historical decrees.

No doubt, it would be quite ineffectual to talk of the redemptive act of the cross and resurrection of Christ as the central *locus theologicus* of God's *oeconomia salutis*, if the *propter nos* and the concrete history of man were not taken into account as well. It is intrinsic to the very meaning of God's saving love – or so we think – that as long as man lives,

---

366. It is, for instance, the conviction of Marafioti, who writes: "Ha un indispensabile *valore funzionale* per impedire che sia compromessa la gratuità della grazia ed eliminare la pretesa della volontà umana di diventare arbitro di tutto. Ma ha una portata teologica *relativa*, anzi decisamente limitata e secondaria" (MARAFIOTI, *Alle origini del teorema della predestinazione* [n. 66], p. 276).

367. We disagree with Marafioti when he says that predestation must not be extrapolated from the theology of grace and must not be judged in the light of God's universal salvific will (Cf. *Ibid.*, p. 276). It is our assumption that the problem of predestination can be thouroughly understood if it is not restricted to the theology of grace but is considered in the light of the different theological perspectives, particularly in that of soteriology.

368. "Die Prädestinationslehre ist eine Explikation der Erfahrung Augustins von der Ohnmacht des Menschen vor Gott, der sich in seiner Verlorenheit an der absoluten Macht Gottes festhält und damit sein Heil nicht im Haltlos-Geschichtlichen, sondern nur in der Zuverlässigkeit des Ewigen verbürgt sieht" (GRESHAKE, *Gnade als konkrete Freiheit* [n. 26], p. 245, n. 64). Beside the personal experience element, which certainly nourished Augustine's comprehension of God, we should not underestimate the influence of Neoplatonism which was also determinant in his understanding of God.

369. Cf. *Ibid.*, p. 265. See also KRAUS, *Vorherbestimmung* [n. 77], p. 54.

and is historically bound in time and space, he remains the object of this love. Indeed "God did not send the Son into the world to condemn the world, but in order that the world might be saved through him" (Jn 3,17). That being the case, we perceive immediately how important it is that predestination be considered not only from the perspective of God's eternal and immutable decrees, but also in its historical and fruitful interplay with God's plan of salvation. The person of Christ is precisely there to remind us where the pivot of this harmonization actually lies, lest the idea of an immutably fixed number of predestined (and damned) opens the door to the reproach of blind fatalism and arbitrary dualism. With respect to this the Pelagians and the Massilians, who had accused the bishop of Hippo of both fatalism and Manichaeism, rightly understood (prescinding from the concrete validity of their accusation and of their alternative solutions) those possible consequences to which Augustine's theological construction on predestination could lead.

6. THE MASSILIANS' APPROACH TO GOD'S UNIVERSAL SALVIFIC WILL AND PREDESTINATION

Not everybody in the Western Church (to limit ourselves to the Latin West) was prepared to accept Augustine's concept of predestination in the way he had defined it. The Massilians were, no doubt, among those who, despite their respect and admiration for the bishop of Hippo, were unwilling to endorse his teaching on absolute grace and original sin[370] and the predestinarian view that it engendered. In a letter addressed by Prosper to the bishop of Hippo[371], we read that the belief was still prevalent in the ecclesiastical milieu of Southern Gaul (where dependence upon Eastern theology remained a determining factor) that God's predestination to salvation must be subordinate to God's prescience. God

---

370. "Ils admettent l'absolue nécessité de la grâce du Christ; ils n'ont pas suivi saint Augustin jusqu'à admettre son absolue gratuité" (SAGE, *La volonté salvifique universelle de Dieu dans la pensée de saint Augustin* [n. 278], p. 117). "Ablehnung der absoluten Prädestination, Bekenntnis zur Allgemeinheit des göttlichen Heilswillens, Verteidigung der traditionellen Lehre von der sittlichen Wahlfreiheit und Wirkkraft auch des gefallenen Menschen: das alles ist offensichtlich gegen den Augustinismus gerichtet, direkt gegen die augustinische Lehre von den Folgen der Erbsünde, indirekt aber auch gegen den augustinischen Erbsündenbegriff selber. Sind doch die Thesen von der Aufhebung der Freiheit durch die Erbschuld sowie vom partikulären Heilswillen nichts anderes als Folgerungen aus der augustinischen Erbsündenidee. Wer diese Folgerungen bestreitet, der leugnet – das hat bereits Prosper richtig erkannt – die Erbsünde selber" (J. GROSS, *Entwicklungsgeschichte des Erbsündendogmas im nachaugustinischen Altertum und in der Vorscholastik (5.-11. Jahrhundert)* [Geschichte des Erbsündendogmas, Bd. II], München-Basel, 1963, p. 34).
371. Cf. Prosper, *Ep.* 225,8 (CSEL, 57), pp. 466-467.

has foreknowledge of those who are going to believe and welcome his saving grace[372].

The Massilians' argument was built on the principle of God's universal salvific will. Cassian's *Conlatio* 13, which tells us quite a lot about the view of the monks and divines of Provence on the subject of grace, does not give us any explicit information about the specific question of predestination. All we find are allusions made to it through the quotation of 1 Tim 2,4 where God's universal salvific will is strongly stated. Cassian describes briefly but poignantly the significance of God's *oeconomia salutis* by asserting that, according to the *propositum Dei* (which is immutable), the human being is not made to perish, but to live for ever[373]. If it is God's will, continues Cassian, that none of his little ones should be lost (cf. Mt 18,14), it would be an enormous blasphemy (*ingens sacrilegium*) to think that He does not wish the salvation of all, and that he limits it to a few[374]. Although not explicitly, Cassian, here, is vigorously countering Augustine's view of the happy few who, set apart from the rest of mankind, have been predestined *secundum Dei propositum* to partake of eternal salvation. Refuting such a restricted view of salvation, the divine of Marseilles stresses the traditionally accepted view that God calls everybody, without exception[375]. Those who will perish are those going towards a destiny they themselves have chosen against God's will. In this light he quotes the sentence of the book of Wisdom where it is said that God *mortem non fecit, nec gaudet in perditione uiuorum* (Wis 1,13)[376]. God cares so much also for those who have chosen to walk towards their eternal perdition, that He does not refrain from lowering himself in order to exert some compulsion upon them, hoping that, either by delaying or by forestalling their deadly choices, they may be willing to leave the wrong path and choose the path of salvation[377]. Thus, while accepting that somebody may decide to follow the way leading to damnation (thus going against God's will, who wishes that all men be saved), Cassian insists on a concerned God who

---

372. "Qui autem credituri sunt quiue in ea fide, quae deinceps per gratiam sit iuuanda, mansuri sunt, praescisse ante mundi constitutionem Deum et eos praedestinasse in regnum suum, quos gratis uocatos dignos futuros electione et de hac vita bono fine excessuros esse praeuiderit" (*Ibid.* 225,3, p. 457).

373. "Propositum namque Dei, quo non ob hoc hominem fecerat ut periret, sed ut in perpetuum uiueret, manet immobile" (Cassian, *Conlatio* 13,7 [SC, 54], p. 155).

374. "Qui enim ut pereat unus ex pusillis non habet uoluntatem, quomodo sine ingenti sacrilegio putandus est non uniuersaliter omnes, sed quosdam saluos fieri uelle pro omnibus? Ergo quicumque pereunt, contra illius pereunt uoluntatem" (*Ibid.*, p. 156).

375. "...cunctos absque ulla exceptione conuocat" (*Ibid.*).

376. Cf. *Ibid.*, pp. 156-157.

377. "...properantes ad mortem retrahit ad salutem" (*Ibid.*, p. 157).

intervenes, at times even forcefully, in order to prevent people from
going astray and perishing. No matter who it is that goes astray, for God
this will always be a loss (*detrimentum*)[378]. In this way the unchangeable
truth about God's will to save and the sovereignty of his grace are
applied to everybody, in the sense that man's inherited fallen state, due
to the fall of Adam, becomes the foundation for a new life in Christ[379].
We can indeed sense the tension underlying Cassian's argument; the difficulty he is wrestling with in wanting to hold together God's saving will
and man's free will, without jeopardizing the importance and necessity
of each.

Cassian is convinced that God's will must not be regarded as an
absolute will that decrees beforehand and irrevocably the destiny of each
individual person. On the contrary, in his eyes God's will should be conceived as acting hand in hand with divine foreknowledge while remaining at the same time in close contact with human free will. In this way
both the Christian principles of individual responsibility, on one side,
and divine impartiality, on the other, could be preserved and respected.
Besides, Cassian affirms that the God who foreknows (*praecognitus*)
what is going to happen, from beginning to end, is a God who adapts
himself not only to the common order and reason, but, somehow, also to
human feelings[380]. Rather than relying exclusively on his own power
(*potentialiter*) and upon the mysterious knowledge (*ineffabilis notitia*) of
his prescience (*praescientia*), God judges people either rejecting them,
by withholding grace from them, or attracting them, by bestowing grace
on them, on the basis of their present actions[381]. The terms *praecognitus*,
praescientia, ineffabilis notitia and *potentialiter*, used by the divine of
Marseilles in combination with one another, is clear evidence that the
"power" of God's inscrutable thought and decree, viz. predestination,
should be equated with "prescience". The fact, however, that divine
foreknowledge takes into account man's actual and historically bound
status, is an indication that God's will to save all men is influenced by

---

378. "Vnum siquidem cuiuslibet interitu ei nascitur detrimentum" (*Ibid.* 16,6, p. 229).
    379. In his work against Nestorius, referring to Rom 5,12 Cassian writes: "Et ideo
cum in omnes mors pertransisset, omnes uita indigebant, ut in Adam scilicet morientes in
Christo uiuerent" (Id., *De incarnatione Domini contra Nestorium* 5,15,3 [CSEL, 17],
p. 324).
    380. "Illud etiam prae omnibus inaestimabilis illa censura nos instruit, quod cum si ei
ante ortum uniuscuiusque praecognitus finis, ita ordine ac actione conmuni et humanis
quodammodo omnia dispensat affectibus" (Id., *Conlatio* 17,25 [SC, 54], p. 278).
    381. "Ut non potentialiter nec secundum praescientiae suae ineffabilem notitiam, sed
secundum praesentes hominum actus uniuersa diiudicans uel respuat unumquemque uel
adtrahat et uel infundat cotidie suam gratiam uel auertat" (*Ibid.*).

the concrete situations in which they find themselves and through which they are able positively to respond to God.

An important feature, connected with Cassian's view on universal salvific will, is the specific role that Jesus Christ plays as mediator, or *pontifex*[382], in the unfolding of God's plan of salvation. He appears as the *redemptor mundi et humanae salutis auctor*[383], as the one who has taken human flesh in order to save mankind and make known to all peoples the wonders of his mysteries[384]. He also gives an example of a virtuous and perfect life[385] – a notion which was emphasized also by the Pelagians[386]. In other words, Jesus Christ is the Son of God who brings life and resurrection to fallen humanity lying in the shadows of death[387], but He is also the second Adam who offers himself as the "paradigm" of the way evil and temptations should be fought so as to attain a perfect life. Jesus Christ is the type or *forma* of this perfection[388]. The fact, continues Cassian, that Jesus himself was tempted to *gula*, *uanagloria* and *superbia*, is an indication that he wanted to set an example of how all must struggle to overcome the lures of the devil[389] and seek perfection.

---

382. See *Ibid.* 14,10, p. 196; *Ibid.* 21,26 (SC, 64), p. 101.

383. Id., *De institutis coenobiorum* 7,23 (SC, 109), p. 324. See also, *Ibid.* 12,17,1, p. 472; Id., *Conlatio* 3,16,1 (SC, 42), p. 160.

384. "... cum postremo dispensationem incarnationis suae pro nostra salute suscepit ac mirabilia mysteriorum suorum in cunctis gentibus dilatauit" (*Ibid.* 1,15, p. 97).

385. See V. CODINA, *El aspecto cristologico en la espiritualidad de Juan Casiano* (OCA, 175), Rome, 1966, pp. 20ff and 54ff.

386. Cf. (Ps.)-Pelagius, *De induratione cordis Pharaonis* 4 (PLS, 1), c. 1508. The *De induratione cordis Pharaonis* was written at the beginning of the 5th century in a Pelagian milieu, but, most probably, not directly ascribable to Pelagius (cf. F.G. NUVOLONE, *Problèmes d'une nouvelle édition du* De Induratione Cordis Pharaonis *attribué à Pélage*, in *REAug* 26 [1980] 105-117, pp. 115-117). As to the importance of the Christ-*exemplum* in Pelagianism, Pirenne writes: "Si dans la sotériologie pélagienne ce rôle rédempteur du Christ est un rôle de base, ce qui importe le plus c'est son rôle de législateur par son exemple et sa doctrine.... S'est par lui que le Père nous explique sa volonté. Le Christ, par son exemple et par sa doctrine reconstruit la nature humaine, lui remontre la voie que par une foi efficace la liberté humaine doit suivre pour atteindre la justice, pour se réaliser.... Le Christ, Dieu donc, dans l'état historique du monde est venu par son exemple et sa doctrine rappeler la voie que l'homme doit suivre.... Quand le Christ devient loi pour lui *[Pelagius]*,... il ne prend jamais cela dans un autre sens que celui de l'imitation du Christ, de la conformité à son exemple" (R. PIRENNE, *La morale de Pélage. Essai historique sur le rôle primordial de la Grâce dans l'enseignement de la théologie morale* [Excerpta ex Dissertatione ad Lauream], Rome, 1961, pp. 42-43 and 44).

387. "Et ille Adam dicitur et iste Adam, ille primus ad ruinam et mortem, hic primus ad resurrectionem et uitam. Per illum omnegenus hominum condemnatur, per istum omne genus hominum liberatur" (Cassian, *Conlatio* 5,6 [SC, 42], p. 193).

388. "Homo ille Dominicus, qui non solum redimere humanum genus, sed etiam praebere uenerat perfectionis formam atque exempla uirtutum" (*Ibid.* 11,13 [SC, 54], p. 118).

389. "... nos quoque quemadmodum temptatorem uincere deberemus suo doceret exemplo" (*Ibid.* 5,6 [SC, 42], p. 193).

The more one imitates the "model", viz. Christ, the more one becomes perfect and obtains salvation[390], and since all men have been made in the image and likeness of God, all men are (in principle) called to salvation by recovering in themselves the beauty and the splendour of this defaced image. It goes without saying that this perspective can only be possible for those who have had the chance of knowing the person of Christ and have been regenerated through baptism.

We must not forget, at this point, that Cassian lived in a monastic setting and wrote for monks who were used to laying great emphasis on human effort and struggle for perfection, considered an indispensable part of the paideutic process of salvation which is already at work here on earth[391]. Conscious of being *athletae* and *milites Christi*[392], they looked at Jesus Christ not simply as a guarantee of salvation, but also as a model to imitate in their quest for a virtuous and holy life. In other words, they regarded salvation (in and through Jesus Christ) as being intimately tied up with their monastic/ascetic commitment[393]. This was

390. For Gregory of Nyssa's "humanistic" solution about salvation being sought through the imitation of Christ, see J. ZACHHUBER, *Human Nature in Gregory of Nyssa. Philosophical Background and Theological Significance* (SVigChr, 46), Leiden-Boston-Cologne, 2000, pp. 190-200. For Gregory's example of the pupil imitating a well-drawn picture set before him, see *supra*, p. 220, n. 152.

391. As Hausherr has shown, for the ancient Christian writers the idea of perfection is included in that of σωτερία, understood as integrity, well being, fulness (in the sense of lack of any infirmity or defect) in the life of the soul that undergoes its ascent to God. Cf. I. HAUSHERR, *Spiritualité monachale et unité chrétienne*, in *Le monachisme orientale* (OCA, 153), Rome, 1958, pp. 15-32, pp. 17-18. In this respect, it is enlightening to note how the main concern of the monks of the desert was "how" to obtain salvation, a concern which was usually set in a very voluntaristic context. See, for instance: "When the holy Abba Antony lived in the desert he was beset by *accidie*, and attacked by many sinful thoughts. He said to God: 'Lord, I want to be saved but these thoughts do not leave me alone; what shall I do in my affliction? How can I be saved (πῶς σωθῶ)? A short while afterwards, when he got up to go out, Antony saw a man like himself sitting at his work, getting up from his work to pray, then sitting down and plaiting a rope, then getting up again to pray. It was an angel of the Lord sent to correct and reassure him. He heard the angel saying to him: 'Do this and you will be saved'. At these words, Antony was filled with joy and courage. He did this, and he was saved (καὶ οὕτως ποιῶν ἐσώζετο)" (*Anthonius* 1, in *Apophthegmata Patrum* [Collectio alphabetica] [PG, 65], c. 76). Also the usual way by which the disciples would address their masters in the desert, sounded as follows: "Give us a word; how are we to be saved? (Εἰπὲ ἡμῖν λόγον, πῶς σωθῶμεν;)" (*Ibid.* 19, c. 81; English translation of both quotations from B. WARD [ed.], *The Sayings of the Desert Fathers. The Alphabetical Collection*, London-Oxford-Kalamazoo, MI, 1975, p. 1 and p. 4). The monks did not simply expect to learn how to avoid sin and spiritual death, but, more importantly, how to make their souls partake of the fulness of divine life already here on earth, by struggling for perfection.

392. See *supra*, p. 150, nn. 275-276.

393. Cassian puts on their guard those who wish to join the monastic life by prospecting a very high profile of the commitment that such a life entails: "Non quia tuam uel omnium salutem non toto desiderio cupiamus amplecti et his qui ad Christum conuerti

seen as a *certamen* in which Christ himself is the *arbiter atque agono-theta*[394], presiding over the fight, measuring the performance of the fighters and granting the prize. The monk is aware that in his struggle against evil he is constantly watched and sustained by Christ, whose gracious presence is not so much that of an *arbiter atque agonotheta* who stands beside the competitors, as of one abiding within man's conscience, whence he follows the course of the struggle[395]. The confidence in the daily wrestle, which is a characteristic of primitive monasticism, stems from this certainty, namely that the help of Christ will never fail to sustain the fight of the believer.

Thus, on a concrete level (and in contrast with Augustine's predestinarian doctrine) the call to salvation becomes for Cassian also a call to perfection which, through the mediation of Christ, is extended to all believers[396]. In Cassian's writings, this call is equivalent to the setting of one's own mind and heart on Jesus Christ and the wholehearted commitment that follows[397]; or to the ability to live in consonance with the grace of the Gospel and the virtue of divine love[398]; or to the evangelical perfection ensuing from total submission to the grace of the Saviour[399]; or to the will of Christ[400]. From these examples we can clearly infer that divine agency and man's commitment are reciprocal, without

cupiunt etiam procul occurrere non optemus, sed ne temere recipientes et nos apud Deum leuitatis et te reum grauioris supplicii faceremus" (Cassian, *De institutis coenobiorum* 4,33 [SC, 109], p. 172). It is likely that Cassian had in mind Origen's description of Jesus as the divine Logos, sent as a physician to sinners, and as a "teacher of divine mysteries" ("διδάσκαλος θείων μυστηρίων": Origen, *Contra Celsum* 3,62 [SC, 136], p. 142) to those who are already pure and are no longer sinning. Origen describes Jesus Christ also as the fullness of animated and living virtue ("ὁ λόγος δέ, καὶ ἀπαξαπλῶς ὁ κύριος, ἡ πᾶσα ἔμψυχος καὶ ζῶσα ἀρετή": Id., *Commentarii in Iohannem* 11,127 [SC, 385], p. 242).

394. Cassian, *Conlatio* 7,22 (SC, 42), p. 265.

395. Cf. Id., *De institutis coenobiorum* 6,9 (SC, 109), p. 272. The image of the Lord as *arbiter* and *agonotheta* is present also in other Church Fathers. Cf., for instance: Tertullian, *De fuga in persecutione* 1,5 (CCL, 2), p. 2136; Cyprian, *Ep.* 8,1 (CCL, 3в), p. 40; Jerome, *Ep.* 71,2 (CSEL, 55), p. 3; Ambrose, *De interpellatione Job et Dauid* 2,3,8 (CSEL, 32/2), p. 238; Augustine, *De ciuitate Dei* 14,9 (CCL, 48), p. 427.

396. "Ad omnem sane aetatem omnemque sexum perfectionis magnificentiam pertinere et uniuersa ecclesiae membra ad conscendandam sublimium meritorum celsitudinem prouocari dicente apostolo: *Sic currite ut comprehendatis [1 Cor 9,24]*" (Cassian, *Conlatio* 21,9 [SC, 64], p. 83).

397. Cf. Id., *De institutis coenobiorum* 5,17 (SC, 109), pp. 218-219.

398. "Quamobrem in nostra hodie situm est potestate, utrum sub euangelii gratia an sub legis uelimus terrore consistere" (Id., *Conlatio* 21,7 [SC, 64], p. 81).

399. Cf. *Ibid.* 21,33, pp. 107-108.

400. "... si perfectionis uiam legitime et secundum uoluntatem Christi fuerimus adgressi, et mortificantes omnia desideria nostra ac uoluntates noxias abscidentes..." (*Ibid.* 24,23, pp. 193-194).

Cassian being preoccupied with drawing theological and systematic distinctions to explain how God and man co-operate, or what exact place and role each occupies in the process of salvation.

Finally, it is very interesting to consider how Cassian interprets Rom 11,33-34, in connection with the motif (largely exploited by Augustine) of the inadequacy of the human mind to fathom the way God eventually works out our salvation[401]. To begin with, the divine of Marseilles, from an entirely different perspective, interprets the Pauline passage in a way which is exactly opposite to that of Augustine. Whereas the bishop of Hippo uses Rom 11,33-34 to underscore the incomprehensibility of God's decrees, and to justify the predestination of the elect, Cassian contends that the inscrutability of God's judgements and the mysterious ways by which He intervenes must not be understood against the background of the predestination of the elect, but in the light of God's universal salvific will, according to which salvation is offered to all men[402]. In order to accomplish his wish, God has chosen to approach human beings through the multifaceted wisdom of his providence and through his merciful love, rather than through the absolute and overwhelming power of his majesty[403]. The positive and optimistic horizon within which the Pauline quotation is interpreted by Cassian sounds an indirect reproach to Augustine's dismal notion of predestination and reprobation. If nobody can pretend to explain the manner by which God acts to bring all men to salvation[404], then, Cassian seems to infer, to conceive of man's salvation as a *reductio ad paucos* would be an even more suspect and unacceptable interpretation. Whereas the bishop of Hippo sacrifices

---

401. Cf. *Ibid.* 13,17 (SC, 54), p. 178.

402. "Per quae euidenter osteditur *inscrutabilia esse iudicia Dei et inuestigabiles uias eius*, quibus ad salutem humanum adtrahit genus" (*Ibid.* 13,15, p. 174). Cassian interprets in the light of a universal salvific will also the third request of the Lord's prayer: "Your will be done on earth, as it is in heaven". After having affirmed that these words can only be appropriately prayed by those who believe that God arranges everything for the good of human beings in a prompt and merciful way, Cassian says that that request can also be intended in the sense of God willing the salvation of all men: "Vel certe taliter accipiendum: uoluntas Dei salus omnium est secundum illam beati Pauli sententiam: *Qui omnes homines uult saluos fieri et ad agnitionem ueritatis uenire*. De qua etiam uoluntate Esaias propheta ex persona Dei Patris *et omnis*, inquit, *uoluntas mea fiet*. Dicentes ergo ei *fiat uoluntas tua sicut in caelo et in terra* hoc eum aliis oramus uerbis, ut sicut hi qui in caelo sunt, ita omnes qui in terra consistunt tua, pater, agnitione saluentur" (*Ibid.* 9,20, p. 58).

403. "Ita multiformis illa sapientia Dei salutem hominum multiplici atque inscrutabili pietate dispensat" (*Ibid.* 13,15, p. 175); "...dispensationis Dei multiplicem largitatem" (*Ibid.* 13,17, p. 178); "Hanc igitur dispensationem atque amorem suum, quem nobis tribuere Dominus indefessa pietate dignatur" (*Ibid.*, p. 179).

404. "...qui ad plenum dispensationes Dei, quibus salutem in hominibus operatur, uel mente concipere uel disserere se posse confidit" (*Ibid.*).

the clear meaning of 1 Tim 2,4 in an overzealous attempt to safeguard God's omnipotence, Cassian prefers to save the traditional exegesis of the Pauline passage, though somehow at the cost of the religious and philosophical notion of divine omnipotence. Above all, however, we believe that Cassian's approach is a clear indication that, before the mystery of God's plans, a confident and positive outlook would match the inner goal of divine merciful and saving love far better than any sombrely restricted view.

From the reports of Prosper and Hilary, we learn that the traditional view, held by Cassian, that God gives each individual the opportunity for salvation, was also shared in the monastic and ecclesiastical milieux of Southern Gaul. They would agree that God's offer of salvation, sealed by the baptismal sacrament of regeneration, becomes effective thanks to the encounter of the divine salvific will with man's will. The gift of salvation is offered either through the natural and written law, or through evangelical preaching[405]. Viewed and interpreted within this framework, the question of universal salvation became the Massilians' *pièce maîtresse* against Augustine's doctrine of predestination. In fact, the bishop of Hippo's restricted exegesis of 1 Tim 2,4 about a definite number of elect and reprobates (an interpretation that they judged unacceptable[406]) became an easy target for their critique. Alongside the traditional standpoint defended by Cassian, and in agreement with the Pelagian view on this particular point[407], they opposed Augustine's interpretation by appealing to the bounty exercised by God towards all men (*uniuersaliter*), whom He calls to salvation without any distinction (*indifferenter*)[408].

Against the Massilians' understanding of universal salvation (and predestination) – a view which was perceived as a real threat to his

405. "Propositum autem uocantis gratiae in hoc omnino definiunt, quod Deus constituerit nullum in regnum suum nisi per sacramentum regenerationis adsumere et ad hoc salutis donum omnes homines uniuersaliter siue per naturalem siue per scriptam legem siue per euangelicam praedicationem uocari" (Prosper, *Ep.* 225,4 [CSEL, 57], p. 460).

406. "...et illud pariter non accipiunt, ut eligendorum reiciendorumque esse definitum numerum nolint atque illius sententiae expositionem non eam, quae a te est deprompta, suscipiant" (Hilary, *Ep.* 226,7 [CSEL, 57], p. 476).

407. That God wills the salvation of all mankind is underlined, for instance, in (Ps).-Pelagius, *De induratione cordis Pharaonis* 34-35 (PLS, 1), cc. 1524-1526. God is no respector of persons. Each one will be judged according to the quality of his own deeds. If God were an *acceptor personarum*, not only would the law have been created in vain, but also Christ's passion and example would have been profitless (*frustra et ipse redemptor noster passus est Christus: Ibid.* 20, c. 1516).

408. "...quia... bonitas *[Dei]* in eo appareat, si neminem repellat a uita, sed indifferenter uniuersos uelit saluos fieri et in agnitionem ueritatis uenire" (Prosper, *Ep.* 225,4 [CSEL, 57], p. 460).

theological construction based upon the doctrine of absolute grace and original sin – Augustine opposed the objection, already employed during the Pelagian controversy, about the destiny of infants who have died prematurely. He points out that the problem of those babies, who die either with or without the gift of baptismal grace, would by itself be enough to jeopardize the Massilians' theory of universal salvation. Such infants, in fact, not having reached the age of reason, could not possibly meet the conditions required of an active and operational will. Undoubtedly one must conclude that they were incapable of coming into contact with God's salvific will by either accepting or refusing it. This, the bishop of Hippo argues, is incontrovertible proof of the inconsistency of the Massilians assumption that God's salvation actually extends to all.

In order to legitimate their viewpoint, the Massilians resorted to using Augustine versus Augustine, viz. some statements belonging to the young Augustine versus the affirmations of the old Augustine. This came about through their appealing to a reply that the bishop of Hippo had elaborated (against the objections raised by Porphyry) about the right time of the incarnation of Christ and the preaching of his gospel[409]. On that occasion, Augustine asserted that Christ came into the world when and where he knew that He and his gospel would not have been rejected by all, but would have been met with some acceptance. Now, alongside this argument, the Massilians suggested an extension of Augustine's answer to Porphyry, affirming that God allows dying infants to be baptized, or not, on account of the future choices and behaviour that they would have made, if they had been given the chance to live longer[410]. Although at first sight the Massilians' argument seems to rely on the traditional assumption according to which God's predestination and foreknowledge were equivalent, on closer inspection it appears to be an outlandish theory (most certainly adopted from Pelagianism[411]), going well beyond such a mere equivalence. In point of fact,

---

409. Cf. Augustine, *Ep.* 102,8-15 (q. 2: *De tempore christianae religionis*) (CSEL, 34/2), pp. 551-558; cf. Id., De *praedestinatione sanctorum* 9,17 (PL, 44), cc. 973-974; Hilary, *Ep.* 226,3 (CSEL, 57), p. 471. See *supra*, p. 160, n. 320.

410. It is from Prosper that we learn about this viewpoint being held by the Massilians. Cf. Prosper, *Ep.* 225,5 (CSEL, 57), pp. 461-462.

411. This hypothesis had already been proposed by the Pelagians and was vigorously rejected by Augustine who labeled such an attempt as *absurdissimum, insulsissimum, dementissimum*: "Quomodo enim praesciuit ea futura, quae illis in infantia morituris, quia praescientia eius falli non potest, praesciuit potius non futura. Aut quid prodest eis, qui rapiuntur ex hac uita, ne malitia mutet intellectum eorum aut ne fictio decipiat animam eorum, si peccatum etiam, quod non est factum, dictum, cogitatum, tamquam commissum fuerit, sic punitur? Quodsi absurdissimum, insulsissimum, dementissimum est"

they introduce a perspective based on the notion of hypothetical future merits (or demerits) belonging to a hypothetical life that, concretely, will never take place. As Augustine rightly understood it, it is a theory about *futura quae non sunt futura*[412]. That being the case, the Massilians' view about the salvation and damnation of respectively baptized and unbaptized infants cannot any longer be said to rest on God's prescience of the real effects of their future choices and behaviour, for these effects will never occur.

Despite the objective weakness contained in the above theory, the Massilians' standpoint is nevertheless broadly valid as an attempt to neutralize Augustine's doctrine of the absolute precedence of grace over man's will, and to counter his theory of the *certus numerus electorum*. In the eyes of the divines of Marseilles, such views entail that man's moral performance is substituted for a kind of fatalism, and also that God must seem an *acceptor personarum* who creates and rewards unjustly the vessels of honour and the vessels of dishonour[413]. Such a view, which they thought was proposed by Augustine, looked to them to be very similar (although under a different form) to the Manichaean teaching of the two natures: that engendered by the principle of good (light) and that engendered by the principle of evil (darkness).

a) Augustine and the Reproach of Fatalism and Manichaeism

The charges of fatalism and Manichaeism brought by the Massilians against Augustine were scarcely original or unusual in the theological panorama of the first quarter of the 5th century. In fact, although "the combatting of Manichean fatalism" was at that time "one of the chief theological interests of contemporary Christians"[414], Manichaeism had also become a general term of abuse, a sort of technical label pinned on any form of suspected dualism or deviation in matters of faith, and was

---

(Augustine, *Contra duas epistulas Pelagianorum* 2,7,16 [CSEL, 60], p. 478). See also Id., *Ep.* 194,9,42 (CSEL, 57), pp. 208-210.

412. Like the Pelagians, also the Massilians will be harshly criticized by Augustine on this point. Cf., for instance: "Quis enim audiat, quod dicuntur parvuli pro suis futuris meritis in ipsa infantili aetate baptizati exire de hac vita; et ideo alii non baptizati in eadem aetate mori, quia et ipsorum praescita sunt merita futura, sed mala; non eorum vitam bonam vel malam Deo remunerante vel damnante, sed nullam?... Sed unde hoc talibus viris in mentem venerit nescio, ut futura quae non sunt futura, puniantur, aut honorentur merita parvulorum" (Id., *De praedestinatione sanctorum* 12,24 [PL, 44], c. 977). See also *Ibid.*13,25 and 14,26.29, cc. 979 and 980.981; Id., *De dono perseuerantiae* 12,31-13,32 (PL, 45), cc. 1011.1012.

413. Cf. Prosper, *Ep.* 225,2-3.6 *passim* (CSEL, 57), pp. 455-459 and 463-464.

414. R.F. EVANS, *Pelagius: Inquiries and Reappraisals*, New York, 1968, p. 22.

often employed by ecclesiastical writers deliberately, just to devalue each other's antagonistic views[415].

Accusations of fatalism and Manichaeism brought against Augustine had first appeared in the Donatist milieu[416], and by the time the Pelagian controversy had reached its peak they had already become a consistent charge laid against him[417]. Of course such a charge did not assume that Augustine was still a member of the Manichaean sect. Even though his past was there (374-383), and could, no doubt, still raise some legitimate suspicions, it was very well known that after his conversion Augustine had turned bitterly against his former correligionists, and the fact that he had known them from within helped him to aim his critiques effectively[418]. What the Pelagians' accusation of "being a Manichee"[419] or of

---

415. This attitude has characterized the Christian controversies of the first centuries. See I. OPELT, *Die Polemik in der christlichen lateinischen Literatur von Tertullian bis Augustin* (BKAW, Neue Folge: Reihe 2, 63), Heidelberg, 1980, pp. 143ff.

416. The Donatists labelled Augustine, as well as some of his friends among the Catholic bishops (like Alypius), as a crypto-Manichee. See J. VAN OORT, *Jerusalem and Babylon. A Study into Augustine's City of God and the Sources of his Doctrine of the Two Cities* (SVigChr, 14), Leiden-New York-Copenhagen-Cologne, 1991, pp. 199-200; P. COURCELLE, *Recherches sur les Confessions de saint Augustin*, 2nd ed., Paris, 1968, pp. 238-245; W.H.C. FREND, *Manichaeism in the Struggle between Saint Augustine and Petilian of Constantine*, in *AugMag*, T. II, Paris, 1955, pp. 859-866. It seems, however, that the accusations brought against Augustine by the Donatists were merely accusations *ad hominem*, driven by the ill-concealed intention of discarding the authority of the once-Manichaean-disciple who was now so staunchly defending orthodox Catholicism against Donatism.

417. See E. CLARK, *The Origenist Controversy. The Cultural Construction of an Early Christian Debate*, Princeton, 1992, pp. 208-209.

418. The question of how much acquaintance Augustine had with Manichaean teaching is still an open one. No doubt he remains the major source of knowledge of Manichaeism outside the Manichaean writings, and that he knew much is shown by his anti-Manichaean works, like the *De moribus ecclesiae catholicae et de moribus Manichaeorum*, the *Contra Fortunatum Manichaeum* and the *Contra Faustum Manichaeum*. This last work is still considered "a *Fundgrube* to anyone studying Manichaeism" (J. VAN OORT, *Mani, Manichaeism and Augustine. The Rediscovery of Manichaeism and Its Influence on Western Christianity*, Tbilisi/Georgia, 1998, p. 43). Generally speaking, the reliability of Augustine's reports on Manichaean teaching is due to the fact that Manichaeism was based on the Scriptures of its founder. For that reason its teaching remained fundamentally the same everywhere, except for some minor variations depending on the different social, cultural and economic background of the various Manichaean communities (see F. DECRET, *Le manichéisme presentait-il en Afrique et à Rome des particularismes régionaux distinctifs?*, in *Aug* 34 [1994] 5-40, p. 40). Yet, the extent of Augustine's acquaintance with the religious tenets of the sect ought to be tempered – as Coyle writes – "by two cautionary remarks. The first is that Augustine's knowledge extended to Western expressions of Manichaeism, the only forms he knew; and the second is that Augustine as a Catholic presbyter and bishop came to learn aspects of Manichaeism which had been beyond the reach of Augustine the Manichaean hearer" (J.K. COYLE, *What Did Augustine Know about Manichaeism When he Wrote His Two Treatises* De moribus?, in J. VAN OORT – O. WERMELINGER – G. WURST [eds.], *Augustine*

preaching "fatalism"[420] actually meant was that a certain Manichaean "tendency" had survived (however unconsciously) in some of Augustine's theological views. Doctrines such as original sin or the *massa damnata* left him open to such a labelling. Thus, in the eyes of the Massilians, the bishop of Hippo had remained a Manichee, especially in as far as the "tendency" of his thought on predestination was concerned. They considered him a Manichee "by implication"[421]. We should, therefore, be careful not to jump to conclusions. Statements such as that the accusations of Manichaeism brought against Augustine were merely "conventional bogeys"[422] are in fact misleading. They were more than that. And even if those accusations turned out to be untenable (*i.e.* just conventional bogeys), they would still remain as a reminder of real uneasiness on the part of Augustine's detractors, whose objections were

and *Manichaeism in the Latin West: Proceedings of the Fribourg-Utrecht Symposium of the International Association of Manichaean Studies* [NHMS, 49], Leiden-Boston-Cologne, 2001, pp. 43-56, pp. 55-56). See also J. VAN OORT, *Augustinus und der Manichäismus*, in A. VAN TONGERLOO (ed.) in collaboration with J. VAN OORT, *The Manichaean NOYΣ. Proceedings of the International Symposium organized in Louvain from 31 July to 3 August 1991* (Manichaean Studies, 2), Louvain, 1995, pp. 289-307. The Pelagians themselves, and Julian of Aeclanum in particular, had come in touch with Augustine's anti-Manichaean writings (see T. BOHLIN, *Die Theologie des Pelagius und ihre Genesis* [AUU, 9], Upsala, 1957, pp. 45-56; P. BROWN, *Pelagius and his Supporters: Aims and Environment*, in *JTS*, new series, 19 [1968] 93-114, p. 104). It is even ascertained that these had exercised some influence on the Pelagians' own attacks against Manichaeism (see G. DE PLINVAL, *Pélage, ses écrits, sa vie et sa réforme. Étude d'histoire littéraire et religieuse*, Lausanne, 1943, p. 151).

419. Julian's blame was rather venomous: "Si mutabit Aethiops pellem suam aut pardus varietatem, ita et tu a Manichaeorum mysteriis elueris" (Julian, *Ad Florum* 4,42 [PL, 45], c. 1361); "Teneat igitur verbi tui lector... sciatque te, fidelem discipulum Manicheorum..." (*Ibid.* 1,66 [CSEL, 85/1], p. 64); "Ceterum Faustus, Manicheorum episcopus, praeceptor tuus..." (*Ibid.* 1,69, p. 76). That Augustine never got completely rid of his Manichaean past is the conviction expressed in A. ADAM, *Das Fortwirken des Manichäismus bei Augustin*, in *ZKG* 69 (1958) 1-25. See also W. GEERLINGS, *Zur Frage des Nachwirkens des Manichäismus in der Theologie Augustins*, in *ZKT* 93 (1971) 45-60.

420. "Nec sub nomine gratiae fatum asserimus" (Augustine, *Contra duas epistulas Pelagianorum* 2,5,9 [CSEL, 60], p. 469). "Vnde *[the fact that grace does not depend on human merits]* autem hoc eis uisum fuerit nobis obicere, quod fatum asseramus sub nomine gratiae" (*Ibid.*, 2,5,10f, pp. 469-470). See also *Ibid.* 2,8,17, p. 479. The same objections can be found in the *De induratione cordis Pharaonis*. See, for instance: "...quicumque igitur... sub gratiae colore fati dogma conatur inducere" ([Ps.]Pelagius, *De induratione cordis Pharaonis* 53 [PLS, 1], c. 1537).

421. "Julian calls Augustine a Manichee, not because he believes him to be consistent in his Manichean views on every point, but because, as he argues, the tendency of Augustine's thought is 'Manichean'. This is Manicheism by implication not by conscious commitment, a manicheism into which a man may slide unawares" (G.R. EVANS, *Augustine on evil*, Cambridge, 1982, p. 139).

422. P. BROWN, *Religion and Society in the Age of St. Augustine*, London, 1972, p. 202.

serious and precise[423]. Augustine's doctrine of *peccatum originale*, for instance, sounded very much like the eternal principle of *malum naturale*[424] (opposed to the equally eternal principle of good) of the Manichaean teaching. In consequence of this reproach, others would follow directed against the Augustinian concept of *natura uitiata*, and against his conviction that the origin of sin should not be looked for in man's free will, but in a "primordial" sin which is at the basis of man's sinfulness, and from which the *concupiscentia sexualis* is originated[425]. These elements were enough for Julian of Aeclanum to blame Augustine for having improperly attributed to *fatum* the place that should be given to *meritum*[426].

According to the Massilians, another feature of Augustine's thought smacking of Manichaeism, was the apparent fatalism lying in the assumption that mankind had been divided into two rival groups, one following God and the other siding with evil. It is most likely that the antithetical and radical dualism of the Manichaean teaching of the two realms of light and darkness, good and evil, exercised an influence on Augustine's doctrine of the two cities/kingdoms, particularly as expounded in *De ciuitate Dei* 11[427]. When it comes to the ripest fruit of

423. About these challenges see, for instance, G.R. Evans, *Neither a Pelagian nor a Manichee*, in *VigChr* 35 (1981) 232-244, pp. 238ff.

424. See M. Lamberigts, *Was Augustine a Manichaean? The Assessment of Julian of Aeclanum*, in Van Oort – Wermelinger – Wurst (eds.), *Augustine and Manichaeism in the Latin West* (n. 418), pp. 113-136, pp. 120ff. Revising his *De Genesi contra Manichaeos*, Augustine refuses to acknowledge that his doctrine of *peccatum originale* is but an echo of the Manichaean principle of eternal evil: "Item in eo quod paulo post dixi: *nullum esse malum naturale*, possunt quaerere similem latebram, nisi hoc dictum ad naturam talem referatur, qualis sine uitio primitus condita est" (Augustine, *Retractationes* 1,10,3 [CCL, 57], p. 32).

425. See Lamberigts, *Was Augustine a Manichaean?* (n. 424), pp. 124-134. See also J. van Oort, *Augustine on Sexual Concupiscence and Original Sin*, in *StPatr* 22, Louvain, 1989, pp. 382-386, where the author stresses that Augustine regards *concupiscentia* as a *motus inmoderatus* or *inordinatus*, which cannot be mastered by the will and which is the result of (or the retribution for) the Forefathers' sin of disobedience. In the eyes of the bishop of Hippo, *concupiscentia* is something "*ex qua et cum qua* man is born" and which must be considered "as a punishment for primordial sin *and* that this primordial sin is transmitted as original sin by means of the sexual desire *[libido]* in copulation" (*Ibid.* p. 384). It is precisely in Augustine's view of *concupiscentia* as *motus inordinatus* (through which original sin is transmitted) that a possible influence of the Manichaean concept of the principle of evil could be detected (*Ibid.* pp. 385f).

426. "Fato fieri quod merito non fit" (Augustine, *Contra Iulianum* 4,8,46 [PL, 44], c. 761). For Julian of Aeclanum's reiterated accusations against Augustine's supposed Manichaeism, see Lamberigts, *Was Augustine a Manichaean?* (n. 424), pp. 113-136.

427. Almost a century ago, Alfaric had expressed the conviction that Augustine had mediated the concept of the two rival groups or cities from Manichaeism: "Cette conception qu'Augustin exposera plus tard très longuement dans la *Cité de Dieu* lui vient des Manichéens" (P. Alfaric, *L'évolution intellectuelle de saint Augustin*, T. I: *Du*

Augustine's doctrine of grace, viz. his concept of predestination, the Massialians would substantially bring about the same reproach, ready to claim that whereas the Augustine who had defended human freedom before 396 was the "Christian" Augustine, the Augustine who wrote on the doctrine on divine election after that date was the "fatalist" and "Manichaean" Augustine, hiding behind Paul's teaching. They would charge the bishop of Hippo with having introduced a *fatalis necessitas*[428], or an *ineuitabilis necessitas*[429], which, by undermining the confidence in one's own achievements, leads human beings to resignation and despair. Once again, according to them, Augustine's doctrine of predestination appeared to be just like the Manichaean view where two different "fields" exist, namely two different created natures, between which human beings are divided. If that were so, then there would be no point in making any effort, since the destiny of each individual would be decided on the basis of the "field" one happens to belong to. Augustine did not let this objection go unanswered[430], although his defence was not entirely convincing to his opponents. On the contrary, it seemed to confirm their objections, viz. that there was an inevitability to everything that exists, and that that inevitability depends on God's decrees.

It must be noted in fact that, although Augustine fought against the pagan notion of *fatum* (according to which the human beings' future *actus, euenta* and *uoluntates* are determined by stars and planets[431]), he actually adopted that notion and christianized it. He was convinced that it could prove useful to the Christian doctrine of grace, provided it was

Manichéisme au Néoplatonisme, Paris, 1918, p. 123, n. 6). See also A. ADAM, *Der manichäische Ursprung der Lehre von den zwei Reichen bei Augustin*, in ID., *Sprache und Dogma. Untersuchungen zu grundproblemen der Kirchengeschichte*, Gütersloh, 1969, pp. 133-140. For a thorough analysis of the Manichaean influence detectable in the *De ciuitate Dei*, see VAN OORT, *Jerusalem and Babylon* (n. 416), pp. 199-234; ID., *Manichaeism in Augustine's* De ciuitate Dei, in E. CAVALCANTI (ed.), *Il* 'De ciuitate Dei'*: l'opera, le interpretazioni, l'influsso*, Rome-Freiburg-Vienna, 1996, pp. 193-214, pp. 200-212.

428. "Sub hoc praedestinationis nomine fatalem quandam induci necessitatem" (Prosper, *Ep.* 225,3 [CSEL, 57], p. 458). Also in Prosper's letter to Rufinus we read: "Dicentes eum *[Augustine]* liberum arbitrium penitus submovere et sub nomine gratiae necessitatem praedicare fatalem" (Id., *Ep. Ad Rufinum* 3,4 [PL, 51], c. 79). He then notes that the Massilians accuse Augustine of Manichaeism on account of his positing "duas humani generis massas, et… duas naturas" (*Ibid.*).

429. Hilary *Ep.* 226,6 (CSEL, 57), p. 475.

430. "Sive nunc recte vivatis, sive non recte, tales eritis postea, quales vos Deus futuros esse praescivit, vel boni si bonos, vel mali si malos" (Augustine, *De dono perseuerantiae* 15,38 [PL, 45], c. 1016).

431. See Id., *De ciuitate Dei* 5,1-11 (CCL, 47), pp. 128-142; *Contra duas epistulas Pelagianorum* 2,5,9-7,16 (CSEL, 60), pp. 468-478. See B. BRUNING, *De l'astrologie à la grâce*, in *Aug(L)* [Mélanges T. J. Van Bavel, T. II] 41 (1991) 575-643, pp. 607-609.

correctly understood as God's eternal *uoluntas* and *potestas* which are at
work in the necessary chain of causes (*ordo causarum*)[432]. In his eyes,
fatum could indeed be taken up and charged with a Christian significance. And that is what Augustine actually did. Stripping it of its astrological determinism by which all that happens in the world is caused by
the movement of heavenly bodies, he made the term *fatum* hinge upon
the concept of *ordo* (or *conexio*) of causes ultimately determined by
God's providence. In his thinking *fatum* is thus related to the will of God
which alone can bring to fulfilment all that, in his foreknowledge, is predestined to be[433]. At the basis of Augustine's semantic modification of
the term *fatum* there is a very precise ontological option that points in
the direction of his predestinarian view: nothing of what exists can be
explained by either the notion of "chance" (*fortuna* or *casus*)[434] or by
man's agency. Everything is part of an order which has always been
known and established in the *nunc stans* of God's eternity. Furthermore,
to reinforce the Christian usage of the term, Augustine points out that
since *fatum* derives from *fari*, it can indeed be thought of as referring to
God's creative and immutable word which is pronounced through
Christ-the-Word over the things that are and shall be[435].

432. "Ordinem autem causarum, ubi uoluntas Dei plurimum potest, neque negamus"
(Augustine, *De ciuitate Dei* 5,9,3 [CCL, 47], p. 138). Prosper would defend Augustine by
giving the same explanation: "Non fato quidquam geri, sed omnia Dei iudicio novimus
ordinari" (Prosper, *Ep. ad Rufinum* 18,19 [PL, 51], c. 88).

433. See C. PARMA, *Pronoia und Providentia: der Vorsehungsbegriff Plotins und
Augustins*, Leiden, 1971, pp. 38-41.

434. Augustine denied any notion of *fortuna* or *casus*: "Multi... omnia enim mala
quae faciunt nolunt sibi tribuere, et incipiunt dicere quia uel fortuna fecit uel fatum
fecit.... Tollat ergo ista de medio qui haec dicit, quia et fortuna uanitas hominum est et
fatum inanitas, et qui putauerit aliquid esse fatum ipse fit fatuus" (Augustine, *Sermo*
16B,1 *[Mai 17]* [CCL, 41], p. 231); "Sed in eisdem tribus libris meis *[De Academicis]*
non mihi placet *totiens me appellasse fortunam*, quamuis non aliquam deam uoluerim hoc
nomine intellegi, sed fortuitum rerum euentum uel in corporis nostri uel in externis bonis
aut malis. Vnde et illa uerba sunt, quae nulla religio dicere prohibet: forte, forsan, fositan,
fortasse, fortuitu, quod tamen totum ad diuinam reuocandum est prouidentiam. Hoc etiam
ibi non tacui dicens: *Etenim fortasse quae uulgo fortuna nominatur, occulto quodam
ordine regitur; nihilque aliud in rebus casum uocamus, nisi cuius ratio et causa secreta
est*. Dixi quidem hoc; uerumtamen penitet me sic illic nominasse fortunam, cum uideam
homines habere in pessima consuetudine, ubi dici debet: hoc Deus uoluit, dicere: hoc
uoluit fortuna" (Id., *Retractationes* 1,1,2 [CCL, 57], p. 7); "Vellem sane, quomodo dix-
eris, nos doceres, quod ea, quae in bonis vel in malis hominum appellantur externa, sicut
divitiae vel paupertas et cetera, casibus ferantur incertis. Etiam haec enim catholica fides
ita demit humanae, ut divinae tribuat potestati" (Id., *Contra secundam Iuliani responsionem opus imperfectum* 3,109 [CSEL, 85/1], p. 530).

435. "Neque fati uocabulo nuncupamus, nisi forte ut fatum a fando dictum intellegamus, id est a loquendo; non enim abnuere possumus esse scriptum in litteris sanctis:
*Semel locutus est Deus, duo haec audiui, quoniam potestas Dei est, et tibi, Domine,
misericordia, qui reddis unicuique secundum opera eius*. Quod enim dictum est: *Semel*

Beside the Christianized meaning of *fatum*[436], Augustine speaks also of the biblical *sors* which he often identifies with divine grace, viz. the eternal *consilium* of his *seueritas* (the just retribution for evildoers) and his *bonitas* (the undue grace bestowed on the good)[437]. In that case *fatum* could also be identified without further ado with God's foreknowledge and predestination (or providence), as well as with the divine and mysterious twofold act of redemption and judgement, *bonitas* and *seueritas*, *gratia* and *iustitia*[438].

The deterministic way in which Augustine has depicted God's election and reprobation does allow us to claim that predestination is in fact the concept he has used in place of the old pagan astrological concept of *fatum*[439]. And yet Augustine could not be called a fatalist in the same way, for instance, we would call a Stoic a fatalist. Not only because he had Christianized the notion of *fatum* and had fought vehemently any form of pagan fatalism, but also because his reasons for fighting it rested on the assumption that Christian faith, however anchored in God's mysterious designs and however dependent on his benevolent grace, requires a concrete, daily commitment that must counter the risk of an irresponsible passivity. Moreover, there is no doubt that the general atmosphere of anxiety and uncertainty about the future which characterized the 5th century (an era in which the downfall of the Roman Empire had become all the more evident, and which Augustine himself had partly witnessed)

---

locutus est, intellegitur 'inmobiliter', hoc est incommutabiliter, 'est locutus', sicut nouit incommutabiliter omnia quae futura sunt et quae ipse facturus est" (Id., *De ciuitate Dei* 5,9,3 [CCL, 47], p. 138). Cf. also: "Si fatum, sicut nonnulli intellexerunt, a fando dictum est, id est a loquendo, Verbum Dei quomodo habet fatum, quando in ipso Verbo omnia sunt quae condita sunt? Non enim aliquid Deus constituit quod ante nesciuit; in Verbo ipsius erat quod factum est" (Id., *Tractatus in Euangelium Ioannis* 37,8 [CCL, 36], p. 336).

436. See BRUNING, *De l'astrologie à la grâce* (n. 431), pp. 622-638.

437. "Dei uero gratia non solum omnia sidera et omnes caelos, uerum etiam omnes angelos supergreditur, deinde fati assertores et bona et mala hominum fato tribuunt; Deus autem in malis hominum merita eorum debita retributione persequitur, bona uero per indebitam gratiam misericordi uoluntate largitur, utrumque faciens non per stellarum temporale consortium, sed per suae seueritatis et bonitatis aeternum altumque consilium" (Augustine, *Contra duas epistulas Pelagianorum* 2,6,12 [CSEL, 60], p. 472).

438. "Al di là del suo rifiuto dell'accusa di fatalismo, si dovrà al tempo stesso riconoscere... la relazione comunque 'fatale' tra la libertà umana e il mistero della assoluta, determinante libertà di Dio e della sua predestinazione, che per Agostino... è l'unica vera *summa causa* irresistibile che crea, illumina e anima, accendendola d'amore, la libertà della creatura" (LETTIERI, *Fato e predestinazione in* De civ. Dei *V,1-11 e* C. duas ep. Pelag. *II,5,9-7,16* [n. 347], pp. 458-459).

439. Smalbrugge shows no doubts about it: "La prédestination, soyons clair, ce n'est rien d'autre que le nom moderne que donnent les chrétiens au vieux Fatum" (M. SMAL-BRUGGE, *Rupture dans l'homme, rupture dans la culture. Quelques réflexions sur le thème de la prédestination chez Augustin*, in *Aug[L]* 50 [2000] 235-256, p. 247).

must have contributed to the lessening of man's self-confidence in favour of a concept of God's grace as an ineluctable *fatum* upon which to cling[440].

Other similarities with, or influences from, Manichaeism could be detected in Augustine's thought. Of no little significance, for example, is the fact that sometimes, when quoting scriptural passages by heart, Augustine seems to recall quotations from Tatian's *Diatessaron*, a work which was regularly used in Manichaean circles[441]. As to the figure of Christ, moreover, a certain relation can be identified in two of the Manichaean forms under which Jesus was venerated: that of the "physician"[442] and that of the "teacher"[443] who brings to men the divine and redeeming γνῶσις. Augustine too talks of *Christus medicus*[444] and *Christus magister*[445] and although in his specific case the background of these motifs should no doubt be looked for in Scripture, in patristic literature and in Neo-Platonism rather than in Manichaeism, we cannot rule out that (at least on the level of reminiscence) there might have been a link also with the latter's teaching[446]. Last but not least, in the field of Augustine's spirituality we might also detect some influence coming

---

440. "L'insicurezza generale, dovuta al nuovo riassetto strutturale dei popoli dell'Occidente che s'incontrarono allora in un clima di belligeranza, di paura, di disfacimento della *ciuitas romana*, rivelò l'assoluta fragilità dell'uomo 'pelagiano' sul piano del concreto esistenziale. L'uomo del secolo V, al credere in se stesso, sostituì l'appoggiarsi a Dio, alla sua grazia, come ad un *fatum ineuitabile*: nacque il predestinazionismo" (V. GROSSI, *La crisi antropologica nel monastero di Adrumeto*, in *Aug* 19 [1979] 103-133, pp. 132-133).

441. See H.C. PUECH, *Das Evangelium des Mani*, in W. SCHNEEMELCHER (ed.), *Neutestamentliche Apokryphen in deutscher Übersetzung*, Bd. I: *Evangelien*, 6th ed., Tübingen, 1990, pp. 320-327; G. QUISPEL, *Mani et la tradition evangélique des judéo-chrétiens*, in *RSR* 60 (1972) 143-150.

442. See V. ARNOLD-DÖBEN, *Die Bildersprache des Manichäismus* (AMRG, 3) Cologne, 1978, pp. 98ff; A. BÖHLIG (ed.) in collaboration with J.P. ASMUSSEN, *Die Gnosis*, Bd. III: *Der Manichäismus*, Zürich-München, 1980, pp. 247, 249 and 255ff. Mani himself was described as a physician: see L.J.R. ORT, *Mani: a Religio-historical Description of his Personality*, Leiden, 1967, pp. 95-101; W.B. OERTER, *Mani als Arzt? Zur Deutung eines manichäischen Bildes*, in V. VAVRINEK (ed.), *From Late Antiquity to Early Byzantium. Proceedings of the Byzantinological Symposium in the 16th Eirene Conference*, Prague, 1985, pp. 219-223, pp. 220-221; J.K. COYLE, *Healing and the 'Physician' in Manichaeism*, in J.K. COYLE – S.C. MUIR (eds.), *Healing in Religion and Society from Hippocrates to the Puritans. Selected Studies* (SRS, 43), New York, 1999, pp. 135-158.

443. See E. ROSE, *Die manichäische Christologie* (StOr, 5) Wiesbaden, 1979, pp. 76ff. Mani too was depicted as a teacher: see ORT, *Mani* (n. 442), p. 255.

444. See W. GEERLINGS, *Christus Exemplum. Studien zur Christologie und Christusverkündigung Augustins* (TTS, 13), Tübingen, 1978, pp. 257-258.

445. See R. ARBESMANN, *The Concept of* Christus medicus *in St. Augustine*, in *Trad* 10 (1954) 1-28.

446. See VAN OORT, *Mani, Manichaeism and Augustine* (n. 418), pp. 48-49.

from the Manichaean (Christian) piety[447]. We know, for instance, that the Manichaean "psalms" (the technical term for "hymns") had attracted him very much[448], and we would not be surprised to find out that some themes dealt with in Manichaean spirituality are also developed by the bishop of Hippo in a similar way[449]. But above all the *Confessiones* seem to be reminiscent of those thorough "confessions" that the Manichaean *auditores* were asked to make once a year during the feast of the *Bêma* (throne)[450].

Following this brief outline of the reasons why Augustine was accused of fatalism, and noting possible similarities between Augustine and Manichaean teaching, we are led to conclude that profound divergencies remain between the two. These divergencies ought to keep us alert and prevent us from formulating hasty (and groundless) equivalences from what might turn out to be "innocent" parallels. This caution should be prompted also by the infancy of Manichaean studies and the complexity of the subjects they are dealing with. As to our particular question, it is sufficient to say that whilst, at first sight, there may appear to be similarities between Augustine's doctrine and Manichaeism, on deeper reflection, differences both in content and in scope appear to be greater. Even when we admit that "considered logically, a number of Augustine's positions may have tended in the same direction as Manichaeism"[451], we are still left doubting whether this "tendency" was inspired by Manichaean teaching itself, or was the result of an independent elaboration, where similar language might suggest direct dependence. This will become more obvious if we consider the particular question of predestination.

447. See *Ibid.*, pp. 38, 43 and 49-53.
448. "...et cantabam carmina" (Augustine, *Confessiones* 3,7,14 [CCL, 27], p. 34).
449. See VAN OORT, *Mani, Manichaeism and Augustine* (n. 418), p. 51.
450. "The prevailing tone, the *cantus firmus* of the *Confessiones*, is gnostic-Manichaean. Here the emphasis is placed on the antithesis of the transitory world of things and the everlasting divine world, on the disunity of temporality and the unity of eternity, on the Call of the Word from the eternal world of Light into the darkness of temporality, on the dualism of the material world as an alien country and the World of Light as the souls' true homeland [See, e.g., a passage like Confessiones 4,12,19]. The extent to which the *Confessiones* are – thetically and antithetically – influenced by Manichaeism has yet to be worked out in detailed studies. The many discoveries in the field of Mani's religion present a unique opportunity now" (*Ibid.*, p. 52).
451. LAMBERIGTS, *Was Augustine a Manichaean?* (n. 424), p. 136.

b) Is Augustine's Theory of Predestination the Result of His Past Adher-
     ence to Manichaeism?

The Pelagians had repeatedly criticized Augustine's view on grace
because, in their eyes, it implied an annihilation of free will[452]. Julian,
especially, was convinced that Augustine was reproducing Manichaean
tenets by maintaining that there is a twofold order of compulsion: one
by which man is compelled *malgré soi* to do evil, and another by which
man, with the help of God, is compelled to do good[453]. Influenced by
polemical invective, Julian even goes so far as to accuse Augustine of
being a Manichee with regard to God's righteousness. The God of
Augustine, he contends, is unrighteous not only because He allows
infants to be born with *peccatum originale*[454], but also because He
allows them to be condemned when they die without being baptized[455].
Worse still, Julian continues, is the fact that such an unrighteousness is
located (unlike the Manichaean dualism) in the one Christian God, who
seems to leave no hope at all for those people whom He judges unworthy of being numbered among the elect[456]. How could it be possible to
hold that only a few people will be singled out by God from the *massa*
peccatorum and that they alone will be allowed to reach salvation[457]?

452. See, for instance, Julian's reaction to Augustine's *Contra duas epistulas Pela-*
gianorum 1,2,4-7 (Julian, *Ad Florum* 1,94 [CSEL, 85/1], pp. 106-108).
453. "Per quod absolute pronuntias humanam naturam unum semper cupere quod
malum est, et velle non posse contrarium, naturam autem Dei malum non posse velle et
ideo, nisi necessitatis suae participem fecerit malam hominum naturam, bonum in ea
actionis esse non posse. Post haec itaque, utrum non multum ames Manicheum, in cordis
tui secreto Deus viderit; quantum tamen ex dogmatum germanitate monstratur, nihil aliud
prorsus egisti, quam ut ordine commutato idem, quod ille affirmarat, astrueres" (*Ibid.*
1,97, p. 113).
454. Cf. *Ibid.* 2,21, pp. 175-176.
455. "Nam et Manicheus subscribit iniquitatem Deo suo, cum eum allegat damnatu-
rum in ultimo die membra quae tradidit; et tu per hoc illum asseris infelicem, per quod
corrumpit gloriam qua cluebat, et persequendo innocentiam, quam creavit, perdidit iustitiam, qua sacerrimus fuit" (*Ibid.* 1,49 [CSEL, 85/1], p. 41).
456. "Ille *[Mani]* enim licet duos induxisset auctores, tamen spem salutis ex ea reliquit parte, qua dixit bonum Deum esse alienissimum ab iniquitate et a crudelitate; tu vero
unum bonum quidem Deum, sed eundem malorum conditorem loquens ut reverentiam
divinitatis, ita spem salutis funditus sustulisti" (*Ibid.* 1,120, p. 136).
457. "Amolire te itaque cum tali Deo tuo de ecclesiarum medio: non est ipse, cui
patriarchae, cui prophetae, cui apostoli crediderunt, in quo speravit et sperat ecclesia
primitivorum, quae conscripta est in caelis; non est ipse, quem credit iudicem rationabilis
creatura, quem spiritus sanctus iuste iudicaturum esse denuntiat. Nemo prudentium pro
tali Domino suum umquam sanguinem fudisset; nec enim merebatur dilectionis affectum,
ut suscipiendae pro se onus imponeret passionis. Postremo iste quem inducis, si esset
uspiam, reus convinceretur esse, non Deus, iudicandus a vero Deo meo, non iudicaturus
pro Deo" (*Ibid.* 1,50, pp. 42-43).

As Magris has clearly shown, there are some texts in Manichaean teaching which, due to its "radical" and "eschatological" dualism[458], might even be understood in a predestinarian way[459] – were it not for the different purpose they acquire when considered in the general (and complex) context of Manichaean doctrine. Let us take, for instance, those statements where it is said that God has planned his *oeconomia salutis* from eternity, by determining beforehand[460] a process that was to unfold itself in three periods of time (or cosmogonical phases): beginning, middle and end[461]. Mani was the only one to have received the revelation

---

458. A "radical" dualism in that it admits the existence *ab aeterno* of two principles (light–darkness/good–evil), and an "eschatological" in that it implies the final destruction of the second principle. Besides, it is also a pro-cosmic dualism in that the cosmos is brought about by the divine principle as a "mechanism" for delivering (and purifying) the divine light which is imprisoned within matter. In this way the cosmos is the means by which the order, harmony and peace of the realm of light is gradually reestablished and its triumph over the realm of darkness becomes definitive (see U. BIANCHI, *Sur le dualisme de Mani*, in A. VAN TONGERLOO – S. GIVERSEN [eds.], *Manichaica Selecta. Studies presented to Professor Julien Ries on the occasion of his seventieth birthday*, Louvain, 1991, pp. 9-17, pp. 9-11).

459. See A. MAGRIS, *Augustins Prädestinationslehre und die manichäischen Quellen*, in VAN OORT – WERMELINGER – WURST (eds.), *Augustine and Manichaeism in the Latin West* (n. 418), pp. 148-160, pp. 151-156.

460. Cf. C.R.C. ALLBERRY (ed.) with a contribution by H. IBSCHER, *A Manichaean Psalm-Book. Part II* (Manichaean Manuscripts in the Chester Beatty Collection, 2), Stuttgart, 1938, p. 7.

461. A brief (and necessarily incomplete) account of the basic elements of the very complex cosmogony of the Manichaean myth (which ultimately tries to solve the perennial and basic question of the existence of evil) can be given as follows. At the beginning of the cosmogonical process the two co-eternal Principles – the principle of good (God) who dwells in the realm of light, and the principle of evil (Satan) who dwells in the realm of darkness – existed completely separated from each other, except for a side of each realm which bordered with the other. The second or middle moment concerns the present condition, which has come about as the result of the cosmic battle caused by the invasion of the darkness-realm into the light-realm. In consequence of this invasion, the defender of the realm of light, the *Ur*-man (or Primal Human), was captured by the evil forces, whereas some of the latter were also captured by the forces of light. From that moment onwards light and darkness, viz. good and evil, became mixed. Some beings were sent out from the realm of light to try and free the Primal Human. In this they succeded, at the cost, however, of some light particles that remained trapped in the darkness. Further steps were taken by the Great Father (or the *Spiritus Vivens*) in order to recapture the imprisoned light. Primarily, the creation of light-collectors (sun and moon) whose goal was to collect the light that had been absorbed by the demons that were captured during the cosmic battle. These demons were in fact enticed to release their light, which was thus transferred back (via the sun and the moon) to the realm of light. The retaliation of the evil principle consisted in the creation of a rival to the Primal Human. The mating of a male and female demon produced the human protoplasts, Adam and Eve, whose aim was to counter the realm of light by keeping as much light as possible entrapped in the visible world by generating offspring. The realm of light, in its turn, reacted to this evil's new tactic by sending Jesus (eventually identified with the bearer of saving knowledge) whose goal was to reveal divine knowledge (γνῶσις) to Adam and Eve, made of both light

of what was, is and shall be[462]. Belief in the pre-existence of the
Manichaean church in the aeons of the kingdom of God[463] may also be
considered as pointing to a predestinarian background, and yet such a
belief was not distinctive of Manichaeism[464]. Even the parable of the
good and bad tree[465], taken from Mt 7,17, could at first sight be interpreted as alluding to two different classes of people: the good, and the
bad. In reality what the parable wants to suggest is that the two principles of light and darkness try to exercise their own power within individuals by fighting against each other[466]. The Manichaean theory of the
"lump" (βῶλος or *globus [horribilis]*)[467] could also offer sufficient reasons for thinking of an underlying eschatological and predestinarian
view. According to this theory, once the universe is destroyed by the
purifying fire, as a result of the final war waged by the realm of light
against the realm of darkness, the light will be definitively separated
from the darkness. Then, whereas the light particles will be released and
saved[468] and the souls of the righteous "glued" to the surface of the
βῶλος, evil matter and its victims (the damned souls) shall be impris-

(soul) and matter (body). The release of light from matter was to continue in this world
through the special agency of the Manichaean Elect. The end or final cosmogonical
moment will come about when this process of releasing light from matter will have
reached its highest pitch. Then a purifying fire will complete the process and destroy the
universe, imprisoning the evil principle and all its substance in the βῶλος or *globus (horribilis)*. See COYLE, *Mani, Manicheism*, in A.D. FITZGERALD (ed.), *Augustine through the
Ages. An Encyclopedia*, Grand Rapids, MI-Cambridge, 1999, pp. 520-525, pp. 521-523.
    462. Cf. *Codex Manichaicus Coloniensis*, in A. HEINRICHS and L. KOENEN (eds.), *Der
Kölner Mani-Kodex (P. Colon. inv. nr. 4780)*, in *ZPE* 19 (1975) 1-85, p. 23. *Turfanfragment M 17*, in F.W. MÜLLER (ed.), *Handschriften-Reste in Estrangelo-Schrift aus Turfan,
Chinesisch-Turkestan* II (SPAW.PH, 2), Berlin, 1904, p. 26.
    463. Cf. ALLBERRY (ed.), *A Manichaean Psalm-Book* (n. 460), pp. 133ff.
    464. The metaphor of the pre-existent Church was used also in orthodox Catholic
milieux. Cf., for instance: "Unde et mystice ait Sara: *conclusit me Dominus ut non
pariam. Intra ergo ad ancillam meam et filium facies ex illa*, ut agnoscas in praedestinatione fuisse semper ecclesiam Dei et paratam fidei fecunditatem..." (Ambrose, *De Abraham* 2,10,74 [CSEL, 32/1], p. 627).
    465. Cf. *Kephalaia* 2, in A. BÖHLIG – H. J. POLOTSKY (eds.), *Kephalaia*, Bd. I/1
(Manichäische Handschriften der Staatlichen Museen Berlin, 1), Stuttgart, 1940, pp. 17.
18. 58; ALLBERRY (ed.), *A Manichaean Psalm-Book* (n. 460), p. 66.
    466. See MAGRIS, *Augustins Prädestinationslehre und die manichäischen Quellen*
(n. 459), p. 153.
    467. Cf. *Kephalaia* 2; 17; 24, in BÖHLIG – POLOTSKY (eds.), *Kephalaia* (n. 465),
pp. 41; 57; 76.
    468. Only a few light particles shall be lost, more precisely those which were still
mingled with evil matter when the latter was forced to withdraw into the βῶλος. See *Turfanfragment M 2*, in F.C. ANDREAS – W.B. HENNING (eds.), *Mitteliranische Manichaica
aus Chinesisch-Turkestan* III, (SPAW.PH, 27), Berlin, 1934, pp. 848-912, pp. 850-851.
Even for the souls of the righteous, however, there exist the possibility of refusing their
salvation. In that case they would doom themselves to eternal perdition (cf. *Ibid.*).

oned in the *globus (horribilis)*, with its opening covered with a huge stone. However, – and this is the main objection against considering the Manichaean concept of salvation as predestinarian –, the righteous souls that are going to be saved are not saved on account of their being pre-destined by the principle of good, but on the basis and on the strength of the human being's will and faith[469].

Furthermore, it must not be forgotten that, according to Mani, all souls partake of the light of the *Ur*-man who was dismembered at the time of the clash between the realms of light and darkness. Every soul, therefore, can freely undertake a journey of repentance and faith through which salvation can be sought. It is obvious that a doctrine of predesti-nation (as Augustine intended it) could not possibly be inferred from these premises[470]. Despite the heavy hindrances that the realm of dark-ness keeps exercising on the spiritual part (light) imprisoned in man[471], Manichaean teaching seems to regard divine election as a chance which is offered to all. Moreover, each individual has a "double" in heaven that has to be rejoined[472]. Retribution and judgement will thus be allot-ted according to each individual's works[473], works which, in their turn, are the result of the commitment of one own's will[474]. This remains operative despite the weakening caused by the pressure exerted on it by the metaphysical struggle. At the same time it is precisely this pressure that, although weighing heavily on each individual, spurs one's free will to make a decision for or against light or darkness. It is man who, ulti-mately, has to choose where to commit himself in the process of the sep-aration of light from darkness[475]. If that is so, then the accusation

469. See MAGRIS, *Augustins Prädestinationslehre und die manichäischen Quellen* (n. 459), p. 154.
470. See ID., *L'idea di destino nel pensiero antico*, Vol. II: *Da Platone a S. Agostino*, Udine, 1985, pp. 830-831.
471. Cf., for instance, *Kephalaia* 85, in BÖHLIG – POLOTSKY (eds.), *Kephalaia* (n. 465), p. 209. For the Manichaean notion of sin, see H.-C. PUECH, *Le Manichéisme. Son fondateur–sa doctrine*, Paris, 1949, pp. 61-62; 169-178; F. DECRET, *Aspects du manichéisme dans l'Afrique romaine. Les controverses de Fortunatus, Faustus et Felix avec saint Augustin*, Paris, 1970, pp. 272-273. 278; 290-291.
472. Cf. *Kephalaia* 90, in BÖHLIG – POLOTSKY (eds.), *Kephalaia* (n. 465), p. 225.
473. Cf. *Ibid.* 39; 59; 89, pp. 105; 150; 222.
474. See R. HAARDT, *Gnosis und Freiheit. 'Die Gnosis ist Freiheit' (Evangelium nach Philippus 132,10). Einige Bemerkungen zur Exposition des Problems*, in *Ex orbe reli-gionum. Studia Geo Widengren*, Vol. I (SHR, 21), Leiden, 1972, pp. 440-448, p. 447.
475. Demaria has rightly noted: "È nell'uomo che deve avvenire la separazione della Luce dalla tenebra, dell'anima dal corpo ed è l'uomo che attua questa separazione seguendo i rigidi precetti dell'etica manichea; è ancora l'uomo che sceglie di compiere o meno questo processo, che è sia materiale sia spirituale. In questo senso il Manicheismo si allontana dallo Gnosticismo che non prevede il libero arbitrio dell'uomo" (S. DEMARIA, *I capitoli LXIX e LXX dei Kephalaia copti manichei. Traduzione e commento* [Archeologia

brought against Manichaeism of being a religion subject to fatalism and totally denying the agency of free will, should be regarded as too simplistic an adaptation of a pattern that was commonly employed in the ancient anti-deterministic polemic. A more nuanced and critical assessment ought thus to be employed regarding free will in Manichaean teaching.

If Manichaeism, as it seems to us, did not share any predestinarian view[476], even less so could the Augustinian theory of predestination be linked with the Manichaean teaching. Magris enumerates three main reasons from which it is possible to infer the Manichaean inbuilt opposition to a predestinarian view[477]. Firstly, according to Manichaeism, the particles of light (the souls of the righteous) are all destined to heaven – with the exception of those very few which remain mingled with evil matter when this is imprisoned in the βῶλος. In Augustine's doctrine, by contrast, Adam's descendants are all born in the *massa damnata*, from which God will single out, from sheer mercy, those He has predestined to salvation. Contrary to the viewpoint of Buonaiuti who had concluded that the Augustinian *massa perditionis* is nothing other than a Christian transposition of the Manichaean βῶλος[478], no equivalence can be established between the two concepts[479]. In fact, however appealing Buonaiuti's contention may be, the differences between the two notions remain great and insuperable. To begin with, the Augustinian theory of predestination, of which the doctrine of the *massa damnata/perditionis/peccatorum* is the ultimate foundation, is infralapsarian. It concerns all men from the point of view of their earthly life. In coming into the world they all partake of Adam's fall, and it is in consequence of that

---

e Storia della Civiltà Egiziana e del Vicino Oriente Antico–Materiali e studi, 3], Imola/Bologna, 1998, p. 12).

476. "Der Manichäer versteht sich nicht als Prädestinierter und darf sich auch nicht als ein solcher verstehen" (MAGRIS, *Augustins Prädestinationslehre und die manichäischen Quellen* [n. 459], p. 156).

477. Cf. *Ibid.*, pp. 156-158.

478. See E. BUONAIUTI, *Manichaeism and Augustine's idea of "massa perditionis"*, in *HTR* 20 (1927) 117-127, pp. 122ff. Buonaiuti was convinced that the Pelagian controversy had forced Augustine's Manichaean past to come to the surface. See also ADAM, *Das Fortwirken des Manichäismus bei Augustin* [n. 419], pp. 16-18.

479. In a note to the *Contra Felicem Manichaeum*, Jourjon points out that the two notions are used independently by both Augustine and Felix. Whereas Augustine employs the term *massa* in the light of his own theological interpretation, Felix speaks of βῶλος according to the Manichaean understanding. There is no indication whatsoever of an attempt, from one side or another, to identify the two notions: "Augustine emploie l'expression *massa* au sens augustinien du terme, devant un Félix qui a évoqué le *globus* manichéen et ni l'un ni l'autre ne donnent l'impression de savoir qu'ils puisent à la même source" (M. JOURJON, *Notes complémentaires* 61, *BA* 17, p. 789).

that they are all worthy to be condemned to eternal death, even though *not* all of them will in fact perish. The metaphor of the βῶλος, instead, rests on a radical dualistic process, whereby only the substances of the evil principle, viz. *all* the darkness (as opposed to the principle of light and its substances), will be gathered and imprisoned in the *globus (horribilis)*, once the final conflagration of the universe has put an end to its mixing with the light. Besides, however connected the two perspectives may be, the Augustinian *massa* is above all a soteriological concept, whereas the manichaean βῶλος is mainly an eschatological one[480]. Secondly, whereas Manichaean righteous souls always risk falling back into the domain of sin and evil[481], in Augustine's predestination theory the *electi* receive with absolute certainty (at times even in spite of themselves) the gift of final perseverance. Thirdly, whereas for Manichaeism the attainment of salvation depends ultimately on man's commitment and right attitude, above all on his adhesion to religious precepts[482], according to Augustine salvation depends essentially on God's grace, on divine predestination *ab aeterno*.

Furthermore, the importance given by Manichaeism to man's agency is no doubt an indication that the concept of nature then entertained was not merely a negative one, and that human nature in particular was not to be seen as intrinsically sinful. Human beings, for the Manichees, are not merely recipients of evil matter, nor are they entirely under the power of the devil. They are also the place where spiritual particles of light are present, although still imprisoned in matter[483]. In other words, man, being a "conflict ridden creature" wherein the two opposing principles face one another, is also the bearer of a positive, godly substance, the light of his soul. The latter is *pars Dei* (or *substantia Dei*)[484], and it

---

480. See A. PINCHERLE, *La formazione teologica di Sant'Agostino*, Rome, 1947, p. 189. It is certainly on the basis of the interrelation of soteriology and eschatology that Lee emphasizes the importance of favouring the study of Augustine's theory of predestination from an eschatological point of view. The importance of such an approach, he contends, becomes evident if we take into account his theory of "cosmic order" as an alternative to the Manichaean theory of the universe as a mixture of good and evil. Moreover, within the framework of the cosmic order of God's creation, the primacy of the determination by divine will would be more easily safeguarded over against the self-determination of man's free will. See LEE, *Augustine, Manichaeism, and the Good* (n. 113), pp. 61ff.

481. Cf. *Kephalaia* 38, in BÖHLIG – POLOTSKY (eds.), *Kephalaia* (n. 465), p. 98.

482. *Turfanfragment* M 2, in ANDREAS–HENNING (eds.), *Mitteliranische Manichaica aus Chinesisch-Turkestan* (n. 468), pp. 850-851.

483. See, for instance, the Manichaean confession schemes in: A. VON LE COQ (ed.), *Chuastvanift, ein Sündenbekenntnis der manichäischen Auditores. Gefunden in Turfan (Chinesisch-Turkestan)*, Berlin, 1911, p. 26.

484. "Augustin hat sich mit der Frage, daß die menschliche Seele *pars dei* nach dem manichäischen Mythos ist, mehrmals auseinandergesetzt" (MAGRIS, *Augustins Prädesti-*

is endowed with a νοῦς[485], thanks to which human beings can free themselves from the dominion of concupiscence and, using free will, can
accomplish moral deeds. In a certain way, therefore, even "the body is a
conditio sine qua non for salvation, since it is the very place where the
nous can demonstrate its triumph over darkness and matter"[486]. No
doubt, this view is in contrast with the accusation brought against
Augustine by Julian of Aeclanum. So Julian cannot have been on such
solid ground[487] as he thought when he attacked the bishop of Hippo for
reviving Manichaean belief in the wickedness of the material nature of
man, seen as a source of sinfulness, through his doctrine of *peccatum
naturale/originale*[488] (or *malum originale*[489]) and the notion of *concupiscentia sexualis*[490]. We should therefore avoid, from a conceptual point of

---

nationslehre und die manichäischen Quellen [n. 459], p. 160, n. 48). Cf., for instance,
Augustine, *Contra Fortunatum Manichaeum* 11-12 (CSEL, 25/1), pp. 89-90; Id., *Contra
Felicem Manichaeum* 2,15-22 (CSEL, 25/2), pp. 844-852. See PUECH, *Le Manichéisme.
Son fondateur–sa doctrine* (n. 471), p. 32; DECRET, *Aspects du manichéisme dans
l'Afrique romaine* [n. 471], pp. 217f.

485. See A. VAN TONGERLOO, *Reflections on the Manichaean ΝΟΥΣ*, in Id. (ed.) in
collaboration with J. VAN OORT, *The Manichaean ΝΟΥΣ* (n. 418), pp. 309-315.

486. H.J.W. DRIJVERS, *Conflict and Alliance in Manichaeism*, in H.G. KIPPENBERG
(ed.), *Struggles of Gods*, Berlin-New York-Amsterdam, 1984, p. 110.

487. One must also be reminded that Julian did not always have a correct knowledge
of Manichaean teaching. For instance, nowhere do we find in Manichaeism the doctrine
of Adam's *Ursünde*, as Julian contends: "Dicunt, inquit *[Iulianus]*, illi Manichei,... quia
primi hominis peccato, id est Adae, liberum arbitrium perierit et nemo iam potestatem
habeat bene uiuendi, sed omnes in peccatum carnis suae necessitate cogantur" (Augustine, *Contra duas epistulas Pelagianorum* 1,2,4 [CSEL, 60], p. 425).

488. Although the expression *peccatum naturale* would serve Julian's purpose better,
in that it recalls the concept of "nature" as something necessary and immutable, the
divine of Aeclanum is well aware that Augustine had substituted the expression *peccatum
originale* for that of *peccatum naturale*: "Ergo iure dicitur, confitearis necesse est, naturale quod Manichaeus finxerat, sed tu nomine commutato originale vocas, interiisse peccatum" (Julian, *Ad Florum* 5,9 [PL, 45], c. 1438).

489. "Perfecte itaque Manichaeus est, qui malum originale defendit" (Id., *Ad Turbantium* 1,78 [CCL, 88], p. 360). "Ambo igitur, tu et Manichaeus, pariter malum naturale
firmatis, id est ambo malam naturam hominum aeque dicitis, sed ille fidelius, tu fraudu-
lentius" (Id., *Ad Florum* 3,154 [CSEL, 85/1], p. 485). "The doctrine of original sin
seemed to Julian to involve the acceptance of the idea that human nature is intrinsically
sinful.... All this smacks of Manichean thinking sufficiently strongly to encourage Julian
to feel that he has solid grounds for his accusation" (G.R. EVANS, *Neither a Pelagian nor
a Manichee, cit.*, p. 239).

490. Manichaeism and Augustine are very negative about the *concupiscentia sexualis*.
In fact they both stress the negativity of the sexual impulse whose inordinateness and
uncontrollability is in their eyes the evident sign of its inherent sinfulness. Sin is transmitted thanks to sexual desire. See J. VAN OORT, *Augustine and Mani on* concupiscentia
sexualis, in J. DEN BOEFT – J. VAN OORT (eds.), *Augustiniana Traiectina. Communications
présentées au Colloque International d'Utrecht 13-14 novembre 1986*, Paris, 1987,
pp. 137-152; ID., *Augustine on Sexual Concupiscence and Original Sin*, in StPatr 22,

view, the temptation to unfairly reduce Manichaeism to a mere "radical" dualism and to make Augustine depend on it[491].

At the end of this short section devoted to the possible links or affinities between Augustine and Manichaeism, in particular between the former's doctrine of predestination and Manichaean dualism, we are left with the conviction that the bishop of Hippo cannot be regarded as a crypto-Manichee, although in more than one aspect of his theology of grace he seems to have remained a Manichee "by implication"[492]. We must accept that due to the long familiarity he had enjoyed with Manichaean teaching, its *Denkformen*, although unconsciously, must have lingered at the back of his mind. Even when the major lines (or "constants") of Augustine's theological construction were laid, the most valuable insights of his past intellectual and religious experience must have continued to exercise some indirect influence. It is hard to believe that traces of the Manichean teaching, with which Augustine had nourished his soul and mind for many years, were not still present in his *Wissenreservoir*[493]. Yet, even if we admit that it probably was so, it does not follow, methodologically speaking, that one should *per se* think of an implied Manichaeism every time Augustine employs a dualistic language to address the different realities of man's existential paradox: life and death, good and evil, grace and free will, salvation and damnation. Besides, dualistic language and phraseology was not the prerogative of Manichaeism. It could be found (and not necessarily in an antithetical

---

Louvain, 1989, pp. 382-386; LAMBERIGTS, *Was Augustine a Manichaean?* (n. 424), pp. 125-132; ID., *Some Critiques on Augustine's View of Sexuality Revisited*, in StPatr 33, Louvain, 1997, pp. 152-161. Lee asserts that there is a direct link between the Manichaean notion of evil as turbulence or random motion and Augustine's concept of *concupiscentia* as *motus inordinatus*. Influenced by Manichaeism Augustine would have more and more identified his notion of *concupiscentia* with the *libido* of the sexual desires, viz. the *concupiscentia carnis* (see LEE, *Augustine, Manichaeism, and the Good* [n. 113], pp. 53-59).

491. "De tous les mots en –isme, le manichéisme est probablement le mot qui est affligé de nos jours de la plus forte réduction conceptuelle. Dans notre usage courant, le manichéisme est celui pour qui il y a le bien et le mal, comme il y a le jour et la nuit, l'eau et le feu. Sans transition, ni mélange. Si au IVe siècle on avait pu en faire une pareille caricature, on ne comprendrait pas qu'Augustin ait pu s'y laisser prendre" (S. LANCEL, *Saint Augustin*, Paris, 1999, p. 56).

492. See *supra*, p. 387, n. 421.

493. "Dabei hat er aus seinem großen Wissenreservoir geschöpft, das er sich aus antiker Philosophie, biblischer und kirklicher Theologie, aber eben auch aus manichäischer Literatur gefüllt hatte, und aus der dialogischen Denktradition und –argumentation der Griechen und Römer" (K. RUDOLPH, *Augustinus Manichaicus–Das Problem von Konstanz und Wandel*, in VAN OORT–WERMELINGER–WURST [eds.], *Augustine and Manichaeism in the Latin West* [n. 418], pp. 1-15, p. 7).

form) in all philosophical or religious systems of antiquity. The language of Christian revelation and Scripture, to which every believer ought to conform, is no exception[494].

494. As a scholar, who has been studying the relationship between Augustine and Manichaeism for a long time, has attentively remarked: "From Manichaean dualism Augustine, strongly influenced by Neoplatonism, moved on to a dualistically coloured phraseology as he found in the Scriptures" (VAN OORT, *Jerusalem and Babylon* [n. 416], p. 226).

CONCLUSION

1. AUGUSTINE'S *GNADENMONERGISMUS* AND CASSIAN'S "HUMANISTIC" APPROACH

If we agree with Augustine that the relationship between grace and free will ought not to be considered as a matter of two equal and complementary truths, it is nevertheless indisputable that in the light of his theory on predestination, what is jeopardised is not only the way that this relationship is kept in place, but the very possibility of it existing. Although he speaks of a co-presence and of a co-operation between the two, the asymmetrical manner by which Augustine brings the two poles together emphasizes the role of sovereign and gratuitous grace at the expense of the significance of free will. The bishop of Hippo became convinced that human existence is subject to God's plan from start to finish. Even though the unfolding of this plan is concretely and historically brought about by men, who perform in the worldly arena as voluntary, though not necessarily conscious, "actors", nothing is really added to or taken away from God's design by this human agency. It is particularly regarding choice in virtue that free will appears to be alienated from its ontological autonomy and absorbed by grace by a process of causality. All of man's good will and virtue is the result of God's will which, in a vertically oriented relationship[1], pre-determines and moves human free will through prevenient grace. Faith itself seems to acquire a "neutral" dimension[2], untouched by man's autonomous desire. It is a gift of God following from his inscrutable predestination[3]. In point of fact, when divine grace is considered at the level of its enactment in a truly free human will – viz. a will delivered from vice and passion by

1. In spite of her heavy criticism of Augustine (which has been defined "un reglèment de comptes": P.-M. HOMBERT, *Gloria gratiae. Se glorifier en Dieu, principe et fin de la théologie augustinienne de la grâce*, Paris, 1996, p. 317, n. 187), it seems to us that Zananiri strikes the right note when she speaks of "une relation verticale-féodale dont Dieu est l'unique arbitre" (M. ZANANIRI, *La controverse sur la prédestination au Vᵉ siècle: Augustin, Cassien et la Tradition*, in P. RANSON [ed.], *Saint Augustin, s. l. s. d.*, p. 251).
2. See M. SMALBRUGGE, *Rupture dans l'homme, rupture dans la culture. Quelques réflexions sur le thème de la prédestination chez Augustin*, in *Aug(L)* 50 (2000) 235-256, p. 254.
3. "Intellegamus ergo vocationem qua fiunt electi: non qui eliguntur quia crediderunt, sed qui eliguntur ut credant" (Augustine, *De praedestinatione sanctorum* 17,34 [PL, 44], c. 985).

divine intervention and now attuned to God –, such grace becomes aligned with and somehow identical to the good-seeking free will. According to Augustine, it is only in the case of evil that man is fully responsible for his will, although it is, even then, not fully free (in the theological sense of freedom) in that the soul will remain subject to passion and vice until it is delivered by divine intervention[4], if and when God so desires. As has been stated, in Augustine's view man is indeed "free in the sense only of being arranged to act in a way which is not subject to external pressures. All men are thus 'free'; the elect are free from serious sins; the damned are free from virtue. The elect are slaves of *caritas*; the damned are slaves of *cupiditas*"[5].

When set against the background of a personal and communal history which seems to be reduced to a mere execution of a divine pre-ordained and pre-determined plan, the uneasiness, the resistance and the opposition of the African and Gallic monks to Augustine's viewpoint, appear fully justified. More specifically, the reaction from the monastic settlements of Southern Gaul is a clear attempt to curb the Augustinian doctrine of the absolute sovereignty of grace, particularly in its predestinarian implications. As has been suggested, it is likely that "if Augustine had never written, we should expect to find Cassian expressing the doctrine of grace in the common manner of Egyptian and Syrian monasticism"[6]. The apparent inconsistency when Cassian speaks of the relationship between divine grace and human free will is in itself an indication of his being forced to give a theoretical explanation of their interplay which, from an experiential point of view, he would have taken for granted. Familiar with the tradition of the Eastern Church and monasticism, Cassian saw the two elements in the light of a "dialogical synergism". There exists such a strong and tight bond of co-operation between grace and free will that their relationship is never univocal, viz. *from* grace *to* human will. On the contrary, the ethical inspiration which is at the basis of ascetic efforts can, at times, come to the fore and become prominent enough to throw light on such co-operation. In spite of the general assertions about the "primacy" of God's grace in Christian

---

4. "Sine Dei gratia nullo modo uoluntas implet humana, quia nec libera dicenda est, quam diu est uincentibus et uincientibus cupiditatis subdita" (Id., *Ep.* 145,2 [CSEL, 44], pp. 267-268).

5. J.M. RIST, *Augustine on Free Will and Predestination*, in *JTS* 20 [1969] 420-447, p. 440. In the light of Augustine's theological construction as a whole, the usual translation of the term *seruus* as "slave" must be nuanced on the level of hermeneutics.

6. O. CHADWICK, *John Cassian. A Study in Primitive Monasticism*, 2nd ed., Cambridge, 1968, p. 111.

life, Eastern theology would not reject the idea of the "priority" of human will when it comes to the actual engagement in the struggle against the cluster of vices and passions that prevent the soul from ascending to God. Yet, as committed Christians, and monks striving for perfection, they were only too aware that there are passions and vices, such as pride, that are too strong to be overcome by the agency of human effort alone, and that in order to be successful, the struggle to overcome them must be sustained by the help of divine grace itself. These prag-matic virtue-seeking-men, led by practical and moral reason, rather than by philosophical and theological speculation, were convinced that God's grace and human will function in an "inclusive" way, without one superseding the other.

Above all Cassian questions Augustine's attempt at systematizing, in terms of competitiveness and absolute primacy, the subtle and often mysterious interaction that characterises the relationship between grace and free will. Cassian himself tries to read the relevant Scripture texts in their polysemantic richness. Convinced that each biblical passage is the fruit of divine revelation, he does not oppose those texts which seem to contradict one another, but acknowledges the truth which they manifest. Above all, he is at pains to avoid an over-speculative approach, since this easily runs the risk of preferring a theological theory to the mysteri-ous character of God's revelation. Having said that, it would be utterly unfair to affirm, as suggested in some quarters[7], that the Massilians' doubt concerning the ability of Augustine's doctrine of grace to solve the dilemma of freedom or fatalism is a symptom of Pelagian mentality. The Massilians' opposition to Augustine reflects a much deeper con-cern; a concern over the "manner" in which the truths of grace and free-dom are reconciled. Whereas for Augustine the manner of their recon-ciliation always depends on the governance of God's grace (*Gnadenmonergismus*), from the Massilians' point of view, there should be some room left for some sort of autarchic human initiative, at least in the initial stages of one's conversion. Prayer too, which the bishop of Hippo always believed to be the result of working grace, was not seen by Cassian as an action that was already pre-empted and shaped by divine intervention, but as an activity which could be performed through man's initiative, in order to elicit the bestowal of grace[8].

---

7. This is the conviction, for instance, of A. TRAPÈ, *Introduzione generale*, in ID., *Sant'Agostino, Grazia e libertà: La grazia e il libero arbitrio, La correzione e la grazia, La predestinazione dei santi, Il dono della perseveranza* (NBA, 20), Rome, 1987, p. CLXIV.

8. Cf., for instance, Cassian, *De institutis coenobiorum* 12,14,2 (SC, 109), p. 468.

These different attitudes, the Augustinian and the Massilian, no doubt owe their origin to an underlying difference of vision regarding human nature and the extent to which it was actually affected by Adam's sin. This was an issue of no little importance in their discussion. Unlike Augustine, whose elaboration of the doctrine of original sin is the basis of his concept of grace and predestination, Cassian's acceptance of creationism, as the explanation to the "origin" of the soul, leaves no room for the extreme consequences brought about by the Augustinian doctrine. For Augustine only the first Adam's sinless nature can properly be called "human nature". As we have seen, at the end of his life he categorically reaffirmed that, when referring to Adam's heirs, the expression was only employed as a metaphor[9]. According to the bishop of Hippo it is only through Christ's redemptive act that man's inherent human capabilities are re-empowered and made *capax Dei* once more. Cassian and the Massilians, on the other hand, referred confidently to the notion of *naturae bonum*, and were more optimistic about the human (moral) action that resulted from it, seeing that, in some instances, it might have a place or role of its own. This is the inherent capability of desiring virtue and good, a capability not totally compromised by Adam's fall. Of course, it goes without saying that the positive value attached to man's initiative is always enveloped within, and ultimately dependent upon God the creator, from whom all goodness comes.

In the light of his doctrine of original sin, Augustine was pessimistic about man's inclination to sin and about his actual, personal sinning. In his eyes, the disharmony apparent in fallen humanity, viz. the struggle between the flesh and the spirit generated by concupiscence, and the conflict within the soul itself (also caused by concupiscence, which is responsible for the internal division of the sinful will), are the unavoidable consequences of original sin. Seen from such a gloomy perspective, he was incapable of regarding this disorder, viz. the result of man's sinful nature, as the starting point for a humanity struggling for virtue, goodness and worthiness before God. Contrary to Augustine's view, however, the Massilians took a more "humanistic" approach and considered the reality of man's fallen nature a prerequisite for divine salvation. Rather than insisting, retrospectively, that original sin is the foundational cause of man's inability to do good (unless assisted by Christ's irresistible grace), they focussed on the concrete demands made of human beings; demands that can lead to a human betterment under the assistance of grace. Concretely, they took into account the constant

9. See *supra*, p. 285, n. 458.

struggle man undergoes between the opposing desires of the flesh and the promptings of the spirit, and regarded this combat as the *locus* where man is able to take the initiative by desiring to re-align himself to God and his commandments. This perspective has, no doubt, the advantage of closely linking together creation and redemption, God's intervention and human responsibility, or, as Augustine would have it, the grace of Adam and the grace of Christ.

Finally, we do not find satisfactory even Augustine's "compatibilist" suggestion, that the ultimate solution to the reconciliation of grace and free will, is the notion of *caritas* or *dilectio* as the source of inspiration for virtuous acts[10]. The bishop of Hippo often invoked this solution, not only as the key to the understanding of his theology of grace, but also as the determining factor of his thought as a whole[11]. He contended that since it does not operate in a coercive way, the *ordo caritatis* neither restrains nor annihilates the agency of human free will. By speaking to the heart rather than the mind, it gently persuades, leading the soul to conversion rather than guilty conviction. Love, as the internal *pondus*[12] of the will, leaves the human being free: free to be touched by God's love, and free to respond by returning it[13]. That being the case, it is remarkable to note that love, as the key to understanding the relationship between grace and free will, suffers a severe blow when it comes to the problem of individual salvation or predestination. Here Augustine seems

10. See *supra*, pp. 245ff. Djuth contends that Augustine's compatibilist solution, with regard to the relationship between grace and free will, is of Stoic provenance. She writes: "Stoic compatibilism, such as that found in the thought of Seneca and Chrysippus, provides the inspiration for the harmony Augustine sees between grace and human freedom. The capacity of free choice, then, is the locus of human and divine activity that intersects in the production of virtuous acts. And since virtuous acts are acts of love, that is, voluntary acts, they remain uncoerced, despite being produced by God" (M. DJUTH, *The Hermeneutics of* De libero arbitrio III*: Are There Two Augustines?*, in StPatr 27, Louvain, 1993, pp. 288-289). See also EAD., *Stoicism and Augustine's Doctrine of Human Freedom after 396*, in J. SCHNAUBELT – F. VAN FLETEREN (eds.), *Augustine: Second Founder of the Faith* (CollAug, 1), New York-Frankfurt a. Mainz-Paris, 1990, pp. 387-401.
11. See T.J. VAN BAVEL, *Love*, in A.D. FITZGERALD (ed.), *Augustine through the Ages. An Encyclopedia*, Grand Rapids, MI – Cambridge, 1999, pp. 509-516; A. TRAPÈ, *Libertà e grazia*, in *Congresso Internazionale su S. Agostino nel XVI Centenario della Conversione, Roma, 15-20 settembre 1986. Atti*, Vol. I (SEAug, 24), Rome, 1987, pp. 189-202, pp. 200-202; ID., *Introduzione generale* (n. 7), pp. LXXXVI-XCI; HOMBERT, *Gloria gratiae* (n. 1), pp. 339 and 576; G. BONNER, *The Desire for God and the Need for Grace in Augustine's Theology*, in *Congresso Internazionale su S. Agostino*, 1987, pp. 203-215, pp. 211f.
12. Cf. Augustine, *Confessiones* 13,9,10 (CCL, 27), pp. 246-247.
13. "...inspiratio dilectionis ut cognita sancto amore faciamus" (Id., *Contra duas epistulas Pelagianorum* 4,5,11 [CSEL, 60], p. 532).

to leave aside the *ordo caritatis* in favour of the *iustitia Dei*, a mysterious and hidden equity, due to which many are not saved. This dismal solution appears to us even more striking when we consider, for instance, Augustine's beautiful commentary on the primacy of love found in the first letter of St. John. It seems a pity that he was struck more by the imperative of divine justice than by the following illuminating words: "God is greater than our hearts" (1 Jn 3,20), and: "Who will separate us from the love of Christ?" (Rom 8,35).

2. DIVINE JUSTICE *VERSUS* DIVINE MERCY, AND OTHER "FALSE NOTES" IN AUGUSTINE'S DOCTRINE OF PREDESTINATION

"Didn't my Lord deliver Daniel, Daniel, Daniel? Didn't my Lord deliver Daniel? Then why not every man?" (*Negro Spiritual*). No doubt questions such as this must have tormented Augustine's mind. The problem was that his efforts were not aimed at understanding "how" all men could indeed be saved, but were aimed instead towards providing answers to the riddle of "why" many would not be saved. Focussing on the absolute sovereignty and necessity of divine grace in attaining salvation (an unavoidable necessity due to Adam's fall and humanity's fellowship with him – *massa damnata*), Augustine comes to the conclusion that grace is not a "right" due to all, and that its dispensation is therefore restricted. If God rescues some from the *massa damnata* in order to justify and save them, He does so purely as an act of mercy. In this way God cannot be said to act unjustly with regard to those He does not save. In the eyes of the bishop of Hippo, justice and mercy are two divine attributes of equal standing which manifest, respectively, God's "due" condemnation of sin and God's "undue" bestowal of grace[14].

The Augustinian dichotomy of justice and mercy could give the impression, as his opponents duly remarked, that he was thinking in Manichaean terms: of a loving and merciful God on one hand, and of the awesome God of geometrical justice and punishment on the other. Augustine's misjudgement rests precisely on his having thought of divine justice as an attribute juxtaposed to that of mercy, and consequently as falling outside the framework of grace. In the light of his doctrine of predestination, the justice of God was seen only in relation to the deserved condemnation of those who are not saved by divine mercy. In

---

14. "Tunc rebus ipsis euidentius apparebit quod in psalmo scriptum est: *Misericordiam et iudicium cantabo tibi Domine [Ps 100,1]*, quia nisi per indebitam misericordiam nemo liberatur, et nisi per debitum iudicium nemo damnatur" (Augustine, *Enchiridion ad Laurentium* 24,94 [CCL, 46], p. 99).

other words, Augustine was not able to integrate divine justice into a soteriological perspective. In his eyes, God's justice has nothing to do with his willingness to extend the promise of salvation to all, but in punishing those deserving of it. In this way God keeps salvation only for those He "wishes" to save. It is as though God did not really desire the salvation of all mankind, so that the severity of his punishment becomes tinged with an even more striking (and shocking) vengeance[15]! In short, Augustine was unable to ask himself the following question: if justice requires punishment for all men (because all have sinned in Adam), why should divine mercy not contain, in its turn, a universal salvation through the second Adam? Or, in other words, why should God exact the punishment of eternal loss/damnation from some people instead of demanding it of all humanity?[16]

We must conclude that, in Augustine's doctrine of predestination, the "unity" of God and of his *oeconomia salutis* is problematic. Even before implying a discrimination on the level of theodicy, the Augustinian theory of predestination produces a metaphysical and logical aporia which cannot be solved. This aporia consists in the impossibility of the predestinarian theory being reconciled with the concept of divine simplicity[17], namely with "the complete absence in God of any distinction, variation, disproportion or inequality"[18]. It would be difficult to believe that Augustine did not see a contradiction between the notion of a God who is *simplex*, on one side, and the notion of a predestinarian, "discriminating" God, on the other. It is most likely that he thought the concept of divine omnipotence (viz. God's absolute will) the most suitable ground on which to base his doctrine of grace, original sin and predestination. Convinced that *totum Deo dandum est*[19] and that man was subject only to the fragility and wretchedness of his fallen nature, he chose to side with God's omnipotence. An "apologist of the rights of God"[20], he stood by the sovereignty of a deity able to determine everything without ever being determined by the will of any creature.

15. "Si omnes a tenebris transferrentur in lucem, in nullo appareret ueritas ultionis" (Id., *De ciuitate Dei* 21,12 [CCL, 48], p. 778).

16. In not positing an equal universality, Augustine does indeed depict a God who is not always equitable, a God who is ultimately "plus digne de la sévérité du droit romain que de la pitié et de la charité de notre Rédempteur" (J.-F. THOMAS, *Saint Augustin s'est-il trompé? Essai sur la prédestination*, Paris, 1959, p. 80).

17. See N. STRAND, *Augustine on Predestination and Divine Simplicity: The Problem of Compatibility*, in StPatr 38, Louvain, 2001, pp. 290-305, p. 302.

18. *Ibid.* p. 290. Cf. Augustine, *De ciuitate Dei* 11,10 (CCL, 48), pp. 330f.

19. Id., *De praedestinatione sanctorum* 7,12 (PL, 44), c. 970.

20. F. CAYRÉ, *La Prédestination dans Saint Augustin. Notes générales*, in ATh(A) 2 (1941) 42-63, p. 56.

However, if Augustine cannot be criticised on account of his option for the primacy of God, nevertheless, when every allowance has been made, we cannot but point out that the view he holds of divine omnipotence seems a more fitting description of a despotic and arbitrary God rather than the Christian God of love. Undoubtedly, the Neoplatonic concept of God (whose self-communication to man is seen as a necessary emanation of the *summum bonum*) can be regarded, at least in part, as responsible for Augustine's view of divine omnipotence. However, one thing is sure: the overriding emphasis given to God's omnipotence seems to neglect the gratuitous initiative taken by God himself in the Incarnation of his Son, Jesus Christ. It is in him and through him that humanity encounters divinity, and is able to see an alternative to human sinfulness. Augustine's way of comprehending God's salvific power with regard to humanity has therefore something to do with his view of God's omnipotence; an omnipotence that (the way it is depicted) seems very close to arbitrariness[21]. By emphasizing God's omnipotent and infallible will over against man's compromised and sinfully oriented freedom[22], and by suggesting that these two realities are in competition, Augustine opened the door to an understanding of divine omnipotence as an overwhelming reality, having more to do with a philosophical idea than with biblical revelation. Entrapped within this unidirectional perspective, he could not but regard the notion of predestination as the best possible explanation of God's absolute ruling vis-à-vis human impotence. Augustine's efforts to safeguard so absolute a theocentrism, where all that matters is the power of divine sovereignty and irresistible grace, was seen to imply, in the eyes of his opponents, that he acknowledged that the *electi* were drawn "to the appropriate stimulus from God in the same inevitable fashion as iron is drawn to a magnet"[23]. If that were so, then, behind the psychological illusion of experiencing a personal freedom, human beings would be in reality subject to moral determinism and deprived of an autonomous metaphysical freedom, which would guarantee the possibility of directing their own will in the way of salvation.

21. "Augustine lacks the conceptual resources to distinguish omnipotence from arbitrariness in God and thereby compromises the workings of the power of God's love, itself a peculiarly Augustinian divine attribute" (J.M. RIST, *Augustine: Ancient Thought Baptized*, Cambridge, 1994, p. 286).

22. "Die totale Entmächtigung des Menschen ... zugunsten der ausschließlichen Macht Gottes" (G. GRESHAKE, *Gnade als konkrete Freiheit. Eine Untersuchung zur Gnadenlehre des Pelagius*, Mainz, 1972, p. 168).

23. RIST, *Augustine on Free Will and Predestination* (n. 5), p. 430.

If that be the case, namely, if nothing occurs in the life of either the elect or the reprobate, other than that already planned by God, what can man achieve except a passive attendance on divine will? Even with regard to virtue and goodness, if God's plan entails the performance of certain deeds by certain people, there is no doubt it will be accomplished. If on the other hand God's plan entails that other people be not actually involved in the outcome of their quest for virtue and goodness, then their only option would be an attitude of passivity. Obviously, Augustine's theory of predestination raises more questions than it solves, questions which ultimately affect the very meaning of life. At this level we feel an instinctive sympathy with the objections raised by the monks of Hadrumetum and Provence. What would be the value of human life, of striving for virtue and fighting against evil, in one word, of ethical commitment, if human destiny has already been decided in a meta-historical realm? What would be the purpose of dispensing praise or rebuke, reward and punishment? And, above all, what would be the criterion for the evaluation of moral acts, said to conform to God's will, if these same acts do not ultimately depend on man's autonomous will, but on a will which is "moved" by God's grace? Not only are these questions left unanswered by Augustine's doctrine of predestination, but they are also magnified in a more dramatic way.

Another problematic question is that concerning the real significance, within God's *oeconomia salutis*, of the gratuitous communication of God's love to all men in and through Christ. According to Augustine's predestinarian theory, there seems to be no room for any reconciliation between God's omnipotent justice and his universal salvific will. On the contrary, the Augustinian notion of election is selective. Ironically enough, the Doctor of Hippo, who had fought against the Pelagian exaltation of man's free will (which in his eyes would not only exalt human ability beyond its capacity, but would ultimately restrict the number of committed Christians to a heroic élite[24]) reached the same conclusion, but from opposite premises, viz. by emphasizing that God's sovereign and omnipotent grace alone is responsible for setting the elect apart. Augustine also expounded the idea of a fixed and unalterable "élite" of predestined, elect called and set apart from the *massa damnata* to be saved by God's eternal decree. We have already hinted at the aporia

24. Determined to combat spiritual elitism, Augustine considered "moral self-advertisement in any form – from Donatists, Pelagians, or orthodox ascetics – ... as theologically ill-founded and socially divisive" (C. LEYSER, *Semi-Pelagianism*, in FITZGERALD [ed.], *Augustine through the Ages* [n. 11], pp. 761-766, p. 763).

such a solution involves regarding the significance of the redemptive act of Christ and his mediation; not to mention the significance of the sacraments, and the Church which dispenses them. Augustine's view of the salvific and regenerative nature of baptism, on one hand, and, on the other, of divine predestination as a determining factor in individual salvation or damnation (independently of the reception of the sacrament of regeneration), reveals an inherent contradiction, as far as his theory of election is concerned. First of all, it makes "morally" unacceptable the idea that innocent infants, dying before baptism, would be condemned to eternal damnation. And secondly, it would make God's grace and salvation exclusively dependent on the performance of the sacrament (viz. baptism) which, although theoretically a *conditio sine qua non* for the attainment of salvation, does not appear, as a matter of fact, ultimately decisive. We come to this conclusion prompted by the observation that, in Augustine's predestinarian view, the power of the sacrament of baptism with regard to baptised adults not elected by God's decree is not decisive, and ultimately remains insignificant. It would seem that, on one hand, the sacrament of regeneration delivers the person concerned from the *massa damnata*, while on the other this person has no guarantee of a future share in eternal bliss. Nor can such a guarantee be looked for in membership of the Church or in one's serious and active engagement in the Christian faith, for even the "faithful" cannot be certain of final perseverance. The good that man accomplishes could, in fact, be only a temporary achievement. Final perseverance in virtue and goodness, as the prerequisite of salvation, is guaranteed only by God's inscrutable and eternal decrees. Augustine's conviction that God's will operates within an "eternal present", in which the effects are produced *hic et nunc*, prevents him from properly taking into account the temporal and historical involvement of God in the person of Jesus Christ, and the ultimate significance of the Church and her sacraments. Moreover, Augustine's vertically oriented doctrine of predestination lacks, as it were, the necessary consideration of the so-called "secondary causes" as being also an undeniable part of the offer of salvation[25] which, thanks to the Incarnation and the Pascal mystery of Christ, is continually bestowed on every human being. Once again, the impasse in which Augustine found himself indicates his inability to express in human terms "the *mode* in which God, the first cause of all that is, works through the secondary causes, in particular our freedom, when creating a world in which some save themselves and others condemn themselves, though no

25. See HOMBERT, *Gloria gratiae* (n. 1), p. 581.

one can accuse God of injustice or favouritism"[26]. There is no doubt that in this matter, Cassian and the Massilians, "though lacking the range and sweep of Augustine's genius", are "truer to Augustine's instincts than Augustine himself"[27].

3. EXEGESIS VIS-À-VIS THEOLOGICAL PRESUPPOSITIONS

Like all the Christian writers of the first centuries, Augustine considered Holy Scripture as the starting point and the essential instrument of his theological reflection. He constantly referred to it in order to bolster his views: from his attempt to explain the relationship between grace and free will, to the issue of the *initium fidei* and the problems of election, predestination and universal salvation[28]. At the beginning of the *De praedestinatione sanctorum*, for instance, Augustine makes it clear that theological questions, such as that of grace, must be tackled and solved in the light of Holy Scripture (*diuina eloquia*) to which Christians must always attentively pay homage[29]. In his eyes it was unacceptable for a Christian not to subdue himself (*non ceditur*) to the authority of Scripture. It is, therefore, through scriptural revelation – viz. from the "point of view of God" – that the *condition humaine* should be approached and understood. Augustine was convinced that this hierarchy, with Scripture firmly in the highest position, should not be overturned[30].

Augustine was also aware of the problem of "right" understanding and interpretation of Scripture, and of how this might give rise to dispute and divergence. He was criticised himself by the Massilians on account of his interpretation of the election of Jacob and the rejection of Esau in Rom 9. They were convinced that Augustine had undertaken a personal exegesis regarding the problem of predestination and universal salvation; an exegesis attuned to his own particular theological viewpoint, rather than to the original meaning intended by Paul and understood by

26. H. RONDET, *Predestination*, in H. RONDET – K. RAHNER, *Predestination*, in *SM* 5, New York-London, 1970, pp. 88-91.

27. BONNER, *The Desire for God and the Need for Grace in Augustine's Theology* (n. 11), p. 215.

28. "Augustin begnügt sich fast ganz damit, aus der Schrift zu zeigen, daß seine Lehre wahr ist und aufrecht erhalten werden muß, ohne weiter auf ihre Vereinbarkeit mit anderen Wahrheiten einzugehen" (K. RAHNER, *Augustin und der Semipelagianismus*, in *ZKT* 62 [1938] 171-196, pp. 194-195).

29. "Ego autem quamvis me moleste ferre confitear, quod divinis eloquiis quibus Dei gratia praedicatur (quae omnino nulla est, si secundum merita nostra datur), tam multis manifestisque non ceditur" (Augustine, *De praedestinatione sanctorum* 1,1 [PL, 44], c. 960).

30. "Non ibi humana, sed diuina occurrat auctoritas" (Id., *De correptione et gratia* 1,1 [CSEL, 92], p. 219).

CONCLUSION

prominent *ecclesiastici*[31]. It must be acknowledged, however, that Augustine's attitude is not a peculiar and isolated one. For him, as well as "for the patristic interpreters, exegesis is not distinct from, but rather is interwoven with theology"[32]. Thus, although constant reference to Holy Scripture constitutes the centre around which Augustine's theological thought is constructed, biblical passages were, at times, interpreted in the light of intuition or presupposition as deemed suitable in solving particular problems. From a methodological point of view it is hard to assess to what extent Augustine drew his theological ideas from Scripture (for instance with regard to predestination and the Pauline understanding of it), and to what extent he tried, instead, to find some basis in Scripture for a theological standpoint peculiarly his own. Since Augustine was a living part of the "formation tradition", it is not easy for us to reach a fair and impartial judgement about his use of each method. Even more so if we acknowledge that Augustine (like all the Fathers of the Church) was not in possession of the historical and critical method to which modern exegesis is accustomed. We will not be exceedingly amazed, therefore, if sometimes Augustine does not hesitate to see in some scriptural texts the necessary substratum to his point of view. What we should be prepared to admit is that some of Augustine's interpretations, besides being alien to the original sense of some specific biblical passages (for which some allowance can be made), show clear traces of an independent approach which detaches itself from the traditional understanding held by his predecessors and contemporaries alike. It may be useful here, to recall a few illustrations. They are taken from the bishop of Hippo's reading of expressions contained in the Pauline letters which, more than any other scriptural book, influenced his doctrine of grace. The intuition (or "revelation") which suddenly struck Augustine as he read 1 Cor 4,7 (*Quid autem habes quod non accepisti?*) convinced him that the sovereignty of grace was the correct hermeneutic for understanding Rom 9 and, more particularly, for understanding faith as a gift from God. The *intentio* of Paul in 1 Cor 4,7, however, was far less pretentious. He simply encouraged in the Corinthians the virtue of humility, and had no intention of sparking a debate as to whether humility was, in

31. Cf. Prosper, *Ep.* 225,3 (CSEL, 57), p. 459. Prosper had warned that at the root of the Massilians' misunderstanding of Augustine's position on grace and predestination, lay the hermeneutical problem of the interpretation of Scripture: "Asserunt quidem haec quibusdam sanctarum scripturarum testimoniis, sed non rationabiliter assumptis" (Id., *Ep. ad Rufinum* 5,6 [PL, 51], c. 80)

32. W.S. BABCOCK, *Introduction*, in ID. (ed.), *Paul and the Legacies of Paul*, Dallas, TX, 1990, pp. 123-140, p. xxii.

fact, a gift of God. And yet this is precisely how Augustine interprets it, bending Paul's *intentio* to the question he is dealing with, viz. the *initium fidei* and final perseverance.

A similar tendencious exegesis can be found in his interpretation of Paul's passage: *in quo omnes peccauerunt* (Rom 5,12). To the Apostle's way of thinking this expression ought to be understood in the light of Rom 5,17 ("If, because of the one man's trespass, death exercised dominion through that one, much more surely will those who receive the abundance of grace and the free gift of righteousness exercise dominion in life through the one man, Jesus Christ"). From Paul's perspective the universal extension of sin was permitted by God so that his universal and gratuitous mercy could be manifested in the redemption brought about in Jesus Christ. It is in this way that Cassian and the Massilians also read and understood this passage[33]. Augustine's interpretation, however, leans towards a grim pessimism. In fact, he lays emphasis on God's punishing justice universally manifested with regard to the *massa damnationis* in which all human beings are enclosed. It is only due to God's gratuitous and merciful (s)election that some are delivered from it.

Augustine also interprets Rom 9,10-29 from a standpoint which does not conform to Paul's original intention. In the context of Rom 9-11, the Apostle metaphorically uses the "corporate" image of Jacob and Esau, representing the two peoples stemming from them, the Israelites and the Edomites respectively, as an historical example of Israel's replacement by the Gentiles[34]; a replacement which must also be seen as part of God's universal plan of salvation. There is absolutely no indication of an eternal rejection of Israel (Paul explicitly refuses to draw such a conclusion: cf. Rom 11,1), nor does Rom 9,10-29 adumbrate an eternal dualistic predestination for individuals, based on election and rejection, choice or abandonment.

Finally, Augustine's restrictive exegesis of 1 Tim 2,4[35], coloured by his doctrine of *certus numerus electorum*, is an example of how the primary thought or *intentio* of the Apostle (viz. its undeniable universal significance) was manipulated by Augustine's different theological view. The problem of God's universal salvific will was never an abstract concept for Paul, and was always rooted in the mystery of Christ's redemption, which enables Christ to become incorporated into the lives of all

33. Cf. Cassian, *Conlatio* 13,7 (SC, 54), p. 156. See *supra*, pp. 274f.
34. See *supra*, pp. 336f.
35. See *supra*, pp. 357-366.

humanity (cf. 1 Cor 2,7; Rom 8,29f; Eph 1,5.11). The determining factor in Pauline theology is ultimately the Christological perspective, with its emphasis on the call for all men to be conformed to Christ and to be justified and glorified according to God's universal plan of salvation. The Massilians' interpretation, unlike that of Augustine, was in line with both the intention of Paul and the traditional understanding of it[36].

In the light of such evidence, which shows how Augustine, in his "theological exegesis", bent or rearranged Scripture to fit his own theological presuppositions, we will describe another aspect of Augustine's methodology, which becomes apparent from time to time. When Augustine is unable to find a reasonable scriptural solution to a particular aspect of God's intervening action in the world, he states that man should simply submit to God's inscrutable design. Such an appeal, however, could also conceal epistemological ambiguity. It is patently unfair, for instance, to appeal to a sovereign God (who acts above and beyond the world and the laws of his creation) simply as a means of supporting one's own controversial answer to that same problematic question. There is no doubt that with regard to the problem of election and predestination Augustine used the argument of God's inscrutable design not as an acknowledgement that such questions are unsolvable, but to support his own solutions. Moreover, to appeal to the mysterious manner in which God deals with humanity (and to invoke a consequent submissive attitude on the part of man) would mean confirming an incompatibility between God's grace and human freedom that would render futile any further effort in seeking and understanding how the two realities might be harmoniously related. The way Augustine inteprets one of his favourite quotations, Rom 11,33 (*O altitudo diuitiarum sapientiae et scientiae Dei! Quam inscrutabilia sunt iudicia eius, et inuestigabiles uiae eius!*)[37], is a clear example of a biased approach. In fact, the inscrutability of God's plan and judgement, before which man should feel an awe filled terror, is used to justify his predestinarian doctrine. By contrast, Paul's appeal in Rom 11,33 is not one of mere resignation; it is an appeal where, by exalting the riches, wisdom and knowledge of God he

36. Cf. Cassian, *Conlatio* 9,20 (SC, 54), pp.155-156; *Ibid.*, 13,7, p. 156; 16,6, p. 229. See *supra*, pp. 379ff.

37. For Augustine's quotation of Rom 11,33 in his writings to the monks of Hadrumetum and Provence, cf. Augustine, *De gratia et libero arbitrio* 22,44 (PL, 44), cc. 909-910; Id., *De correptione et gratia* 8,17.18.19 (CSEL, 92), pp. 237, 239 and 240; *De praedestinatione sanctorum* 6,11 and 8,16 (PL, 44), cc. 969 and 973; *De dono perseverantiae* 11,25 and 12,30 (PL, 45), cc. 1007 and 1011. See also the references to Rom 9,20 ("O homo, tu quis es qui respondeas Deo?"): Id., *De correptione et gratia* 8,17 (CSEL, 92), p. 237; *De praedestinatione sanctorum* 8,14.16 and 15,30 (PL, 44), cc. 971, 973 and 982; *De dono perseuerantiae* 8,17 and 12,30 (PL, 45), cc.1003 and 1011.

is able to show how God manifests his love to all humanity[38], even though his ways are often impenetrable by our human understanding. There is a positive thread that unites the "depth" of God's agency and the "incapability" of man to penetrate it. Divine judgement emanates from the depths of riches, wisdom and knowledge of God's love at work in the salvation history of mankind. Once again, it is Cassian and the Massilians who interpret Paul correctly regarding the understanding we should have of God's unfathomable judgement in apportioning his saving love and mercy[39]. Whereas Augustine appealed to God's mystery in order to safeguard the absolute primacy and power of grace with regard to the sombre outcome of his predestinarian theory, the more optimistic view of the Massilians allowed them to see, in God's mysterious plans, the manifestation of his love and mercy which came to fulfilment through the universal mediation of Jesus Christ.

To conclude, we can confidently affirm that, for Augustine, Holy Scripture was not only the source of his theological construction, but also the *locus* from which biblical passages were drawn and re-interpreted to fit his theological presuppositions. In this sense we can indeed speak of an Augustinian "theological exegesis". No doubt, the controversial discussions in which Augustine was engaged played an important role in his thought and in the formulation of his doctrine vis-à-vis the use of Scripture. It is, in fact, within a polemic framework that he is often pushed to search for the meaning of Christian doctrine. Although such a remark can in no way be taken as a justification of Augustine's peculiar interpretation of some scriptural passages, the external pressure he endured in the heat of several controversies may help us to better grasp his inner preoccupation, viz. the clarification and defence of the Christian faith and what he believed to be Christian tenets, such as his doctrine of predestination.

4. THE WEIGHT OF TRADITION AND PERSONAL AUTHORITY

According to Burns, "in a fifth-century perspective, Augustinianism was innovation or, more likely, aberration"[40]. If the first conclusion in

---

38. "Angesichts des Geschickes Israels, seiner Erwählung, seines Falles und seiner eschatologischen Rettung, aber auch angesichts des Geschickes der Heiden, das mit dem Israels aufs engste verflochten ist, angesichts also des weltweiten richtenden und erbarmenden Handelns Gottes kann der Apostel nicht anders, als in den Ruf ausbrechen, der Gottes abgründige Fülle, Weisheit und Liebeserkenntnis rühmt" (H. SCHLIER, *Der Römerbrief* [HTK, 6], Freiburg-Basel-Wien, 1977, p. 345).

39. See *supra*, p. 145, n. 255, and p. 382.

40. J.P. BURNS, *The Atmosphere of Election. Augustinianism as Common Sense*, in *JECS* 2 (1994) 325-339, p. 325.

this statement needs nuancing and the second is difficult to accept, it is nevertheless and without doubt Augustine's original genius that, in spite of the many external influences he experienced, impresses us[41]. In fact, the resistance of the monks of Hadrumetum and the opposition of those in Southern Gaul brought about the clash between commonly accepted Church tradition (especially the rich legacy of Greek theology) and some of the innovative views put forward by the bishop of Hippo. There is substantial agreement among scholars that Augustine's familiarity with Scripture (although often interpreted in too personal a way) was not paralleled by an equal knowledge of the theological tradition of the Church. More precisely, his knowledge appears particularly scanty in the area of the Greek theological inheritance[42]. We might well question whether Augustine's position regarding grace, election and free will might not have been different had he read Rufinus' Latin version of Origen's balanced presentation of Rom 9-11 (*De principiis* 3)[43]. Such a lacuna is clear evidence of Augustine's limited connections with the Greek theological world; a world that had deeply influenced the Massilians.

It is striking to see the extent to which Augustine, rather than being preoccupied with building up a *réservoir* of authorities he could refer to in order to back his argumentation, shows his independent confidence in exploring new ground and suggesting new solutions. Besides, he seems quite confident that his theological *opus* was going to have a great influence on future generations of Christian writers[44]. So that, if on the one

---

41. "Kein Stadium seines Lebensganges (...) ohne Wirkung für ihn geblieben ist. Allein auch von hier aus vermag man schliesslich nicht, der Eigenart dieses Mannes völlig gerecht zu werden" (A. VON HARNACK, *Monasticism, Its Ideals and History*, New York, 1895, pp. 62-63).

42. See G. BARTELINK, *Die Beeinflussung Augustins durch die griechischen Patres*, in J. DEN BOEFT – J. VAN OORT (eds.), *Augustiniana Traiectina. Communications présentées au Colloque International d'Utrecht 13-14 novembre 1986*, Paris, 1987, pp. 9ff.

43. There seems to be evidence, however, that Augustine "did indeed read and react to Rufinus's translation of Origen's *Commentary on Romans* by about 411" (C.P. BAMMEL, *Augustine, Origen and the Exegesis of St. Paul*, in *Aug* 32 [1992] 341-368, p. 342). As to Origen's *De principiis* 3, we may as well recall that, surprisingly enough, in the very midst of the Origenist controversy (A.D. 400), Jerome (by then turned into a fervent anti-Origenist) advised Paulinus of Nola that his question about the hardening of Pharaoh's heart (a question concerning the relationship between free will and God's predetermination) was answered in Origen's *De principiis* (cf. Jerome, *Ep.* 85,2-3 [CSEL, 54], pp. 136-137). This alone speaks volumes about the enduring influence exercised by Origen despite the attacks brought against his thought. See E.A. CLARK, *The Origenist Controversy. The Cultural Construction of an Early Christian Debate*, Princeton, NJ, 1992, p. 35 *et passim*.

44. "By the preparation of the *Retractationes* and by Possidius' autorship of the *Life of Augustine* and his compilation of the little pamphlet we call his *indiculum* of Augustine's writings, Augustine left this world with a more secure claim on future readers'

hand, we recognise a significant lack of support from ecclesiastical tradition for Augustine's more controversial views, on the other hand, the bishop of Hippo felt certainly that he could also rely on his "own" authority; an authority which, even during his life, was recognised in and outside Africa alike[45]. Augustine's thinking on grace and predestination, above all, shows how a peculiarly novel touch in doctrinal matters found a breakthrough thanks to the personal authority enjoyed by the bishop of Hippo. As already mentioned, Augustine himself recalls the decisive "revelation" that came to him after studying 1 Cor 4,7[46]. Obviously the "internal" decisiveness of such a revelation cannot be checked, any more than his exegetical interpretation of this passage can be proved. And yet, it was this revelation that caused an innovative turn in Augustine's doctrine of grace and predestination; a theory so original to him and so largely dismissive of tradition that it cannot be taken in any way as "the" teaching of the Church. It is quite likely that Vincent of Lérins alluded to this "revelatory" encounter of Augustine with 1 Cor 4,7, when he spoke ironically of those who are convinced that true faith, after centuries of concealment, has eventually been revealed to them alone[47]. As to the specific issue of authority and tradition, raised by the Massilians in connection with Augustine's extreme views on grace, it has to be seen as the outcome of their unwillingness to assent to an unfamiliar and uncongenial exegesis regarding election, predestination and universal salvation; exegesis which was not supported by any of the reputable Christian authors of the Church[48]. The Massilians' underlying assumption was that the "certainty" of a commonly held opinion was what really mattered. In connection with the rigidities of his doctrine of grace, Augustine was, in their eyes, a lone and somewhat eccentric voice.

---

attention than any other writer of his age" (J.J. O'DONNELL, *The Authority of Augustine*, in *AugSt* 22 [1991] 7-35, p. 16). We should, nevertheless, consider as sincere the proviso Augustine himself put forward: "... neminem velim sic amplecti omnia mea, ut me sequatur, nisi in iis in quibus me non errasse perspexerit" (Augustine, *De dono perseuerantiae* 21,55 [PL, 45], cc. 1027-1028).

45. Hilary speaks of Augustine's "reuerentissima auctoritas" (Hilary, *Ep.* 226,10 [CSEL, 57], p. 480).

46. Cf. Augustine, *De praedestinatione sanctorum* 4,8 (PL, 44), c. 966. See *supra*, p. 158, n. 311.

47. "Audias etenim quosdam ipsorum dicere: Venite, o insipientes et miseri, qui uulgo catholici uocitamini, et discite fidem ueram, quam praeter nos nullus intellegit, quae multis ante saeculis latuit, nuper uero reuelata et ostensa est" (Vincent of Lérins, *Commonitorium* 21,7 [CCL, 64], p. 176).

48. Cassian's expression "ab omnibus catholicis patribus definitur" (Cassian, *Conlatio* 13,18 [SC, 54], p. 180), is reminiscent of Vincent of Lérins famous rule of authenticity (cf. *supra*, p. 146, n. 258).

The divergent opinions of the Massilians and Augustine were, above
all, the result of the Eastern tradition that had been embraced by the
monks of Provence vis-à-vis the novel ideas of Augustine on grace. It is
not always clear through which channels Cassian and his associates
received their theological culture, nor can we detect a direct, literal
dependence on any particular Christian author. It is mainly the development of a specific *forma mentis*, the intellectual and ideological ties and
the way different issues are tackled and understood, that points to the
Massilians' relationship to, and strict dependence on, Eastern theology.
No doubt, the role played by the monastic milieux of Egypt and Palestine in their "living" transmission of the fundamental truths of Christian
belief, lived out in asceticism and particularly indebted (through Evagrius) to Origenist insights and spirituality, made a permanent impression on Cassian. This influence can be seen in the way the cosmic and
"paideutic" salvation process in Christ unfolds, in the mankind's co-
operation with it, and the centrality of Jesus as the model of man's struggle for perfection[49]. In his turn, Cassian shared his learning and experience of the East with the brethren of Provence.

Similarities can be detected also between Massilianism and Pelagianism; similarities that might lead us to think that there was a direct influence of the latter on the former, but which should be traced back to a
common pre-Pelagian heritage. In our understanding, what the monks of
Hadrumetum and the Massilians shared with the Pelagians was an optimistic view of the basic goodness of nature. This belief issued in ascetic
energy; an energy that lay at the core of their Christian and monastic
commitment. We can presume that the ascetic writings of Pelagius (*e.g.*,
his *Epistula ad Demetriadem*) must have been read, and profitably so, in
monastic establishments, without the monks necessarily sharing the
underlying theological presuppositions to the full[50]. In addition, we
should not forget that the emphasis the monks put on ascetic effort,
although nourished by Christian revelation, also found fertile ground
outside Christianity, particularly in the Greek philosophical moral tradition (Neo-Stoicism *in primis*), which continued to exercise considerable
influence within the ranks of the Church[51].

49. See *supra*, pp. 379f.
50. We may well underline, once again, that, generally speaking, the Massilians's
affinity with Augustine's views was much greater and that there was more agreement
with it than disagreement. Augustine stood certainly nearer to them than Pelagius and his
satellites.
51. For instance, the rhetorical formation of those learned aristocrats who, after having fled from Northern Gaul, had joined the monastic settlements of Provence, was a formation "à forte coloration stoïcienne" (J.-P. WEISS, *Le sémi-pelagianisme se réduit-il à*

5. *Homo monasticus in saeculo:* Micro- and Macro-Contextuality

That Cassian was a *homo monasticus*, and wrote in that capacity, goes without saying. What is not so obvious, however, is the underlying motivation of his words, and the inspiration that nurtured both his life and writing. His critique of Augustine's *Gnadenmonergismus*, and his attempt to save some small part of the autonomy of man's free will in the process of adhesion to God, was a logical consequence of his *monastica uiuendi forma*; a way of life which sought to safeguard the role of asceticism and the part that human self-initiative plays in it[52]. In the Massilians' eyes, God's universal offer of salvation was not "one way" phenomenon; on the contrary, it involved man's assent, achieved through daily struggle against the vices and passions that would hinder his ascent to God. In other words, they nourished the belief that divine grace would not superimpose itself on man in an absolute and overriding manner.

It is clearly evident that the framework provided by Augustinian theological reflection and the Cassianic/Massilian one were quite different. Although they certainly agreed that pride and self-centredness are major obstacles to the ascent of the soul to God, they disagreed on one particular idea. Whereas, for the bishop of Hippo, any step in the direction of the good (and of God) could be confidently taken in the knowledge that the origin of the desire for this step was the love of God and the gift of the Holy Spirit at work in the soul, Cassian and the Massilians believed that the ascetic commitment of the monks, their desire to adhere to God's commands as well as their effort (*industria, labor, conatus*) in following them, were in no way contrary to, but in complete accordance with, the divine grace required for the attainment of perfection[53]. Guided by an underlying *raison pratique* or a "practical ethos" which kept them alert for fear "that experience would not play a sufficient part in the formulation of theological position"[54], Cassian and the Massilians strongly underlined the importance of the interaction of grace and human striving. This interaction seemed to find clear expression in their monastic

---

une réaction contre Augustin et l'augustinisme de la première génération?, in *Congresso Internazionale su S. Agostino nel XVI Centenario della Conversione. Atti*, Vol. I [SEAug, 24], Rome, 1987, pp. 465-481, p. 481).

52. "Gnade u. Freiheit sind nicht (wie bei Augustinus) identisch, sondern voneinander abgesetzt, womit genug Raum für das asketische Bemühen gegeben ist" (S.K. Frank, *Johannes Cassianus*, in *RAC* 18 [1997] 414-426, c. 421).

53. Cf., for instance, Cassian, *De institutis coenobiorum* 12,11-16 *passim* (SC, 109), pp. 464-472.

54. P. Rousseau, *Ascetics, Authority, and the Church in the Age of Jerome and Cassian*, Oxford, 1978, p. 231.

commitment, and was naturally favoured in a cenobitic context. In point of fact, the task of conversion or self-reform, as experienced by the monks of Southern Gaul, was not simply a matter of personal concern, as it was for hermits, but a task they thought better undertaken within the regulated and disciplined communal framework of a community founded in the ascetic tradition and in obedience and submission to the authoritative judgements of a supervisor or superior[55]. To stress the ascetic/cenobitic background of the monks of Southern Gaul (and of those of Hadrumetum) is of paramount importance in contextualising their resistance to Augustine. Rather than a contest, carried out on the level of metaphysical and theological speculation, their confrontation must ultimately be seen against the basic misunderstanding of the metaphor of "agonism", viz. of the meaning of ascetic struggle. Whereas Augustine was suspicious of any overtly confident attitude with regard to human potentialities and their role in co-operating with God, for the perfection of the soul[56], the ascetics of both Hadrumetum and Marseilles were suspicious of his concept of overwhelming grace. They saw that such a view could lead to a dangerous passivity which was in complete opposition to the ascetic/monastic structures they were accustomed to.

It goes without saying that the monks' zeal for perfection was best expressed not in terms of passivity, but of active commitment; a commitment described linguistically in terms such as *agon* or *militia* (combat/contest); terms alive with military or athletic connotation. This metaphor was already present in the New Testament (cf. 1 Cor 9,24ff; Eph 6,11ff; Phil 3,12-14; 2 Tim 2,3-5 and 4,7.8), and was soon applied to the martyrs[57] and, after the *pax Constantiniana*, to the "new martyrs", viz. the monks. The strong ascetic content of their *propositum* was considered to be the most suitable means of achieving the perfection of faith witnessed to in the blood of the martyr[58]. This image of the monk as

55. Although Cassian shared in Augustine's concern about the moral dangers of elitism, his response "was not to distrust the ascetic project itself, but to make all the more exacting and precise the means of assessing a person's integrity" (C. LEYSER, *Semi-Pelagianism* [n. 23], p. 764).
56. "Augustine seems to have been worried that if he allowed anyone, even with God's help, to reach a state of achieved perfection in this life, the help would become unnecessary" (RIST, *Augustine on Free Will and Predestination* [n. 5], p. 426).
57. See, for instance; "Vocati sumus ad militiam Dei ... Nemo miles ad bellum cum deliciis uenit, nec de cubiculo ad aciem procedit, sed de papilionibus expeditis et substrictis, ubi omnis duritia et inbonitas et insuauitas constitit ... Proinde uos, benedicti, quodcumque hoc durum est, ad exercitationem uirtutum animi et corporis deputate. Bonum agonem subituri estis..." (Tertullian, *Ad martyras* 3 [CCL, 1], p. 5).
58. See *supra*, p. 49.

miles or *athleta Christi* made its appearance also in Gaul at the very beginning of monasticism. Sulpicius Severus tells the story of the soldier Martin (the forerunner of the Gallic monks) who asked the emperor for permission to leave the army in order to serve (viz. *to fight* for) God. With great confidence, as well as courage, he proclaimed his newly found identity with the following words: "I am a soldier of Christ"[59]. This image of *miles* can be found in the writings of Cassian too. In his monastic regulations, the *De institutis coenobiorum*, the monk is described from the outset as a *miles Christi*, dressed in his soldier's outfit and ready to fight the enemy at any time[60]. As seen above[61], terms such as *miles (Christi)*, *militia Christi/spiritalis*, *athleta*, as well as *agon*, *certamen*, *conluctatio* keep recurring in the works of the divine of Marseilles when describing the monk's engagement in the continuous battle against passion and vice. This same confident *esprit de conquête*, based on voluntary effort and a quest for perfection in conjunction with God's salvific presence, can also be found in the monastery of Lérins. Eucherius, for instance, could not refrain from remarking that the *fuga mundi* of the Lérinian monks was so advanced, that the will to sin, as well as its performance, had become almost foreign to them[62]. Although doubtless a hyperbole, such a statement betrays the optimistic confidence of the monks regarding the capacity of human free will to co-operate with divine grace at the level of moral struggle and in the quest for perfection. This confidence in no way contradicted the belief that, ultimately, everything depends on God's grace.

Furthermore, the vigilant readiness for strenuous effort was regarded as the best antidote to the persistent temptation to lassitude and idleness (*torpor* or *tepor*)[63], and the most suitable way to enter the kingdom of God. Cassian stresses this conviction using the words of Abba Abraham who, basing himself on Mt 11,12 (*Regnum enim caelorum uim patitur, et uiolenti diripiunt illud*), affirms: "It is not the lazy, the negligent, the lax, the fastidious or the weak who seize the kingdom of heaven, but the violent (...) who exercise a noble violence (...) upon their own soul and

---

59. "Patere ut ... militem Deo ... Christi ego miles sum" (Sulpicius Severus, *Vita Martini* 4,3 [SC, 133], p. 260).

60. "Itaque monachum ut militem Christi in procinctu semper belli positum accinctis lumbis iugiter oportet incedere" (Cassian, *De institutis coenobiorum* 1,1,1 [SC, 109], p. 36).

61. See *supra*, p. 150.

62. "Qui alieni sunt ab illo reipublicae humanae tumultu, sepositi, quieti, silentes; nec magis absunt a voluntate peccandi quam a facultate" (Eucherius, *De laude eremi* 31 [PL, 50], c. 708).

63. See *supra*, p. 144, n. 245.

who, by a praiseworthy pillage, snatch it away from every pleasure in present things. By the Lord's words they are declared excellent pillagers, and with plundering of this sort they gain violent entrance into the kingdom of heaven"[64]. What better place could be found for the soul's purification and its ascent to God, than a supporting, well disciplined and self contained community? What better environment than the monastic, cenobitic establishment for meeting the demands of Christian faith in a precise and enduring way? Although the monks of Hadrumetum and of Southern Gaul were simply trying to live to the full their Christian call, they were certainly aware, as are all living in a strongly ascetic context, that they constituted a sort of *tête de pont* within the ecclesiastical body; a "specialized" élite treading the path that every Christian should in theory be treading, as the surest way to salvation. Naturally, the context provided in a monastic settlement, be it the community of Hadrumetum or those of Provence, gave a sense of purpose and a direction that the mass of ordinary lay Christians could not possibly experience to the same degree. The vast majority of fairly uneducated lay people, far from being concerned with the quest for perfection, were wrestling with the day to day problem of how to combine their ordinary lives with a minimum faithfulness to Christian commandments. Augustine's own congregation, probably little different from the other congregations scattered across Christendom, was not so much concerned with renunciation and the high demands of the ascetic life, as with the rather pragmatic preoccupation of not straying too far from the norms laid by the Church. No doubt, such contextual differences played a role in forming the opinions held by Augustine and the Massilians when it came to the question of the intervening action of grace.

Here we must also take into account the general context in which both the Church and the Roman Empire found themselves at the beginning of the 5th century. Following the "establishment" of Christianity in the Constantinian and Theodosian times, the Church lost that sharp sense of social belonging and separateness that had characterised it when the frequently persecuted Christian faith was considered *illicita*. After Christianity became the "established" religion, and conversions an every-day-affair (often dictated by opportunism and rewarding in terms of social integration) there developed a sense of security and ease. The strong

---

64. "Regnum enim caelorum non desides, non remissi, non delicati, non teneri, sed uiolenti diripiunt ... qui ... animae suae praeclaram inferunt uiolentiam, qui direptione laudabili omni eam praesentium rerum uoluptate fraudantes uoce dominica egregii direptores pronuntiantur et per huiuscemodi rapinam regnum caelorum uiolenter inuadunt" (Cassian, *Conlatio* 24,26 [SC, 64], p. 203).

feeling of responsibility and commitment, typical of any minority group, that had characterised the pre-Constantinian Church, abated[65]. To use Burns' words, "the Church no longer considered itself an island of religious and moral purity in a sea of idolatry and corruption. Its rituals, baptism and eucharist, no longer established and limited a social body, protecting and preserving the whole community from the pollution of the Roman world"[66]. The shift from a close knit feeling of belonging and participation, in matters of faith and religion, to a more individual attitude, is shown by the changing approach to baptism. By the beginning of the 5th century it had become a consolidated custom to postpone baptism and opt for a life long catechumenate, a sort of "no man's land" without the obligations pertaining to "new life" in Christ. In this state the pleasures of the "old life" could still be enjoyed without worrying too much about one's own behaviour. For many, baptism had become a postponed commitment, something to take seriously only before death (if the timing was right!), in order to make sure that sins were forgiven and access to the kingdom of heaven assured. Furthermore, beside the situation of the Church in general, we must not forget that also the Roman Empire found itself in difficulty at the beginning of the 5th century, due to a crumbling structure and the threat of invasions. No doubt the crumbling social structure was partly due to the decadence of the Roman Empire itself which, by this time, was closely aligned with the religious structures of Christianity.

The way this state of affairs was tackled was undoubtedly influenced by the respective environment and worldview of Augustine and of the monastic establishments. Since the pastoral work of Augustine, as a bishop, was mainly concerned with ordinary Christians (or cathecumens) living amid uncertainty and irrationality, we should not be surprised to find him seeking solutions to provide a "safe haven" in a sea of incoherence and insecurity, both on the ecclesial and the social level. The *De ciuitate Dei,* a work in which Augustine attempted to clarify Christianity's ambiguous relationship with the temporal order, by establishing the radical transcendence of Christianity vis-à-vis the Roman Empire[67], bears traces of this general, often dramatic insecurity which affected both society and the Church. Augustine's reaction, whilst stressing the

65. See D. PRAET, *Explaining the Christianization of the Roman Empire. Older Theories and Recent Developments,* in *SE* 33 (1992-1993) 5-119.

66. J.P. BURNS, *The Atmosphere of Election: Augustinianism as Common Sense,* in *JECS* 2 (1994) 325-339, p. 336.

67. See E.L. FORTIN, *Civitate Dei, De,* in FITZGERALD (ed.), *Augustine through the Ages* (n. 11), pp. 196-202.

mysterious co-habitation of both the Godly and earthly cities, points to the inscrutability of God's providence in leading human history to its final goal, regardless of hindrance and constant contradiction. It is also against this background that we should understand his doctrine of pre-destination, a doctrine which emphasizes the incomprehensibility of God's mysterious intervening action in history. This doctrine was an extreme formulation of a *certa, immutabilis* and *efficacissima* divine omnipotence with regard to humanity, and rested solely on Augustine's theological assumption of mankind's inherited fallibility and vitiated nature; on the visible contradictions of history, and on his observation that many people were not touched *stricto sensu* by God's grace (*e.g.*, unbaptised children and pagans/heathens). Conversely, the monastic communities, relying on a severe masculine ideal of Christian asceti-cism, which resulted in a high moral standard, offered a different and contrasting picture. The ascetics of Hadrumetum and Southern Gaul, who had devoted themselves to a life long struggle for the transforma-tion of the soul, were not so much concerned with the atmosphere of uncertainty present in both Church and society at large, as with the effort of avoiding any uncertainty which might possibly undermine their *propositum*, viz. their journey of ascent to God through the purification of body and soul and the acquisition of virtue. Set apart from worldly affairs and events[68], the monks' daily life was marked by a twofold expectancy. On the one hand, they had a firm grasp of the equitable and fair demands made by God to all mankind, and realised the expectation on them to fulfil these demands, and, on the other hand, they were con-fident that God would eventually reward their efforts. Thus, whereas many, Augustine included, had lost confidence in man's capacity to take an active part in the cosmic process of salvation, and were now looking for sure and definitive answers in the providence of God, the homes of monastic asceticism, such as Hadrumetum and the settlements of South-ern Gaul, kept the flame of "humanism" alive. Their optimism was not influenced by the general pessimism of the times, and for this very rea-son it stood out as something quite remarkable. If nothing else, it was a clear indication of their belief in the role that man must always play in

---

68. "Cassian äußert sich nicht direkt zum damaligen *Zeitgeschehen* ... Außere Bedrängnis kann nach ihm ein Anstoß zur Mönchsberufung werden. Cassian regt an, moralisch indifferente Gegebenheiten dieser Welt so zu handhaben, daß sie für das Streben nach Gott nützlich sind. ... Cassin Anliegen war es, schon gegenwärtig im asketischen Kampf die 'Welt' zu überwinden und sich auf das Reich Gottes auszurichten. So erscheint bei ihm das Leben in der mönchischen Gemeinschaft deutlich als ein Rück-zug von der Welt" (G. SUMMA, *Geistliche Unterscheidung bei Johannes Cassian* [StSSpTh, 7], Würzburg, 1992, p. 243).

the process of (his own) salvation, no matter what the climate of the Church or world.

6. *EXITUS*

The resistance/opposition of the monastic settlements of Hadrumetum and Southern Gaul to Augustine's address was ultimately due to the impossibility of finding a rational solution to the "unique" and "mysterious" relationship between grace and free will. We do not possess suitable categories or analogies to pin-point the exact "manner" in which such relationship takes place. Seen separately, no one can question their existence and their place in the life of the believer, for they are without doubt present by way of reason and experience. It is when we try to relate them one to another that difficulties arise, particularly in reconciling their interaction. It is indeed as if we were holding two ends of a chain, without being able to see how all the links that make up the chain are joined together[69]. We are left with an aporia beyond our grasp, to which neither Augustine's solutions, the expression of an excessive apologia of the "rights of God", nor the Massilians' ideas, directed mainly at saving "something" of the human rights, are completely satisfactory. Even the Massilians' approach, in fact, though more "humanistic" and significant in the way it took into account the issue of freedom and free will (viz. from a practical, psychological and moral point of view), and in spite of its sensible course, can be seen as no more than another argument which ultimately leaves the dilemma still unsolved.

There is an image, however, which Cassian uses to illustrate the tension (a tension experienced by every Christian) between the need for decisive commitment to God's commandments and a confidence in God's gracious intervening action and his universal offer of salvation. The image is that of the funambulist or tightrope walker. This image can be seen as a useful metaphor for those who have abandoned the things of the world in order wholeheartedly to seek the Lord[70]. Interestingly,

69. Cf. Bossuet's quotation, *supra*, p. 139, n. 223. "L'*excès* d'Augustin – writes Solignac – plutôt que son 'erreur', a été de prétendre avoir saisi quelques autres maillons non sans reconnaître que les plus secrets lui échappaient" (A. SOLIGNAC, *Les excès de l' "intellectus fidei" dans la doctrine d'Augustin sur la grâce*, in *NRT* 110 [1998] 825-849, p. 843).
70. "Recte igitur sanctos, qui memoriam Dei stabiliter retinentes quasi per extentas in sublime lineas suspenso feruntur incessu, schoenobatis, quos uulgo funambulos uocant, dixerim conparandos, qui summam suae salutis ac uitae in angustissimo funiculi illius tramite conlocantes atrocissimam se mortem protinus incursuros esse non ambigunt, si uel exigua pes eorum titubatione deuiauerit aut modum illius salutaris directionis excesserit" (Cassian, *Conlatio* 23,9 [SC, 64], p. 151).

Cassian accentuates the inner tension and ability (the *ars mirifica*, the *cauta atque sollicita moderatio*)[71] that guide the performance of the funambulist, rather than the danger he faces[72]. This same intensity and tension should sustain the Christian search for perfection[73]. Although the believer cannot succeed in reaching a state of perfection unaided (for he will ultimately need the help of divine grace to achieve it), the desire for perfection is motivated by man's own desire for commitment in encountering and forming a relationship with God. In this way we see "that the theological affirmation of the gratuity of grace need not entail a potential lapse into idleness, just as growth in virtue need not lead to hubristic illusions of perfectibility"[74].

To conclude, the Cassianic metaphor of the funambulist illustrates the underlying wisdom or *raison pratique* of the monks of Hadrumetum and Southern Gaul, and it is a reminder of the concept of the *uia media* (or *uia regia*)[75], a concept which enjoyed widespread consensus in monastic circles[76]. It is along this middle path, and by the careful avoidance of extremes, that a process of integration and unification (*et–et*), rather than one of confrontation and antinomy (*aut–aut*), is maintained. The ascetics of the day saw this as the best way forward in their quest for perfection. This was a way that linked free will with grace, and human existence with divine transcendence, in a synergetic and harmonious fashion. It was, without doubt, an attempt to "humanize" the otherwise tragic substance of Christian faith. Their enlightening insight continues to this day.

---

71. *Ibid.*

72. John Chrysostom, for instance, who employing the same image compares the rope-dancer to the Christian who has to walk along the narrow path of divine commandments, stresses mostly the fatal danger that could be invited by a relaxation (cf. John Chrysostom, *Homiliae in Oziam [In illud, uidi Dominum]* 3,2 [SC, 277], p. 112).

73. "Cassien (...) achève de faire sienne cette image en déplaçant l'accent de l'évidence du péril encouru à la tension intérieure commune au funambule et au saint" (E. REBILLARD, *Quasi funambuli. Cassien et la controverse pélagienne sur la perfection*, in *REAug* 40 [1994] 197-210, p. 208).

74. T.A. SMITH, *Agonism and Antagonism: Metaphor and the Gallic Resistance to Augustine*, in *StPatr* 38, Louvain, 2001, pp. 283-289.

75. "... uia regia monachum docet semper incedere..." (Cassian, *Conlatio* 2,2 [SC, 42], p. 113); "...sed itinere plano ac uia regia semper incedens..." (*Ibid.* 6,9, p. 228). Cf. also *Ibid.* 24,25 (SC, 64), p. 198; Id., *De institutis coenobiorum* 11,4, (SC, 109), p. 430.

76. See M. DJUTH, *Royal Way*, in FITZGERALD (ed.), *Augustine through the Ages* (n. 11), pp. 735-737; C.M. KASPER, *Theologie und Askese. Die Spiritualität des Inselmönchtums von Lérins im 5. Jahrhundert* (BGAM, 40), Münster, 1991 ("Stütze der *via regia*").

EPILOGUE

The Second Phase of Massilianism
From the Death of Augustine (430) to the 2nd Council of Orange (529)

Were the monks of Hadrumetum and of Southern Gaul defenders of a lost cause? Did their concern for a "humanistic" theology simply succumb to Augustine's more powerful thought? History tells us that it was not so. Since the issues at stake had not received any doctrinal approval in one sense or another, even after the death of Augustine (430) and, a few years later, the death of Cassian (ca. 435), the opposing parties continued their intellectual contest. Prosper, the leading figure of the Augustinian party in Gaul, travelled to Rome with Hilary in 431 to gain the support of Caelestinus I. The success was slight. The pope did not take any definitive doctrinal decision about the questions that provoked so much discussion in Southern Gaul, and the lack of precision in the letter he addressed to the Gallic bishops (in which he praised Augustine and urged peace)[1], made it possible for Vincent of Lérins to twist the interpretation into praise of the Massilians for their defence of truth against innovation[2].

Vincent's partisan interpretation is a clear sign that the debate in Provence had not subsided, and after his return to Marseilles Prosper realised it was still necessary for him to defend Augustine's teaching on grace and predestination. He threw himself headlong into the heat of the controversy. Firstly, changing from defensive tactics (present in his letter to Augustine [*Ep.* 225]) to the offensive, he violently attacked Cassian, the leader and mentor of the opposite camp. Cassian's *Conlatio* 13 was singled out for special criticism in the *De gratia Dei et libero arbitrio contra Collatorem*[3]. At the same time Prosper's counterattack was

---

1. Cf. Caelestinus, *Ep. ad episcopos Galliarum* (PL, 50), cc. 528-530.

2. "Ait enim in epistula, quam Gallorum sacerdotibus misit arguens eorum coniuentiam quod antiquam fidem silentio destituentes *profanas nouitates* exsurgere paterentur: *Merito*, inquit, *causa nos respicit, si silentio foueamus errorem.Ergo corripiantur huiusmodi; non sit his liberum habere pro uoluntate sermonem.* Hic aliquis fortasse addubitet, quinam sint illi, quos habere prohibeat liberum pro uoluntate sermonem, uetustatis praedicatores an nouitatis adinuentores. ... Ergo haec fuit beati Caelestini beata sententia, ut non uetustas cessaret obruere nouitatem, sed potius nouitas desineret incessere uetustatem" (Vincent of Lérins, *Commonitorium* 32,4-7 [CCL, 64], p. 193)

3. Prosper, *De gratia Dei et libero arbitrio contra Collatorem* (PL, 51), cc. 213-276.

directed against anti-Augustinian pamphlets caricaturing some aspects of the bishop of Hippo's doctrine of grace. The result was the redaction of two *Responsiones*, the *Pro Augustino responsiones ad capitula obiectionum Gallorum calumniantium*[4] and the *Pro Augustino responsiones ad capitula obiectionum Vincentianarum*[5], whereas a third one, the *Pro Augustino responsiones ad excerpta Genuensium*[6], falls outside the polemical context. In the first *Responsio* (written against a group of Gallic theologians, probably belonging to the milieux of Marseilles and Lérins, and certainly sympathisers with the anti-Augustinian movement) Prosper replies first by discussing their objections and then by re-stating his answer using fifteen sentences taken from Augustine himself. The main, underlying objection of these Gallic theologians was the attribution to the bishop of Hippo of the idea that predestination consists in the pre-determination of men, on the part of God, to good or evil, in such a way that when good deeds are performed it is the power of grace that acts in the will, whereas when evil deeds are done the will acts without the help of grace[7]. The second *Responsio* deals with some objections probably raised by Vincent of Lérins[8] (or by some other monastic theologian of Provence)[9] against some aspects of Augustine's theology of grace. In short, such objections contest what they take to be the bishop of Hippo's depiction of the two *massae* in which humanity is divided: the one destined to salvation, and the other to damnation. Furthermore they represent Augustine as denying that God really wishes all men to be saved, that Christ did not die for all, and that the evil done by those who are not predestined is willed by God (who is responsible for it)[10], so

4. Id., *Pro Augustino responsiones ad capitula obiectionum Gallorum calumniantium* (PL, 51), cc. 155-174.
5. Id., *Pro Augustino responsiones ad capitula obiectionum Vincentianarum* (PL, 51), cc. 177-186.
6. Id., *Pro Augustino responsiones ad excerpta Genuensium* (PL, 51), cc. 187-202.
7. Cf., for instance: "Praedestinationem autem Dei sive ad bonum, sive ad malum, in hominibus operari ineptissime dicitur, ut ad utrumque homines quaedam necessitas videatur impellere, cum in bonis voluntas sit intelligenda de gratia, in malis autem voluntas intelligenda sine gratia" (Id., *Pro Augustino responsiones ad capitula obiectionum Gallorum calumniantium* 6 [PL, 51], c. 161).
8. It is possible that these objections were indeed raised by Vincent of Lérins, although this indication is known to us only from Prosper's rebuttal. See M. VESSEY, *Vincent of Lérins*, in A.D. FITZGERALD, *Augustine through the Ages. An Encyclopedia*, Grand Rapids, MI – Cambridge, 1999, p. 870.
9. "Ces 'objections' traduisent visiblement une réaction exaspérée des moines de Provence contre la doctrine augustinienne de la prédestination, du moins telle qu'ils la comprenaient. Même si Vincent n'en est pas l'auteur, il doit être compté parmi les membres du mouvement" (A. SOLIGNAC, *Semipélagiens*, in *DSp* 14 [1990] 556-568, c. 561).
10. Cf., for instance, the following quotation: "Quod nolit Deus, ut omnes catholici in fide catholica perseverent, sed velit ut magna exinde pars apostatet ... magna pars sanctorum a sanctitatis proposito ruat" (Prosper, *Pro Augustino responsiones ad capitula*

much so that when they pray to God with the words of the Lord's prayer ("Your will be done"), they are asking for their eternal perdition. No doubt the Vincentian objections are far more radical than the Gallic ones, and introduce a basic pessimism with regard to the semantic meaning of predestination. The third *Responsio*, as already stated, was not so much a controversial writing as a serene and clarifying answer to two priests of Genoa, Camillus and Theodore, who had been puzzled by a number of passages they had read in Augustine's *De pradestinatione sanctorum* and *De dono perseuerantiae*. Asked to clarify some obscure points, Prosper assembled a dossier of Augustinian texts taken from those two same writings of the bishop of Hippo mentioned above, and concerning questions such as the *initium fidei*, the vocation of the elect and the gratuity of the gift of perseverance.

As a member of the anti-Augustinian party, we must mention Vincent of Lérins who, besides being the probable author of the *Obiectiones*, against which Prosper reacted, is also the author of the *Commonitorium* (written soon after the Council of Ephesus [431]) whose level of anti-Augustinianism is still debated[11]. It is, however, most likely that its central tenet about how to determine catholic orthodoxy[12], reflects the veneration for tradition which played so great a role in the monastic settlements of Southern Gaul. In that sense, and within this framework, the *Commonitorium* can indeed be seen as the manifestation of the Gallic "local resistance to the perceived 'novelty' of Augustine's doctrine of predestination"[13]. Close to the caricature of predestination made by the *Obiectiones Vincentianae* is the *Praedestinatus*[14]. This work (whose author has not been identified with certainty), was written between 432 and 440, and does not belong to the monastic and ecclesiastical milieu of Southern Gaul[15]. Among other things, the anonymous author stresses

---

obiectionum Vincentianarum 8-9 [PL, 51], c. 182). "Quod adulteria et corruptelae virginum sacrarum ideo contingant, quia illas Deus ad hoc praedestinavit ut caderent" (*Ibid.* 10, cc. 182-183).

11. See *supra*, p. 118, n. 117.

12. "In ipsa item catholica ecclesia magnopere curandum est, ut id teneamus quod ubique, quod semper, quod ab omnibus creditum est" (VINCENT OF LÉRINS, *Commonitorium* 2,5 [CCL, 64], p. 149).

13. M. VESSEY, Opus Imperfectum. *Augustine and His Readers, 426-435* A.D., in *VigChr* 52 (1998) 264-285, p. 870.

14. Arnobius Iunior (attributed to), *Praedestinatus* (CCL, 25B). See É. AMANN, *Praedestinatus*, in *DTC* 12/2 (1935) 2775-2780; F.-M. ABEL, *Le* Praedestinatus *et le pélagianisme*, in *RTAM* 35 (1968) 5-25.

15. "Même s'il vient d'un autre milieu, le *Praedestinatus* est à rapprocher, pour ce qui concerne la doctrine, du mouvement provençal. Il en est de même pour l'*Hypomnesticon* ... qui, à l'inverse, est une défense des vues d'Augustin" (SOLIGNAC, *Semipélagiens* [n. 9], c. 561).

God's universal salvific will[16], a certain priority of good will over grace[17], the value of human effort[18], and the capacity of infralapsarian free will to desire and pursue the good[19], together with the necessity of grace in order effectively to attain salvation[20].

With the death of Cassian, which occurred in ca. 435, the debate cooled; not only because the most illustrious among the Massilians had died, but also because, upon his death, Prosper himself left Provence to return to Rome. Once in Rome, Prosper would temper his polemic, as the very title of his work *De uocatione omnium gentium*[21] clearly witnesses. It is very interesting to see how the once staunch defender of Augustine's doctrine of grace now moves towards a more flexible position. This is an even more remarkable shift when we consider that, confronted with Augustine's restricted interpretation of salvation, on one hand, and the Massilians' stress on the universality of God's salvific will, on the other, Prosper's work not only affirms God's universal salvific will and the idea of a general grace given to all, but it is also "the earliest Christian work to address the question of the salvation of nonbelievers"[22]. To steer a middle course between the bishop of Hippo and the Massilians, Prosper separates the doctrine of gratuitous and sovereign grace from that of predestination. As Amann remarks, in the *De uocatione omnium gentium* the fervent disciple of Augustine tempers the rigidities of the master, coming closer, with regard to the question of universal salvation, to the position of the Massilians, although he remains essentially faithful to the Augustinian doctrine of the absolute gratuity of grace, even at the beginning of one's conversion[23].

As we mentioned above, during the first phase of the controversy between Augustine's defenders and the Gallic theologians, there was no formal condemnation of the views held by the Massilians, so that the two parties continued to stick to their own position, even when the confrontation lay dormant. It would not be long, after the middle of the 5th century to be precise, before a further phase in the Massilian reaction would be marked through the writings of *Faustus of Riez*[24]. Abbot of

16. Arnobius Iunior (attributed to), *Praedestinatus* 3,3 (CCL 25B), p. 67.
17. *Ibid.* 3,12, pp. 86-87.
18. *Ibid.* 3,15-17, pp. 92-96.
19. *Ibid.* 3,27-30, pp. 112-116.
20. *Ibid.* 3,21-23, pp. 103-108.
21. Prosper, *De uocatione omnium gentium* (PL, 51), cc. 647-722.
22. M.P. McHugh, *Prosper of Aquitaine*, in Fitzgerald (ed.), *Augustine through the Ages* (n. 8), p. 685.
23. See É. Amann, *Semi-Pélagiens*, in DTC XIV/2 (1941) 1796-1850, c. 1832.
24. See C. Tibiletti, *Libero arbitrio e grazia in Fausto di Riez*, in *Aug* 19 [1979] 259-285; Id., *La salvezza umana in Fausto di Riez*, in *Orpheus* n. s. 1 (1980) 371-390;

Lérins from 434 to 460, and bishop of Riez from 460 up to his death, in ca. 495, he wrote a treatise, the *De gratia*[25], to refute the errors of Lucidus[26], a priest of the diocese of Riez who taught that Christ did not die for all men, and that men were predestined from eternity either to eternal life or to eternal death. This work offers us a very interesting and solid synthesis of the continuing optimistic position held in the monastic and ecclesiastical milieux of Southern Gaul on the question of predestination, and the relationship between grace and free will. Faustus condemns the Pelagian view, which he sees as unilaterally stressing the role and effort of free will and its possibilities to the detriment of grace, and also the view of his adversaries (Augustine *in primis*, although he is not explicitly mentioned) who insist instead on *sola gratia* for salvation[27]. Truth, Faustus contends, sails between these two errors, as between Scylla and Carybdis[28]. In fact, to deny the place and role of free will, and not that of grace, is to exclude man from the *seruitutis officium*[29], as well as to accept a double predestination (*ad mortem et ad uitam*), and to empty prayer of all hope (*spem intercludit orandi*)[30]. Faustus gives a well reasoned *plaidoyer* of free will, stating that to regard it as entirely compromised by Adam's fall would be to equate man with animals; whereas man's free will *in amore innocentiae uel operatione iustitiae uel in corporis sanctificatione consistit*[31]. The *liberum arbitrium* was, no doubt, weakened (*infirmatum*) by the fall, but it did not become impossible for it to desire what is virtuous and good. Human beings can reach this, as climbers do, struggling to reach the peak of a mountain, *suo labore et sudore per adiutorii patrocinium*[32]. Moreover, free will cannot

R.J. HOWARD COLLINS, *Faustus von Reji*, in *TRE* 11 (1983) 63-67; M. SIMONETTI, *Fausto di Riez*, in *DPAC* 1 (1983) 1336-1338; SOLIGNAC, *Semipélagiens* (n. 9), cc. 562-564; R.H. WEAVER, *Divine Grace and Human Agency. A Study of the Semi-Pelagian Controversy* (PatMS, 15), Macon, GA, 1996, pp. 165-180; T.A. SMITH, *Faustus of Riez*, in FITZGERALD (ed.), *Augustine through the Ages* (n. 8), pp. 356-358; C. LEYSER, *Semi-Pelagianism*, in FITZGERALD [ed.], *Augustine through the Ages* (n. 8), pp. 764f.
    25. Faustus of Riez, *De gratia* (CSEL, 21). See T.A. SMITH, *"De Gratia": Faustus of Riez's Treatise on Grace and Its Place in the History of Theology*, Notre Dame/IN, 1990.
    26. See É. AMANN, *Lucidus*, in *DTC* 9 (1926) 1020-1024.
    27. "Hic *[Pelagius]* iudicii sui perdidit sanitatem dum arbitrii libertatem integram praedicat et inlaesam, sicut illi qui eam ex toto asserunt fuisse euacuatam. Hoc itaque loco gemini inter se conluctantur errores, quorum unus solam gratiam, alter solum laborem relicto tramite atque mensura ueritatis insinuat" (Faustus of Riez, *De gratia* 1,1 [CSEL, 21], p. 7). Cf. also *Ibid.* 3, pp. 14f.
    28. *Ibid.* 1,1, p. 7.
    29. "Nam qui negat gratiae adsociandum famuli laboris conatum, subtrahit homini seruitutis officium" (*Ibid.* 3, p. 15).
    30. *Ibid.*
    31. *Ibid.* 7, p. 23.
    32. *Ibid.* 8, p. 25.

be said to be capable of evil only; on the contrary the *uasa contumeliae* can become *uasa honoris*[33]. It is worth noting the interpretation he gives to Rom 9,20 (*ex eadem massa*) where he emphasizes that according to God's will there is only one *massa*; the division into two *massae* is a division made by man's will[34]. Prescience comes before predestination and must be distinguished from it, while divine election is based on God's foreknowledge of one's future merits[35]. Faustus talks again of the freedom man is endowed with, by stating that, being created in the image of the Trinitarian God (and not in that of the coming Christ) freedom is inherent in human beings, thanks to that first grace by which man was created in God's image[36]. The "image" is distinguished from the "likeness" of God. Whereas the "image" pertains to all, even to evildoers who continue to possess it in a blurred manner (*licet a se et in se decoloratam*)[37], the "likeness" only belongs to the virtuous[38]. These are the main points of Faustus' *De gratia*, a work which indeed can be said to represent the ideology of the monastic/ecclesiastical milieu of Southern Gaul, and which can be seen as the last well thought-out attempt to curb the Augustinian influence about the questions of grace and predestination.

Faustus' *De gratia* met with no opposition, especially in Gaul[39]. However, when a group of eastern theologians, the so-called Scythian monks[40] (whose ideas on grace reflected the Augustinian view) read Faustus' treatise, they raised some questions about its orthodoxy. They first sought clarifications by Possessor[41], an African bishop exiled to Constantinople, who, in his turn, asked Rome for instructions. Pope Hormisdas remained neutral about Faustus' writing and suggested that

33. *Ibid.* 10-11, pp. 32-40.

34. "Inter haec dum dicit *ex eadem massa*, quicumque duas generis humani massas esse arbitrabaris, unam sacra ex lectione cognosce, duas autem facit prauitas studiorum et diuersitas uoluntatum" (*Ibid.* 12, p. 44).

35. "Praescientia itaque regendo praenoscit, postmodum praedestinatio retribuenda describit: illa praeuidit merita, haec praeordinat praemia; praescientiam ad potentiam, praedestinatio ad iustitiam pertinet" (*Ibid.* 2,3, p. 63).

36. "Quae cum ita sunt, inesse homini licet adtenuatam uoluntatis propriae libertatem minime dubitabis, si primam gratiam, qua a Deo est honoratus, inspexeris. Imago ergo Dei homo dicitur, quia ei indulgenter ac dignanter inseruit ueritas iustitiam, ratio sapientiam, perennitas aeternitatem" (*Ibid.* 2,9, p. 78).

37. *Ibid.*, p. 79.

38. *Ibid.*

39. According to Amann, the influence of the monastery of Lérins (as well as that of Marseilles) was so great in Gaul that no one dared contest Faustus' doctrine. See AMANN, *Semi-Pélagiens* (n. 23), c. 1837.

40. They were a group of monks who became involved in discussions between Rome and Constantinople. See *Ibid.*, cc. 1838-1840.

41. See *Possessor*, in A. MANDOUZE *et al.*, *Prosopographie chrétienne du Bas-Empire*, T. I: *Prosopographie de l'Afrique Chrétienne (303-533)*, Paris, 1982, p. 889.

the monks should read the documents (*capitula*) kept in the Roman Curia, plus Augustine's *De praedestinatione sanctorum* and *De dono perseuerantiae*. Not satisfied, and still doubting Faustus' orthodoxy, the Scythian monks turned to some African bishops who had fled to Sardinia under pressure from the Arian Vandals.

The most outstanding figure of this group was *Fulgentius of Ruspe*[42]. A good theologian, and strongly influenced by the theology of Augustine, he set out to refute Faustus' doctrine. The result of his undertaking are the following writings: the *Contra Faustum* (now lost), the *Ad Monimum*[43], and the *De ueritate praedestinationis ad Ioannem presbyterum et Venerium diaconum*[44]. Even so, the anti-Augustinian controversy in Gaul might have gone on indefinitely, had not a variety of reasons eventually given the upper hand to the Augustinian party. One of the key considerations here was undoubtedly the influence exercised by Julian Pomerius[45]. A rhetorician of African origin, Pomerius happened to be in Arles when Caesarius (the future bishop of Arles)[46] was also there (497/498), after he had left Lérins on health reasons. Pomerius became mentor of Caesarius, and the latter soon shared the great esteem in which his teacher held Augustine, whom he highly praised[47] and whose works he knew very well. Caesarius, who became bishop of Arles in 503, is the one who prepared the 2nd Council of Orange (529), whose aim was to settle, from a dogmatic point of view, the questions raised by the Massilian movement. It is hardly surprising that Caesarius, the natural ally of the Augustinian party in Gaul, was the chief architect especially of the *Praefatio* and the *Definitio fidei* produced by the council[48]. However, it must not be forgotten that Caesarius was also a pupil of Lérins. This is shown by his sermons which, besides the Augustinian doctrine, reveal that he also assimilated the teaching of Cassian, whom he had read extensively[49].

Thanks to Caesarius' conversance with both Augustinian and Cassianic literature, and thanks to his influential leadership, the Council of

42. See *Fulgentius of Ruspe*, in *Ibid.*, pp. 507-513; P. LANGLOIS, *Fulgentius*, in *RAC* 8 (1972) 632-661; R.J. HOWARD COLLINS, *Fulgentius von Ruspe*, in *TRE* 11 (1983) 723-727; WEAVER, *Divine Grace and Human Agency* (n. 24), pp. 182-196; T. SMITH, *Fulgentius of Ruspe*, in FITZGERALD (ed.), *Augustine through the Ages* (n. 8), pp. 373-374.

43. Fulgentius of Ruspe, *Ad Monimum* (CCL, 91), pp. 1-64.

44. Id., *De ueritate praedestinationis ad Ioannem presbyterum et Venerium diaconum* (CCL, 91), pp. 458-548.

45. See G. FRITZ, *Pomère*, in *DTC* 12/2 (1935) 2537-2543.

46. See T. O'LOUGHLIN, *Caesarius of Arles*, in FITZGERALD (ed.), *Augustine through the Ages* (n. 8), pp. 115-116.

47. Cf. Pomerius, *De uita contemplatiua* 3,31,6 (PL, 59), cc. 516-517.

48. Cf. *Concilium Arausicanum, Concilia Galliae A. 511–A. 695* (CCL, 148A), pp. 55-64. See WEAVER, *Divine Grace and Human Agency* (n. 24), pp. 225-232.

49. Cf. LEYSER, *Semi-Pelagianism* (n. 24), p. 765.

Orange was able to bring to an eirenic end the Gallic controversy. In fact, if the twenty-five decrees of the council sanction a moderate Augustinianism as the teaching of the Church on grace, they also "nuance, rather than delete the 'middle way' consensus on the issue on grace characteristic of the Gallic Church"[50]. On the one hand, they rejected the theory of the *naturae bonum* persisting after original sin, stating that man needs the grace of God in order to adhere to his commandments, and reasserted that faith, in its *initium* and in its *augmentum*, together with all acts leading to salvation, is anticipated and caused by God's grace[51]. On the other hand, they insisted upon the coexistence and co-operation of grace and free will, even though they left unsolved the exact mode of their relationship. Interestingly enough, the invitation to make fruitful efforts (*si fideliter laborare uoluerint*) by co-operating with Christ's grace for our salvation[52], apart from being an apparently clear concession to the monastic milieux of Southern Gaul, is also an implicit rejection of Augustine's theory of irresistible grace. Predestination to evil is strongly denied also, so much so that an anathema is pronounced against all those who hold such an enormity (*tantum mali*)[53]. In this way the *definitio fidei* of the Council of Orange subscribed to the belief that God's redemptive will is and remains the decisive factor of the *oeconomia salutis*. Overall, the council was a success[54]. The peace of the Gallic Church was not to be further disturbed by confrontation over these issues, until the middle of the 9th century with the case of the radical Augustinian Gottschalk of Aachen. But that belongs to another historical period and to a different context.

"BONUM CERTAMEN CERTAVI,
CURSUM CONSUMMAVI,
FIDEM SERVAVI"
(2 Tim 4,7)

---

50. *Ibid.*
51. Cf. *Concilium Arausicanum, Concilia Galliae A. 511–A. 695* (CCL, 148A), pp. 56ff.
52. Cf. *Definitio fidei*, in *Ibid.*, p.63.
53. *Ibid.*
54. Perhaps, as it has been suggested by Solignac, "pour tenir compte de 'l'autre tradition', la valeur dogmatique du concile d'Orange demanderait à être réévaluée; il faudrait situer ses décisions dans leur contexte historique et par rapport à la perspective différente (mais complémentaire) d'Hilaire, Grégoire de Nysse et Jean Chrysostome" (SOLIGNAC, *Semipélagiens* [n. 9], c. 567).

I. INDEX OF BIBLICAL REFERENCES AND CITATIONS

1. OLD TESTAMENT

2. NEW TESTAMENT

II. INDEX OF ANCIENT AUTHORS

1. AUGUSTINE

2. ANCIENT WRITERS

III. INDEX OF MODERN AUTHORS

IV. SELECTIVE INDEX OF NAMES, PLACES AND SUBJECTS

BIBLIOTHECA EPHEMERIDUM THEOLOGICARUM LOVANIENSIUM

SERIES I

* = Out of print

*1. *Miscellanea dogmatica in honorem Eximii Domini J. Bittremieux*, 1947.

*2-3. *Miscellanea moralia in honorem Eximii Domini A. Janssen*, 1948.

*4. G. PHILIPS, *La grâce des justes de l'Ancien Testament*, 1948.

*5. G. PHILIPS, *De ratione instituendi tractatum de gratia nostrae sanctificationis*, 1953.

6-7. *Recueil Lucien Cerfaux. Études d'exégèse et d'histoire religieuse*, 1954. 504 et 577 p. Cf. *infra*, nᵒˢ 18 et 71 (t. III).   25 € par tome

8. G. THILS, *Histoire doctrinale du mouvement œcuménique*, 1955. Nouvelle édition, 1963. 338 p.   4 €

*9. *Études sur l'Immaculée Conception*, 1955.

*10. J.A. O'DONOHOE, *Tridentine Seminary Legislation*, 1957.

*11. G. THILS, *Orientations de la théologie*, 1958.

*12-13. J. COPPENS, A. DESCAMPS, É. MASSAUX (ed.), *Sacra Pagina. Miscellanea Biblica Congressus Internationalis Catholici de Re Biblica*, 1959.

*14. *Adrien VI, le premier Pape de la contre-réforme*, 1959.

*15. F. CLAEYS BOUUAERT, *Les déclarations et serments imposés par la loi civile aux membres du clergé belge sous le Directoire (1795-1801)*, 1960.

*16. G. THILS, *La «Théologie œcuménique». Notion-Formes-Démarches*, 1960.

17. G. THILS, *Primauté pontificale et prérogatives épiscopales. «Potestas ordinaria» au Concile du Vatican*, 1961. 103 p.   2 €

*18. *Recueil Lucien Cerfaux*, t. III, 1962. Cf. *infra*, n° 71.

*19. *Foi et réflexion philosophique. Mélanges F. Grégoire*, 1961.

*20. *Mélanges G. Ryckmans*, 1963.

21. G. THILS, *L'infaillibilité du peuple chrétien «in credendo»*, 1963. 67 p.   2 €

*22. J. FÉRIN & L. JANSSENS, *Progestogènes et morale conjugale*, 1963.

*23. *Collectanea Moralia in honorem Eximii Domini A. Janssen*, 1964.

24. H. CAZELLES (ed.), *De Mari à Qumrân. L'Ancien Testament. Son milieu. Ses écrits. Ses relectures juives* (Hommage J. Coppens, I), 1969. 158*-370 p.   23 €

*25. I. DE LA POTTERIE (ed.), *De Jésus aux évangiles. Tradition et rédaction dans les évangiles synoptiques* (Hommage J. Coppens, II), 1967.

26. G. THILS & R.E. BROWN (ed.), *Exégèse et théologie* (Hommage J. Coppens, III), 1968. 328 p.   18 €

*27. J. COPPENS (ed.), *Ecclesia a Spiritu sancto edocta. Hommage à Mgr G. Philips*, 1970. 640 p.

28. J. COPPENS (ed.), *Sacerdoce et célibat. Études historiques et théologiques*, 1971. 740 p.   18 €

29. M. DIDIER (ed.), *L'évangile selon Matthieu. Rédaction et théologie*, 1972. 432 p.   25 €
*30. J. KEMPENEERS, *Le Cardinal van Roey en son temps*, 1971.

SERIES II

31. F. NEIRYNCK, *Duality in Mark. Contributions to the Study of the Markan Redaction*, 1972. Revised edition with Supplementary Notes, 1988. 252 p.   30 €
32. F. NEIRYNCK (ed.), *L'évangile de Luc. Problèmes littéraires et théologiques*, 1973. *L'évangile de Luc – The Gospel of Luke*. Revised and enlarged edition, 1989. x-590 p.   55 €
33. C. BREKELMANS (ed.), *Questions disputées d'Ancien Testament. Méthode et théologie*, 1974. *Continuing Questions in Old Testament Method and Theology*. Revised and enlarged edition by M. VERVENNE, 1989. 245 p.   30 €
34. M. SABBE (ed.), *L'évangile selon Marc. Tradition et rédaction*, 1974. Nouvelle édition augmentée, 1988. 601 p.   60 €
35. B. WILLAERT (ed.), *Philosophie de la religion – Godsdienstfilosofie. Miscellanea Albert Dondeyne*, 1974. Nouvelle édition, 1987. 458 p.   60 €
36. G. PHILIPS, *L'union personnelle avec le Dieu vivant. Essai sur l'origine et le sens de la grâce créée*, 1974. Édition révisée, 1989. 299 p.   25 €
37. F. NEIRYNCK, in collaboration with T. HANSEN and F. VAN SEGBROECK, *The Minor Agreements of Matthew and Luke against Mark with a Cumulative List*, 1974. 330 p.   23 €
38. J. COPPENS, *Le messianisme et sa relève prophétique. Les anticipations vétérotestamentaires. Leur accomplissement en Jésus*, 1974. Édition révisée, 1989. XIII-265 p.   25 €
39. D. SENIOR, *The Passion Narrative according to Matthew. A Redactional Study*, 1975. New impression, 1982. 440 p.   25 €
40. J. DUPONT (ed.), *Jésus aux origines de la christologie*, 1975. Nouvelle édition augmentée, 1989. 458 p.   38 €
41. J. COPPENS (ed.), *La notion biblique de Dieu*, 1976. Réimpression, 1985. 519 p.   40 €
42. J. LINDEMANS & H. DEMEESTER (ed.), *Liber Amicorum Monseigneur W. Onclin*, 1976. XXII-396 p.   25 €
43. R.E. HOECKMAN (ed.), *Pluralisme et œcuménisme en recherches théologiques. Mélanges offerts au R.P. Dockx, O.P.*, 1976. 316 p.   25 €
44. M. DE JONGE (ed.), *L'évangile de Jean. Sources, rédaction, théologie*, 1977. Réimpression, 1987. 416 p.   38 €
45. E.J.M. VAN EIJL (ed.), *Facultas S. Theologiae Lovaniensis 1432-1797. Bijdragen tot haar geschiedenis. Contributions to its History. Contributions à son histoire*, 1977. 570 p.   43 €
46. M. DELCOR (ed.), *Qumrân. Sa piété, sa théologie et son milieu*, 1978. 432 p.   43 €
47. M. CAUDRON (ed.), *Faith and Society. Foi et société. Geloof en maatschappij. Acta Congressus Internationalis Theologici Lovaniensis 1976*, 1978. 304 p.   29 €

68. N. LOHFINK (ed.), *Das Deuteronomium. Entstehung, Gestalt und Botschaft / Deuteronomy: Origin, Form and Message*, 1985. XI-382 p.   50 €
69. P.F. FRANSEN, *Hermeneutics of the Councils and Other Studies*. Collected by H.E. MERTENS & F. DE GRAEVE, 1985. 543 p.   45 €
70. J. DUPONT, *Études sur les Évangiles synoptiques*. Présentées par F. NEIRYNCK, 1985. 2 tomes, XXI-IX-1210 p.   70 €
71. *Recueil Lucien Cerfaux*, t. III, 1962. Nouvelle édition revue et complétée, 1985. LXXX-458 p.   40 €
72. J. GROOTAERS, *Primauté et collégialité. Le dossier de Gérard Philips sur la Nota Explicativa Praevia (Lumen gentium, Chap. III)*. Présenté avec introduction historique, annotations et annexes. Préface de G. THILS, 1986. 222 p.   25 €
73. A. VANHOYE (ed.), *L'apôtre Paul. Personnalité, style et conception du ministère*, 1986. XIII-470 p.   65 €
74. J. LUST (ed.), *Ezekiel and His Book. Textual and Literary Criticism and their Interrelation*, 1986. X-387 p.   68 €
75. É. MASSAUX, *Influence de l'Évangile de saint Matthieu sur la littérature chrétienne avant saint Irénée*. Réimpression anastatique présentée par F. NEIRYNCK. *Supplément: Bibliographie 1950-1985*, par B. DEHAND-SCHUTTER, 1986. XXVII-850 p.   63 €
76. L. CEYSSENS & J.A.G. TANS, *Autour de l'Unigenitus. Recherches sur la genèse de la Constitution*, 1987. XXVI-845 p.   63 €
77. A. DESCAMPS, *Jésus et l'Église. Études d'exégèse et de théologie*. Préface de Mgr A. HOUSSIAU, 1987. XLV-641 p.   63 €
78. J. DUPLACY, *Études de critique textuelle du Nouveau Testament*. Présentées par J. DELOBEL, 1987. XXVII-431 p.   45 €
79. E.J.M. VAN EIJL (ed.), *L'image de C. Jansénius jusqu'à la fin du XVIIIe siècle*, 1987. 258 p.   32 €
80. E. BRITO, *La Création selon Schelling. Universum*, 1987. XXXV-646 p.   75 €
81. J. VERMEYLEN (ed.), *The Book of Isaiah – Le livre d'Isaïe. Les oracles et leurs relectures. Unité et complexité de l'ouvrage*, 1989. X-472 p.   68 €
82. G. VAN BELLE, *Johannine Bibliography 1966-1985. A Cumulative Bibliography on the Fourth Gospel*, 1988. XVII-563 p.   68 €
83. J.A. SELLING (ed.), *Personalist Morals. Essays in Honor of Professor Louis Janssens*, 1988. VIII-344 p.   30 €
84. M.-É. BOISMARD, *Moïse ou Jésus. Essai de christologie johannique*, 1988. XVI-241 p.   25 €
84ᴬ. M.-É. BOISMARD, *Moses or Jesus: An Essay in Johannine Christology*. Translated by B.T. VIVIANO, 1993, XVI-144 p.   25 €
85. J.A. DICK, *The Malines Conversations Revisited*, 1989. 278 p.   38 €
86. J.-M. SEVRIN (ed.), *The New Testament in Early Christianity – La réception des écrits néotestamentaires dans le christianisme primitif*, 1989. XVI-406 p.   63 €
87. R.F. COLLINS (ed.), *The Thessalonian Correspondence*, 1990. XV-546 p.   75 €
88. F. VAN SEGBROECK, *The Gospel of Luke. A Cumulative Bibliography 1973-1988*, 1989. 241 p.   30 €

89. G. THILS, *Primauté et infaillibilité du Pontife Romain à Vatican I et autres études d'ecclésiologie*, 1989. XI-422 p. 47 €
90. A. VERGOTE, *Explorations de l'espace théologique. Études de théologie et de philosophie de la religion*, 1990. XVI-709 p. 50 €
*91. J.C. DE MOOR, *The Rise of Yahwism: The Roots of Israelite Monotheism*, 1990. *Revised and Enlarged Edition*, 1997. XV-445 p.
92. B. BRUNING, M. LAMBERIGTS & J. VAN HOUTEM (eds.), *Collectanea Augustiniana. Mélanges T.J. van Bavel*, 1990. 2 tomes, XXXVIII-VIII-1074 p. 75 €
93. A. DE HALLEUX, *Patrologie et œcuménisme. Recueil d'études*, 1990. XVI-887 p. 75 €
94. C. BREKELMANS & J. LUST (eds.), *Pentateuchal and Deuteronomistic Studies: Papers Read at the XIIIth IOSOT Congress Leuven 1989*, 1990. 307 p. 38 €
95. D.L. DUNGAN (ed.), *The Interrelations of the Gospels. A Symposium Led by M.-É. Boismard – W.R. Farmer – F. Neirynck, Jerusalem 1984*, 1990. XXXI-672 p. 75 €
96. G.D. KILPATRICK, *The Principles and Practice of New Testament Textual Criticism. Collected Essays*. Edited by J.K. ELLIOTT, 1990. XXXVIII-489 p. 75 €
97. G. ALBERIGO (ed.), *Christian Unity. The Council of Ferrara-Florence: 1438/39 – 1989*, 1991. X-681 p. 75 €
98. M. SABBE, *Studia Neotestamentica. Collected Essays*, 1991. XVI-573 p. 50 €
99. F. NEIRYNCK, *Evangelica II: 1982-1991. Collected Essays*. Edited by F. VAN SEGBROECK, 1991. XIX-874 p. 70 €
100. F. VAN SEGBROECK, C.M. TUCKETT, G. VAN BELLE & J. VERHEYDEN (eds.), *The Four Gospels 1992. Festschrift Frans Neirynck*, 1992. 3 volumes, XVII-X-X-2668 p. 125 €

SERIES III

101. A. DENAUX (ed.), *John and the Synoptics*, 1992. XXII-696 p. 75 €
102. F. NEIRYNCK, J. VERHEYDEN, F. VAN SEGBROECK, G. VAN OYEN & R. CORSTJENS, *The Gospel of Mark. A Cumulative Bibliography: 1950-1990*, 1992. XII-717 p. 68 €
103. M. SIMON, *Un catéchisme universel pour l'Église catholique. Du Concile de Trente à nos jours*, 1992. XIV-461 p. 55 €
104. L. CEYSSENS, *Le sort de la bulle Unigenitus. Recueil d'études offert à Lucien Ceyssens à l'occasion de son 90ᵉ anniversaire*. Présenté par M. LAMBERIGTS, 1992. XXVI-641 p. 50 €
105. R.J. DALY (ed.), *Origeniana Quinta. Papers of the 5th International Origen Congress, Boston College, 14-18 August 1989*, 1992. XVII-635 p. 68 €
106. A.S. VAN DER WOUDE (ed.), *The Book of Daniel in the Light of New Findings*, 1993. XVIII-574 p. 75 €
107. J. FAMERÉE, *L'ecclésiologie d'Yves Congar avant Vatican II: Histoire et Église. Analyse et reprise critique*, 1992. 497 p. 65 €

108. C. Begg, *Josephus' Account of the Early Divided Monarchy (AJ 8, 212-420). Rewriting the Bible*, 1993. IX-377 p. 60 €
109. J. Bulckens & H. Lombaerts (eds.), *L'enseignement de la religion catholique à l'école secondaire. Enjeux pour la nouvelle Europe*, 1993. XII-264 p. 32 €
110. C. Focant (ed.), *The Synoptic Gospels. Source Criticism and the New Literary Criticism*, 1993. XXXIX-670 p. 75 €
111. M. Lamberigts (ed.), avec la collaboration de L. Kenis, *L'augustinisme à l'ancienne Faculté de théologie de Louvain*, 1994. VII-455 p. 60 €
112. R. Bieringer & J. Lambrecht, *Studies on 2 Corinthians*, 1994. XX-632 p. 75 €
113. E. Brito, *La pneumatologie de Schleiermacher*, 1994. XII-649 p. 75 €
114. W.A.M. Beuken (ed.), *The Book of Job*, 1994. X-462 p. 60 €
115. J. Lambrecht, *Pauline Studies: Collected Essays*, 1994. XIV-465 p. 63 €
116. G. Van Belle, *The Signs Source in the Fourth Gospel: Historical Survey and Critical Evaluation of the Semeia Hypothesis*, 1994. XIV-503 p. 63 €
117. M. Lamberigts & P. Van Deun (eds.), *Martyrium in Multidisciplinary Perspective. Memorial L. Reekmans*, 1995. X-435 p. 75 €
118. G. Dorival & A. Le Boulluec (eds.), *Origeniana Sexta. Origène et la Bible/Origen and the Bible. Actes du Colloquium Origenianum Sextum, Chantilly, 30 août – 3 septembre 1993*, 1995. XII-865 p. 98 €
119. É. Gaziaux, *Morale de la foi et morale autonome. Confrontation entre P. Delhaye et J. Fuchs*, 1995. XXII-545 p. 68 €
120. T.A. Salzman, *Deontology and Teleology: An Investigation of the Normative Debate in Roman Catholic Moral Theology*, 1995. XVII-555 p. 68 €.
121. G.R. Evans & M. Gourgues (eds.), *Communion et Réunion. Mélanges Jean-Marie Roger Tillard*, 1995. XI-431 p. 60 €
122. H.T. Fleddermann, *Mark and Q: A Study of the Overlap Texts*. With an *Assessment* by F. Neirynck, 1995. XI-307 p. 45 €
123. R. Boudens, *Two Cardinals: John Henry Newman, Désiré-Joseph Mercier*. Edited by L. Gevers with the collaboration of B. Doyle, 1995. 362 p. 45 €
124. A. Thomasset, *Paul Ricœur. Une poétique de la morale. Aux fondements d'une éthique herméneutique et narrative dans une perspective chrétienne*, 1996. XVI-706 p. 75 €
125. R. Bieringer (ed.), *The Corinthian Correspondence*, 1996. XXVII-793 p. 60 €
126. M. Vervenne (ed.), *Studies in the Book of Exodus: Redaction – Reception – Interpretation*, 1996. XI-660 p. 60 €
127. A. Vanneste, *Nature et grâce dans la théologie occidentale. Dialogue avec H. de Lubac*, 1996. 312 p. 45 €
128. A. Curtis & T. Römer (eds.), *The Book of Jeremiah and its Reception – Le livre de Jérémie et sa réception*, 1997. 331 p. 60 €
129. E. Lanne, *Tradition et Communion des Églises. Recueil d'études*, 1997. XXV-703 p. 75 €

130. A. DENAUX & J.A. DICK (eds.), *From Malines to ARCIC. The Malines Conversations Commemorated*, 1997. IX-317 p. 45 €
131. C.M. TUCKETT (ed.), *The Scriptures in the Gospels*, 1997. XXIV-721 p. 60 €
132. J. VAN RUITEN & M. VERVENNE (eds.), *Studies in the Book of Isaiah. Festschrift Willem A.M. Beuken*, 1997. XX-540 p. 75 €
133. M. VERVENNE & J. LUST (eds.), *Deuteronomy and Deuteronomic Literature. Festschrift C.H.W. Brekelmans*, 1997. XI-637 p. 75 €
134. G. VAN BELLE (ed.), *Index Generalis ETL / BETL 1982-1997*, 1999. IX-337 p. 40 €
135. G. DE SCHRIJVER, *Liberation Theologies on Shifting Grounds. A Clash of Socio-Economic and Cultural Paradigms*, 1998. XI-453 p. 53 €
136. A. SCHOORS (ed.), *Qohelet in the Context of Wisdom*, 1998. XI-528 p. 60 €
137. W.A. BIENERT & U. KÜHNEWEG (eds.), *Origeniana Septima. Origenes in den Auseinandersetzungen des 4. Jahrhunderts,* 1999. XXV-848 p. 95 €
138. É. GAZIAUX, *L'autonomie en morale: au croisement de la philosophie et de la théologie*, 1998. XVI-760 p. 75 €
139. J. GROOTAERS, *Actes et acteurs à Vatican II*, 1998. XXIV-602 p. 75 €
140. F. NEIRYNCK, J. VERHEYDEN & R. CORSTJENS, *The Gospel of Matthew and the Sayings Source Q: A Cumulative Bibliography 1950-1995*, 1998. 2 vols., VII-1000-420* p. 95 €
141. E. BRITO, *Heidegger et l'hymne du sacré*, 1999. XV-800 p. 90 €
142. J. VERHEYDEN (ed.), *The Unity of Luke-Acts*, 1999. XXV-828 p. 60 €
143. N. CALDUCH-BENAGES & J. VERMEYLEN (eds.), *Treasures of Wisdom. Studies in Ben Sira and the Book of Wisdom. Festschrift M. Gilbert*, 1999. XXVII-463 p. 75 €
144. J.-M. AUWERS & A. WÉNIN (eds.), *Lectures et relectures de la Bible. Festschrift P.-M. Bogaert*, 1999. XLII-482 p. 75 €
145. C. BEGG, *Josephus' Story of the Later Monarchy (AJ 9,1–10,185)*, 2000. X-650 p. 75 €
146. J.M. ASGEIRSSON, K. DE TROYER & M.W. MEYER (eds.), *From Quest to Q. Festschrift James M. Robinson*, 2000. XLIV-346 p. 60 €
147. T. RÖMER (ed.), *The Future of the Deuteronomistic History*, 2000. XII-265 p. 75 €
148. F.D. VANSINA, *Paul Ricœur: Bibliographie primaire et secondaire - Primary and Secondary Bibliography 1935-2000*, 2000. XXVI-544 p. 75 €
149. G.J. BROOKE & J.D. KAESTLI (eds.), *Narrativity in Biblical and Related Texts*, 2000. XXI-307 p. 75 €
150. F. NEIRYNCK, *Evangelica III: 1992-2000. Collected Essays*, 2001. XVII-666 p. 60 €
151. B. DOYLE, *The Apocalypse of Isaiah Metaphorically Speaking. A Study of the Use, Function and Significance of Metaphors in Isaiah 24-27*, 2000. XII-453 p. 75 €
152. T. MERRIGAN & J. HAERS (eds.), *The Myriad Christ. Plurality and the Quest for Unity in Contemporary Christology*, 2000. XIV-593 p. 75 €
153. M. SIMON, *Le catéchisme de Jean-Paul II. Genèse et évaluation de son commentaire du Symbole des apôtres*, 2000. XVI-688 p. 75 €

154. J. Vermeylen, *La loi du plus fort. Histoire de la rédaction des récits davidiques de 1 Samuel 8 à 1 Rois 2*, 2000. xiii-746 p. 80 €
155. A. Wénin (ed.), *Studies in the Book of Genesis. Literature, Redaction and History*, 2001. xxx-643 p. 60 €
156. F. Ledegang, *Mysterium Ecclesiae. Images of the Church and its Members in Origen*, 2001. xvii-848 p. 84 €
157. J.S. Boswell, F.P. McHugh & J. Verstraeten (eds.), *Catholic Social Thought: Twilight of Renaissance*, 2000. xxii-307 p. 60 €
158. A. Lindemann (ed.), *The Sayings Source Q and the Historical Jesus*, 2001. xxii-776 p. 60 €
159. C. Hempel, A. Lange & H. Lichtenberger (eds.), *The Wisdom Texts from Qumran and the Development of Sapiential Thought*, 2002. xii-502 p. 80 €
160. L. Boeve & L. Leijssen (eds.), *Sacramental Presence in a Postmodern Context*, 2001. xvi-382 p. 60 €
161. A. Denaux (ed.), *New Testament Textual Criticism and Exegesis. Festschrift J. Delobel*, 2002. xviii-391 p. 60 €
162. U. Busse, *Das Johannesevangelium. Bildlichkeit, Diskurs und Ritual. Mit einer Bibliographie über den Zeitraum 1986-1998*, 2002. xiii-572 p. 70 €
163. J.-M. Auwers & H.J. de Jonge (eds.), *The Biblical Canons*, 2003. lxxxviii-718 p. 60 €
164. L. Perrone (ed.), *Origeniana Octava. Origen and the Alexandrian Tradition*, 2003. Forthcoming.
165. R. Bieringer, V. Koperski & B. Lataire (eds.), *Resurrection in the New Testament. Festschrift J. Lambrecht*, 2002. xxxi-551 p. 70 €
166. M. Lamberigts & L. Kenis (eds.), *Vatican II and Its Legacy*, 2002. xii-512 p. 65 €
167. P. Dieudonné, *La Paix clémentine. Défaite et victoire du premier jansénisme français sous le pontificat de Clément IX (1667-1669)*, 2003. xxxix-302 p. 70 €
168. F. García Martínez, *Wisdom and Apocalypticism in the Dead Sea Scrolls and in the Biblical Tradition*, 2003. xxxiv-491 p. 60 €
169. D. Ogliari, *Gratia et Certamen: The Relationship between Grace and Free Will in the Discussion of Augustine with the So-Called Semipelagians*, 2003. lvii-468 p. 75 €
170. G. Cooman, M. van Stiphout & B. Wauters (eds.), *Zeger Van Espen at the Crossroads of Canon Law, History, Theology and Church-State Relations*. Forthcoming.
171. B. Bourgine, *L'herméneutique théologique de Karl Barth. Exégèse et dogmatique dans le quatrième volume de la Kirchliche Dogmatik*, 2003. xxii-548 p. 75 €

PRINTED ON PERMANENT PAPER • IMPRIME SUR PAPIER PERMANENT • GEDRUKT OP DUURZAAM PAPIER - ISO 9706

N.V. PEETERS S.A., WAROTSTRAAT 50, B-3020 HERENT